Lecture Notes in Computer Science 6980

Commenced Publication in 1973
Founding and Former Series Editors:
Gerhard Goos, Juris Hartmanis, and Jan va

T0074327

Xavier Boyen   Xiaofeng Chen (Eds.)

Provable Security

5th International Conference, ProvSec 2011
Xi'an, China, October 16-18, 2011
Proceedings

 Springer

Volume Editors

Xavier Boyen
Palo Alto Research Center
Palo Alto, CA 94304, USA
E-mail: xb@boyen.org

Xiaofeng Chen
Xidian University
School of Telecommunications Engineering
Xi'an, 710071, China
E-mail: xfchen@xidian.edu.cn

ISSN 0302-9743   e-ISSN 1611-3349
ISBN 978-3-642-24315-8   e-ISBN 978-3-642-24316-5
DOI 10.1007/978-3-642-24316-5
Springer Heidelberg Dordrecht London New York

Library of Congress Control Number: 2011936538

CR Subject Classification (1998): E.3, C.2, K.6.5, D.4.6, J.1, K.4.4

LNCS Sublibrary: SL 4 – Security and Cryptology

Typesetting: Camera-ready by author, data conversion by Scientific Publishing Services, Chennai, India

Printed on acid-free paper

Springer is part of Springer Science+Business Media (www.springer.com)

Preface

The Fifth International Conference on Provable Security (ProvSec 2011) was held in Xi'an, China, October 16–18, 2011. This volume contains papers that were accepted to the academic track of the conference. The Program Committee also invited two distinguished researchers to deliver their keynote talks. The first speaker was Jens Groth from University College London, UK. His talk was entitled "Optimal Structure-Preserving Signatures." The second speaker was Vipul Goyal from Microsoft Research, India. His talk was entitled "Secure Composition of Cryptographic Protocols."

The conference received 75 submissions this year. Each paper was assigned to four referees and we tried our best to ensure that each paper received a thorough and fair review. We are indebted to the members of the Program Committee and the external reviewers for all their hard work. The committee accepted 22 regular papers and 4 short papers to be included in the conference program. These proceedings contain revised versions of the accepted papers. While revisions are expected to take the referees' comments into account, this was not enforced and the authors bear full responsibility for the content of their papers.

In addition to the academic track, the conference hosted a non-archival technical track whose papers were also carefully selected from among the submissions.

It is our pleasure to thank the General Chair Hui Li, the Publicity Co-chairs Qingqi Pei and Yueyu Zhang, and the Chair of the Organizing Committee Weiyi Yin for their great help and support in putting this conference together. We also appreciate the developer of the EasyChair conference system which we used for this conference. Special thanks for Ilsun You and Fatos Xhafa for their great support. Finally, we are grateful to the National Natural Science Foundation of China (NSFC), Key Laboratory of Computer Networks and Information Security, Ministry of Education, Xidian University for sponsoring the conference.

October 2011

Xavier Boyen
Xiaofeng Chen

ProvSec 2011

5th International Conference on Provable Security

October 16–18, Xi'an, China

Sponsored by
The National Natural Science Foundation of China (NSFC)
Key Laboratory of Computer Networks and Information Security,
Ministry of Education, Xidian University, China

General Chair

Hui Li   Xidian University, China

Program Co-chairs

Xavier Boyen   PARC, USA
Xiaofeng Chen   Xidian University, China

Program Committee

Joonsang Baek   KUSTAR, UAE
Feng Bao   Institute for Infocomm Research, Singapore
Dario Catalano   Università di Catania, Italy
Kefei Chen   Shanghai Jiaotong University, China
Liqun Chen   Hewlett-Packard Laboratories, UK
Sherman S.M. Chow   University of Waterloo, Canada
Dengguo Feng   Chinese Academy of Sciences, China
Marc Fischlin   Darmstadt University of Technology, Germany
Matthew Green   The Johns Hopkins University, USA
Yupu Hu   Xidian University, China
Xinyi Huang   Institute for Infocomm Research, Singapore
Kwangjo Kim   KAIST, Korea
Noboru Kunihiro   University of Tokyo, Japan
Kaoru Kurosawa   Ibaraki University, Japan
Fabien Laguillaumie   University of Caen, France
Jin Li   Guangzhou University, China
Benoit Libert   Université Catholique de Louvain, Belgium
Jianfeng Ma   Xidian University, China
Wojciech Mazurczyk   Warsaw University of Technology, Poland
Yi Mu   University of Wollongong, Australia

David Naccache	École normale supérieure, France
Claudio Orlandi	Bar Ilan University, Israel
Olivier Pereira	UCL, Belgium
Josef Pieprzyk	Macquarie University, Australia
Kouichi Sakurai	Kyushu University, Japan
Palash Sarkar	Indian Statistical Institute, India
Alice Silverberg	University of California, Irvine, USA
Ron Steinfeld	Macquarie University, Australia
Willy Susilo	University of Wollongong, Australia
Tsuyoshi Takagi	Future University-Hakodate, Japan
Damien Vergnaud	École normale supérieure, France
Huaxiong Wang	Nanyang Technological University, Singapore
Duncan Wong	City University of Hong Kong, China
Qianhong Wu	Universitat Rovira i Virgili, Spain
Shouhuai Xu	University of Texas at San Antonio, USA
Bo Yang	South China Agricultural University, China
Ilsun You	Korean Bible University, Korea
Fangguo Zhang	Sun Yan-Sen Univeristy, China
Rui Zhang	Tokyo University of Science, Japan
Yunlei Zhao	Fudan University, China
Yuliang Zheng	University of North Carolina at Charlotte, USA
Jianying Zhou	Institute for Infocomm Research, Singapore

Steering Committee

Feng Bao	Institute for Infocomm Research, Singapore
Xavier Boyen	PARC, USA
Yi Mu	University of Wollongong, Australia
Josef Pieprzyk	Macquarie University, Australia
Willy Susilo	University of Wollongong, Australia

Publicity Co-chairs

Qingqi Pei	Xidian University, China
Yueyu Zhang	Xidian University, China

Organizing Committee

Weiyi Yin	Xidian University, China
Yuanyuan Zuo	Xidian University, China
Fengrong Zhang	Xidian University, China
Yinghui Zhang	Xidian University, China

External Reviewers

Au, Man Ho
Bhattacharyya, Rishiraj
Brzuska, Christina
Canard, Sébastien
Castagnos, Guilhem
Chang, Donghoon
Chatterjee, Sanjit
Chen, Jie
Chen, Yu
Choudhury, Ashish
Chu, Cheng-Kang
Dagdelen, Özgür
Deng, Yi
Di Raimondo, Mario
Fan, Jia
Fiore, Dario
Furukawa, Jun
Gao, Wei
Guo, Fuchun
Han, Jinguang
Hanaoka, Goichiro
Hanatani, Yoshikazu
Herranz, Javier
Hirose, Shoichi
Iwata, Tetsu
Kawai, Yutaka
Keller, Marcel
Lai, Junzuo
Li, Fagen
Li, Ximing
Liu, Joseph
Long, Yu

Lv, Xixiang
Ma, Sha
Ma, Xu
Mandell Freeman, David
Mao, Xianping
Matsuda, Takahiro
Mawet, Sophie
Meiklejohn, Sarah
Meldgaard, Sigurd
Mitsunari, Shigeo
Naito, Yusuke
Nandi, Mridul
Nishide, Takashi
Nordholdt, Peter
Ogata, Wakaha
Onete, Maria Cristina
Orumiehchiha, Ali
  Mohammad
Pan, Jiaxin
Pandey, Omkant
Pastro, Valerio
Pehlivanoglu, Serdar
Peng, Kun
Peters, Thomas
Phong, Le Trieu
Qian, Haifeng
Qin, Bo
Wang, Qinglong
Ramanna, Somindu
Schroeder, Dominique
Sen Gupta, Sourav
Jiang, Shaoquan

Singh, Shashank
Steine, Asgeir
Su, Chunhua
Sun, Weiwei
Sur, Chul
Tan, Xiao
Teranishi, Isamu
Visconti, Ivan
Wan, Junzhou
Wan, Yanchun
Wang, Liangliang
Wang, Ping
Wang, Yongtao
Weng, Jian
Wu, Wei
Wu, Yongdong
Xu, Lingling
Yamada, Shota
Yang, Dexin
Yang, Yanjiang
Yoneyama, Kazuki
Yu, Yong
Zhang, Lei
Zhang, Liangfeng
Zhang, Mingwu
Zhang, Yun
Zhang, Zongyang
Zhao, Xingwen
Zheng, Qingji
Zhu, Huafei

Table of Contents

Cryptographic Protocols

Security Models and Framework

Key Agreement

Optimal Structure-Preserving Signatures

Jens Groth

University College London, UK
`j.groth@ucl.ac.uk`

Abstract. Structure preservation captures the notion of pairing-based schemes that rely on generic group operations and where the components are group elements. Their structural properties make it easy to compose them with other pairing-based schemes.

In this talk, we will take a closer look at structure-preserving signatures. The structure preserving property allows us to analyze the efficiency of signature schemes in the generic group model. Using the generic group model to analyze the efficiency of a cryptographic scheme stands in contrast to the more common usage of the generic group model to rule out certain types of attack. We will show that structure-preserving signatures need to consist of at least 3 group elements.

We also discuss recent constructions of structure-preserving signatures that consist of 3 group elements. These constructions match our lower bounds, thus giving us provably optimal structure-preserving signatures.

Keywords: Structure-preserving pairing-based cryptography, digital signatures, generic group model, lower bounds.

X. Boyen and X. Chen (Eds.): ProvSec 2011, LNCS 6980, p. 1, 2011.

Secure Composition of Cryptographic Protocols

Vipul Goyal

Microsoft Research, India
vipul@microsoft.com

1 Talk Overview

General positive results for secure computation were obtained more than two decades ago. These results were for the setting where each protocol execution is done in isolation. With the proliferation of the network setting (and especially the internet), an ambitious effort to generalize these results and obtain concurrently secure protocols was started. However it was soon shown that designing secure protocols in the concurrent setting is unfortunately impossible in general. In this talk, we will first describe the so called chosen protocol attack. This is an explicit attack which establishes general impossibility of designing secure protocols in the concurrent setting. The negative results hold for the so called plain model where there is no trusted party, no honest majority, etc.

On the other hand, several *positive* results for protocols composition have been established in various related settings (which are either weaker or incomparable). A few examples are the setting of resettable computation (where the parties may not be able to keep state during the protocol execution and may be run several times with the same random tape), bounded concurrent secure computation (where there is an apriori bound on the total number of concurrent sessions), standalone protocol execution with man-in-the-middle (i.e., the setting of non-malleable protocols), the single input setting (where the honest party uses the same input in all polynomially unbounded concurrent protocol executions), etc.

We will survey known results as well various open problems in each of the above settings. We also given an overview of an emerging technique which has been used to construct secure protocols in several of these settings. We will focus on the plain model throughout the talk.

X. Boyen and X. Chen (Eds.): ProvSec 2011, LNCS 6980, p. 2, 2011.
© Springer-Verlag Berlin Heidelberg 2011

Secure Two-Party Computation over a Z-Channel

Paolo Palmieri and Olivier Pereira

Université catholique de Louvain
UCL Crypto Group, ICTEAM Institute
Place du Levant 3, B-1348 Louvain-la-Neuve, Belgium
{paolo.palmieri,olivier.pereira}@uclouvain.be

Abstract. In secure two-party computation, two mutually distrusting parties are interested in jointly computing a function, while preserving the privacy of their respective inputs. However, when communicating over a clear channel, security against computationally unbounded adversaries is impossible. Thus is the importance of noisy channels, over which we can build Oblivious Transfer (OT), a fundamental primitive in cryptography and the basic building block for any secure multi-party computation. The noisy channels commonly used in current constructions are mostly derived from the Binary Symmetric Channel (BSC), which is modified to extend the capabilities of an attacker. Still, these constructions are based on very strong assumptions, in particular on the error probability, which makes them hard to implement.

In this paper, we provide a protocol achieving oblivious transfer over a Z-channel, a natural channel model in various contexts, ranging from optical to covert communication. The protocol proves to be particularly efficient for a large range of error probabilities p (e.g., for $0.17 \leq p \leq 0.29$ when a security parameter $\varepsilon = 10^{-9}$ is chosen), where it requires a limited amount of data to be sent through the channel. Our construction also proves to offer security against unfair adversaries, who are able to select the channel probability within a fixed range. We provide coding schemes that can further increase the efficiency of the protocol for probabilities distant from the range mentioned above, and also allow the use of a Z-channel with an error probability greater than 0.5. The flexibility and the efficiency of the construction make an actual implementation of oblivious transfer a more realistic prospect.

Keywords: Oblivious transfer, secure multi-party computation, information theoretic security, cryptography on noisy channels.

1 Introduction

Oblivious Transfer (OT), introduced by Rabin in 1981 [14], is a primitive of primary importance in the field of secure multi-party computation and, more generally, cryptography: any secure computation can be built on top of a secure OT protocol [10]. In this paper we present a protocol achieving OT on

X. Boyen and X. Chen (Eds.): ProvSec 2011, LNCS 6980, pp. 3–15, 2011.
© Springer-Verlag Berlin Heidelberg 2011

a *Z-channel*, a communication channel that, while being closely related to the most commonly used ones, has never been used for this purpose. We also show the greater flexibility our construction has in comparison to current protocols, being able to accept any error probability p, and allowing an adversary large control over p itself.

Secure multi-party computation deals with the problem of mutually distrusting players interested in jointly compute a function, while preserving the privacy of their respective inputs. In the information-theoretic setting, where protocols must be secure against computationally unbounded adversaries, security cannot be generally achieved without any further assumption. However, multi-party computation can be achieved when some form of noise in the communication is available, which, in turn, allows for the construction of oblivious transfer. Since OT can be built using almost any noisy channel [5], the most interesting research question is what form of noise offers the best flexibility and efficiency, and could therefore be used in the prospect of an actual implementation.

The two players involved in an oblivious transfer protocol are generally divided into a sender and a receiver. The sender knows a set of secret input values, and is interested in communicating to the receiver a smaller subset, selected according to the latter's choice. After a successful execution of the protocol, the receiver learns the chosen inputs but gets no information about the others, while the sender remains oblivious of the receiver's selection.

The first protocol to implement oblivious transfer on a noisy channel was provided by Crépeau and Kilian in 1988 [4]. The construction is based on the *binary symmetric channel* (BSC), which flips with a fixed probability each bit sent though it. Security is guaranteed by privacy amplification, while the use of error correction codes assures the correctness of the results. Results were later improved and generalized in [3,5,12]. However, strong requirements are imposed by the construction: the players must have perfect knowledge of the statistics of the channel, such as the error probability, which can not change during protocol execution. Damgård et al. tried to weaken these requirements by introducing the *unfair noisy channels* in 1999 [7]. The name comes from the "unfair" advantage given to an adversary, who is able to arbitrarily choose the error probability of the channel within a certain range. Results were improved by widening the range of acceptable probabilities in a following paper in 2004 [6]. Wullschleger further extended the concept of unfair noisy channel by introducing two new channel models, the *weak erasure channel* and the *weak binary symmetric channel* [16]. The two new primitives aim to be more general by lessening the security assumptions. For instance, they take into account the possibility, for a dishonest sender, to learn with a small probability if a bit was or not affected by the channel noise (being flipped in the case of the weak BSC, or lost in the case of the weak erasure channel).

Although it has been shown that oblivious transfer can be built from almost any noisy channel, we still lack a clear understanding of what properties a noisy channel needs to be best suited for efficient protocols. This knowledge is of primary importance if we are to build better protocols and thus achieve actual implementation.

1.1 The Z-Channel

In a 1980 correspondence on the IEEE Transactions on Information Theory, Golomb succinctly describes the mutual information and capacity of the Z-channel [8]. A Z-channel is a discrete memoryless channel with two input symbols (x_1, x_2) and two output symbols (y_1, y_2). The noise in the channel is determined by its error probability p. The conditional probabilities of receiving a given output based on a given input are expressed by the following matrix:

$$\begin{pmatrix} P(y_1|x_1) & P(y_2|x_1) \\ P(y_1|x_2) & P(y_2|x_2) \end{pmatrix} = \begin{pmatrix} 1 & 0 \\ p & 1-p \end{pmatrix}.$$

In the following, we use the name Z-channel to refer to a binary Z-channel, where $(x_1, x_2) = (0, 1)$ and $(y_1, y_2) = (0, 1)$. Using these symbols, the behavior of the Z-channel closely resemble that of a binary symmetric channel, except for the fact that the noise is affecting the communication asymmetrically (see Fig. 1). In practice, we can transmit a "0" through the channel noiselessly, while sending a "1" we have a probability p that it will be received as a "0".

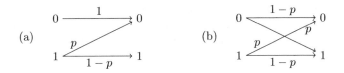

Fig. 1. A Z-channel (a) and a standard Binary Symmetric Channel (b)

We observe that using the correct encoding, a Z-channel with crossover probability $p = \frac{1}{2}$ is in fact equivalent to a Rabin OT (which in turn is equivalent to an erasure channel with $p = \frac{1}{2}$), where the sender sends a secret bit b, which is received with probability $\frac{1}{2}$ and lost otherwise, and remains oblivious as to whether the bit reached the receiver or not. We can achieve this by sending the bit string "01" for $b = 0$ and "10" for $b = 1$. The receiver is able to decode the bit if the string is received correctly, but learns no information about it if she receives the string "00" instead.

The Z-channel appears as a natural model of various types of communications, from optical communications [1], to various forms of covert communications [11].

1.2 Contribution

While we know that noise is essential to achieve security in multi-party computation, we still lack the understanding of how the properties of a particular noisy channel affect the efficiency and security of oblivious transfer protocols. This paper aims at showing how a careful selection of a noisy channel is needed in order to achieve secure multi-party computation efficiently.

To do so we provide a protocol implementing oblivious transfer on a simple channel model, the Z-channel. This channel has interesting properties: contrary to the binary symmetric and erasure channels, only part of the input symbols are affected by the noise, allowing the receiver to interpret some (but not all) of the output symbols with certainty. For the other symbols, the receiver has no way to recover the original information with certainty. This provides us with the ambiguity needed for the security of the construction.

We show how these channel properties can be exploited to build an oblivious transfer protocol that can accommodate any non-zero value of the flipping probability p of the Z-channel and, interestingly, can offer security as long as this probability is known to lie in any fixed range. This contrasts with the case of the unfair BSC (UNC) channel studied by Damgård et al. [7,6], for which it is known that OT is impossible to achieve as soon as the range of acceptable flipping probabilities increases too much. In general, we show that an unfair Z-channel, which allows the adversary to choose the probability of the channel within a range, behaves much better than an unfair BSC: oblivious transfer can be achieved for any fixed range, and our protocol is efficient for ranges larger than the possibility range of a UNC.

Following the terminology of Imai et al. [9], our protocol achieves an oblivious transfer rate of $\frac{1}{4}$. We also demonstrate how this efficiency and flexibility can be further improved for specific channel parameters and concrete security bounds, through the use of different coding strategies and protocol modifications.

1.3   Outline of the Paper

Section 2 contains some useful definitions and preliminary notions that are needed in the following. In particular, we give a security definition for oblivious transfer. Section 3 describes the basic version of our protocol for achieving OT on a Z-channel, and proves the security of this protocol in the semi-honest model. In Section 4, we introduce the unfair version of the Z-channel, and we analyze the efficiency of our construction. We also demonstrate how different coding strategies and protocol modifications can be used to improve the efficiency of concrete instances of our protocol.

2   Preliminaries

Many different flavors of oblivious transfer exist, and they have all been proved equivalent by Crépeau [2]. In the following, when using the name oblivious transfer, we will be referring to a *binary 1-out-of-2 oblivious transfer* protocol, where a sender, Sam, has two bits b_0 and b_1, while a receiver, Rachel, has a choice bit c. After a successful execution of such a protocol, three conditions must be satisfied: the receiver party knows the value of the selected bit b_c (correctness); the receiver party learns nothing about the value of the other bit b_{1-c} (security for Sam); the sender party learns nothing about the choice bit c (security for Rachel) [4].

A useful way of measuring the knowledge an adversary has on a secret bit of information is the *prediction advantage*. Prediction advantage measures the advantage the adversary has in guessing the secret bit by using all the available information.

Definition 1. [15] *Let P_{XY} be a distribution over $\{0,1\} \times \mathcal{Y}$. The maximal bit prediction advantage of X from Y for a function f is*

$$\text{PredAdv}\,(X \mid Y) = 2 \cdot \max_f \Pr\left[f\left(Y\right) = X\right] - 1 \ . \tag{1}$$

All the information that is available to a player during an execution of the protocol is called the *view* of the player.

2.1   A Security Definition for Oblivious Transfer

Using the concept of prediction advantage, the three conditions that form the security of an oblivious transfer protocol can be formally defined, leading to a security definition for OT. Such a definition can be found in [13]. We will use it in the following to prove the security of our construction.

Definition 2. [13] *A protocol Π between a sender and a receiver, where the sender inputs $(b_0, b_1) \in \{0,1\}$ and outputs nothing, and the receiver inputs $c \in \{0,1\}$ and outputs S, securely computes 1-2 oblivious transfer with an error of at most ε, assuming that U and V represent the sender and receiver views respectively, if the following conditions are satisfied:*

- (Correctness) *If both players are honest, we have*

$$Pr\left[S = b_c\right] \geq 1 - \varepsilon \ . \tag{2}$$

- (Security for Sam) *For an honest sender and an honest (but curious) receiver we have*

$$\text{PredAdv}\,(b_{1-c} \mid V, c) \leq \varepsilon \ . \tag{3}$$

- (Security for Rachel) *For an honest receiver and an honest (but curious) sender we have*

$$\text{PredAdv}\,(c \mid U, b_0, b_1) \leq \varepsilon \ . \tag{4}$$

3   Oblivious Transfer over a Z-Channel

Our construction differs from standard oblivious transfer protocols for the binary symmetric channel for the fact that it does not require the use of error correcting codes (ECC's). This is due to the fact that some output symbols can always be interpreted correctly, thanks to the Z-channel properties (a "1" output symbol always come from a "1" input). The ambiguity needed to assure the security of the construction is however guaranteed by the fact that we cannot correct errors in other output symbols (a "0" output symbol can come either from a "0" or a "1" input).

3.1   Protocol

The protocol is a sequence of three different stages. The first stage is called *precomputation*, and is performed by the sender. During this stage, the sender selects, according to some prescribed distribution, a set of bit pairs to be sent on the Z-channel.

The communication between the sender and the receiver takes place in the second stage (*communication*). The precomputed set is sent to the receiver through the Z-channel. The interaction then proceeds by exchanging on a clear channel the information needed to construct the encoded version of the secret bits b_0 and b_1, that are subsequently sent to the receiver.

During the third and last stage, called *postcomputation*, the receiver computes the value of the chosen bit b_c.

Protocol 1. The three phases described below happen sequentially.

Precomputation. The sender Sam selects n pairs of bits $s_i := (c_i, c_i')$ such that $c_i \oplus c_i' = 1$ for all $i \in [1, n]$. Knowledge of the value of n is shared between the parties.

Communication. The sender Sam and the receiver Rachel can communicate over a Z-channel with error probability p and over a clear channel.

1. Sam sends the pairs $s_1, \ldots s_n$ to Rachel through the Z-channel.
2. Rachel receives a sequence of n pairs of bits $r_i := (d_i, d_i')$, with $i \in [1, n]$, somehow similar to the s_i pairs.
3. Rachel arbitrarily selects two sequences I_c and I_{1-c}, where c is her choice bit, each composed of $\frac{n}{2}$ unique indices $i \in [1, n]$, where $i \in I_c$ if and only if $d_i \neq d_i'$, that is, if the pair (c_i, c_i') has not been modified during the transmission. When she selected enough elements for I_c, Rachel puts all the other indices i in I_{1-c}, regardless of the content of (d_i, d_i') and sends the two sets back to Sam on a clear channel. If instead there are less than $\frac{n}{2}$ indices that she can put in I_c, she aborts the protocol.
4. Sam receives the two sequences of indices (I_0, I_1) and builds two strings e_0, e_1 such that the i-th bit of e_b has value 0 if and only if $\left(c_{I_{b[i]}}, c'_{I_{b[i]}}\right) = (0, 1)$ where $I_{b[i]}$ is the i-th index in I_b. Then Sam chooses two universal hash functions h_0 and h_1 whose output is 1-bit long for any input. He computes

$$f_0 = (b_0 \oplus h_0(e_0)) \ , \quad f_1 = (b_1 \oplus h_1(e_1)) \ , \tag{5}$$

and sends f_0, f_1, h_0, h_1 to Rachel via a clear channel.

Postcomputation. The receiver Rachel builds the string e_c using the same procedure used by Sam when building (e_0, e_1) but using $\left(d_{I_{c[i]}}, d'_{I_{c[i]}}\right)$ instead of $\left(c_{I_{b[i]}}, c'_{I_{b[i]}}\right)$. Then she computes

$$b_c = (f_c \oplus h_c(e_c)) \ . \tag{6}$$

We observe that this protocol follows the general pattern of OT-protocols from noisy channels [3,5,12]. First, it somehow builds an erasure channel (this is the purpose of the precomputation stage). Then this erasure channel is used a number of times to realize OT.

3.2   Security in the Semi-honest Scenario

In the *semi-honest model* the players act in a honest-but-curious way. In practice, they follow the protocol, but try to use all the information they can get during the protocol execution to get extra knowledge. We can also say that in a semi-honest scenario, the adversary is *passive*: she follows the protocol, but outputs her entire view [15].

We now show the security of the protocol when the probability p is in the interval $\left(0, \frac{1}{2}\right)$. In the next section, we will show how to relax this requirement in order to deal with any probability p in the interval $(0, 1)$.

Theorem 1. *The protocol described in Section 3.1 securely computes 1-2 oblivious transfer with error probability ε when it is executed on a Z-channel with error probability p, where $0 < p < \frac{1}{2}$, and with the security parameter n satisfying:*

$$n > \max\left(\frac{-2\log\left(\varepsilon\right)}{(1 - 2p)^2}, \frac{\log\left(\frac{\varepsilon}{2}\right)}{\log\left(1 - \frac{p}{2}\right)}\right) \quad . \tag{7}$$

Proof. We prove that our construction is secure by showing that each of the three security conditions for an oblivious transfer protocol is satisfied.

Correctness. When transmitted through a binary Z-channel, each pair (c_i, c'_i) is received correctly except with probability p, and Rachel is able to decide whether she received that pair correctly: the pair has been modified by the channel only if $c_i = c'_i = 0$.

The protocol is correct, that is, Rachel is able to build the sequence I_c correctly if at least $\frac{n}{2}$ pairs have been delivered without errors; we call this event Correct. This Correct event happens with the following probability:

$$\Pr\left[\mathsf{Correct}\right] = \sum_{k=\frac{n}{2}}^{n} \binom{n}{k} (1 - p)^k \, p^{n-k} \geq 1 - e^{-2n\left(\frac{1}{2} - p\right)^2} \quad , \tag{8}$$

where the inequality follows from the Chernoff bound.

Security for Sam. The aim of a curious Rachel is to learn the value of b_{1-c}. Let us call this event Success. Rachel has two ways of achieving it: by decoding e_{1-c} on the correct inputs (let us call this event DecodeE), or by not doing so. So, we have that $\Pr\left[\mathsf{Success}\right] = \Pr\left[\mathsf{Success} \wedge \mathsf{DecodeE}\right] + \Pr\left[\mathsf{Success} \wedge \neg\mathsf{DecodeE}\right]$. The latter probability is upper-bounded by $\frac{1}{2}$, due to the properties of a universal hash function, while the former is upper-bounded by $\Pr\left[\mathsf{DecodeE}\right]$. In the following, we evaluate that probability.

Rachel needs to learn the value of all the bits in e_{1-c}. For each bit, she has two ways of doing so:

1. By computing the value. This is possible if $d_i \neq d'_i$ for the pair of bits r_i corresponding to the bit in e_{1-c} she wants to learn. We call this event NoAmbiguity.
2. By guessing the value. This is necessary if she cannot directly compute it, that is, if $d_i = d'_i = 0$ for the corresponding pair of bits. Let us call this event Ambiguity, and note that it is complementary to the event NoAmbiguity.

The first case happens with probability $(1 - p)$. Therefore, Rachel will be able to decode the whole string e_{1-c} without any guessing with probability $(1 - p)^n$.

In the second case, which happens with probability $\Pr[\text{Ambiguity}] = 1 - \Pr[\text{NoAmbiguity}]$, Rachel has no information about which pair (c_i, c'_i) of weight 1 was sent. Therefore Rachel has to guess the value of the bit by tossing a coin, with a probability to succeed equal to $\frac{1}{2}$.

Overall, for any bit pair r_i she will select the correct value for the bit in e_{1-c} with probability $\left(\frac{p}{2} + (1 - p)\right) = 1 - \frac{p}{2}$. Since the hash function can be correctly evaluated only if all the guesses are correct, we have

$$\Pr[\text{DecodeE}] = \left(1 - \frac{p}{2}\right)^n . \tag{9}$$

Therefore we have

$$\Pr[\text{Success}] \leq \frac{1}{2} + \left(1 - \frac{p}{2}\right)^n . \tag{10}$$

Security for Rachel. The Z-channel does not give any feedback to the sender as to what errors it introduces in a message transmitted through it. Since Rachel distinguishes the sets I_c and I_{1-c} from the bits flipped by the channel, from Sam's point of view the distribution of (I_0, I_1) is independent of c.

Combining the two results of the correctness and security for Sam sections of the proof by extracting n in the two inequalities, and using the definition of prediction advantage, we obtain the two arguments of the maximum function in the theorem statement.   □

We observe that the bounds provided here are also valid for similar channels on which OT is built through a simple reduction to the binary erasure channel (e.g., the *binary discrete-time delaying channel* considered in [13]).

4   Efficiency and Resistance to Unfair Adversaries

Our construction exhibits a particularly low sensitivity of the n parameter to the value of the probability p for a given security bound ε, in a wide range of values of p. We believe that this is a very useful feature of using a Z-channel for realizing OT, as the precise channel characteristics are often difficult to evaluate when communication is achieved between a sender and a receiver who do not trust each other.

A concrete depiction of the bounds of Theorem 1 is provided in Fig. 2. Our protocol is particularly efficient when the probability p is around 0.25 (the optimal value has little sensitivity to fluctuations of the ε parameter: it ranges from 0.2486 to 0.2462 when ε ranges from 10^{-6} to 10^{-15}).[1] Just 163 bit pairs are sufficient to guarantee a security of $\varepsilon = 10^{-9}$ at the optimal probability $p = 0.2473$. More importantly, the graph in Fig. 2 shows that the number of bit pairs n can be kept low for large ranges of p and reasonable values of ε. For instance, for $\varepsilon = 10^{-9}$, transmitting 250 pairs of bits on the Z-channel is enough to realize OT for $0.17 \leq p \leq 0.29$, and the even larger range of $0.04 \leq p \leq 0.40$ only requires $n = 1060$.

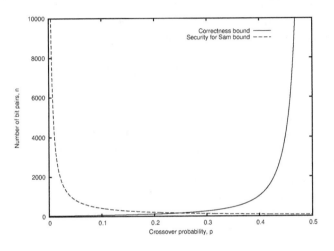

Fig. 2. n as a function of p for $\varepsilon = 10^{-9}$

4.1   Unfair Z-Channel

The large acceptable ranges discussed above also imply that our construction behaves considerably well when the adversary is given the advantage of choosing the channel probability within a certain range. Following the definition in [7], an unfair Z-channel with parameters γ and δ, where $\gamma, \delta \leq \frac{1}{2}$, is a Z-channel with an error probability $p \in [\gamma, \delta]$ that is set by the adversary but is not known by the honest players, who have access to the values of γ and δ only. Therefore, a protocol implementing OT over an unfair Z-channel must work for any p in this range.

The concept of unfair Z-channel gives the graph in Fig. 2 a new meaning: the area comprised between the two functions is also the largest acceptable range for a given n, where the security for Sam bound is equivalent to the minimum γ, and the correctness bound is the maximum δ. This result is particularly interesting if compared to the best known achievable ranges for the unfair BSC (UNC) [6].

---

[1] Note that these values are actually as precise as the Chernoff bound that we used in the proof on Theorem 1.

While in the case of the UNC oblivious transfer can not be achieved as soon as the difference between δ and γ becomes too large, namely if $\delta \geq 2\gamma (1 - \gamma)$, in the unfair Z-channel OT is possible for any fixed range. The largest possible range for the UNC has a width of 0.125, with $\gamma = 0.25$ and $\delta = 0.375$, but such an interval can not be achieved by any of the current protocols. As we have seen before, for the relatively small $n = 1060$ our construction offers security for a maximum range as wide as 0.36.

4.2 Efficiency

For input messages longer than one bit, the efficiency of the protocol proposed in Section 3.1 can be increased by using privacy amplification techniques (see Crépeau [3] for instance). Following the terminology of Imai et al. [9], we can observe that, by letting n grow to infinity on a Z-channel with probability $p = \frac{1}{2}$, the I_{1-c} sequence will only contain indices for which the corresponding (c_i, c_i') pair is unknown from r_i. As a result, it is possible to realize the oblivious transfer of messages of $\frac{n}{2}$ bits by exchanging $2n$ bits on the Z-channel, achieving an oblivious transfer rate of $\frac{1}{4}$.

This rate is however an asymptotic notion, and is only useful for the exchange of longer messages. We now investigate improvements on the efficiency of our protocol for concrete parameters (i.e., concrete values of ε and n).

Usually, it is not possible to choose the characteristics of the Z-channel that one uses. This suggests the use of coding strategies that could let the parties emulate a Z-channel with probability $p \approx 0.25$ from a Z-channel exhibiting a very different crossover probability.

Emulating a Z channel with lower crossover probability. Suppose first that a Z-channel with crossover probability $p \gg 0.25$ is available (including the case where $p > 0.5$, as long as $p < 1$). Using a simple repetition code is actually enough to emulate a Z-channel with lower crossover probability.

Suppose indeed that, instead of selecting c_i and c_i' as bits, we select them as sequences of m repeated bits. A sequence of m zeros will always be delivered as it is, while a sequence of m ones can be delivered as an arbitrary bit string of length m. However, as long as that bit string contains a single 1, the receiver can be sure that a sequence of m "1" was actually sent. So, ambiguity happens only if all the m "1" are flipped during transmission. This happens with probability p^m, which is always smaller than p for $m > 1$.

As a result, a m repetition code allows emulating a Z-channel with crossover probability p^m from a Z-channel with crossover probability p. This also provides a way to use our protocol on a Z-channel with $p > \frac{1}{2}$.

Emulating a Z channel with larger crossover probability. Suppose now that a Z-channel with crossover probability $p \ll 0.25$ is available. We can then decide to encode each "1" bit to be sent on the Z-channel as a sequence of l "1", and each "0" bit as a sequence of $(l - 1)$ "1" with a "0" placed in an arbitrary position unknown to the receiver. Now, a "1" will only be recognized as it if none of its l

bits is modified while going through the channel. This happens with probability $(1-p)^l$, which allows emulating a Z-channel with probability $1-(1-p)^l$, which is larger than p for any $l > 1$.

These two codes can always be combined in order to emulate a Z-channel with the desired crossover probability with arbitrary precision. For instance, we could choose to encode a "1" as a sequence of $m \cdot l$ "1", and a "0" as a sequence of $l-1$ blocks of m "1" among which a block of m "0" is inserted, which would provide a Z-channel with crossover probability $1-(1-p^m)^l$.

These two codes however come at the price of each time increasing the number of bits to be transmitted on the Z-channel by a factor $m \cdot l$, and one may wonder whether this is actually compensated by the possibility to use a lower number n of pairs. This actually becomes the case when the probability p leaves the efficient range mentioned above.

Let us consider for instance a Z-channel with crossover probability $p = 0.4$. A number of pairs $n = 1037$ is needed to reach a security margin $\varepsilon = 10^{-9}$ with our basic protocol. However, applying our first code with $m = 2$ allows emulating a Z-channel with crossover probability $p^2 = 0.16$, for which a security parameter $n = 246$ is needed, improving the efficiency of our protocol by a factor larger than 2.

In general, for a Z-channel with probability p, we have a minimum number of bit pairs n for a given security bound ε. It is convenient to use an m-l-coding strategy if the number of bit pairs needed after applying the coding scheme is

$$n' < \frac{n}{m \cdot l} \ . \tag{11}$$

Since we have, for a given security bound ε, an optimal probability p_{opt} and the respective minimum number of bit pairs n_{opt}, the combinations of m and l that could provide for a convenient m-l-coding scheme are those for which $n > n_{\mathrm{opt}} \cdot m \cdot l$, from which we have $m \cdot l < \frac{n}{n_{\mathrm{opt}}}$. By simply iterating through the limited number of possibilities, we can find the best n'. Then, subtracting this n' to n, we get the measure of the improvement we get by using the associated l-m-coding scheme, calculated in number of bit pairs. For probabilities $p > 0.37$, the gain quickly becomes consistent. There is also a (very) modest gain for low probabilities, namely for $0 < p \le 0.002$, where the number of saved packets reaches, for example, the value of 51 for $p = 0.0001$.

A different strategy to increase the efficiency of the protocol without using coding schemes is to modify the size of the index sets I_0 and I_1. This strategy is effective when the observed probability of the channel is higher than the optimal value. By reducing the size of the sets I_0 and I_1, we are able to tolerate a larger number of errors introduced by the channels, effectively moving the correctness bound to the right of the graph. However, we are at the same time increasing the minimum number of errors needed to guarantee the security for Sam, moving the relative bound to the right too. In practice, if $r = |I| - |\overline{I}|$ is the difference between the cardinality of regular set I, $\frac{n}{2}$, and that of the reduced set of size $|\overline{I}|$, we have a probability that Rachel will be able to correctly decode the selected bit (correctness) $\sum_{k=\frac{n}{2}-r}^{n} \binom{n}{k} (1-p)^k p^{n-k}$. Using Hoeffding's inequality we can bound that probability to $\leq \exp\left(-2n\left(\frac{1}{2}-p-\frac{r}{n}\right)^2\right)$. Her probability of being able to correctly decode both bits is instead $\leq \frac{1}{2} + \left(\frac{1+p}{2}\right)^{n-2r}$.

5   Conclusion

In this paper we consider the use of the Z-channel for implementing oblivious transfer. This simple communication channel models the functioning of various real-life communication methods, ranging from optical to covert communication. The Z-channel features an unusual property for a noisy channel: only part of the information sent through it is affected by the noise, so the receiver can always interpret correctly some of the output symbols. This particular characteristic eliminates the need for error correction codes, which, in other constructions, limit considerably the range of error probabilities acceptable for secure computation.

Our construction follows the common strategy of constructing some form of erasure channel, which is then repeatedly used to implement OT. Thanks to an efficient reduction of the Z-channel to a binary erasure channel, the protocol exhibits a low sensitivity to the channel characteristics. The parties are less constrained by exact knowledge of the channel statistics, and for a very large range of error probabilities, $0.17 < p < 0.29$, a total of 500 bits transmitted through the channel is sufficient to guarantee a security of $\varepsilon = 10^{-9}$ (Fig. 2). This is particularly useful when confronted to unfair adversaries, who are able to select the channel probability within a certain range $[\gamma, \delta]$. Over a Z-channel, security against unfair behavior is possible for any fixed range, while the unfair BSC introduced by Damgård et al. [7,6] can not achieve OT as soon as the range is larger than $\delta \geq 2\gamma(1-\gamma)$, with a maximum possible width of 0.125. A total of 2120 bits transmitted over a Z-channel is instead sufficient to guarantee security for any probability in the range $[0.04, 0.4]$, for $\varepsilon = 10^{-9}$.

The efficiency of the construction can be further increased by using a combination of two coding schemes, presented in the last section of the paper. A combined m-l-coding strategy, where m and l are the parameters of the schemes, can reduce any Z-channel with probability p to a Z-channel with error probability $1 - (1 - p^m)^l$. This allows the use of channels whose error probability is greater than 0.5. Moreover, when confronted with a channel with a probability distant from the optimal range, the parties can decide to opt for the use of a coding strategy in order to increase the efficiency of the protocol. The factor by which the communication over a Z-channel is increased $(m \cdot l)$ is widely compensated by the reduced repetition number n that the more efficient probability allows for. This is especially evident for any $p > 0.37$.

Acknowledgments. This research work was supported by the SCOOP Action de Recherche Concertées. Olivier Pereira is a Research Associate of the F.R.S.-FNRS.

References

1. Baumert, L.D., McEliece, R.J., Rumsey, H.: Coding for optical channels. In: JPL Deep Space Network Progress Report, vol. 42-49, pp. 70–77 (1978)
2. Crépeau, C.: Equivalence between two flavours of oblivious transfers. In: Pomerance, C. (ed.) CRYPTO 1987. LNCS, vol. 293, pp. 350–354. Springer, Heidelberg (1988)
3. Crépeau, C.: Efficient cryptographic protocols based on noisy channels. In: Fumy, W. (ed.) EUROCRYPT 1997. LNCS, vol. 1233, pp. 306–317. Springer, Heidelberg (1997)
4. Crépeau, C., Kilian, J.: Achieving oblivious transfer using weakened security assumptions (extended abstract). In: FOCS, pp. 42–52. IEEE, Los Alamitos (1988)
5. Crépeau, C., Morozov, K., Wolf, S.: Efficient unconditional oblivious transfer from almost any noisy channel. In: Blundo, C., Cimato, S. (eds.) SCN 2004. LNCS, vol. 3352, pp. 47–59. Springer, Heidelberg (2005)
6. Damgård, I.B., Fehr, S., Morozov, K., Salvail, L.: Unfair noisy channels and oblivious transfer. In: Naor, M. (ed.) TCC 2004. LNCS, vol. 2951, pp. 355–373. Springer, Heidelberg (2004)
7. Damgård, I., Kilian, J., Salvail, L.: On the (Im)possibility of basing oblivious transfer and bit commitment on weakened security assumptions. In: Stern, J. (ed.) EUROCRYPT 1999. LNCS, vol. 1592, pp. 56–73. Springer, Heidelberg (1999)
8. Golomb, S.W.: The limiting behavior of the z-channel. IEEE Transactions on Information Theory 26(3), 372–372 (1980)
9. Imai, H., Morozov, K., Nascimento, A.: On the oblivious transfer capacity of the erasure channel. In: Proceedings of 2006 International Symposium on Information Theory (ISIT), pp. 1428–1431. IEEE, Los Alamitos (2006)
10. Kilian, J.: Founding cryptography on oblivious transfer. In: STOC, pp. 20–31. ACM, New York (1988)
11. Moskowitz, I.S., Greenwald, S.J., Kang, M.H.: An analysis of the timed z-channel. IEEE Transactions on Information Theory 44(7), 3162–3168 (1998)
12. Nascimento, A.C.A., Winter, A.: On the oblivious-transfer capacity of noisy resources. IEEE Transactions on Information Theory 54(6), 2572–2581 (2008)
13. Palmieri, P., Pereira, O.: Building oblivious transfer on channel delays. In: Lai, X., Yung, M., Lin, D. (eds.) Inscrypt 2010. LNCS, vol. 6584, pp. 125–138. Springer, Heidelberg (2011)
14. Rabin, M.O.: How to exchange secrets by oblivious transfer. Technical Report TR-81, Aiken Computation Laboratory, Harvard University (1981) (manuscript)
15. Wullschleger, J.: Oblivious-transfer amplification. In: Naor, M. (ed.) EUROCRYPT 2007. LNCS, vol. 4515, pp. 555–572. Springer, Heidelberg (2007)
16. Wullschleger, J.: Oblivious transfer from weak noisy channels. In: Reingold, O. (ed.) TCC 2009. LNCS, vol. 5444, pp. 332–349. Springer, Heidelberg (2009)

Precise Time and Space Simulatable Zero-Knowledge

Ning Ding and Dawu Gu

Department of Computer Science and Engineering
Shanghai Jiao Tong University, China
{dingning,dwgu}@sjtu.edu.cn

Abstract. Traditionally, the definition of zero-knowledge states that an interactive proof of $x \in L$ provides zero (additional) knowledge if the view of any *polynomial-time* verifier can be reconstructed by a *polynomial-time* simulator. Since this definition only requires that the worst-case running-time of the verifier and simulator are polynomials, zero-knowledge becomes a worst-case notion.

In STOC'06, Micali and Pass proposed a new notion of precise zero-knowledge, which captures the idea that the view of any verifier in every interaction can be reconstructed in (almost) the same time (i.e., the view can be "indistinguishably reconstructed"). This is the strongest notion among the known works towards precislization of the definition of zero-knowledge.

However, as we know, there are two kinds of resources (i.e. time and space) each algorithm consumes in computation. Although the view of a verifier in the interaction of a precise zero-knowledge protocol can be reconstructed in almost the same time, the simulator may run in very large space while at the same time the verifier only runs in very small space. In this case it is still doubtful to take indifference for the verifier to take part in the interaction or to run the simulator. Thus the notion of precise zero-knowledge may be still insufficient. This shows that precislization of the definition of zero-knowledge needs further investigation.

In this paper, we propose a new notion of precise time and space simulatable zero-knowledge (PTSSZK), which captures the idea that the view of any verifier in each interaction can be reconstructed *not only* in the same time, *but also* in the same space. We construct the first PTSSZK proofs and arguments with simultaneous linear time and linear space precisions for all languages in **NP**. Our protocols do not use noticeably more rounds than the known precise zero-knowledge protocols.

Keywords: Zero-Knowledge, Precise Zero-Knowledge, Proofs of Knowledge.

1 Introduction

Zero-knowledge proofs were introduced by Goldwasser, Micali and Rackoff [12]. Their definition essentially states that an interactive proof of $x \in L$ provides zero (additional) knowledge if, for any efficient verifier V^*, the view of V^* in

X. Boyen and X. Chen (Eds.): ProvSec 2011, LNCS 6980, pp. 16–33, 2011.

the interaction can be "indistinguishably reconstructed" by an efficient simulator S -interacting with no one- on just input x. Since efficiency is formalized as polynomial-time, a worst-case notion, zero-knowledge too automatically becomes a worst-case notion. The refinement of [11] (Sec. 4.4.4.2) calls for a tighter coupling between the expected running-time of V^* and that of S: a proof is zero-knowledge with tightness $t(\cdot)$ if there exists a fixed polynomial $p(\cdot)$ such that the expected running-time of $S(x)$ is upper-bounded by $t(|x|)$ times the expected running-time of $V^*(x)$ plus $p(|x|)$.

Micali and Pass [13] argued, however, that such coupling may still be insufficient, even when the tightness function is a constant and the polynomial $p(\cdot)$ is identically 0. Consider a family of malicious verifiers $\{V_i^*\}_{i \in \mathbb{N}}$, in which on input an instance $x \in \{0,1\}^n$, V_i^* takes n^{10i} computational steps with probability $\frac{1}{n}$, and n steps in the rest of the time. Since the expected running-time of V_i^* is $\Theta(n^{10i-1})$, zero-knowledge with optimal tightness only requires that V_i^*'s view be simulated in expected time $\Theta(n^{10i-1})$. Assume S always takes $\Theta(n^{10i-1})$ time to reconstruct V_i^*'s view. Then in the viewpoint of [11], it is indistinguishable for V_i^* to get out and interact with the prover or to stay home and run S for granted. However, by interacting with P, V_i^* will almost always execute n steps of computation, while (in absence of extra guarantees) running the simulator might always cause him to invest n^{10i-1} steps of computation, which tends to infinite as i tends to infinite. Is the view of V_i^* "reconstructed indistinguishably"? This discussion shows that we need a stronger notion of zero-knowledge.

Hence [13] put forward a notion of precise zero-knowledge. This notion captures the idea that prover provides a zero-knowledge proof of $x \in L$ if the view v of any verifier in an interaction with the prover about x can be reconstructed in (almost) the same time. Informally, by [13] a proof system is zero-knowledge with $p(n, y)$ (time) precision if for every verifier V^*, S's running-time in outputting a view is bounded by $p(n, \mathsf{T})$ whenever V^*'s running-time on this view is T. Following this notion, [13] constructed $\omega(\log n)$-round (resp. $\omega(1)$-round) (non-black-box) zero-knowledge proofs and arguments with linear (resp. polynomial) precision for all languages in **NP**.

Further, [13] showed there do not exist black-box zero-knowledge protocols with polynomial precision for languages outside **BPP**, and [15] showed the simulators of Barak's non-black-box zero-knowledge arguments [1] cannot provide polynomial precision. To achieve precise time simulation, [13,15] developed a method, called the "cut-off" technique. That is, the simulator S still needs to rewind a verifier V^* to extract secret information, but in the first run it records V^*'s running-time (steps) and then in the second run it uses this time to bound V^*'s computing, i.e., S emulates V^* for at most such time (steps). If V^* needs more time then S terminates its computing. It can be seen this simulation strategy uses verifiers in a non-black-box way.

However, as we know, there are two kinds of resources (i.e. time and space) each algorithm consumes in computation. Although the notion of precise zero-knowledge is quite strong, it investigates precise simulation only with respect to the *running-time* of the simulator and verifier, regardless of their *running-space.* Consider a family of malicious verifiers $\{V_i^*\}_{i \in \mathbb{N}}$, in which on input an instance $x \in \{0,1\}^n$ (for sufficiently large n's), V_i^* takes n^{10i} computational steps and n^c space for some $c > 0$ (note that an n^c-space machine may take at most $n2^{\Theta(n^c)}$ time, which is greater than n^{10i} for arbitrary i when n is large enough). Zero-knowledge with linear (time) precision only requires that V_i^*'s view be simulated in time $\Theta(n^{10i})$. Assume S always takes $\Theta(n^{10i})$ time, but n^i space, to reconstruct V_i^*'s view. In this case in the viewpoint of [13], it is indistinguishable for V_i^* to take part in the interaction or run the simulator. But it can be seen that (for sufficiently large n's) V_i^*'s running-space in the interaction is n^c, while the simulator needs n^i space to reconstruct V_i^*'s view, which is greater than any predetermined polynomial in n^c as i tends to infinite. Thus, *is it really "indistinguishable" for V_i^* to interact with the prover or to run the simulator?*

The above discussion shows the notion of precise zero-knowledge may be still insufficient and precislization of the definition of zero-knowledge needs further investigation. A natural (and maybe the strongest) avenue for extending precise zero-knowledge is to require that views be reconstructed *not only* in the same time, *but also* in the same space. In this paper we will try to pursue this avenue and to construct zero-knowledge proof systems which are precisely simulatable in this sense.

1.1   Our Results

We put forward a new notion of precise time and space simulatable zero-knowledge (PTSSZK), which strengthens the notion of precise zero-knowledge [13] by additionally requiring the space used in reconstructing the view of a verifier is also almost the same as that of the verifier in the interaction. Informally, we say a proof system is zero-knowledge with time precision $p_t(n,y)$ and space precision $p_s(n,y)$ if for every verifier V^* the simulator S's running-time and running-space in reconstructing a view are always respectively bounded by $p_t(n, \mathsf{T})$ and $p_s(n, \mathsf{S})$ whenever V^*'s running-time and running-space on this view are respectively T and S.

Since V^* and S are usually required to run in polynomial-time, it is less meaningful if $p_t(n,y)$ or $p_s(n,y)$ is super-polynomial in n or y, or else it is meaningful. To the best of our knowledge, all the known zero-knowledge protocols for languages outside **BPP** cannot obtain simultaneous meaningful time and space precisions. We construct the first PTSSZK proofs and arguments with simultaneous meaningful time and space precisions for all languages in **NP**. The formal results are shown as follows.

Theorem 1. *Assume the existence of constant-round perfectly-hiding commitments. Then for every language $L \in$ **NP***
1. there exist $\omega(\log^3 n)$-round zero-knowledge proofs with time precision $p_t(n,y)$ = $poly(n) + O(y)$ and space precision $p_s(n,y) = poly(n) + O(y)$ for L.
2. there exist $\omega(\log n)$-round zero-knowledge proofs with time precision $p_t(n,y) = poly(n) + poly(n)O(y)$ and space precision $p_s(n,y) = poly(n) + O(y)$ for L.

Theorem 2. *Assume the existence of one-way functions. Then for every language $L \in \mathbf{NP}$,*

1. there exist $\omega(\log^3 n)$-round zero-knowledge arguments with time precision $p_t(n, y) = poly(n) + O(y)$ and space precision $p_s(n, y) = poly(n) + O(y)$ for L.

2. there exist $\omega(\log n)$-round zero-knowledge arguments with time precision $p_t(n, y) = poly(n) + poly(n)O(y)$ and space precision $p_s(n, y) = poly(n) + O(y)$ for L.

Comments. We give some comments on our results.

1. We stress that our results can hold in general computational models. (Of course, the precise quantities of the $poly(n)$s depend on the underlying model.) Although this work concerns the precision of simulation, we are oblivious of the details how machines work and of definitions of the complexity measures of time and space. That is, we don't need to explicitly refer to any concrete machine model and definitions of the complexity measures of the two types of resource in that model.

2. Our precisions are pure in the sense that the simulator S's running-time (resp. running-space) are only related to V^*'s running-time T (resp. V^*'s running-space S), regardless of S (resp. T).

3. In Theorem 1 (or Theorem 2), the summand $poly(n)$ in p_t depends on both L and the primitives in our constructions (e.g. commitments and one-way functions). The coefficient $poly(n)$ in p_t (using $\omega(\log n)$ rounds) is independent of L, but to depend on the primitives. The $poly(n)$ in p_s depends on both L and the primitives. We did not try to minimize the $poly(n)$ in p_s by letting our simulators employ subtle strategies for space recycling, as our primary interest is just to obtain a fixed polynomial. The constant coefficients in O-notation of p_t, p_s are independent of both L and the primitives.

4. We obtain simultaneous *linear* time precision (using $\omega(\log^3 n)$ rounds) and *linear* space precision.

Our Technique. Our constructions follow the paradigm used in [15] (based on [13]). To construct precise zero-knowledge protocols, [15] first constructed some proofs of knowledge with time precisions by using the "cut-off" technique and then constructed the desired precise zero-knowledge protocols based on them. As aforementioned, the simulators in [15] (as extractor in the proofs of knowledge) in the first run record V^*'s (as prover in the proofs of knowledge) running-time (steps) and then in the second run use this time to bound V^*'s computing, i.e., they emulate V^* for at most such time (steps) and if V^* needs more time then they terminate its computing. Since this (original) "cut-off" technique only concerns V^*'s running-time, the simulators in [15] cannot automatically provide simultaneous meaningful time and space precisions. Remark 3 in Section 4 shows an example that the two types of precision indeed cannot be obtained by using the original "cut-off" technique.

We extend the "cut-off" technique to present an improved extraction strategy and thus construct the proofs of knowledge with simultaneous meaningful time and space precisions. (This shows our simulators use verifiers in the non-black-box way.) Based on these proofs of knowledge, we achieve the PTSSZK protocols.

To extract secret information our simulators not only record V^*'s running-time (steps), but also record its running-space in the first run. In the second run our simulators emulate V^* for at most such steps, times a factor, and keep track of V^*'s running-space. If V^* needs more time or more space than the recorded space (in size) in the rewind, our simulators terminate its computing. Remark 4 in Section 4 shows the usage of the factor for the time in the rewind is necessary, or else our simulator cannot succeed in extraction for any V^*. Since there is one more necessary condition w.r.t. space for our simulators to succeed in extraction, we shall present more subtle probability analysis of successful extraction, which is the technical novelty of this work.

Outline of This Paper. We assume familiar with the notions of negligible functions (we use $\mathsf{neg}(n)$ to denote an unspecified negligible function), computational indistinguishability, interactive proofs [12] and arguments [5], commitment schemes [3], zero-knowledge [12], witness-indistinguishability [9], proofs of knowledge [8,2,16]. Refer to [11] for their refined definitions and constructions.

In Section 2, we present the new notion of PTSSZK. In Section 3 we present the high-level proofs of our results assuming the existence of the proofs of knowledge with simultaneous time and space precisions. In Section 4, we present the constructions of the desired proofs of knowledge and complete the entire proofs.

2   The New Notion

Counting Time and Space. If M is a probabilistic (non-interactive) machine, denote by M_r the deterministic one obtained by fixing M's random coins to r, by $\mathsf{T}_{M_r(x)}$ and $\mathsf{S}_{M_r(x)}$ the running-time and running-space of M_r on input x. (As aforementioned, we herein don't explicitly refer to any machine model and definitions of the complexity measures of running-time and running-space. Each of general models and the appropriate definitions of the complexity measures in it are suitable for this paper.)

Assume (P, V) uses κ-round prover's messages. For any interactive machine V^* with auxiliary input z (w.l.o.g. assume V^* is deterministic), denote by $v = (x, z, (m_1, m_2, ..., m_\kappa))$ V^*'s view. Denote by $\mathsf{T}_{V^*}(v)$ and $\mathsf{S}_{V^*}(v)$ the running-time and running-space of V^* on input x and letting the jth message received be m_j, $1 \leq j \leq \kappa$. For convenience of statement, we will always consider V^* to have x, z hardwired and refer the view of V^* to $(m_1, m_2, ..., m_\kappa)$ in the rest of this paper (similarly for any P^*).

Definition 1. (PTSSZK) *Let (P, V) be an interactive proof (argument) for a language $L = L(R)$, $p_t : N \times N \rightarrow N$ and $p_s : N \times N \rightarrow N$ be two monotonically increasing 2-variate functions. We say that (P, V) is computational zero-knowledge, or just zero-knowledge, with time precision p_t and space precision p_s if there exists a probabilistic polynomial-time algorithm S, called precise simulator, such that for every polynomial-sized V^* and every $\{(x, w)\} \in R$ the following conditions hold:*
1. The output of $S(x, V^*)$ is computationally indistinguishable from the view of V^* in an execution of $(P(w), V^*)(x)$.

2. For every sufficiently long $r \in \{0, 1\}^*$, let v be the view generated by $S_r(x, V^*)$. Then $T_{S_r(x,V^*)} \leq p_t(n, T_{V^*}(v))$ and $S_{S_r(x,V^*)} \leq p_s(n, S_{V^*}(v))$.

Remark 1. If we only require the running-time of S and V^* satisfy the constraint $p_t(n, y)$, regardless of the constraint $p_s(n, y)$ for their running-space, this is essentially the definition of precise zero-knowledge given in [13].

It can be seen a main task of constructing a PTSSZK protocol is to construct a precise simulator S. To output a simulated view, S usually needs to invoke an interaction in which it acts as prover on one hand and emulates V^* to output verifier's messages on the other hand. To make the analysis of S's running-space accurately, we make the following specifications on the decomposition of running-space of S when emulating V^* (which are quite general).

Specifications. For our simulator S, $S_{S_r(x,V^*)}$ consists of three parts: (1) the space needed to emulate V^*, (2) the predetermined space (decided by the protocol) needed to store the communicated messages (notice that V^*'s computation is emulated by S and thus if S detects V^* tries to send a message longer than what the protocol specifies it aborts) and (3) the space needed to perform the prover's strategy and extraction etc.

Time and Space Cost in Emulation. For universal machine S, we assume there are two universal constants l_1, l_2 satisfying that the time taken by S in emulating V^* on view v is $l_1 T_{V^*}(v)$ (refer to [13]), and the space taken by S in emulating V^* on v (i.e. part 1 described in the previous paragraph) is $l_2 S_{V^*}(v)$.

3   High-Level Proofs of Our Results

In this and next section we prove Theorem 1 and Theorem 2. This section only presents the high-level constructions of the desired protocols. To do this we present a new primitive in Section 3.1, called precise time and space emulatable proofs/arguments of knowledge (PTSEPOK/PTSEAOK). In Section 3.2, we present the PTSSZK proofs and arguments under the assumption of the existence of the PTSEPOKs and PTSEAOKs. In Section 4 we will present the detailed constructions of the required PTSEPOKs and PTSEAOKs and thus complete the entire proofs.

3.1   PTSEPOKs and PTSEAOKs

The notions of PTSEPOKs and PTSEAOKs capture the idea that for any prover P^* and any x, (1) the joint view of P^* and the honest verifier V and (2) the witness for $x \in L$ whenever V's view is accepting, can be simultaneously reconstructed (by an emulator-extractor) in the time and space almost identical to those taken by P^* on the reconstructed view. The formal description is shown as follows.

Definition 2. *(PTSEPOK/PTSEAOK) Let $L = L(R)$, (P, V) be an interactive proof (argument) for L, $p_t : N \times N \rightarrow N$ and $p_s : N \times N \rightarrow N$ be two* *monotonically increasing 2-variate functions. We say (P,V) is a proof (argument) of knowledge with time precision p_t and space precision p_s if there exists a probabilistic polynomial-time algorithm E, called precise emulator-extractor, satisfying that for every polynomial-sized prover P^* and for every $x \in \{0,1\}^n$ the following conditions hold:*

1. Let $(\text{view}_{P^*}, \text{view}_V, w)$ denote the output of $E(x, P^*)$. Then $(\text{view}_{P^*}, \text{view}_V)$ is identically distributed to the joint view in the interaction of $(P^*, V)(x)$. Further, if with non-negligible probability p' view_V is a convincing view, then w is a witness for $x \in L$ with probability $p' - \text{neg}(n)$.

2. For every sufficiently long $r \in \{0,1\}^*$ let $(v_{P^*}, v_V, w) \leftarrow E_r(x, P^*)$. Then $T_{E_r(x,P^*)} \leq p_t(n, T_{P^*}(v_{P^*}))$ and $S_{E_r(x,P^*)} \leq p_s(n, S_{P^*}(v_{P^*}))$.

Remark 2. To be a building block of our PTSSZK protocols, a PTSEPOK (or PTSEAOK) (P,V) should have one more property, i.e. (perfect) WI. That is, (P,V) should additionally satisfy that for every polynomial-sized V^* and for every x, w_1, w_2 where $(x, w_1) \in R$ and $(x, w_2) \in R$ V^*'s view in the interacting with $P(x, w_1)$ is (identical to) computationally indistinguishable from its view in the interacting with $P(x, w_2)$.

3.2   The Constructions

Claim 1. *Assume there exist constant-round perfectly-hiding commitments and m'-round perfectly WI PTSEAOKs with time precision $poly(n) + O(y)$ (resp. $poly(n) + O(ny)$) and space precision $poly(n) + O(y)$ for each **NP** relation. Then for every language $L \in$ **NP**, there exists an $m' + O(1)$-round zero-knowledge proof with time precision $p_t(n, y) = poly(n) + O(y)$ (resp. $poly(n) + poly(n)O(y)$) and space precision $p_s(n, y) = poly(n) + O(y)$ for L.*

Proof. Our protocol is depicted in Protocol 1 where Com is a constant-round perfectly-hiding commitment given in e.g. [14,6]. We show the protocol has all the required properties.

Completeness and Soundness. First, it is obvious completeness holds. Second, by perfect WI of the PTSEAOK, it holds that the whole stage 1 is still a perfectly-hiding commitment. Thus we deduce that when reaching stage 2 the prover has no idea about the value of challenge σ. In other words, even though the cheating prover reaches the second stage after seeing all messages in the first stage, the messages in the second stage are independent of the verifier's messages in stage 1. So a cheating prover violating the soundness of our protocol can be transformed to a full power cheating prover violating the soundness of the n parallel executions of Blum's proof. Thus soundness holds.

Simulator S. For every polynomial-sized V^* and $x \in L$, S works as follows: It first emulates V^* to the commitment c. Then S uses the strategy of the emulator-extractor E of the PTSEAOK to generate $(\text{view}_{V^*1}, \text{view}_{P1}, (\sigma, s))$. (Strictly speaking, the input to E should be c and V^*'s code as Definition 2 requires, not the residual V^* after sending c. But since the essential way that E uses (the residual) V^* is to emulate it, as next section shows, our statement

Public Input: $x \in \{0,1\}^n$ (statement to be proved is "$x \in L$").   **Auxiliary Input to Prover:** w, a witness for $x \in L$.
Stage 1: $V \to P$: V chooses $\sigma \in_R \{0,1\}^n$, $s \in_R \{0,1\}^{\mathrm{poly}(n)}$ and sends $\mathsf{c} = \mathsf{Com}(\sigma; s)$. Then V proves to P via the perfectly WI PTSEAOK of the statement: there exist values σ and s such that $\mathsf{c} = \mathsf{Com}(\sigma; s)$.
Stage 2: $P \to V$: P proves to V in the (slightly modified) n parallel repetitions of Blum's proof [4] that $x \in L$, in which V opens c and uses the string σ as its challenge.

Protocol 1. *The PTSSZK proof for L.*

is still correct.) If view_{P1} is not a convincing view, S terminates the interaction. Otherwise, the extracted σ is that one V^* chose. Then to generate the view in stage 2, S adopts the honest prover strategy using the knowledge of the verifier challenge σ to interact with V^*. Denote by view_{V^*2} the simulated view of V^* in stage 2. Let T (resp. S) denote V^*'s running-time (resp. running-space) on $\mathsf{view}_{V^*1} \circ \mathsf{view}_{V^*2}$, where "$\circ$" denotes concatenation.

Output Distribution. First, the view output by E is identical to that of stage 1 in the real interaction. Second, knowing the challenge in advance makes S's output in stage 2 computationally indistinguishable from a real view of V^* in stage 2, ensured by Blum's simulation strategy. Third, we have when the simulation proceeds to the second stage the event that S can extract σ and V^* opens σ in stage 2 occurs with probability $1 - \mathsf{neg}(n)$, ensured by the binding property of Com. Combining these facts and using a hybrid argument, we infer S's output is computationally indistinguishable from the real view of V^*.

Running-Time. By the time precision of the PTSEAOK, it takes S at most $\mathrm{poly}(n) + O(\mathsf{T})$ time (resp. $\mathrm{poly}(n) + \mathrm{poly}(n)O(\mathsf{T})$, where the latter $\mathrm{poly}(n)$ is $|\mathsf{c}|$) to finish the simulation of stage 1. In stage 2 it takes S a $\mathrm{poly}(n)$ time to perform the honest prover's strategy and $O(\mathsf{T})$ time to emulate V^*. Consequently, there is a $p_t(n, y)$ as required satisfying S's running-time is bounded by $p_t(n, \mathsf{T})$.

Running-Space. By the space precision of the PTSEAOK, S's running-space in stage 1 is less than $\mathrm{poly}(n) + O(\mathsf{S})$ (this $\mathrm{poly}(n)$ is within $|(\mathsf{view}_{V^*1}, \mathsf{view}_{P1}, (\sigma, s) | + \mathrm{poly}(|\mathsf{c}|)$, where the latter poly is that one in the space precision of the PTSEAOK). Second, S's running-space in stage 2 is less than $\mathrm{poly}(n) + O(\mathsf{S})$ (this $\mathrm{poly}(n)$ denotes the space needed to perform the honest prover's strategy and store the view of stage 2). Consequently, there is a $p_s(n, y)$ as required satisfying S's running-space is bounded by $p_s(n, \mathsf{S})$. The claim follows. □

Claim 2. *Assume there exist one-way functions and m'-round WI PTSEPOKs with time precision $\mathrm{poly}(n) + O(y)$ (resp. $\mathrm{poly}(n) + O(ny)$) and space precision $\mathrm{poly}(n) + O(y)$ for each* **NP** *relation. Then for every language $L \in$* **NP***, there exists an $m' + O(1)$-round zero-knowledge argument with time precision $p_t(n, y) = \mathrm{poly}(n) + O(y)$ (resp. $\mathrm{poly}(n) + \mathrm{poly}(n)O(y)$) and space precision $p_s(n, y) = \mathrm{poly}(n) + O(y)$ for L.*

Public Input: $x \in \{0, 1\}^n$ (statement to be proved is "$x \in L$").
Auxiliary Input to Prover: w, a witness for $x \in L$.

Stage 1: $V \to P$: V chooses $r_1, r_2 \in_R \{0, 1\}^n$ and sends $v_1 = f(r_1)$, $v_2 = f(r_2)$.
Then V proves to P via the WI PTSEPOK of the statement: either there exists a r_1
s.t. $v_1 = f(r_1)$ or there exists a r_2 s.t. $v_2 = f(r_2)$.

Stage 2: $P \to V$: P proves to V in the n parallel repetitions of Blum's proof that
$x \in L$ or there exists a r_1 s.t. $v_1 = f(r_1)$ or there exists a r_2 s.t. $v_2 = f(r_2)$.

Protocol 2. *The PTSSZK argument for L.*

Proof. Our protocol is shown in Protocol 2, where f is a one-way function.
Since it is an instantiation of Feige and Shamir's protocol [10], completeness
and computational soundness hold. The simulator S works in almost the same
way described in the previous proof. The difference is that what S obtains by
running E in stage 1 is r_1 or r_2 and then S uses r_1 or r_2 as a witness for the
combined statement to finish the interaction of stage 2. The desired time and
space precisions are also satisfied by using the same analysis in the previous
proof. Lastly, we know the view output by E is identical to that of stage 1 in the
real interaction, and the protocol in stage 2 is WI. Moreover, when the simulation
proceeds to stage 2, S can extract r_1 or r_2 with probability $1 - \mathsf{neg}(n)$. Then S's
output is computationally indistinguishable from the real view of V^*.   □

In the high-level proofs, many details of S are hidden in E. In next section we
will construct the required PTSEPOKs and PTSEAOKs, in which the key task
is to present all the details of E.

4   Constructions of the PTSEPOKs and PTSEAOKs

This section is devoted to the constructions of the required PTSEPOKs and
PTSEAOKs. The emphasis is the probability analysis of successful extraction of
E. (Since it is actually a partial strategy of S, E also follows the specifications
on running-space shown in Section 2). We illustrate the constructions of the
PTSEPOKs in detail and then show the PTSEAOKs can be obtained similarly.
We also show two remarks on E's extraction strategy and its comparison with
the original "cut-off" technique in [15].

Claim 3. *Assume there exist one-way functions. Then for each* **NP** *relation R
there exists an $\omega(\log^3 n)$-round WI PTSEPOK with time precision $p_t(n, y) =
poly(n) + O(y)$ and space precision $p_s(n, y) = poly(n) + O(y)$ for R.*

Proof. Instantiate the commitment scheme in Blum's proof for R with a constant-
round perfectly-binding commitment scheme. This proof is special-sound in the
sense that there is a polynomial-time algorithm, denoted Ex_R, which given the

public input x and two different valid transcripts w.r.t. a common commitment can compute a witness w for x. We call the n parallel repetitions of this proof the atomic protocol. Let (P, V) denote the $m = \omega(\log^3 n)$ sequential repetitions of the atomic protocol, in each of which P proves to V the knowledge of a witness for x. We will show (P, V) is a WI PTSEPOK with the required properties. It can be seen that completeness and soundness hold and WI is preserved. Thus we only need to construct a precise emulator-extractor E for (P, V), as the following shows.

The Construction of E. For any polynomial-sized (deterministic) P^* (we only need to consider polynomial-sized provers) and x, and for each $i \in \{1, \cdots, m\}$:

Step i.1. E adopts the honest verifier's strategy to interact with P^* in the ith atomic protocol to output the joint view (this is the first run, used to gather the joint view), and at the same time records P^*'s running-time and running-space. If P^* sends an invalid message in this atomic protocol, E halts outputting $\perp$. Otherwise let r_i denote E's challenge in this atomic protocol, v_i denote the current prover's view prior to r_i (exclusive). Let t_i denote P^*'s running-time in computing the response on receiving r_i, s_i denote (*the size* of) P^*'s running-space on view $\mathsf{v}_i \circ r_i$.

Step i.2. If the witness has not been extracted, E performs the extraction (this is the second run only for extraction). It rewinds P^* to the point where r_i is supposed to be sent, and chooses a new challenge $r_i' \in_R \{0, 1\}^n$ and sends r_i' to P^*, and recycles the space used in emulating P^* of the previous rewinds. It emulates P^* for at most $2t_i$ steps, and at the same time keeps track of P^*'s running-space on view $\mathsf{v}_i \circ r_i'$ and checks whether it is within s_i. If P^* can output a response to r_i' within $2t_i$ time and its running-space on $\mathsf{v}_i \circ r_i'$ is within s_i, E computes a witness w by running Ex_R (in the case that the response is valid and $r_i' \neq r_i$ or else E proceeds to next atomic protocol). Otherwise, E cuts off P^*'s computing and proceeds to next atomic protocol. (If $i = m$, E performs the extraction and halts outputting w if it has been extracted.)

Properties of E. Let $(\mathsf{view}_{P^*}, \mathsf{view}_V)$ be the joint view output by E. By E's strategy in the first run, we have $(\mathsf{view}_{P^*}, \mathsf{view}_V)$ is identical to the joint view in a real interaction of $(P^*, V)(x)$. Let T and S denote the running-time and running-space of P^* on view_{P^*} respectively. Hence we only need to show E has the following properties.

Running-Time. Since P^*'s running-time in the rewind of the ith atomic protocol is at most $2t_i$, $1 \leq i \leq m$, P^*'s running-time in all rewind runs is no more than $2 \cdot \sum_{i \in [1,m]} t_i < 2\mathsf{T}$. Then it takes E $O(\mathsf{T})$ time to emulate P^* in the entire simulation. Further, sending prover's messages, checking if a transcript is accepting, and extracting a witness for two accepting transcripts, can be done in a fixed polynomial time. Thus E's running-time is bounded by $\mathrm{poly}(n) + O(\mathsf{T})$.

Running-Space. First, it takes E $O(\mathsf{S})$ space to emulate P^*'s computing on view_{P^*}. Second, by the recycling strategy, it also takes E $O(\mathsf{S})$ space to emulate all P^*'s computing on $\mathsf{v}_i \circ r_i'$ for $1 \leq i \leq m$. Third, besides emulating P^*, E needs a more fixed polynomial space to carry out other computing and store the joint view. Thus E's running-space is bounded by $\mathrm{poly}(n) + O(\mathsf{S})$.

Extractable Probability. Let Accept (resp. Reject) denote the event that view_V is an accepting (resp. rejective) view. Let Suc denote the event E succeeds in extraction. Then what we need to prove is $\Pr[\mathsf{Suc}|\mathsf{Accept}] = 1 - \mathsf{neg}(n)$ if $\Pr[\mathsf{Accept}]$ is non-negligible. On the occurrence of Reject, we can regard the extraction as successful with probability 1, i.e. $\Pr[\mathsf{Suc}|\mathsf{Reject}] = 1$ (note since E is a partial strategy of S, if E's view is rejective then S terminates the simulation and the view output by S is still identical to the real view). Thus if we are able of proving $\Pr[\mathsf{Suc}] = 1 - \mathsf{neg}(n)$, $\Pr[\mathsf{Accept}]\Pr[\mathsf{Suc}|\mathsf{Accept}] + \Pr[\mathsf{Reject}]\Pr[\mathsf{Suc}|\mathsf{Reject}] = 1 - \mathsf{neg}(n)$. We have $\Pr[\mathsf{Accept}](1 - \Pr[\mathsf{Suc}|\mathsf{Accept}]) = \mathsf{neg}(n)$. Since $\Pr[\mathsf{Accept}]$ is non-negligible, $\Pr[\mathsf{Suc}|\mathsf{Accept}] = 1 - \frac{\mathsf{neg}(n)}{\Pr[\mathsf{Accept}]} = 1 - \mathsf{neg}(n)$. Consequently, to prove $\Pr[\mathsf{Suc}|\mathsf{Accept}] = 1 - \mathsf{neg}(n)$, we only need to show $\Pr[\mathsf{Suc}] = 1 - \mathsf{neg}(n)$. Actually, this is true, ensured by Claim 4. The claim follows.   □

Before proceeding to Claim 4, we show two remarks on E's extraction strategy and its comparison with the original "cut-off" technique in [15]. If we modify E by only requiring it cuts off P^*'s computing in the second run of each atomic protocol iff P^* cannot output a response to r_i' within t_i time, then this is the original "cut-off" technique. Notice that there are two differences between it and the extraction strategy herein. The main difference is that E herein uses the "cut-off" technique by simultaneously considering P^*'s running-time and running-space instead of P^*'s running-time alone. Another difference is that E herein allows P^* to run $2t_i$ time at most in the second run instead of t_i time. In Remark 3, we show the original "cut-off" technique cannot obtain simultaneous meaningful time and space precisions. In Remark 4, we show the time for P^* to run in the second run cannot be reduced to t_i (if we require that the space for it to run is at most s_i). That is, it is necessary for E to allow P^* to run t_i times a factor (e.g. 2) steps in the second run.

Remark 3. We now show if E adopts the original "cut-off" technique, although it can of course obtain linear time precision it cannot obtain any meaningful space precision. To this end we need to show for any meaningful $p_s(n, y)$ there exists a P^* satisfying E's running-space is more than $p_s(n, \mathsf{S})$ with non-zero probability even if m can be any arbitrary polynomial. (Actually, we can show a stronger negative result that there exists a P^* satisfying E's running-space is more than $p_s(n, \mathsf{S})$ with non-negligible probability.)

First consider a prover P' defined below. P' proceeds just as the honest prover P, except that P' receives a random 2-wise independent hash function $h : \{0, 1\}^n \rightarrow \{0, 1\}^n$ as the auxiliary input. Let $Q(n)$ be a polynomial bound on the running-space of P. Then in the 1st atomic protocol on receiving a challenge (r_1 or r_1') P' applies h to this challenge and generates a random string a. If the first $\log n$ bits of a are not zeros, P' executes some instructions to consume $p_s(n, Q(n))^2$ more space. Otherwise, it also executes some dummy instructions to consume the same time but no more space. Then, it proceeds to do what P would on a challenge and also executes some instructions (which don't consume any more space), if needed, to adjust its running-time in this step to be same in answering different challenges. In all the residual atomic protocols, P' behaves identically to P.

In the 1st atomic protocol, since P'''s running-time on different challenges are always identical, there is no possibility for E to cut off P'''s computing in the second run and thus the extraction always succeeds in case of $r_1 \neq r_1'$. However, it can be seen the event that P'''s running-space on view $v_1 \circ r_1$ is less than $Q(n)$ and its running-space on view $v_1 \circ r_1'$ is at least $p_s(n, Q(n))^2$ occurs with probability $\frac{1}{n}(1 - \frac{1}{n})$. Thus E's running-space is more than $p_s(n, S)$ with probability at least $\frac{1}{n}(1 - \frac{1}{n})$. By an averaging argument, there exists at least one auxiliary input $z = h$ resulting in the event occurs with that probability. Let P^* be P' having z hardwired and then P^* is the desired one.

Remark 4. Now we show the factor (i.e. 2) for t_i in E's strategy in the second run cannot be eliminated. That is, we show if we bound the time and space for a prover to run in the second run are respectively t_i and s_i, then there exists a P^* such that E fails in extraction with non-negligible probability even if m can be any arbitrary polynomial.

Consider a prover P^* defined below. P^* proceeds just as P, except that the following differences. According to P^*'s running-time and running-space, all the $N = 2^n$ challenges in $\{0,1\}^n$ can be divided into $n^{co} > m$ disjoint classes, ordered in an arbitrary way, each of which has $\frac{N}{n^{co}}$ challenges, such that for $1 \leq i \leq m$ when executing the ith atomic protocol (the view prior to this atomic protocol is then fixed): 1. besides doing what P would, P^* also executes some instructions to ensure its running-time (resp. running-space) on any of the challenges (resp. the generated view concatenated with any of the challenges) from the same class are identical; 2. if denote by $t_i^{(j)}$ (resp. $s_i^{(j)}$) P^*'s running-time (resp. running-space) on any challenge (resp. the generated view concatenated with any challenge) from the jth class, then $t_i^{(1)} < t_i^{(2)} < \cdots < t_i^{(n^{co})}$ but $s_i^{(1)} > s_i^{(2)} > \cdots > s_i^{(n^{co})}$.

Hence for each i a sufficient condition for the extraction to fail in the ith atomic protocol is that r_i and r_i' are chosen from two different classes, which occurs with probability $n^{co} \cdot \frac{1}{n^{co}} \cdot (1 - \frac{1}{n^{co}}) = 1 - \frac{1}{n^{co}}$. Thus the extraction fails in all the m atomic protocols with probability at least $(1 - \frac{1}{n^{co}})^m = O((\frac{1}{e})^{m/n^{co}}) > c'$ for a constant $0 < c' < 1$.

Claim 4. *The E described in the proof of Claim 3 succeeds in extraction with probability $1 - \mathsf{neg}(n)$.*

Proof. If there exists an i satisfying that the extraction always succeeds in the first i atomic protocols for all outcomes of E's coins used in the first and second runs of these protocols, the claim of course holds. Thus in the following we prove this claim by assuming for all i's there are some outcomes of the E's coins resulting in the extraction fails in the first i atomic protocols.

Fix any outcome of such E's coins that result in the extraction fails in the first $i - 1$ atomic protocols. Let us analyze the probability of successful extraction in the ith atomic protocol. We will present a uniform lower bound for this probability when further fixing any outcome of E's coins used in this atomic protocol before sending the challenge (r_i). (Thus view v_i is determined.) In the case P^* outputs an invalid message on view v_i, the probability of successful extraction is 1. Thus we only need to consider the case the extraction can reach the step E sends the challenge as follows.

We first (re)highlight some crucial random variables. Let r_i (resp. r_i') denote the random challenge in $\{0,1\}^n$ sent to P^* in the first (resp. second) run. Let t_i (resp. t_i') denote P^*'s running-time in answering r_i (resp. r_i') in the first (resp. second) run. Let s_i (resp. s_i') denote (the size of) P^*'s running-space on view $v_i \circ r_i$ (resp. $v_i \circ r_i'$). Since coins E uses are independent, we have that r_i and r_i' are independently identically distributed (i.i.d.), t_i and t_i' are i.i.d., s_i and s_i' are i.i.d..

If P^* outputs a valid response to r_i in the first run, a necessary and sufficient condition for the extraction to succeed is that $s_i' \leq s_i, t_i' \leq 2t_i, r_i \neq r_i'$ and P^* can output a valid response to r_i' in the second run. Otherwise, the extraction is regarded as successful. If we set t_i, s_i (resp. t_i', s_i') the values that are respectively greater than 2 times P^*'s maximal running-time and P^*'s maximal running-space when P^* outputs an invalid response in the first (resp. second) run, then in the former case the necessary and sufficient condition can be reduced to $s_i' \leq s_i, t_i' \leq 2t_i, r_i \neq r_i'$ and in the latter case $s_i' \leq s_i, t_i' \leq 2t_i$ can be satisfied too. This means $s_i' \leq s_i, t_i' \leq 2t_i, r_i \neq r_i'$ can be used as a uniform sufficient condition for the extraction to succeed.

Thus assuming P^*'s running-time and running-space are bounded by $\frac{1}{4}n^c - 1$ for some non-predetermined constant $c > 0$ and for sufficiently large n's (the coefficients $\frac{1}{4}$ and -1 were chosen only for notational convenience), we set $t_i = \frac{1}{2}n^c - 1$ and $s_i = \frac{1}{4}n^c$ (resp. $t_i' = \frac{1}{2}n^c - 1$ and $s_i' = \frac{1}{4}n^c$) if P^* outputs an invalid response in the first (resp. second) run. Hence, by the analysis in the above paragraph, the probability the extraction succeeds is at least $\Pr[s_i' \leq s_i, t_i' \leq 2t_i, r_i \neq r_i']$. Thus, our main task in this proof is to present a lower bound for this probability.

Since $\Pr[s_i' \leq s_i, t_i' \leq 2t_i, r_i \neq r_i'] \geq 1 - \Pr[s_i' > s_i] - \Pr[t_i' > 2t_i] - \Pr[r_i = r_i']$, and $\Pr[r_i = r_i'] = 2^{-n}$, we only need to evaluate $\Pr[s_i' > s_i]$ and $\Pr[t_i' > 2t_i]$.

It follows from the symmetry property that $\Pr[s_i' < s_i] = \Pr[s_i < s_i']$. Since $\Pr[s_i' < s_i] + \Pr[s_i < s_i'] + \Pr[s_i = s_i'] = 1$, we have $2 \cdot \Pr[s_i' > s_i] < 1$. Thus, $\Pr[s_i' > s_i] < \frac{1}{2}$. For the same reason, $\Pr[t_i' < t_i] = \frac{1}{2} - \frac{1}{2}\Pr[t_i = t_i']$, $\Pr[t_i' \leq t_i] = \frac{1}{2} + \frac{1}{2}\Pr[t_i = t_i']$.

Let $\delta(n) = (\frac{1}{m})^{1/3}$. ($m(n) = \omega(\log^3 n)$, shown in the proof of Claim 3.) Then $\delta(n) = \frac{1}{\omega(\log n)}$. In the following we divide the evaluation of $\Pr[t_i' \leq 2t_i]$ and $\Pr[s_i' \leq s_i, t_i' \leq 2t_i, r_i \neq r_i']$ into two cases. Before proceeding we first define some notations and variables.

Notations and Variables. We define the following notations and variables.
(1) We use $t(u)$ to denote the value of t_i when the challenge to P^* is $u \in \{0,1\}^n$ in the first run. (Equivalently, $t(u)$ is the value of t_i' when the challenge to P^* is u in the second run.) We order the $N = 2^n$ challenges in $\{0,1\}^n$ as $u_1, u_2, \cdots, u_N$ in an arbitrary way only if this order satisfies $t(u_1) \leq t(u_2) \leq \cdots \leq t(u_N)$. We also write $u_1 < u_2 < \cdots < u_N$ by this order, and say u_1 is less than u_2, u_2 is

less than u_3 and so on. Then when we say "choose the minimal challenge from set $U \subset \{0,1\}^n$, denoted u" we mean the chosen $u \in U$ is less than any one in $U - \{u\}$. For simplicity, let a_k denote $t(u_k)$, $1 \le k \le N$. (a_k's may not be mutually different and $1 \le a_k < \frac{1}{2}n^c$ for each k.)

(2) For each u_k, we define a set A_k corresponding to u_k as $A_k \overset{\text{def}}{=} \{u \in \{0,1\}^n : a_k \le t(u) \le 2a_k\}$.

(3) For each u_k, we define N_k as the cardinal number of the set $\{u \in \{0,1\}^n : t(u) = a_k\}$. It is clear that $|A_k| \ge N_k$ for each k.

Case 1. Assume there is a k_0 satisfying $\frac{N_{k_0}}{N} \ge \delta(n)$. Let $B \overset{\text{def}}{=} \{k \in [1, N] : t(u_k) = a_{k_0}\}$. Then $N_{k_0} = |B| = N_k$ for each $k \in B$. Since r_i is independent of t'_i, $\Pr[t_i = t'_i] = \sum\limits_{k \in [1, N]} \Pr[r_i = u_k, t'_i = a_k] \ge \sum\limits_{k \in B} \Pr[r_i = u_k, t'_i = a_k] = \sum\limits_{k \in B} \frac{1}{N} \cdot$
$\frac{N_{k_0}}{N} = \frac{N_{k_0}}{N} \frac{N_{k_0}}{N} \ge \delta^2$.

Thus, $\Pr[t'_i \le 2t_i] \ge \Pr[t'_i \le t_i] = \frac{1}{2} + \frac{1}{2}\Pr[t_i = t'_i] \ge \frac{1}{2} + \frac{1}{2}\delta^2$. Then $\Pr[t'_i > 2t_i] \le \frac{1}{2} - \frac{1}{2}\delta^2$. Hence, $\Pr[s'_i \le s_i, t'_i \le 2t_i, r_i \ne r'_i] > 1 - \frac{1}{2} - (\frac{1}{2} - \frac{1}{2}\delta^2) - 2^{-n} = \frac{1}{2}\delta^2 - 2^{-n}$.

Case 2. Assume $\frac{N_k}{N} < \delta(n)$ for all k's. Since $\Pr[t'_i \le 2t_i] = \Pr[t'_i < t_i] + \Pr[t_i \le t'_i \le 2t_i] = \frac{1}{2}(1 - \Pr[t_i = t'_i]) + \Pr[t_i \le t'_i \le 2t_i]$, to evaluate $\Pr[t'_i \le 2t_i]$ we first compute $\Pr[t_i \le t'_i \le 2t_i]$, which is actually the main part of this case.

Our fundamental approach to computing $\Pr[t_i \le t'_i \le 2t_i]$ is that we construct a decomposition $\{D_1, \cdots, D_H\}$ of the sample space for some integer $H > 0$, and compute $\Pr[t_i \le t'_i \le 2t_i | D_h]$ for $1 \le h \le H$ and then apply the formula of total probability to evaluate $\Pr[t_i \le t'_i \le 2t_i]$. Thus, in the following we will show how to construct the desired decomposition and compute the conditional probabilities.

We first show what D_1 is. Choose the minimal challenge from $\{0,1\}^n$, denoted $u_{k_{11}}$, $1 \le k_{11} \le N$. ($k_{11} = 1$ actually.) If $A_{k_{11}}$ doesn't contain $\{0,1\}^n$, then choose the minimal challenge from $\{0,1\}^n - A_{k_{11}}$, denoted $u_{k_{12}}$, $1 \le k_{12} \le N$. If $A_{k_{11}} + A_{k_{12}}$ (note that $A_{k_{11}} \cap A_{k_{12}} = \phi$) still doesn't contain $\{0,1\}^n$, continue to choose the minimal challenge from $\{0,1\}^n - A_{k_{11}} - A_{k_{12}}$, denoted $u_{k_{13}}$, $1 \le k_{13} \le N$, and proceed. Since $\{0,1\}^n$ is finite, using this selection method we can finally obtain a sequence of challenges $\{u_{k_{11}}, \cdots, u_{k_{1d_1}}\}$ for some $d_1 > 0$, satisfying $\sum\limits_{j \in [1,d_1]} A_{k_{1j}} = \{0,1\}^n$ (note that $A_{k_{1j}}$'s are disjoint). Let D_1 denote the event of $r_i \in \{u_{k_{11}}, \cdots, u_{k_{1d_1}}\}$, D_1^* denote $\{u_{k_{11}}, \cdots, u_{k_{1d_1}}\}$.

Let us evaluate the value of d_1. Since $a_1, \cdots, a_N$ are bounded by $\frac{1}{2}n^c$, and $a_{k_{11}} < 2a_{k_{11}} < a_{k_{12}} < 2a_{k_{12}} < \cdots < a_{k_{1d_1}} < 2a_{k_{1d_1}}$, we have $a_{k_{11}} \cdot 2^{d_1 - 1} < a_{k_{1d_1}} < \frac{1}{2}n^c$. Hence $d_1 < c\log n$. Further, as $\sum\limits_{j \in [1,d_1]} A_{k_{1j}} = \{0,1\}^n$, there is a K_1, $1 \le K_1 \le d_1$, satisfying $|A_{k_{1K_1}}| \ge \max[\frac{N}{d_1}, N_{k_{1K_1}}]$. Then,

$$\Pr[t_i \leq t'_i \leq 2t_i | D_1] = \frac{1}{\Pr[D_1]} \Pr[t_i \leq t'_i \leq 2t_i, D_1]$$

$$= \frac{1}{\Pr[D_1]} \sum_{j \in [1, \, d_1]} \Pr[r_i = u_{k_{1j}}, a_{k_{1j}} \leq t'_i \leq 2a_{k_{1j}}]$$

$$= \frac{1}{\Pr[D_1]} \sum_{j \in [1, \, d_1]} \Pr[r_i = u_{k_{1j}}] \cdot \Pr[a_{k_{1j}} \leq t'_i \leq 2a_{k_{1j}}]$$

$$= \sum_{j \in [1, \, d_1]} \Pr[r_i = u_{k_{1j}} | D_1] \cdot \Pr[a_{k_{1j}} \leq t'_i \leq 2a_{k_{1j}}]$$

$$\geq \sum_{j \in [1, \, d_1] - \{K_1\}} \frac{1}{d_1} \frac{N_{k_{1j}}}{N} + \frac{1}{d_1 N} \max[\frac{N}{d_1}, N_{k_1 K_1}]$$

$$= \sum_{j \in [1, \, d_1]} \frac{1}{d_1} \frac{N_{k_{1j}}}{N} + \frac{1}{d_1 N} \max[\frac{N}{d_1} - N_{k_1 K_1}, 0]$$

If D_1 equals the sample space, the decomposition has only one element D_1. Otherwise, we need to construct D_2 by using the similar way in constructing D_1. Choose the minimal challenge from $\{0,1\}^n - D_1^*$, denoted $u_{k_{21}}$, $1 \leq k_{21} \leq N$. If $A_{k_{21}}$ doesn't contain $\{0,1\}^n - D_1^*$, then choose the minimal challenge from $\{0,1\}^n - D_1^* - A_{k_{21}}$, denoted $u_{k_{22}}$, $1 \leq k_{22} \leq N$. If $A_{k_{21}} + A_{k_{22}}$ still doesn't contain $\{0,1\}^n - D_1^*$, continue this selection. Finally, using this selection method we obtain a sequence of challenges $\{u_{k_{21}}, \cdots, u_{k_{2d_2}}\}$ for some $d_2 > 0$ satisfying $\sum_{j \in [1, d_2]} A_{k_{2j}}$ contains $\{0,1\}^n - D_1^*$. Let D_2 denote the event of $r_i \in \{u_{k_{21}}, \cdots, u_{k_{2d_2}}\}$, D_2^* denote $\{u_{k_{21}}, \cdots, u_{k_{2d_2}}\}$. Similarly, we have $d_2 < c \log n$.

As $\sum_{j \in [1, d_2]} A_{k_{2j}} \supset \{0,1\}^n - D_1^*$ and $|D_1^*| = d_1$, there is a K_2, $1 \leq K_2 \leq d_2$, satisfying $|A_{k_2 K_2}| \geq \max[\frac{N - d_1}{d_2}, N_{k_2 K_2}]$. Then in the same way,

$$\Pr[t_i \leq t'_i \leq 2t_i | D_2] = \sum_{j \in [1, \, d_2]} \Pr[r_i = u_{k_{2j}} | D_2] \cdot \Pr[a_{k_{2j}} \leq t'_i \leq 2a_{k_{2j}}]$$

$$\geq \sum_{j \in [1, \, d_2]} \frac{1}{d_2} \frac{N_{k_{2j}}}{N} + \frac{1}{d_2 N} \max[\frac{N - d_1}{d_2} - N_{k_2 K_2}, 0]$$

We now turn to describe the general case. Assume we have constructed $D_1 \cdots$, D_{h-1} for some $h > 0$. If $D_1 + \cdots + D_{h-1}$ equals the sample space, the decomposition is $\{D_1 \cdots, D_{h-1}\}$. Otherwise, we need to construct D_h. Using the same selection method, we can select a sequence of challenges $\{u_{k_{h1}}, \cdots, u_{k_{hd_h}}\}$ for some $d_h > 0$, $1 \leq k_{h1}, \cdots, k_{hd_h} \leq N$, satisfying $\sum_{j \in [1, d_h]} A_{k_{hj}}$ contains $\{0,1\}^n - D_1^* - \cdots - D_{h-1}^*$. Let D_h denote the event of $r_i \in \{u_{k_{h1}}, \cdots, u_{k_{hd_h}}\}$, D_h^* denote $\{u_{k_{h1}}, \cdots, u_{k_{hd_h}}\}$. Similarly, we have $d_h < c \log n$.

As $\sum_{j \in [1, d_h]} A_{k_{hj}} \supset \{0,1\}^n - D_1^* - \cdots - D_{h-1}^*$, there is a K_h, $1 \leq K_h \leq d_h$, satisfying $|A_{k_h K_h}| \geq \max[\frac{N - d_1 - \cdots - d_{h-1}}{d_h}, N_{k_h K_h}]$. Thus,

$$\Pr[t_i \leq t'_i \leq 2t_i | D_h] = \sum_{j \in [1, d_h]} \Pr[r_i = u_{k_{hj}} | D_h] \cdot \Pr[a_{k_{hj}} \leq t'_i \leq 2a_{k_{hj}}]$$

$$\geq \sum_{j \in [1, d_h]} \frac{1}{d_h} \frac{N_{k_{hj}}}{N} + \frac{1}{d_h N} \max[\frac{N - d_1 - \cdots - d_{h-1}}{d_h} - N_{k_{hK_h}}, 0]$$

Since the sample space is finite, the construction of the decomposition will halt certainly. Namely, there is a number H satisfying $\sum_{h \in [1, H]} D_h$ contains the sample space. Thus the desired decomposition is $\{D_1, \cdots, D_H\}$. It can be seen $\{D_1^*, \cdots, D_H^*\}$ is actually a decomposition of $\{0, 1\}^n$, which shows k_{hj}'s for all $1 \leq h \leq H, 1 \leq j \leq d_h$ are a permutation of $1, \cdots, N$. Consequently, by the formula of total probability,

$$\Pr[t_i \leq t'_i \leq 2t_i] = \sum_{h \in [1, H]} \Pr[D_h] \cdot \Pr[t_i \leq t'_i \leq 2t_i | D_h]$$

$$\geq \sum_{h \in [1, H]} \frac{d_h}{N} \cdot \{ \sum_{j \in [1, d_h]} \frac{1}{d_h} \frac{N_{k_{hj}}}{N} + \frac{1}{d_h N} \max[\frac{N - d_1 - \cdots - d_{h-1}}{d_h} - N_{k_{hk_h}}, 0] \}$$

$$= \sum_{h \in [1, H]} \sum_{j \in [1, d_h]} \frac{N_{k_{hj}}}{N^2} + \sum_{h \in [1, H]} \frac{1}{N^2} \max[\frac{N - d_1 - \cdots - d_{h-1}}{d_h} - N_{k_{hK_h}}, 0]$$

$$= \sum_{k \in [1, N]} \frac{N_k}{N^2} + \sum_{h \in [1, H]} \frac{1}{N^2} \max[\frac{N - d_1 - \cdots - d_{h-1}}{d_h} - N_{k_{hK_h}}, 0]$$

$$= \Pr[t_i = t'_i] + \sum_{h \in [1, H]} \frac{1}{N^2 d_h} \max[N - d_1 - \cdots - d_{h-1} - N_{k_{hK_h}} d_h, 0]$$

In the last step of the above formula, we use the fact $\sum_{k \in [1, N]} \frac{N_k}{N^2} = \Pr[t_i = t'_i]$. This is so because $\Pr[t_i = t'_i] = \sum_{k \in [1, N]} \Pr[r_i = u_k, t'_i = a_k] = \sum_{k \in [1, N]} \Pr[r_i = u_k]$ $\cdot \Pr[t'_i = a_k] = \sum_{k \in [1, N]} \frac{N_k}{N^2}$. Now let us evaluate the second item at the right hand of the last equal sign in the above formula. Since $N_{k_{hK_h}} < \delta N$ (by the assumption of Case 2), $N_{k_{hK_h}} d_h < \delta d_h N < c\delta \log nN$. Let γ denote $c\delta \log n$ and then $\gamma(n) = o(1)$. Then $N_{k_{hK_h}} d_h < \gamma N$ for $1 \leq h \leq H$. Thus (for sufficiently large n's),

$$\text{The second item} = \sum_{h \in [1, H]} \frac{1}{N^2 d_h} \cdot \max[N - d_1 - \cdots - d_{h-1} - N_{k_{hK_h}} d_h, 0]$$

$$> \frac{1}{N^2 c \log n} \cdot \sum_{h \in [1, H]} \max[N - d_1 - \cdots - d_{h-1} - \gamma N, 0]$$

$$> \frac{1}{N^2 c \log n} \cdot \sum_{h \in [1, H]} \max[(1 - \gamma)N - (h - 1)c \log n, 0]$$

Denote by H' the largest integer satisfying $(1-\gamma)N - (h-1)c\log n \geq 0$ for $1 \leq h \leq H'$. Then $H' = \lfloor \frac{1-\gamma}{c\log n} N \rfloor + 1$. Thus (for sufficiently large n's),

$$\text{The second item} > \frac{1}{N^2 c\log n} \cdot \sum_{h\in[1,\,H']} \{(1-\gamma)N - (h-1)c\log n\} > \frac{1}{N^2 c\log n} \cdot$$

$$\frac{(1-\gamma)^2}{c\log n} N^2 - \frac{1}{N^2 c\log n} \sum_{h\in[1,\,H']} (h-1)c\log n = \frac{(1-\gamma)^2}{(c\log n)^2} - \frac{1}{N^2} \frac{H'(H'-1)}{2}$$

$$\geq \frac{(1-\gamma)^2}{(c\log n)^2} - \frac{1}{2N^2}\{\frac{(1-\gamma)^2 N^2}{(c\log n)^2} + \frac{1-\gamma}{c\log nN}\} = \frac{1}{2}\frac{(1-\gamma)^2}{(c\log n)^2} - \frac{1-\gamma}{2N^3 c\log n}$$

$$> \frac{1}{4c^2 \log^2 n} > \delta^2$$

Thus, $\Pr[t_i \leq t_i' \leq 2t_i] > \Pr[t_i = t_i'] + \delta^2$. Consequently, $\Pr[t_i' \leq 2t_i] = \Pr[t_i' < t_i] + \Pr[t_i \leq t_i' \leq 2t_i] > \frac{1}{2}(1 - \Pr[t_i = t_i']) + \Pr[t_i = t_i'] + \delta^2 = \frac{1}{2} + \frac{1}{2}\Pr[t_i = t_i'] + \delta^2 > \frac{1}{2} + \delta^2$.

Then $\Pr[t_i' > 2t_i] < \frac{1}{2} - \delta^2$. Hence in Case 2, $\Pr[s_i' \leq s_i, t_i' \leq 2t_i, r_i \neq r_i'] > 1 - \frac{1}{2} - (\frac{1}{2} - \delta^2) - 2^{-n} = \delta^2 - 2^{-n}$.

Combining the results of Cases 1 and 2 (and the case the extraction cannot reach the step E sends r_i), we conclude that for any outcome of E's coins used in the ith atomic protocol prior to r_i the extraction succeeds with probability at least $\frac{1}{2}\delta^2 - 2^{-n}$. This means the extraction succeeds in this atomic protocol with probability at least $\frac{1}{2}\delta^2 - 2^{-n}$. Namely, the extraction fails with probability at most $1 - \frac{1}{2}\delta^2 + 2^{-n}$. It follows from $m = \frac{1}{\delta^3}$ that the extraction fails in all atomic protocols with probability at most $(1 - \frac{1}{2}\delta^2 + 2^{-n})^m = O(e^{-1/(2\delta)}) = \mathsf{neg}(n)$. $\square$

Claim 5. *Assume there exist one-way functions. Then for each* **NP** *relation R there exists an $\omega(\log n)$-round WI PTSEPOK with time precision $poly(n)+O(ny)$ and space precision $poly(n) + O(y)$ for R.*

Proof. The proof can be referred to the full version of this paper [7]. $\square$

Claim 6. *Assume there exist constant-round perfectly-hiding commitments. Then for each* **NP** *relation R there exists an $\omega(\log^3 n)$-round (resp. $\omega(\log n)$-round) perfectly WI PTSEAOK with time precision $poly(n)+O(y)$ (resp. $poly(n)+O(ny)$) and space precision $poly(n) + O(y)$ for R.*

Proof. Instantiate the commitment scheme in Blum's proof for R with a constant-round perfectly-hiding commitment scheme. Then using the proofs of Claim 3, Claim 4 and Claim 5, we infer this claim holds. Details are omitted. $\square$

Combining Claim 6 with Claim 1, we have Theorem 1 follows. Combining Claim 3 and Claim 5 with Claim 2, we have Theorem 2 follows.

Acknowledgments. This work is supported by China Postdoctoral Science Foundation funded project (20100480595), Shanghai Postdoctoral Scientific

Program (11R21414500) and Major Program of Shanghai Science and Technology Commission (10DZ1500200). Thanks to the anonymous reviewers of ProvSec 2011 for their useful comments and suggestions.

References

1. Barak, B.: How to go beyond the black-box simulation barrier. In: Proc. 42nd FOCS, pp. 106–115. IEEE, Los Alamitos (2001)
2. Bellare, M., Goldreich, O.: On defining proofs of knowledge. In: Brickell, E.F. (ed.) CRYPTO 1992. LNCS, vol. 740, pp. 390–420. Springer, Heidelberg (1993)
3. Blum, M.: Coin flipping by phone. In: Proc. 24th Computer Conference, pp. 133–137. IEEE, Los Alamitos (1982)
4. Blum, M.: How to prove a theorem so no one else can claim it. In: Proc. the International Congress of Mathematicians, Berkeley, California, USA, pp. 1444–1451 (1986)
5. Brassard, G., Chaum, D., Crépeau, C.: Minimum disclosure proofs of knowledge. J. Comput. Syst. Sci. 37(2), 156–189 (1988)
6. Damgård, I., Pedersen, T., Pfitzmann, B.: On the existence of statistically hiding bit commitment schemes and fail-stop sigantures. In: Stinson, D.R. (ed.) CRYPTO 1993. LNCS, vol. 773, pp. 250–265. Springer, Heidelberg (1994)
7. Ding, N., Gu, D.: Precise time and space simulatable zero-knowledge (2009), http://eprint.iacr.org/2009/429
8. Feige, U., Fiat, A., Shamir, A.: Zero-knowledge proofs of identity. Journal of Cryptology 1(2), 77–94 (1988)
9. Feige, U., Shamir, A.: Witness indistinguishability and witness hiding protocols. In: Proc. 22nd STOC, pp. 416–426. ACM, New York (1990)
10. Feige, U., Shamir, A.: Zero knowledge proofs of knowledge in two rounds. In: Brassard, G. (ed.) CRYPTO 1989. LNCS, vol. 435, pp. 526–544. Springer, Heidelberg (1990)
11. Goldreich, O.: Foundations of cryptography - basic tools. Cambridge University Press, Cambridge (2001)
12. Goldwasser, S., Micali, S., Rackoff, C.: The knowledge complexity of interactive proof-systems. In: Proc. 17th STOC, pp. 291–304. ACM, New York (1985)
13. Micali, S., Pass, R.: Local zero knowledge. In: Proc. 38th STOC, pp. 306–315. ACM, New York (2006)
14. Naor, M., Yung, M.: Universal one-way hash functions and their cryptographic applications. In: Proc. 21st STOC, pp. 33–43. ACM, New York (1989)
15. Pass, R.: A precise computational approach to knowledge. Dissertation for the Doctoral Degree. MIT, Cambridge (2006)
16. Tompa, M., Woll, H.: Random self-reducibility and zero-knowledge interactive proofs of possession of information. In: Proc. 28th FOCS, pp. 472–482. IEEE, Los Alamitos (1987)

Weak Oblivious Transfer from Strong One-Way Functions

Keisuke Tanaka, Akihiro Yamada, and Kenji Yasunaga

Tokyo Institute of Technology

Abstract. We consider weak oblivious transfer (OT) from strong one-way functions and the paradigm of transforming unconditionally secure protocols in Maurer's bounded storage model into computational secure protocols in the random oracle model. Weak OT is secure against adversaries which have a quadratic resource gap to honest parties. We prove that the random oracle can be replaced with strong one-way functions in the OT protocol. We construct an OT protocol achieving quadratic security from strong one-way functions.

1 Introduction

In modern cryptography, it is important to prove that constructed primitives and protocols are secure. Reduction to computational assumptions is one of the general methods to prove that the primitives and the protocols are secure. For some cryptographic primitives (e.g. private key encryption, pseudo-random generators, bit commitment), several ways of the reduction to weak assumptions are known.

Oblivious transfer (OT) is one of the fundamental cryptographic primitives. OT was first introduced by Rabin [22] and their variations have been studied in several works [24][18][11]. In this paper, we consider the one-out-of-two variant of OT proposed by Even, Goldreich, and Lempel [7], which is shown to be equivalent to Rabin's OT by Crépeau [5] and more useful. The one-out-of-two OT is a protocol between two players: a sender (Alice and a receiver (Bob). Alice has two secrets s_0 and s_1, and Bob has a choice bit c. Bob wishes to receive one out of the two secrets that he chooses (i.e., s_c) without Alice learning c, while Alice wants to ensure that Bob receives only one of the two secrets. OT can be applied to a wide variety of protocols [18][8]. In particular, secure multi-party computation can be based on the security of OT. The constructions of OT require some computational assumptions such as the difficulty of factoring numbers, computing discrete logarithms, and the existence of enhanced trapdoor permutations [22][21][7].

The weakest assumption that is commonly used in cryptography is the existence of one-way functions. If such functions do not exist, any private/public primitives do not exist [15]. Furthermore, the existence of OT cannot be reduced to that of one-way permutations in black-box constructions [16][23]. Therefore, we consider a weaker variant of OT based on one-way functions.

We study the case in which there exists a quadratic gap between the computational resources of honest parties and the adversary. The security achieved in such a setting is called *quadratic security*. In the standard setting, the gap between the computational resources should be super-polynomial. We here describe the quadratic security

X. Boyen and X. Chen (Eds.): ProvSec 2011, LNCS 6980, pp. 34–51, 2011.
© Springer-Verlag Berlin Heidelberg 2011

using a key-exchange protocol as an example. In a key-exchange protocol, the two honest parties exchange messages and share a common secret key. The standard security guarantees that any adversary that can obtain the secret key needs to compute in super-polynomial time. Since the time complexity of the honest parties is bounded by some polynomial, there is a super-polynomial gap between the computational resources of the honest parties and the adversary. In the quadratic security, if the honest parties can share the secret key in some polynomial time T, then any adversary needs to compute in at least T^2 time to obtain the secret key. Thus, there is a quadratic gap between the computational resources of the honest parties and the adversary rather than a super-polynomial gap.

A key-exchange protocol with quadratic security has been studied by Biham, Goren, and Ishai [2]. They proposed a protocol based on strong one-way functions. Barak and Mahmoody-Ghidary [1] showed that the quadratic gap of the key-exchange protocol in the random oracle model is optimal. Therefore, it is significant to study cryptographic protocols with quadratic security.

1.1 Our Contribution

We present a construction of an OT protocol with quadratic security from a strong one-way function. In our protocol, we use an exponentially strong one-way function. Note that we do not require any trapdoor for one-way functions. The key-exchange protocol presented in [2] also uses such strong one-way functions. Our OT protocol can send an $O(\log k)$-bit secret, where k is the security parameter. We note that our OT protocols only achieve quadratic security for adversary Bob, but they achieve perfect security for adversary Alice. A corresponding situation can make the protocol appealing for situation where Alice is run on a powerful server and Bob is run on a mobile device.

We consider a malicious adversary rather than semi-honest one. In the standard setting, which requires a super-polynomial gap, a malicious OT can be constructed from a semi-honest OT in a black-box way [17][14]. However, a loss of efficiency in the construction is a very sensitive problem in the setting of quadratic security. Therefore, in this paper, we directly construct a malicious OT protocol.

Our protocol is based on Merkle's puzzles [20], the OT protocol in the bounded storage model [6], a standard error-correcting technique, and the paradigm of transforming an unconditionally secure protocol in the bounded storage model into a computationally secure protocol based on strong one-way functions.

A similar transformation was presented for key-exchange protocols [2], and we consider an application of this transformation to OT. First we construct an OT protocol in the random oracle model based on that in the bounded storage model [6]. Second, we replace the random oracle with a strong one-way permutation. Finally, we construct an OT protocol with quadratic security based on strong one-way functions. One problem in replacing a one-way permutation with one-way functions is that one-way functions do not have the 1-to-1 property. Thus, one might consider that we could apply the same technique as in [2] to our protocol. However, it does not work for OT in a simple way. The reason stems from the fact that one of the two parties, Alice and Bob, in the OT protocol can be an adversary. This situation is different from a key-exchange protocol, in which Alice and Bob are always honest, and the adversary is a third party other than them. In addition, we need to consider a malicious adversary rather than semi-honest one. If we apply the technique in [2] to OT protocols in a straightforward way, then a malicious adversary Bob can obtain both of the two secrets that Alice holds, and this breaks the security of OT. Therefore, in order to circumvent this problem, we use an error-correcting technique to our OT protocol. Due to this technique, our OT protocol achieves the desired functionality and security.

2   Preliminaries

For an integer n, we denote by $[n]$ the set $\{1, \ldots, n\}$. We denote by U_n the uniform distribution over $\{0, 1\}^n$. For $\ell \leq n$, we write $\binom{[n]}{\ell}$ to denote the set of all subsets $T \subseteq [n]$ with $|T| = \ell$. We write $f(n) = \tilde{O}(g(n))$ if there exists some constant c such that $f(n) = O(g(n) \log^c(g(n)))$. An algorithm is called $T(n)$-*bounded* if the running time on n-bit input is upper bounded by $T(n)$. A function $\epsilon(n)$ is called *negligible* if for any constant $c > 0$, $\epsilon(n) < 1/n^c$ for sufficiently large n. We denote by $\text{negl}(n)$ some negligible function in n. We write $p = \text{poly}(n)$ if $p(\cdot)$ is some polynomial in n. We say that ϵ is *bounded away from* c if $\epsilon(n) \leq c - 1/p(n)$ for some polynomial p for sufficiently large n. We write $x \circ y$ to denote the concatenation operation of x and y.

2.1   Encoding Subsets, Min-Entropy and Strong Extractor

We encode sets into binary strings in the protocols. The following methods are used in [3] and [6]. Using Lemma 1, we can encode $\binom{[n]}{\ell}$ by binary strings of length $\lceil \log \binom{n}{\ell} \rceil$.

Lemma 1 ([4]). *For every integer $\ell \leq n$ there is a 1-to-1 mapping $E : \binom{[n]}{\ell} \to \left[\binom{n}{\ell}\right]$ such that both E and E^{-1} can be computed in time polynomial in n.*

Definition 1 (Dense encoding of subsets). *For every integer $\ell \leq n$ let E be the mapping from Lemma 1. We set $t_m = \lfloor 2^m / \binom{n}{\ell} \rfloor$ where m is an integer such that $m \geq \lceil \log \binom{n}{\ell} \rceil$. We define the mapping $E_m : \binom{[n]}{\ell} \times [t_m] \to \{0, 1\}^m$ as $E_m(S, i) = (i - 1)\binom{n}{\ell} + E(S)$ (every subset S is mapped to t_m different m bit strings).*

Min-entropy is a variant of Shannon's entropy. It measures the randomness of a random variable or a probability distribution in the worst case. We use an extractor, which is a function that generates uniformly random outputs from high min-entropy distributions. These are also used in [3] and [6]. We review the definitions.

Definition 2 (Min-entropy). *For a distribution X over a probability space Ω, the min-entropy of X is defined as*

$$H_\infty(X) = \min_{x \in \Omega} \log(1/\Pr[X = x]).$$

If $H_\infty(X) \geq k$, X is called k-source.

Definition 3 (Statistical distance). *Two distributions P and Q over a probability space Ω are ϵ-close if for every $A \subseteq \Omega$,*

$$\left| \Pr_{x \leftarrow P}[x \in A] - \Pr_{x \leftarrow Q}[x \in A] \right| \leq \epsilon.$$

We write $P \overset{\epsilon}{\equiv} Q$ if P and Q are ϵ-close. If $\epsilon = 0$, we write $P \equiv Q$.

Definition 4 (Strong extractor). *A function* Ext $: \{0,1\}^n \times \{0,1\}^d \rightarrow \{0,1\}^m$ *is a (k, ϵ)-strong extractor if for every k-source X over $\{0,1\}^n$, the distribution $(\text{Ext}(X,Y),Y)$ is ϵ-close to (U_m, Y), where Y is the uniform distribution over $\{0,1\}^d$ and U_m is independent of Y.*

We note that in the standard extractor, which is not strong, the random variables $(\text{Ext}(X,Y),Y)$ and (U_m, Y) are replaced by $\text{Ext}(X,Y)$ and U_m, respectively.

2.2 One-Way Functions and Hard-Core Predicates

Our OT protocol uses strong one-way functions, hard-core predicates, and hard predicates. The following definitions are also used in [2].

Definition 5 (One-way function). *An efficiently computable function $f : \{0,1\}^* \rightarrow \{0,1\}^*$ is (T, ϵ) one-way if for any $T(n)$-bounded adversary A, every sufficiently large n, and the uniform distribution U_n,*

$$\Pr_{x \in U_n}[f(A(1^n, f(x))) = f(x)] < \epsilon(n).$$

We note that a standard one-way function is $(n^c, \frac{1}{n^c})$ one-way for every constant $c > 1$.

Definition 6 (Hard-core predicate). *An efficiently computable function $g : \{0,1\}^* \rightarrow \{0,1\}$ is a (T, ϵ) hard-core predicate for f if for any $T(n)$-bounded adversary A and sufficiently large n,*

$$\Pr_{x \in U_n, r \in U_n}[A(f(x), r) = g(x, r)] < \frac{1}{2} + \epsilon(n).$$

Definition 7 (Hard predicate). *An efficiently computable function $P : \{0,1\}^* \rightarrow \{0,1\}$ is a (T, ϵ) hard predicate if for any $T(n)$-bounded adversary A and sufficiently large n,*

$$\Pr_{x \in U_n}[A(f(x)) = P(x)] < \frac{1}{2} + \epsilon(n).$$

Definition 8 (Multi-source hard-core predicate). *An efficiently computable function $H : \{0,1\}^* \rightarrow \{0,1\}$ is a (T, ϵ) multi-source hard-core predicate (MSHCP) for f if there exist two polynomial $t(\cdot)$ and $s(\cdot)$ such that for any $T(n)$-bounded adversary A and sufficiently large n,*

$$\Pr_{x_1,\dots,x_{t(n)} \in U_n, r \in U_{s(n)}}[A(1^n, f(x_1), \cdots, f(x_{t(n)}), r) = H(x_1 \cdots x_{t(n)}, r)] < \frac{1}{2} + \epsilon(n).$$

We use Lemmas 2, 3 and 4 to prove the security of our protocols (OWP/OWFs Protocol). Using these lemmas, we can prove that the probability that Bob obtains both of Alice's two secrets is at most $1/\text{poly}(k)$, where k is the security parameter. We can show that this probability is $\text{negl}(k)$ by using dream Yao's XOR lemma (Conjecture 1; see also [2] and [10]). However, we do not know how to prove that this probability is $\text{negl}(k)$ without this conjecture.

Lemma 2 (Goldreich-Levin [9]). *If f is a (T, ϵ) one-way function, then $\text{IP}(x, r) = \langle x, r \rangle$ is a (T', ϵ') hard-core predicate for f with $T'(n) = T(n) \cdot \frac{\epsilon^4}{n^3}$ and $\epsilon'(n) = 4\epsilon(n)$, where $\langle x, r \rangle$ is the inner product modulo 2.*

Lemma 3 (Yao's XOR lemma). *If P is a (T, ϵ) hard predicate and it is possible to efficiently sample from distribution $(U_n, P(U_n))$, then for any $\mu(n)$ and $t = \text{poly}(n)$, $P^{(t)}(x_1, \ldots, x_t) = \oplus_{i=1}^{t} P(x_i)$ is a (T', ϵ') hard predicate with $T' = T \cdot \frac{\mu^2}{\text{poly}(n)} - \text{poly}(n)$ and $\epsilon' = (2\epsilon)^t + \mu$.*

Conjecture 1 (Dream Yao's XOR lemma [2]). If P is a (T, ϵ) hard predicate for some ϵ that is bounded away from $\frac{1}{2}$ and it is possible to efficiently sample from the distribution $(U_n, P(U_n))$, then there exists a constant $c < 1$, a negligible function $\mu(\cdot)$ and some function $\eta(\cdot)$ that is bounded away from 1 such that for any $t = \text{poly}(n)$, $P^{(t)}(x_1, \ldots, x_t) = \oplus_{i=1}^{t} P(x_i)$ is a (T', ϵ') hard predicate with $T' = T \cdot 2^{-o(n)}$ and $\epsilon' = 2^{cn} \cdot \eta^t + \mu(2^n)$.

Lemma 4 ([2]). *For any $\delta < 1$, every $(2^{n(1-\delta)}, \frac{1}{16})$ one-way function has a (T, ϵ) MSHCP with the following T and ϵ:*

- *$T = 2^{n(1-\delta)}/\text{poly}(n)$ $\epsilon = \frac{1}{\text{poly}(n)}$ using $\mu = O(\epsilon)$*
- *$T = 2^{n(1-\delta-\tau)}/\text{poly}(n)$ $\epsilon = 2^{-\tau n/2}$ using $\mu = O(2^{-\tau n/2})$*
- *$T = 2^{n(1-\delta)}/2^{o(n)}$ $\epsilon = \text{negl}(2^n)$ assuming the dream XOR lemma*

We note that our OT protocol uses a collection $\mathcal{F}$ of $(2^{n(1-\delta)}, \frac{1}{16})$ one-way functions, and $\mathcal{F}$ can be constructed from a collection of $(2^{n(1-\delta)}, \frac{1}{32})$ one-way functions and an pairwise independent family of hash functions [2].

Definition 9 (Collection of one-way functions). *A (T, ϵ) one-way collection $\mathcal{F} = \bigcup F_n$ of functions is a family of functions $F_n = \{f_i : \{0, 1\}^n \to \{0, 1\}^* \mid i \in I_n\}$ such that*

Easy to sample and compute: *There exist two PPT algorithms G and F such that $G(1^n)$ outputs an index $i \in I_n$, where $I_n \subseteq \{0, 1\}^{\ell(n)}$ and $\ell(n)$ is a polynomial, and for $x \in \{0, 1\}^n$, $F(i, x)$ evaluates $f_i(x)$.*

Hard to invert: *For every $T(n)$-bounded adversary A and sufficiently large n,*

$$\Pr_{i \in G(1^n), x \in U_n} [f_i(A(1^n, i, f_i(x))) = f_i(x)] < \epsilon(n).$$

We say that $\mathcal{F}$ is almost 1-to-1 if the probability $f_i \in F_n$ is not 1-to-1 is bounded by $2^{-\Omega(n)}$.

Lemma 5 ([2]). *If there exists a (T, ϵ) one-way function $f : \{0, 1\}^{9n} \to \{0, 1\}^*$ with $T \geq 2^{\frac{n}{3}}, \epsilon \leq 2^{-\frac{n}{3}}$, and $T/\epsilon \geq 2^{9n(1-\delta)}$ then there exists a $(2^{n(1-10\delta)}, \frac{1}{32})$ one-way collection of functions $\mathcal{F} = \bigcup F_n$ that is almost 1-to-1.*

2.3 Oblivious Transfer

We now formally define "weak" oblivious transfer, where "weak" means that malicious player's (either Alice or Bob) computational resources are bounded. First we define malicious strategies for Alice and Bob. In the definition below (Definitions 10 and 11), the computational resources for Alice is weaker than those for Bob.

Definition 10 (Malicious strategy for Alice). *A (malicious) strategy A^* for Alice is an $\tilde{O}(k)$-bounded interactive machine with inputs $s_0, s_1 \in \{0, 1\}^{u(k)}$, where k is the security parameter and $u(\cdot)$ is a polynomial. That is, A^* receives s_0, s_1, interacts with B, and in each stage may compute the next message as any function of its inputs, its randomness, and messages it received so far. The view of A^* when interacting with B who holds input c, denoted by $\text{view}_{A^*}^{\langle A^*, B \rangle}(s_0, s_1; c)$, consists of its local output.*

Definition 11 (d-bounded strategy for Bob). *A d-bounded strategy B^* for Bob is an $O(k^{d'})$-bounded interactive machine with input $c \in \{0, 1\}$ for any constant $d' < d$. B^* receives c, interacts with A, and in each stage may compute the next message as any function of its inputs, its randomness, and messages it received so far. The view of B^* when interacting with A who holds input s_0 and s_1, denoted by $\text{view}_{B^*}^{\langle A, B^* \rangle}(s_0, s_1; c)$, consists of its local output.*

Definition 12 (C-consistent). *Two pairs $\bar{s} = (s_0, s_1)$ and $\bar{s}' = (s_0', s_1')$ are c-consistent if $s_c = s_c'$.*

Definition 13 (Oblivious transfer). *A protocol $\langle A, B \rangle$ is a (d, ϵ)-secure oblivious transfer (OT) protocol if for a security parameter k it is a protocol in which Alice inputs two secrets $s_0, s_1 \in \{0, 1\}^{u(k)}$ and Bob inputs a choice bit $c \in \{0, 1\}$, and that satisfies:*

Functionality: *If Alice and Bob follow the protocol, then for any s_0, s_1 and c,*
  – *The protocol does not abort with probability at least $1 - \text{negl}(k)$.*
  – *If the protocol ends then Bob outputs s_c with probability at least $1 - \text{negl}(k)$, whereas Alice outputs nothing.*
Security for Bob: *The view of any strategy A^* for Alice is independent of c. That is, for every s_0 and s_1:*

$$\left\{ \text{view}_{A^*}^{\langle A, B^* \rangle}(s_0, s_1; c) \mid c = 0 \right\} \equiv \left\{ \text{view}_{A^*}^{\langle A, B^* \rangle}(s_0, s_1; c) \mid c = 1 \right\}.$$

(d, ϵ)-**Security for Alice:** *For every d-bounded strategy B^* for Bob with input c, there is a random variable C defined by the end of the setup stage, which is the stage that Alice does not use her secrets (s_0, s_1) for computation, such that for every two pairs $\bar{s}$ and $\bar{s}'$ that are C-consistent,*

$$\left\{ \text{view}_{B^*}^{\langle A, B^* \rangle}(\bar{s}; c) \right\} \overset{\epsilon}{\equiv} \left\{ \text{view}_{B^*}^{\langle A, B^* \rangle}(\bar{s}'; c) \right\}.$$

2.4 Interactive Hashing

Our OT protocols use an interactive hashing protocol, in which only Bob has input and both Alice and Bob obtain the same output without Alice learning the input. Below we give the definitions of interactive hashing and describe the protocol which was presented in [6]. The protocol is called 4M-IH Protocol. The work [6] shows that the 4M-IH Protocol satisfies the definitions of interactive hashing (Definitions 15 and 16). We note that the 4M-IH protocol achieves security against unbounded adversaries.

Definition 14 (2^k-to-1 **hash functions**). *A hash function* $h : \{0, 1\}^m \rightarrow \{0, 1\}^{m-k}$ *is* 2^k-*to-1 if for every output of h there are exactly* 2^k *pre-images. That is,* $|h^{-1}(z)| = 2^k$ *for every* $z \in \{0, 1\}^{m-k}$.

One simple way for constructing a 2^k-to1 hash function is to take a permutation on m-bit strings and omit the last k bits of its output.

Definition 15 (Interactive hashing). *A protocol* $\langle A, B \rangle$ *is called an* interactive hashing protocol *if it is an efficient protocol between Alice with no input and Bob with input string* $W \in \{0, 1\}^m$. *At the end of the protocol both Alice and Bob output a (succinct representation of a) 2-to-1 function* $h : \{0, 1\}^m \rightarrow \{0, 1\}^{m-1}$ *and two values* $W_0, W_1 \in \{0, 1\}^m$ *(in the dictionary order) such that* $h(W_0) = h(W_1) = h(W)$. *Let* $e \in \{0, 1\}$ *be such that* $W_e = W$. *Furthermore, if the distribution of the string* W_{1-e} *over the randomness of the two parties is* η *-close to uniform, then the protocol is called* η-uniform interactive hashing *(or simply uniform interactive hashing if* $\eta = 0$).

Definition 16 (Security of interactive hashing). *An interactive hashing protocol is* se-cure for B *if for every unbounded deterministic strategy* A^*, *if* h, W_0, W_1 *are the outputs of the protocol between an honest Bob with input W and* A^*, *then*

$$\left\{ \text{view}_{A^*}^{\langle A^*, B \rangle}(W) \mid W = W_0 \right\} \equiv \left\{ \text{view}_{A^*}^{\langle A^*, B \rangle}(W) \mid W = W_1 \right\}.$$

An interactive hashing protocol is (s, ρ)-secure for A *if for every* $S \subseteq \{0, 1\}^m$ *of size at most* 2^s, *every unbounded deterministic strategy* B^*, *if* h, W_0, W_1 *are the outputs of the protocol, then*

$$\Pr[W_0 \in S \cap W_1 \in S] < \rho.$$

where the probability is taken over the randomness of A and B^*.

An interactive hashing protocol is (s, ρ)-secure *if it is secure for B and* (s, ρ)-secure *for A.*

4M-IH Protocol presented in [6] uses an η-almost t-wise independent permutation constructed in [13]. We describe the protocol below.

Definition 17 (η-almost t-wise independent permutation). *An* η-almost t-wise inde-pendent permutation *is a procedure that takes as input a seed of* ℓ *bits and outputs a description of an efficiently computable permutation in* S_{2^m}, *where* S_{2^m} *is the family of all permutations on m-bit string, with the property that a uniformly chosen seed induces a distribution* $\Pi_{t,\eta}$ *on permutations such that for any t strings* $x_1, \cdots, x_t \in \{0, 1\}^m$:

$$\{\pi(x_1), \cdots, \pi(x_t)\}_{\pi \leftarrow \Pi_{t,\eta}} \overset{\eta}{\equiv} \{\pi(x_1), \cdots, \pi(x_t)\}_{\pi \leftarrow U_{S_m}},$$

where U_{S_m} *is the uniform distribution over* S_{2^m}.

4M-IH Protocol [6]

Common Input: parameters m and s.
   Let $v = s - \log m$.
   A family Π of η-almost t-wise independent permutation $\pi : \{0, 1\}^m \to \{0, 1\}^m$. Set
   $t = m$ and $\eta = (\frac{1}{2^v})^t$.
   A family G of 2-wise independent 2-1 hash functions $g : \{0, 1\}^{m-v} \to \{0, 1\}^{m-v-1}$.
   A family H of 2-1 hash functions $h : \{0, 1\}^m \to \{0, 1\}^{m-1}$ defined as:

$$h(x) \stackrel{def}{=} \pi(x)_1 \circ \cdots \circ \pi(x)_v \circ g(\pi(x)_{v+1}, \cdots, \pi(x)_m)$$

   where $\pi(x)_i$ denotes the ith bit of $\pi(x)$.
Input of Alice: $\perp$.
Input of Bob: $W \in \{0, 1\}^m$
   – Alice randomly chooses $\pi \in \Pi$ and sends π to Bob.
   – Bob computes $\pi(W) = z_1, \ldots, z_m$ and sends $\pi'(W) = z_1, \ldots, z_v$ to Alice (let π'
     denote π when truncated in its first v bits).
   – Alice randomly chooses $g \in G$ and sends g to Bob.
   – Bob sends $g(z_{v+1}, \ldots, z_m)$ to Alice.
   – Alice and Bob output W_0, W_1 such that
     $h(W_0) = h(W_1) = h(W)$.

Lemma 6 ([6]). *For all s and m such that $s \geq \log m + 2$, 4M-IH Protocol is an*
$(s, 2^{-(m-s)O(\log m)})$-*secure η'-uniform interactive hashing protocol for*
$\eta' = (2^{-(s-\log m-1)})^m < 2^{-m}$. *Furthermore, the protocol runs in time polynomial in m.*

Due to lack of space, we omit security proof of Lemma 6 (see [6]).

2.5   Error-Correcting Codes

Our protocol based on one-way functions uses an error-correcting code.

Definition 18. *An error-correcting code* (Enc, Dec) *consists of two functions* Enc :
$\{0, 1\}^k \to \{0, 1\}^n$ *and* Dec : $\{0, 1\}^n \to \{0, 1\}^k$ *such that for any $x \in \{0, 1\}^k$, we have*
Dec(Enc(x)) = x.

Lemma 7 ([19]). *There exists an error-correcting code* (Enc, Dec) *such that* Enc_H :
$\{0, 1\}^{3n} \to \{0, 1\}^{4n}$ *and* $Dec_H : \{0, 1\}^{4n} \to \{0, 1\}^{3n}$, *and for any $x \in \{0, 1\}^{4n}$ we have*
$Dec_H(Enc_H(x) + e) = x$ *for any $e \in \{0, 1\}^{4n}$ with Hamming weight less than δn for some*
constant δ. Furthermore, both Enc_H and Dec_H run in time polynomial in n.

3   The Protocol in the Random Oracle Model

3.1   Description of ROM Protocol

We describe our OT protocol in the random oracle model (ROM Protocol) below. The
protocol uses the following tools, a random permutation, a strong extractor, and an interactive hashing protocol. For simplicity, we assume that k is a power of 2. For arbitrary
k, we can think $\log k$ as $\lceil \log k \rceil$ instead. For simplicity, we use $s_0, s_1 \in \{0, 1\}^{\log k}$ and
$\ell = \frac{1}{2} \cdot \log^4 k$. For arbitrary $u = \text{poly}(\log k)$, we can use $s_0, s_1 \in \{0, 1\}^{\log k}$, $\ell = \frac{1}{2} \cdot \log^4 k$,
$\mathcal{A}$ and $\mathcal{B}$ of size $k \log^2 k$ as $s_0, s_1 \in \{0, 1\}^u$ and $\ell = \frac{1}{2} \cdot u^2 \cdot \log^2 k$, $\mathcal{A}$ and $\mathcal{B}$ of size $k\sqrt{2\ell}$
instead.

ROM Protocol

For security parameter k, we use an oracle to compute a random permutation $f : [k^2] \rightarrow [k^2]$ and a random predicate $g : [k^2] \rightarrow \{0, 1\}$. We set $\ell = \frac{1}{2} \cdot \log^4 k$ and $m = 10\ell \cdot \lceil \log(k \log^2 k) \rceil$.

Input of Alice: Two secrets $s_0, s_1 \in \{0, 1\}^{\log k}$.
Input of Bob: A choice bit $c \in \{0, 1\}$.
Setup stage:
- Alice chooses a set $\mathcal{A}$ of k^2-bit random strings of size $k \log^2 k$, and queries the oracle on these inputs and sends $f(\mathcal{A}) = \{f(a) \mid a \in \mathcal{A}\}$ to Bob.
- Bob chooses a set $\mathcal{B}$ of k^2-bit random strings of size $k \log^2 k$, and queries the oracle on these inputs to obtain $f(\mathcal{B})$. If $|f(\mathcal{A}) \cap f(\mathcal{B})| < \ell$, then Bob aborts. Otherwise, Bob randomly chooses ℓ common outputs $c_1, \ldots, c_\ell \in f(\mathcal{A}) \cap f(\mathcal{B})$ and sorts $c_1, \ldots, c_\ell$ by the dictionary order.
  Bob randomly chooses $p \in [t_m]$ such that t_m is as in Definition 1 and computes $W = E_m(f(C), p)$, where $f(C) = \{c_1, \ldots, c_\ell\}$.
- Alice and Bob run 4M-IH Protocol, where Bob's input is W. Both Alice and Bob interactively obtain h, W_0, W_1 such that $h(W_0) = h(W_1) = h(W)$
  Alice computes two sets $f(C_0), f(C_1) \subseteq f(\mathcal{A})$ such that $W_0 = E_m(f(C_0), p)$ and $W_1 = E_m(f(C_1), p)$. If W_0 or W_1 is not a valid encoding, i.e., there is no such $f(C_0)$ or $f(C_1)$, then abort.
- Bob chooses e such that $W_e = W$, and sends $\hat{e} = e \oplus c$ to Alice.
- Alice computes $C_0, C_1, g(C_0)$ and $g(C_1)$, where $C_i = \{x \mid f(x) \in f(C_i)\}$ and $g(C_i) = \{g(x) \mid x \in C_i\}$ for $i \in \{0, 1\}$, and sorts the elements in the two sets $g(C_0)$ and $g(C_1)$ by the dictionary order.

Transfer stage:
- For $i = 0, 1$, Alice chooses a seed Y_i uniformly at random and computes $Z_i = \mathrm{Ext}(\mathcal{G}(C_i), Y_i) \oplus s_{i \oplus \hat{e}}$, where $\mathcal{G}(C_i)$ is defined as $\mathcal{G}(C_i) = (g_1 \oplus \cdots \oplus g_{\frac{1}{2}\log^2 k}) \circ (g_{\frac{1}{2}\log^2 k+1} \oplus \cdots \oplus g_{\log^2 k}) \circ \cdots \circ (g_{\ell-(\frac{1}{2}\log^2 k-1)} \oplus \cdots \oplus g_\ell)$, where $g_1, \ldots g_\ell \in g(C_i)$. Alice sends to Bob (Y_0, Z_0, Y_1, Z_1).
- Bob computes $C_e = \{x \mid f(x) \in f(C)\}$ and $\mathcal{G}(C_e)$, and then sorts the elements in $\mathcal{G}(C_e)$ by the dictionary order. Then Bob obtains $s_c = \mathrm{Ext}(\mathcal{G}(C_e), Y_e) \oplus Z_e$.

We note that if Alice and Bob follow ROM Protocol, then the protocol requires $\tilde{O}(k)$ running time for both of them. Using an efficient sorting algorithm, they can choose the sets $\mathcal{A}$ and $\mathcal{B}$, sort the sets $f(\mathcal{A}) \cap f(\mathcal{B}), g(C_0), g(C_1)$, and $\mathcal{G}(C_e)$ in $\tilde{O}(k)$ time, and query to the random oracles in $O(k)$ time. Alice and Bob can perform the interactive hashing protocol and compute the strong extractor in polynomial time in the input length. Since the input length of the interactive hashing is $|W| = O(m)$ and that of the extractor is $O(|\mathcal{G}(C_i)|) = O(\log^2 k)$, they can perform and compute in poly$(\log k)$ time. Therefore, they can run ROM Protocol in total $\tilde{O}(k)$ time.

Theorem 1. *Given an oracle to a random function $f : \{0, 1\}^* \rightarrow \{0, 1\}$, there exists a $(2, \epsilon)$ oblivious transfer protocol with $\epsilon = \mathrm{negl}(k)$.*

The proof of this theorem is given in the next section.

3.2   Functionality and Security Proofs

Lemma 8. *ROM Protocol is a* $(2, \epsilon)$ *OT protocol with* $\epsilon = \text{negl}(k)$ *if the extractor is* (k_E, ϵ_E)*-strong for* $k_E \geq \lambda \cdot \log k$ *and* $\epsilon_E = \text{negl}(k)$*, where* λ *is a constant, and the interactive hashing protocol is* (2^{-m})*-uniform and* (ψ, ρ)*-secure for* $\psi \leq m - \ell$ *and* $\rho = \text{negl}(k)$*.*

Lemma 8 follows from Lemmas 9, 10, and 11.

Functionality of ROM Protocol

Lemma 9. *For ROM Protocol that satisfies the parameters in Lemma 8, if Alice and Bob follow the protocol with input* $s_0, s_1 \in \{0, 1\}^{\log k}$ *and* $c \in \{0, 1\}$*, then the following holds.*

- *The protocol does not abort with probability* $1 - 2^{-\Omega(\ell)}$;
- *If the protocol does not abort, then Bob's output is* s_c.

Proof. We first show that the protocol does not abort with high probability. The protocol aborts only if $|f(\mathcal{A}) \cap f(\mathcal{B})| < \ell$ or at least one of W_0 and W_1 is not a valid encoding. We show that $|f(\mathcal{A}) \cap f(\mathcal{B})| \geq \ell$ with high probability. For every fixed $f(\mathcal{A})$, since $f(\mathcal{B})$ is a set of random strings, the expected size of $|f(\mathcal{A}) \cap f(\mathcal{B})|$ is $(k \log^2 k)^2 / k^2 \geq \log^4 k = 2\ell$. By Chernoff bound, the probability of $|f(\mathcal{A}) \cap f(\mathcal{B})| < \ell$ is at most $2^{-\Omega(\ell)}$. Next we show that the probability that at least one of W_0 and W_1 is not a valid encoding is small. Since W_e was chosen by Bob, W_e is a valid encoding. By the property of interactive hashing, W_{1-e} is (2^{-m})-close to the uniform distribution over $\{0, 1\}^m$. By Lemma 3.3 in [6], the probability that a uniformly random string in $\{0, 1\}^m$ is not a valid encoding is at most $|f(\mathcal{A})| \cdot 2^{-m} \leq \binom{k^2}{\ell} \cdot 2^{-m} \leq 2^{-\ell-1}$. Therefore, the probability that the protocol aborts is bounded by $2^{-\Omega(\ell)} + 2^{-m} + 2^{-\ell-1} \leq 2^{-\Omega(\ell)}$.

We show that if the protocol does not abort, then Bob outputs s_c. Since Bob knows C_e, he can always compute $\text{Ext}(g(C_e), Y_e)$ and subsequently use it to decrypt the value Z_e. Then we have

$$\text{Ext}(\mathcal{G}(C_e), Y_e) \oplus Z_e = \text{Ext}(\mathcal{G}(C_e), Y_e) \oplus (s_{e \oplus \hat{e}} \oplus \text{Ext}(\mathcal{G}(C_e), Y_e))$$
$$= s_{e \oplus \hat{e}}$$
$$= s_c.$$

Security for Bob

Lemma 10. *ROM Protocol that satisfies the parameters in Lemma 8 is secure for Bob.*

Proof. We show that the view of any strategy A^* for Alice is independent of c. Fix the randomness of A^*. We show a bijection between pairs of $(\mathcal{B}, c)$ and $(\mathcal{B}', 1 - c)$, where $\mathcal{B}$ and $\mathcal{B}'$ are chosen randomly by honest Bob and c is his input. That is, we show that, for each pair $(\mathcal{B}, c)$ that is consistent with the view of A^*, there exists a unique pair $(\mathcal{B}', 1-c)$ such that $(\mathcal{B}', 1 - c)$ is consistent with the same view A^*. There are two possibilities for a view of A^*:

- The protocol aborts before the step in which Bob sends the value $\hat{e} = c \oplus e$ to Alice. In this case, the view of A^* is totally independent of c. We can map every consistent $\mathcal{B}$ to itself $\mathcal{B}' = \mathcal{B}$. Clearly $(\mathcal{B}, c)$ and $(\mathcal{B}', 1 - c)$ are consistent with the view of A^*.

- Alice receives the message $\hat{e} = c \oplus e$ sent by Bob. Let $(\mathcal{B}, c)$ be a pair consistent with the view of A^*. Then, $f(\mathcal{B})$ is a random set such that $f(C) \subseteq f(\mathcal{A}) \cap f(\mathcal{B})$ and $W_e = E_m(f(C), p)$. Since f is a permutation, $\mathcal{B}$ is also a random set such that $C \subseteq \mathcal{A} \cap \mathcal{B}$. Since the protocol has not aborted, it follows from the property of the interactive hashing that there is a unique random set C' such that $W_{1-e} = E_m(f(C'), p)$. If we set $\mathcal{B}'$ to be $\mathcal{B}' = \mathcal{B} \backslash C \cup C'$, then $(\mathcal{B}', 1 - c)$ is consistent with the view of A^*. Therefore we get a bijection.

Since there is a bijection between pairs $(\mathcal{B}, c)$ and $(\mathcal{B}', 1 - c)$, the view of A^* for Alice is independent of c.

Security for Alice

Lemma 11. *ROM Protocol that satisfies the parameters in Lemma 8 is $(2, \epsilon)$-secure for Alice for $\epsilon = \mathrm{negl}(k)$.*

Proof. Fix a 2-bounded strategy B^* with an input c. We need to show that there exists a random variable C defined by the end of Setup stage such that for every two pairs of secrets $\bar{s} = (s_0, s_1)$ and $\bar{s}' = (s_0', s_1')$ that are C-consistent, the view of B^* when the input of Alice is $\bar{s}$ is ϵ-close to that when the input is $\bar{s}'$. In ROM Protocol, the secrets s_0, s_1 are only involved in Transfer stage, and they are sent to Bob as $Z_i = \mathrm{Ext}(\mathcal{G}(C_i), Y_i) \oplus s_i$ for $i \in \{0, 1\}$. Thus, it is sufficient to show that Z_{1-C} is close to the uniform distribution from the view of B^*. To show this, we prove that $\mathcal{G}(C_{1-C})$ has enough entropy from the view of B^*. From the security of the interactive hashing, with probability at least $1 - \rho$, B^* obtain no information about $\mathcal{G}(C_{1-C})$ in the interactive hashing. Let assume that such an event happens. Without loss of generality, we assume that B^* makes at most $\frac{k^2}{3}$ different oracle queries. The first bit of $\mathcal{G}(C_{1-C})$ is $g_1 \oplus \cdots \oplus g_{\frac{1}{2} \log^2 k}$. If B^* did not query the oracle for at least one of $g_1, \ldots, g_{\frac{1}{2} \log^2 k}$, then the first bit of $\mathcal{G}(C_{1-C})$ is uniformly distributed, since g_j is an output of a random predicate g. We bound the probability that B^* makes all the elements $g_1, \ldots, g_{\frac{1}{2} \log^2 k}$. Suppose $g_j = g(x_j)$ for $j \in [\frac{1}{2} \log^2 k]$. Let X_j be an event that B^* queries x_j to the oracle. Since g is a random predicate that maps k^2 bits to 1 bit, we have that $\Pr[X_j] \leq 1/k^2$ and thus $\Pr[\bigcup_j X_j] \leq \log^2 k/(2k^2)$. This means that the probability that the first bit of $\mathcal{G}(C_{1-C})$ is not uniformly distributed is at most $\log^2 k/(2k^2)$. The same argument holds for any other bit of $\mathcal{G}(C_{1-C})$. For $i \in [\log k]$, let Y_i be a random variable that takes 1 if an event $\bigcup_j X_{i \cdot (\frac{1}{2} \log^2 k) + j}$ happens and 0 otherwise. Namely, $Y_i = 0$ means that the i-th bit of $\mathcal{G}(C_{1-C})$ is uniformly distributed. Then, the probability that $\mathcal{G}(C_{1-C})$ is a $(\lambda \cdot \log k)$-source is at least $\Pr[\sum_i Y_i \leq (1 - \lambda) \log k]$. By Chernoff bound, since $\mathrm{E}[\sum_i Y_i] = \log^2 k \cdot \mathrm{E}[Y_1] \leq \ell/k^2$, we have $\Pr[\sum_i Y_i > (1 - \lambda) \log k] \leq 2^{-\Omega(\log^2 k)}$. Thus, with probability at least $1 - 2^{-\Omega(\log^2 k)}$, $\mathcal{G}(C_{1-C})$ is a $(\lambda \cdot \log k)$-source, and hence $\mathrm{Ext}(\mathcal{G}(C_{1-C}), Y_{1-C})$ is ϵ_E-close to the uniform distribution. Therefore, the statistical distance between the view of B^* when the input of Alice is $\bar{s}$ and that when $\bar{s}'$ is at most $2(\rho + \epsilon_E + 2^{-\Omega(\log^2 k)}) = \mathrm{negl}(k)$.

Replacing Random Permutation with Random Function. We can replace a random permutation with a random function in ROM Protocol using the same technique described in the proof of Theorem 2 in [12]. Thus, Theorem 1 follows from Lemma 8.

4   The Protocol from One-Way Permutations

4.1   Description of OWP Protocol

We construct a protocol with quadratic security based on a one-way permutation. We consider to replace the random oracle with a one-way permutation in ROM Protocol. Note that our protocol relies on a (T, ϵ) one-way permutation with $T(n) \geq 2^{\log k}$. For simplicity, we assume that k is a power of 2, and use $s_0, s_1 \in \{0, 1\}^{\log k}$. For arbitrary $u = \text{poly}(\log k)$, we can use $s_0, s_1 \in \{0, 1\}^{\log k}$ and $\ell = t \cdot \log^2 k$ as $s_0, s_1 \in \{0, 1\}^u$ and $\ell = t \cdot u$ instead.

OWP Protocol

For a security parameter k, we use a one-way permutation $f : \{0, 1\}^{2 \log k} \rightarrow \{0, 1\}^{2 \log k}$ for which H is a (T, ϵ_H) MSHCP with $T = 2^{2(1-\delta) \cdot \log k}$ for a positive constant $\delta < 1$. We set $\ell = t \cdot \log^2 k$ and $m = 10\ell \cdot \lceil \log(k \sqrt{2\ell}) \rceil$, where $t = t(\log k)$ is some polynomial for H as in Definition 8. Also let $s = s(\log k)$ be some polynomial for H as in Definition 8.

Input of Alice: Two secrets $s_0, s_1 \in \{0, 1\}^{\log k}$.
Input of Bob: A choice bit $c \in \{0, 1\}$.
Setup stage:
   - Alice chooses a set $\mathcal{A}$ of $2 \log k$-bit random strings of size $\lceil k \sqrt{2\ell} \rceil$ and a set $\mathcal{R}_i$ of s-bit random strings of size $\log^2 k$ for $i = 0, 1$, and computes $f(\mathcal{A}) = \{f(a) \mid a \in \mathcal{A}\}$ and sends them to Bob.
   - Bob chooses a set $\mathcal{B}$ of $2 \log k$-bit random strings of size $\lceil k \sqrt{2\ell} \rceil$, and computes $f(\mathcal{B}) = \{f(b) \mid b \in \mathcal{B}\}$. If $|f(\mathcal{A}) \cap f(\mathcal{B})| < \ell$, then Bob aborts. Otherwise, Bob randomly chooses ℓ common outputs $c_1, \dots, c_\ell \in f(\mathcal{A}) \cap f(\mathcal{B})$.
     Bob randomly chooses $p \in [t_m]$ such that t_m is as in Definition 1 and computes $W = E_m(f(C), p)$, where $f(C) = \{c_1, \dots, c_\ell\}$.
   - Alice and Bob run 4M-IH Protocol, where Bob's input is W. Both Alice and Bob interactively obtain h, W_0, W_1 such that $h(W_0) = h(W_1) = h(W)$.
     Alice computes two sets $f(C_0), f(C_1) \subseteq f(\mathcal{A})$ such that $W_0 = E_m(f(C_0), p)$ and $W_1 = E_m(f(C_1), p)$. If W_0 or W_1 is not a valid encoding, then abort.
   - Bob chooses e such that $W_e = W$, and sends $\hat{e} = e \oplus c$ to Alice.
   - For $i = 0, 1$, Alice computes C_i and $\mathcal{H}(C_i, \mathcal{R}_i)$, where $C_i = \{x \mid f(x) \in f(C_i)\}$ and $\mathcal{H}(C_i, \mathcal{R}_i) = H(x_1, \dots, x_t, r_1) \circ H(x_{t+1}, \dots, x_{2t}, r_2) \circ \cdots \circ H(x_{\ell-t+1}, \dots, x_\ell, r_{\log^2 k})$, where $x_1, \dots x_\ell \in C_i, r_1, \dots r_{\log^2 k} \in \mathcal{R}_i$. Alice sorts the elements in $\mathcal{H}(C_0, \mathcal{R}_0)$ and $\mathcal{H}(C_1, \mathcal{R}_1)$ by the dictionary order.
Transfer stage:
   - For $i = 0, 1$, Alice chooses a seed Y_i uniformly at random and computes $Z_i = \text{Ext}(\mathcal{H}(C_i, r_i), Y_i) \oplus s_{i \oplus \hat{e}}$. Alice sends to Bob (Y_0, Z_0, Y_1, Z_1).

- Bob computes $C_e = \{x \mid f(x) \in f(C)\}$ and $\mathcal{H}(C_e, r_e)$, and then sorts the elements in $\mathcal{H}(C_e, r_e)$ by the dictionary order. Then Bob obtains $s_c = \text{Ext}(\mathcal{H}(C_e, r_e), Y_e) \oplus Z_i$.

We note that if Alice and Bob follow OWP Protocol, then they can run it in total $\tilde{O}(k)$ time. This follows from a similar argument as ROM Protocol.

Theorem 2. *If there exists a* $(2^{2\log k(1-\delta)}, \frac{1}{16})$ *one-way permutation for* $\delta < \frac{1}{2}$, *then there exists a* (d, ϵ)-*secure oblivious transfer protocol for the following* d *and* ϵ:

- $d = 2 \cdot (1 - \delta)$ $\epsilon = \frac{1}{\log^c k}$ for any constant c
- $d = 2 \cdot (1 - \delta - \tau)$ $\epsilon = k^{-\tau}$ for any $\tau < 1 - \delta$
- $d = 2 \cdot (1 - \delta)$ $\epsilon = \text{negl}(k)$ assuming the dream XOR lemma

4.2 Functionality and Security Proofs

We first show the following lemma.

Lemma 12. *OWP Protocol is a* $(2, \epsilon)$ *OT protocol with* $\epsilon = 2\epsilon_H \cdot \log^2 k + \text{negl}(k)$ *if* H *is* (T, ϵ_H) *MSHCP, the extractor is* (k_E, ϵ_E)-*strong for* $k_E \geq \lambda \cdot \log^2 k$ *and* $\epsilon_E = \text{negl}(k)$, *where* λ *is a constant, and the interactive hashing protocol is* (2^{-m})-*uniform and* (ψ, ρ)-*secure for* $\psi \leq m - \ell, \rho = \text{negl}(k)$.

Theorem 2 can be proven by this lemma and Lemma 4. Lemma 12 follows from Lemmas 13, 14, and 15.

Functionality of OWP Protocol

Lemma 13. *For OWP Protocol that satisfies in Lemma 12, if Alice and Bob follow the protocol with input* $s_0, s_1 \in \{0, 1\}^{\log k}$ *and* $c \in \{0, 1\}$, *then the following holds.*

- *The protocol does not abort with probability* $1 - 2^{-\Omega(\ell)}$;
- *If the protocol does not abort, then Bob's output is* s_c.

We can show this lemma by almost the same argument as the proof of Lemma 10. Hence we omit the proof.

Security for Bob

Lemma 14. *OWP Protocol that satisfies the parameters in Lemma 12 is secure for Bob.*

Since the proof is almost the same as Lemma 9, we omit the proof.

Security for Alice

Lemma 15. *OWP Protocol that satisfies the parameters in Lemma 12 is* $(2, \epsilon)$-*secure for Alice with* $\epsilon = 2\epsilon_H \cdot \log^2 k + \text{negl}(k)$.

Proof. Fix a 2-bounded strategy B^* with an input c. We need to show that there exists a random variable C defined by the end of Setup stage such that for every two pairs of secrets $\bar{s} = (s_0, s_1)$ and $\bar{s}' = (s_0', s_1')$ that are C-consistent, the view of B^* when the input of Alice is $\bar{s}$ is ϵ-close to that when the input is $\bar{s}'$. By the same reason as in Lemma 11, it is sufficient to show that $\mathcal{H}(C_{1-c}, \mathcal{R}_{1-c})$ has enough entropy from the view of B^*. In the case of ROM Protocol (Lemma 11), we show that $\mathcal{G}(C_{1-c})$ has enough entropy. The difference is that, in OWP Protocol, $\mathcal{H}(C_{1-c}, \mathcal{R}_{1-c})$ consists of the outputs of MSHCP, while in ROM Protocol, $\mathcal{G}(C_{1-c})$ consists of the outputs of the random predicate g. Since H is (T, ϵ_H) MSHCP and $|\mathcal{H}(C_{1-c}, \mathcal{R}_{1-c})| = \log^2 k$, the difference is at most $\epsilon_H \cdot \log^2 k$. Therefore, by the same argument as in the proof of Lemma 11, the statistical distance between the view of B^* when the input of Alice is $\bar{s}$ and that when $\bar{s}'$ is at most $2(\rho + \epsilon_E + 2^{-\Omega(\log^2 k)} + \epsilon_H \cdot \log^2 k) \leq \epsilon$.

5   The Protocol from One-Way Functions

5.1   Description of OWFs Protocol

We describe our OT protocol based on one-way functions (OWFs Protocol) below. The protocol uses the following tools, a collection of one-way functions, an interactive hashing protocol, a strong extractor, and an error-correcting code.

In OWFs Protocol, Alice first randomly chooses two random strings σ_0 and σ_1, which are the same length as s_0 and s_1. Then Alice encodes σ_0, σ_1 to $\sigma_0' \sigma_1'$ using an error-correcting code. Alice and Bob run the basic protocol several times. In the one basic protocol, they run setup stage several times. Bob's output of the t'th basic protocol is the t'th bit of the encoded string σ_c'. If Bob collects almost of all outputs of the basic protocols, then Bob can decode the strings σ_c' to σ_c which Alice made, and by using it, get Alice's input s_c.

For simplicity, we assume that k is a power of 2. In OWFs Protocol, for simple description, we set the length of the secrets (s_0 and s_1) with $\log^2 k$ while that of the previous ROM/OWP Protocol with $\log k$. For arbitrary $u = \text{poly}(\log k)$, we can use $u = \log^2 k$ and $u' = \frac{4}{3} \log^2 k$ as $u = \text{poly}(\log k)$ and $u' = \frac{4}{3} u$ instead.

OWFs Protocol

For a security parameter k, we use a collection $\mathcal{F} = \bigcup F_{(2 \log k)}$ of one-way functions, 4M-IH Protocol with input length $m = 10\ell \cdot \lceil \log k \sqrt{2\ell} \rceil$, a randomness extractor, and an error-correcting code (Enc, Dec) with Enc : $\{0, 1\}^u \to \{0, 1\}^{u'}$, where $\ell = \frac{1}{2} \cdot \log^2 k$, $u = \log^2 k$, and $u' = \frac{4}{3} \log^2 k$.

Input of Alice: Two secrets $s_0, s_1 \in \{0, 1\}^u$.
Input of Bob: A choice bit $c \in \{0, 1\}$.
Encoding stage:
  - Alice chooses two random strings $\sigma_0, \sigma_1 \in \{0, 1\}^u$, and computes $\sigma_0' = \text{Enc}(\sigma_0)$ and $\sigma_1' = \text{Enc}(\sigma_1)$.
  For each $t \in [u']$, Alice and Bob run the following basic protocol.

The basic protocol for t :

Alice and Bob run Setup stage for each $s \in [\log k]$, and then run Combining stage.

Setup stage for s :

- Alice chooses a set $\mathcal{A}$ of $2 \log k$-bit random strings of size $k \log k$, two random strings $r_0, r_1 \in \{0, 1\}^\ell$, and $f_i \in F_{(2 \log k)}$. Alice computes $f_i(\mathcal{A}) = \{f_i(x) \mid x \in \mathcal{A}\}$ and sends it to Bob.
- Bob chooses a set $\mathcal{B}$ of $2 \log k$-bit random strings of size $k \log k$, and computes $f_i(\mathcal{B}) = \{f_i(x) \mid x \in \mathcal{B}\}$. If $|f_i(\mathcal{A}) \cap f_i(\mathcal{B})| < \ell$, then Bob aborts. Otherwise, Bob randomly chooses ℓ common outputs $c_1, \ldots, c_\ell \in f(\mathcal{A}) \cap f(\mathcal{B})$. Bob randomly chooses $p \in [t_m]$ such that t_m is as in Definition 1 and computes $W = E_m(f_i(C), p)$, where $f_i(C) = \{c_1, \ldots, c_\ell\}$.
- Alice and Bob run the 4M-IH Protocol, where Bob's input is W. Both Alice and Bob interactively obtain h, W_0, W_1 such that $h(W_0) = h(W_1) = h(W)$. Alice computes two sets $f(C_0), f(C_1) \subseteq f(\mathcal{A})$ such that $W_0 = E_m(f(C_0), p)$ and $W_1 = E_m(f(C_1), p)$. If W_0 or W_1 is not a valid encoding, then abort.
- Bob chooses e such that $W_e = W$, and sends $\hat{e}_s = e \oplus c$ to Alice.
- Alice computes C_0, C_1 and sorts the elements by the dictionary order, where $C_j = \{x \mid f_i(x) \in f(C_j)\}$ for $j \in \{0, 1\}$, Alice randomly chooses two indices $i_0, i_1 \in [\ell]$ such that $c_{i_0} \in C_0 \setminus C_1$ and $c_{i_1} \in C_1 \setminus C_0$, computes $v_0^s = \mathrm{IP}(c_{i_0}, r_0)$ and $v_1^s = \mathrm{IP}(c_{i_1}, r_1)$ and sends (i_0, i_1) to Bob.
- Bob computes $v_{\hat{e}_s}^s = \mathrm{IP}(c_{\hat{e}_s}, r_{\hat{e}_s})$.

Combining stage:

- Alice computes $V_0^t = v_{\hat{e}_1}^1 \oplus v_{\hat{e}_2}^2 \oplus \cdots \oplus v_{\hat{e}_{\log k}}^{\log k}$, $V_1^t = v_{(1-\hat{e}_1)}^1 \oplus v_{(1-\hat{e}_2)}^2 \oplus \cdots \oplus v_{(1-\hat{e}_{\log k})}^{\log k}$.
- Bob computes $V_c^t = v_c^1 \oplus v_c^2 \oplus \cdots \oplus v_c^{\log k}$.

Transfer stage:

- For $i = 0, 1$, Alice computes $V_i = (V_i^1 \circ V_i^2 \circ \cdots \circ V_i^{u'})$ and $V_i' = V_i \oplus \sigma_i'$, and chooses a random seed Y_i and computes $Z_i = \mathrm{Ext}(\sigma_i, Y_i) \oplus s_i$. Then Alice sends (V_0', Z_0, V_1', Z_1) to Bob.
- Bob computes $\hat{\sigma}_c' = V_c' \oplus (V_c^1 \circ V_c^2 \circ \cdots \circ V_c^{\log k})$ and $\sigma_c = \mathrm{Dec}(\hat{\sigma}_c')$, and obtains $s_c = \mathrm{Ext}(\sigma_c, Y_c) \oplus Z_c$.

We note that if Alice and Bob follow OWFs Protocol, then the protocol requires $\tilde{O}(k)$ running time for them. In Encoding stage, Alice can choose strings and encode them in $\mathrm{poly}(u) = \mathrm{poly}(\log k)$ time. In Setup stage for each Basic protocol, Alice and Bob can choose the sets $\mathcal{A}$ and $\mathcal{B}$, sort the sets $f_i(\mathcal{A}) \cap f_i(\mathcal{B})$, choose elements i_0 and i_1, and compute v_0^s, v_1^s and $v_{\hat{e}_s}^s$ in $\tilde{O}(k)$. Alice and Bob can perform 4M-IH Protocol in polynomial time in the input length, that is, $\mathrm{poly}(\log k)$ time. Since, they run Setup stage $s = \log k$ times and compute V_0^t, Z_1^t and Z_c^t in Combining stage in $O(s) = O(\log k)$, they perform the basic protocol in total $\tilde{O}(k)$ time. They can perform Transfer stage in $\mathrm{poly}(\log k)$ time. Therefore, they can run OWFs Protocol in total $\tilde{O}(k)$ time.

Theorem 3. *For any $\delta < 1/10$, If there exists a (T, ϵ) one-way functions with $T \geq 2^{2 \log k/3}$, $\epsilon \leq 2^{-(2 \log k/3)}$, and $T/\epsilon \geq 2^{18 \log k(1-\delta)}$, then there exists a (d, ϵ)-secure oblivious transfer protocol for the following d and ϵ:*

- $d = 2 \cdot (1 - 10\delta)$ $\quad \epsilon = \frac{1}{\log^c k}$ $\quad$ for any constant c
- $d = 2 \cdot (1 - 10\delta - \tau)$ $\epsilon = k^{-\tau}$ $\quad$ for any $\tau < 1 - \delta$
- $d = 2 \cdot (1 - 10\delta)$ $\quad \epsilon = \text{negl}(k)$ assuming the dream XOR lemma

5.2 Functionality and Security Proofs

We first show the following lemma:

Lemma 16. *OWFs Protocol is a $(2, \epsilon)$ OT protocol with $\epsilon = \epsilon_F \cdot \text{poly}(\log k) + \text{negl}(k)$ if $\mathcal{F}$ is a (T, ϵ_F) one-way collection of function that is almost 1-to-1, the extractor is (k_E, ϵ_E)-strong for $k_E \geq \lambda \cdot \log^2 k$ and $\epsilon_E = \text{negl}(k)$, where λ is a constant, the interactive hashing protocol is (2^{-m})-uniform and (ψ, ρ)-secure for $\psi \leq m - \ell, \rho = \text{negl}(k)$, and the error-correcting code is as presented in Lemma 7.*

Theorem 3 can be proven by this lemma and Lemma 5. Lemma 16 follows from Lemmas 17, 18, 19.

Functionality of the OWFs Protocol

Lemma 17. *For OWFs Protocol that satisfies in Lemma 16, if Alice and Bob follow the protocol with input $s_0, s_1 \in \{0, 1\}^{\log k}$ and $c \in \{0, 1\}$, then the following holds.*

- *The protocol does not abort with probability $1 - 2^{-\Omega(\ell)}$;*
- *If the protocol does not abort, then Bob's output is s_c with probability $1 - \text{negl}(k)$.*

Proof. The protocol aborts only in running Setup stage of the basic protocol. Since OWFs Protocol performs Setup stage $\text{poly}(\log k)$ times, it follows from the same argument as in the case of ROM/OWP Protocol that the probability that the protocol aborts is $\text{negl}(k)$.

Next we show that, if the protocol does not abort, the output of Bob is s_c with probability at least $1 - \text{negl}(k)$. Bob can output s_c if he can compute $\text{Ext}(\sigma_c, Y_c)$ correctly, which happens if $\text{Dec}(\hat{\sigma}'_c) = \sigma'_c$. For each $t \in [u']$, the probability that the value of V_c^t that Bob holds differs from that of Alice is at most $\log k / k^2$. Thus, the expected number of errors contained in $\hat{\sigma}'_c$ is $\log^3 k / k^2$. Since Dec can correct $\Omega(\log^2 k)$ errors in $\hat{\sigma}'_c$, we can show by using Chernoff bound that the probability that $\text{Dec}(\hat{\sigma}'_c) = \sigma'_c$ is at least $1 - \text{negl}(k)$.

Security for Bob

Lemma 18. *OWFs Protocol that satisfies the parameters in Lemma 16 is secure for Bob.*

Proof. Bob uses his secret c only in the iteration of Setup stage. By the same argument as in ROM/OWP Protocol, Alice has no information about c in the information theoretic sense. Therefore, the lemma follows.

The Proof of Security for Alice

Lemma 19. *OWFs Protocol that satisfies the parameters in Lemma 16 is $(2, \epsilon)$-secure for Alice with $\epsilon = 2\epsilon_F \cdot \text{poly}(\log k) + \text{negl}(k)$*

Proof. For a 2-bounded strategy B^* with an input c, we need to show that there exists a random variable C defined by the end of Setup stage such that for every two pairs of secrets $\bar{s} = (s_0, s_1)$ and $\bar{s}' = (s_0', s_1')$ that are C-consistent, the view of B^* when the input of Alice is $\bar{s}$ is ϵ-close to that when the input is $\bar{s}'$. As in the case of ROM/OWP Protocol, it is sufficient to show that the input to the extractor, σ_{1-C}, has enough entropy.

First we show that the probability that Bob can obtain some bit of both σ_C' and σ_{1-C}' is small. To obtain a bit of both σ_C' and σ_{1-C}', he need to break either the interactive hashing or the one-wayness of f_i for all $\log k$ iterations of Setup stage. That probability is at most $(\frac{1}{2} + \epsilon_F + \rho)^{\text{poly}(\log k)} \leq \epsilon_F \cdot \text{poly}(\log k)$. Therefore, the probability that Bob obtains some bit of both σ_C' and σ_{1-C}' is at most $\epsilon_F \cdot \text{poly}(\log k)$.

Thus, if Bob obtains σ_C' correctly, then he performs the basic protocol with input C at least $\frac{1}{2}u'$ times out of u' times. This means that he performs the basic protocol with input $1 - C$ at most $\frac{1}{2}u'$ times. By a similar argument as is the proof of Lemma 11, σ_{1-C} has entropy $\geq \frac{3}{4}u$. Hence the entropy of σ_C' is at least $\frac{3}{4}u - \frac{1}{2}u' = \frac{1}{12}u = \Omega(\log^2 k)$.

Therefore, the statistical distance between the view of B^* when the input of Alice is $\bar{s}$ and that when $\bar{s}'$ is at most $2(\epsilon_F \cdot \text{poly}(\log k) + \epsilon_E) \leq \epsilon$.

6 Conclusions and Open Problems

We have proposed an OT protocol with quadratic security from strong one-way functions. In our OT protocol (OWFs Protocol), Bob obtains the two secret with probability $1/\text{poly}(k)$. We do not know the way of improving this probability to $\text{negl}(k)$ without dream Yao's XOR lemma. In order to do this, we believe that we must use other techniques: other error-correcting codes, extractors. Thus, these techniques may improve probability $\text{negl}(k)$ and remain hardness.

Another issue is on optimality. In [1], it is shown that the key-exchange protocol with quadratic security is optimal in the random oracle model. Therefore, it may be able to prove that an OT protocol with quadratic security is optimal in the random oracle model.

Acknowledgement. We are very grateful to Dr. Claudio Orlandi for helpful suggestions and comments. We would also like to thank the anonymous referees for very valuable comments.

References

1. Barak, B., Mahmoody-Ghidary, M.: Merkle Puzzles Are Optimal – An $O(n^2)$-query Attack on Any Key Exchange from a Random Oracle. In: Halevi, S. (ed.) CRYPTO 2009. LNCS, vol. 5677, pp. 374–390. Springer, Heidelberg (2009)
2. Biham, E., Goren, Y.J., Ishai, Y.: Basing Weak Public-Key Cryptography on Strong One-Way Functions. In: Canetti, R. (ed.) TCC 2008. LNCS, vol. 4948, pp. 55–72. Springer, Heidelberg (2008)
3. Cachin, C., Crépeau, C., Marcil, J.: Oblivious Transfer with a Memory-Bounded Receiver. In: Proceedings of FOCS 1998, pp. 493–502 (1998)
4. Cover, T.M.: Enumerative Source Encoding. IEEE Transaction on Information Theory, 73–77 (1973)

5. Crépeau, C.: Equivalence between Two Flavours of Oblivious Transfers. In: Pomerance, C. (ed.) CRYPTO 1987. LNCS, vol. 293, pp. 350–354. Springer, Heidelberg (1988)
6. Ding, Y.Z., Harnik, D., Rosen, A., Shaltiel, R.: Constant-Round Oblivious Transfer in the Bounded Storage Model. In: Naor, M. (ed.) TCC 2004. LNCS, vol. 2951, pp. 446–472. Springer, Heidelberg (2004)
7. Even, S., Goldreich, O., Lempel, A.: A Randomized Protocol for Signing Contracts. Communications of the ACM, 637–647 (1985)
8. Gertner, Y., Kannan, S., Malkin, T.: The Relationship between Public Key Encryption and Oblivious Transfer. In: Proceedings of FCCS 2000, pp. 325–335 (2000)
9. Goldreich, O.: Foundation of Cryptography Basic Tools, pp. 64–78. Cambridge University Press, Cambridge (2001)
10. Goldreich, O., Nisan, N., Wigderson, A.: On Yao's XOR lemma. Technical Report TR95-50 (1995)
11. Goldreich, S., Micali, O., Wigderson, A.: How to Play Any Mental Game - A Completeness Theorem for Protocols with Honest Majority. In: 19th ACM Symposium on the Theory of Computing, pp. 218–229 (1987)
12. Goren, Y.: Basing Weak Public-Key Cryptography on Strong One-Way Functions. M.Sc. Thesis, Technion (2006)
13. Gowers, W.T.: An Almost m-wise Independent Random Permutation of the Cube. Combinatorics, Probability and Computing, 119–130 (1996)
14. Haitner, I.: Semi-honest to Malicious Oblivious Transfer—The Black-Box Way. In: Canetti, R. (ed.) TCC 2008. LNCS, vol. 4948, pp. 412–426. Springer, Heidelberg (2008)
15. Impagliazzo, R., Ruby, M.: One-Way Functions Are Essential for Complexity-Based Cryptography. In: Proceedings of FOCS 1989, pp. 230–235 (1989)
16. Impagliazzo, R., Rudich, S.: Limits on the Provable Consequences of One-Way Permutations. In: Proceedings of STOC 1989, pp. 44–61 (1989)
17. Ishai, Y., Kushilevitz, E., Lindell, Y., Petrank, E.: Black-Box Constructions for Secure Computation. In: Proceedings of STOC 2006, pp. 531–540 (2006)
18. Kilian, J.: Founding Cryptography on Oblivious Transfer. In: 20th ACM Symposium on the Theory of Computing, pp. 20–31 (1988)
19. MacWilliams, F.J., Sloane, N.J.A.: The Theory of Error-Correcting Codes. North-Holland, Amsterdam (1977)
20. Merkle, R.C.: Secure Communications over Insecure Channels. Communications of the ACM, 294–299 (1978)
21. Naor, M., Pinkas, B.: Efficient Oblivious Transfer Protocols. In: Proceedings of SODA 2001, pp. 448–457 (2001)
22. Rabin, M.: How to Exchange Secrets by Oblivious Transfer. Technical Report TR-81 (1981)
23. Reingold, O., Trevisan, L., Vadhan, S.P.: Notions of Reducibility between Cryptographic Primitives. In: Naor, M. (ed.) TCC 2004. LNCS, vol. 2951, pp. 1–20. Springer, Heidelberg (2004)
24. Yao, A.C.: How to Generate and Exchange Secrets. In: 27th IEEE Symposium on Theory of Computing, pp. 218–229 (1986)

Simulatable Adaptive Oblivious Transfer with Statistical Receiver's Privacy

Bingsheng Zhang

University of Tartu, Estonia
zhang@ut.ee

Abstract. During an adaptive oblivious transfer (OT), a sender has n private documents, and a receiver can adaptively fetch k documents from them such that the sender learns nothing about the receiver's selection and the receiver learns nothing more than those k documents. Most recent fully simulatable adaptive OT schemes are based on so-called "assisted decryption" or "blind decryption". In this paper, we revisit another technique, "blind permute-decryption", for designing adaptive OT. We propose an efficient generic fully simulatable oblivious transfer framework with statistical receiver's privacy that based on "blind permute-decryption" together with three concrete installations. The first one is based on Elgamal, so the corresponding OT is secure under classical DDH assumption. The second one is based on Paillier, so the corresponding OT is secure under Decisional n-th Residuosity assumption. Besides, we introduce an extended zero-knowledge proof framework with several applications.

Keywords: Adaptive oblivious transfer, Zero-knowledge Proof, fully simulatable security.

1   Introduction

Oblivious Transfer (OT) plays an important role in secure two-party computation, e.g. oblivious database manipulations. As a primitive, 1-out-of-2 oblivious transfer, denoting as OT_1^2, is a two-party protocol that used in many applications, such as Branching Program (BP) based cryptocomputing protocols [IP07]. Adaptive oblivious transfer, denoting as $\mathsf{OT}_{k\times1}^n$, is introduced by Naor and Pinkas in [NP99]. During an $\mathsf{OT}_{k\times1}^n$ protocol, a sender has n private documents, and a receiver can adaptively fetch k documents from them such that the sender learns nothing about the receiver's selection and the receiver learns nothing more than those k documents. In the ideal world, the sender sends $m_1, \cdots, m_n$ to a Trusted Third Party (**TTP**), and the receiver adaptively fetches m_{σ_i} from **TTP**, where the i-th index σ_i depends on $m_{\sigma_1}, \cdots, m_{\sigma_{i-1}}$. Many previous OT schemes in the literature, e.g. [CT05, Lip05], satisfy so-called half-simulation security. However, this security definition is vulnerable [NP99]; therefore, this paper will focus on fully simulatable $\mathsf{OT}_{k\times1}^n$ schemes. In particular, we are investigating a generic $\mathsf{OT}_{k\times1}^n$ framework that does not require a certain encryption scheme, so it is not limited to any concrete cryptographic assumption. Moreover, our two example schemes in this paper do not use bilinear group for efficiency.

X. Boyen and X. Chen (Eds.): ProvSec 2011, LNCS 6980, pp. 52–67, 2011.
© Springer-Verlag Berlin Heidelberg 2011

1.1   Related Work

Figure. 1 lists several existing $OT^n_{k \times 1}$ schemes, together with our proposed schemes for comparison. In 2007, Camenisch, Neven and shelat [CNS07] proposed an $OT^n_{k \times 1}$ under the q-strong Diffie-Hellman and q-power Decisional Diffie-Hellman assumptions in bilinear groups. They used signatures as a key ingredient in their scheme. Later, Green and Hohenberger [GH07] showed an $OT^n_{k \times 1}$ in random oracle model under Decisional Bilinear Diffie-Hellman assumption. In their scheme, the sender encrypts message m_i by identity-based encryption under identity i. The receiver executes a blind key extraction protocol such that he can obliviously obtain the secret key of any identity. In 2008, Green and Hohenberger [GH08] introduced another OT that achieves UC security in common reference string model, using Groth-Sahai non-interactive zero-knowledge proof for pairing product equations. The scheme is based on the decisional linear and q-Hidden LRSW assumptions. Jarecki and Liu [JL09] simplified the Camenisch et al. construction to a fully simulatable OT based on the Composite Decisional Residuosity and q-Decisional Diffie-Hellman Inversion assumptions. The scheme uses $pk = g^x$ and $c_i = m_i \cdot g^{1/(x+i)}$, and $g^{1/(x+i)}$ is Dodis-Yampolskiy verifiable pseudorandom function on input i [DY05]. The blind decryption is based on PRF with input i, and the protocol is the first efficient fully-simulatable OT without bilinear pairing. Rial, Kohlweiss and Preneel [RKP09] presented an adaptive priced OT that achieves UC security using "assisted decryption". In a priced OT, the receiver's privacy is still protected, even if the documents are paid at unique prices. The scheme is based on Decisional Linear, q-Triple Diffie-Hellman, and q-Hidden Strong Diffie-Hellman assumptions. Recently, Kurosawa and Nojima [KN09] gave adaptive OT constructions simple computational assumptions. Later, Kurosawa, Nojima and Phong [KNP10] improved the scheme [KN09] by increasing the complexity of initialization phase. In 2011, Green and Hohenberger [GH10] proposed another fully simulatable OT under Decisional 3-party Diffie-Hellman assumption. Very recently, *independent to this work*, Kurosawa, Nojima and Phong [KNP11] generalized their result in [KNP10] to various schemes with different assumptions.

1.2   Our Contributions

We proposed an extended zero-knowledge framework, and we enumerated several direct applications, including ZK argument for correct encryption, re-encryption, shuffle, etc. We also introduced a new efficient adaptive oblivious transfer framework with statistical receivers privacy that based on blind permute-decryption. Its communication cost is $\mathcal{O}(n + k) = \mathcal{O}(n)^1$ in initialization phase and $\mathcal{O}(1)$ in each transfer phase. In the first concrete installation, we use standard Elgamal encryption as building block, so the corresponding $OT^n_{k \times 1}$ achieves fully simulatable security under classical DDH assumption. The second concrete example scheme is based on Paillier encryption, so the corresponding $OT^n_{k \times 1}$ achieves fully simulatable security under Decisional n-th Residuosity assumption. What are the new contributions over the existing paper [KNP10]?

---

[1] By definition, $k \leq n$; otherwise, the OT is trivial, for the client is allowed to fetch the entire database if he/she wants.

Table 1. Survey On recent $\mathsf{OT}^n_{k\times 1}$ schemes. Ignore $\log n$ trivial factor in communication complexity

Scheme	Init Cost	Transfer Cost	Assumption	Security
Folklore	—	$\mathcal{O}(n)$	general assumptions	Full Sim
[KN09]	$\mathcal{O}(n)$	$\mathcal{O}(n)$	Decisional n-th Residuosity/DDH	Full Sim
[NP99]	—	$\mathcal{O}(n)$	DDH + OT^2_1	Half Sim
[KNP10]	$\mathcal{O}(n)$	$\mathcal{O}(1)$	DDH	Full Sim
[CNS07]	$\mathcal{O}(n)$	$\mathcal{O}(1)$	q-Power DDH + q-Strong DH	Full Sim
[GH08]	$\mathcal{O}(n)$	$\mathcal{O}(1)$	Decision Linear + q-Hidden LRSW	UC
[JL09]	$\mathcal{O}(n)$	$\mathcal{O}(1)$	Comp. Dec. Residuosity + q-DDHI	Full Sim
[RKP09]	$\mathcal{O}(n)$	$\mathcal{O}(1)$	DLIN + q-Hidden SDH + q-TDH	UC
[GH10]	$\mathcal{O}(n)$	$\mathcal{O}(1)$	Decision 3-Party DH + DLIN	Full Sim
[KNP11]	$\mathcal{O}(n)$	$\mathcal{O}(1)$	DDH/d-Linear/DCR/QR/LWE	Full Sim
Sect. 3.4	$\mathcal{O}(n)$	$\mathcal{O}(1)$	DDH	Full Sim
Sect. 3.5	$\mathcal{O}(n)$	$\mathcal{O}(1)$	Decisional n-th Residuosity	Full Sim

Paper [KNP10] proposed the idea of shuffle based OT and gave ZK shuffle argument under DDH assumption. We improve it further to blind-permute re-encryption that gives statistical receivers privacy, and we gave generic ZK argument for correct blind-permute re-encryption that does not require a certain encryption scheme, so it is not limited to any concrete cryptographic assumption. (cf. Sect. 3.2, below) Hence, we can extend their OT scheme to generic $\mathsf{OT}^n_{k\times 1}$ framework, which is suitable for most IND-CPA secure encryptions. Moreover, in paper [GH10], the authors gave critical comments on [KNP10], claiming that shuffle-based OT does not satisfy standard fully simulatable security definition, for it leaks information if the receiver submits repeated queries. As a response, we offer a simple solution to the issue, and it is also adaptable to [KNP10] scheme. we use dummy-document technique in initialization phase to make our $\mathsf{OT}^n_{k\times 1}$ framework fulfill standard security definition with additional cost of $\mathcal{O}(k)$ at initialization phase.

2   Preliminaries

2.1   Zero-Knowledge Proof and Σ-Protocol

We follow the definitions described in [CDM00a, BG93]. A pair of interactive algorithms $(\mathcal{P}, \mathcal{V})$, called a prover and a verifier is a proof of knowledge for a relation $\mathcal{R} = \{(\alpha, \beta)\} \subseteq \{0, 1\}^* \times \{0, 1\}^*$ with knowledge error $\kappa \in [0, 1]$ if for all $(\alpha, \beta) \in \mathcal{R}$, $\mathcal{V}(\alpha)$ accepts a conversation with $\mathcal{P}(\beta)$ with probability 1, and there exists a polynomial time knowledge extractor $\mathcal{E}$ such that if a cheating prover $\hat{\mathcal{P}}$ has probability ε of convincing $\mathcal{V}$ to accept α, then $\mathcal{E}$ outputs a witness β for α with probability $\varepsilon - \kappa$ via rewindable black-box access to $\hat{\mathcal{P}}$.

A proof system $(\mathcal{P}, \mathcal{V})$ is computational honest-verifier zero-knowledge if there exists a p.p.t. simulator $\mathcal{S}$ such that for any $(\alpha, \beta) \in \mathcal{R}$, the outputs of $\mathcal{V}(\alpha)$ after interacting with $\mathcal{P}(\beta)$ or with $\mathcal{S}(\alpha)$ are computationally indistinguishable. It is possible to transform an honest-verifier zero-knowledge proof system to a general zero-knowledge one, e.g. [CDM00b]. Therefore, our ZK argument will be honest-verifier zero-knowledge throughout the paper.

A Σ-Protocol for language $\mathcal{L}$ is a proof system $(\mathcal{P}, \mathcal{V})$ where the conversation is a tuple (α, β, γ), where $\mathcal{P}$ outputs α and $\mathcal{V}$ gives a random challenge β, and then $\mathcal{P}$ replies γ. $\mathcal{V}$ accepts if $\phi(x, \alpha, \beta, \gamma) = 1$, where ϕ is a predicate function. A Σ-protocol must satisfy three security properties: correctness, special soundness and special honest-verifier zero knowledge. A Σ-protocol is correct when an honest prover convinces an honest verifier with probability $1 - k^{-w(1)}$. A Σ-protocol has the special soundness property when from two accepted views (α, β, γ) and $(\alpha, \beta', \gamma')$, where $\beta \neq \beta'$, one can efficiently recover a witness w such that $w \rightarrow x \in \mathcal{R}$. A Σ-protocol has the special honest-verifier zero-knowledge property if there exists a p.p.t. simulator $\mathcal{S}$ that can output a tuple $(\alpha^*, \beta^*, \gamma^*)$ that will be accepted and such the distribution of $(\alpha^*, \beta^*, \gamma^*)$ is computationally indistinguishable from the distribution of accepted views between an honest prover and an honest verifier.

2.2 Security Definition (Fully Simulation Security)

We recap the same security definition that used in papers [NP99, CNS07, GH10]. Let tuple $(\mathcal{S}_I, \mathcal{R}_I, \mathcal{S}_T, \mathcal{R}_T)$ be the adaptive oblivious transfer $\mathrm{OT}^n_{k \times 1}$. Denote S_*, R_* as state values. During the initialization phase, the sender executes $S_0 \leftarrow \mathcal{S}_I(m_1, \cdots, m_n)$, and the receiver executes $R_0 \leftarrow \mathcal{R}_I()$. During the i-th transfer phase, $1 \leq i \leq k$, the sender executes $S_i \leftarrow \mathcal{S}_T(S_{i-1})$, and the receiver executes $(R_i, m^*_{\sigma_i}) \leftarrow \mathcal{R}_T(R_{i-1}, \sigma_i)$, where $1 \leq \sigma_i \leq n$ is the index of the message to be received. $m^*_{\sigma_i} = m_{\sigma_i}$ if successes, $m^*_{\sigma_i} = \bot$ if fails. The security of an $\mathrm{OT}^n_{k \times 1}$ scheme is defined in real-world/ideal-world paradigm with static corruption, i.e. the adversary $\mathcal{A}$ can only choose to corrupt either the sender or the receiver at the beginning of the experiments.

Real Experiment. In experiment $\mathbf{Real}_{\hat{\mathbf{S}}, \hat{\mathbf{R}}}(n, k, m_1, \cdots, m_n, \Sigma)$, the presumably cheating sender $\hat{\mathbf{S}}$ is given messages $(m_1, \cdots, m_n)$ as input and interacts with the presumably cheating receiver $\hat{\mathbf{R}}(\Sigma)$, where Σ is a selection algorithm that on input messages $m_{\sigma_1}, \cdots, m_{\sigma_{i-1}}$, outputs the index σ_i of the next message to be queried. In the initialization phase, $\hat{\mathbf{S}}$ and $\hat{\mathbf{R}}$ output the initial states S_0 and R_0. In the i-th transfer phase, for $1 \leq i \leq k$, the sender runs $S_i \leftarrow \hat{\mathbf{S}}(S_{i-1})$, and the receiver runs $(R_i, m'_i) \leftarrow \hat{\mathbf{R}}(R_{i-1})$, where m'_i is not necessary equal to m_i. After the k-th transfer, the output of the experiment $\mathbf{Real}_{\hat{\mathbf{S}}, \hat{\mathbf{R}}}$ is the tuple (S_k, R_k).

We define the honest sender algorithm $\mathbf{S}$ as the one that runs $\mathcal{S}_I(m_1, \cdots, m_n)$ in the initialization phase, runs $\mathcal{S}_T()$ during each transfer phase, and returns $S_k = \varepsilon$ as its final output. The honest receiver algorithm $\mathbf{R}$ runs $\mathcal{R}_I()$ in the initialization phase, runs $\mathcal{R}_T(R_{i-1}, \sigma_i)$ during the i-th transfer phase, where the index σ_i is generated by Σ, and returns $R_k = (m_{\sigma_1}, \cdots, m_{\sigma_k})$ as its final output.

Ideal Experiment. In experiment $\mathbf{Ideal}_{\hat{\mathbf{S}}', \hat{\mathbf{R}}'}(n, k, m_1, \cdots, m_n, \Sigma)$, the presumably cheating sender $\hat{\mathbf{S}}'$ and the presumably cheating receiver $\hat{\mathbf{R}}'$ communicate with the ideal functionality $\mathcal{F}_{OT}^{n \times 1}$. In the initialization phase, $\hat{\mathbf{S}}'(m_1, \cdots, m_n)$ sends messages $m_1^*, \cdots, m_n^*$ to $\mathcal{F}_{OT}^{n \times 1}$. In the i-th transfer phase, for $1 \leq i \leq k$, $\hat{\mathbf{R}}'(\Sigma)$ sends to $\mathcal{F}_{OT}^{n \times 1}$ an index σ_i^*. $\mathcal{F}_{OT}^{n \times 1}$ then sends a tag 'Received' to $\hat{\mathbf{S}}'$, and $\hat{\mathbf{S}}'$ replies a bit $b_i \in \{0, 1\}$ to $\mathcal{F}_{OT}^{n \times 1}$. If $b_i = 1$ and $\sigma_i^* \in \{1, \cdots, n\}$, $\mathcal{F}_{OT}^{n \times 1}$ sends $m_{\sigma_i^*}^*$ to $\hat{\mathbf{R}}'$; otherwise, it sends $\perp$ to $\hat{\mathbf{R}}'$. After the k-th transfer, the output of the experiment $\mathbf{Ideal}_{\hat{\mathbf{S}}', \hat{\mathbf{R}}'}$ is the tuple (S_k, R_k).

Similarly, we define the honest sender algorithm $\mathbf{S}'(m_1, \cdots, m_n)$ as the one that sends $m_1, \cdots, m_n$ to $\mathcal{F}_{OT}^{n \times 1}$ in the initialization phase, sends $b_i = 1$ during each transfer phase, and returns $S_k = \varepsilon$ as its final output. The honest receiver $\mathbf{R}'$ submits the indices σ_i that generated by Σ to $\mathcal{F}_{OT}^{n \times 1}$, and returns $R_k = (m_{\sigma_1}, \cdots, m_{\sigma_k})$ as its final output.

Denote $\mathrm{poly}(\cdot)$ as a polynomially-bounded function. The security is defined as follows.

Sender Security. An $\mathsf{OT}_{k \times 1}^n$ is sender-secure if for every real-world p.p.t. receiver $\hat{\mathbf{R}}$, there exists an ideal-world p.p.t. receiver $\hat{\mathbf{R}}'$ such that for any $n = \mathrm{poly}(\kappa)$, any $k \in [0, n]$, any messages $(m_1, \cdots, m_n)$, any selection algorithm Σ, and every p.p.t. distinguisher $\mathbf{D}$:

$$\mathbf{Real}_{\mathbf{S}, \hat{\mathbf{R}}}(n, k, m_1, \cdots, m_n, \Sigma) \overset{c}{\approx} \mathbf{Ideal}_{\mathbf{S}', \hat{\mathbf{R}}'}(n, k, m_1, \cdots, m_n, \Sigma)$$

Receiver Security. An $\mathsf{OT}_{k \times 1}^n$ is receiver-secure if for every real-world p.p.t. receiver $\hat{\mathbf{S}}$, there exists an ideal-world p.p.t. receiver $\hat{\mathbf{S}}'$ such that for any $n = \mathrm{poly}(\kappa)$, any $k \in [0, n]$, any messages $(m_1, \cdots, m_n)$, any selection algorithm Σ, and every p.p.t. distinguisher $\mathbf{D}$:

$$\mathbf{Real}_{\hat{\mathbf{S}}, \mathbf{R}}(n, k, m_1, \cdots, m_n, \Sigma) \overset{c}{\approx} \mathbf{Ideal}_{\hat{\mathbf{S}}', \mathbf{R}'}(n, k, m_1, \cdots, m_n, \Sigma)$$

Definition 1. *We say a fully simulatable* $\mathsf{OT}_{k \times 1}^n$ *is secure iff it achieves both sender and receiver security.*

3   Fully Simulatable $\mathsf{OT}_{k \times 1}^n$ with Statistical Receiver's Privacy

Kurosawa, Nojima and Phong [KNP10] proposed a fully simulatable $\mathsf{OT}_{k \times 1}^n$ under DDH Assumption, and we are going to show our improved construction, which gives us a fully simulatable $\mathsf{OT}_{k \times 1}^n$ framework with statistical receiver's privacy if the underlying encryption scheme is IND-CPA secure. We are going to introduce a new technique called "blind-permute decryption". First, we will give the definition about blind-permute re-encryption as follows.

Definition 2. *We say the set of ciphertexts* $\{c_i' = E(m_i'; r_i')\}$ *is blind-permute re-encryption of the set of ciphertexts* $\{c_i = E(m_i; r_i)\}$ *if and only if* $\exists \pi \forall i \exists \{(u_i, v_i)\}$: $m_i' = f_1(m_{\pi(i)}, u_{\pi(i)}) \wedge r_i' = f_2(r_{\pi(i)}, v_{\pi(i)})$, *where* π *is a permutation,* $(\forall x) f_1(x, r_1 \overset{\$}{\leftarrow} \Omega_1)$ *has uniform distribution and* $(\forall y) f_2(y, r_2 \overset{\$}{\leftarrow} \Omega_2)$ *has uniform distribution.*

In our scheme, we also require f_1 to be invertible, i.e. $\forall (x, r) : x = f_1^{-1}(f_1(x, r), r)$. One possible blind-permute re-encryption example based on Elgamal encryption could be $\{c_i = (g^{r_i}, m_i \cdot h^{r_i})\}$ and $\{c'_i = (g^{r'_i}, m'_i \cdot h^{r'_i})\}$, where $m'_i = m_{\pi(i)} \cdot g^{u_{\pi(i)}}$ and $r'_i = r_{\pi(i)} + v_{\pi(i)}$. During a blind permute-decryption protocol, Alice sends Bob a set of ciphertexts; Bob performs blind-permute re-encryption on the ciphertexts and sends back to Alice; Alice then blind-decrypts them.

3.1 Extended Zero-Knowledge Proof Framework

A well-known zero-knowledge proof framework for proof of knowledge (ZK-PoK) is based on homomorphic commitments. The prover $\mathcal{P}$ knows a secret s, and he publishes com(s). To prove knowledge of s, $\mathcal{P}$ first commits a randomizer r and sends $\alpha := \text{com}(r)$ to the verifier $\mathcal{V}$. The verifier $\mathcal{V}$ picks a challenge $\beta := b \leftarrow \{0, 1\}$. If $b = 0$, $\mathcal{P}$ opens com(r); if $b = 1$, $\mathcal{P}$ opens com$(s \circ r) := \text{com}(s) \bullet \text{com}(r)$, where $\bullet$ is homomorphic commitment operation and $(\forall s)X = s \circ r \stackrel{\$}{\leftarrow} \Omega$ has uniform distribution. $\mathcal{V}$ accepts the proof if he can successfully verify the commitment either com(r) or com$(s \circ r)$, according to b. We repeat the proof κ times to amplify the soundness property. The well-known Fiat-Shamir identification protocol uses com$(s) := s^2$ based on quadratic residue problem. Most homomorphic commitments can be used in this framework, for instance, one can use Pedersen Commitment for perfect hiding.

We would like to extend this zero-knowledge proof framework to be suitable for generalised-associative functions. Its definition is given as following.

Definition 3. *Let $\mathcal{S}_1, \mathcal{S}_2, \mathcal{S}_3$ be three sets. We say functions $f : \mathcal{S}_1 \times \mathcal{S}_2 \rightarrow \mathcal{S}_3$, $g : \mathcal{S}_3 \times \mathcal{S}_2 \rightarrow \mathcal{S}_3$ and $h : \mathcal{S}_2 \times \mathcal{S}_2 \rightarrow \mathcal{S}_2$ are generalised-associative if and only if*

$$\forall x_i, y_i \in \mathcal{S}_i : g(f(x_1, x_2), y_2) = f(x_1, h(x_2, y_2))$$

Additionally, we require g, f, h have the following properies. Given $x \in \mathcal{S}_1$ and $f(x, y \stackrel{\$}{\leftarrow} \mathcal{S}_2)$, there is no p.p.t. algorithm to output correct y with significant probability. Similarly, given $x \in \mathcal{S}_3$ and $g(x, y \stackrel{\$}{\leftarrow} \mathcal{S}_2)$, there is no p.p.t. algorithm to output correct y with significant probability. Given $x \in \mathcal{S}_2$, the distribution of $D := h(x, r \stackrel{\$}{\leftarrow} \mathcal{S}_2)$ and the distribution of $D' : r' \stackrel{\$}{\leftarrow} \mathcal{S}_2$ are computationally indistinguishable.

In the ZK proof framework, $c_0 := x_1$ is public information. The prover $\mathcal{P}$ outputs statement $c_1 := f(x_1, x_2)$ and he wants to convince the verifier $\mathcal{V}$ that he knows x_2. (Namely, $\mathcal{P}$ has correctly performed function f with private input x_2.) $\mathcal{P}$ first randomly picks $y_2 \in \mathcal{S}_2$ and outputs $\alpha := g(c_1, y_2)$. The verifier $\mathcal{V}$ outputs a challenge $\beta := b \leftarrow \{0, 1\}$. If $b = 0$, $\mathcal{P}$ publishes $\gamma_0 := y_2$; if $b = 1$, $\mathcal{P}$ publishes $\gamma_1 := h(x_2, y_2)$. $\mathcal{V}$ accepts the proof if either $\alpha = g(c_1, \gamma_0)$ is correct or $\alpha = f(c_0, \gamma_1)$ is correct, according to b. It is obvious that there exists a p.p.t. simulator, and we skip the construction details here. In order to have knowledge extractor $\mathcal{E}$, we also require that h has inverse function, i.e. there exists h^{-1}. Therefore, we can extract secret $x_2 = h^{-1}(\gamma_0, \gamma_1)$. Again, repeat κ times for reasonable soundness.

3.2   Applications

ZK Argument for Correct Encryption, Re-encryption and Ciphertext Manipulation. For encryption, given message m and public key pk, the prover $\mathcal{P}$ outputs a ciphertext C, and he wants to convince the verifier $\mathcal{V}$ that (m, C) is a valid plaintext-ciphertext pair. Follow our framework, $c_1 = f(m, r) := E_{pk}(m; r)$ and $c_2 = g(f(m, r), r')$ is defined as $E_{pk}(m; r)E_{pk}(0; r')$ for additive homomorphic schemes or $E_{pk}(m; r)E_{pk}(1; r')$ for multiplicative homomorphic schemes. By homomorphic property, we have $c_2 = E_{pk}(m; r \circ r')$, where $\circ$ depends on concrete schemes. For brevity, take additive homomorphic as an example. The correctness of encryption is equivalent to prove that the prover knows r. Assume that both $\mathcal{P}$ and $\mathcal{V}$ knows $c_0 := m$; otherwise, $\mathcal{P}$ also publishes c_0. $\mathcal{P}$ outputs statement c_1, and starts ZK proof as follows. $\mathcal{P}$ randomly chooses r' and sends $\alpha := c_2$, and then $\mathcal{V}$ picks challenge $\beta := b \leftarrow \{0, 1\}$. If $b = 0$, $\mathcal{P}$ reveals $\gamma_0 := r'$; if $b = 1$, $\mathcal{P}$ reveals $\gamma_1 := r \circ r'$. $\mathcal{V}$ accepts the proof if either $c_2 = c_1 \cdot E_{pk}(0; r')$ or $c_2 = c_0 \cdot E_{pk}(0; r \circ r')$, according to b. Repeat κ times with different randomizer r'. Similarly, we can prove re-encryption or double re-encryption, e.g. the one used in [AW07]. If m is also private, the prover $\mathcal{P}$ can first publish a template, e.g. $T := E_{pk}(1; 1)$, such that everyone can verify. Then $\mathcal{P}$ proves that he knows m, r to re-encrypt T to $c_1 := E_{pk}(m; r)$. More importantly, we can prove correctness of ciphertext manipulation with similar approach, such as $E_{pk}(a; r)E_{pk}(b; r')$.

ZK Argument for Correct Shuffle and Blind-permute Re-encryption. Take Elgamal encryption as an example, the prover $\mathcal{P}$ outputs $c_0 := \{E_{pk}(m_i; r_i)\}$ and $c_1 := \{E_{pk}(m_{\pi(i)}\alpha_{\pi(i)}; r_{\pi(i)} + r'_{\pi(i)})\} \leftarrow \{E_{pk}(m_{\pi(i)}; r_{\pi(i)})E_{pk}(\alpha_{\pi(i)}; r'_{\pi(i)})\}$ for private $\pi, \{\alpha_i\}, \{r'_i\}$, and he wants to convince the verifier $\mathcal{V}$ that c_1 is blind-permute re-encryption of c_0. To prove the knowledge of $\pi, \{\alpha_i\}, \{r'_i\}$, the prover $\mathcal{P}$ randomly chooses $\sigma, \{\beta_i\}, \{t_i\}$ and performs blind-permutate re-encryption again. $\mathcal{P}$ then outputs $\alpha := c_2 := \{E_{pk}(m_{\sigma\pi(i)}\alpha_{\sigma\pi(i)}\beta_{\sigma\pi(i)}; r_{\sigma\pi(i)} + r'_{\sigma\pi(i)} + t_{\sigma\pi(i)})\}$. The verifier $\mathcal{V}$ picks a challenge $\beta := b \leftarrow \{0, 1\}$. If $b = 0$, the prover $\mathcal{P}$ reveals $\sigma, \{\beta_{\sigma\pi(i)}\}, \{t_{\sigma\pi(i)}\}$ between c_1 and c_2; if $b = 1$, $\mathcal{P}$ reveals $\sigma \circ \pi, \{\alpha_{\sigma\pi(i)}\beta_{\sigma\pi(i)}\}, \{r'_{\sigma\pi(i)} + t_{\sigma\pi(i)}\}$ between c_0 and c_2. The verifier $\mathcal{V}$ check either (c_1, c_2) is blind-permute re-encryption or (c_0, c_2) is blind-permute re-encryption, according to b. Denote $c_{j,i}$ for the i-th ciphertext in c_j, where $j \in \{0, 1, 2\}$ and $i \in \{1, \cdots, n\}$. For example, to check whether (c_1, c_2) is blind-permute re-encryption, $\mathcal{V}$ checks whether $c_{2,i} = c_{1,\sigma(i)} \cdot E_{pk}(\beta_{\sigma\pi(i)}; t_{\sigma\pi(i)})$ for $i \in \{1, \cdots, n\}$. Similarly, after repeating κ times for different tuples $(\sigma, \{\beta_i\}, \{t_i\})$, $\mathcal{V}$ believes that (c_0, c_1) is indeed blind-permute re-encryption. Set randomizers α_i, β_i to constant 1, we get ZK argument for standard shuffle.

ZK Range Proof. Let $E_{pk}(*, *)$ be an additively homomorphic encryption scheme. First of all, we are going to show the ZK argument for $E_{pk}(b; *)$, where $b \in \{0, 1\}$. Since we have shown ZK argument for correct shuffle, one can first create a template $(C_0 := E_{pk}(0; r_0), C_1 := E_{pk}(1; r_1)$ and reveal r_0, r_1 so that everyone can check (C_0, C_1). The prover $\mathcal{P}$ outputs encryptions $\{B_i := E_{pk}(b_i)\}$, and he proves that each B_i is a correct re-encryption of C_0 or C_1 by using standard disjunction technique of Sigma protocols. If we apply this proof based on generalized paillier cryptosystem [DJ01], we can directly transfer Lipmaa's PIR [Lip05] to OT_1^n by adding our ZK range proof for the receiver's inputs. For general arbitrary range $x \in [L, R]$, it is sufficient to prove $x \in [0, Y]$, where $Y = R - L$. One can apply additive combinatorics that used in [LAN02]:

$$[0, Y] = \sum_{i=0}^{\lfloor \log_2 Y \rfloor} \lfloor \frac{Y + 2^i}{2^{i+1}} \rfloor * [0, 1]$$

Alternatively, we can disassemble Y to $t_0, \cdots, t_k$, where $Y = \sum_{i=0}^{k} t_i$ and $t_i = 2^{e_i} - 1$ for some $e_i \geq 0$. To prove $t_i \in [0, 2^{e_i} - 1]$, the prover just encrypts e_i bits separately $c_j := E_{pk}(u_j, *)$ for $0 \leq j \leq e_i - 1$, and $\mathcal{P}$ proves each $u_j \in \{0, 1\}$. $t_i = \sum_{j=0}^{e_i} 2^j u_j$.

3.3   Generic Fully Simulatable $OT_{k \times 1}^n$ Framework

We are going to propose a generic fully simulatable $OT_{k \times 1}^n$ framework that uses homomorphic encryption schemes. We use the technique "blind-permute decryption". During the protocol, the sender first sends ciphertexts of documents to the receiver, and the receiver perform a blind-permute re-encryption and sends them back to the sender. After that, in each transfer phase, the receiver simply asks the sender to decrypt the corresponding ciphertext. Of course, zero-knowledge proofs are necessary for correctness. The framework consists of two parts: OT_{init} and $OT_{transfer}$. (cf. Fig. 1 and Fig. 2, below)

Security. Our framework is fully simulatable $OT_{k \times 1}^n$ with statistical receiver's privacy if the underlying encryption scheme is IND-CPA secure. We use dummy documents to deal with repeated-query issue that mentioned in [GH10]. If someone wants even

---

OT_{init} of Generic Fully Simulatable $OT_{k \times 1}^n$ Framework

Sender's input: $\{m_1, \cdots, m_n\}$.
Sender's output: S_0.
Receiver's output: R_0.

1. The Sender **S** generates a key pair (sk, pk), and he sends pk to the receiver **R**.
2. **S** proves to **R** that he knows sk by ZK-PoK.
3. **S** encrypts $c_i := E_{pk}(m_i; r_i)$ for $i \in \{1, \ldots, n\}$, and he encrypts k dummy documents $c_i := E_{pk}(1; r_i)$ for $i \in \{n + 1, \ldots, n + k - 1\}$. **S** sends $\{c_i\}$ to **R**.
4. **S** proves to **R** that the encryption is correct by ZK-PoK, e.g. prove that c_i is re-encryption of $E_{pk}(1; 1)$ by ZK-PoK 3.2.
5. **R** picks permutation π and randomizers $\{\alpha_i\}, \{r_i'\}$. He performs blind-permute re-encryption from $\{c_i\}$ to $\{C_i := c_{\pi(i)} \bullet E_{pk}(\alpha_{\pi(i)}; r_{\pi(i)}')\}$ for $i \in \{1, \ldots, n + k - 1\}$, where $\bullet$ depends on concrete encryption schemes.
6. **R** proves correctness of blind-permute re-encryption by ZK-PoK proof in Sec. 3.2.
7. Set $S_0 := (\{C_i\}, (sk, pk))$ and $R_0 := (pk, \{C_i\}, \{\alpha_i\}, \pi, DB[n] = \{\})$.

Fig. 1. OT_{init} of Generic Fully Simulatable $OT_{k \times 1}^n$ Framework

---

The i-th OT$_{transfer}$ of Generic Fully Simulatable OT$_{k\times 1}^n$ Framework

Sender's input: S_{i-1}.
Receiver's iutput: R_{i-1}, σ_i.
Sender's output: S_i.
Receiver's output: m_{σ_i}, R_i.

1. The receiver **R** parses R_{i-1} to $pk, \{C_i\}, \{\alpha_i\}, \pi$ and DB.
2. If $DB[\sigma_i]$ has record, set $\sigma_i' = n + i$; otherwise, set $\sigma_i' = \sigma_i$.
3. **R** sends $q = \pi^{-1}(\sigma_i')$ to the sender **S**.
4. **S** computes $Y_q = D_{sk}(C_q)$ and sends to **R**. He proves the decryption is correct by ZK-PoK.
5. $m_{\sigma_i'} = Y_q \circledast \alpha_{\sigma_i'}$, where $\circledast$ depends on concrete encryption scheme.
6. Set $S_i := S_{i-1}$. If $\sigma_i' \in [1, n]$, $DB[\sigma_i'] = m_{\sigma_i'}$. Update $R_i := (pk, \{C_i\}, \{\alpha_i\}, \pi, DB)$. Set $m_{\sigma_i} = DB[\sigma_i]$.

Fig. 2. OT$_{transfer}$ of Generic Fully Simulatable OT$_{k\times 1}^n$ Framework

stronger privacy, [GIKM98] shows that there is a transformation of any PIR or OT scheme into information theoretic sender's privacy with the cost of increasing the number of servers (senders), introducing the assumption of a separation between the servers.

Theorem 1. *The proposed* OT$_{k\times 1}^n$ *framework (shown in Figure 1 and 2) is statistically secure against the sender corruption.*

Proof. We show that for every real-world cheating p.p.t. sender $\hat{S}$ there exists an ideal-world cheating p.p.t. sender $\hat{S}'$ such that for every distinguisher D:

$$\mathbf{Real}_{\hat{S},\mathbf{R}}(n, k, m_1, \cdots, m_n, \Sigma) \overset{\$}{\approx} \mathbf{Ideal}_{\hat{S}',\mathbf{R}'}(n, k, m_1, \cdots, m_n, \Sigma)$$

Considering a sequence of games $G_0, \cdots, G_5$, where Game $G_0 = \mathbf{Real}_{\hat{S},\mathbf{R}}$ and Game $G_5 = \mathbf{Ideal}_{\hat{S}',\mathbf{R}'}$. We define

$$Adv[D] = |Pr[D(X) = 1 : X \overset{\$}{\leftarrow} \mathbf{Ideal}_{\hat{S}',\mathbf{R}'}] - Pr[D(X) = 1 : X \overset{\$}{\leftarrow} \mathbf{Real}_{\hat{S},\mathbf{R}}]|$$

Game G_0: The real-world experiment $\mathbf{Real}_{\hat{S},\mathbf{R}}$. By definition, $Pr[D(X) = 1 : X \overset{\$}{\leftarrow} G_0] = Pr[D(X) = 1 : X \overset{\$}{\leftarrow} \mathbf{Real}_{\hat{S},\mathbf{R}}]$.

Game G_1: Game G_1 is the same as Game G_0 except the following. In initialization phase, the receiver uses the knowledge extractor of the ZK-PoK to extract sk and $\{r_i\}$ from $\hat{S}$. If extraction fails, then the protocol aborts. Since the failure probability is negligible, $Pr[D(X) = 1 : X \overset{\$}{\leftarrow} G_1] \approx Pr[D(X) = 1 : X \overset{\$}{\leftarrow} G_0]$.

Game G_2: Game G_2 is the same as Game G_1 except the following. In initialization phase, the receiver uses the ZK-PoK simulator for blind-permute re-encryption proof. Thus, $Pr[D(X) = 1 : X \overset{\$}{\leftarrow} G_2] \approx Pr[D(X) = 1 : X \overset{\$}{\leftarrow} G_1]$.

Game G_3: Game G_3 is the same as Game G_2 except the following. In initialization phase, the receiver computes $\{C_i\} = E_{pk}(\hat{r}_i, *)$, where $\hat{r}_i$ is randomly chosen, and sends them to the sender. Since the distribution of $\{C_i\}$ is unchanged, $Pr[D(X) = 1 : X \xleftarrow{\$} G_3] = Pr[D(X) = 1 : X \xleftarrow{\$} G_2]$.

Game G_4: Game G_4 is the same as Game G_3 except the following. In each transfer phase, the receiver maintains a set Q that stores all queried indices. Each time, the receiver picks a random index q such that $q \notin Q$. He adds q to Q and sends q to the sender. Since the view is unchanged, $Pr[D(X) = 1 : X \xleftarrow{\$} G_4] = Pr[D(X) = 1 : X \xleftarrow{\$} G_3]$.

Game G_5: The ideal-world experiment $\mathbf{Ideal}_{\hat{\mathbf{S}}', \mathbf{R}'}$ in which an ideal-world sender $\hat{\mathbf{S}}'$ uses the real-world sender $\hat{\mathbf{S}}$ as a black-box as follows.

1. After receiving $(m_1, \cdots, m_n)$, $\hat{\mathbf{S}}'$ forwards them to $\hat{\mathbf{S}}$.
2. $\hat{\mathbf{S}}'$ acts as the receiver and plays Game G_4 with $\hat{\mathbf{S}}$.
3. In the initialization phase, $\hat{\mathbf{S}}'$ decrypts $\{c_i\}$ to obtain $\{m_i^*\}$ with the sk and $\{r_i\}$ extracted in Game G_1. He then sends $(m_1^*, \cdots m_n^*)$ to $\mathcal{F}_{OT}^{n \times 1}$.
4. In each transfer phase, if $\hat{\mathbf{S}}$ behaved in an acceptable way, then $\hat{\mathbf{S}}'$ sends $b = 1$ to $\mathcal{F}_{OT}^{n \times 1}$. Otherwise, $\hat{\mathbf{S}}'$ sends $b = 0$ to $\mathcal{F}_{OT}^{n \times 1}$.

To sum up, it is easy to see that $Adv(D) = |Pr[D(X) = 1 : X \xleftarrow{\$} G_5] - Pr[D(X) = 1 : X \xleftarrow{\$} G_0]|$ is negligible. $\square$

Theorem 2. *The proposed $OT_{k \times 1}^n$ framework (shown in Figure 1 and 2) is secure against the receiver corruption if the underlying encryption scheme is IND-CPA secure.*

Proof. We show that for every real-world cheating p.p.t. receiver $\hat{\mathbf{R}}$ there exists an ideal-world cheating p.p.t. receiver $\hat{\mathbf{R}}'$ such that for every distinguisher D:

$$\mathbf{Real}_{\mathbf{S}, \hat{\mathbf{R}}}(n, k, m_1, \cdots, m_n, \Sigma) \overset{c}{\approx} \mathbf{Ideal}_{\mathbf{S}', \hat{\mathbf{R}}'}(n, k, m_1, \cdots, m_n, \Sigma)$$

Again, we consider a series of hybrid games $G_0, \cdots, G_5$, where Game $G_0 = \mathbf{Real}_{\mathbf{S}, \hat{\mathbf{R}}}$ and Game $G_5 = \mathbf{Ideal}_{\mathbf{S}', \hat{\mathbf{R}}'}$. We define

$$Adv[D] = |Pr[D(X) = 1 : X \xleftarrow{\$} \mathbf{Ideal}_{\mathbf{S}', \hat{\mathbf{R}}'}] - Pr[D(X) = 1 : X \xleftarrow{\$} \mathbf{Real}_{\mathbf{S}, \hat{\mathbf{R}}}]|$$

Game G_0: The real-world experiment $\mathbf{Real}_{\mathbf{S}, \hat{\mathbf{R}}}$. By definition, $Pr[D(X) = 1 : X \xleftarrow{\$} G_0] = Pr[D(X) = 1 : X \xleftarrow{\$} \mathbf{Real}_{\mathbf{S}, \hat{\mathbf{R}}}]$.

Game G_1: Game G_1 is the same as Game G_0 except the following. In the initialization phase, the sender uses the knowledge extractor of the ZK-PoK for blind-permute re-encryption proof to extract π, $\{\alpha_i\}$, $\{r_i'\}$ from $\mathcal{A}$. If extraction fails, then the protocol aborts. In each transfer phase, the sender extracts the index $\sigma_i = \pi(q)$. Since the failure probability is negligible, $Pr[D(X) = 1 : X \xleftarrow{\$} G_1] = Pr[D(X) = 1 : X \xleftarrow{\$} G_0]$.

Game G_2: Game G_2 is the same as Game G_1 except the following. In each transfer phase, if $\sigma_i \in [1, n]$, the sender computes $Y_q = m_{\sigma_i} \circledast^{-1} \alpha_{\sigma_i}$, where $\circledast$ operation depends on concrete encryption schemes; otherwise, he computes $Y_q = 1 \circledast^{-1} \alpha_{\sigma_i}$. Since it is identical, $Pr[D(X) = 1 : X \xleftarrow{\$} G_2] = Pr[D(X) = 1 : X \xleftarrow{\$} G_1]$.

Game G_3: Game G_3 is the same as Game G_2 except the following. In each transfer phase, the sender uses simulator of the ZK-PoK to prove that the decryption is correct. Thus, $Pr[D(X) = 1 : X \xleftarrow{\$} G_3] \approx Pr[D(X) = 1 : X \xleftarrow{\$} G_2]$.

Game G_4: Game G_4 is the same as Game G_3 except the following. In the initialization phase, the sender replaces c_i with $E_{pk}(\gamma_i)$, where γ_i is randomly chosen. Due to indistinguishability of ciphertexts, $Pr[D(X) = 1 : X \xleftarrow{\$} G_4] \approx Pr[D(X) = 1 : X \xleftarrow{\$} G_3]$.

Game G_5: The ideal-world experiment $\mathbf{Ideal}_{S', \hat{R}'}$ in which an ideal-world receiver $\hat{R}'$ uses the real-world receiver $\hat{R}$ as a black-box as follows.

1. $\hat{R}'$ acts as the sender and plays Game G_4 with $\hat{R}$.
2. In each transfer phase, if $\sigma_i \in [1, n]$, where σ_i is extracted in Game G_1, $\hat{R}'$ sends σ_i to $\mathcal{F}_{OT}^{n \times 1}$ and fetches m_{σ_i} from $\mathcal{F}_{OT}^{n \times 1}$. If if $\sigma_i \in [n+1, n+k-1]$, $\hat{R}'$ sends random $\hat{\sigma}_i \leftarrow \{1, \cdots, n\}$ to $\mathcal{F}_{OT}^{n \times 1}$, and prepare dummy document '1'. Therefore, he can reply Y_q as in Game G_2 with knowledge $\pi, \{\alpha_i\}, \{r'_i\}$ that extracted in Game G_1.

To sum up, it is easy to see that $Adv(\mathcal{Z}) = |Pr(G_0) - Pr(G_5)|$ is negligible.   □

Theorem 3. *The proposed $OT_{k \times 1}^n$ framework (shown in Figure 1 and 2) is fully simulatable secure with statistical receivers privacy if the underlying encryption scheme is IND-CPA secure.*

Proof. By Definition 1, the proposed $OT_{k \times 1}^n$ framework is fully simulatable secure due to both Theorem. 1 and Theorem. 2.

Efficiency. In terms of efficiency, the scheme uses k additional dummy documents in the initialization phase. OT_{init} costs $\mathcal{O}(n + k)$ communication complexity, and $OT_{transfer}$ costs $\mathcal{O}(1)$ communication complexity, here we ignore trivial factor $\log n$. However, by definition, $k \in [0, n]$, so it does not increase communication complexity asymptotically. The storage requirement for both receiver and sender are $\mathcal{O}(n + k) = \mathcal{O}(n)$. So that the storage requirement is also asymptotically the same as most existing schemes.

3.4 $OT_{k \times 1}^n$ Based on Elgamal Encryption

The first concrete scheme that we are going to show uses Elgamal encryption, and OT_{init} and $OT_{transfer}$ of this scheme are depicted in Fig. 3 and Fig. 4, respectively.

OT_{init} of Fully Simulatable $OT_{k \times 1}^n$ Based On Elgamal

Common input: A multiplicative cyclic group G of order q with generator g.
Sender's input: $\{m_1, \cdots, m_n\}$.
Sender's output: S_0.
Receiver's output: R_0.

1. The Sender **S** chooses $x \in \mathbb{Z}_q$ to generate a key pair $(sk := x, pk := h = g^x)$, and he sends pk to the receiver **R**.
2. **S** proves to **R** that he knows x by Schnorr's ZK-PoK [Sch91].
3. For $j \in \{n + 1, \cdots, n + k - 1\}$, set dummy documents $m_j = 1$. **S** picks $(r_1, \cdots, r_{n+k-1}) \in \mathbb{Z}_q^{n+k-1}$, and encrypts $c_i := (c_{1,i}, c_{2,i}) = (g^{r_i}, m_i \cdot h^{r_i})$ for $i \in \{1, \ldots, n + k - 1\}$. **S** sends $\{c_i\}$ to **R**.
4. **R** picks permutation π and randomizers $\{\alpha_i \in G\}, \{r_i' \in \mathbb{Z}_q\}$. He performs blind-permute re-encryption from $\{c_i\}$ to $\{C_i := (C_{1,i}, C_{2,i})\} = \{(c_{1,\pi(i)} g^{r'_{\pi(i)}}, c_{2,\pi(i)} h^{r'_{\pi(i)}} \alpha_{\pi(i)})\}$.
5. **R** proves correctness of blind-permute re-encryption by ZK-PoK proof in Sec. 3.2.
6. Set $S_0 := (\{C_i\}, x)$ and $R_0 := (h, \{C_i\}, \{\alpha_i\}, \pi, DB[n] = \{\})$.

Fig. 3. OT_{init} of Fully Simulatable $OT_{k \times 1}^n$ Based On Elgamal

---

The i-th $OT_{transfer}$ of Fully Simulatable $OT_{k \times 1}^n$ Based On Elgamal

Common input: A multiplicative cyclic group G of order q with generator g.
Sender's input: S_{i-1}.
Receiver's iutput: R_{i-1}, σ_i.
Sender's output: S_i.
Receiver's output: m_{σ_i}, R_i.

1. The receiver **R** parses R_{i-1} to $h, \{C_i\}, \{\alpha_i\}, \pi$ and DB.
2. If $DB[\sigma_i]$ has record, set $\sigma_i' = n + i$; otherwise, set $\sigma_i' = \sigma_i$. **R** sends $q = \pi^{-1}(\sigma_i')$ to the sender **S**.
3. **S** computes $Y_q = C_{1,q}^x$ and sends to **R**.
4. **S** proves $(g, h, C_{1,q}, Y_q)$ is a DDH-tuple [Cha90].
5. **R** set $m_{\sigma_i'} = C_{2,q} \cdot Y_q^{-1} \cdot \alpha_{\sigma_i'}^{-1}$.
6. Set $S_i := S_{i-1}$. If $\sigma_i' \in [1, n]$, $DB[\sigma_i'] = m_{\sigma_i'}$. Update $R_i := (pk, \{C_i\}, \{\alpha_i\}, \pi, DB)$. Set $m_{\sigma_i} = DB[\sigma_i]$.

Fig. 4. $OT_{transfer}$ of Fully Simulatable $OT_{k \times 1}^n$ Based On Elgamal

---

Security

Theorem 4. *The proposed $OT_{k \times 1}^n$ scheme that based on Elgamal (shown in Figure 3 and 4) is fully simulatable secure with statistical receiver's privacy under the DDH assumption.*

OT$_{init}$ of Fully Simulatable OT$_{k \times 1}^n$ Based On Paillier

Sender's input: $\{m_1, \cdots, m_n\}$.
Sender's output: S_0.
Receiver's output: R_0.

1. The Sender **S** chooses large primes p, q and computes $n = pq$.
2. For $j \in \{n + 1, \cdots, n + k - 1\}$, set dummy documents $m_j = 1$. **S** picks $(r_1, \cdots, r_{n+k-1}) \in (\mathbb{Z}_n^*)^{n+k-1}$, and encrypts $c_i := (n + 1)^{m_i} r_i^n \mod n^2$ for $i \in \{1, \ldots, n + k - 1\}$. **S** sends $\{c_i\}$ and n to the receiver **R**.
3. **S** proves that $f_n(x) = x^n \mod n$ is bijective by ZK-PoM [KN09].
4. **S** proves that he knows r_i for each c_i such that $c_i \mod n = r_i^n \mod n$ by ZK-PoK [KN09].
5. **R** picks permutation π and randomizers $\{\alpha_i \in \mathbb{Z}_n\}, \{r_i' \in \mathbb{Z}_n^*\}$. He performs blind-permute re-encryption from $\{c_i\}$ to $\{C_i := c_{\pi(i)} \cdot (n + 1)^{\alpha_{\pi(i)}} {r_{\pi(i)}'}^n\} = \{(n + 1)^{m_{\pi(i)} + \alpha_{\pi(i)}} (r_{\pi(i)} r_{\pi(i)}')^n\}$.
6. **R** proves correctness of blind-permute re-encryption by ZK-PoK proof in Sec. 3.2.
7. Set $S_0 := (\{C_i\}, p, q)$ and $R_0 := (n, \{C_i\}, \{\alpha_i\}, \pi, DB[n] = \{\})$.

Fig. 5. OT$_{init}$ of Fully Simulatable OT$_{k \times 1}^n$ Based On Paillier

---

The i-th OT$_{transfer}$ of Fully Simulatable OT$_{k \times 1}^n$ Based On Paillier

Sender's input: S_{i-1}.
Receiver's iutput: R_{i-1}, σ_i.
Sender's output: S_i.
Receiver's output: m_{σ_i}, R_i.

1. The receiver **R** parses R_{i-1} to $n, \{C_i\}, \{\alpha_i\}, \pi$ and DB.
2. If $DB[\sigma_i]$ has record, set $\sigma_i' = n + i$; otherwise, set $\sigma_i' = \sigma_i$. **R** sends $q = \pi^{-1}(\sigma_i')$ to the sender **S**.
3. **S** computes $Y = (C_q \mod n)^{1/n} \mod n$ and computes U such that

$$Y^n = (C_q \mod n) + Un \mod n^2 \qquad (1)$$

4. **S** sends U to **R** and proves that he knows Y satisfying eq. 1 by ZK-PoK [CDM00a].
5. **R** set $T := (r_{\sigma_i'} r_{\sigma_i'}')^n = (C_q \mod n) + Un \mod n^2$ and computes $m_{\sigma_i'}$ from $C_q, T, \alpha_{\sigma_i'}$.
6. Set $S_i := S_{i-1}$. If $\sigma_i' \in [1, n]$, $DB[\sigma_i'] = m_{\sigma_i'}$. Update $R_i := (pk, \{C_i\}, \{\alpha_i\}, \pi, DB)$. Set $m_{\sigma_i} = DB[\sigma_i]$.

Fig. 6. OT$_{transfer}$ of Fully Simulatable OT$_{k \times 1}^n$ Based On Paillier

Proof (Sketch). Similar to the proof of our framework, in the Game G_1 against the sender corruption, the receiver use knowledge extractor to extract x such that $h = g^x$. In the Game G_2 against the receiver corruption, the sender computes $Y_q = c_{2,\pi(q}h^{r_{\pi(q)}'} m_{\pi(q)}^{-1}$, and in the Game G_3 against the receiver corruption, the sender uses simulator of the ZK-PoM to prove $(g, h, c_{1,\pi(q)}g^{r'_{\pi(q)}}, Y_q)$ is a DDH-tuple. It is easy to see that $\mathsf{OT}^n_{k \times 1}$ scheme (shown in Figure 3 and 4) is secure against both the sender and receiver corruptions.

3.5 $\mathsf{OT}^n_{k \times 1}$ Based on Paillier Encryption

We use Paillier encryption in our second $\mathsf{OT}^n_{k \times 1}$ scheme. Again, OT_{init} and $\mathsf{OT}_{transfer}$ of this scheme are depicted in Fig. 5 and Fig. 6, respectively.

Security

Theorem 5. *The proposed* $\mathsf{OT}^n_{k \times 1}$ *scheme that based on Paillier (shown in Figure 5 and 6) is fully simulatable secure with statistical receiver's privacy under the Decisional n-th Residuosity assumption.*

Proof (Sketch). Similar to the proof of our framework, it is easy to see that $\mathsf{OT}^n_{k \times 1}$ scheme (shown in Figure 5 and 6) is secure against both sender and receiver corruptions.

4   Conclusions and Discussion

In this paper, we have proposed an extended ZK-PoK framework with several useful applications. We revisited the technique called "blind-permute decryption" and constructed an efficient $\mathsf{OT}^n_{k \times 1}$ framework. It achieves fully simulatable security with statistical receiver's privacy if the underlying encryption scheme is IND-CPA secure. We gave two examples: the first one was based on Elgamal encryption and the second one was based on Paillier encryption. We used dummy-document technique to make shuffle-based OT fulfill standard security definition that is also adaptable to [KNP10] scheme. Of course, the $\mathsf{OT}^n_{k \times 1}$ schemes based on many other homomorphic encryption schemes, such as BGN encryption [BGN05] and BBS encryption [BBS04], can be constructed according to our framework. Their ZK-proofs can be sometimes much more efficient due to bilinear properties, and a great amount of available NIZK arguments allow us to construct non-rewinding simulators. One can simply convert our scheme to UC-secure $\mathsf{OT}^n_{k \times 1}$ in CRS-hybrid model, by replacing our ZK argument with NIZK argument for blind-permute re-encryption. Since $k \leq n$, there are enough "free" documents to query when the receiver is asked to query an already fetched document, why it is necessary to introduce dummy documents? The difference occurs when the receiver is honest-but-curious, for he/she cannot get more information than those documents that the environment asked to query. Whereas, if the protocol allows the receiver to query random document(s), he/she will get extra real document(s).

Acknowledgments. The author is supported by Estonian Science Foundation, grant #8058, the European Regional Development Fund through the Estonian Center of Excellence in Computer Science (EXCS) and ICT doctoral school. Most of this work was done while the author was working at Cybernetica AS.

References

[AW07]   Adida, B., Wikström, D.: How to shuffle in public. In: Vadhan, S.P. (ed.) TCC 2007.
            LNCS, vol. 4392, pp. 555–574. Springer, Heidelberg (2007) 3.2

[BBS04]   Boneh, D., Boyen, X., Shacham, H.: Short Group Signatures. In: Franklin, M. (ed.)
            CRYPTO 2004. LNCS, vol. 3152, pp. 227–242. Springer, Heidelberg (2004) 4

[BG93]   Bellare, M., Goldreich, O.: On Defining Proofs of Knowledge. In: Brickell, E.F.
            (ed.) CRYPTO 1992. LNCS, vol. 740, pp. 390–420. Springer, Heidelberg (1993)
            2.1

[BGN05]   Boneh, D., Goh, E.-J., Nissim, K.: Evaluating 2-DNF Formulas on Ciphertexts. In:
            Kilian, J. (ed.) TCC 2005. LNCS, vol. 3378, pp. 325–342. Springer, Heidelberg
            (2005) 4

[CDM00a]   Cramer, R., Damgård, I.B., MacKenzie, P.D.: Efficient Zero-Knowledge Proofs
            of Knowledge without Intractability Assumptions. In: Imai, H., Zheng, Y. (eds.)
            PKC 2000. LNCS, vol. 1751, pp. 354–373. Springer, Heidelberg (2000) 2.1, 4

[CDM00b]   Cramer, R., Damgård, I.B., MacKenzie, P.D.: Efficient Zero-Knowledge Proofs
            of Knowledge without Intractability Assumptions. In: Imai, H., Zheng, Y. (eds.)
            PKC 2000. LNCS, vol. 1751, pp. 354–373. Springer, Heidelberg (2000) 2.1

[Cha90]   Chaum, D.: Zero-Knowledge Undeniable Signatures. In: Damgård, I.B. (ed.)
            EUROCRYPT 1990. LNCS, vol. 473, pp. 458–464. Springer, Heidelberg (1991)
            4

[CNS07]   Camenisch, J., Neven, G., Shelat, A.: Simulatable Adaptive Oblivious Transfer. In:
            Naor, M. (ed.) EUROCRYPT 2007. LNCS, vol. 4515, pp. 573–590. Springer, Hei-
            delberg (2007) 1.1, 1, 2.2

[CT05]   Chu, C.-K., Tzeng, W.-G.: Efficient oblivious transfer schemes with adaptive and
            non-adaptive queries. In: Vaudenay, S. (ed.) PKC 2005. LNCS, vol. 3386, pp. 172–
            183. Springer, Heidelberg (2005) 1

[DJ01]   Damgård, I., Jurik, M.: A generalisation, a simplification and some applications of
            paillier's probabilistic public-key system. In: Kim, K.-c. (ed.) PKC 2001. LNCS,
            vol. 1992, pp. 119–136. Springer, Heidelberg (2001) 3.2

[DY05]   Dodis, Y., Yampolskiy, A.: A Verifiable Random Function with Short Proofs and
            Keys. In: Vaudenay, S. (ed.) PKC 2005. LNCS, vol. 3386, pp. 416–431. Springer,
            Heidelberg (2005) 1.1

[GH07]   Green, M., Hohenberger, S.: Blind Identity-Based Encryption and Simulatable
            Oblivious Transfer. In: Kurosawa, K. (ed.) ASIACRYPT 2007. LNCS, vol. 4833,
            pp. 265–282. Springer, Heidelberg (2007) 1.1

[GH08]   Green, M., Hohenberger, S.: Universally Composable Adaptive Oblivious Transfer.
            In: Pieprzyk, J. (ed.) ASIACRYPT 2008. LNCS, vol. 5350, pp. 179–197. Springer,
            Heidelberg (2008) 1.1, 1

[GH10]   Green, M., Hohenberger, S.: Practical adaptive oblivious transfer from
            simple assumptions. Cryptology ePrint Archive, Report 2010/109 (2010),
            http://eprint.iacr.org/ 1.1, 1, 1.2, 2.2, 3.3

[GIKM98]   Gertner, Y., Ishai, Y., Kushilevitz, E., Malkin, T.: Protecting data privacy in pri-
            vate information retrieval schemes. In: Proceedings of the Thirtieth Annual ACM
            Symposium on Theory of Computing, STOC 1998, pp. 151–160. ACM, New York
            (1998) 3.3

[IP07]   Ishai, Y., Paskin, A.: Evaluating Branching Programs on Encrypted Data. In: Vad-
            han, S.P. (ed.) TCC 2007. LNCS, vol. 4392, pp. 575–594. Springer, Heidelberg
            (2007) 1

[JL09]   Jarecki, S., Liu, X.: Efficient Oblivious Pseudorandom Function with Applications to Adaptive OT and Secure Computation of Set Intersection. In: Reingold, O. (ed.) TCC 2009. LNCS, vol. 5444, pp. 577–594. Springer, Heidelberg (2009) 1.1, 1

[KN09]   Kurosawa, K., Nojima, R.: Simple Adaptive Oblivious Transfer without Random Oracle. In: Matsui, M. (ed.) ASIACRYPT 2009. LNCS, vol. 5912, pp. 334–346. Springer, Heidelberg (2009) 1.1, 1, 3, 4

[KNP10]   Kurosawa, K., Nojima, R., Le Phong, T.: Efficiency-Improved Fully Simulatable Adaptive OT under the DDH Assumption. In: Garay, J.A., De Prisco, R. (eds.) SCN 2010. LNCS, vol. 6280, pp. 172–181. Springer, Heidelberg (2010) 1.1, 1.2, 1, 3, 4

[KNP11]   Kurosawa, K., Nojima, R., Le Phong, T.: Generic fully simulatable adaptive oblivious transfer. In: Lopez, J., Tsudik, G. (eds.) ACNS 2011. LNCS, vol. 6715, pp. 274–291. Springer, Heidelberg (2011) 1.1, 1

[LAN02]   Lipmaa, H., Asokan, N., Niemi, V.: Secure vickrey auctions without threshold trust. In: Blaze, M. (ed.) FC 2002. LNCS, vol. 2357, pp. 87–101. Springer, Heidelberg (2003) 3.2

[Lip05]   Lipmaa, H.: An oblivious transfer protocol with log-squared communication, pp. 314–328 (2005) 1, 3.2

[NP99]   Naor, M., Pinkas, B.: Oblivious Transfer with Adaptive Queries. In: Wiener, M. (ed.) CRYPTO 1999. LNCS, vol. 1666, p. 791. Springer, Heidelberg (1999) 1, 1, 2.2

[RKP09]   Rial, A., Kohlweiss, M., Preneel, B.: Universally composable adaptive priced oblivious transfer. In: Shacham, H., Waters, B. (eds.) Pairing 2009. LNCS, vol. 5671, pp. 231–247. Springer, Heidelberg (2009) 1.1, 1

[Sch91]   Schnorr, C.P.: Efficient signature generation by smart cards. Journal of Cryptology 4, 161–174 (1991) 2

Verifiable Security of Boneh-Franklin Identity-Based Encryption[*]

Gilles Barthe, Federico Olmedo, and Santiago Zanella Béguelin

IMDEA Software Institute, Madrid, Spain
{Gilles.Barthe,Federico.Olmedo,Santiago.Zanella}@imdea.org

Abstract. Identity-based encryption (IBE) allows one party to send ciphered messages to another using an arbitrary identity string as an encryption key. Since IBE does not require prior generation and distribution of keys, it greatly simplifies key management in public-key cryptography. Although the concept of IBE was introduced by Shamir in 1981, constructing a practical IBE scheme remained an open problem for years. The first satisfactory solution was proposed by Boneh and Franklin in 2001 and constitutes one of the most prominent applications of pairing-based cryptography. We present a game-based machine-checked reduction of the security of the Boneh-Franklin IBE scheme to the Bilinear Diffie-Hellman assumption, and analyze its tightness by providing an exact security bound. Our proof simplifies and clarifies the original proof by Boneh and Franklin and can be automatically verified by running a trusted checker.

Keywords: Bilinear Diffie-Hellman problem, Boneh-Franklin scheme, CertiCrypt, iddentity-based encryption, pairing-based cryptography, verifiable security.

1 Introduction

Identity-based cryptography is an approach to public-key cryptography in which public keys can be arbitrary identity strings associated to users, e.g. their email addresses. Identity-based cryptography significantly reduces the cost and complexity of managing a public-key infrastructure because, in contrast to standard public-key systems, it does not require prior distribution and generation of keys. Although the concept of identity-based cryptography was introduced by Shamir in 1984 [14] and identity-based signature schemes are relatively easy to construct, a solution to the problem of building a practical identity-based encryption scheme eluded cryptographers for years. The first satisfactory solution to this problem was proposed by Boneh and Franklin in 2001 [7] using the Weil pairing, and constitutes one of the most prominent applications of pairing-based

---

[*] Partially funded by European Project FP7-256980 NESSoS, French project ANR SESUR-012 SCALP, Spanish project TIN2009-14599 DESAFIOS 10, and Madrid Regional project S2009TIC-1465 PROMETIDOS.

X. Boyen and X. Chen (Eds.): ProvSec 2011, LNCS 6980, pp. 68–83, 2011.

cryptography. Boneh and Franklin proved that this scheme is secure against chosen-ciphertext attacks in the Random Oracle Model (ROM) under the Bilinear Diffie-Hellman assumption. The proof proceeds in two stages: first, an identity-based scheme BasicIdent is introduced and proved secure against chosen-plaintext attacks; second, the BasicIdent scheme is transformed into a scheme that is secure against chosen-ciphertext attacks by applying a variant of the Fujisaki-Okamoto transformation [11]. A flaw in the second part of this proof was discovered and fixed by Galindo [12]. Although, fortunately, in this case the fix did not require to modify the scheme or the underlying assumption, this shows that some degree of wariness is needed when evaluating provable security arguments.

Boneh and Boyen [6] and Waters [16] subsequently proposed other provably-secure IBE schemes that admit reductions in the standard model; Bellare and Ristenpart [5] improve on the security bound of Waters' scheme by removing artificial abort steps from the proof. Over the last decade, more sophisticated schemes have emerged, such as hierarchical [13] and anonymous [8] IBE schemes. As the security proofs for such schemes are getting more and more involved, it becomes increasingly difficult to assess the correctness of the mathematical arguments, or the tightness of the concrete security bounds.

Verifiable security [1, 2] is an emerging approach to provable security that advocates using state-of-the-art tools to build fully formalized, independently verifiable proofs of security of cryptographic systems. This approach has been applied to prominent cryptographic constructions, including proofs of chosen-ciphertext security of OAEP encryption [2] and unforgeability of FDH signatures [17]. In this paper we follow this approach and use CertiCrypt [1] to build a machine-checked game-based proof of the security of Boneh-Franklin BasicIdent scheme. Our main contributions are the following: 1) We extend the CertiCrypt framework with primitive operations for bilinear maps and mechanisms to reason about their algebraic properties; 2) We formalize a game-based proof of the security of Boneh-Franklin BasicIdent scheme that is simpler than the original one; 3) We analyze the tightness of the reduction and obtain an exact security bound that coincides with the one in the original proof. To the best of our knowledge, the proof presented here constitutes the first machine-checked proof of a pairing-based cryptographic scheme, and paves the way to formally analyze the provable security of other pairing-based constructions.

2   An Introduction to CertiCrypt

CertiCrypt [1] is a framework for building and verifying game-based proofs of cryptographic systems that adopts a code-based view of games. CertiCrypt is built on top of the general-purpose proof assistant Coq [15], that has been used effectively for verifying intricate results from mathematics and computer science.

The core of CertiCrypt is a formalization of the probabilistic programming language used to represent games; the syntax of games is defined as follows:

$$
\begin{array}{llll}
\mathcal{I} ::= \mathcal{V} \leftarrow \mathcal{E} & \text{deterministic assignment} & \mathcal{C} ::= \text{skip} & \text{nop} \\
\quad | \;\; \mathcal{V} \xleftarrow{\$} \mathcal{DE} & \text{random assignment} & \quad | \;\; \mathcal{I};\, \mathcal{C} & \text{sequence} \\
\quad | \;\; \text{if } \mathcal{E} \text{ then } \mathcal{C} \text{ else } \mathcal{C} & \text{conditional} \\
\quad | \;\; \text{while } \mathcal{E} \text{ do } \mathcal{C} & \text{while loop} \\
\quad | \;\; \mathcal{V} \leftarrow \mathcal{P}(\mathcal{E}, \ldots, \mathcal{E}) & \text{procedure call}
\end{array}
$$

where $\mathcal{V}$ is a set of variables, $\mathcal{E}$ a set of expressions, $\mathcal{DE}$ is a set of expressions that represent distributions from which values can be sampled in random assignments, and $\mathcal{P}$ is a set of procedures that includes oracles and adversaries. Adversaries are formalized as procedures with unknown code; the only requirement is that adversaries execute in probabilistic polynomial-time and comply with an interface that specifies a read/write access policy to global variables. The semantics of a game G is given by a function $[\![G]\!] : \mathcal{M} \to \mathcal{D}(\mathcal{M})$ which yields for any initial memory m, mapping program variables to values, the (sub-)distribution of final memories resulting from executing G starting from m. We denote by $\Pr[G, m : A]$ the probability of event A occurring after executing game G in an initial memory m.

In order to formalize security proofs, CertiCrypt provides support for most common reasoning patterns used in game-based proofs. In particular, CertiCrypt supports program optimizations that are commonly used in bridging steps in game-based proofs, such as game simplifications like expression propagation, procedure call inlining, code motion, and dead code elimination. More importantly, CertiCrypt provides a mechanization of the Fundamental Lemma of Game-Playing (see Appendix A), that allows to bound the difference in the probability of an event in two different games by the probability of a designated failure event. This allows to analyze simulation-based reductions that are not tight by bounding the gap by the probability of failure of the simulation.

Following a foundational approach to verification, the soundness of all the above reasoning mechanisms is verified formally in the Coq proof assistant. This is done using a relational Hoare logic, which manipulates judgments of the form

$$\models G_1 \sim G_2 : \Psi \Rightarrow \Phi$$

where G_1, G_2 are games and Ψ, Φ are binary relations over program memories. The above judgment is valid if for any initial memories m_1 and m_2 satisfying the pre-condition $m_1 \; \Psi \; m_2$, the distributions $[\![G_1]\!] \, m_1$ and $[\![G_2]\!] \, m_2$ are related by the lifting of relation Φ to distributions. We refer the reader to [3, 1] for an appropriate definition of lifting and a more thorough description of the logic. Relational Hoare Logic subsumes observational equivalence, which is obtained by restricting pre- and post-conditions in judgments to equality relations on subsets of program variables.

Relational logic can be used to prove claims about the probability of events in games by using the following rules:

$$\frac{m_1 \; \Psi \; m_2 \qquad \models \mathsf{G}_1 \sim \mathsf{G}_2 : \Psi \Rightarrow \Phi \qquad \Phi \to (A\langle 1\rangle \leftrightarrow B\langle 2\rangle)}{\Pr\left[\mathsf{G}_1, m_1 : A\right] = \Pr\left[\mathsf{G}_2, m_2 : B\right]}$$

$$\frac{m_1 \; \Psi \; m_2 \qquad \models \mathsf{G}_1 \sim \mathsf{G}_2 : \Psi \Rightarrow \Phi \qquad \Phi \to (A\langle 1\rangle \to B\langle 2\rangle)}{\Pr\left[\mathsf{G}_1, m_1 : A\right] \leq \Pr\left[\mathsf{G}_2, m_2 : B\right]}$$

We represent relations on states as first-order formulae over tagged program variables; we use the tags $\langle 1\rangle$ and $\langle 2\rangle$ to distinguish between the value of a variable or formula in the left and right-hand side program, respectively, and $=_X$ to denote the binary relation that relates memories that coincide on variables in set X.

CertiCrypt inherits two essential features from the Coq proof assistant. First, since Coq is a general-purpose proof assistant, CertiCrypt is modular and extensible and can be used to reason about arbitrary mathematical constructions. In particular the language of expressions that games manipulate can be extended by the user. We take advantage of this characteristic and extend the language of expressions with values denoting elements of groups and a primitive operator that denotes a bilinear map; we enrich the simplification mechanism of CertiCrypt to compute normal forms of expressions involving this operator. Second, since any Coq proof can be automatically verified using a small and trustworthy type checker, and the reasoning principles that are supported by CertiCrypt are proved sound with respect to the semantics of games, the correctness of a machine-checked proof can be reduced to a small trusted base. This trusted base includes the security statement and the formalization of the semantics of games, but not the proof itself, which is verified by the Coq type checker.

3 Preliminaries

3.1 Bilinear Maps and Bilinear Diffie-Hellman Assumption

Let $\mathbb{G}_1$ and $\mathbb{G}_2$ be two cyclic groups of prime order q. In the remainder, we use additive notation for $\mathbb{G}_1$ and multiplicative notation for $\mathbb{G}_2$. Moreover, we let $\mathbb{G}_1^+ = \mathbb{G}_1 \setminus \{0\}$, and $\mathbb{Z}_q^+ = \{1, .., q-1\}$. An *admissible bilinear map* is a polynomially computable function $\hat{e} : \mathbb{G}_1 \times \mathbb{G}_1 \to \mathbb{G}_2$ satisfying the following two conditions:

Bilinearity: for any $P, Q \in \mathbb{G}_1$ and $a, b \in \mathbb{Z}$, $\hat{e}(aP, bQ) = \hat{e}(P, Q)^{ab}$;
Non-degeneracy: for any generator P of $\mathbb{G}_1$, $\hat{e}(P, P)$ is a generator of $\mathbb{G}_2$.

The Bilinear Diffie-Hellman (BDH) problem is a variant of the computational Diffie-Hellman problem: given a quadruple of uniformly chosen values (P, aP, bP, cP) the goal is to compute $\hat{e}(P, P)^{abc}$. The BDH assumption on a family of groups equipped with an admissible bilinear map can be formalized in terms of the following probabilistic game:

$$\textbf{Game } \mathsf{G}_{\mathsf{BDH}} : P \xleftarrow{\$} \mathbb{G}_1^+; \; a, b, c \xleftarrow{\$} \mathbb{Z}_q^+; \; z \leftarrow \mathcal{B}(P, aP, bP, cP)$$

We define the advantage of an algorithm $\mathcal{B}$ in solving BDH as

$$\mathbf{Adv}_{\mathsf{BDH}}^{\mathcal{B}} = \Pr\left[\mathsf{G}_{\mathsf{BDH}} : z = \hat{e}(P, P)^{abc}\right]$$

The BDH assumption holds if the advantage of every probabilistic polynomial-time procedure $\mathcal{B}$ is a negligible function of a security parameter that determines the order of the groups in the family.

3.2 Identity-Based Encryption

In a typical setting, an IBE scheme involves a trusted third party, the Private Key Generator (PKG). The PKG generates the scheme public parameters and a master private key. On request of users, the PKG derives from the master key the private decryption key associated to a public identity by running an extraction algorithm. More formally, an IBE scheme is defined as follows.

Definition 1 (Identity-Based Encryption scheme). *An identity-based encryption scheme is specified by a quadruple of algorithms* (Setup, $\mathcal{EX}, \mathcal{E}, \mathcal{D}$)*:*

Setup: *Given a security parameter η, the* Setup *algorithm generates the public parameters of the scheme and a master private key;*
Extract: *Given a master key mk and a public identity $id \in \{0,1\}^{\star}$, $\mathcal{EX}(mk, id)$ computes the corresponding decryption key sk;*
Encrypt: *Given a public identity id and a message m, $\mathcal{E}(id, m)$ computes a ciphertext c corresponding to the encryption of m under id;*
Decrypt: *Given a private decryption key sk and ciphertext c, $\mathcal{D}(sk, c)$ returns either the plaintext corresponding to the decryption of c, if it is a valid ciphertext, or a distinguished value $\perp$ otherwise.*

Definition 2 (BasicIdent scheme). *Let $\mathbb{G}_1$, $\mathbb{G}_2$ be two (families of) cyclic groups of prime order q equipped with a bilinear map $\hat{e} : \mathbb{G}_1 \times \mathbb{G}_1 \rightarrow \mathbb{G}_2$, and let $\mathcal{H}_1 : \{0,1\}^{\star} \rightarrow \mathbb{G}_1^{+}$, $\mathcal{H}_2 : \mathbb{G}_2 \rightarrow \{0,1\}^n$ be two hash functions for some $n \in \mathbb{N}$. BasicIdent is defined by the following algorithms:*

$$\begin{aligned}
\mathsf{Setup}(\eta) \quad &: \quad P \xleftarrow{\$} \mathbb{G}_1^{+}; \ a \xleftarrow{\$} \mathbb{Z}_q^{+}; \ P_{pub} \leftarrow aP; \ \mathsf{return} \ ((P, P_{pub}), a) \\
\mathcal{EX}(a, id) \quad &: \quad Q_{id} \leftarrow \mathcal{H}_1(id); \ \mathsf{return} \ aQ_{id} \\
\mathcal{E}(id, m) \quad &: \quad Q_{id} \leftarrow \mathcal{H}_1(id); \ c \xleftarrow{\$} \mathbb{Z}_q^{+}; \ m' \leftarrow \mathcal{H}_2(e(Q_{id}, P_{pub})^c); \\
&\qquad \mathsf{return} \ (cP, m \oplus m') \\
\mathcal{D}(sk, (u, v)) &: \quad \mathsf{return} \ v \oplus \mathcal{H}_2(\hat{e}(sk, u))
\end{aligned}$$

Definition 3 (Semantic security against chosen-plaintext attacks).
The semantic security of an IBE scheme against chosen-plaintext attacks is defined by means of the following probabilistic experiment parametrized by an adversary $\mathcal{A}$:

$$\begin{aligned}
&\textbf{Game } \mathsf{G}_{IND\text{-}ID\text{-}CPA} : \\
&(\mathsf{params}, mk) \leftarrow \mathsf{Setup}(\eta); \\
&(m_0, m_1, id_{\mathcal{A}}) \leftarrow \mathcal{A}_1(\mathsf{params}); \\
&b \xleftarrow{\$} \{0, 1\}; \\
&c \leftarrow \mathcal{E}(id_{\mathcal{A}}, m_b); \\
&b_{\mathcal{A}} \leftarrow \mathcal{A}_2(c)
\end{aligned}$$

The two phases of the adversary $\mathcal{A}$ are modelled by two procedures $\mathcal{A}_1$ and $\mathcal{A}_2$ that can communicate through shared variables and have oracle access to a private-key extraction oracle (but not to a decryption oracle). In the first phase, $\mathcal{A}_1$ chooses two plaintexts and a challenge identity id_A, while in the second phase $\mathcal{A}_2$ outputs a guess b_A for b. During the second phase of the experiment $\mathcal{A}_2$ is not allowed to query id_A to the extraction oracle. The IND-ID-CPA-advantage of $\mathcal{A}$ is defined as

$$\mathbf{Adv}^{\mathcal{A}}_{IND\text{-}ID\text{-}CPA} \overset{def}{=} \left| \Pr\left[\mathsf{G}_{IND\text{-}ID\text{-}CPA} : b = b_A\right] - \frac{1}{2} \right|$$

An IBE scheme is semantically secure if every probabilistic polynomial-time adversary $\mathcal{A}$ has only a negligible advantage.

4   Security of the Boneh-Franklin BasicIdent Scheme

We prove that BasicIdent is semantically secure against chosen-plaintext attacks in the Random Oracle Model under the Bilinear-Diffie Hellman assumption on the underlying map $\hat{e}(\cdot, \cdot)$. The formal security statement is specified in terms of the IND-ID-CPA experiment instantiated to the BasicIdent scheme and appears at the bottom of Figure 1. It takes the form of an implication, whose premise fixes the class of adversaries considered. Specifically, the statement considers any well-formed IND-ID-CPA adversary $\mathcal{A}$ that makes at most $q_{\mathcal{H}_1}$ queries to oracle $\mathcal{H}_1$, at most $q_{\mathcal{H}_2}$ queries to oracle $\mathcal{H}_2$, and exactly $q_{\mathcal{EX}}$ queries to oracle $\mathcal{EX}$, and that does not query the $\mathcal{EX}$ oracle with the identity id_A it chooses to attack. An adversary $\mathcal{A}$ is well-formed if it does not read or write any global variables besides its own. The conclusion of the statement upper bounds the advantage of the adversary $\mathcal{A}$ in terms of the advantage of an algorithm $\mathcal{B}$ in solving the BDH problem. The code of an algorithm $\mathcal{B}$ that uses $\mathcal{A}$ as a subroutine and achieves the bound in the statement is given in the next section. Theorem 1 summarizes in simpler terms the result that we prove, which coincides with the one given in [7, Theorem 4.1].

Theorem 1 (IND-ID-CPA security of BasicIdent). *Let $\mathcal{A}$ be an adversary against the IND-ID-CPA security of BasicIdent. Suppose $\mathcal{A}$ executes within time t_A and makes at most $q_{\mathcal{H}_1} > 0$ queries to $\mathcal{H}_1$, $q_{\mathcal{H}_2} > 0$ queries to $\mathcal{H}_2$, and exactly $q_{\mathcal{EX}} > 0$ queries to the extraction oracle $\mathcal{EX}$. Then, there exists an algorithm $\mathcal{B}$ that executes within time $t_B = O(t_A)$ such that*

$$\mathbf{Adv}^{\mathcal{B}}_{BDH} \geq \mathbf{Adv}^{\mathcal{A}}_{IND\text{-}ID\text{-}CPA} \frac{2\ q^{q_{\mathcal{EX}}}_{\mathcal{EX}}}{q_{\mathcal{H}_2}\ (1 + q_{\mathcal{EX}})^{1 + q_{\mathcal{EX}}}} \geq \mathbf{Adv}^{\mathcal{A}}_{IND\text{-}ID\text{-}CPA} \frac{2\ \exp(-1)}{q_{\mathcal{H}_2}\ (1 + q_{\mathcal{EX}})}$$

The proof is organized as a sequence of games (the sequence is given as input to CertiCrypt); an outline is given in Figures 2-4. In the figure, each game is shown alongside the code of the oracles made available to adversary $\mathcal{A}$ and global variables are typeset in boldface. Fragments of code displayed inside a box appear only in the game whose name is surrounded by the matching box.

Game $\mathsf{G}_{\mathsf{IND\text{-}ID\text{-}CPA}}$:	**Oracle** $\mathcal{EX}(id)$:	**Oracle** $\mathcal{H}_1(id)$:
$L_1, L_2, L_3 \leftarrow \mathsf{nil}$;	if $id \notin L_3$ then	if $id \notin \mathsf{dom}(L_1)$ then
$P \xleftarrow{\$} \mathbb{G}_1^+;\ a \xleftarrow{\$} \mathbb{Z}_q^+$;	$\quad L_3 \leftarrow id :: L_3$	$\quad R \xleftarrow{\$} \mathbb{G}_1^+$;
$P_{pub} \leftarrow aP$;	$\quad Q \leftarrow \mathcal{H}_1(id)$;	$\quad L_1(id) \leftarrow R$
$(m_0, m_1, id_\mathcal{A}) \leftarrow \mathcal{A}_1(P, P_{pub})$;	$\quad$return aQ	return $L_1(id)$
$d \xleftarrow{\$} \{0, 1\}$;		
$y \leftarrow \mathcal{E}(id_\mathcal{A}, m_d)$;		**Oracle** $\mathcal{H}_2(r)$:
$d_\mathcal{A} \leftarrow \mathcal{A}_2(y)$		if $r \notin \mathsf{dom}(L_2)$ then
		$\quad m \xleftarrow{\$} \{0, 1\}^n$;
		$\quad L_2(r) \leftarrow m$
		return $L_2(r)$

$$\forall \mathcal{A}.\ \mathsf{WF}(\mathcal{A}) \wedge \Pr\left[\mathsf{G}_{\mathsf{IND\text{-}ID\text{-}CPA}} : id_\mathcal{A} \notin L_3 \wedge |L_1| \le q_{\mathcal{H}_1} \wedge |L_2| \le q_{\mathcal{H}_2} \wedge |L_3| = q_{\mathcal{EX}}\right] = 1$$

$$\implies \exists \mathcal{B}.\ \mathbf{Adv}_{\mathsf{BDH}}^{\mathcal{B}} \ge \mathbf{Adv}_{\mathsf{IND\text{-}ID\text{-}CPA}}^{\mathcal{A}}\ \frac{2q_{\mathcal{EX}}^{q_{\mathcal{EX}}}}{q_{\mathcal{H}_2}(1 + q_{\mathcal{EX}})^{1 + q_{\mathcal{EX}}}}$$

Fig. 1. Formal statement of the IND-ID-CPA security of BasicIdent

The initial game of the sequence is the game $\mathsf{G}_{\mathsf{IND\text{-}ID\text{-}CPA}}$ appearing in Figure 1. In the first transition from game $\mathsf{G}_{\mathsf{IND\text{-}ID\text{-}CPA}}$ to game G_1, we inline the encryption of the challenge ciphertext and extend the state of oracle $\mathcal{H}_1$ by instrumenting its code with a list J that keeps track of the order of queries. In addition, for each of the $q_{\mathcal{H}_1}$ possible queries to $\mathcal{H}_1$, we toss a coin and store the result in a list T. The coins are sampled independently following a Bernoulli distribution true $\oplus_p$ false, that assigns true with probability p and false with probability $1 - p$. We prove that games $\mathsf{G}_{\mathsf{IND\text{-}ID\text{-}CPA}}$ and G_1 are observationally equivalent with respect to d and d_A, and thus:

$$\Pr\left[\mathsf{G}_{\mathsf{IND\text{-}ID\text{-}CPA}} : d = d_\mathcal{A}\right] = \Pr\left[\mathsf{G}_1 : d = d_\mathcal{A}\right] \tag{1}$$

Consider the following event:

$$\mathsf{Guessed} \stackrel{\mathsf{def}}{=} T[J(id_\mathcal{A})] \wedge \forall id \in L_3.\ \neg T[J(id)]$$

Since the events $d = d_\mathcal{A}$ and Guessed are trivially independent, we have that

$$\Pr\left[\mathsf{G}_1 : d = d_\mathcal{A} \wedge \mathsf{Guessed}\right] = \Pr\left[\mathsf{G}_1 : d = d_\mathcal{A}\right]\ \Pr\left[\mathsf{G}_1 : \mathsf{Guessed}\right]$$

Furthermore, a straightforward calculation gives

$$\Pr\left[\mathsf{G}_1 : \mathsf{Guessed}\right] = p(1 - p)^{q_{\mathcal{EX}}} \tag{2}$$

In game G_2, we hoist the loop that samples the $q_{\mathcal{H}_1}$ coins in T to the beginning of the game and change the way oracle $\mathcal{H}_1$ answers to queries. To answer the i-th hash query, $\mathcal{H}_1$ chooses uniformly a value $v \in \mathbb{Z}_q^+$ and replies according to the i-th entry in T: if it is true, replies with bvP, where b is uniformly chosen at the beginning of the game; otherwise replies with vP. Since the value v acts as a one-time pad, in both cases the answers are distributed uniformly and independently from previous queries, and are thus perfectly indistinguishable

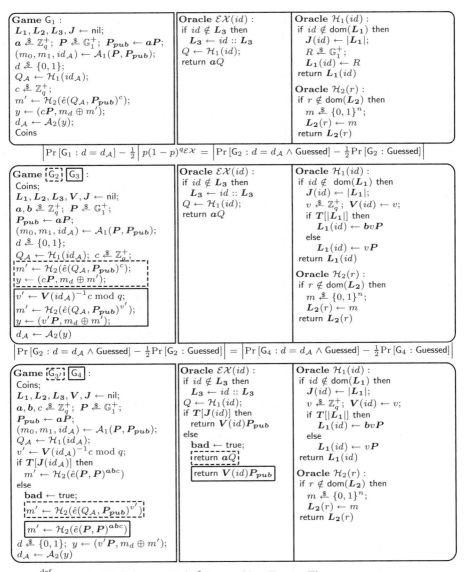

Game G_1 :
$L_1, L_2, L_3, J \leftarrow$ nil;
$a \xleftarrow{\$} \mathbb{Z}_q^+; \ P \xleftarrow{\$} \mathbb{G}_1^+; \ P_{pub} \leftarrow aP;$
$(m_0, m_1, id_\mathcal{A}) \leftarrow \mathcal{A}_1(P, P_{pub});$
$d \xleftarrow{\$} \{0,1\};$
$Q_\mathcal{A} \leftarrow \mathcal{H}_1(id_\mathcal{A});$
$c \xleftarrow{\$} \mathbb{Z}_q^+;$
$m' \leftarrow \mathcal{H}_2(\hat{e}(Q_\mathcal{A}, P_{pub})^c);$
$y \leftarrow (cP, m_d \oplus m');$
$d_\mathcal{A} \leftarrow \mathcal{A}_2(y);$
Coins

Oracle $\mathcal{EX}(id)$:
if $id \notin L_3$ then
$\quad L_3 \leftarrow id :: L_3$
$\quad Q \leftarrow \mathcal{H}_1(id);$
return aQ

Oracle $\mathcal{H}_1(id)$:
if $id \notin \mathsf{dom}(L_1)$ then
$\quad J(id) \leftarrow |L_1|;$
$\quad R \xleftarrow{\$} \mathbb{G}_1^+;$
$\quad L_1(id) \leftarrow R$
return $L_1(id)$

Oracle $\mathcal{H}_2(r)$:
if $r \notin \mathsf{dom}(L_2)$ then
$\quad m \xleftarrow{\$} \{0,1\}^n;$
$\quad L_2(r) \leftarrow m$
return $L_2(r)$

$$\left| \Pr\left[G_1 : d = d_\mathcal{A}\right] - \tfrac{1}{2} \right| \, p(1-p)^{q_{\mathcal{EX}}} = \left| \Pr\left[G_2 : d = d_\mathcal{A} \wedge \mathsf{Guessed}\right] - \tfrac{1}{2}\Pr\left[G_2 : \mathsf{Guessed}\right] \right|$$

Game $\boxed{G_2}$ $\boxed{G_3}$:
Coins;
$L_1, L_2, L_3, V, J \leftarrow$ nil;
$a, b \xleftarrow{\$} \mathbb{Z}_q^+; \ P \xleftarrow{\$} \mathbb{G}_1^+;$
$P_{pub} \leftarrow aP;$
$(m_0, m_1, id_\mathcal{A}) \leftarrow \mathcal{A}_1(P, P_{pub});$
$d \xleftarrow{\$} \{0,1\};$
$Q_\mathcal{A} \leftarrow \mathcal{H}_1(id_\mathcal{A}); \ c \xleftarrow{\$} \mathbb{Z}_q^+;$
$m' \leftarrow \mathcal{H}_2(\hat{e}(Q_\mathcal{A}, P_{pub})^c);$
$y \leftarrow (cP, m_d \oplus m');$
$v' \leftarrow V(id_\mathcal{A})^{-1} c \bmod q;$
$m' \leftarrow \mathcal{H}_2(\hat{e}(Q_\mathcal{A}, P_{pub})^{v'});$
$y \leftarrow (v'P, m_d \oplus m');$
$d_\mathcal{A} \leftarrow \mathcal{A}_2(y)$

Oracle $\mathcal{EX}(id)$:
if $id \notin L_3$ then
$\quad L_3 \leftarrow id :: L_3$
$\quad Q \leftarrow \mathcal{H}_1(id);$
return aQ

Oracle $\mathcal{H}_1(id)$:
if $id \notin \mathsf{dom}(L_1)$ then
$\quad J(id) \leftarrow |L_1|;$
$\quad v \xleftarrow{\$} \mathbb{Z}_q^+; \ V(id) \leftarrow v;$
$\quad$ if $T[|L_1|]$ then
$\quad\quad L_1(id) \leftarrow bvP$
$\quad$ else
$\quad\quad L_1(id) \leftarrow vP$
return $L_1(id)$

Oracle $\mathcal{H}_2(r)$:
if $r \notin \mathsf{dom}(L_2)$ then
$\quad m \xleftarrow{\$} \{0,1\}^n;$
$\quad L_2(r) \leftarrow m$
return $L_2(r)$

$$\left| \Pr\left[G_2 : d = d_\mathcal{A} \wedge \mathsf{Guessed}\right] - \tfrac{1}{2}\Pr\left[G_2 : \mathsf{Guessed}\right] \right| = \left| \Pr\left[G_4 : d = d_\mathcal{A} \wedge \mathsf{Guessed}\right] - \tfrac{1}{2}\Pr\left[G_4 : \mathsf{Guessed}\right] \right|$$

Game $\boxed{G_3}$ $\boxed{G_4}$:
Coins;
$L_1, L_2, L_3, V, J \leftarrow$ nil;
$a, b, c \xleftarrow{\$} \mathbb{Z}_q^+; \ P \xleftarrow{\$} \mathbb{G}_1^+;$
$P_{pub} \leftarrow aP;$
$(m_0, m_1, id_\mathcal{A}) \leftarrow \mathcal{A}_1(P, P_{pub});$
$Q_\mathcal{A} \leftarrow \mathcal{H}_1(id_\mathcal{A});$
$v' \leftarrow V(id_\mathcal{A})^{-1} c \bmod q;$
if $T[J(id_\mathcal{A})]$ then
$\quad m' \leftarrow \mathcal{H}_2(\hat{e}(P, P)^{abc})$
else
$\quad$ **bad** $\leftarrow$ true;
$\quad m' \leftarrow \mathcal{H}_2(\hat{e}(Q_\mathcal{A}, P_{pub})^{v'})$
$\quad m' \leftarrow \mathcal{H}_2(\hat{e}(P, P)^{abc})$
$d \xleftarrow{\$} \{0,1\}; \ y \leftarrow (v'P, m_d \oplus m');$
$d_\mathcal{A} \leftarrow \mathcal{A}_2(y)$

Oracle $\mathcal{EX}(id)$:
if $id \notin L_3$ then
$\quad L_3 \leftarrow id :: L_3$
$\quad Q \leftarrow \mathcal{H}_1(id);$
$\quad$ if $T[J(id)]$ then
$\quad\quad$ return $V(id)P_{pub}$
$\quad$ else
$\quad\quad$ **bad** $\leftarrow$ true;
$\quad\quad$ return aQ
$\quad$ return $V(id)P_{pub}$

Oracle $\mathcal{H}_1(id)$:
if $id \notin \mathsf{dom}(L_1)$ then
$\quad J(id) \leftarrow |L_1|;$
$\quad v \xleftarrow{\$} \mathbb{Z}_q^+; \ V(id) \leftarrow v;$
$\quad$ if $T[|L_1|]$ then
$\quad\quad L_1(id) \leftarrow bvP$
$\quad$ else
$\quad\quad L_1(id) \leftarrow vP$
return $L_1(id)$

Oracle $\mathcal{H}_2(r)$:
if $r \notin \mathsf{dom}(L_2)$ then
$\quad m \xleftarrow{\$} \{0,1\}^n;$
$\quad L_2(r) \leftarrow m$
return $L_2(r)$

$\mathrm{Coins} \stackrel{\text{def}}{=} T \leftarrow$ nil; while $|T| < q_{\mathcal{H}_1}$ do $(t \xleftarrow{\$} \mathrm{true} \oplus_p \mathrm{false}; \ T \leftarrow t :: T)$

Fig. 2. Outline of the proof of IND-ID-CPA security of BasicIdent

$\left|\Pr\left[\mathsf{G}_4 : d = d_{\mathcal{A}} \wedge \mathsf{Guessed}\right] - \frac{1}{2}\Pr\left[\mathsf{G}_4 : \mathsf{Guessed}\right]\right| = \left|\Pr\left[\mathsf{G}_5 : d = d_{\mathcal{A}} \wedge \mathsf{Guessed}\right] - \frac{1}{2}\Pr\left[\mathsf{G}_5 : \mathsf{Guessed}\right]\right|$

$\left|\Pr\left[\mathsf{G}_5 : d = d_{\mathcal{A}} \wedge \mathsf{Guessed}\right] - \frac{1}{2}\Pr\left[\mathsf{G}_5 : \mathsf{Guessed}\right]\right| = \left|\Pr\left[\mathsf{G}_6 : d = d_{\mathcal{A}} \wedge \mathsf{Guessed}\right] - \frac{1}{2}\Pr\left[\mathsf{G}_6 : \mathsf{Guessed}\right]\right|$

Fig. 3. Outline of the proof of IND-ID-CPA security of BasicIdent

from those of a random oracle. We prove this by first proving the validity of the following algebraic equivalence:

$$\models R \xleftarrow{\$} \mathbb{G}_1^+; \ v \leftarrow (\log R / \log Q) \bmod q \sim v \xleftarrow{\$} \mathbb{Z}_q^+; \ R \leftarrow vQ : \Psi \Rightarrow \Phi$$

where

$$\Psi \overset{\text{def}}{=} Q\langle 1 \rangle = Q\langle 2 \rangle \wedge \ \log Q\langle 1 \rangle \neq 0 \qquad \Phi \overset{\text{def}}{=} =_{\{v,R\}}$$

We then apply this equivalence twice to show that no matter what branch is taken in the conditional in $\mathcal{H}_1$, the value of $L_1(id)$ will be uniformly distributed. In one case, we take $Q = bP$, while in the other we simply take $Q = P$. We conclude that

$$\Pr\left[\mathsf{G}_1 : \mathsf{Guessed}\right] = \Pr\left[\mathsf{G}_2 : \mathsf{Guessed}\right] \tag{3}$$

$$\Pr\left[\mathsf{G}_1 : d = d_{\mathcal{A}} \wedge \mathsf{Guessed}\right] = \Pr\left[\mathsf{G}_2 : d = d_{\mathcal{A}} \wedge \mathsf{Guessed}\right] \tag{4}$$

$$2\left|\Pr[G_6 : d = d_{\mathcal{A}} \wedge \mathsf{Guessed}] - \tfrac{1}{2}\Pr[G_6 : \mathsf{Guessed}]\right| \le \Pr[G_6 : \mathsf{S}] = \Pr[G_7 : \mathsf{S}]$$

Game $\boxed{G_7}$ $\boxed{G_7}$:	Oracle $\mathcal{EX}(id)$:	Oracle $\mathcal{H}_1(id)$:
Coins;	if $id \notin L_3$ then	if $id \notin \mathrm{dom}(L_1)$ then
$L_1, L_2, L_3, V, J \leftarrow$ nil;	$\quad L_3 \leftarrow id :: L_3$	$\quad J(id) \leftarrow \lvert L_1 \rvert$;
$a,b,c \overset{\$}{\leftarrow} \mathbb{Z}_q^+;\ P \overset{\$}{\leftarrow} \mathbb{G}_1^+;$	$\quad Q \leftarrow \mathcal{H}_1(id);$	$\quad v \overset{\$}{\leftarrow} \mathbb{Z}_q^+;\ V(id) \leftarrow v;$
$P_{pub} \leftarrow aP;\ \boxed{m^* \overset{\$}{\leftarrow} \{0,1\}^n;}$	return $V(id)P_{pub}$	$\quad$ if $T[\lvert L_1 \rvert]$ then $L_1(id) \leftarrow bvP$
$(m_0, m_1, id_{\mathcal{A}}) \leftarrow \mathcal{A}_1(P, P_{pub});$		$\quad$ else $L_1(id) \leftarrow vP$
$Q_{\mathcal{A}} \leftarrow \mathcal{H}_1(id_{\mathcal{A}});$		return $L_1(id)$
$v' \leftarrow V(id_{\mathcal{A}})^{-1}c \bmod q;$		
$d \overset{\$}{\leftarrow} \{0,1\};$		Oracle $\mathcal{H}_2(r)$:
$\boxed{y \leftarrow (v'P, m_d \oplus m^*);}$		if $r = \hat{e}(P,P)^{abc}$ then
		$\quad$ bad $\leftarrow$ true;
$\boxed{R \overset{\$}{\leftarrow} \{0,1\}^n;\ y \leftarrow (v'P, R);}$		if $r \notin \mathrm{dom}(L_2)$ then
$d_{\mathcal{A}} \leftarrow \mathcal{A}_2(y)$		$\quad\quad m \overset{\$}{\leftarrow} \{0,1\}^n;\ L_2(r) \leftarrow m$
		$\quad$ else $m \leftarrow L_2(r)$
		else
		$\quad$ if $r \notin \mathrm{dom}(L_2)$ then
		$\quad\quad m \overset{\$}{\leftarrow} \{0,1\}^n;\ L_2(r) \leftarrow m$
		$\quad$ else $m \leftarrow L_2(r)$
		return m

$$q_{\mathcal{H}_2}^{-1}\Pr[G_7 : \mathsf{S}] \le \Pr\left[G_{\mathsf{BDH}} : z = \hat{e}(P,P)^{abc}\right]$$

Game G_{BDH} :	Oracle $\mathcal{EX}(id)$:	Oracle $\mathcal{H}_1(id)$:
$P \overset{\$}{\leftarrow} \mathbb{G}_1^+;\ a,b,c \overset{\$}{\leftarrow} \mathbb{Z}_q^+;$	if $id \notin L_3$ then	if $id \notin \mathrm{dom}(L_1)$ then
$z \leftarrow \mathcal{B}(P, aP, bP, cP)$	$\quad L_3 \leftarrow id :: L_3$	$\quad v \overset{\$}{\leftarrow} \mathbb{Z}_q^+;\ V(id) \leftarrow v;$
	$\quad Q \leftarrow \mathcal{H}_1(id);$	$\quad$ if $T[\lvert L_1 \rvert]$ then $L_1(id) \leftarrow vP'$
$\mathcal{B}(P_0, P_1, P_2, P_3)$:	return $V(id)P_{pub}$	$\quad$ else $L_1(id) \leftarrow vP$
Coins;		return $L_1(id)$
$L_1, L_2, L_3, V \leftarrow$ nil;		
$P \leftarrow P_0;\ P_{pub} \leftarrow P_1;\ P' \leftarrow P_2;$		Oracle $\mathcal{H}_2(r)$:
$(m_0, m_1, id_{\mathcal{A}}) \leftarrow \mathcal{A}_1(P, P_{pub});$		if $r \notin \mathrm{dom}(L_2)$ then
$Q_{\mathcal{A}} \leftarrow \mathcal{H}_1(id_{\mathcal{A}});$		$\quad m \overset{\$}{\leftarrow} \{0,1\}^n;\ L_2(r) \leftarrow m$
$v' \leftarrow V(id_{\mathcal{A}})^{-1};$		else $m \leftarrow L_2(r)$
$R \overset{\$}{\leftarrow} \{0,1\}^n;\ y \leftarrow (v'P_3, R);$		return m
$d_{\mathcal{A}} \leftarrow \mathcal{A}_2(y);$		
$i \overset{\$}{\leftarrow} [1..\lvert L_2 \rvert];$ return $\mathrm{fst}(L_2[i])$		

Fig. 4. Outline of the proof of IND-ID-CPA security of BasicIdent

Game G_3 is obtained from game G_2 by padding the random value c used to encrypt m_d with the value $V(id_{\mathcal{A}})^{-1}$. To justify this transformation we prove that the assertion $0 < V(id_{\mathcal{A}}) < q$ holds just before sampling c in G_3, and apply the rule:

$$\vDash x \overset{\$}{\leftarrow} \mathbb{Z}_q^+;\ y \leftarrow zx \bmod q \sim y \overset{\$}{\leftarrow} \mathbb{Z}_q^+;\ x \leftarrow z^{-1}y \bmod q$$
$$: (=_{\{z\}} \wedge\ 0 < z\langle 2 \rangle < q) \implies =_{\{x,y,z\}}$$

to show that the distribution of the challenge ciphertext y is the same in both games. To prove the above assertion, we first show that

$$\forall id \in \mathrm{dom}(L_1).\ 0 < V(id) < q$$

is an invariant of $\mathcal{A}_1$ that it is established right after the initialization of L_1 and that after making the oracle call $\mathcal{H}_1(id_{\mathcal{A}})$, the public key $id_{\mathcal{A}}$ necessarily belongs to the domain of L_1. Therefore we have

$$\Pr[G_2 : \mathsf{Guessed}] = \Pr[G_3 : \mathsf{Guessed}] \tag{5}$$
$$\Pr[G_2 : d = d_{\mathcal{A}} \wedge \mathsf{Guessed}] = \Pr[G_3 : d = d_{\mathcal{A}} \wedge \mathsf{Guessed}] \tag{6}$$

In game G_4 we "inject" the challenge $\hat{e}(\boldsymbol{P}, \boldsymbol{P})^{abc}$ into the ciphertext y and we change the simulation of the extraction oracle to eliminate its dependency on the private master key $\boldsymbol{a}$. The former is achieved by replacing the bitstring m' used to pad m_d with $\mathcal{H}_2\left(\hat{e}(\boldsymbol{P}, \boldsymbol{P})^{abc}\right)$, whereas the latter is achieved by replacing the return expression of oracle $\mathcal{H}_1$ with $\boldsymbol{V}(id)\,\boldsymbol{P_{pub}}$.

Observe that if the coin $\boldsymbol{T}[\boldsymbol{J}(id_{\mathcal{A}})]$ used to decide how the hash value $\mathcal{H}_1(id_{\mathcal{A}})$ is computed is true, then $\hat{e}(\boldsymbol{Q_{\mathcal{A}}}, \boldsymbol{P_{pub}})^{v'} = \hat{e}(\boldsymbol{P}, \boldsymbol{P})^{abc}$. Furthermore, if for every extraction query id we have $\boldsymbol{T}[\boldsymbol{J}(id)] = \mathsf{false}$, then $\boldsymbol{a}\mathcal{H}_1(id) = \boldsymbol{V}(id)\boldsymbol{P_{pub}}$. This motivates the introduction of a hybrid game $G_{3'}$, for which we prove the following invariant:

$$(\boldsymbol{P_{pub}} = \boldsymbol{aP} \wedge\ \boldsymbol{L_3} \subseteq \mathrm{dom}(\boldsymbol{L_1}) \wedge\ \forall id \in \mathrm{dom}(\boldsymbol{L_1}).\ 0 < \boldsymbol{V}(id) < q)\langle 1\rangle \wedge$$
$$(\forall id \in \mathrm{dom}(\boldsymbol{L_1}).\ \boldsymbol{L_1}(id) = \mathsf{if}\ \boldsymbol{T}[\boldsymbol{J}(id)]\ \mathsf{then}\ \boldsymbol{bV}(id)\boldsymbol{P}\ \mathsf{else}\ \boldsymbol{V}(id)\boldsymbol{P})\,\langle 1\rangle$$

from which we can prove that

$$\Pr\left[G_3 : d = d_{\mathcal{A}} \wedge \mathsf{Guessed}\right] = \Pr\left[G_{3'} : d = d_{\mathcal{A}} \wedge \mathsf{Guessed}\right]$$

Now, games $G_{3'}$ and G_4 differ only on code appearing after the flag **bad** is set and we can apply the Fundamental Lemma to prove that

$$\Pr\left[G_{3'} : d = d_{\mathcal{A}} \wedge \mathsf{Guessed} \wedge \neg\mathbf{bad}\right] = \Pr\left[G_4 : d = d_{\mathcal{A}} \wedge \mathsf{Guessed} \wedge \neg\mathbf{bad}\right]$$

Observe that $\mathsf{Guessed} \Rightarrow \neg\mathbf{bad}$ is a post-condition of both $G_{3'}$ and G_4, and therefore

$$\Pr\left[G_{3'} : d = d_{\mathcal{A}} \wedge \mathsf{Guessed}\right] = \Pr\left[G_4 : d = d_{\mathcal{A}} \wedge \mathsf{Guessed}\right]$$

Finally by transitivity we have

$$\Pr\left[G_3 : d = d_{\mathcal{A}} \wedge \mathsf{Guessed}\right] = \Pr\left[G_4 : d = d_{\mathcal{A}} \wedge \mathsf{Guessed}\right] \tag{7}$$

and analogously,

$$\Pr\left[G_3 : \mathsf{Guessed}\right] = \Pr\left[G_4 : \mathsf{Guessed}\right] \tag{8}$$

In game G_5 we eagerly sample the hash value $\boldsymbol{m^\star}$ that $\mathcal{H}_2$ gives in response to query $\hat{e}(\boldsymbol{P}, \boldsymbol{P})^{abc}$. To formally justify this transformation we use the logic of swapping statements presented in [4], which constitutes a general technique to reason about inter-procedural code motion and can be readily specialized to deal with this kind of bridging step. The logic yields equations

$$\Pr\left[G_4 : \mathsf{Guessed}\right] = \Pr\left[G_5 : \mathsf{Guessed}\right] \tag{9}$$
$$\Pr\left[G_4 : d = d_{\mathcal{A}} \wedge \mathsf{Guessed}\right] = \Pr\left[G_5 : d = d_{\mathcal{A}} \wedge \mathsf{Guessed}\right] \tag{10}$$

Our goal now is to make explicit that the message used to pad m_d during its encryption is $\boldsymbol{m^\star}$. Note that just inlining in G_5 the call to $\mathcal{H}_2$ made when encrypting the challenge ciphertext would result in the inclusion of the conditional statement

$$\mathsf{if}\ \hat{e}(\boldsymbol{P}, \boldsymbol{P})^{abc} \notin \mathrm{dom}(\boldsymbol{L_2})\ \mathsf{then}\ \boldsymbol{L_2}(\hat{e}(\boldsymbol{P}, \boldsymbol{P})^{abc}) \leftarrow \boldsymbol{m^\star}$$

which depends on $\hat{e}(P, P)^{abc}$, while we want to efficiently simulate an environment for $\mathcal{A}$ in terms of only P, aP, bP, and cP. We therefore introduce an intermediate game $G_{6'}$, where the oracle $\mathcal{H}_2$ does not store in its memory the answer to a $\hat{e}(P, P)^{abc}$ query.

The equivalence between games G_5 and $G_{6'}$ is proved by inlining the call to oracle $\mathcal{H}_2$ in G_5 and by means of the following relational invariant

$$I_{5 \to 6'} \stackrel{\text{def}}{=} \left(\hat{e}(P, P)^{abc} \in \text{dom}(L_2) \Rightarrow L_2\left(\hat{e}(P, P)^{abc}\right) = m^\star\right)\langle 1 \rangle \wedge$$
$$\forall x \neq \hat{e}(P, P)^{abc}\langle 1 \rangle. \ L_2\langle 1 \rangle(x) = L_2\langle 2 \rangle(x)$$

The equivalence between games $G_{6'}$ and G_6 relies on the dual invariant

$$I_{6' \to 6} \stackrel{\text{def}}{=} \left(\hat{e}(P, P)^{abc} \in \text{dom}(L_2) \Rightarrow L_2\left(\hat{e}(P, P)^{abc}\right) = m^\star\right)\langle 2 \rangle \wedge$$
$$\forall x \neq \hat{e}(P, P)^{abc}\langle 1 \rangle. \ L_2\langle 1 \rangle(x) = L_2\langle 2 \rangle(x)$$

From these two equivalences we have

$$\Pr[G_5 : \text{Guessed}] = \Pr[G_6 : \text{Guessed}] \tag{11}$$

$$\Pr[G_5 : d = d_{\mathcal{A}} \wedge \text{Guessed}] = \Pr[G_6 : d = d_{\mathcal{A}} \wedge \text{Guessed}] \tag{12}$$

Observe that if in game G_6 the value $\hat{e}(P, P)^{abc}$ is never queried to $\mathcal{H}_2$, then the second component of the challenge y looks completely random to the adversary. This motivates the definition of game G_7, where we also recover the usual implementation of $\mathcal{H}_2$ as a random oracle. To prove this, we introduce an intermediate game $G_{7'}$ that computes the challenge y given to the adversary as in game G_6, but whose implementation of oracle $\mathcal{H}_2$ is the same as in G_7. This results in two games G_6 and $G_{7'}$ that are syntactically identical except at program points where the flag **bad** is set. By the Fundamental Lemma we have

$$\Pr[G_6 : d = d_{\mathcal{A}} \wedge \text{Guessed} \wedge \neg S \wedge \neg \text{bad}]$$
$$= \Pr[G_{7'} : d = d_{\mathcal{A}} \wedge \text{Guessed} \wedge \neg S \wedge \neg \text{bad}]$$

where S is an event defined as

$$S \stackrel{\text{def}}{=} \hat{e}(P, P)^{abc} \in \text{dom}(L_2)$$

Additionally, we prove that $\neg S \Rightarrow \neg \text{bad}$ is an invariant of both G_6 and $G_{7'}$, and thus

$$\Pr[G_6 : d = d_{\mathcal{A}} \wedge \text{Guessed} \wedge \neg S] = \Pr[G_{7'} : d = d_{\mathcal{A}} \wedge \text{Guessed} \wedge \neg S]$$

We next prove that

$$\Pr[G_{7'} : d = d_{\mathcal{A}} \wedge \text{Guessed} \wedge \neg S] = \Pr[G_7 : d = d_{\mathcal{A}} \wedge \text{Guessed} \wedge \neg S]$$

using the following algebraic property of exclusive-or, known as *optimistic sampling*:

$$\vDash m^\star \xleftarrow{\$} \{0,1\}^n; R \leftarrow m_d \oplus m^\star \sim R \xleftarrow{\$} \{0,1\}^n; m^\star \leftarrow m_d \oplus R$$
$$: \ =_{\{m_d\}} \implies \ =_{\{m_d, m^\star, R\}}$$

This, together with the previous equation implies

$$\Pr\left[\mathsf{G}_6 : d = d_{\mathcal{A}} \wedge \mathsf{Guessed} \wedge \neg\mathsf{S}\right] = \Pr\left[\mathsf{G}_7 : d = d_{\mathcal{A}} \wedge \mathsf{Guessed} \wedge \neg\mathsf{S}\right] \qquad (13)$$

Analogously, we have

$$\Pr\left[\mathsf{G}_6 : \mathsf{Guessed} \wedge \neg\mathsf{S}\right] = \Pr\left[\mathsf{G}_7 : \mathsf{Guessed} \wedge \neg\mathsf{S}\right] \qquad (14)$$

$$\Pr\left[\mathsf{G}_6 : \neg\mathsf{S}\right] = \Pr\left[\mathsf{G}_7 : \neg\mathsf{S}\right] \qquad (15)$$

In game G_7 the challenge y becomes independent of the random bit d. Since the guess $d_{\mathcal{A}}$ of the adversary is now completely independent from d, the probability of the guess being correct can be proven to be exactly $1/2$, and hence

$$\Pr\left[\mathsf{G}_7 : d = d_{\mathcal{A}} \wedge \mathsf{Guessed} \wedge \neg\mathsf{S}\right] = \frac{1}{2}\Pr\left[\mathsf{G}_7 : \mathsf{Guessed} \wedge \neg\mathsf{S}\right] \qquad (16)$$

The final game $\mathsf{G}_{\mathsf{BDH}}$ constitutes the desired reduction of the security of the scheme to the BDH assumption. We prove the equivalence between G_7 and $\mathsf{G}_{\mathsf{BDH}}$ by coalescing the branches of the conditional in oracle $\mathcal{H}_2$, inlining the call $z \leftarrow \mathcal{B}(P, aP, bP, cP)$, and removing dead code. This equivalence gives

$$\Pr\left[\mathsf{G}_7 : \hat{e}(\boldsymbol{P}, \boldsymbol{P})^{\boldsymbol{abc}} \in \mathsf{dom}(\boldsymbol{L_2})\right] = \Pr\left[\mathsf{G}_{\mathsf{BDH}} : \hat{e}(P, P)^{abc} \in \mathsf{dom}(\boldsymbol{L_2})\right] \qquad (17)$$

To relate the advantage $\mathbf{Adv}^{\mathcal{A}}_{\mathsf{IND\text{-}ID\text{-}CPA}}$ of adversary $\mathcal{A}$ in the initial game with the advantage $\mathbf{Adv}^{\mathcal{B}}_{\mathsf{BDH}}$ of $\mathcal{B}$ in the final game we first claim that

$$\Pr\left[\mathsf{G}_6 : \mathsf{Guessed} \wedge \hat{e}(\boldsymbol{P}, \boldsymbol{P})^{\boldsymbol{abc}} \in \mathsf{dom}(\boldsymbol{L_2})\right] \geq 2\,\mathbf{Adv}^{\mathcal{A}}_{\mathsf{IND\text{-}ID\text{-}CPA}}\,p(1-p)^{q_{\varepsilon x}} \qquad (18)$$

In Appendix B we show that combining equations (3)–(14) and (16), one gets the inequality

$$\Pr\left[\mathsf{G}_6 : \mathsf{Guessed} \wedge \hat{e}(\boldsymbol{P}, \boldsymbol{P})^{\boldsymbol{abc}} \in \mathsf{dom}(\boldsymbol{L_2})\right]$$

$$\geq 2\left|\Pr\left[\mathsf{G}_1 : d = d_{\mathcal{A}} \wedge \mathsf{Guessed}\right] - \frac{1}{2}\Pr\left[\mathsf{G}_1 : \mathsf{Guessed}\right]\right|$$

Inequality (18) follows from Equations (1), (2) and the independence of the events $d = d_{\mathcal{A}}$ and $\mathsf{Guessed}$ in G_1.

We conclude from Equations (15) and (17):

$$\begin{aligned}
\mathbf{Adv}^{\mathcal{B}}_{\mathsf{BDH}} &= \Pr\left[\mathsf{G}_{\mathsf{BDH}} : z = \hat{e}(P, P)^{abc}\right] \\
&\geq q_{\mathcal{H}_2}^{-1}\Pr\left[\mathsf{G}_{\mathsf{BDH}} : \hat{e}(P, P)^{abc} \in \boldsymbol{L_2} \wedge |\boldsymbol{L_2}| \leq q_{\mathcal{H}_2}\right] \\
&= q_{\mathcal{H}_2}^{-1}\Pr\left[\mathsf{G}_7 : \hat{e}(\boldsymbol{P}, \boldsymbol{P})^{\boldsymbol{abc}} \in \mathsf{dom}(\boldsymbol{L_2})\right] \\
&= q_{\mathcal{H}_2}^{-1}\Pr\left[\mathsf{G}_6 : \hat{e}(\boldsymbol{P}, \boldsymbol{P})^{\boldsymbol{abc}} \in \mathsf{dom}(\boldsymbol{L_2})\right] \\
&\geq q_{\mathcal{H}_2}^{-1}\Pr\left[\mathsf{G}_6 : \mathsf{Guessed} \wedge \hat{e}(\boldsymbol{P}, \boldsymbol{P})^{\boldsymbol{abc}} \in \mathsf{dom}(\boldsymbol{L_2})\right] \\
&\geq 2\,q_{\mathcal{H}_2}^{-1}\,\mathbf{Adv}^{\mathcal{A}}_{\mathsf{IND\text{-}ID\text{-}CPA}}\,p(1-p)^{q_{\varepsilon x}}
\end{aligned}$$

The bound in the statement of the theorem is obtained by taking

$$p = \frac{1}{1 + q_{\varepsilon x}}$$

which maximizes the factor $p(1-p)^{q_{\varepsilon x}}$. □

5   Conclusion and Future Work

Identity-based cryptography is an active field of public-key cryptography. We have demonstrated that the emerging approach promoted by verifiable security naturally applies to identity-based schemes by building a fully formal, independently verifiable proof of the BasicIdent scheme of Boneh and Franklin. Overall, the formal proof is about 3,500 lines of Coq, while our extension of CertiCrypt required about 1,800 lines. Our proof is more detailed and simpler than the original proof. Since we were not able to reproduce some of the arguments in [7] (e.g. Claim 1), we were compelled to find alternative arguments that resulted in a more compact proof.

A natural follow-up to the work presented here is to formally prove that the application of the Fujisaki-Okamoto transformation to the Boneh-Franklin BasicIdent scheme yields an IND-ID-CCA-secure scheme—this can be done generically for any IND-ID-CPA-secure scheme. Another interesting possibility is to weaken the ROM assumption in the security proof of BasicIdent: when instantiated using e.g. the Weil pairing, the proof assumes the hash function $\mathcal{H}_1$ behaves like a random oracle into an elliptic curve. We could instead assume just the existence of a random oracle into the field over which the elliptic curve is defined, and use it to build a function that is indifferentiable from a random oracle into the elliptic curve as shown by Brier et al. [10], thus recovering the same result under a weaker assumption.

Other research directions include developing mathematical libraries for pairings, such as the Weil pairing or the Tate pairing, and proving the security of other pairing-based systems, such as the Boneh-Boyen [6] and Waters [16] IBE schemes, or the Boneh-Lynn-Shacham signature scheme [9].

References

1. Barthe, G., Grégoire, B., Heraud, S., Zanella Béguelin, S.: Formal certification of ElGamal encryption. In: Degano, P., Guttman, J., Martinelli, F. (eds.) FAST 2008. LNCS, vol. 5491, pp. 1–19. Springer, Heidelberg (2009)
2. Barthe, G., Grégoire, B., Lakhnech, Y., Zanella Béguelin, S.: Beyond provable security verifiable IND-CCA security of OAEP. In: Kiayias, A. (ed.) CT-RSA 2011. LNCS, vol. 6558, pp. 180–196. Springer, Heidelberg (2011)
3. Barthe, G., Grégoire, B., Zanella Béguelin, S.: Formal certification of code-based cryptographic proofs. In: 36th ACM SIGPLAN-SIGACT Symposium on Principles of Programming Languages, POPL 2009, pp. 90–101. ACM, New York (2009)
4. Barthe, G., Grégoire, B., Zanella Béguelin, S.: Programming language techniques for cryptographic proofs. In: Kaufmann, M., Paulson, L.C. (eds.) ITP 2010. LNCS, vol. 6172, pp. 115–130. Springer, Heidelberg (2010)
5. Bellare, M., Ristenpart, T.: Simulation without the artificial abort: Simplified proof and improved concrete security for Waters' IBE scheme. In: Joux, A. (ed.) EUROCRYPT 2009. LNCS, vol. 5479, pp. 407–424. Springer, Heidelberg (2009)
6. Boneh, D., Boyen, X.: Secure identity based encryption without random oracles. In: Franklin, M. (ed.) CRYPTO 2004. LNCS, vol. 3152, pp. 197–206. Springer, Heidelberg (2004)

7. Boneh, D., Franklin, M.: Identity-based encryption from the Weil pairing. SIAM J. Comput. 32(3), 586–615 (2003)
8. Boneh, D., Gentry, C., Hamburg, M.: Space-efficient identity based encryption without pairings. In: 48th Annual IEEE Symposium on Foundations of Computer Science, FOCS 2007, pp. 647–657. IEEE Computer Society, Los Alamitos (2007)
9. Boneh, D., Lynn, B., Shacham, H.: Short signatures from the Weil pairing. Journal of Cryptology 17, 297–319 (2004)
10. Brier, E., Coron, J.-S., Icart, T., Madore, D., Randriam, H., Tibouchi, M.: Efficient indifferentiable hashing into ordinary elliptic curves. In: Rabin, T. (ed.) CRYPTO 2010. LNCS, vol. 6223, pp. 237–254. Springer, Heidelberg (2010)
11. Fujisaki, E., Okamoto, T.: How to enhance the security of public-key encryption at minimum cost. In: Imai, H., Zheng, Y. (eds.) PKC 1999. LNCS, vol. 1560, p. 634. Springer, Heidelberg (1999)
12. Galindo, D.: Boneh-Franklin Identity Based Encryption Revisited. In: Caires, L., Italiano, G.F., Monteiro, L., Palamidessi, C., Yung, M. (eds.) ICALP 2005. LNCS, vol. 3580, p. 102. Springer, Heidelberg (2005)
13. Horwitz, J., Lynn, B.: Toward hierarchical identity-based encryption. In: Knudsen, L.R. (ed.) EUROCRYPT 2002. LNCS, vol. 2332, pp. 466–481. Springer, Heidelberg (2002)
14. Shamir, A.: Identity-based cryptosystems and signature schemes. In: Blakely, G.R., Chaum, D. (eds.) CRYPTO 1984. LNCS, vol. 196, pp. 47–53. Springer, Heidelberg (1985)
15. The Coq development team: The Coq Proof Assistant Reference Manual Version 8.3. (2010), http://coq.inria.fr
16. Waters, B.: Efficient identity-based encryption without random oracles. In: Cramer, R. (ed.) EUROCRYPT 2005. LNCS, vol. 3494, p. 557. Springer, Heidelberg (2005)
17. Zanella Béguelin, S., Grégoire, B., Barthe, G., Olmedo, F.: Formally certifying the security of digital signature schemes. In: 30th IEEE symposium on Security and Privacy, S&P 2009, pp. 237–250. IEEE Computer Society, Los Alamitos (2009)

A   Fundamental Lemma of Game-Playing

Lemma 1 (Fundamental Lemma). *Let G_1, G_2 be two games and let A, B, and F be events. If* $\Pr\left[G_1 : A \wedge \neg F\right] = \Pr\left[G_2 : B \wedge \neg F\right]$, *then*

$$\left|\Pr\left[G_1 : A\right] - \Pr\left[G_2 : B\right]\right| \leq \max(\Pr\left[G_1 : F\right], \Pr\left[G_2 : F\right])$$

Proof.

$$
\begin{aligned}
&\left|\Pr\left[G_1 : A\right] - \Pr\left[G_2 : B\right]\right| \\
&= \left|\Pr\left[G_1 : A \wedge F\right] + \Pr\left[G_1 : A \wedge \neg F\right] - \Pr\left[G_2 : B \wedge F\right] - \Pr\left[G_2 : B \wedge \neg F\right]\right| \\
&= \left|\Pr\left[G_1 : A \wedge F\right] - \Pr\left[G_2 : B \wedge F\right]\right| \\
&\leq \max(\Pr\left[G_1 : A \wedge F\right], \Pr\left[G_2 : B \wedge F\right]) \\
&\leq \max(\Pr\left[G_1 : F\right], \Pr\left[G_2 : F\right])
\end{aligned}
$$

A syntactic criterion can be applied to discharge the hypothesis of the lemma for the case where $A = B$ and $F = \mathbf{bad}$. The hypothesis can be automatically established by inspecting the code of both games: it holds if their code differs only after program points setting the flag **bad** to true and **bad** is never reset to false afterwards. Note also that if both games terminate with probability 1, then $\Pr\left[G_1 : \mathbf{bad}\right] = \Pr\left[G_2 : \mathbf{bad}\right]$, and that if, for instance, only game G_2 terminates with probability 1, it must be the case that $\Pr\left[G_1 : \mathbf{bad}\right] \leq \Pr\left[G_2 : \mathbf{bad}\right]$.

B   Derived Equations

From Equations (13), (14) and (16) we can prove the following two inequalities:

$$
\begin{aligned}
\Pr\left[\mathsf{G}_6 : d = d_{\mathcal{A}} \wedge \mathsf{Guessed}\right] &\geq \Pr\left[\mathsf{G}_6 : d = d_{\mathcal{A}} \wedge \mathsf{Guessed} \wedge \neg\mathsf{S}\right] \\
&= \Pr\left[\mathsf{G}_7 : d = d_{\mathcal{A}} \wedge \mathsf{Guessed} \wedge \neg\mathsf{S}\right] \\
&= \frac{1}{2}\Pr\left[\mathsf{G}_7 : \mathsf{Guessed} \wedge \neg\mathsf{S}\right] \\
&= \frac{1}{2}\Pr\left[\mathsf{G}_6 : \mathsf{Guessed} \wedge \neg\mathsf{S}\right] \\
&= \frac{1}{2}\Pr\left[\mathsf{G}_6 : \mathsf{Guessed}\right] - \frac{1}{2}\Pr\left[\mathsf{G}_6 : \mathsf{Guessed} \wedge \mathsf{S}\right]
\end{aligned}
$$

and

$$
\begin{aligned}
\Pr\left[\mathsf{G}_6 : d = d_{\mathcal{A}} \wedge \mathsf{Guessed}\right] & \\
&= \Pr\left[\mathsf{G}_6 : d = d_{\mathcal{A}} \wedge \mathsf{Guessed} \wedge \mathsf{S}\right] + \Pr\left[\mathsf{G}_6 : d = d_{\mathcal{A}} \wedge \mathsf{Guessed} \wedge \neg\mathsf{S}\right] \\
&\leq \Pr\left[\mathsf{G}_6 : \mathsf{Guessed} \wedge \mathsf{S}\right] + \Pr\left[\mathsf{G}_7 : d = d_{\mathcal{A}} \wedge \mathsf{Guessed} \wedge \neg\mathsf{S}\right] \\
&= \Pr\left[\mathsf{G}_6 : \mathsf{Guessed} \wedge \mathsf{S}\right] + \frac{1}{2}\Pr\left[\mathsf{G}_7 : \mathsf{Guessed} \wedge \neg\mathsf{S}\right] \\
&= \Pr\left[\mathsf{G}_6 : \mathsf{Guessed} \wedge \mathsf{S}\right] + \frac{1}{2}\Pr\left[\mathsf{G}_6 : \mathsf{Guessed} \wedge \neg\mathsf{S}\right] \\
&= \frac{1}{2}\Pr\left[\mathsf{G}_6 : \mathsf{Guessed}\right] + \frac{1}{2}\Pr\left[\mathsf{G}_6 : \mathsf{Guessed} \wedge \mathsf{S}\right]
\end{aligned}
$$

which together with Equations (3)-(12) imply

$$
\Pr\left[\mathsf{G}_6 : \mathsf{Guessed} \wedge \mathsf{S}\right] \geq 2 \left| \Pr\left[\mathsf{G}_1 : d = d_{\mathcal{A}} \wedge \mathsf{Guessed}\right] - \frac{1}{2}\Pr\left[\mathsf{G}_1 : \mathsf{Guessed}\right] \right|
$$

Efficient Ciphertext Policy Attribute-Based Encryption with Constant-Size Ciphertext and Constant Computation-Cost

Cheng Chen, Zhenfeng Zhang, and Dengguo Feng

State Key Laboratory of Information Security, Institute of Software, Chinese
Academy of Sciences, Beijing, 100190, China
{chencheng,zfzhang,feng}@is.iscas.ac.cn

Abstract. Attribute-based encryption provides good solutions to the problem of anonymous access control by specifying access policies among private keys or ciphertexts over encrypted data. In ciphertext-policy attribute-based encryption (CP-ABE), each user is associated with a set of attributes, and data is encrypted with access structures on attributes. A user is able to decrypt a ciphertext if and only if his attributes satisfy the ciphertext access structure. CP-ABE is very appealing since the ciphertext and data access policies are integrated together in a natural and effective way.

Most current CP-ABE schemes incur large ciphertext size and computation costs in the encryption and decryption operations which depend at least linearly on the number of attributes involved in the access policy. In this paper, we present two new CP-ABE schemes, which have both constant-size ciphertext and constant computation costs for a non-monotone **AND** gate access policy, under chosen plaintext and chosen ciphertext attacks. The security of first scheme can be proven CPA-secure in standard model under the decision n-BDHE assumption. And the security of second scheme can be proven CCA-secure in standard model under the decision n-BDHE assumption and the existence of collision-resistant hash functions. Our scheme can also be extended to the decentralizing multi-authority setting.

Keywords: Attribute-based encryption, chosen ciphertext security, efficiency.

1 Introduction

When one wants to share sensitive data, he should establish a specific access control policy determining who can obtain the data. Traditional access control by employing a trusted server to store data locally has the drawback that it is increasingly difficult to guarantee the security of data: access control servers may become accessible to hackers if the network of the organization is not well protected. For these reasons we would like to require that sensitive data is stored in an encrypted form so that it will remain private even if a server is compromised. The data resource providers can encrypt the data under the recipient's

X. Boyen and X. Chen (Eds.): ProvSec 2011, LNCS 6980, pp. 84–101, 2011.

public key such that only the recipients, with knowledge of his private key, can decrypt it. However, in many applications, we need to share data according to an encryption policy without prior knowledge of who will be receiving the data. Furthermore, the relationship between resources and users is more ad-hoc and dynamic, resource providers and users are not in the same security domain, and the resource providers may not know the exact identities of all other people who should be able to access the data. In the application scenario, the users are usually identified by their characteristics or attributes, such as his age, job, company, expertise, etc., rather than predefined identities. The access control policy specifies which claims need to be satisfied in order to grant access to the data. For instance the claim could be "older than". Therefore, the traditional identity-based access control models are not effective and fine-grained, and access policies system based on attribute credentials needs to be made.

In 2005, Sahai and Waters [23] proposed a solution to the above problem that they called attribute-based encryption (ABE). In an ABE system, a party encrypting data can specify access policy to the data as a boolean formula over a set of attributes. Each user in the system will be issued a private key from an authority that reflects their attributes (or credentials). A user will be able to decrypt a ciphertext if the attributes associated with their private key satisfy the access policy ascribed to the ciphertext. A crucial property of ABE systems is the resistance of collusion attacks: if multiple users collude, they should not be able to decrypt a ciphertext if none of the users could decrypt it on their own.

Subsequently, Goyal, Pandey, Sahai and Waters [14] formulate two complimentary forms of ABE: key-policy ABE, where a ciphertext is associated to a list of attributes, and a secret key is associated to a policy for decryption; and ciphertext-policy ABE, where secret keys are associated to a list of attributes (i.e. credentials of that user) and ciphertexts are associated to policies for decryption. A construction of a key-policy ABE scheme was proposed in [14]. The ciphertext-policy scenario was first studied in [4]. Later, ABE schemes with non-monotone access structures was investigated by [10,22].

Since the introduction of attribute-based encryption, several ABE schemes [4,8,10,13,22,21,18,19,24] have been proposed. In most of the ABE proposals, the size of ciphertext and the computation costs in encryption and decryption operations depend (at least) linearly on the number of attributes involved in the access policy. This fact can limit the applications of ABE in real life. If we consider for the case of large number attributes involving in the access policy, the bandwidth for the communication and the overhead in the encryption and decryption operations will be a bottleneck of the applications.

Chosen-ciphertext security (CCA) is considered as an important notion of security for public key encryption schemes [1,6,9,12,28,17]. Some previous ABE schemes [10,14,21,15] use CHK technique [9] to obtain a CCA-secure extension from a CPA-secure scheme in the standard model. The main idea of [10] is to associate one-time signature keys with each encryption operation. A message is encrypted using additional attributes corresponding to the bit-string representation of the verification key. The decryption algorithm runs the signature verification algorithm to check the validity of the ciphertext. This technique incurs additional overhead that the length of ciphertext and the computing costs depend linearly on the length of the very key. Recently, a generic construction of CCA-secure ABE was given by Yamada et al. in [27]. They propose eight generic conversions that transform CPA-secure ABE to CCA-secure ABE. For the small attribute universe case, [27] uses a similar strategy as [10] [21] to achieve CCA-secure ABE scheme. In contrast, it is easy to achieve CCA security in the random oracle model by applying Fujisaki-Okamoto transformation [12].

In an ABE scheme, users' private keys are usually issued by a central authority that would need to verify all the attributes or credentials it issued for each user in the system. Such deployment may not be entirely realistic, in that it assumes the existence of a single trusted party who monitors all attributes and issues all decryption keys. Instead, there are different entities responsible for monitoring different attributes of a person, e.g. the Department of Motor Vehicles tests whether one can drive, a university can certify a student, etc.. In [8], Chase proposed a multi-authority ABE scheme which supports different authorities operating simultaneously, each issues secret keys for a different set of attributes. However, in Chase's construction, each authority which holds a secret that is powerful enough to decrypt every ciphertexts in the system, and the set of authorities is pre-determined. Chase and Chow [7] resolved the key-escrow problem by proposing a multi-authority ABE in which no single party holds such a powerful master secret key. But the set of authorities is fixed ahead of time, and they must interact during the system setup. Lewko and Waters [20] proposed a decentralizing ABE system, in which a party can simply act as an authority by creating a public key and issuing private keys to different users that reflect their attributes, and different authorities can function entirely independently. A global identifier is used to "link" private keys that were issued to the same user by different authorities. A user can encrypt data over attributes issued from any chosen set of authorities. This makes the system more robust.

Our contribution. In this paper, we first propose a CPA-secure non-monotone access structure CP-ABE scheme whose ciphertext size and computation costs are constant (regardless of the number of underlying attributes) for an AND gate access policy. Compared with previous CP-ABE schemes, our basic CP-ABE scheme achieves better performance in terms of encryption and decryption operations, and the security can be proved under a well-established assumption in the standard model. Apart from this, the basic scheme can be extended to be CCA-secure in the standard model without losing its efficiency, i.e., the CCA-secure extension still has both constant ciphertext size and computation costs in the encryption and decryption operations. Comparing with previous work [10,14,21,15] using CHK technique to achieve CCA-secure in the standard model, our scheme is significantly efficient.

In the two CP-ABE schemes, a public key element and a master secret key element are specified for each attribute value. A random group element is chosen by the key generator for a user associated with a set of attributes, and varies among different users. In the secret key generation phase, each master secret key element is used to produce user's secret key element corresponding to one of the user's attribute values. The encryptor can aggregate the corresponding attribute values' public key elements to encrypt the plaintext. And each user whose attributes set satisfies the access policy can also aggregate the corresponding secret key elements to decrypt the ciphertext. By this technique, we can pool n attributes to "one" aggregated attribute in the encryption and decryption operations in an AND gate access policy. The secret key elements from different users can not be pooled together to decrypt the ciphertext, and the collusion attacks can be prevented. Finally, we show that our schemes can be easily extended to the decentralizing setting like [20]. There is no requirement for any global coordination other than the creation of an initial set of common reference parameters.

Related Work. The first CP-ABE scheme whose ciphertexts are constant-size is proposed in [11], which admits only (n, n)-threshold decryption policies, i.e., users who have fixed n attributes can decrypt a ciphertext. Another constant-size ciphertext CP-ABE scheme is proposed in [15], and works for the (t, n)-threshold case, where users authorized to decrypt are those who hold at least t attributes among a certain universe of attributes, for some threshold t chosen by the sender, and the encryption operation requires $n + t + 1$ exponentiations and the decryption operation requires $O(t^2)$ exponentiations. The scheme admits however monotone threshold access structures, and the security is reduced to an augmented assumption (aMSE-DDH). Recently, [2] uses a new efficient identity-based revocation mechanism to construct the first KP-ABE scheme allowing for expressive non-monotonic access structures with constant ciphertext size. The KP-ABE scheme has quadratic private key size. The exponentiation computations in encryption operations are linear with the number of attributes involved. The exponentiation computations in decryption operations are linear with the number of attributes in an access structure.

Most previous constructions of ABE systems have been proven to be selectively secure. Lewko et al.[18] first obtain full security by adapting the dual system encryption technique [25] to the ABE case. Okamoto and Takashima [21] present a fully secure ABE scheme under a well-established assumption. The scheme in [20] is fully secure as well.

2   Preliminary

We present a few facts related to groups with efficiently computable bilinear maps. Let $\mathbb{G}$ and $\mathbb{G}_T$ be two multiplicative cyclic groups of prime order p. Let g be a generator of $\mathbb{G}$ and $e : \mathbb{G} \times \mathbb{G} \to \mathbb{G}_T$ be a bilinear map such that $e(g, g) \neq 1$, and for any $u, v \in \mathbb{Z}_p$ it holds that $e(g^u, g^v) = e(g, g)^{uv}$. We say that $\mathbb{G}$ is a bilinear group if the group operation in $\mathbb{G}$ and the bilinear map $e : \mathbb{G} \times \mathbb{G} \to \mathbb{G}_T$ are both efficiently computable. Notice that the map e is symmetric since $e(g^u, g^v) = e(g, g)^{uv} = e(g^v, g^u)$.

The security proof of our schemes base on the decision n-BDHE assumption which is introduced and shown to be hard by Boneh et al. [5] in the generic group model.

Definition 1. *Let $\mathbb{G}$ be bilinear group of prime order p as defined above, and g, h two independent generators of $\mathbb{G}$. Denote $\overrightarrow{y}_{g,\alpha,n} = (g_1, g_2, \ldots, g_n, g_{n+2}, \ldots, g_{2n})$ $\in \mathbb{G}^{2n-1}$, where $g_i = g^{\alpha^i}$ for some unknown $\alpha \in \mathbb{Z}_p^*$. An algorithm $\mathcal{B}$ that outputs $\nu \in \{0, 1\}$ has advantage ϵ in solving the n-BDHE problem if*

$$\left| Pr\Big[\mathcal{B}(g, h, \overrightarrow{y}_{g,\alpha,n}, e(g_{n+1}, h)) = 1 \Big] - Pr\Big[\mathcal{B}(g, h, \overrightarrow{y}_{g,\alpha,n}, Z) = 1 \Big] \right| \geqslant \epsilon$$

where the probability is over the random choice of g, h in $\mathbb{G}$, the random choice $\alpha \in \mathbb{Z}_p^*$, the random choice of $Z \in \mathbb{G}_T$, and the random bits consumed by $\mathcal{B}$. We say that the decision n-BDHE assumption holds in $\mathbb{G}$ is if no polynomial algorithm has advantage at least ϵ in solving the n-BDHE problem.

3   Ciphertext Policy ABE

3.1   Syntactic Definition of CP-ABE

Intuitively, an access structure is a rule $\mathbb{W}$ that returns either 0 or 1 given a set of attributes S. We say that S satisfies $\mathbb{W}$ (written $S \models \mathbb{W}$) if and only if $\mathbb{W}$ answers 1 on S. As mentioned above, access structures may be boolean expressions, threshold trees, etc. In our context, we focus on the AND gate access policy.

A ciphertext policy attribute-based encryption (CP-ABE) system consists of four fundamental algorithms: **Setup**, **Encrypt**, **KeyGen** and **Decrypt**.

Setup(κ, U). The algorithm takes as input a security parameter κ and an attribute universe description U. It outputs a public key PK and a master key MK. The public key is made public. The master key is kept secret by the central authority, and is used to generate users' secret keys.

KeyGen(MK, S). The algorithm takes as input the master key MK and a set of attributes $S \subseteq U$. It returns a secret key SK associated with S.

Encrypt(PK, M, $\mathbb{W}$). The algorithm takes as input the public key PK, a message M and an access structure $\mathbb{W}$. It returns a ciphertext CT such that a secret key generated from attribute set S can be used to decrypt CT if and only if S satisfies $\mathbb{W}$.

Decrypt(PK, CT, SK). The algorithm takes as input the public key PK, a ciphertext CT, which contains an access policy $\mathbb{W}$, and a secret key SK, which is a private key for a set of attributes S. It returns the message M if the set of attributes S satisfies the access structure $\mathbb{W}$.

3.2   CPA Security Game for CP-ABE

We now describe a selective security model against chosen plaintext attacks for ciphertext-policy ABE schemes. In the selective security model, the adversary will choose to be challenged on an encryption to an access structure $\mathbb{W}^*$ before **Setup** and can ask for any private keys corresponding to the set of attributes S such that S does not satisfy $\mathbb{W}^*$. We now present the CPA-CP-ABE game as follows.

Init. The adversary chooses the challenge access structure $\mathbb{W}^*$ and gives it to the challenger.

Setup. The challenger runs the **Setup** algorithm and gives the adversary PK.

Phase 1. The adversary submits a set of attributes S for a **KeyGen** query. Provided $S \nvDash \mathbb{W}^*$, the challenger answers with a secret key SK for S. These queries can be repeated adaptively.

Challenge. The adversary submits two messages M_0 and M_1 of equal length. The challenger chooses $\mu \in \{0, 1\}$ at random and encrypts M_μ under $\mathbb{W}^*$. The resulting ciphertext CT^* is given to the adversary.

Phase 2. The adversary can continue to make queries as Phase 1.

Guess. Finally, the adversary outputs a guess μ' of μ.

The advantage of an adversary Adv in the CPA-CP-ABE game is defined as $Pr[\mu' = \mu] - \frac{1}{2}$.

Definition 2. *A ciphertext-policy attribute-based encryption scheme is CPA-secure if all polynomial time adversaries have at most a negligible advantage in the CPA-CP-ABE game.*

Notice, the CPA-CP-ABE game captures the indistinguishability of messages as standard and the collusion-resistance of secret keys, namely, the adversary cannot generate a new secret key for a new set of attributes by combining their secret keys.

3.3   Basic Construction

In this section, we present a CPA-secure CP-ABE scheme. The construction is inspired by a primitive referred to as aggregatable signature-based broadcast proposed in [26].

For notational simplicity, let the attribute universe be $U = \{A_1, A_2, \ldots, A_n\}$ for some natural number n. We have $2n$ attribute values since each attribute A_i has 2 values: A_i^+ and A_i^-, where A_i^+ denotes the user has A_i, and A_i^- denotes the user does not have A_i or A_i is not a proper attribute of this user. For ease of presentation, we map attribute value A_i^+ to i , A_i^- to $\neg i$ as literals. In this section, we consider access structure $\mathbb{W}$ that consist of a single AND gate whose inputs are literals. This is denoted $\bigwedge_{i \in I} \underline{i}$, where $I \subseteq U$ and every $\underline{i}$ is a literal (i.e., i or $\neg i$).

Setup(U). Takes as input a security parameter κ, the algorithm randomly chooses $r_1, r_2, \ldots, r_{2n} \in \mathbb{Z}_p^*$, and $x_1, x_2, \ldots, x_{2n} \in \mathbb{G}$. For $k = 1, 2, \ldots, 2n$, set $u_k = g^{-r_k}$ and $h_k = e(x_k, g)$.

The public key is $PK := \{\langle u_k, h_k \rangle \mid k = 1, 2, \ldots, 2n\}$.

The master secret key is $MK := \{\langle r_k, x_k \rangle | k = 1, 2, \ldots, 2n\}$.

Intuitively, the public key elements $\langle u_i, h_i \rangle$ and $\langle u_{i+n}, h_{i+n} \rangle$ correspond to the positive, negative types of each attribute A_i respectively.

Encrypt(PK, M, $\mathbb{W}$). The encryption algorithm encrypts a message $M \in \mathbb{G}_T$ under an AND gate $\mathbb{W} = \bigwedge_{i \in I} \underline{i}$, where $\underline{i} \in \{i, \neg i\}$, and I is the set of attributes index consisting of all the attributes specified in the encryption. The encryption algorithm first selects a random number $s \in \mathbb{Z}_p^*$ and aggregates all the public key elements corresponding to the attribute values to generate an aggregated public key $\langle u_I, h_I \rangle = \langle \prod_{i \in I} u_{\underline{i}}, \prod_{i \in I} h_{\underline{i}} \rangle$, where for each $i \in I$,

$$
\langle u_{\underline{i}}, h_{\underline{i}} \rangle = \begin{cases} \langle u_i, h_i \rangle = \langle g^{-r_i}, e(x_i, g) \rangle, & \text{if } \underline{i} = i, \\ \langle u_{i+n}, h_{i+n} \rangle = \langle g^{-r_{i+n}}, e(x_{i+n}, g) \rangle, & \text{if } \underline{i} = \neg i. \end{cases}
$$

Then, it calculates $C_1 = g^s, C_2 = u_I^s, C_3 = M h_I^s$.

The algorithm outputs $CT = (\mathbb{W}, C_1, C_2, C_3)$ as the ciphertext.

KeyGen(MK, S). The key generation algorithm takes as input a set of attributes S and outputs a secret key that identifies with that set. Every $i \notin S$ is considered a negative attribute. The algorithm first randomly chooses $v \in \mathbb{G}$ for each user. Then for each $i \in \{1, 2, \ldots, n\}$ the algorithm computes with v and the master key element $\langle r_i, x_i \rangle$ of the positive attribute value A_i^+ to obtain $\sigma_i = x_i v^{r_i}$, if $i \in S$; the algorithm computes with v under the master key element $\langle r_{i+n}, x_{i+n} \rangle$ of the negative attribute value A_i^- to obtain $\sigma_i = x_{i+n} v^{r_{i+n}}$, if $i \notin S$. In both cases, the output can be verified by $e(\sigma_i, g) \cdot e(v, u_{\underline{i}}) = h_{\underline{i}}$.

The secret key is defined as $SK := \langle v, \{\sigma_i | i \in \{1, 2, \ldots, n\}\} \rangle$.

Decrypt(PK, CT, SK). Suppose the ciphertext is of the form $CT := (\mathbb{W}, C_1, C_2, C_3)$, where $\mathbb{W} = \bigwedge_{i \in I} \underline{i}$. The decryption algorithm first checks whether $S \models \mathbb{W}$ when receiving the ciphertext. If not, the decryption algorithm returns $\perp$. The secret key is of the form $SK := \langle v, \{\sigma_i | i \in \{1, 2, \ldots, n\}\} \rangle$. The decryption algorithm aggregates the secret key elements corresponding to the attribute values in I to generate $sk = \langle v, \sigma = \prod_{i \in I} \sigma_i \rangle$. Then, the decryption algorithm computes $M = C_3/(e(v, C_2) \cdot e(\sigma, C_1))$, and outputs M as the plaintext.

3.4   CPA Security Proof

We now prove that the proposed scheme is secure against chosen-plaintext attack in the standard model under the decision n-BDHE assumption.

Theorem 1. *Suppose the decisional n-BDHE assumption holds in $\mathbb{G}$. Then no polynomial time adversary can win the CPA-CP-ABE game defined in section 3.2 with non-negligible probability.*

Proof. Suppose that an adversary *Adv* can win the CPA-CP-ABE game with advantage ϵ for a CP-ABE scheme whose attribute universe U has n attributes. We can construct a simulator *Sim* that uses a n-BDHE challenge to simulate all the requested service for adversary *Adv*. Then *Sim* uses output of *Adv* to solve the decision n-BDHE assumption.

Let $\nu \in \{0,1\}$ be selected at random. *Sim* takes as input a random n-BDHE challenge $(g, h, \overrightarrow{y}_{g,\alpha,n}, T)$, where $\overrightarrow{y}_{g,\alpha,n} = (g_1, g_2, \ldots, g_n, g_{n+2}, \ldots, g_{2n}) \in \mathbb{G}^{2n-1}$, and $T = e(g_{n+1}, h)$ if $\nu = 1$, and T is a random element in $\mathbb{G}_T$ if $\nu = 0$.

The simulator *Sim* now plays the role of challenger in the CPA-CP-ABE game, and interacts with *Adv* as follows.

Init. During the initial phase, *Sim* receives a challenge gate $\mathbb{W}^* = \bigwedge_{i \in I^*} \underline{i}$ specified by the adversary *Adv*. Since $\{A_i | i \in I^*\} \subseteq U$, we have $|I^*| \leq n$. We denote the attribute index in I^* by $I^* = \{i_1, i_2, \ldots, i_m\}$, where $m = |I^*|$ is the number of attributes specified in the challenge access structure $\mathbb{W}^*$.

Setup. The simulator *Sim* randomly selects $j^* \in \{1, 2, \ldots, m\}$, and also chooses at random $r'_k \in \mathbb{Z}_p^*$, $x_k \in \mathbb{G}$ for $k = 1, 2, \ldots, 2n$, and $r_{i_j}, a_{i_j} \in \mathbb{Z}_p^*$ for $j = 1, 2, \ldots, m$.

For $i \in I^* - \{j^*\}$, *Sim* constructs public key elements (u_{i_j}, h_{i_j}) for the positive attribute value $A_{i_j}^+$, and public key elements (u_{i_j+n}, h_{i_j+n}) for the negative attribute value $A_{i_j}^-$, according to the following cases:

(1) If $i_j = i_j$, then compute

$$(u_{i_j}, h_{i_j}) = (g^{r_{i_j}} g_{n+1-i_j}^{-1}, e(g,g)^{a_{i_j}}), \quad (u_{i_j+n}, h_{i_j+n}) = (g^{-r'_{i_j}+n}, e(x_{i_j+n}, g)).$$

(2) If $i_j = \neg i_j$, then compute

$$(u_{i_j}, h_{i_j}) = (g^{-r'_{i_j}}, e(x_{i_j}, g)), \quad (u_{i_j+n}, h_{i_j+n}) = (g^{r_{i_j}} g_{n+1-i_j}^{-1}, e(g,g)^{a_{i_j}}).$$

For $i = i_{j^*}$, *Sim* constructs the public key element $(u_{i_{j^*}}, h_{i_{j^*}})$ of the positive attribute value $A_{i_{j^*}}^+$, and the public key element $(u_{i_{j^*}+n}, h_{i_{j^*}+n})$ of the negative attribute value $A_{i_{j^*}}^-$ as follows.

(1) If $i_{j^*} = i_{j^*}$, then compute

$$(u_{i_{j^*}}, h_{i_{j^*}}) = \left(g^{r_{i_{j^*}}} \prod_{k \in I^*-\{j^*\}} g_{n+1-k}, \; e(g,g)^{a_{i_{j^*}}} e(g,g)^{\alpha^{n+1}}\right),$$

$$(u_{i_{j^*}+n}, h_{i_{j^*}+n}) = \left(g^{-r'_{i_{j^*}+n}}, e(x_{i_{j^*}+n}, g)\right).$$

(2) If $i_{j^*} = \neg i_{j^*}$, then compute

$$(u_{i_{j^*}}, h_{i_{j^*}}) = \left(g^{-r'_{i_{j^*}}}, e(x_{i_{j^*}}, g)\right),$$

$$(u_{i_{j^*}+n}, h_{i_{j^*}+n}) = \left(g^{r_{i_{j^*}}} \prod_{k \in I^* - \{j^*\}} g_{n+1-k}, \; e(g,g)^{a_{i_{j^*}}} e(g,g)^{\alpha^{n+1}}\right).$$

For $i \notin I^*$, Sim computes $(u_i, h_i) = (g^{-r_i'}, e(x_i, g))$, $(u_{i+n}, h_{i+n}) = (g^{-r_{i+n}'}, e(x_{i+n}, g))$.

Phase 1. Adv can submit a few sets $S \subseteq U$ in a secret key query, where $S \nvDash \mathbb{W}^* = \bigwedge_{i \in I^*} i$.

There must exist $i_j \in I^*$ such that: either $A_{i_j} \in S$ and $i_j = \neg i_j$, or $A_{i_j} \notin S$ and $i_j = i_j$. Without loss of generality, we assume that S only has one literal i_j that doesn't satisfy the access structure $\mathbb{W}^*$ and $A_{i_j} \notin S$ and $i_j = i_j$. Sim randomly selects $z \in \mathbb{Z}_p^*$ and sets $v = g_{i_j} g^z$. The value g_{i_j} is hidden by blinding factor g^z.

For i_j, Sim computes the secret key element as $\sigma_{i_j} = x_{i_j+n} (g_{i_j} g^z)^{r_{i_j}'+n}$.

For $i \neq i_j$, the value of σ_i is calculated according to the following cases:

(1) If $i = i_k \in I^* - \{j^*\}$ $(k \neq j^*)$, compute $\sigma_i = g^{a_{i_k}} (g_{i_j})^{r_{i_k}} g_{n+1-i_k+i_j} (u_{i_k})^{-z}$.
    The correctness of σ_i can be verified as:

$$e(\sigma_i, g) e(v, u_{i_k}) = e(g^{a_{i_k}} (g_{i_j})^{r_{i_k}} g_{n+1-i_k+i_j} (u_{i_k})^{-z}, g) e(g_{i_j} g^z, u_{i_k})$$
$$= e(g,g)^{a_{i_k}} \equiv h_{i_k}$$

(2) If $i = i_{j^*}$, compute $\sigma_i = g^{a_{i_{j^*}}} (g_{i_j})^{r_{i_{j^*}}} (\prod_{k \in I^* - \{j^*\}}^{k \neq i_j} g_{n+1-k+i_j}^{-1})(u_{i_{j^*}})^{-z}$.
    The correctness of $\sigma_i = \sigma_{i_{j^*}}$ can be verified as:

$$e(\sigma_{i_{j^*}}, g) e(v, u_{i_{j^*}})$$
$$= e(g^{a_{i_{j^*}}} (g_{i_j})^{r_{i_{j^*}}} (\prod_{\substack{k \in I^* - \{j^*\} \\ }}^{k \neq i_j} g_{n+1-k+i_j}^{-1})(u_{i_{j^*}})^{-z}, g) e(g_{i_j} g^z, u_{i_{j^*}})$$
$$= e(g,g)^{a_{i_{j^*}}} e(g,g)^{\alpha^{n+1}} \equiv h_{i_{j^*}}.$$

(3) If $i \notin I^*$, compute
    (a) $\sigma_i = x_i (g_{i_j} g^z)^{r_i'}$, if $i = i$;
    (b) $\sigma_i = x_{i+n} (g_{i_j} g^z)^{r_{i+n}'}$, if $i = \neg i$.

Sim answers with the secret key $SK = \langle v, \{\sigma_i | i \in \{1, 2, \ldots, n\}\}\rangle$ for S.

Challenge. Adv runs the CPA-CP-ABE game under the the aggregated public encryption key.

We denote $a_{I^*} = a_{i_1} + a_{i_2} + \ldots + a_{i_m}$, $r_{I^*} = r_{i_1} + r_{i_2} + \ldots + r_{i_m}$. It follows that the aggregated public encryption key is $\langle u_{I^*}, h_{I^*}\rangle$, where

$$u_{I^*} = u_{i_{j^*}} \underbrace{\prod_{k \in I^* - \{j^*\}} u_k}_{} = \left(g^{r_{i_{j^*}}} \underbrace{\prod_{k \in I^* - \{j^*\}} g_{n+1-k}}_{}\right) \underbrace{\prod_{k \in I^* - \{j^*\}} g^{r_k} g_{n+1-k}^{-1}}_{} = g^{r_{I^*}},$$

$$h_{I^*} = h_{i_{j^*}} \underbrace{\prod_{k \in I^* - \{j^*\}} h_k}_{} = e(g,g)^{a_{i_{j^*}}} e(g,g)^{\alpha^{n+1}} \underbrace{\prod_{k \in I^* - \{j^*\}} e(g,g)^{a_k}}_{} = e(g,g)^{a_{I^*} + \alpha^{n+1}}.$$

For the aggregated public key $\langle u_{I^*}, h_{I^*} \rangle$, the decryption keys corresponding to each member are not revealed. Hence, Sim can challenge Adv as follows. Adv submits two messages M_0 and M_1 of equal length. Sim chooses $\mu \in \{0,1\}$ at random. Then Sim computes the challenge ciphertext

$$CT^* = \left(\mathbb{W}^*, C_1^* = h, C_2^* = h^{r_{I^*}}, C_3^* = M_\mu T e(g,h)^{a_{I^*}}\right).$$

The challenge ciphertext is a valid encryption of M_μ whenever $T = e(g_{n+1}, h)$. On the other hand, when T is uniform and independent in $\mathbb{G}_T$, the challenge ciphertext C^* is independent of μ in the Adv 's view.

Guess. If Adv outputs a correct guess after the **Challenge** phase, Sim answers 1 in the n-BDHE game to guess that $T = e(g_{n+1}, h)$. Otherwise, Sim answers 0 to indicate that it believes T is a random group element in $\mathbb{G}_T$. If $T = e(g_{n+1}, h)$, then CT is a valid ciphertext, the simulator Sim gives a perfect simulation so we have that

$$Pr\left[Sim(g, h, \overrightarrow{y}_{g,\alpha,n}, e(g_{n+1}, h)) = 1\right] = 1/2 + \epsilon$$

If T is a random group element, the message M_μ is completely hidden from the adversary, and we have

$$Pr\left[Sim(g, h, \overrightarrow{y}_{g,\alpha,n}, Z) = 1\right] = 1/2$$

Therefore, Sim can play the decisional n-BDHE game with non-negligible advantage. This concludes the proof of Theorem 1. $\square$

3.5   Performance Comparison

It is reasonable to measure the performance of CPA-secure CP-ABE schemes in this class in several ways: the computation costs of encryption and decryption operations, the ciphertext length, the flexibility of access policy, the size of the public key and private key. In this section, we compare the efficiency and security of the proposed ABE scheme with some existing CPA-secure CP-ABE schemes.

In Table 1 we present a brief comparison of some existing CP-ABE schemes, where t denotes the number of attributes involved in the access policy, and r denotes the number of attributes the user has. The bit-length of the expression of access policy is ignored here. In Table 1, **ex** stands for an exponentiation operation, and **p** stands for a pairing operation. The computational costs over $\mathbb{Z}_p$ is ignored as usual. The conclusion we would like to draw from this comparison is the following. Our scheme is efficient in the ciphertext size and the overhead of encryption and decryption operations since they do not depend on the number of the underlying attributes. Beyond that, the security proof is under a well-established assumption, n-BDHE, in the standard model.

Table 1. Comparison with existing ciphertext policy ABE schemes

	Enc.	Dec.	Ciphertext Length	Expressiveness	Assumption
CN[10]	$(n+2)\mathbf{ex}$	$(n+1)\ \mathbf{p}$	$|\mathbb{G}_T| + (n+1)|\mathbb{G}|$	non-monotone AND gates	DBDH
Wat[24]	$(2t+2)\ \mathbf{ex}$	$(2t+1)\ \mathbf{p}$	$|\mathbb{G}_T| + (2t+1)|\mathbb{G}|$	monotone linear structure	PBDHE
EM+[11]	$(t+2)\ \mathbf{ex}$	$2\mathbf{p}+\ 2\mathbf{ex}$	$|\mathbb{G}_T| + 2|\mathbb{G}|$	monotone (n,n) threshold scheme	DBDH
ZH[29]	$2\ \mathbf{ex}$	$2t\mathbf{p} + 1$	$|\mathbb{G}_T| + 2|\mathbb{G}|$	non-monotone AND gates	n-BDHE
HLR[15]	$(n+t+1)\mathbf{ex}$	$3\mathbf{p} + (t^2)\mathbf{ex}$	$|\mathbb{G}_T| + 2|\mathbb{G}|$	monotone (t,n) threshold scheme	aMSE-DDH
AL1[3]	$4\mathbf{ex}$	$3\mathbf{p} + (n-1)\mathbf{ex}$	$|\mathbb{G}_T| + 2|\mathbb{G}|$	inner-product	n-BDHE
AL2[3][1]	$15\mathbf{ex}$	$9\mathbf{p} + (n+1)\mathbf{ex}$	$|\mathbb{G}_T| + 9|\mathbb{G}|$	inner-product	n-BDHE, DLIN
Our Scheme	$3\mathbf{ex}$	$2\mathbf{p}$	$|\mathbb{G}_T| + 2|\mathbb{G}|$	non-monotone AND gates	n-BDHE

4   CCA-Secure Extension

In [14,10,27], the general technique of [9] is applied to obtain a CCA-secure ABE extension for the small attribute universe. The main idea is to associate one-time signature keys $\langle K_v, K_s \rangle$ with each encryption operation, in which the message M is encrypted using additional attributes corresponding to each bit-string representation of K_v. This incurs an additional overhead that is linear in the length of K_v.

In this section we present an efficient CCA-secure CP-ABE construction with a small attribute universe. The construction is motivated by [1,17]. Compared with the previous schemes[14,10,27], our construction is very simple and compact: the increase of ciphertext size and public key size are small, and computation costs are also small both in encryption and decryption operations.

We now give the CCA-secure construction as a set of four algorithms.

Setup(U). Select at random $r_1, r_2, \ldots, r_{2n} \in \mathbb{Z}_p^*$ and $x_1, x_2, \ldots, x_{2n}, \delta_1, \delta_2, \delta_3 \in \mathbb{G}$. Let $u_k := g^{-r_k}$ and $h_k := e(x_k, g)$ for each $k \in \{1, 2, \ldots, 2n\}$. Choose a collision-resistant hash function $H : \{0,1\}^* \to \mathbb{Z}_p^*$.
   The public key is $PK := (\{\langle u_k, h_k \rangle | k \in \{1, 2, \ldots, 2n\}\}, \delta_1, \delta_2, \delta_3, H)$
   The master key is $MK := \{\langle r_k, x_k \rangle | k \in \{1, 2, \ldots, 2n\}\}$.

Encrypt$(PK,\ M,\ \mathbb{W})$. The encryption algorithm encrypts a message $M \in \mathbb{G}_T$ under an AND gate $\mathbb{W} = \bigwedge_{i \in I} \underline{i}$, where $\underline{i} \in \{i, \neg i\}$. The algorithm first selects random number $s, t \in \mathbb{Z}_p^*$ and aggregates all the the public key elements corresponding to the attribute values to generate an aggregated public key $\langle u_I, h_I \rangle = \langle \prod_{i \in I} u_{\underline{i}}, \prod_{i \in I} h_{\underline{i}} \rangle$. Then, it calculates

$$C_1 = g^s, C_2 = u_I^s, C_3 = Mh_I^s, C_4 = (\delta_1^c \delta_2^t \delta_3)^s,$$

where $c = H(\mathbb{W}, C_1, C_2, C_3)$. The ciphertext is $CT := (\mathbb{W}, C_1, C_2, C_3, C_4, t)$.

---
[1] AL2[3] is the only scheme in the table can achieve full security.

KeyGen(MK, S). The key generation algorithm takes as input a set of attributes S and outputs a key that identifies with that set. The algorithm first randomly chooses $v \in \mathbb{G}$ for each user. Then for each $i \in \{1, 2, \ldots, n\}$ the algorithm computes with v under the master key element $\langle r_i, x_i \rangle$ of the positive attribute value A_i^+ to obtain $\sigma_i = x_i v^{r_i}$, if $i \in S$; the algorithm computes with v under the master key element $\langle r_{i+n}, x_{i+n} \rangle$ of the negative attribute value A_i^- to obtain $\sigma_i = x_{i+n} v^{r_{i+n}}$, if $i \notin S$.

The secret key is defined as $SK := \langle v, \{\sigma_i | i \in \{1, 2, \ldots, n\}\}\rangle$.

Decrypt(PK, CT, SK). The decryption algorithm takes as input a ciphertext CT with access structure $\mathbb{W}$ and a private key for a set S. Suppose the ciphertext is of the form $CT = (\mathbb{W}, C_1, C_2, C_3, C_4, t)$, where $\mathbb{W} = \bigwedge_{i \in I} \underline{i}$. The algorithm first checks whether $S \models \mathbb{W}$. If not, the algorithm returns $\bot$. Otherwise, it checks whether the ciphertext CT is consistent. For a correctly generated ciphertext CT, we have that

$$e(g, C_4) = e(C_1, \delta_1^c \delta_2^t \delta_3), e(g, C_2) = e(C_1, \prod_{i \in I} u_i).$$

If the equation does not hold, return $\bot$. Otherwise, CT is consistent, and the algorithm continues to decrypt. The secret key is of the form $SK := \langle v, \{\sigma_i | i \in \{1, 2, \ldots, n\}\}\rangle$. First, the algorithm aggregates the secret key elements corresponding to the attribute values in I to generate $sk = \langle v, \sigma = \prod_{i \in I} \sigma_i \rangle$. Then, the decryption algorithm computes $M = C_3/(e(v, C_2) \cdot e(\sigma, C_1))$, and outputs M as the plaintext.

Theorem 2. *Suppose the decisional n-BDHE assumption holds and collision-resistant hash function exists. Then no poly-time adversary can break the CCA-CP-ABE game.*

Proof. The CCA security game for CP-ABE and the proof of Theorem 2 is given in the appendix.

4.1   Performance Considerations

The CCA-secure extension still has constant ciphertext size and computation costs: the length of ciphertext is $|\mathbb{G}_T| + 3|\mathbb{G}| + |\mathbb{Z}_p|$; the encryption requires 6 exponentiation computations, and the decryption process requires 4 pairing evaluations. Compared with the basic scheme, the public key extension consists of 3 additional elements of group $|\mathbb{G}|$. There is no increase over the secret key. Compared with other generic constructions for CCA-secure CP-ABE with the small attribute universe in the standard model [10,27], our CCA-secure scheme does not need to introduce a additional dummy attributes set corresponding to the bit-string representation of the verification key. Further more, if we use generic conversions [27] to transform a constant-size ciphertext CP-ABE schemes [3,15] to be CCA-secure, the new schemes may no longer have constant-size ciphertext, since the conversion in small attribute universe case will add new gates in the access policy. However, the existing constant-size ciphertext CP-ABE [3,15,11,29] schemes are all restricted (a single gate or threshold) in the access policy over the small attribute universe. As far as we know, expressive CP-ABE with constant-size ciphertext is still a challenging problem. Therefore, the generic conversions [27] do not seem to guarantee the ciphertext size still be constant after transforming to CCA-secure on the existing CP-ABE schemes.

5   Multi-authority Extension

We briefly outline how we extend our schemes to the decentralizing multi-authority setting [20]. In our schemes, each user has a unique secret key component v. Each attribute value corresponds to a master secret key element $\langle r_i, x_i \rangle$ and a public key element $\langle u_i, h_i \rangle$. The authority uses the master secret key element $\langle r_i, x_i \rangle$ to issue a secret key element $x_i v^{r_i}$ for the user whose secret key component is v. In the multi-authority setting, each attribute is assigned to one authority, and each authority may control multiple attributes. Each user has a unique global identity GID "link" secret key elements together that are issued to the same user by different authorities. To extend our schemes to the multi-authority setting, each user first obtains a unique global identity in the global setup phase. Then we can replace each user's secret key component v by a hash function value $H(GID)$ which is generated from the his global identity GID (The hash function maps global identities GID to elements of $\mathbb{G}$). For the attribute A_i, the corresponding authority chooses $\langle r_i, x_i \rangle$ as its secret key element and publishes $\langle u_i, h_i \rangle$ as its public key element $\langle r_i, x_i \rangle$ in the authority setup phase. In the key generation phase, the authority can create a secret key element $x_i H(GID)^{r_i}$ for the user who has GID as his global identity. Finally, a user can encrypt data in terms of an AND gate over attribute values issued from any chosen set of authorities. And the decryptor can use a collection of secret key elements corresponding to attribute values and his global identity to decrypt the ciphertext. This multi-authority system does not require any central authority. We thus avoid the performance bottleneck incurred by relying on a central authority, which makes the system more scalable. We also avoid placing absolute trust in a single designated entity which must remain active and uncorrupted throughout the lifetime of the system. In the multi-authority system, any party can become an authority and there is no requirement for any global coordination other than the creation of an initial set of common reference parameters.

6   Conclusion

In this paper, we propose a chosen plaintext secure and a chosen ciphertext secure CP-ABE schemes which have constant-size ciphertext and constant computation costs for a non-monotone AND gate access policy. The computation costs overhead (including the exponentiation and pairing operation in both encryption and decryption operations) and the ciphertext length are independent of the number of attributes involved in the access policy. The security of both schemes can be proved in standard model under a well-established assumption.

In the future work, it would be interesting to construct a constant-size ciphertext and constant computation costs CP-ABE scheme with more expressive access structures.

Acknowledgment. The work is supported by the National Natural Science Foundation of China (60873261), and the National Basic Research Program (973) of China (2007CB311202).

References

1. Abe, M., Cui, Y., Imai, H., Kiltz, E.: Efficient Hybrid Encryption from Id-based Encryption. Cryptology ePrint Archive, Report 2007/023 (2007)
2. Attrapadung, N., Libert, B., de Panafieu, E.: Expressive Key-Policy Attribute-Based Encryption with Constant-Size Ciphertexts. In: Catalano, D., Fazio, N., Gennaro, R., Nicolosi, A. (eds.) PKC 2011. LNCS, vol. 6571, pp. 90–108. Springer, Heidelberg (2011)
3. Attrapadung, N., Libert, B.: Functional Encryption for Inner Product: Achieving Constant-Size Ciphertexts with Adaptive Security or Support for Negation. In: Nguyen, P.Q., Pointcheval, D. (eds.) PKC 2010. LNCS, vol. 6056, pp. 384–402. Springer, Heidelberg (2010)
4. Bethencourt, J., Sahai, A., Waters, B.: Ciphertext-Policy Attribute-Based Encryption. In: 2007 IEEE Symposium on Security and Privacy, pp. 321–334. IEEE Press, Los Alamitos (2007)
5. Boneh, D., Boyen, X., Goh, E.-J.: Hierarchical Identity Based Encryption with Constant Size Ciphertext. In: Cramer, R. (ed.) EUROCRYPT 2005. LNCS, vol. 3494, pp. 440–456. Springer, Heidelberg (2005)
6. Boyen, X., Mei, Q., Waters, B.: Direct Chosen Ciphertext Security from Identity-based Techniques. In: CCS 2005: 12th Conference on Computer and Communications Security, Alexandria, Virginia, USA, November 7-11, pp. 320–329. ACM Press, New York (2005)
7. Chase, M., Chow, S.S.M.: Improving Privacy and Security in Multi-Authority Attribute-Based Encryption. In: ACM Conference on Computer and Communication Security 2009, pp. 195–203. ACM, New York (2009)
8. Chase, M.: Multi-authority Attribute Based Encryption. In: Vadhan, S.P. (ed.) TCC 2007. LNCS, vol. 4392, pp. 515–534. Springer, Heidelberg (2007)
9. Canetti, R., Halevi, S., Katz, J.: Chosen-Ciphertext Security from Identity-Based Encryption. In: Cachin, C., Camenisch, J.L. (eds.) EUROCRYPT 2004. LNCS, vol. 3027, pp. 207–222. Springer, Heidelberg (2004)
10. Cheung, L., Newport, C.: Provably Secure Ciphertext Policy ABE. In: ACM Conference on Computer and Communication Security 2007, pp. 456–465. ACM, New York (2007)
11. Emura, K., Miyaji, A., Nomura, A., Omote, K., Soshi, M.: A Ciphertext-Policy Attribute-Based Encryption Scheme with Constant Ciphertext Length. In: Bao, F., Li, H., Wang, G. (eds.) ISPEC 2009. LNCS, vol. 5451, pp. 13–23. Springer, Heidelberg (2009)
12. Fujisaki, E., Okamoto, T.: How to Enhance the Security of Public-Key Encryption at Minimum Cost. In: Imai, H., Zheng, Y. (eds.) PKC 1999. LNCS, vol. 1560, pp. 53–68. Springer, Heidelberg (1999)

13. Goyal, V., Jain, A., Pandey, O., Sahai, A.: Bounded Ciphertext Policy Attribute Based Encryption. In: Aceto, L., Damgård, I., Goldberg, L.A., Halldórsson, M.M., Ingólfsdóttir, A., Walukiewicz, I. (eds.) ICALP 2008, Part II. LNCS, vol. 5126, pp. 579–591. Springer, Heidelberg (2008)
14. Goyal, V., Pandey, O., Sahai, A., Waters, B.: Attribute-based Encryption for Fine-grained Access Control of Encrypted Data. In: ACM Conference on Computer and Communication Security 2006, pp. 89–98. ACM, New York (2006)
15. Herranz, J., Laguillaumie, F., Ràfols, C.: Constant Size Ciphertexts in Threshold Attribute-Based Encryption. In: Nguyen, P.Q., Pointcheval, D. (eds.) PKC 2010. LNCS, vol. 6056, pp. 19–34. Springer, Heidelberg (2010)
16. Katz, J., Sahai, A., Waters, B.: Predicate Encryption Supporting Disjunctions, Polynomial Equations, and Inner Products. In: Smart, N.P. (ed.) EUROCRYPT 2008. LNCS, vol. 4965, pp. 146–162. Springer, Heidelberg (2008)
17. Lai, J., Deng, R.H., Liu, S., Kou, W.: Efficient CCA-Secure PKE from Identity-Based Techniques. In: Pieprzyk, J. (ed.) CT-RSA 2010. LNCS, vol. 5985, pp. 132–147. Springer, Heidelberg (2010)
18. Lewko, A., Okamoto, T., Sahai, A., Takashima, K., Waters, B.: Fully Secure Functional Encryption: Attribute-Based Encryption and (Hierarchical) Inner Product Encryption. In: Gilbert, H. (ed.) EUROCRYPT 2010. LNCS, vol. 6110, pp. 62–91. Springer, Heidelberg (2010)
19. Lewko, A., Sahai, A., Waters, B.: Revocation Systems with Very Small Private Keys. In: 2010 IEEE Symposium on Security and Privacy (2010)
20. Lewko, A., Waters, B.: Decentralizing Attribute-Based Encryption. In: Paterson, K.G. (ed.) EUROCRYPT 2011. LNCS, vol. 6632, pp. 568–588. Springer, Heidelberg (2011)
21. Okamoto, T., Takashima, K.: Fully Secure Functional Encryption with General Relations from the Decisional Linear Assumption. In: Rabin, T. (ed.) CRYPTO 2010. LNCS, vol. 6223, pp. 191–208. Springer, Heidelberg (2010)
22. Ostrovsky, R., Sahai, A., Waters, B.: Attribute-based Encryption with Non-monotonic Access Structures. In: ACM Conference on Computer and Communication Security 2007, pp. 195–203. ACM, New York (2007)
23. Sahai, A., Waters, B.: Fuzzy Identity-Based Encryption. In: Cramer, R. (ed.) EUROCRYPT 2005. LNCS, vol. 3494, pp. 457–473. Springer, Heidelberg (2005)
24. Waters, B.: Ciphertext-Policy Attribute-Based Encryption: An Expressive, Efficient, and Provably Secure Realization. In: Catalano, D., Fazio, N., Gennaro, R., Nicolosi, A. (eds.) PKC 2011. LNCS, vol. 6571, pp. 90–107. Springer, Heidelberg (2011)
25. Waters, B.: Dual System Encryption: Realizing Fully Secure IBE and HIBE under Simple Assumptions. In: Halevi, S. (ed.) CRYPTO 2009. LNCS, vol. 5677, pp. 619–636. Springer, Heidelberg (2009)
26. Wu, Q., Mu, Y., Susilo, W., Qin, B., Domingo-Ferrer, J.: Asymmetric Group Key Agreement. In: Joux, A. (ed.) EUROCRYPT 2009. LNCS, vol. 5479, pp. 153–170. Springer, Heidelberg (2009)
27. Yamada, S., Attrapadung, N., Hanaoka, G., Kunihiro, N.: Generic Constructions for Chosen-Ciphertext Secure Attribute Based Encryption. In: Catalano, D., Fazio, N., Gennaro, R., Nicolosi, A. (eds.) PKC 2011. LNCS, vol. 6571, pp. 90–107. Springer, Heidelberg (2011)
28. Zhang, R.: Tweaking TBE/IBE to PKE Transforms with Chameleon Hash Functions. In: Katz, J., Yung, M. (eds.) ACNS 2007. LNCS, vol. 4521, pp. 323–339. Springer, Heidelberg (2007)
29. Zhou, Z., Huang, D.: On Efficient Ciphertext-Policy Attribute Based Encryption and Broadcast Encryption. Cryptology ePrint Archive, Report 2010/395 (2010)

A   CCA Security Game for CP-ABE

A ciphertext policy ABE scheme is said to be CCA-secure if no probabilistic polynomial-time adversaries have non-negligible advantage in the CCA-CP-ABE game defined as follows. The security game of the definition is under the selective structure model since the target access structure is chosen before the **Setup** phase. We now give the CCA-CP-ABE game.

Init. The adversary chooses the challenge access structure $\mathbb{W}^*$ and gives it to the challenger.

Setup. The challenger runs the **Setup** algorithm and gives the adversary PK.

Phase 1. The adversary makes, adaptively, any combination of secret key and decryption queries.

   Secret Key Query. The adversary submits a set of attributes S for a **Key-Gen** query. Provided $S \nvDash \mathbb{W}^*$, challenger answers with a secret key SK for S.

   Decryption Query. The adversary submits a ciphertext CT encrypted under $\mathbb{W}$. The challenger decrypts the ciphertext CT by the secret key whose attribute set satisfies $\mathbb{W}$, and returns the result to the adversary.

Challenge. The adversary submits two messages M_0 and M_1 of equal length. The challenger chooses $\mu \in \{0, 1\}$ at random and encrypts M_μ under $\mathbb{W}^*$. The resulting ciphertext CT^* is given to the adversary.

Phase 2. Same as **Phase 1**, but with the natural constraint that the adversary does not request the decryption of CT.

Guess. The adversary outputs a guess μ' of μ.
   The advantage of an adversary Adv in this game is defined as $Pr[\mu' = \mu] - \frac{1}{2}$.

Definition 3. *A ciphertext-policy attribute-based encryption scheme is CCA-secure if all polynomial time adversaries have at most a negligible advantage in the CCA-CP-ABE game.*

B   Proof of Theorem 2

Proof. We prove that the scheme proposed in section 4 is CCA-secure using a similar strategy to our proof of the CPA-secure scheme. Some details of the CCA-secure proof can be given almost exactly in the same way as the proof of Theorem 1. We thus omit them here and focus on the differences. Suppose adversary Adv can win the CCA-CP-ABE game with advantage ϵ for the scheme whose attribute universe U has n attributes. We can construct a simulator Sim that uses a n-BDHE challenge to simulate all the requested service for adversary Adv. Then Sim uses the output of Adv to solve the decision n-BDHE assumption.
   $\nu \in \{0, 1\}$ is selected at random. Sim takes as input a random n-BDHE challenge $(g, h, \overrightarrow{y}_{g,\alpha,n}, T)$, where $\overrightarrow{y}_{g,\alpha,n} = (g_1, g_2, \ldots, g_n, g_{n+2}, \ldots, g_{2n}) \in \mathbb{G}^{2n-1}$

and T is $e(g_{n+1}, h)$ if $\nu = 1$ or a random element $Z \in \mathbb{G}_T$. The simulator Sim now plays the role of challenger in the CCA-CP-ABE game.

Init. The phase will be the same as the **Init** phase in the proof of Theorem 1.

Setup. The phase will be the same as the **Setup** phase in the proof of Theorem 1, except that Sim randomly selects $\phi_2, \phi_3, \varphi_1, \varphi_2, \varphi_3 \in \mathbb{Z}_p^*$ to compute $\delta_1 = g_1 g^{\varphi_1}$, $\delta_2 = g_1^{\phi_2} g^{\varphi_2}$, $\delta_3 = g_1^{\phi_3} g^{\varphi_3}$. We point the fact that $\delta_1, \delta_2, \delta_3$ are distributed randomly due to the $g^{\varphi_1}, g^{\varphi_2}, g^{\varphi_3}$, respectively.

Phase 1: Secret Key Query. The secret key query phase will be the same as the **Phase 1: Secret Key Query** phase in the proof of Theorem 1.

Phase 1: Decryption Query. Adv submits a ciphertext $CT := (\mathbb{W} = \bigwedge_{i \in I} \underline{i}$, $C_1, C_2, C_3, C_4, t)$. Sim first computes $c = H(\mathbb{W}, C_1, C_2, C_3)$ and checks whether the ciphertext is consistent:

$$e(g, C_4) = e(C_1, \delta_1^c \delta_2^t \delta_3), e(g, C_2) = e(C_1, \prod_{i \in I} u_{\underline{i}})$$

If not, output $\perp$.

Check whether $c + t\phi_2 + \phi_3 = 0$. If so, Sim aborts and randomly outputs a bit, else computes $\omega = c + t\phi_2 + \phi_3, \psi = C_1^{c\varphi_1 + t\varphi_2 + \varphi_3}$. Then, Sim outputs $C_3 / (e((\frac{C_4}{\psi})^{-\omega}, g_n) \cdot e(g, g)^{a_I})$, where $a_I = a_{i_1} + a_{i_2} + \ldots + a_{i_m}$.

Challenge. Adv runs the CCA-CP-ABE game under the the aggregated public encryption key. For the aggregated public key $\langle u_{I^*}, h_{I^*} \rangle$, the decryption keys corresponding to each member are not revealed. Hence, Sim can challenge Adv as follows. Adv submits two messages M_0 and M_1 of equal length. Sim chooses $\mu \in \{0, 1\}$ at random. It sets $t^* = -(c^* + \phi_3)/\phi_2$, where $c^* = H(\mathbb{W}^*, C_1^*, C_2^*, C_3^*)$. Then Adv computes the challenge ciphertext

$$CT^* = (\mathbb{W}^*, C_1^* = h, C_2^* = (h)^{r_{I^*}}, C_3^* = M_\mu T e(g, h)^{a_{I^*}},$$
$$C_4^* = (h)^{\varphi_1 - t^* \varphi_2 + \varphi_3}, t^* = -(c^* + \phi_3)/\phi_2)$$

where $r_{I^*} = r_{i_1} + r_{i_2} + \ldots + r_{i_m}$.

Since ϕ_2, ϕ_3 is completely hidden by φ_2, φ_3 in δ_2, δ_3 from the Adv, $t^* = -(c^* + \phi_3)/\phi_2$ is uniform distribution in Adv's view. Therefore, the challenge ciphertext is a valid encryption of M_μ with the correct distribution whenever $T = e(g_{n+1}, h)$. On the other hand, when T is uniform in $\mathbb{G}_T$, the challenge ciphertext CT^* is independent of μ in Adv's view.

Phase 2: Secret Key Query. Same as **Phase 1: Secret Key Query**

Phase 2: Decryption Query. Adv continues to adaptively issue decryption query $CT = (\mathbb{W}^*, C_1, C_2, C_3, C_4, t)$, Sim performs the following steps:

1. Check if $CT = CT^*$. If so, output $\perp$.
2. Check if CT is consistent. If not, output $\perp$.

3. Check if $c^* = H(\mathbb{W}^*, C_1, C_2, C_3)$, Sim aborts and randomly outputs a bit. Note that, if Adv is able to produce such a ciphertext $CT \neq CT^*$, this represents a collision in the hash function H, and so the probability that this event occurs is Adv_A^{CR}.

4. Check whether $c + t\phi_2 + \phi_3 = 0$. If so, Sim aborts and randomly outputs a bit, else Sim responds as in query **Phase 1: Decryption Query**. Observe that the values α, ϕ_2, ϕ_3 are completely hidden by blinding factors φ_1, φ_2, φ_3, respectively. Adv could not obtain any information about α, ϕ_2, ϕ_3 from the decryption queries. The probability that $c + t\phi_2 + \phi_3 = 0$ occurs is at most $1/p$.

Guess. If Adv outputs a correct guess after the **Challenge** phase, Sim answers 1 in the n-BDHE game to guess that $T = e(g_{n+1}, h)$. Otherwise, Sim answers 0 to indicate that it believes T is a random group element in $\mathbb{G}_T$. If $T = e(g_{n+1}, h)$, then CT is a valid ciphertext, the simulator Sim gives a perfect simulation so we have that

$$Pr[Sim(g, h, \overrightarrow{y}_{g,\alpha,n}, e(g_{n+1}, h)) = 1] = 1/2 + \epsilon - Adv_A^{CR} - Q_D/p$$

where Q_D is the number of decryption queries Adv makes.

If T is a random choice, then C_3^* is completely random from the view of Adv. Therefore $\mu' \neq \mu$ holds with probability exactly $1/2$, regardless of the distribution on μ'. Hence,

$$Pr[Sim(g, h, \overrightarrow{y}_{g,\alpha,n}, Z) = 1] = 1/2$$

Putting the two pieces together, we know that the advantage of Sim solving the n-BDHE problem is Adv_{Sim}^{n-BDHE}, where

$$Adv_{Sim}^{n-BDHE} \geq 1/2(\epsilon - Adv_A^{CR} - Q_D/p)$$

Due to existence of collision-resistant hash function, Adv_A^{CR} is negligible. Q_D/p is negligible in information theory. Therefore, Sim can play the decisional n-BDHE game with non-negligible advantage. This concludes the proof of Theorem 2. □

Fully Distributed Broadcast Encryption

Qianhong Wu[1,2], Bo Qin[1,3], Lei Zhang[4], and Josep Domingo-Ferrer[1]

[1] Universitat Rovira i Virgili, Dept. of Comp. Eng. and Maths
UNESCO Chair in Data Privacy, Tarragona, Catalonia
{qianhong.wu,bo.qin,josep.domingo}@urv.cat
[2] Key Lab. of Aerospace Information Security and Trusted Computing
Ministry of Education, School of Computer, Wuhan University, China
[3] Dept. of Maths, School of Science, Xi'an University of Technology, China
[4] Software Engineering Institute
East China Normal University, Shanghai, China
leizhang@sei.ecnu.edu.cn

Abstract. Broadcast encryption schemes rely on a centralized authority to generate decryption keys for each user. It is observed that, when a broadcast encryption scheme is deployed for secret escrows, a dishonest dealer can read the escrowed secrets without leaving any witnesses. We present a new broadcast encryption paradigm referred to as fully distributed broadcast encryption (FDBE) without suffering from this vulnerability. In the new paradigm, there are multiple dealers, and by contacting a number of them equal to a threshold or more, any user can join the system; then the secrets can be encrypted to any subset of users and only the intended receivers can decrypt, while an attacker cannot get any information about the encrypted message even if the attacker controls all the users outside the receiver set and corrupts some dealers, provided that the number of corrupted dealers is less than a threshold. We realize the first fully distributed broadcast encryption scheme which is proven secure under the decision Bilinear Diffie-Hellman Exponentiation assumption in the standard model. A variant is also shown to achieve sub-linear complexity in terms of public key, decryption key and ciphertext, comparable to up-to-date regular broadcast encryption schemes without robustness and strong security against misbehaving dealers.

Keywords: Broadcast encryption, Bilinear pairing, Provable security, Secrets escrow, Access control.

1 Introduction

Broadcasting is one of the most useful, versatile communication paradigms in distributed computing with many applications. Broadcast encryption (BE) [1] is a cryptographic primitive securing broadcast communication. In a setup phase, a dealer generates and privately distributes decryption keys to n users; then a sender can send a message to a dynamically chosen subset of receivers $\mathbb{R} \subseteq \{1, \cdots, n\}$ in such a way that only users in $\mathbb{R}$ can decrypt the ciphertext. Broadcast encryption schemes in the literatures can be classified into two categories:

X. Boyen and X. Chen (Eds.): ProvSec 2011, LNCS 6980, pp. 102–119, 2011.

symmetric key broadcast encryption and public key broadcast encryption. In the symmetric key setting, only the trusted center generates all the secret keys and broadcasts messages to users. Hence, only the key generation center can be the broadcaster. In the public key setting, in addition to the secret keys for each user, the trusted center also generates a public key for all the users so that any one can play the role of a broadcaster or sender.

Related Work. Fiat and Naor [1] first formalized broadcast encryption in the symmetric key setting and proposed a systematic method of broadcast encryption. The earlier broadcast encryption systems include a collusion bound: if an attacker compromises a number of users greater than the bound, the system no longer guarantees security even for encryptions solely sent to uncompromised users. Subsequent efforts were devoted to improve efficiency. Wallner *et al.* [2] and Wong [3] independently discovered the logical-tree-hierarchy scheme for group multicast. The parameters of the original schemes are improved in further work [4, 5]. Further improvements [7, 8, 9] reduced the decryption key size. Dodis and Fazio [10] extended the subtree difference method into a public-key broadcast system for a small size public key. D'Arco and Stinson's distributed BE scheme also follows this research line [11]. The state of the art is presented in [12] along this research line.

Public-key based BE schemes are more versatile in practice since it allows any one knowing the public key to broadcast safely. This avoids re-establishing the BE system for different applications. In the public key setting, Naor and Pinkas presented [13] the first public key broadcast encryption scheme. Their system is not collusion-resistant. If more than this threshold of users are revoked, then the scheme will be insecure and hence not fully collusion-resistant. Subsequently, by exploiting newly developed bilinear paring technologies, a fully collusion-resistant public key broadcast encryption was presented [14] which has $\mathcal{O}(\sqrt{n})$ complexity in key size, ciphertext size and computation cost, where n is the maximum allowable number of potential receivers. A recent scheme [15] reduces the key size and ciphertexts, although it has the same asymptotical complexity of sub-linear overhead as in [14]. The up-to-date schemes were presented in [16, 17, 18] which strengthen the security concept of public key BE schemes. However, as to system complexity, the sub-linear barrier $\mathcal{O}(\sqrt{n})$ has not yet been broken.

There are several extensions of the conventional BE notion. These variations can be easily mixed with our FDBE as they also make use of a threshold. But, unlike our motivation of removing the trust on the dealer in BE schemes, the efforts in the these variations have been devoted to achieving flexible decryption. These variants of BE systems were usually referred to as threshold broadcast encryption [19], dynamic threshold encryption [20, 21] or *ad hoc* threshold encryption [22, 23]. In such systems, a sender can choose a subset of receivers and a threshold, such that only a number of receivers equal to the threshold or more in the receiver set can cooperatively decrypt the ciphertext. An attacker controlling all the users outside the receiver set and some users in the receiver set cannot decrypt, provided that the number of corrupted users in the receiver set is less than the threshold. The state of the extensions was presented in [24] which achieves adaptive security and short ciphertexts.

Our Contribution. Existing BE systems rely on a fully trusted dealer that can reveal all the secrets encrypted by the senders without leaving any witnesses. This is not desirable in some applications. To relieve from the heavy dependance on the centralized dealer, we present a new notion referred to as fully distributed broadcast encryption (FDBE). In an FDBE system, each of multiple dealers has a public key and a combination (i.e., a simple multiplication operation in our instantiation) of each dealer's public key produces the system BE public key; by contacting a number of dealers equal to a threshold t or more, any user can obtain a decryption key; then any sender can send secret messages to any chosen users and only the intended users can decrypt. We define an attacker who can adaptively corrupt users and some dealers. Strong security is guaranteed if such a powerful attacker cannot decrypt the ciphertext, provided that the corrupted users are not in the receiver set and the number of corrupted dealers is less than the threshold. This implies that FDBE preserves security even if some dealers and users are corrupted, which is a desirable security property to remove the trust on the dealer and to preserve secrecy against compromised subscribers in BE systems. By exploiting pairings, we realize the first provably secure FDBE scheme under the decision Bilinear Diffie-Hellman Exponentiation (BDHE) assumption in the standard model (*i.e.* without using random oracles). The resulting scheme has sub-linear complexity in terms of public key, decryption key and ciphertext per user. This is comparable to up-to-date regular BE schemes which have no robustness or strong security against compromised dealers. Finally, we discuss the application of our FDBE notion to robust secrets escrow and controllable access to sensitive information.

2   Preliminaries

2.1   Bilinear Pairings and Assumptions

Our schemes are implemented in bilinear pairing groups [25]. Let PairGen be an algorithm that, on input a security parameter 1^λ, outputs a tuple $\Upsilon = (p, \mathbb{G}, \mathbb{G}_T, e)$, where $\mathbb{G}$ and $\mathbb{G}_T$ have the same prime order p, and $e : \mathbb{G} \times \mathbb{G} \to \mathbb{G}_T$ is an efficient non-degenerate bilinear map such that $e(g, g) \neq 1$ for any generator g of $\mathbb{G}$, and for all $u, v \in \mathbb{Z}$, it holds that $e(g^u, g^v) = e(g, g)^{uv}$.

The security of the schemes that we propose in this paper relies on the decision BDHE problem. The corresponding decision BDHE assumption is shown to be sound and used [18, 26, 27]. The decision BDHE assumption in $\mathbb{G}$ is as follows.

Definition 1 (Decision BDHE Assumption). *Let $\mathbb{G}$ and $\mathbb{G}_T$ be groups of order p with bilinear map $e : \mathbb{G} \times \mathbb{G} \to \mathbb{G}_T$, and let g be a generator for $\mathbb{G}$. Let n be a nonnegative integer and let $\beta, \gamma \leftarrow \mathbb{Z}_p$ and $b \leftarrow \{0, 1\}$. If $b = 0$, set $Z = e(g, g)^{\beta^{n+1}\gamma}$; else, set $Z \leftarrow \mathbb{G}_T$. The problem instance consists of*

$$\{g^\gamma, Z\} \cup \{g^{\beta^i} : i \in [0, n] \cup [n + 2, 2n]\}$$

The Decision BDHE problem is to guess b. An attacker $\mathcal{A}$ wins if it correctly guesses b and its advantage is defined by $Adv_{BDHE_{\mathcal{A},n}}(\lambda) = |\Pr[\mathcal{A} \ wins] - \frac{1}{2}|$. The Decision BDHE assumption states that, for any polynomial-time probabilistic attacker $\mathcal{A}$, $Adv_{BDHE_{\mathcal{A},n}}(\lambda)$ is negligible in λ.

2.2   Shamir's Secret Sharing Scheme

Our system exploits Shamir's (t, T)-threshold secret sharing scheme [28], which is briefly reviewed here. Let $\mathbb{Z}_p$ be a finite field with $p > T$ and $\xi \in \mathbb{Z}_p$ be the secret to be shared. A dealer picks a polynomial $f(\alpha)$ of degree at most $t-1$ at random, whose free term is the secret ξ, that is, $f(0) = \xi$. The polynomial $f(\alpha)$ can be written as $f(\alpha) = \xi + a_1\alpha + \cdots + a_{t-1}\alpha^{t-1} \mod p$, where $a_1, \cdots, a_{t-1} \in \mathbb{Z}_p$ are randomly chosen. Each shareholder k is assigned a known index $k \in \{1, \cdots, T\}$ and the dealer privately sends to shareholder k a share $\xi_k = f(k)$. Then any t holders in set $\mathbb{A} \subset \{1, \cdots, T\}$ can recover the secret $\xi = f(0)$ by interpolating their shares $\xi = f(0) = \sum_{k \in \mathbb{A}} \xi_k \lambda_k = \sum_{k \in \mathbb{A}} f(k) \lambda_k$, where $\lambda_k = \prod_{\ell \in \mathbb{A}}^{\ell \neq k} \frac{\ell}{\ell - k}$ are the Lagrange coefficients. Actually, shareholders in $\mathbb{A}$ can reconstruct the polynomial $f(\alpha) = \sum_{k \in \mathbb{A}} f(k)(\prod_{\ell \in \mathbb{A}}^{\ell \neq k} \frac{\ell - \alpha}{\ell - k})$.

3   Fully Distributed Broadcast Encryption

We first model FDBE systems and then formalize the security definitions in FDBE schemes. An attacker is allowed to adaptively corrupt some dealers and users before requesting the challenge ciphertext. This seems appropriate to capture powerful attackers against FDBE schemes.

3.1   Modeling FDBE Systems

For simplicity, we define FDBE as a key encapsulation mechanism. An FDBE system consists of the following polynomial-time algorithms:

- Setup(1^λ): This algorithm sets up the system. It takes as input a security parameter λ and outputs the global system parameters, including the number T of dealers, the threshold t, the number N of possible users, and the number n of the actual receivers of a broadcast. We denote the system parameters by π.
- DKeyGen(k, π): This key generation algorithm is run by each dealer $k \in \{1, \cdots, T\}$ to generate her public/private key pair. A dealer takes as input the system parameters π, her index $k \in \{1, \cdots, T\}$, and outputs $\langle X_k, x_k \rangle$ as her public/private key pair[1].

---

[1] In this definition, we distinguish the terms of private key, master secret key, decryption key share and decryption key. A private key is generated and held by a dealer. A master secret key is held by a dealer and it is jointly computed from the private keys of the dealers. A decryption key share is held by a user and it is computed from the private key of one dealer. A decryption key is held by a user and it is computed from that user's decryption key shares.

- BEKeyGen($X_1, \cdots, X_T$): This publicly computable algorithm generates the FDBE public encryption key. It takes as input all the dealers' public keys $X_1, \cdots, X_T$, and it outputs the FDBE public key PK.
- MSKeyGen($x_1, \cdots, x_T$): This is an interactive algorithm running among the dealers. It takes as input each dealer's private key, and it outputs S_k as dealer k's master secret key.
- UKeyGen(k, S_k, i): This algorithm is run by a dealer for index $k \in \{1, \cdots, T\}$ to generate a decryption key share for user $i \in \{1, \cdots, N\}$. For dealer k, the algorithm takes as input the dealer's index $k \in \{1, \cdots, T\}$ and master secret key S_k, and the user's index $i \in \{1, \cdots, N\}$, and it outputs $s_{i,k}$ as user i's decryption key share from dealer k. Denote user i's decryption key shares from dealers $k \in \mathbb{A} \subseteq \{1, \cdots, T\}$ by $s_{i,\mathbb{A}}$.
- DKeyGen($i, s_{i,\mathbb{A}}$): This algorithm is run by each user to generate his decryption key. For user i, the algorithm takes as input the user's index $i \in \{1, \cdots, N\}$ and received decryption key shares $s_{i,\mathbb{A}}$, and it outputs d_i as the user's decryption key if $|\mathbb{A}| \geq t$.
- Encryption($\mathbb{R}, PK$): This algorithm is run by a sender to send messages to chosen users. It takes as input a recipient set $\mathbb{R} \subseteq \{1, \cdots, N\}$ and the FDBE public key PK. It outputs a pair $\langle Hdr, sk \rangle$, where Hdr is called the header and sk is the secret session key to encrypt messages. Let $\mathcal{E}_{sym}$ be a symmetric encryption scheme with key space $\mathbb{K}$, and $E(\cdot)$ and $D(\cdot)$ be the encryption and decryption algorithms, respectively. Let M be a message to be broadcast to the set $\mathbb{R}$, and let $C = E(M, sk)$ be the encryption of M under the session key $sk \in \mathbb{K}$. The information broadcast to users in $\mathbb{R}$ consists of $(\mathbb{R}, Hdr, C)$.
- Decryption($\mathbb{R}, i, d_i, Hdr, PK$): This algorithm allows each user in the receiver set to decrypt the message encryption key sk hidden in the header. It takes as input the receiver set $\mathbb{R}$, an index $i \in \{1, \cdots, N\}$, the receiver's secret key d_i, a header Hdr. If $i \in \mathbb{R}$, then the algorithm outputs the message encryption key sk. The key sk can then be used to decrypt C to obtain M by computing $M = D(C, sk)$.

3.2   Security Definitions

An FDBE scheme is correct if any user in the receiver set can decrypt a valid header, provided that the user has obtained sufficient decryption key shares from the dealers. A formal definition follows.

Definition 2 (Correctness). *An FDBE scheme is correct if for all $\mathbb{R} \subseteq \{1, \cdots, N\}$, all $\mathbb{A} \subseteq \{1, \cdots, T\}$ ($|\mathbb{A}| \geq t$), all $k \in \{1, \cdots, T\}$, $(X_k, x_k) \leftarrow DKeyGen(k, \pi)$, $PK \leftarrow BEKeyGen(X_1, \cdots, X_T)$, $S_k \leftarrow MSKeyGen(x_1, \cdots, x_T)$, $s_{i,k} \leftarrow UKeyGen(k, S_k, i)$, $d_i \leftarrow DKeyGen(i, s_{i,\mathbb{A}})$, $\langle Hdr, sk \rangle \leftarrow Encryption(\mathbb{R}, PK)$, then $Decryption(\mathbb{R}, i, d_i, Hdr, PK) = sk$ for any $i \in \mathbb{R}$.*

We concentrate on adaptive security against corrupted dealers and users. For simplicity, we define security against chosen-plaintext attacks which are readily extended to capture chosen-ciphertext attacks. As usual, the attacker is allowed to see all the public data including the system parameters, each dealer's public key and the FDBE public key in an FDBE scheme. To capture *adaptive* security, the attacker is also allowed to adaptively ask for the private keys and master secret keys of several dealers, and the decryption key shares and the decryption keys of some users before choosing the set of indices that it wishes to attack. Formally, adaptive security in an MBDE scheme is defined using the following game between an attacker $\mathcal{A}$ and a challenger $\mathcal{CH}$. Both $\mathcal{CH}$ and $\mathcal{A}$ are given λ as input.

- **Setup.** The challenger runs $Setup(1^\lambda)$ to obtain the system parameters. The challenger gives the public system parameters to the attacker.
- **Corruption.** Attacker $\mathcal{A}$ can access all the public keys of the dealers and the FDBE public key. $\mathcal{A}$ can adaptively request the private keys and the master secret keys of dealers for some indices $i \in \{1, \cdots, T\}$, with a constraint that the number of the queried indices must be less than t. $\mathcal{A}$ can also adaptively request the decryption key shares and the decryption keys of users for some indices $i \in \{1, \cdots, N\}$.
- **Challenge.** At some point, $\mathcal{A}$ specifies a challenge set $\mathbb{R}^*$, such that for the decryption key of any user i queried in the corruption step, we have that $i \notin \mathbb{R}^*$ and, for any $i \in \mathbb{R}^*$, $\mathcal{A}$ has requested at most $t-1$ decryption key shares. The challenger sets $\langle Hdr^*, sk_0 \rangle \leftarrow Encryption(\mathbb{R}^*, PK)$ and $sk_1 \leftarrow \mathbb{K}$. It sets $b \leftarrow \{0,1\}$ and gives (Hdr^*, sk_b) to $\mathcal{A}$.
- **Guess.** Attacker $\mathcal{A}$ outputs a guess bit $b' \in \{0,1\}$ for b and wins the game if $b = b'$.

We define $\mathcal{A}$'s advantage in attacking the FDBE system with security parameter λ as $Adv^{FDBE}_{\mathcal{A},n,N,t,T}(1^\lambda) = |\Pr[b = b'] - \frac{1}{2}|$.

Definition 3 (Adaptive security). *We say that an FDBE scheme is adaptively secure if, for any polynomial-time algorithm $\mathcal{A}$, we have that $Adv^{FDBE}_{\mathcal{A},n,N,t,T}(1^\lambda)$ is negligible in λ.*

Similarly to conventional BE systems [18], another useful security definition is referred to as *semi-adaptive* security. In this game the attacker must commit to a set $\tilde{\mathbb{R}} \subseteq \mathbb{R}$ of indices at the *Initialization* phase. The attacker cannot query for the decryption key for any $i \in \tilde{\mathbb{R}}$. She can query for the decryption key shares for $i' \in \tilde{\mathbb{R}}$ but the queried decryption key shares must be less than t. She has to choose a target group $\mathbb{R}^*$ for the challenge ciphertext that is a subset of $\tilde{\mathbb{R}}$. A semi-adaptive attacker is weaker than an adaptive attacker, but stronger than a non-adaptive attacker since the attacker's choice of which subset of $\tilde{\mathbb{R}}$ to attack can be adaptive.

Remark 1. One may note that, although the attacker may be allowed to adaptively corrupt the dealers, their corruption is passive: a corrupted dealer will follow the protocol except that she will leak all her secret values and internal state information to the attacker. One may also define a stronger attacker by allowing a corrupted dealer to deviate from the protocol arbitrarily. This kind of attackers can be generally defeated by requiring the dealers to prove (in a zero-knowledge manner) that they have correctly followed the protocol in each step during the protocol execution. Hence, we concentrate on passive corruption in this paper.

3.3   Transforming Semi-adaptive Security to Adaptive Security

Recently, Gentry and Waters developed a modular proof approach [18] for adaptive security in regular BE systems with the two-key simulation technique [29]. We observe that this idea can also be employed to convert any semi-adaptively secure FDBE system into an adaptively secure system. The cost is doubling ciphertexts. Given a semi-adaptively secure FDBE system $FDBE_{SA}$ consists of algorithms: $Setup_{SA}$, $DKeyGen_{SA}$, $BEKeyGen_{SA}$, $MSKeyGen_{SA}$, $UKeyGen_{SA}$, $DKeyGen_{SA}$, $Encryption_{SA}$, $Decryption_{SA}$, we can build an adaptively secure $FDBE_A$ system as follows.

- Setup(1^λ): Run $Setup_{SA}(1^\lambda)$ and obtain π including parameters $T, t, 2n, N$. This implies that if the underlying $FDBE_{SA}$ allows $2n$ users, then the adaptive variant allows n users.
- DKeyGen(k, π): For $k = 1, \cdots, T$, Run $(X_k, x_k) \leftarrow DKeyGen_{SA}(k, \pi)$. Output (X_k, x_k) as dealer k's public/private key pair.
- BEKeyGen($X_1, \cdots, X_T$): Run $PK \leftarrow BEKeyGen_{SA}(X_1, \cdots, X_T)$. Output PK as the public broadcast encryption key.
- MSKeyGen($x_1, \cdots, x_T$): Run $(S'_1, \cdots, S'_T) \leftarrow MSKeyGen_{SA}(x_1, \cdots, x_T)$. Run a multiparty Mental Poker protocol [6] to generate random n-bit string $\theta \leftarrow \{0,1\}^n$. Set $S_k = (S'_k, \theta)(k = 1, \cdots, T)$. Output S_k as dealer k's master secret key. Denote the i-th bit of θ by θ_i.
- UKeyGen(k, S_k, i): Run $s'_{i,k} \leftarrow UKeyGen_{SA}(k, S'_k, 2i - \theta_i)$. Set $s_{i,k} = (s'_{i,k}, \theta_i)$. Output $s_{i,k}$ as user i's decryption key share from dealer k. Denote $s'_{i,\mathbb{A}} = \{s'_{i,k} | k \in \mathbb{A}\}$.
- DKeyGen($i, s_{i,\mathbb{A}}$): Run $d'_i \leftarrow DKeyGen_A(i, s'_{i,\mathbb{A}})$. Set $d_i = (d'_i, \theta_i)$. Output d_i as user i's decryption key.
- Encryption($\mathbb{R}, PK$): Generate a random set of $|\mathbb{R}|$ bits: $\zeta \leftarrow \{\zeta_i \leftarrow \{0,1\} : i \in \mathbb{R}\}$. Randomly choose $sk \leftarrow \mathbb{K}$. Set

$$\mathbb{R}_0 \leftarrow \{2i - \zeta_i : i \in \mathbb{R}\}, \qquad \langle Hdr_0, sk_0 \rangle \leftarrow Encryption_{SA}(\mathbb{R}_0, PK);$$
$$\mathbb{R}_1 \leftarrow \{2i - (1 - \zeta_i) : i \in \mathbb{R}\}, \langle Hdr_1, sk_1 \rangle \leftarrow Encryption_{SA}(\mathbb{R}_1, PK).$$

  Set

$$C_0 \leftarrow E(M, sk_0), C_1 \leftarrow E(M, sk_1), Hdr \leftarrow \langle Hdr_0, C_0, Hdr_1, C_1, \zeta \rangle.$$

  Output $\langle Hdr, sk \rangle$.
- Decryption($\mathbb{R}, i, d_i, Hdr, PK$): Parse d_i as (d'_i, θ_i) and Hdr as $\langle Hdr_0, C_0, Hdr_1, C_1, \zeta \rangle$. Set $\mathbb{R}_0, \mathbb{R}_1$ as above. Run

$$sk_{\theta_i \oplus \zeta_i} \leftarrow Decryption_{SA}(\mathbb{R}_{\theta_i \oplus \zeta_i}, i, d'_i, Hdr_{\theta_i \oplus \zeta_i}, PK), sk = D(C_{\theta_i \oplus \zeta_i}, sk_{\theta_i \oplus \zeta_i}).$$

  Output sk.

We briefly compare the Gentry-Waters conversion for regular BE systems with ours for FDBE systems. In the Gentry-Waters conversion for regular BE systems, each user is associated two potential secret decryption keys; however, the dealer gives the user only one of the two. An encryptor (who does not know which secret key the receiver possesses) encrypts the ciphertext twice, one for each key. The main benefit of this idea is that a simulator will have decryption keys for every user, and then it can always correctly answer the corruption queries from the attacker, hence circumventing the need of guessing of the target set in advance.

In our conversion, we employ a similar idea to associate one user with two potential decryption keys (corresponding to the FDBE public key) which can be reconstructed from the decryption key shares from the dealers. The difference is that, since there are multiple dealers, we allow multiple dealers to decide which decryption key a user can reconstruct. Then the encryptor and the users can do the same as in the Gentry-Waters conversion. It is easy to see that, from the perspective of a security proof, the two conversions are identical. This is due to the fact that, in the security proof of a regular BE system, a simulator will generate all the system parameters, the BE public key, the master secret key and the decryption keys on behalf of the dealer. In the context of FDBE systems, the simulator will do the same job on behalf of multiple dealers. In both cases, the attacker only communicates with the simulator. There is no difference for the attacker to communicate with the simulator in a regular BE or an FDBE system. Hence, the proof of the Gentry-Waters conversion can be trivially extended for the following theorem.

Theorem 1. *Let $\mathcal{A}$ be an adaptive attacker against* FDBE$_A$. *Then, there exist algorithms* $\mathcal{B}_1, \mathcal{B}_2, \mathcal{B}_3$, *and* $\mathcal{B}_4$, *each running in about the same time as* $\mathcal{A}$, *such that*

$$Adv^{\mathrm{FDBE}_A}_{\mathcal{A},n,N,t,T}(\lambda) \leq Adv^{\mathrm{FDBE}_{S}A}_{\mathcal{B}_1,2n,N,t,T}(\lambda) + Adv^{\mathrm{FDBE}_{S}A}_{\mathcal{B}_2,2n,N,t,T}(\lambda) + Adv^{\mathcal{E}_{sym}}_{\mathcal{B}_3}(\lambda) + Adv^{\mathcal{E}_{sym}}_{\mathcal{B}_4}(\lambda),$$

where $Adv^{\mathcal{E}_{sym}}_{\mathcal{B}}(\lambda)$ *is the advantage of an attacker* $\mathcal{B}$ *breaking the underlying symmetric encryption scheme.*

Proof. It is omitted to avoid repetition.

4   Basic FDBE with Short Ciphertext

In this section, we propose a basic FDBE construction. The construction is built on the known Shamir secret sharing scheme [28] and the recent Gentry-Waters BE scheme [18]. The basic scheme has constant-size ciphertexts and is proven to be secure without using random oracles.

In the following proposed FDBE system, we assume that there are T dealers and n users. The T dealers jointly generate the public broadcast encryption key. By interacting with t dealers, for some threshold $t \leq T$, a user can obtain a secret decryption key. A sender can send confidential messages to any subset of the n users and only the chosen users can decrypt.

- **Setup.** Let `PairGen` be an algorithm that, on input a security parameter 1^λ, outputs a tuple $\Upsilon = (p, \mathbb{G}, \mathbb{G}_T, e)$, where $\mathbb{G}$ and $\mathbb{G}_T$ have the same prime order p, and $e : \mathbb{G} \times \mathbb{G} \rightarrow \mathbb{G}_T$ is an efficient non-degenerate bilinear map. Let $h_1, \cdots, h_n$ be randomly chosen from $\mathbb{G}$. The system parameters are $\pi = (\Upsilon, g, h_1, \cdots, h_n, t, T, n, N)$. For convenience, we denote $g = h_0$.
- **Broadcast key generation.** Each dealer k for $k = 1, \cdots, T$ generates a secret polynomial

$$f_k(\alpha) = x_k + a_{k,1}\alpha + \cdots + a_{k,t-1}\alpha^{t-1} \mod p,$$

where the randomly chosen $(x_k, a_{k,1}, \cdots, a_{k,t-1}) \in \mathbb{Z}_p^t$ is the private key of dealer k. Dealer k computes

$$X_k = e(g, g)^{x_k}, S_{k,\ell} = g^{f_k(\ell)} (\ell = 1, \cdots, T).$$

X_k is published as dealer k's public key. Dealer k privately sends $S_{k,\ell}$ to dealer ℓ. The public broadcast encryption key is

$$PK = \prod_{k=1}^{T} e(g, g)^{x_k} = e(g, g)^{x_1 + \cdots + x_T} \stackrel{\text{def}}{=} e(g, g)^x.$$

After receiving the secret key shares from other dealers, dealer k can extract her master secret key by computing $S_k = g^{f_1(k)} \cdots g^{f_T(k)} = g^{f_1(k) + \cdots + f_T(k)}$.
- **Decryption key distribution.** When receiving user i's request for a decryption key share $s_{i,k}$, the dealer k randomly chooses $r_{i,k} \in \mathbb{Z}_p$ and outputs:

$$s_{i,k} = \langle s_{i,0,k}, \cdots, s_{i,i-1,k}, s_{i,i,k}, s_{i,i+1,k}, \cdots, s_{i,n,k} \rangle$$

$$= \langle g^{-r_{i,k}}, h_1^{r_{i,k}}, \cdots, h_{i-1}^{r_{i,k}}, S_k h_i^{r_{i,k}}, h_{i+1}^{r_{i,k}}, \cdots, h_n^{r_{i,k}} \rangle.$$

Assume that user i has received decryption key shares $\{s_{i,k}\}_{k \in \mathbb{A}}$ from a set $\mathbb{A}$ of at least t dealers. The user i's decryption key is denoted by

$$d_i = \langle d_{i,0}, \cdots, d_{i,i-1}, d_{i,i}, d_{i,i+1}, \cdots, d_{i,n} \rangle.$$

We show each user can recover his/her decryption key with the received decryption key shares. Note that

$$g^{x_\ell} = g^{\sum_{k \in \mathbb{A}} f_\ell(k)\lambda_k}, \quad \text{and} \quad g^x = g^{\sum_{\ell=1}^{T} x_\ell} = g^{\sum_{\ell=1}^{T} \sum_{k \in \mathbb{A}} f_\ell(k)\lambda_k},$$

where λ_k is the Lagrange coefficient of Shamir's secret sharing scheme. Denote $r_i = \sum_{k \in \mathbb{A}} r_{i,k}\lambda_k$. It follows that

$$h_i^{r_j} = h_j^{\sum_{k \in \mathbb{A}} r_{i,k}\lambda_k} \quad \text{for} \quad j = 0, \cdots, n.$$

Hence, by respectively computing $d_{i,j} = \prod_{k \in \mathbb{A}} s_{i,j,k}^{\lambda_k}$, the received $s_{i,j,k}$'s in a multiplication way, the user i can reconstruct his/her decryption key[2]

$$d_i = \langle d_{i,0}, \cdots, d_{i,i-1}, d_{i,i}, d_{i,i+1}, \cdots, d_{i,n} \rangle$$
$$= \langle g^{-r_i}, h_1^{r_i}, \cdots, h_{i-1}^{r_i}, g^x h_i^{r_i}, h_{i+1}^{r_i}, \cdots, h_n^{r_i} \rangle.$$

- **Broadcast encryption.** For a receiver set $\mathbb{R}$, randomly pick γ in $\mathbb{Z}_p$ and compute

$$Hdr = (c_1, c_2) : c_1 = g^\gamma, c_2 = (\prod_{j \in \mathbb{R}} h_j)^\gamma.$$

Set $sk = e(g,g)^{x\gamma}$ and output $\langle Hdr, sk \rangle$. Send $\langle \mathbb{R}, Hdr \rangle$ to receivers.
- **Broadcast decryption.** If $i \in \mathbb{R}$, user i can extract sk from Hdr with his decryption key d_i by computing

$$e(d_{i,i} \prod_{j \in \mathbb{R} \setminus \{i\}} d_{i,j}, c_1) e(d_{i,0}, c_2) = e(\prod_{j \in \mathbb{R}} d_{i,j}, c_1) e(d_{i,0}, c_2)$$

$$= e(g^x (\prod_{j \in \mathbb{R}} h_j)^{r_i}, g^\gamma)(g^{-r_i}, (\prod_{j \in \mathbb{R}} h_j)^\gamma) = e(g,g)^{x\gamma} = sk.$$

Theorem 2. *Let $\mathcal{A}$ be a semi-adaptive attacker breaking the above system with advantage ϵ in time τ. Then, there is an algorithm $\mathcal{B}$ breaking the BDHE assumption with advantage ϵ' in time τ', such that*

$$\epsilon' \geq \frac{1}{C_T^{t-1}} \epsilon, \tau' \leq \tau + \mathcal{O}(2\tau_{Pair} + (n^2 T^2 + T^4 + n^3)\tau_{Exp}),$$

where τ_{Pair} denotes the overhead to compute a pairing, and τ_{Exp} denotes the time complexity to compute one exponentiation without differentiating exponentiations in different groups.

We note that in Algorithm $\mathcal{B}$ there is an advantage loss by a factor $\frac{1}{C_T^{t-1}}$ w.r.t. Algorithm $\mathcal{A}$. However, since T and t are usually small, e.g., $T \leq 10$, $t \leq 5$, the loss factor is $\frac{1}{C_T^{t-1}} \approx 10^{-3}$, which is not significant in practice.

5   Discussions

5.1   FDBE with Adaptive Security

The above construction only achieves semi-adaptive security. However, by applying the generic transformation from semi-adaptive security to fully-adaptive security in Section 3.3, the above scheme can be readily improved to meet fully-adaptive security, at the cost of doubling ciphertexts.

---

[2] If the user contacts a different set $\mathbb{A}'$ of at least t dealers, the user will recover another decryption key of the form $d_i' = \langle d_{i,0}', \cdots, d_{i,i-1}', d_{i,i}', d_{i,i+1}', \cdots, d_{i,n}' \rangle = \langle g^{-r_i'}, h_1^{r_i'}, \cdots, h_{i-1}^{r_i'}, g^x h_i^{r_i'}, h_{i+1}^{r_i'}, \cdots, h_n^{r_i'} \rangle$. They are equivalent for decryption. Furthermore, d_i' can be viewed as randomization of d_i and it can also be reconstructed by properly randomized shares from dealers in $\mathbb{A}$. Here, we say that a vector v' is a randomization of vector $v = (v_o, v_1, \cdots, v_n)$ by $\delta \in Z_p$ if $v' = (v_o g^\delta, v_1 h_1^\delta, \cdots, v_n h_n^\delta)$.

5.2   Tradeoff between Ciphertexts and Keys

In the above basic FDBE construction, the public broadcast key requires $\mathcal{O}(n)$ elements (by taking into account the system parameters), the decryption key of each user consists of $\mathcal{O}(n)$ elements and the ciphertext is $\mathcal{O}(1)$ size. In the following, we illustrate an efficient tradeoff between the decryption keys and ciphertexts.

Let $n_1 + \cdots + n_J = n$ and divide the maximal receiver group $\{i_1, \cdots, i_n\}$ into J subgroups each of which hosts at most n_j receivers in the j-th subgroup. Then when a sender wants to broadcast to a set of users $\mathbb{R} \subseteq \{i_1, \cdots, i_n\}$, the sender can concurrently apply our basic FDBE scheme to each subgroup $\mathbb{R}_j = \mathbb{R} \cap \{n_1 + \cdots + n_{j-1} + 1, \cdots, n_1 + \cdots + n_{j-1} + n_j\}$. After employing this approach, the public broadcast key, the decryption key of each user, and the ciphertext all consist of $\mathcal{O}(\sqrt{n})$ elements if $n_i = \cdots = n_J$ and $J = \sqrt{n}$.

This tradeoff approach is also applicable to the above adaptively secure variant. Hence, the resulting adaptively secure FDBE scheme has sub-linear complexity, i.e., $\mathcal{O}(\sqrt{n})$ size public keys, decryption keys and ciphertexts. This performance is comparable to the up-to-date conventional broadcast schemes [14, 16, 17, 18] which have also sub-linear complexity $\mathcal{O}(\sqrt{n})$.

5.3   Applications

The FDBE primitive has some promising applications. One of them is to enable robust and flexible access control of sensitive documents. For instance, unauthorized distribution of submissions to some conference has been an issue. Our FDBE can provide a solution to this problem. In first step, several co-chairs jointly initialize an FDBE system and distribute decryption keys to the committee members. In the second step, the authors provide the title and abstract of their submissions to the conference chairs. Then the chairs assign the review tasks to the committee members according to their bids and return the indices (i.e., one-time pseudonyms) of the reviewers to the authors. Finally, the authors encrypt their full submissions so that only assigned reviewers can read the full submissions. With this approach, unauthorized distribution will be greatly limited since any submission can only be accessed by the designated reviewers.

Another application is to support online pay-per-view movies against dishonest dealers using the D'Arco-Stinson framework [11]. Unlike the D'Arco-Stinson solution which employs symmetric-key BE scheme, our scheme is public key based and the system does not need to be re-established in case of premiere of a new movie. The movie producer only needs to know the indices of the new subscribers. Also, since our scheme is collusion resistant, the end users (together with at most $t - 1$ misbehaving dealers) cannot collude to decrypt and watch the movie if they are not subscribers of the corresponding movie.

6   Conclusion

To relieve from the dependence on the trustability of the single dealer in existing BE systems, we presented the new FDBE notion. In an FDBE system, multiple dealers jointly generate the BE public key; by contacting a number of dealers equal to a threshold or more, any user can obtain a secret decryption key; then a sender can send secret messages to any chosen users and only the intended users can decrypt. No attacker can decrypt, even if the attacker controls all the users outside the receiver set and corrupts some dealers, provided that the number of corrupted dealers is less than the threshold. We realized the first FDBE scheme proven to be secure under recognized assumptions. We also show how to implement our FDBE scheme for practical applications.

Acknowledgments. The authors are partly supported by by the EU 7FP through project "DwB", the Spanish Government through projects CTV-09-634, PTA2009-2738-E, TSI-020302-2010-153, PT-430000- 2010-31, TIN2009-11689, CONSOLIDER INGENIO 2010 "ARES" CSD2007-0004 and TSI2007-65406-C03-01, by the Government of Catalonia under grant SGR2009-1135, and by the Chinese NSF projects 60970115, 60970116, 61003214 and 61021004. The authors also acknowledge support by the Fundamental Research Funds for the Central Universities of China to Project 3103004, Beijing Municipal Natural Science Foundation to Project 4112052 and Shaanxi Provincial Education Department through Scientific Research Program 2010JK727. The fourth author is partially supported as an ICREA-Acadèmia researcher by the Catalan Government. The authors are with the UNESCO Chair in Data Privacy, but this paper does not necessarily reflect the position of UNESCO nor does it commit that organization.

References

1. Fiat, A., Naor, M.: Broadcast encryption. In: Stinson, D.R. (ed.) CRYPTO 1993. LNCS, vol. 773, pp. 480–491. Springer, Heidelberg (1994)
2. Wallner, D.M., Harder, E.J., Agee, R.C.: Key Management for Multicast: Issues and Architectures. RFC Archives, #RFC2627 (1999)
3. Wong, C.K., Gouda, M., Lam, S.: Secure Group Communications Using Key Graphs. IEEE/ACM Trans. Netw. 8(1), 16–30 (2000)
4. Canetti, R., Garay, J., Itkis, G., Micciancio, D., Naor, M., Pinkas, B.: Multicast Security: A Taxonomy and Some Efficient Constructions. In: IEEE INFOCOM 1999, vol. 2, pp. 708–716. IEEE Press, New York (1999)
5. Canetti, R., Malkin, T., Nissim, K.: Efficient Communication-Storage Tradeoffs for Multicast Encryption. In: Stern, J. (ed.) EUROCRYPT 1999. LNCS, vol. 1592, pp. 459–474. Springer, Heidelberg (1999)
6. Golle, P.: Dealing Cards in Poker Games. In: ITCC 2005, vol. 1, pp. 506–511. IEEE Press, Las Vegas (2005)
7. Halevy, D., Shamir, A.: The LSD Broadcast Encryption Scheme. In: Yung, M. (ed.) CRYPTO 2002. LNCS, vol. 2442, pp. 47–60. Springer, Heidelberg (2002)
8. Goodrich, M.T., Sun, J.Z., Tamassia, R.: Efficient Tree-Based Revocation in Groups of Low-State Devices. In: Franklin, M. (ed.) CRYPTO 2004. LNCS, vol. 3152, pp. 511–527. Springer, Heidelberg (2004)
9. Sherman, A.T., McGrew, D.A.: Key Establishment in Large Dynamic Groups using One-way Function Trees. IEEE Trans. Softw. Eng. 29(5), 444–458 (2003)

10. Dodis, Y., Fazio, N.: Public Key Broadcast Encryption for Stateless Receivers. In: Feigenbaum, J. (ed.) DRM 2002. LNCS, vol. 2696, pp. 61–80. Springer, Heidelberg (2003)

11. D'Arco, P., Stinson, D.R.: Fault Tolerant and DistributedBroadcast Encryption. In: Joye, M. (ed.) CT-RSA 2003. LNCS, vol. 2612, pp. 263–280. Springer, Heidelberg (2003)

12. Cheon, J.H., Jho, N.S., Kim, M.H., Yoo, E.S.: Skipping, Cascade, and Combined Chain Schemes for Broadcast Encryption. IEEE Trans. Inf. Theory 54(11), 5155–5171 (2008)

13. Naor, M., Pinkas, B.: Efficient Trace and Revoke Schemes. In: Frankel, Y. (ed.) FC 2000. LNCS, vol. 1962, pp. 1–20. Springer, Heidelberg (2001)

14. Boneh, D., Gentry, C., Waters, B.: Collusion Resistant Broadcast Encryption with Short Ciphertexts and Private Keys. In: Shoup, V. (ed.) CRYPTO 2005. LNCS, vol. 3621, pp. 258–275. Springer, Heidelberg (2005)

15. Park, J.H., Kim, H.J., Sung, M.H., Lee, D.H.: Public Key Broadcast Encryption Schemes With Shorter Transmissions. IEEE Trans. on broadcasting 54(3), 401–411 (2008)

16. Boneh, D., Sahai, A., Waters, B.: Fully Collusion Resistant Traitor Tracing with Short Ciphertexts and Private Keys. In: Vaudenay, S. (ed.) EUROCRYPT 2006. LNCS, vol. 4004, pp. 573–592. Springer, Heidelberg (2006)

17. Boneh, D., Waters, B.: A Fully Collusion Resistant Broadcast, Trace, and Revoke System. In: Juels, A., Wright, R.-N., De Capitani di, V.S. (eds.) ACM CCS 2006, pp. 211–220. ACM Press, New York (2006)

18. Gentry, C., Waters, B.: Adaptive Security in Broadcast Encryption Systems (with Short Ciphertexts). In: Joux, A. (ed.) EUROCRYPT 2009. LNCS, vol. 5479, pp. 171–188. Springer, Heidelberg (2009)

19. Daza, V., Herranz, J., Morillo, P., Ràfols, C.: CCA2-Secure Threshold Broadcast Encryption with Shorter Ciphertexts. In: Susilo, W., Liu, J.K., Mu, Y. (eds.) ProvSec 2007. LNCS, vol. 4784, pp. 35–50. Springer, Heidelberg (2007)

20. Ghodosi, H., Pieprzyk, J., Safavi-Naini, R.: Dynamic Threshold Cryptosystems: A New Scheme in Group Oriented Cryptography. In: Pragocrypt 1996, pp. 370–379. CTU Publishing House (1996)

21. Lim, C.H., Lee, P.J.: Directed Signatures and Application to Threshold Cryptosystems. In: Lomas, M. (ed.) Security Protocols 1996. LNCS, vol. 1189, pp. 131–138. Springer, Heidelberg (1997)

22. Daza, V., Herranz, J., Morillo, P., Ràfols, C.: Ad-hoc Threshold Broadcast Encryption with Shorter Ciphertexts. Electronic Notes in Theoretical Computer Science 192(22), 3–5 (2008)

23. Delerablée, C., Pointcheval, D.: Dynamic Threshold Public-Key Encryption. In: Wagner, D. (ed.) CRYPTO 2008. LNCS, vol. 5157, pp. 317–334. Springer, Heidelberg (2008)

24. Qin, B., Wu, Q., Zhang, L., Domingo-Ferrer, J.: Threshold Public-Key Encryption with Adaptive Security and Short Ciphertexts. In: Soriano, M., Qing, S., López, J. (eds.) ICICS 2010. LNCS, vol. 6476, pp. 62–76. Springer, Heidelberg (2010)

25. Boneh, D., Franklin, M.: Identity Based Encryption from the Weil Pairing. SIAM J. of Computing 32(3), 586–615 (2003)

26. Boneh, D., Boyen, X., Goh, E.-J.: Hierarchical Identity Based Encryption with Constant Size Ciphertext. In: Cramer, R. (ed.) EUROCRYPT 2005. LNCS, vol. 3494, pp. 440–456. Springer, Heidelberg (2005)

27. Wu, Q., Mu, Y., Susilo, W., Qin, B., Domingo-Ferrer, J.: Asymmetric Group Key Agreement. In: Joux, A. (ed.) EUROCRYPT 2009. LNCS, vol. 5479, pp. 153–170. Springer, Heidelberg (2009)
28. Shamir, A.: How to Share a Secret. Communications of the ACM 22, 612–613 (1979)
29. Katz, J., Wang, N.: Efficiency Improvements for Signature Schemes with Tight Security Reductions. In: Jajodia, S., Atluri, V., Jaeger, T. (eds.) ACM CCS 2003, pp. 155–164. ACM Press, New York (2003)
30. Gennaro, R., Jarecki, S., Krawczyk, H., Rabin, T.: Secure Distributed Key Generation for Discrete-Log Based Cryptosystems. J. Cryptology 20(1), 51–83 (2007)
31. Pedersen, T.P.: A Threshold Cryptosystem without a Trusted Party. In: Davies, D.W. (ed.) EUROCRYPT 1991. LNCS, vol. 547, pp. 522–526. Springer, Heidelberg (1991)

Appendix: Proof of Theorem 2

The proof outline is as follows. We construct an algorithm $\mathcal{B}$ to break an instance of the $BDHE$ assumption by invoking Attacker $\mathcal{A}$ against our scheme as a black box. $\mathcal{B}$ is given an instance of the $BDHE$ challenge. With it, $\mathcal{B}$ simulates the system parameters, the public keys of the dealers, private keys and secret key shares of corrupted dealers, and the decryption key shares of the users which the attacker may query for. The simulated data are indistinguishable from those generated in a real scheme from the viewpoint of the attacker, so that the attacker does not know she is interacting with a simulator. Then $\mathcal{B}$ uses $\mathcal{A}$'s guess to solve the $BDHE$ challenge. This contradicts the $BDHE$ assumption. Accordingly, such a successful attacker against our FDBE scheme does not exist and our scheme is secure.

Proof. $\mathcal{B}$ receives the BDHE challenge instance, which includes g^γ, Z and the set $\{g^{\beta^i} : i \in [0, n] \cup [n + 2, 2n]\}$.

Init. $\mathcal{A}$ commits to a set $\bar{\mathbb{R}} \subseteq [1, n]$. $\mathcal{A}$ is allowed to obtain the system parameters, each dealer's public key (and the public broadcast encryption key), the private keys of the corrupted dealers, the private key shares of the corrupted dealers from both corrupted and non-corrupted dealers, the decryption key and the decryption key shares of the users in $[1, n] \setminus \bar{\mathbb{R}}$, and less than t decryption key shares of any user in $\bar{\mathbb{R}}$.

Setup. $\mathcal{B}$ generates $y_0, \cdots, y_n \leftarrow \mathbb{Z}_p$. It sets $h_i = g^{y_i}$ for $i \in \bar{\mathbb{R}}$, $h_i = g^{y_i + \beta^i}$ for $i \in [1, n] \setminus \bar{\mathbb{R}}$. $\mathcal{B}$ outputs $\pi = (\Upsilon, g, h_1, \cdots, h_n, t, T, n, N)$ as the system parameters. Clearly, due to the randomness of y_i, π has the same distribution as that in the real scheme and the simulation of the system parameters is perfect.

Public key simulation. $\mathcal{B}$ randomly chooses $k^* \in \{1, \cdots, T\}$ and denote $\overline{K^*} = \{1, \cdots, T\} \setminus \{k^*\}$. For $k \neq k^*$, $\mathcal{B}$ randomly chooses $x_k \in \mathbb{Z}_p$ and computes $X_k = e(g, g)^{x_k}$. For $k = k^*$, define $x_{k^*} = y_0 \beta^{n+1}$ which is unknown to $\mathcal{B}$. However, $\mathcal{B}$ can compute the public key for dealer k^* by computing $X_{k^*} = e(g, g)^{x_{k^*}} = e(g^\beta, g^{\beta^n})^{y_0}$. For a dealer $k \in \{1, \cdots, T\}$, her public key is X_k. The public BE key is

$$PK = \prod_{k=1}^{t} e(g,g)^{x_k} = e(g,g)^{(x_1+\cdots+x_{k^*-1}+x_{k^*+1}+\cdots+x_T)+y_0\beta^{n+1}} \overset{\text{Def}}{=} e(g,g)^x.$$

It is easy to see that, due to the randomness of x_k and y_0, X_k and PK are well-formed and have the same distribution as those in the real scheme. The simulation of each dealer's public key and the public broadcast encryption key[3] is also perfect.

Simulation of private keys of corrupted dealers. $\mathcal{B}$ guesses $t-1$ dealers for indices $\ell \in \tilde{\mathbb{A}}$ that $\mathcal{A}$ might corrupt. $\mathcal{B}$ follows the real scheme to generate the secret keys of the corrupted dealers for indices $\ell \in \tilde{\mathbb{A}}$, where $\tilde{\mathbb{A}}$ contains at most $t-1$ dealers. Without loss of generality, we assume that $|\tilde{\mathbb{A}}| = t-1$. Indeed, if $|\tilde{\mathbb{A}}| < t-1$, $\mathcal{B}$ can query other corrupted dealers on behalf of the attacker $\mathcal{A}$. For a corrupted dealer $\ell \in \tilde{\mathbb{A}}$, $\mathcal{B}$ randomly chooses $a_{\ell,1}, \cdots, a_{\ell,t-1} \in \mathbb{Z}_p$ and sets $f_\ell(\alpha) = x_\ell + a_{\ell,1}\alpha + \cdots + a_{\ell,t-1}\alpha^{t-1} \mod p$. If $\mathcal{A}$ queries private keys of dealers outside $\tilde{\mathbb{A}}$, $\mathbb{B}$ declares FAILURE and aborts the game. Else, the simulation is perfect. The probability of FAILURE is at most $1 - \frac{1}{C_T^{t-1}}$.

Simulation of secret key shares of corrupted dealers. Since the attacker is allowed access to the secret key shares held by a corrupted dealer $\ell \in \tilde{\mathbb{A}}$, $\mathcal{B}$ needs to simulate the key shares $S_{k,\ell}$ of the corrupted dealers $k \in \tilde{\mathbb{A}}$ and the non-corrupted dealers $k \notin \tilde{\mathbb{A}}$.

If $k \neq k^*$, $\mathcal{B}$ follows the real scheme to generate the secret key share $S_{k,\ell} = g^{f_k(\ell)} (\ell \in \tilde{\mathbb{A}}, k \neq k^*)$ which is sent to corrupted dealer ℓ by a dealer $k \neq k^*$. If $k = k^*$, $\mathcal{B}$ randomly chooses $S_{k^*,\ell} \in \mathbb{G}$.

From Shamir's secret sharing scheme (see Section 2.2 above), there exists a $(t-1)$-degree polynomial $f_{k^*}(\alpha)$ in $\mathbb{Z}_p$ such that $S_{k^*,\ell} = g^{f_{k^*}(\ell)}$. However, since the attacker can only know at most $t-1$ shares, $f_{k^*}(\ell')$ for $\ell' \notin \tilde{\mathbb{A}}$ is uniformly random from the attacker's perspective. Hence, the simulation of the secret key shares of corrupted dealers is perfect.

After simulating the corrupted dealer ℓ's secret key shares $S_{k,\ell}$ from all the other dealers, the master secret key of the corrupted dealer $\ell \in \tilde{\mathbb{A}}$ is:

$$S_\ell = S_{k^*,\ell} \prod_{k=1}^{T,k\neq k^*} S_{k,\ell} = g^{f_{k^*}(\ell)} \prod_{k=1}^{T,k\neq k^*} g^{f_k(\ell)} = g^{f_1(k)+\cdots f_T(k)},$$

which is clearly well-formed and perfectly simulated.

---

[3] Here, the uniform randomness of x in $\mathbb{Z}_p$ (and accordingly, the public broadcast encryption key $PK = e(g,g)^x$ in $\mathbb{G}_T$) also relies on our assumption that the corrupted dealers will follow the protocol, although they may leak their secrets and internal state information to the attacker (refer to Remark 1). If the dealers are corrupted before the key generation phase and deviate from the key generation sub-protocol, the corrupted dealers can bias $x = x_1 + x_2 + \cdots + x_T$ from uniform randomness using Gennaro et al.'s attack [30]. This deviation does not raise serious security flaws but leaves a gap in the simulation. This can be addressed by letting the dealers commit to their secret polynomials before the key generation phase and use the information-theoretic verifiable secret sharing scheme [31] to replace Shamir's secret sharing scheme. For more details about the attack and the fix, please refer to [30].

Decryption key share simulation. $\mathcal{B}$ can simulate the decryption key shares of users for indices $i \in [1, n] \setminus \bar{\mathbb{R}}$. Since the decryption key can be recovered from the decryption key shares, we do not need to specifically simulate the decryption key for users in $[1, n] \setminus \bar{\mathbb{R}}$.

The decryption key share can be from corrupted dealers $k \in \tilde{\mathbb{A}}$ and non-corrupted dealers $k \notin \tilde{\mathbb{A}}$. For corrupted dealers $k \in \tilde{\mathbb{A}}$, $\mathcal{B}$ does as in the real scheme. That is, $\mathcal{B}$ randomly chooses $r_{i,k} \in \mathbb{Z}_p$ and outputs the corrupted user i's decryption key share $s_{i,k} = \langle s_{i,0,k}, \cdots, s_{i,i-1,k}, s_{i,i,k}, s_{i,i+1,k}, \cdots, s_{i,n,k} \rangle = \langle g^{-r_{i,k}}, h_1^{r_{i,k}}, \cdots, h_{i-1}^{r_{i,k}}, S_j h_i^{r_{i,k}}, h_{i+1}^{r_{i,k}}, \cdots, h_n^{r_{i,k}} \rangle$.

For non-corrupted dealers $k \notin \tilde{\mathbb{A}}$, $\mathcal{B}$ also needs to simulate the corrupted user i's decryption key share:

$$s_{i,k} = \langle s_{i,0,k}, \cdots, s_{i,i-1,k}, s_{i,i,k}, s_{i,i+1,k}, \cdots, s_{i,n,k} \rangle_{k \notin \tilde{\mathbb{A}}}.$$

Here, the simulation must guarantee that, for any subset $\mathbb{A}$ with t indices in $\{1, \cdots, T\}$, a valid decryption key for corrupted user i can be reconstructed:

$$\left(\prod_{k \in \mathbb{A}} s_{i,0,k}^{\lambda_k}, \prod_{k \in \mathbb{A}} s_{i,1,k}^{\lambda_k}, \cdots, \prod_{k \in \mathbb{A}} s_{i,n,k}^{\lambda_k} \right).$$

$\mathcal{B}$ finishes the simulation for this case in three steps. In the first step, $\mathcal{B}$ generates a trial but valid decryption key d_i for user i. In the second step, $\mathcal{B}$ determines a trial but valid decryption key share from each non-corrupted dealer such that any t shares can be used to recover d_i. In the third step, $\mathcal{B}$ randomizes the decryption shares obtained from the second step and sends the randomized shares to the corrupted user i. After the third step, user i will recover different valid decryption keys if the user uses different sets of t shares (see Footnote 2). The third step ensures that the simulated decryption shares are distributed and work as the shares in the real world. In the following, we show how $\mathcal{B}$ can finish the three steps.

We begin with the first step. To generate a valid decryption key for corrupted user $i \in [1, n] \setminus \bar{\mathbb{R}}$, $\mathcal{B}$ randomly chooses $z_i \leftarrow \mathbb{Z}_p$ and formally sets $r_i = z_i - y_0 \beta^{n+1-i}$. It outputs

$$d_i = \langle d_{i,0}, \cdots, d_{i,n} \rangle : d_{i,0} = g^{-r_i}, d_{i,i} = g^x h_i^{r_i}, d_{i,j} = h_j^{r_i} (\forall j \neq i).$$

Clearly, d_i is well-formed and has the same distribution as that in the real scheme. Furthermore, notice that $\mathcal{B}$ can compute all these terms from the BDHE challenge instance, in particular

$$d_{i,i} = g^x h_i^{r_i} = g^{(x_1 + \cdots + x_{k^* - 1} + x_{k^* + 1} + \cdots + x_T) + y_0 x^{n+1} + (y_i + \beta^i)(z_i - y_0 \beta^{n+1-i})}$$
$$= g^{x_1 + \cdots + x_{k^* - 1} + x_{k^* + 1} + \cdots + x_T} \times g^{y_0 \beta^{n+1} + y_i z_i - y_i y_0 \beta^{n+1-i} + \beta^i z_i - y_0 \beta^{n+1}}$$
$$= g^{(x_1 + \cdots + x_{k^* - 1} + x_{k^* + 1} + \cdots + x_T) + y_i z_i - y_i y_0 \beta^{n+1-i} + \beta^i z_i}$$

which can be computed as the β^{n+1} term in the exponent cancels out. This finishes the first step.

Then we move to the second step to let $\mathcal{B}$ determine a trial but valid decryption key share from each non-corrupted dealer such that any t shares can be used to recover d_i. To this end, for $j = 0, \cdots, n$, $\mathcal{B}$ needs to find $(B_{i,j,0}, B_{i,j,1},$

$\cdots, B_{i,j,t-1}) \in \mathbb{G}^t$ to compute the function $F_{i,j}(\alpha) = B_{i,j,0}B_{i,j,1}^{\alpha} \cdots B_{i,j,t-1}^{\alpha^{t-1}}$ such that, $d_{i,j} = \prod_{k \in \mathbb{A}} s_{i,j,k}^{\lambda_k} = \prod_{k \in \mathbb{A}} F_{i,j}(k)^{\lambda_k}$. Note that $F_{i,j}(\alpha)$ is uniquely determined by any t pairs $(\alpha, F_{i,j}(\alpha))$. Specifically, $\mathcal{B}$ can use the $t-1$ pairs $(k, F_{i,j}(k))$ from corrupted dealers $k \in \tilde{\mathbb{A}}$ and the pair $(0, F_{i,j}(0)) = (0, B_{i,j,0})$ in which $F_{i,j}(0)$ is the j-th component $d_{i,j}$ of the corrupted user i's decryption key vector. Then $\mathcal{B}$ can obtain $(B_{j,0}, B_{j,1}, \cdots, B_{j,t-1})$ by solving the following t-variable linear equations in $\mathbb{G}$ for $k \in \tilde{\mathbb{A}} \cup \{0\}$: $s_{i,j,k} = F_{i,j}(k) = B_{i,j,0}B_{i,j,1}^{k} \cdots B_{i,j,t-1}^{k^{t-1}}$, where $s_{i,j,0} = B_{i,j,0} = d_{i,j}$.

After obtaining $(B_{j,0}, B_{j,1}, \cdots, B_{j,t-1})$, for a non-corrupted dealer $k \notin \tilde{\mathbb{A}}$, $\mathcal{B}$ can obtain the corrupted user i's decryption key share

$$s'_{i,k} = \langle s'_{i,0,k}, \cdots, s'_{i,i-1,k}, s'_{i,i,k}, s'_{i,i+1,k}, \cdots, s'_{i,n,k} \rangle_{k \notin \tilde{\mathbb{A}}}$$

by computing $s'_{i,j,k} = F_{i,j}(k) = B_{i,j,0}B_{i,j,1}^{k} \cdots B_{i,j,t-1}^{k^{t-1}}$ for $k \in \{1, \cdots, T\} \setminus \tilde{\mathbb{A}}$. According to Shamir's secret sharing scheme, any t shares can be used to recover d_i. This finishes the second step.

Finally, $\mathcal{B}$ moves to the third step and randomizes the computed decryption key shares. $\mathcal{B}$ randomly chooses $\delta_{i,k} \in \mathbb{Z}_p$ and randomizes $s'_{i,j,k}$ (see Footnote 1) by computing

$$s_{i,k} = \langle s'_{i,0,k}h_0^{\delta_{i,k}}, \cdots, s'_{i,i-1,k}h_{i-1}^{\delta_{i,k}}, s'_{i,i,k}h_i^{\delta_{i,k}}, s'_{i,i+1,k}h_{i+1}^{\delta_{i,k}}, \cdots, s'_{i,n,k}h_n^{\delta_{i,k}} \rangle_{k \notin \tilde{\mathbb{A}}},$$

where $h_0 \overset{\text{Denote}}{=} g$. This finishes the third step. Then all the corrupted users' decryption key shares from non-corrupted dealers are well-formed and have the same distribution as those in the real scheme. Note that the decryption key shares from corrupted dealers are computed as those in the real scheme. Hence, the simulation of all the decryption key shares for corrupted users is perfect.

$\mathcal{B}$ also needs to simulate $t - 1$ decryption key shares for non-corrupted users. If the decryption key share is from a corrupted dealer, $\mathcal{B}$ generates it as in the real scheme. Else if the decryption key share is from a non-corrupted dealer k, since the attacker can only obtain $t - 1$ decryption key shares and the Shamir's secret sharing scheme is information theoretically secure, these decryption key shares are information-theoretically independent of the decryption key of non-corrupted user i and the master secret key of non-corrupted dealer k. Hence, $\mathcal{B}$ can also follow the real scheme without knowing the master secret key. That is, $\mathcal{B}$ can perfectly simulate these decryption key shares by randomly choosing $S'_k \in \mathbb{G}, r'_{i,k} \in \mathbb{Z}_p$ and outputting user i's decryption key share

$$s_{i,k} = \langle g^{-r'_{i,k}}, h_1^{r'_{i,k}}, \cdots, h_{i-1}^{r'_{i,k}}, S'_k h_i^{r'_{i,k}}, h_{i+1}^{r'_{i,k}}, \cdots, h_n^{r'_{i,k}} \rangle.$$

This finishes all the simulated services provided to the attacker.

Challenge. $\mathcal{A}$ chooses a subset $\mathbb{R}^* \subset \bar{\mathbb{R}}$. $\mathcal{B}$ sets

$$Hdr = (c_1, c_2) : c_1 = g^{\gamma}, c_2 = (\prod_{j \in \mathbb{R}^*} h_j)^{\gamma}.$$

$\mathcal{B}$ sets $sk \leftarrow Z$ and sends $\langle Hdr, sk \rangle$ to $\mathcal{A}$. Notice that $\mathcal{B}$ can compute these terms from the instance. c_1 and sk come directly from the instance. $\mathcal{B}$ can compute c_2 since it knows $\log_g(h_i)$ for all $i \in \mathbb{R}^*$; in particular,

$$c_2 = (\prod_{j \in \mathbb{R}^*} h_j)^{\gamma} = (\prod_{j \in \mathbb{R}^*} g^{y_j})^{\gamma} = (g^{\gamma})^{\sum_{j \in \mathbb{R}^*} y_j}.$$

Guess. Eventually, $\mathcal{A}$ outputs a bit b'. $\mathcal{B}$ sends b' to the BDHE challenger.

Success probability. We compute the advantage of $\mathcal{B}$ to break the BDHE assumption. Assume that $\mathcal{B}$ does not declare FAILURE during the semi-adaptive game. When $b = 0$ in the semi-adaptive game, (Hdr, sk) is generated according to the same distribution as in the real world. This is also true in $\mathcal{B}$'s simulation: when $b = 0, sk = e(g,g)^{x\gamma}$, and so the challenge is a valid ciphertext under randomness γ. When $b = 1$ in the semi-adaptive game, $\langle Hdr, sk' \rangle$ is generated as in the real world, but sk' is replaced by $sk \leftarrow \mathbb{K}$, and $\langle Hdr, sk \rangle$ is sent to the attacker. This distribution is identical to that of $\mathcal{B}$'s simulation, where Hdr is valid for randomness γ, but $sk = Z$ is a uniformly random element of $\mathbb{G}_T$. From this, we see that $\mathcal{B}$'s advantage in deciding the BDHE instance is precisely $\mathcal{A}$'s advantage against FDBE if $\mathcal{B}$ does not declare FAILURE during the semi-adaptive game. By taking into account the simulation failure, $\mathcal{B}$'s advantage to break the BDHE assumption is $\varepsilon' \geq \frac{1}{C_T^{t-1}} \epsilon$.

Time complexity. The additional overhead for $\mathcal{B}$ is to simulate the answers that $\mathcal{A}$ may query. In the Setup stage, $\mathcal{B}$ needs $n + 1$ exponentiations in $\mathbb{G}$. In the Public key simulation, $\mathcal{B}$ needs n exponentiations and two pairing operations to compute $e(g,g)$ and $e(g^{\beta}, g^{\beta^n})$. In the Simulation of private keys of corrupted dealers, $\mathcal{B}$ only needs to sample $(t-1)^2$ elements from $\mathbb{Z}_p$. This overhead is negligible, compared to the exponentiations. In the Simulation of secret key shares of corrupted dealers, $\mathcal{B}$ needs $(T-1)(t-1)$ exponentiations in $\mathbb{G}$, $O(t)$ multiplications and additions in $\mathbb{Z}_p$. The multiplications and additions can be neglected, compared to the exponentiations. In the Decryption key simulation, $\mathcal{B}$ needs at most $(n-1)(n+1)(t-1)$ exponentiations in $\mathbb{G}$ to compute the decryption key shares from the corrupted dealers, $(n-1)(n+1)$ exponentiations in $\mathbb{G}$ to compute the trial decryption key for corrupted users (there are at most $n-1$ corrupted users), $O((t-1)t^3)$ exponentiations in $\mathbb{G}$ for the $(t-1)$ t-variable linear equations, $(t-1)(n-t+1)(n+1)t$ exponentiations in $\mathbb{G}$ to compute the decryption key shares from the non-corrupted dealers, at most $(n-1)(n-t+1)(n+1)$ exponentiations in $\mathbb{G}$ to randomize these decryption key shares, and at most $(t-1)n^2$ exponentiations to simulate the decryption key shares of the non-corrupted users. In the Challenge stage, $\mathcal{B}$ needs one exponentiation in $\mathbb{G}$ to compute the challenge ciphertext. Let τ_{Pair} denote the overhead to compute a pairing, and τ_{Exp} denote the time complexity to compute one exponentiation without differentiation of exponentiations in different groups. Note that $1 \leq t \leq T$. By summing up all of them, the time complexity of $\mathcal{B}$ is $\tau' \leq \tau + \mathcal{O}(2\tau_{\text{Pair}} + (n^2 T^2 + T^4 + n^3)\tau_{\text{Exp}})$. This completes the proof.

Efficient Identity-Based Signcryption in the Standard Model

Fagen Li[1,2], Fahad Bin Muhaya[3], Mingwu Zhang[2], and Tsuyoshi Takagi[2]

[1] School of Computer Science and Engineering,
University of Electronic Science and Technology of China, Chengdu 611731, China
[2] Institute of Mathematics for Industry,
Kyushu University, Fukuoka 819-0395, Japan
[3] Prince Muqrin Chair for IT Security,
King Saud University, Riyadh, Saudi Arabia
fagenli@uestc.edu.cn

Abstract. Signcryption is a cryptographic primitive that fulfills both the functions of digital signature and public key encryption simultaneously, at a cost significantly lower than that required by the traditional signature-then-encryption approach. Signcryption has been shown to be useful in many applications, such as electronic commerce, mobile communications and smart cards. Recently, three identity-based signcryption schemes in the standard model were proposed. However, the three schemes are broken soon. How to construct a secure identity-based signcryption scheme in the standard model is still an open problem. In this paper, we solve this problem and propose an efficient identity-based signcryption scheme in the standard model. We prove that our scheme has the indistinguishability against adaptive chosen ciphertext attacks under the modified decisional bilinear Diffie-Hellman assumption and the existential unforgeability against adaptive chosen messages attacks under the computational Diffie-Hellman assumption.

Keywords: Identity-based cryptography, signcryption, standard model.

1 Introduction

In 1984, Shamir [1] introduced the concept of identity-based cryptography (IBC). The distinguishing property of IBC is that a user's public key can be any binary string, such as an email address that can identify the user. This removes the need for senders to look up the recipient's public key before sending out an encrypted message. IBC is supposed to provide a more convenient alternative to conventional public key infrastructure (PKI). Several practical identity-based signature (IBS) schemes have been devised since 1984 [2,3] but a satisfying identity-based encryption (IBE) scheme only appeared in 2001 [4]. It was devised by Boneh and Franklin and cleverly uses bilinear maps (the Weil or Tate pairing) over supersingular elliptic curves.

X. Boyen and X. Chen (Eds.): ProvSec 2011, LNCS 6980, pp. 120–137, 2011.

Signcryption, first proposed by Zheng [5], is a cryptographic primitive that fulfills both the functions of digital signature and public key encryption simultaneously, at a cost significantly lower than that required by the traditional signature-then-encryption approach. The performance advantage of signcryption over the signature-then-encryption method makes signcryption useful in many applications, such as electronic commerce, mobile communications and smart cards. Zheng gave two signcryption schemes based on the discrete logarithm problem without security proof. Zheng's signcryption was only proven secure by Baek, Steinfeld and Zheng [6] who described a formal security model in a multi-user setting. One of the shortcomings of Zheng's schemes is that its non-repudiation procedure is inefficient since they are based on interactive zero-knowledge proof. To achieve simple and safe non-repudiation procedure, Bao and Deng [7] introduced a signcryption scheme that can be verified by a sender's public key. Furthermore, Steinfeld and Zheng [8] and Malone-Lee and Mao [9] proposed efficient signcryption schemes based on integer factorization and using RSA, respectively.

A recent direction is to merge the concepts of IBC and signcryption to design efficient identity-based signcryption (IBSC) schemes. Malone-Lee [10] gave the first IBSC scheme in 2002. Libert and Quisquater [11] pointed out that Malone-Lee's scheme is not semantically secure and proposed three IBSC schemes. However, the properties of public verifiability and forward security are mutually exclusive in the their schemes. They also gave an open problem to design an efficient IBSC scheme providing both public verifiability and forward security. Soon, this open problem was solved by Chow et al. [12]. Boyen [13] presented an IBSC scheme that provides not only public verifiability and forward security but also ciphertext unlinkability and anonymity. Chen and Malone-Lee [14] improved Boyen's scheme in efficiency. In [15], Barreto et al. constructed the most efficient IBSC scheme to date. In 2010, Selvi, Vivek and Rangan [16] proposed a new IBSC scheme that provides both public verifiability and third party verification. However, all of these IBSC schemes are provably secure in the random oracle model [17]. Random oracle model is a formal model in analyzing cryptographic schemes, where a hash function is considered as a black-box that contains a random function. However, it has been shown that security in the random oracle model does not imply the security in the real world [18,19]. So it is important to design provably secure IBSC schemes in the standard model, i.e., without resorting to the random oracle heuristic.

1.1   Related Work

In 2009, Yu et al. [20] proposed an IBSC scheme in the standard model. Yu et al.'s scheme is based on Waters' IBE scheme [21] and Paterson and Schuldt's IBS scheme [22]. However, in 2010, Jin, Wen and Du [23] pointed out that Yu et al.'s scheme does not have the indistinguishability against adaptive chosen ciphertext attacks (IND-CCA2). In Yu et al.'s scheme, the signature on the plaintext is visible in the ciphertext. So an adversary can simply verify the signature on plaintexts m_0 and m_1 produced during the IND-CCA2 game and find out which one matches to the challenge ciphertext. Jin, Wen and Du also proposed an improved IBSC scheme. Unfortunately, Li, Liao and Qin [24] pointed out that the Jin-Wen-Du scheme has neither the IND-CCA2 security nor the existential unforgeability against adaptive chosen messages attacks (EUF-CMA). For the IND-CCA2 security, in the Jin-Wen-Du scheme, when receiving the challenge ciphertext $\sigma^* = (\sigma_1^*, \sigma_2^*, \sigma_3^*, \sigma_4^*, \sigma_5^*)$, the adversary can randomly chooses $r' \in Z_p$ and generate a new ciphertext $\sigma_1' = \sigma_1^*$, $\sigma_2' = \sigma_2^*$, $\sigma_3' = \sigma_3^*$, $\sigma_4' = \sigma_4^*(u' \prod_{i \in \mathcal{U}_A} u_i)^{r'}$ and $\sigma_5' = \sigma_5^* g^{r'}$. That is, the adversary modify the random number of the sender's secret key to obtain a new ciphertext. For the EUF-CMA security, in the Jin-Wen-Du scheme, different M and R can generate the same $\mathcal{M}$. So the adversary can generate easily a signcryption for new message. In 2010, Zhang [25] also gave an improvement of Yu et al.'s scheme. However, we find Zhang's improvement is not IND-CCA2 secure either. An adversary can first guess that m_0 is the signcrypted message in the challenge ciphertext σ^*. Then the adversary computes $\hat{R} = \sigma_1^* \cdot m_0^{-1}$, $\hat{t} = H_1(m_0 || \hat{R})$ and $\hat{\tilde{m}} = H_2(g^{\hat{t}} h^{\sigma_6^*})$. Finally, the adversary checks if the signature equation holds using $\hat{\tilde{m}}$. If the signature equation holds, then m_0 is the plaintext for the challenge ciphertext. Otherwise m_1 is the plaintext for the challenge ciphertext.

In conclusion, all the IBSC schemes in the standard model are broken. Therefore, how to construct a secure IBSC scheme in the standard model is still an open problem. The research on this topic is very important and significant.

1.2   Our Contribution

In this paper, we propose an efficient IBSC scheme in the standard model by using Kiltz and Vahlis's IBE scheme [26] and Paterson and Schuldt's IBS scheme [22]. We prove that our scheme is IND-CCA2 secure under the modified decisional bilinear Diffie-Hellman assumption and is EUF-CMA secure under the computational Diffie-Hellman assumption.

1.3   Paper Organization

The rest of this paper is organized as follows. We introduce the preliminary work in Section 2. We give the formal model of IBSC in Section 3. An efficient IBSC scheme is proposed in Section 4. We analyze the proposed scheme in Section 5. Finally, the conclusions are given in Section 6.

2   Preliminaries

In this section, we briefly describe the basic definition of bilinear pairings and some complexity assumptions. We refer the reader to [4,11,12,15,21,22] for more details.

2.1 Bilinear Maps

Let G and G_T be two multiplicative cyclic groups of prime order p. Let g be a generator of G. The map $\hat{e} : G \times G \to G_T$ is said to be an admissible map if the following three conditions hold true:

- $\hat{e}$ is bilinear, i.e. $\hat{e}(g^a, g^b) = \hat{e}(g, g)^{ab}$ for all $a, b \in Z_p$.
- $\hat{e}$ is non-degenerate, i.e. $\hat{e}(g, g) \neq 1$.
- $\hat{e}$ is efficiently computable.

2.2 Complexity Assumptions

Given two groups G and G_T of the same prime order p, a bilinear map $\hat{e} : G \times G \to G_T$ and a generator g of G, the decisional bilinear Diffie-Hellman (DBDH) problem in $(G, G_T, \hat{e})$ is to decide whether $T = \hat{e}(P, P)^{abc}$ given (g, g^a, g^b, g^c) and an element $T \in G_T$. Here a, b and c are random elements in Z_p.

Kiltz and Vahlis [26] gave modified DBDH problem that provides the adversary with the element g^{b^2}. They used the modified DBDH problem to construct an IBE scheme in the standard model. We describe this problem as follows.

Given two groups G and G_T of the same prime order p, a bilinear map $\hat{e} : G \times G \to G_T$ and a generator g of G, the modified decisional bilinear Diffie-Hellman (mDBDH) problem in $(G, G_T, \hat{e})$ is to decide whether $T = \hat{e}(P, P)^{abc}$ given $(g, g^a, g^b, g^{b^2}, g^c)$ and an element $T \in G_T$. Here a, b and c are random elements in Z_p. We define the advantage of an adversary $\mathcal{C}$ against the mDBDH problem like this

$$Adv(\mathcal{C}) = |\Pr[\mathcal{C}(g, g^a, g^b, g^{b^2}, g^c, T) = 1] - \Pr[\mathcal{C}(g, g^a, g^b, g^{b^2}, g^c, \hat{e}(g, g)^{abc}) = 1]|.$$

Definition 1. *The (ϵ_{mdbdh}, t)-mDBDH assumption holds if no t-polynomial time adversary $\mathcal{C}$ has advantage at least ϵ_{mdbdh} in solving the mDBDH problem.*

Given a group G of prime order p and a generator g of G, the computational Diffie-Hellman (CDH) problem in G is to compute g^{ab} given (g, g^a, g^b) for $a, b \in Z_p$.

Definition 2. *The (ϵ_{cdh}, t)-CDH assumption holds if no t-polynomial time adversary $\mathcal{C}$ has advantage at least ϵ_{cdh} in solving the CDH problem.*

Definition 3. *A hash function H is (ϵ_H, t)-collision resistant if no t-polynomial time adversary $\mathcal{C}$ has advantage at least ϵ_H in find two different messages m_1 and m_2 such that $H(m_1) = H(m_2)$.*

3 Formal Model of Identity-Based Signcryption

In this section, we describe the definition and security notions for IBSC.

3.1   Definition

An IBSC scheme consists of the following four algorithms [10].

- **Setup:** Given a security parameter k, the private key generator (PKG) generates the system's public parameters par and a master secret key msk. The PKG publishes par and keeps msk to itself.
- **Extract:** Given an identity id, the PKG computes the corresponding secret key sk_{id} and sends it to its owner in a secure way.
- **Signcrypt:** Let Alice's identity be id_A and Bob's identity be id_B. To send a message m to the receiver Bob, Alice computes **Signcrypt**(m, sk_A, id_B) to obtain the ciphertext c. Here $sk_A = $ **Extract**(id_A, msk).
- **Unsigncrypt:** When receiving c, Bob computes **Unsigncrypt**(c, id_A, sk_B) and obtains the plaintext m or the symbol $\perp$ if c is an invalid ciphertext between Alice and Bob. Here $sk_B = $ **Extract**(id_B, msk).

These algorithms should satisfy the standard consistency constraint of IBSC, i.e. if

$$c = \textbf{Signcrypt}(m, sk_A, id_B),$$

then

$$m = \textbf{Unsigncrypt}(c, id_A, sk_B).$$

3.2   Security Notions

An IBSC scheme should satisfy two basic security notions. These notions are the IND-CCA2 security and EUF-CMA security.

For the IND-CCA2 security, we consider the following game played between a challenger $\mathcal{C}$ and an adversary $\mathcal{A}$.

Initial: $\mathcal{C}$ runs the **Setup** algorithm with a security parameter k and sends the system parameters par to $\mathcal{A}$.

Phase 1: $\mathcal{A}$ performs a polynomially bounded number of queries (these queries may be made adaptively, i.e., each query may depend on the answer to the previous queries). The types of queries are described below.

- Key extraction queries: $\mathcal{A}$ chooses an identity id. $\mathcal{C}$ sends the result of $sk_{id} = $ **Extract**(id, msk) to $\mathcal{A}$.
- Signcryption queries: $\mathcal{A}$ chooses two identities id_A and id_B, and a plaintext m. $\mathcal{C}$ first computes the secret key $sk_A = $ **Extract**(id_A, msk) and then sends the ciphertext $c = $ **Signcrypt**(m, sk_A, id_B) to $\mathcal{A}$.
- Unsigncryption queries: $\mathcal{A}$ chooses two identities id_A and id_B, and a ciphertext c. $\mathcal{C}$ computes the secret key $sk_B = $ **Extract**(id_B, msk) and sends the result of **Unsigncrypt**(c, id_A, sk_B) to $\mathcal{A}$ (this result can be the $\perp$ symbol if c is an invalid ciphertext)

Challenge: $\mathcal{A}$ decides when Phase 1 ends. $\mathcal{A}$ generates two equal length plaintexts, m_0 and m_1, and two identities, id_A^* and id_B^*, on which it wants to be challenged. It cannot have asked the secret key corresponding to id_B^* in Phase 1.

$\mathcal{C}$ takes a random bit γ from $\{0, 1\}$ and computes $c^* = \mathbf{Signcrypt}(m_\gamma, sk_A^*, id_B^*)$ which is sent to $\mathcal{A}$.

Phase 2: $\mathcal{A}$ can ask a polynomially bounded number of queries adaptively again as in Phase 1. This time, it cannot make a key extraction query on id_B^* and cannot make an unsigncryption query on c^* to obtain the corresponding plaintext.

Guess: $\mathcal{A}$ produces a bit γ' and wins the game if $\gamma' = \gamma$.

The advantage of $\mathcal{A}$ is defined as $Adv(\mathcal{A}) = |\Pr[\gamma' = \gamma] - 1/2|$, where $\Pr[\gamma' = \gamma]$ denotes the probability that $\gamma' = \gamma$.

Definition 4. *An IBSC scheme is $(\epsilon_{sc}, t, q_k, q_s, q_u)$-IND-CCA2 secure if no probabilistic t-polynomial time adversary $\mathcal{A}$ has advantage at least ϵ_{sc} after at most q_k key extraction queries, q_s signcryption queries and q_u unsigncryption queries in the IND-CCA2 game.*

For the EUF-CMA security, we consider the following game played between a challenger $\mathcal{C}$ and an adversary $\mathcal{F}$.

Initial: $\mathcal{C}$ runs the **Setup** algorithm with a security parameter k and sends the system parameters *par* to $\mathcal{F}$.

Attack: $\mathcal{F}$ performs a polynomially bounded number of queries just like in the IND-CCA2 game.

Forgery: $\mathcal{F}$ produces a new triple (c', id_A', id_B') for a message m' (i.e. a triple that was not produced by the signcryption oracle), where the secret key of id_A' was not asked for during the Attack phase and wins the game if the result of **Unsigncrypt**(c', id_A', id_B') is not the $\bot$ symbol.

The advantage of $\mathcal{F}$ is defined as the probability that it wins.

Definition 5. *An IBSC scheme is $(\epsilon_{sc}, t, q_k, q_s, q_u)$-EUF-CMA secure if no probabilistic t-polynomial time adversary $\mathcal{F}$ has advantage at least ϵ_{sc} after at most q_k key extraction queries, q_s signcryption queries and q_u unsigncryption queries in the EUF-CMA game.*

4   An Efficient Identity-Based Signcryption Scheme

In this section, we present an IBSC scheme in the standard model by using Kiltz and Vahlis's IBE scheme [26] and Paterson and Schuldt's IBS scheme [22]. Let $id = (id_1, \ldots, id_{n_{id}}) \in \{0, 1\}^{n_{id}}$ be an identity and $\pi = (\pi_1, \ldots, \pi_{n_m}) \in \{0, 1\}^{n_m}$ be a message. Here n_{id} is the number of bits required to represent an identity id and n_m is the number of bits required to represent a message π. Note that the message π is not the plaintext m. Our IBSC scheme consists of the following four algorithms.

- **Setup:** Given a security parameter k, the PKG chooses two multiplicative cyclic groups G and G_T of prime order p, a generator g of G and a bilinear map $\hat{e} : G \times G \to G_T$. The PKG chooses $\alpha, w \in G$ randomly and computes $z = \hat{e}(\alpha, g)$. Additionally, the PKG chooses random values $u', v' \in G$

and vectors $U = (u_i)$, $V = (v_i)$ of length n_{id} and n_m, respectively, whose elements are chosen at random from G. We also need two hash functions $H_1 : G \rightarrow Z_p^*$ and $H_2 : \{0,1\}^* \rightarrow \{0,1\}^{n_m}$. $SE = (E, D)$ is a secure one-time symmetric-key encryption scheme [27] with key space $\mathcal{K} = G_T$. Two functions $H_3 : \{0,1\}^{n_{id}} \rightarrow G$ and $H_4 : \{0,1\}^{n_m} \rightarrow G$ are defined as follows, respectively.

$$H_3(id) = u' \prod_{i=1}^{n_{id}} u_i^{id_i} \quad \text{and} \quad H_4(\pi) = v' \prod_{i=1}^{n_m} v_i^{\pi_i}$$

Note that this kind of functions are used to construct IBE scheme by Waters in [21]. The PKG publishes system parameters

$$par = \{G, G_T, \hat{e}, g, w, z, u', U, v', V, H_1, H_2, H_3, H_4, SE\}$$

and keeps the master secret key α to itself.

- **Extract:** Given an identity id, the PKG chooses $s \in Z_p^*$ randomly and computes the secret key sk_{id} as follows.

$$sk_{id} = (sk_1, sk_2, sk_3) = (\alpha \cdot H_3(id)^s, g^s, w^s)$$

Let id_A be Alice's identity and id_B be Bob's identity. The secret key of Alice is

$$sk_A = (sk_{A1}, sk_{A2}, sk_{A3}) = (\alpha \cdot H_3(id_A)^{s_A}, g^{s_A}, w^{s_A})$$

and the secret key of Bob is

$$sk_B = (sk_{B1}, sk_{B2}, sk_{B3}) = (\alpha \cdot H_3(id_B)^{s_B}, g^{s_B}, w^{s_B}).$$

- **Signcrypt:** To send a message m to Bob, Alice follows the steps below.
  1. Choose $r \in Z_p^*$ randomly.
  2. Compute $c_1 = g^r$.
  3. Compute $t = H_1(c_1)$.
  4. Compute $c_2 = sk_{A2}$.
  5. Compute $K = z^r$.
  6. Compute $c_3 = E_K(m)$.
  7. Compute $c_4 = (H_3(id_B) \cdot w^t)^r$.
  8. Compute $\pi = H_2(c_1, c_2, c_3, c_4)$.
  9. Compute $c_5 = sk_{A1} \cdot H_4(\pi)^r \cdot c_4$.
  The ciphertext is $c = (c_1, c_2, c_3, c_4, c_5)$.
- **Unsigncrypt:** When receiving $c = (c_1, c_2, c_3, c_4, c_5)$, Bob follows the steps below.
  1. Compute $\pi = H_2(c_1, c_2, c_3, c_4)$ and $t = H_1(c_1)$.
  2. Check if the following equation holds:

$$\hat{e}(c_5, g) = z \cdot \hat{e}(H_3(id_A), c_2) \cdot \hat{e}(H_4(\pi) \cdot H_3(id_B) \cdot w^t, c_1). \tag{1}$$

If Eq.(1) holds, compute

$$K = \frac{\hat{e}(c_1, sk_{B1} \cdot sk_{B3}^t)}{\hat{e}(c_4, sk_{B2})}, \qquad (2)$$

and return the message $m = D_K(c_3)$. Otherwise, the ciphertext is not valid and return $\perp$.

As compared with previous IBSC schemes [20,23,25], our scheme has the following two differences.

1. We sign $\pi = H_2(c_1, c_2, c_3, c_4)$ instead of plaintext m. So an adversary cannot verify the signature on plaintexts m_0 and m_1 produced during the IND-CCA2 game and find out which one matches to the challenge ciphertext.
2. We include $c_2 = sk_{A2}$ in computing $\pi = H_2(c_1, c_2, c_3, c_4)$. So an adversary cannot modify the random number of the sender's secret key to obtain a new ciphertext.

5   Analysis of the Scheme

In this section, we analyze the consistency, security and efficiency of our scheme.

5.1   Consistency

Now we verify the consistency of our scheme. For Eq.(1), we have

$$\hat{e}(c_5, g) = \hat{e}(sk_{A1} \cdot H_4(\pi)^r \cdot c_4, g) = \hat{e}(\alpha \cdot H_3(id_A)^{s_A} \cdot (H_4(\pi) \cdot H_3(id_B) \cdot w^t)^r, g)$$
$$= \hat{e}(\alpha, g) \cdot \hat{e}(H_3(id_A), g^{s_A}) \cdot \hat{e}(H_4(\pi) \cdot H_3(id_B) \cdot w^t, g^r)$$
$$= z \cdot \hat{e}(H_3(id_A), c_2) \cdot \hat{e}(H_4(\pi) \cdot H_3(id_B) \cdot w^t, c_1)$$

For Eq.(2), we have

$$\frac{\hat{e}(c_1, sk_{B1} \cdot sk_{B3}^t)}{\hat{e}(c_4, sk_{B2})} = \frac{\hat{e}(g^r, \alpha \cdot H_3(id_B)^{s_B} \cdot (w^{s_B})^t)}{\hat{e}((H_3(id_B) \cdot w^t)^r, g^{s_B})}$$
$$= \frac{\hat{e}(g^r, \alpha) \cdot \hat{e}(g^r, H_3(id_B)^{s_B} \cdot (w^{s_B})^t)}{\hat{e}((H_3(id_B) \cdot w^t)^r, g^{s_B})}$$
$$= \frac{\hat{e}(\alpha, g)^r \cdot \hat{e}(g^r, (H_3(id_B) \cdot w^t)^{s_B})}{\hat{e}((H_3(id_B) \cdot w^t)^r, g^{s_B})}$$
$$= \hat{e}(\alpha, g)^r = z^r = K$$

5.2   Security

We prove that our scheme satisfies the IND-CCA2 security and EUF-CMA security by the following Theroems 1 and 2. In addition, our scheme also satisfies the public verifiability. Anyone can verify the validity of a ciphertext by Eq.(1).

Theorem 1. *Our IBSC scheme is $(\epsilon_{sc}, t, q_k, q_s, q_u)$-IND-CCA2 secure in the standard model if the (ϵ_{mdbdh}, t)-mDBDH assumption holds, H_1 and H_2 are (ϵ_{H_1}, t) and (ϵ_{H_2}, t) are collision resistant hash functions, respectively, such that*

$$\epsilon_{sc} \leq \epsilon_{mdbdh} + \epsilon_{H_1} + \epsilon_{H_2} + \frac{q_k + q_u + 3}{p} + \frac{q_s}{p^2},$$

where t is the processing time, q_k is the number of key extraction queries, q_s is the number of signcryption queries and q_u is the number of unsigncryption queries.

Proof. See the appendix A. □

Theorem 2. *Our IBSC scheme is $(\epsilon_{sc}, t, q_k, q_s, q_u)$-EUF-CMA secure in the standard model assuming Paterson and Schuldt's signature scheme is $(\epsilon_{sc}, t', q_k, q_s)$ existential unforgeable such that $t' = t + q_k C_k + q_s C_s + q_u C_u$, where q_k is the number of key extraction queries, q_s is the number of signcryption queries, q_u is the number of unsigncryption queries, C_k is the key extract cost of IBSC scheme, C_s is the signcryption cost of IBSC scheme and C_u is the unsigncryption cost of IBSC scheme.*

Proof. See the appendix B. □

5.3   Performance and Security Comparison

We compare the major computational cost and security properties of our scheme with those of Yu et al.'s scheme [20], the Jin-Wen-Du scheme [23] and Zhang's scheme [25] in Table 1. We consider the costly operations which include multiplications in G (GMul), exponentiations in G (GExp), multiplications in G_T (G_TMul), exponentiations in G_T (G_TExp), inversion in G_T (G_TInv) and pairing operations (Pairing).

In the table, we represent the total number of pairing computations in the form of $x(+y)$ where y is the number of operations that are independent of the message and can be pre-computed and cached for subsequent uses. For security properties, we consider the IND-CCA2 and EUF-CMA security. From Table 1, we can see that our scheme is as efficient as existing schemes. However, Yu et al.'s scheme, the Jin-Wen-Du scheme and Zhang's scheme are not IND-CCA2 secure. The Jin-Wen-Du scheme is not EUF-CMA secure either. Our scheme is both IND-CCA2 secure and EUF-CMA secure.

Table 1. Performance and security comparison

	GMul	GExp	G_TMul	G_TExp	G_TInv	Pairing	IND-CCA2	EUF-CMA
[20]	$2n_{id} + 2n_m + 1$	3	5	1	1	7(+2)	No	Yes
[23]	$2n_{id} + 2n_m + 1$	3	5	1	1	7(+2)	No	No
[25]	$2n_{id} + 2n_m + 3$	7	5	1	2	7(+2)	No	Yes
Ours	$3n_{id} + 2n_m + 6$	6	3	1	1	5	Yes	Yes

6 Conclusions

In this paper, we proposed an efficient IBSC scheme in the standard model. We proved that our scheme is IND-CCA2 secure under the mDBDH assumption and is EUF-CMA secure under the CDH assumption. It is an interesting problem to design more efficient IBSC schemes in the standard model.

Acknowledgements. We would like to thank the anonymous reviewers for their valuable comments and suggestions. This work is supported by the National Natural Science Foundation of China (Grant Nos. 60803133, 60873233, 61073176, 61003230 and 61003232), the Fundamental Research Funds for the Central Universities, and the NPST Program by King Saud University (Grant No. 09-INF851-02).

References

1. Shamir, A.: Identity-based cryptosystems and signature schemes. In: Blakely, G.R., Chaum, D. (eds.) CRYPTO 1984. LNCS, vol. 196, pp. 47–53. Springer, Heidelberg (1985)
2. Fiat, A., Shamir, A.: How to prove yourself: Practical solutions to identification and signature problems. In: Odlyzko, A.M. (ed.) CRYPTO 1986. LNCS, vol. 263, pp. 186–194. Springer, Heidelberg (1987)
3. Guillou, L.C., Quisquater, J.-J.: A "Paradoxical" identity-based signature scheme resulting from zero-knowledge. In: Goldwasser, S. (ed.) CRYPTO 1988. LNCS, vol. 403, pp. 216–231. Springer, Heidelberg (1990)
4. Boneh, D., Franklin, M.: Identity-based encryption from the weil pairing. In: Kilian, J. (ed.) CRYPTO 2001. LNCS, vol. 2139, pp. 213–229. Springer, Heidelberg (2001)
5. Zheng, Y.: Digital signcryption or how to achieve cost (Signature & encryption) $<<$ cost(Signature) + cost(Encryption). In: Kaliski Jr., B.S. (ed.) CRYPTO 1997. LNCS, vol. 1294, pp. 165–179. Springer, Heidelberg (1997)
6. Baek, J., Steinfeld, R., Zheng, Y.: Formal proofs for the security of signcryption. Journal of Cryptology 20(2), 203–235 (2007)
7. Bao, F., Deng, R.H.: A signcryption scheme with signature directly verifiable by public key. In: Imai, H., Zheng, Y. (eds.) PKC 1998. LNCS, vol. 1431, pp. 55–59. Springer, Heidelberg (1998)
8. Steinfeld, R., Zheng, Y.: A signcryption scheme based on integer factorizatio. In: Okamoto, E., Pieprzyk, J.P., Seberry, J. (eds.) ISW 2000. LNCS, vol. 1975, pp. 308–322. Springer, Heidelberg (2000)
9. Malone-Lee, J., Mao, W.: Two birds one stone: Signcryption using RSA. In: Joye, M. (ed.) CT-RSA 2003. LNCS, vol. 2612, pp. 211–225. Springer, Heidelberg (2003)
10. Malone-Lee, J.: Identity based signcryption. Cryptology ePrint Archive, Report 2002/098 (2002), http://eprint.iacr.org/2002/098
11. Libert, B., Quisquater, J.J.: A new identity based signcryption schemes from pairings. In: 2003 IEEE Information Theory Workshop, Paris, France, pp. 155–158 (2003)
12. Chow, S.S.M., Yiu, S.M., Hui, L.C.K., Chow, K.P.: Efficient forward and provably secure ID-based signcryption scheme with public verifiability and public ciphertext authenticity. In: Lim, J.-I., Lee, D.-H. (eds.) ICISC 2003. LNCS, vol. 2971, pp. 352–369. Springer, Heidelberg (2004)

13. Boyen, X.: Multipurpose identity-based signcryption: a swiss army knife for identity-based cryptography. In: Boneh, D. (ed.) CRYPTO 2003. LNCS, vol. 2729, pp. 383–399. Springer, Heidelberg (2003)

14. Chen, L., Malone-Lee, J.: Improved identity-based signcryption. In: Vaudenay, S. (ed.) PKC 2005. LNCS, vol. 3386, pp. 362–379. Springer, Heidelberg (2005)

15. Barreto, P.S.L.M., Libert, B., McCullagh, N., Quisquater, J.-J.: Efficient and provably-secure identity-based signatures and signcryption from bilinear maps. In: Roy, B. (ed.) ASIACRYPT 2005. LNCS, vol. 3788, pp. 515–532. Springer, Heidelberg (2005)

16. Selvi, S.S.D., Sree Vivek, S., Pandu Rangan, C.: Identity based public verifiable signcryption scheme. In: Heng, S.-H., Kurosawa, K. (eds.) ProvSec 2010. LNCS, vol. 6402, pp. 244–260. Springer, Heidelberg (2010)

17. Bellare, M., Rogaway, P.: Random oracles are practical: a paradigm for designing efficient protocols. In: 1st ACM Conference on Computer and Communications Security, Fairfax, Virginia, USA, pp. 62–73 (1993)

18. Bellare, M., Boldyreva, A., Palacio, A.: An uninstantiable random-oracle-model scheme for a hybrid-encryption problem. In: Cachin, C., Camenisch, J. (eds.) EUROCRYPT 2004. LNCS, vol. 3027, pp. 171–188. Springer, Heidelberg (2004)

19. Canetti, R., Goldreich, O., Halevi, S.: The random oracle methodology, revisited. Journal of the ACM 51(4), 557–594 (2004)

20. Yu, Y., Yang, B., Sun, Y., Zhu, S.: Identity based signcryption scheme without random oracles. Computer Standards & Interfaces 31(1), 56–62 (2009)

21. Waters, B.: Efficient identity-based encryption without random oracles. In: Cramer, R. (ed.) EUROCRYPT 2005. LNCS, vol. 3494, pp. 114–127. Springer, Heidelberg (2005)

22. Paterson, K.G., Schuldt, J.C.N.: Efficient identity-based signatures secure in the standard model. In: Batten, L.M., Safavi-Naini, R. (eds.) ACISP 2006. LNCS, vol. 4058, pp. 207–222. Springer, Heidelberg (2006)

23. Jin, Z., Wen, Q., Du, H.: An improved semantically-secure identity-based signcryption scheme in the standard model. Computers & Electrical Engineering 36(3), 545–552 (2010)

24. Li, F., Liao, Y., Qin, Z.: Analysis of an identity-based signcryption scheme in the standard model. IEICE Transactions on Fundamentals of Electronics, Communications and Computer Sciences E94-A (1), 268–269 (2011)

25. Zhang, B.: Cryptanalysis of an identity based signcryption scheme without random oracles. Journal of Computational Information Systems 6(6), 1923–1931 (2010)

26. Kiltz, E., Vahlis, Y.: CCA2 secure IBE: Standard model efficiency through authenticated symmetric encryption. In: Malkin, T. (ed.) CT-RSA 2008. LNCS, vol. 4964, pp. 221–238. Springer, Heidelberg (2008)

27. Cramer, R., Shoup, V.: Design and analysis of practical public-key encryption schemes secure against adaptive chosen ciphertext attack. SIAM Journal on Computing 33(1), 167–226 (2003)

28. Shoup, V.: Sequences of games: a tool for taming complexity in security proofs. Cryptology ePrint Archive, Report 2004/332 (2004), http://eprint.iacr.org/2004/332

29. Shoup, V.: OAEP reconsidered. In: Kilian, J. (ed.) CRYPTO 2001. LNCS, vol. 2139, pp. 239–259. Springer, Heidelberg (2001)

Appendix

A   Proof of Theorem 1

Proof. The theorem proceeds by reductionist proof. That is, We assume that an adversary $\mathcal{A}$ can break our scheme in the sense of IND-CCA2 security in the standard model, then one can construct an algorithm $\mathcal{C}$ which solves the mDBDH problem with advantage ϵ_{mdbdh}. Let G and G_T be two multiplicative cyclic groups of prime order p. Let g be a generator of G. Let $\hat{e} : G \times G \to G_T$ be the bilinear map. We assume that $\mathcal{C}$ receives a random instance $(g, g^a, g^b, g^{b^2}, g^c, T)$ of the mDBDH problem. Its goal is to decide whether $T = \hat{e}(g, g)^{abc}$ or not. $\mathcal{C}$ will run $\mathcal{A}$ as a subroutine and act as $\mathcal{A}$'s challenger in the IND-CCA2 game.

Initial: $\mathcal{C}$ sets $l_u = q_k + q_s + q_u$ and $l_v = q_s + q_u$, and randomly chooses two integers k_u and k_v, with $0 \le k_u \le n_{id}$ and $0 \le k_v \le n_m$. $\mathcal{C}$ sets $f_u = 4l_u$ and $f_v = 4l_v$. $\mathcal{C}$ then chooses an integer $x' \in Z_{l_u}$ randomly and a vector $\boldsymbol{X} = (x_i)$ of length n_{id}, whose elements are chosen at random from Z_{l_u}. Likewise, $\mathcal{C}$ chooses an integer $z' \in Z_{l_v}$ randomly and a vector $\boldsymbol{Z} = (z_j)$ of length n_m, whose elements are chosen at random from Z_{l_v}. $\mathcal{C}$ chooses an integer $y' \in Z_{f_u}$ and vector $\boldsymbol{Y} = (y_i)$ of length n_{id}, whose elements are chosen at random from Z_{f_u}. Lastly, $\mathcal{C}$ chooses an integer $w' \in Z_{f_v}$ and vector $\boldsymbol{W} = (w_j)$ of length n_m, whose elements are chosen at random from Z_{f_v}. We define the following two pairs of functions for an identity $id = (id_1, \ldots, id_{n_{id}}) \in \{0,1\}^{n_{id}}$ and a message $\pi = (\pi_1, \ldots, \pi_{n_m}) \in \{0,1\}^{n_m}$ respectively:

$$F(id) = x' + \sum_{i=1}^{n_{id}} x_i^{id_i} \quad \text{and} \quad J(id) = p - f_u k_u + y' + \sum_{i=1}^{n_{id}} y_i^{id_i},$$

$$K(\pi) = z' + \sum_{j=1}^{n_m} z_j^{\pi_j} \quad \text{and} \quad L(\pi) = p - f_v k_v + w' + \sum_{j=1}^{n_m} w_j^{\pi_j}.$$

Let $c_1^* = g^c$ and $t^* = H_1(c_1^*)$. $\mathcal{C}$ constructs a set of public parameters for the IBSC scheme by making the following assignments:

$$w = g^b, z = \hat{e}(g^a, g^b)$$
$$u' = (g^a)^{p - f_u k_u + y'}(g^b)^{-t^*} g^{x'}, u_i = g^{x_i}(g^a)^{y_i} \quad 1 \le i \le n_{id}$$
$$v' = (g^a)^{p - f_v k_v + w'} g^{z'}, v_j = g^{z_j}(g^a)^{w_j} \quad 1 \le j \le n_m$$

From the perspective of the adversary, the distribution of the public parameters is identical to the real construction. Furthermore, this assignment means that the master secret key will be $\alpha = g^{ab}$ and that for any identity id and a message π, the equations

$$H_3(id) = u' \prod_{i=1}^{n_{id}} u_i^{id_i} = g^{F(id)}(g^a)^{J(id)}(g^b)^{-t^*}$$

and

$$H_4(\pi) = v' \prod_{j=1}^{n_m} v_j^{\pi_j} = g^{K(\pi)}(g^a)^{L(\pi)}$$

hold. Let H_1 and H_2 are two collision resistant hash functions and $SE = (E, D)$ be a secure one-time symmetric-key encryption scheme with key space $\mathcal{K} = G_T$. $\mathcal{C}$ gives system parameters

$$par = \{G, G_T, \hat{e}, g, w, z, u', \mathbf{U}, v', \mathbf{V}, H_1, H_2, H_3, H_4, SE\}$$

to $\mathcal{A}$.

Phase 1: In this phase, $\mathcal{A}$ performs a polynomially bounded number of key extraction queries, signcryption queries and unsigncryption queries in an adaptive manner. $\mathcal{C}$ answers these queries in the following way.

– Key extraction queries: when $\mathcal{A}$ asks a query for the secret key of an identity id, if $J(id) \neq 0 \mod Z_{f_u}$, $\mathcal{C}$ chooses a random $s' \in Z_p^*$ and computes $sk_{id} = (sk_1, sk_2, sk_3)$ as follows.

$$sk_1 = (g^a)^{s' \cdot J(id)}(g^b)^{-\frac{F(id)}{J(id)} - s't^*}(g^{b^2})^{\frac{t^*}{J(id)}}g^{s' \cdot F(id)}$$
$$sk_2 = (g^b)^{-\frac{1}{J(id)}}g^{s'}$$
$$sk_3 = (g^{b^2})^{-\frac{1}{J(id)}}(g^b)^{s'}$$

Let $s = s' - \frac{b}{J(id)}$. Then we can see that (sk_1, sk_2, sk_3) is a valid secret key of id since

$$sk_1 = (g^a)^{s' \cdot J(id)}(g^b)^{-\frac{F(id)}{J(id)} - s't^*}(g^{b^2})^{\frac{t^*}{J(id)}}g^{s' \cdot F(id)}$$
$$= (g^a)^{s \cdot J(id) + b}(g^b)^{-\frac{F(id)}{J(id)} - st^* - \frac{bt^*}{J(id)}}(g^{b^2})^{\frac{t^*}{J(id)}}g^{s \cdot F(id) + \frac{b \cdot F(id)}{J(id)}}$$
$$= (g^a)^{s \cdot J(id) + b}(g^b)^{-st^*}g^{s \cdot F(id)} = g^{ab}((g^a)^{J(id)}(g^b)^{-t^*}g^{F(id)})^s$$
$$= g^{ab}(g^{F(id)}(g^a)^{J(id)}(g^b)^{-t^*})^s = \alpha \cdot H_3(id)^s$$
$$sk_2 = (g^b)^{-\frac{1}{J(id)}}g^{s'} = (g^b)^{-\frac{1}{J(id)}}g^{s + \frac{b}{J(id)}} = g^s$$
$$sk_3 = (g^{b^2})^{-\frac{1}{J(id)}}(g^b)^{s'} = (g^{b^2})^{-\frac{1}{J(id)}}(g^b)^{s + \frac{b}{J(id)}} = (g^b)^s = w^s$$

On the other hand, if $J(id) = 0 \mod Z_{f_u}$, the above computation cannot be performed and the simulator will abort.

– Signcryption queries: at any time $\mathcal{A}$ can perform a signcryption query for a plaintext m and identities id_A and id_B. If $J(id_A) \neq 0 \mod Z_{f_u}$, $\mathcal{C}$ computes the secret key sk_A corresponding to id_A by running a key extraction query algorithm and then can simply run the algorithm **Signcrypt**(m, sk_A, id_B). If $J(id_A) = 0 \mod Z_{f_u}$ and $J(id_B) \neq 0 \mod Z_{f_u}$, $\mathcal{C}$ first computes the secret key $sk_B = (sk_{B1}, sk_{B2}, sk_{B3}) = (\alpha \cdot H_3(id_B)^{s_B}, g^{s_B}, w^{s_B})$ corresponding to id_B and then follows the steps below.
  1. Choose $r \in Z_p^*$ randomly.
  2. Compute $c_1 = sk_{B2}$.

3. Compute $t = H_1(c_1)$.
4. Compute $c_2 = g^r$.
5. Compute $K = 1/\hat{e}(g^r, sk_{B2})$.
6. Compute $c_3 = E_K(m)$.
7. Compute $c_4 = g^r \cdot sk_{B1} \cdot sk_{B3}^t$.
8. Compute $\pi = H_2(c_1, c_2, c_3, c_4)$.
9. If $L(\pi) = 0 \bmod Z_{f_v}$, proceed to next step, else go to step 1.
10. Compute $c_5 = sk_{B1} \cdot H_3(id_A)^r \cdot (sk_{B2})^{K(\pi)} \cdot sk_{B3}^t$.

$\mathcal{C}$ sends $(c_1, c_2, c_3, c_4, c_5)$ to $\mathcal{A}$. We show the correctness of this simulation. Since $L(\pi) = 0 \bmod Z_{f_v}$, we have $H_4(\pi) = g^{K(\pi)}$. So we have

$$
\begin{aligned}
\hat{e}(c_5, g) &= \hat{e}(sk_{B1} \cdot H_3(id_A)^r \cdot (sk_{B2})^{K(\pi)} \cdot sk_{B3}^t, g) \\
&= \hat{e}(\alpha \cdot H_3(id_B)^{s_B} \cdot H_3(id_A)^r \cdot (g^{s_B})^{K(\pi)} \cdot (w^{s_B})^t, g) \\
&= \hat{e}(\alpha, g) \cdot \hat{e}(H_3(id_A), g^r) \cdot \hat{e}(g^{K(\pi)} \cdot H_3(id_B) \cdot w^t, g^{s_B}) \\
&= z \cdot \hat{e}(H_3(id_A), c_2) \cdot \hat{e}(H_4(\pi) \cdot H_3(id_B) \cdot w^t, c_1).
\end{aligned}
$$

That is, Eq.(1) holds. In addition, we have

$$
K = \frac{\hat{e}(c_1, sk_{B1} \cdot sk_{B3}^t)}{\hat{e}(c_4, sk_{B2})} = \frac{\hat{e}(sk_{B2}, sk_{B1} \cdot sk_{B3}^t)}{\hat{e}(g^r \cdot sk_{B1} \cdot sk_{B3}^t, sk_{B2})} = \frac{1}{\hat{e}(g^r, sk_{B2})}.
$$

That is, Eq.(2) holds. If $J(id_A) = 0 \bmod Z_{f_u}$ and $J(id_B) = 0 \bmod Z_{f_u}$, $\mathcal{C}$ fails and stops.

- Unsigncryption queries: at any time $\mathcal{A}$ can perform an unsigncryption query for a ciphertext $c = (c_1, c_2, c_3, c_4, c_5)$ for identities id_A and id_B. $\mathcal{C}$ first checks if $c_1 = c_1^*$ holds. If $c_1 = c_1^*$, the simulation aborts. Otherwise $\mathcal{C}$ follows the steps below.
  1. Compute $\pi = H_2(c_1, c_2, c_3, c_4)$ and $t = H_1(c_1)$.
  2. Check if the following equation holds:

$$
\hat{e}(c_5, g) = z \cdot \hat{e}(H_3(id_A), c_2) \cdot \hat{e}(H_4(\pi) \cdot H_3(id_B) \cdot w^t, c_1). \tag{3}
$$

If Eq.(3) does not hold, $\mathcal{C}$ rejects the ciphertext. Otherwise, $\mathcal{C}$ does the following step 3 or step 4.

  3. If $J(id_B) \neq 0 \bmod Z_{f_u}$, $\mathcal{C}$ first computes the $sk_B = (sk_{B1}, sk_{B2}, sk_{B3})$ corresponding to id_B by running the key extraction query algorithm. Then $\mathcal{C}$ computes

$$
K = \frac{\hat{e}(c_1, sk_{B1} \cdot sk_{B3}^t)}{\hat{e}(c_4, sk_{B2})}
$$

and returns the message $m = D_K(c_3)$ to $\mathcal{A}$.

  4. If $J(id_B) = 0 \bmod Z_{f_u}$, $\mathcal{C}$ computes

$$
K = \hat{e}(\frac{c_4}{c_1^{F(id_B)}}, g^a)^{(t-t^*)^{-1}} \tag{4}
$$

and returns the message $m = D_K(c_3)$.

The correctness of Eq.(4) can be verified by the following equations.

$$K = \hat{e}\left(\frac{c_4}{c_1^{F(id_B)}}, g^a\right)^{(t-t^*)^{-1}} = \hat{e}\left(\frac{(H_3(id_B) \cdot w^t)^r}{c_1^{F(id_B)}}, g^a\right)^{(t-t^*)^{-1}}$$

$$= \hat{e}\left(\frac{(g^{F(id_B)}(g^b)^{-t^*}(g^b)^t)^r}{g^{r \cdot F(id_B)}}, g^a\right)^{(t-t^*)^{-1}}$$

$$= \hat{e}((g^b)^{(t-t^*)}, g^a)^{r(t-t^*)^{-1}}$$

$$= \hat{e}(g^b, g^a)^r = z^r$$

Challenge: After the number of queries in Phase 1, $\mathcal{A}$ outputs two plaintexts m_0 and m_1 together with two identities id_A^* and id_B^* on which it wishes to be challenged. $\mathcal{C}$ chooses a random bit γ from $\{0, 1\}$ and signcrypts m_γ. If $J(id_A^*) = 0 \bmod Z_{f_u}$, then $\mathcal{C}$ fails and stops. Otherwise, it computes the secret key $sk_A^* = (sk_{A1}^*, sk_{A2}^*, sk_{A3}^*)$ corresponding to id_A^* by running the key extraction query algorithm. If $J(id_B^*) \neq 0 \bmod Z_{f_u}$ or $L(\pi^*) \neq 0 \bmod Z_{f_v}$, then $\mathcal{C}$ fails and stops. Otherwise, the ciphertext $c^* = (c_1^*, c_2^*, c_3^*, c_4^*, c_5^*)$ of m_γ can be constructed as follows:

1. Compute $c_1^* = g^c$.
2. Compute $t^* = H_1(c_1^*)$.
3. Compute $c_2^* = sk_{A2}^*$.
4. Compute $K = T$.
5. Compute $c_3^* = E_K(m_\gamma)$.
6. Compute $c_4^* = (g^c)^{F(id_B^*)}$.
7. Compute $\pi^* = H_2(c_1^*, c_2^*, c_3^*, c_4^*)$.
8. Compute $c_5^* = sk_{A1}^* \cdot (g^c)^{K(\pi^*)} \cdot c_4^*$.

Here T is $\mathcal{C}$'s candidate for the mDBDH problem. $\mathcal{C}$ sends the ciphertext c^* to $\mathcal{A}$

Phase 2: $\mathcal{A}$ can ask a polynomially bounded number of queries adaptively again as in Phase 1. This time, it cannot make a key extraction query on id_B^* and cannot make an unsigncryption query on c^* to obtain the corresponding plaintext.

Guess: The adversary $\mathcal{A}$ produces a bit $\gamma' \in \{0, 1\}$. If $\gamma' = \gamma$, $\mathcal{C}$ returns 1 that denotes $T = \hat{e}(g, g)^{abc}$, otherwise returns 0 that denotes $T \neq \hat{e}(g, g)^{abc}$.

This completes the simulation of the attacks game of IBSC between $\mathcal{C}$ and $\mathcal{A}$.

Now we analyze the success probability of $\mathcal{C}$. We adopted the Shoup's technique [28] which define a sequence of games. We will use the following useful lemma from [29].

Lemma 1. *Let E, E', and F be events defined on a probability space such that $\Pr[E \wedge \neg F] = \Pr[E' \wedge \neg F]$. Then we have*

$$|\Pr[E] - \Pr[E']| \leq \Pr[F].$$

The sequence of games starts from game G_0 to game G_7, where G_0 is the original attack game and G_7 gives no advantage to $\mathcal{A}$. Let E_i be the event that $\gamma' = \gamma$ in the game G_i for $0 \leq i \leq 7$. Then, we have

$$Adv(\mathcal{A}) = |\Pr[E_0] - 1/2|$$

and the sequence of games are described as follows.

Game G_1 (Eliminate the correct guess of c_1 in Phase 1). In this game, we modify game G_0 by reject an unsigncryption query for a ciphertext $c = (c_1, c_2, c_3, c_4, c_5)$ in Phase 1 if $c_1 = c_1^*$. $\mathcal{C}$ fails and stops. Since $\mathcal{A}$ has no information about $c_1 = c_1^*$ from the challenge ciphertext c^*, the probability of this type of ciphertext submitted by the adversary $\mathcal{A}$ is at most $\frac{q_u}{p}$. So, by Lemma 1, we have $|\Pr[E_1] - \Pr[E_0]| \le \frac{q_u}{p}$.

Game G_2 (Eliminate hash collision of H_1). In this game, we modify game G_1 by reject an unsigncryption query for a ciphertext $c = (c_1, c_2, c_3, c_4, c_5)$ if $c_1 \ne c_1^*$ and $t = t^*$, where $t = H_1(c_1)$. In this case, $\mathcal{C}$ fails and stops. The probability of this rejection is negligible with the probability ϵ_{H_1} as the chance of finding $t = t^*$ with $c_1 \ne c_1^*$ is ϵ_{H_1}. So, by Lemma 1, we have $|\Pr[E_2] - \Pr[E_1]| \le \epsilon_{H_1}$.

Game G_3 (Eliminate hash collision of H_2). In this game, we modify game G_2 by reject an unsigncryption query for a ciphertext $c = (c_1, c_2, c_3, c_4, c_5)$ if $(c_1, c_2, c_3, c_4) \ne (c_1^*, c_2^*, c_3^*, c_4^*)$ and $\pi = \pi^*$, where $\pi = H_2(c_1, c_2, c_3, c_4)$. In this case, $\mathcal{C}$ fails and stops. The probability of this rejection is negligible with the probability ϵ_{H_2} as the chance of finding $\pi = \pi^*$ with $(c_1, c_2, c_3, c_4) \ne (c_1^*, c_2^*, c_3^*, c_4^*)$ is ϵ_{H_2}. So, by Lemma 1, we have $|\Pr[E_3] - \Pr[E_2]| \le \epsilon_{H_2}$.

Game G_4 (Eliminate $J(id) = 0 \bmod Z_{f_u}$ in key extraction query). In this game, we modify game G_3 by reject a key extraction query for an identity id if $J(id) = 0 \bmod Z_{f_u}$. $\mathcal{C}$ fails and stops. The probability of this type of identity submitted by $\mathcal{A}$ is at most $\frac{q_k}{p}$. So, by Lemma 1, we have $|\Pr[E_4] - \Pr[E_3]| \le \frac{q_k}{p}$.

Game G_5 (Eliminate $J(id_A) = 0 \bmod Z_{f_u}$ and $J(id_B) = 0 \bmod Z_{f_u}$ in signcryption query). In this game, we modify game G_4 by reject a signcryption query for a plaintext m and identities id_A and id_B if $J(id_A) = 0 \bmod Z_{f_u}$ and $J(id_B) = 0 \bmod Z_{f_u}$. $\mathcal{C}$ fails and stops. The probability of this type of identity submitted by $\mathcal{A}$ is at most $\frac{q_s}{p^2}$. So, by Lemma 1, we have $|\Pr[E_5] - \Pr[E_4]| \le \frac{q_s}{p^2}$.

Game G_6 (Eliminate $J(id_A^*) = 0 \bmod Z_{f_u}$ or $J(id_B^*) \ne 0 \bmod Z_{f_u}$ or $L(\pi^*) \ne 0 \bmod Z_{f_v}$ in challenge phase). In this game, we modify game G_5 by reject an challenge for two paintexts m_0, m_1 and two identities id_A^* and id_B^* in challenge phase if $J(id_A^*) = 0 \bmod Z_{f_u}$ or $J(id_B^*) \ne 0 \bmod Z_{f_u}$ or $L(\pi^*) \ne 0 \bmod Z_{f_v}$. $\mathcal{C}$ fails and stops. The probability of this type of m_0, m_1 and id_A^*, id_B^* submitted by $\mathcal{A}$ is at most $\frac{3}{p}$. So, by Lemma 1, we have $|\Pr[E_6] - \Pr[E_5]| \le \frac{3}{p}$.

Game G_7 (Modify the challenge ciphertext). In this game, we modify game G_6 by replacing c_3^* with $E_T(m_\gamma)$ (T is a random element in G_T) in challenge phase. Since $E_T(m_\gamma)$ is independent of the challenge bit γ and no information about γ is given to $\mathcal{A}$. Hence $\Pr[E_7] = 1/2$. Because game G_7 and game G_6 are equal unless $\mathcal{A}$ can distinguish $e(g, g)^{abc}$ from the random element T in G_T. Therefore, we have $|\Pr[E_7] - \Pr[E_6]| \le \epsilon_{mdbdh}$.

Combine the results from the above games, we have

$$\epsilon_{sc} \le \epsilon_{mdbdh} + \epsilon_{H_1} + \epsilon_{H_2} + \frac{q_k + q_u + 3}{p} + \frac{q_s}{p^2}.$$

This completes the proof of Theorem 1.

B   Proof of Theorem 2

Proof. The proof of this theorem proceeds by reductionist proof. If an adversary $\mathcal{F}$ is able to break the $(\epsilon_{sc}, t, q_k, q_s, q_u)$-EUF-CMA security in our IBSC scheme, then one can construct an algorithm $\mathcal{C}$ that can break $(\epsilon_{sc}, t', q_k, q_s)$-EUF-CMA security in Paterson and Schuldt's signature scheme [22]. We first review Paterson and Schuldt's signature scheme to make our proof clear.

Let $id = (id_1, \ldots, id_{n_{id}}) \in \{0,1\}^{n_{id}}$ be an identity and $\pi = (\pi_1, \ldots, \pi_{n_m}) \in \{0,1\}^{n_m}$ be a message. Here n_{id} is the number of bits required to represent an identity id and n_m is the number of bits required to represent a message π. Paterson and Schuldt's signature scheme consists of the following four algorithms.

- **Setup:** Given a security parameter k, the PKG chooses two multiplicative cyclic groups G and G_T of prime order p, a generator g of G and a bilinear map $\hat{e} : G \times G \to G_T$. The PKG chooses $\delta \in Z_p^*$ and $g_2 \in G$ randomly and computes $g_1 = g^\delta$. Additionally, the PKG chooses random values $u', v' \in G$ and vectors $\boldsymbol{U} = (u_i)$, $\boldsymbol{V} = (v_i)$ of length n_{id} and n_m, respectively, whose elements are chosen at random from G. We also need a hash function $H_2 : \{0,1\}^* \to \{0,1\}^{n_m}$. Two functions $H_3 : \{0,1\}^{n_{id}} \to G$ and $H_4 : \{0,1\}^{n_m} \to G$ are defined as follows, respectively.

$$H_3(id) = u' \prod_{i=1}^{n_{id}} u_i^{id_i} \quad \text{and} \quad H_4(\pi) = v' \prod_{i=1}^{n_m} v_i^{\pi_i}$$

The PKG publishes system parameters

$$par_{ps} = \{G, G_T, \hat{e}, g, g_1, g_2, u', \boldsymbol{U}, v', \boldsymbol{V}, H_2, H_3, H_4\}$$

and keeps the master secret key g_2^δ to itself.
- **Extract:** Given an identity id, the PKG chooses $s \in Z_p^*$ randomly and computes the secret key sk_{id} as follows.

$$sk_{id} = (sk_1, sk_2) = (g_2^\delta \cdot H_3(id)^s, g^s)$$

- **Sign:** To sign a message m, the signer with identity id follows the steps below.
  1. Choose $r \in Z_p^*$ randomly.
  2. Compute $c_1 = g^r$.
  3. Compute $c_2 = sk_2$.
  4. Compute $\pi = H_2(m)$.
  5. Compute $c_5 = sk_1 \cdot H_4(\pi)^r$.
  The signature of message m is $c = (c_1, c_2, c_5)$.
- **Verify:** A verifier accepts c if and only if the following equation holds:

$$\hat{e}(c_5, g) = \hat{e}(g_2, g_1) \cdot \hat{e}(H_3(id), c_2) \cdot \hat{e}(H_4(\pi), c_1).$$

Now we begin to describe the simulation process of the EUF-CMA game between $\mathcal{C}$ and $\mathcal{F}$.

Initial: Given Paterson and Schuldt's signature system parameters $par_{ps} = \{G, G_T, \hat{e}, g, g_1, g_2, u', \boldsymbol{U}, v', \boldsymbol{V}, H_2, H_3, H_4\}$, $\mathcal{C}$ chooses $x \in Z_p^*$ randomly and sets $w = g^x$ and $z = \hat{e}(g_1, g_2)$. Let $H_1 : G \to Z_p^*$ be one hash function and $SE = (E, D)$ be a secure one-time symmetric-key encryption scheme with key space $\mathcal{K} = G_T$. $\mathcal{C}$ gives $par = \{G, G_T, \hat{e}, g, w, z, u', \boldsymbol{U}, v', \boldsymbol{V}, H_1, H_2, H_3, H_4, SE\}$ to $\mathcal{F}$.

Attack: When $\mathcal{F}$ makes a key extraction for an identity id, $\mathcal{C}$ make a key extraction query on id to its own key extraction oracle to obtain (sk_1, sk_2). Then $\mathcal{C}$ computes $sk_3 = sk_2^x = (g^s)^x = (g^x)^s = w^s$ and sends (sk_1, sk_2, sk_3) to $\mathcal{F}$. Since we set $z = \hat{e}(g_1, g_2) = \hat{e}(g^\delta, g_2) = \hat{e}(g, g_2^\delta)$, the master secret key g_2^δ in Paterson and Schuldt's signature scheme is equivalent to the master secret key α in our IBSC scheme. So, $g_2^\delta \cdot H_3(id)^s$ in Paterson and Schuldt's signature scheme is equivalent to $\alpha \cdot H_3(id)^s$ in our IBSC scheme. Thefore, the simulation of key extraction query is correct. When $\mathcal{F}$ makes a signcryption query for a plaintext m and identities id_A and id_B, $\mathcal{C}$ computes the secret key sk_A according to the above method and then simply runs the algorithm **Signcrypt**(m, sk_A, id_B). When $\mathcal{F}$ makes an unsigncryption query for a ciphertext c for identities id_A and id_B, $\mathcal{C}$ computes the secret key sk_B according to the above method and then simply runs the algorithm **Unsigncrypt**(c, id_A, sk_B).

Forgery: $\mathcal{F}$ outputs a forgery $c' = (c_1', c_2', c_3', c_4', c_5')$ for a new message m' for a sender id_A and a receiver id_B. $\mathcal{C}$ outputs $c'' = (c_1', c_2', c_5'/c_4')$ is a valid signature on a new message $m'' = H_2(c_1', c_2', c_3', c_4')$ for the sender id_A. Therefore, $\mathcal{C}$ is able to forge a signature for Paterson and Schuldt's signature scheme, which is contrary to the conclusion in [22]. Paterson and Schuldt's signature scheme is proved to be EUF-CMA secure under the computational Diffie-Hellman assumption [22].

Furthermore, it is easy to see that the time to forge Paterson and Schuldt's signature scheme is $t' = t + q_k C_k + q_s C_s + q_u C_u$.

This completes the proof of Theorem 2.

Toward Compact Public Key Encryption Based on CDH Assumption via Extended Twin DH Assumption

Yoshikazu Hanatani[1,2], Hirofumi Muratani[1], and Tomoko Yonemura[1]

[1] Toshiba Corporation,Komukai Toshiba-cho 1, Saiwai-ku,
Kawasaki-shi, Kanagawa 212-8582, Japan
yoshikazu.hanatani@toshiba.co.jp
[2] The University of Electro-Communications, Chofugaoka 1-5-1, Chofu-shi,
Tokyo 182-8585, Japan

Abstract. IND-CCA secure public key encryption schemes based on the CDH assumption in the standard model use a hardcore function as a key derivation function for a shared key. Therefore, many secret and public key size are necessary for sending a sufficiently long shared key. Yamada et al. [17,16] and Haralambiev et al. [12] proposed efficient public key encryption schemes based on the CDH assumption. Moreover, they proposed a method that drastically reduces the secret and the public key sizes by using a bilinear map, and they also proposed IND-CCA secure public key encryption based on the bilinear DH assumption. Unfortunately, many secret and public key sizes are still necessary in general cyclic groups that lack known efficient bilinear map.

In this paper, we propose a compact public key scheme based on the CDH assumption in the standard model. The public and secret key sizes are trivially reduced by sending several block of the ciphertext. By using batch verification, our scheme succeeded in reducing the ciphertext size compared with that in the case of the trivially extended scheme. To prove IND-CCA security of our scheme, we define a new computational assumption, namely, the extended hashed strong twin Diffie-Hellman assumption. Moreover, we construct an extended trapdoor test to simulate a decisional oracle, and prove that if the CDH assumption holds and the hash function is the hardcore function for DH key, then the extended hashed strong twin DH assumption also holds. Our reducing technique is also applicable to other schemes [17,16,15] based on the CDH assumption.

Keywords: CDH Assumption, Extended Strong Twin DH Assumption, Extended Trapdoor Test, Public Key Encryption, KEM, IND-CCA Security.

1 Background

Nowadays, public key encryption schemes based on various computational assumptions are proposed. From the viewpoint of security, it is preferable that the computational assumptions are weak (i.e. practical). Construction of secure public key encryption under weaker assumptions is important, and is intensively studied.

Cramer and Shoup were the first to propose a practical public key encryption scheme [7] without the random oracle [2]. Moreover, they generalized the result, and proposed a universal hash proof system [8]. Unfortunately, their framework strongly depended on hardness of decisional assumptions (e.g. DDH assumption [3]).

X. Boyen and X. Chen (Eds.): ProvSec 2011, LNCS 6980, pp. 138–153, 2011.
© Springer-Verlag Berlin Heidelberg 2011

The CDH assumption [3], which is hardness of a search problem, is a weaker assumption than the DDH assumption. For a long time, construction of an IND-CCA secure public key encryption scheme based on the CDH assumption in the standard model was an open problem. Since 2008, Cash et al. [6] and Hanaoka et al. [11] have independently solved the open problem. Both schemes [6,11] use a hardcore function [10,5,4] as a key derivation function for a shared key. Therefore, in both schemes, many secret and public key sizes were necessary for sending a sufficiently long shared key (e.g. 128 bits).

Since 2010 Yamada et al. [17,16] and Haralambiev et al. [12] have independently proposed CDH assumption-based public key encryption schemes whose ciphertext sizes were constant, and both secret and public key sizes were reduced by improving the scheme of [6]. The public and secret key sizes of [17,12,16] were increased by the shared key size. On the other hand, schemes that drastically reduced public and secret key sizes by using bilinear map were also proposed [17,12,16], and their IND-CCA security was based on the bilinear DH assumption. Unfortunately, their reducing technique by the bilinear map does not apply to unknown general cyclic groups to computing of efficient bilinear maps.

Wee [15] proposed an extractable hash proof system, and presented the CDH-based public key encryption whose secret and public key sizes were constant, and whose ciphertext size depended on a shared key size. His construction offers a trade-off between the key sizes and the ciphertext size when compared with Halarambiev's scheme [12].

Many public and secret key sizes or many ciphertext size are necessary for the public key encryption schemes based on the CDH assumption. The sizes should be reduced to facilitate widespread use in real systems.

Our Contributions. In this paper, we propose a public key encryption scheme with shorter public and secret keys, which CCA-security can be proven in the standard model under the CDH assumption. We reduce public and secret key sizes and ciphertext size by combining the trade-off relation that Wee pointed out [15] and the batch verification technique [9,1]. Namely, our scheme achieves a milder trade-off relation between the keys sizes and the ciphertext size than other CDH-based schemes [6,12,17,16,15].

Our scheme is based on Haralambiev's scheme [12]. The ciphertext of Haralambiev's scheme is composed by one element for computing the shared key, and two elements for checking whether the element is correctly computed. Our scheme reduces public and secret key sizes that depend on the shared key size to half by increasing the element for computing the shared key to two. The trivially extended scheme has four elements for checking the ciphertext. Then, we reduce the number of elements of the ciphertext from four to three by using the batch verification. Therefore, our scheme is more efficient for sending two pairs of Haralambiev's ciphertext.

To prove IND-CCA security of our scheme, we introduce a new computational assumption as the extended hashed strong twin Diffie-Hellman assumption. Moreover, we construct an extended trapdoor test to simulate a decisional oracle, and prove that if the CDH assumption holds and the hash function is the hardcore function for DH key, then the extended hashed strong twin DH assumption also holds. Then we give the proof that our scheme satisfies IND-CCA security under the CDH assumption in the standard model.

Our reducing technique can easily be applied to other schemes such as [17,16,15].

Organization. The remainder of this is organized as follows. In section 2, we introduce the definition of IND-CCA and computational assumptions. In section 3, we define the extended hashed strong twin DH assumption, and prove that the assumption is equivalent to the CDH assumption. In section 4, we present the proposed scheme and give its security proof via the extended hashed strong twin DH assumption. In section 5, we compare our scheme and other schemes based on the CDH assumption. In section 6 we conclude.

2   Preliminary

In this section, we introduce the definition of KEM, its security model and the computational assumption.

2.1   Key Encapsulation Mechanism (KEM)

A KEM consists of the following three algorithms.

KeyGen: Takes the security parameter 1^k as input, and outputs a public key pk and a secret key sk.

Encapsulate: Takes a public key pk as input, and outputs (C, K) where C is a ciphertext and K is a shared key for data encryption.

Decapsulate: Takes the secret key sk, the public key pk, and a ciphertext C as input, and outputs a shared key K for data encryption.

2.2   IND-CCA Security for KEM

Indistinguishability against adaptive chosen ciphertext attack (IND-CCA security) for KEM is defined as the following game between an adversary $\mathcal{A}$ and a challenger C. Let q_D be the number of decryption queries.

Setup: C runs KeyGen(1^k), and obtains a public key pk and a secret key sk. Then C gives pk to $\mathcal{A}$.

Challenge: C runs Encapsulate(pk), and obtains (ψ^*, K^*). Next, C chooses $b \xleftarrow{R} \{0, 1\}$. C sets $K_0 \leftarrow K^*$ and sets K_1 as a random bit-string whose length is the same as K^*. Then, C sends the challenge ciphertext (ψ^*, K_b) to $\mathcal{A}$.

Decrypt: $\mathcal{A}$ adaptively queries a ciphertext ψ to C at most q_D times. Then C returns Decapsulate(sk, pk, ψ).

Guess: $\mathcal{A}$ guesses b, and outputs $b' \in \{0, 1\}$.

If $b' = b$ and ψ^* is never queried to C, $\mathcal{A}$ wins the game. We define IND-CCA advantage for KEM Π of $\mathcal{A}$ as

$$\text{AdvCCA}_{\Pi, \mathcal{A}} = |Pr[b' = b] - 1/2|.$$

Definition 1. *(IND-CCA security for KEM) We say that a KEM Π is an IND-CCA secure scheme, if for all PPT $\mathcal{A}$, $\text{AdvCCA}_{\Pi, \mathcal{A}}$ is negligible in terms of security parameter k.* □

2.3 Computational Diffie-Hellman Assumption

Let $\mathbb{G}$ be a multiplicative group generated by g with prime order q. Define

$$dh(X, Y) := Z, \text{ where } X = g^x, Y = g^y, \text{ and } Z = g^{xy}.$$

The computational Diffie-Hellman (CDH) problem is the problem of computing $dh(X, Y)$ where random $X, Y \in \mathbb{G}$.

Definition 2. *(CDH Assumption) We say that the CDH assumption holds on $\mathbb{G}$, if for all PPT $\mathcal{A}$, $\mathcal{A}$'s advantage $|\Pr[\mathcal{A}(g, X, Y) = dh(X, Y)]|$ is negligible in terms of security parameter k.* □

2.4 Hardcore Function for the Diffie-Hellman Key

Let $f_{gl} : \mathbb{G} \times \{0, 1\}^u \to \{0, 1\}^v$ be Goldreich-Levin's hardcore function [10] for $dh(X, Y)$ with randomness space $\{0, 1\}^u$ and range $\{0, 1\}^v$, where u and v are suitable integers depending on the given group representation.

The following version of the Goldreich-Levin theorem is given as the theorem 9 of [6]. The proof of this version involves combining the original analysis [10] with Shoup's self-correcter [13].

Theorem 1. *[6] Let $\mathbb{G}$ be a prime-order multiplicative group, and g be a generator of $\mathbb{G}$. Suppose that $\mathcal{A}_{gl}$ is a PPT algorithm such that $\mathcal{A}(g, X_1, Y, R, k)$ distinguishes $k = f_{gl}(dh(X_1, Y), R)$ from a uniform string with non-negligible advantage, for random $X_1, Y \in \mathbb{G}$ and random $R \in \{0, 1\}^u$. Then there exists a probabilistic polytime algorithm $\mathcal{A}_{dh}$ that computes $dh(X_1, Y)$ with non-negligible probability for random X_1, Y.* □

Other examples of hardcore functions for DH key are given in [5,4].

2.5 Target Collision-Resistant Hash Function

Let $\mathsf{TCR} : \mathbb{G} \to \mathbb{Z}_q$ be a hash function, and let $\mathcal{A}$ be an algorithm, and $\mathcal{A}$'s advantage $AdvTCR_{\mathcal{A}}$ be $\Pr[\mathsf{TCR}(c^*) = \mathsf{TCR}(c) \wedge c \neq c^* : c^* \leftarrow \mathbb{G}; c \leftarrow \mathcal{A}(c^*)]$.

Definition 3. *We say TCR is target collision-resistant hash function, if for all PPT $\mathcal{A}$, $\mathcal{A}$'s advantage is negligible in terms of security parameter k.* □

3 Extended Strong Twin Diffie-Hellman Assumption

In this section, we define new computational assumptions to which the strong twin DH assumption [6] is extended. They differ in terms of their decision oracles used by adversaries. The extended strong twin DH assumption is artificial, but it is reduced to the CDH assumption if the hash function is a hardcore function.

Definition 4. *(Extended Twin DH Predicate) For $X_1, X_2, \hat{Y}_1, \hat{Y}_2, \hat{Z}_1, \hat{Z}_2, \hat{Z}_3 \in \mathbb{G}$, $e \in [|\mathbb{G}|]$, define the predicate*

$$e2dhp(X_1, X_2, \hat{Y}_1, \hat{Y}_2, \hat{Z}_1, \hat{Z}_2, \hat{Z}_3, e) :=$$
$$(dh(X_1, \hat{Y}_1) = \hat{Z}_1 \wedge dh(X_2, \hat{Y}_2) = \hat{Z}_2 \wedge dh(X_1^e, \hat{Y}_2) \cdot dh(X_2, \hat{Y}_1) = \hat{Z}_3).$$

Definition 5. *(Extended Strong Twin DH Assumption)* $\mathcal{A}^O$ *is given random* $X_1, X_2, Y \overset{R}{\leftarrow}$ $\mathbb{G}$, *along with access to a decision oracle* O *for the predicate* $e2dhp(X_1, X_2, \cdot, \cdot, \cdot, \cdot, \cdot, \cdot)$, *which on input* $(\hat{Y}_1, \hat{Y}_2, \hat{Z}_1, \hat{Z}_2, \hat{Z}_3, e)$, *returns* $e2dhp(X_1, X_2, \hat{Y}_1, \hat{Y}_2, \hat{Z}_1, \hat{Z}_2, \hat{Z}_3, e)$. *Here,* $\mathcal{A}^O$ *chooses* e *from* $\mathbb{Z}_q$ *at random, and sends the same* e *to all oracle access.*

We say that extended strong twin DH assumption holds on $\mathbb{G}$, *if for all PPT* $\mathcal{A}^O$, $\mathcal{A}^O$*'s advantage* $|\Pr[\mathcal{A}^O(g, X_1, X_2, Y) = dh(X_1, Y)]|$ *is negligible in terms of security parameter* k. □

Definition 6. *(Extended Hashed Strong Twin Diffie-Hellman Assumption)* $\mathcal{A}^O$ *is given random* $X_1, X_2, Y \overset{R}{\leftarrow} \mathbb{G}$, *a hash function* $H: \mathbb{G} \rightarrow \{0,1\}^\nu$ *and* $L \in \{0,1\}^\nu$, *along with access to a decision oracle* O *for the predicate* $e2dhp(X_1, X_2, \cdot, \cdot, \cdot, \cdot, \cdot, \cdot)$, *which for input* $(\hat{Y}_1, \hat{Y}_2, \hat{Z}_1, \hat{Z}_2, \hat{Z}_3, e)$, *returns* $e2dhp(X_1, X_2, \hat{Y}_1, \hat{Y}_2, \hat{Z}_1, \hat{Z}_2, \hat{Z}_3, e)$. *Here,* $\mathcal{A}^O$ *chooses* e *from* $\mathbb{Z}_q$ *at random, and sends the same* e *to all oracle access. Let* $U_\nu \overset{R}{\leftarrow} \{0,1\}^\nu$ *be uniformly random.*

We say that extended hashed strong twin DH assumption holds on $\mathbb{G}$ *and* H, *if for all PPT* $\mathcal{A}^O$, $\mathcal{A}^O$*'s advantage*

$$|\Pr[\mathcal{A}^O(g, X_1, X_2, Y, H, H(dh(X_1, Y))) = 0] - \Pr[\mathcal{A}^O(g, X_1, X_2, Y, H, U_\nu)) = 0]|$$

is terms of negligible in security parameter k. □

We can evaluate $e2dhp(X_1, X_2, \hat{Y}_1, \hat{Y}_2, \hat{Z}_1, \hat{Z}_2, \hat{Z}_3, e)$ for each $(\hat{Y}_1, \hat{Y}_2, \hat{Z}_1, \hat{Z}_2, \hat{Z}_3, e)$ by using (x_1, y_1) where $X_1 = g^{x_1}, X_2 = g^{x_2}$. The following theorem 2 is an extended version of the tarpdoor test [6]. Theorem 2 gives the method of computing the same value as $e2dhp(X_1, X_2, \hat{Y}_1, \hat{Y}_2, \hat{Z}_1, \hat{Z}_2, \hat{Z}_3, e)$ with overwhelming probability without x_1, x_2.

Remark 1. The theorem 2 holds even if $\mathcal{A}^O$ chooses e from $\mathbb{Z}_q$ at arbitrary distribution, and sends different e in each oracle access. We restricted $\mathcal{A}^O$ by the definition 5 and 6, because the restricted $\mathcal{A}^O$ is sufficient to prove that our scheme is IND-CCA secure under the CDH assumption.

Theorem 2. *(Extended Trapdoor Test) Let* $\mathbb{G}$ *be a multiplicative group with prime order* q, *and* g *is a generator of* $\mathbb{G}$. *Suppose* X_1, r, s, e *are mutually independent random variables, where* X_1 *takes values in* $\mathbb{G}$, *and each of* r, s, e *is uniformly distributed over* $\mathbb{Z}_q$, *and define the random variable* $X_2 \leftarrow g^s/X_1^r$. *Further, suppose that* $\hat{Y}_1, \hat{Y}_2, \hat{Z}_1, \hat{Z}_2, \hat{Z}_3$ *are random variables taking values in* $\mathbb{G}$, *each of which is defined as some function of* X_1 *and* X_2. *Then we have:*

1. X_2 *is uniformly distributed over* $\mathbb{G}$;
2. X_1 *and* X_2 *are independent;*
3. *If* $X_1 = g^{x_1}$ *and* $X_2 = g^{x_2}$, *then the probability that the truth value of*

$$\hat{Z}_1^r \hat{Z}_2^{e/r} \hat{Z}_3 = \hat{Y}_1^s \hat{Y}_2^{es/r}, \tag{1}$$

does not agree with the truth value of

$$\hat{Z}_1 = \hat{Y}_1^{x_1} \wedge \hat{Z}_2 = \hat{Y}_2^{x_2} \wedge \hat{Z}_3 = \hat{Y}_1^{x_2} \hat{Y}_2^{ex_1} \tag{2}$$

is at most $2/q$, *if the equation (2) holds, then the equation (1) certainly holds.* □

Proof. $s = rx_1 + x_2$ because $X_2 = g^s/X_1^r$. The integers r and s are chosen uniformly at random from $\mathbb{Z}_q$, then X_2 is uniformly distributed over $\mathbb{G}$. And X_1, r, s are mutually independent random variables, then X_1, X_2, r are mutually independent.

To prove 3., we consider the condition on values of X_1 and X_2 are fixed. In the resulting conditional probability space, r is uniformly distributed over $\mathbb{Z}_q$, whereas $e, x_1, x_2, \hat{Y}_1, \hat{Y}_2, \hat{Z}_1, \hat{Z}_2$, and $\hat{Z}_3$ are fixed. If the equation (2) holds, then by multiplying together the three equations in the equation (2), we see that the equation (1) certainly holds. Conversely, if the equation (2) does not hold, we show that the equation (1) holds with probability of at most $2/q$. Transforming the equation (1) by using $s = rx_1 + x_2$, we obtain

$$\left(\frac{\hat{Z}_1}{\hat{Y}_1^{x_1}}\right)^r \left(\frac{\hat{Z}_2}{\hat{Y}_2^{x_2}}\right)^{e/r} = \frac{\hat{Y}_1^{x_2}\hat{Y}_2^{ex_1}}{\hat{Z}_3}. \tag{3}$$

If $\hat{Z}_1 = \hat{Y}_1^{x_1}$, $\hat{Z}_2 = \hat{Y}_2^{x_2}$, and $\hat{Z}_3 \neq \hat{Y}_1^{x_2}\hat{Y}_2^{ex_1}$, then the equation (3) does not hold. Therefore, we consider the case $(\hat{Z}_1 \neq \hat{Y}_1^{x_1}, \hat{Z}_2 \neq \hat{Y}_2^{x_2})$ or $(\hat{Z}_1 \neq \hat{Y}_1^{x_1}, \hat{Z}_2 = \hat{Y}_2^{x_2})$ or $(\hat{Z}_1 = \hat{Y}_1^{x_1}, \hat{Z}_2 \neq \hat{Y}_2^{x_2})$. Observe that the equation (3) is equivalent to

$$\left(\left(\frac{\hat{Z}_1}{\hat{Y}_1^{x_1}}\right)^{r^2} \cdot \left(\frac{\hat{Z}_2}{\hat{Y}_2^{x_2}}\right)^e\right)^{1/r} = \frac{\hat{Y}_1^{x_2}\hat{Y}_2^{ex_1}}{\hat{Z}_3}. \tag{4}$$

In the cases of $(\hat{Z}_1 \neq \hat{Y}_1^{x_1}, \hat{Z}_2 = \hat{Y}_2^{x_2})$ or $(\hat{Z}_1 = \hat{Y}_1^{x_1}, \hat{Z}_2 \neq \hat{Y}_2^{x_2})$, the left-hand side of the equation (4) is a random element of $\mathbb{G}$ since r is uniformly distributed over $\mathbb{Z}_q$, but the right-hand side is a fixed element of $\mathbb{G}$. Therefore, the equation (3) holds with probability $1/q$ in these cases.

Next, we consider the case of $(\hat{Z}_1 \neq \hat{Y}_1^{x_1}, \hat{Z}_2 \neq \hat{Y}_2^{x_2})$. r^2 is uniformly distributed over the set of quadratic residues $QR_q = \{r^2 | r \in \mathbb{Z}_q\}$ on $\mathbb{Z}_q$. The number of the elements of QR_q is $q/2$, then $(\hat{Z}_1/\hat{Y}_1^{x_1})^{r^2}$ in the left-hand side of the equation (4) takes $(q-1)/2$ kinds of random values over $\mathbb{G}$. That means the left-hand side of the equation (4) takes at least $q/2$ kinds of random values over $\mathbb{G}$, even if $(\hat{Z}_2/\hat{Y}_2^{x_2})^e$ in the left-hand side of the equation (4) is fixed. Thus, the equation (3) holds with probability of at most $2/q$ in this case.

Therefore, the probability that the equation (1) holds but the equation (2) does not hold is at most $2/q$. ∎

The following theorem is led from the theorem 2 and the theorem 1. The theorem 3 means the CDH assumption holds if and only if the extended hashed strong DH assumption holds where the hash function is a hardcore function for the DH key.

Theorem 3. *Let $\mathbb{G}$ be a prime-order multiplicative group, and g is a generator of $\mathbb{G}$. Let $X_1, X_2, Y \overset{R}{\leftarrow} \mathbb{G}$ be random group elements, $R \overset{R}{\leftarrow} \{0,1\}^\nu$, and let $K = f_{gl}(dh(X_1, Y), R)$. Let $U_\nu \overset{R}{\leftarrow} \{0,1\}^\nu$ be uniformly random. Suppose there exists a PPT algorithm $\mathcal{A}$ having access to an oracle computing $e2dhp(X_1, X_2, \cdot, \cdot, \cdot, \cdot, \cdot, \cdot)$ and distinguishing the distributions*

$$\Delta_{\mathsf{dh}} = (g, X_1, X_2, Y, K, R) \text{ and } \Delta_{\mathsf{rand}} = (g, X_1, X_2, Y, U_\nu, R)$$

with non-negligible advantage. Then there exists a PPT algorithm $\mathcal{B}$ computing $dh(X_1, Y)$ on input (g, X_1, Y) with non-negligible success probability.   □

Proof sketch. Let $\mathcal{A}_{gl}$ be a PPT algorithm of the theorem 1. $\mathcal{A}$ of the theorem 3 is $\mathcal{A}_{gl}$ that additionally gets as input a random $X_2 \in \mathbb{G}$ and has access to oracle computing $2dhp(X_1, X_2, \hat{Y}_1, \hat{Y}_2, \hat{Z}_1, \hat{Z}_2, \hat{Z}_3, e)$ for $(\hat{Y}_1, \hat{Y}_2, \hat{Z}_1, \hat{Z}_2, \hat{Z}_3, e)$ of its choosing. To prove the theorem 3, it is sufficient that we can compute X_2 and $2dhp(X_1, X_2, \cdot, \cdot, \cdot, \cdot, \cdot, \cdot)$ by using (g, X, Y), which is the input of $\mathcal{B}$.

$\mathcal{B}$ chooses $r, s \in \mathbb{Z}_q$ uniformly at random, and computes $X_2 \leftarrow g^s/X_1^r$. When $\mathcal{A}$ sends $(\hat{Y}_1, \hat{Y}_2, \hat{Z}_1, \hat{Z}_2, \hat{Z}_3, e)$ to the oracle, $\mathcal{B}$ checks whether $\hat{Z}_1^s \hat{Z}_2^{e/r} \hat{Z}_3 = \hat{Y}_1^s \hat{Y}_2^{es/r}$ holds or not, and returns the results. From the theorem 2, $\mathcal{B}$ can correctly answer with overwhelming probability.   ∎

The following theorem is also led from the theorem 2. The theorem 4 means the CDH assumption holds if and only if the extended strong DH assumption holds. The proof of the theorem 4 is almost the same as the proof of the theorem 3.

Theorem 4. *Let $\mathbb{G}$ be a prime-order multiplicative group, and g is a generator of $\mathbb{G}$. Let $X_1, X_2, Y \xleftarrow{R} \mathbb{G}$ be random group elements. Suppose there exists a PPT algorithm $\mathcal{A}$ having access to an oracle computing $e2dhp(X_1, X_2, \cdot, \cdot, \cdot, \cdot, \cdot, \cdot)$, and $\mathcal{A}$ computes $dh(X_1, Y)$ with non-negligible advantage. Then there exists a PPT algorithm $\mathcal{B}$ computing $dh(X_1, Y)$ on input (g, X_1, Y) with non-negligible success probability.*   □

4   Proposed Scheme

We propose a key encapsulation mechanism to reduce the number of public and secret keys by increasing the number of elements for generating a shared key from 1 to 2. Haralambiev's scheme [12] can send a shared key of at most nv bits by one ciphertext, and our scheme can also send a shared key of at most nv bits by one ciphertext. We prove CCA security of our scheme under the extended strong hashed twin DH assumption. From the theorem 1 and 3, we can show that the extended twin DH assumption is reduced to the CDH assumption. Therefore, our scheme can be reduced to the CDH assumption. For simplicity, we assume n is even number as follows.

4.1   Algorithms (KEM$_{e2dh}$)

Let g be a generator of a multiplicative group $\mathbb{G}$ whose order is prime q. Let TCR : $\{0, 1\}^* \leftarrow \mathbb{Z}_q$ be a target collision-resistant hash function, and $f_{gl} : \mathbb{G} \times \{0, 1\}^u \rightarrow \{0, 1\}^v)$ be a hardcore function for the DH key.

KeyGen(1^k). Choose a random generator $g \xleftarrow{R} \mathbb{G}$, randomness $R \leftarrow \{0, 1\}^v$ for f_{gl}, and TCR. Compute $n = \kappa/v$ where κ is a shared key size. Then choose $x, x', y, y', z_i \xleftarrow{R} \mathbb{Z}_q$, and compute $X \leftarrow g^x, X' \leftarrow g^{x'}, Y \leftarrow g^y; Y' \leftarrow g^{y'}, Z_i \leftarrow g^{z_i}$ for all i such that $1 \le i \le n/2$. Set a public key $\mathsf{pk} = (g, X, X', Y, Y', \{Z_i\}_{i=1,...,n/2}, R, \mathsf{TCR})$ and a secret key $\mathsf{sk} = (x, x', y, y', \{z_i\}_{i=1,...,n/2})$, and return $(\mathsf{pk}, \mathsf{sk})$.

Encapsulate(pk). On input of a public key pk, choose $r_1, r_2 \overset{R}{\leftarrow} \mathbb{Z}_q$ uniformly at random. Then, compute $C_0 \leftarrow g^{r_1}, \hat{C}_0 \leftarrow g^{r_2}, t \leftarrow \mathsf{TCR}(C_0, \hat{C}_0), C_1 \leftarrow (X^t X')^{r_1}; \hat{C}_1 \leftarrow (Y^t Y')^{r_2}$, $C_2 \leftarrow (X^t X')^{r_2} (Y^t Y')^{r_1}$, and $k_{1,i} \leftarrow f_{gl}(Z_i^{r_1}, R), k_{2,i} \leftarrow f_{gl}(Z_i^{r_2}, R)$ for all i such that $1 \leq i \leq n/2$. Set $K \leftarrow k_{1,1} \| k_{2,1} \| \ldots \| k_{1,n/2} \| k_{2,n/2}$, and return a ciphertext $(C_0, \hat{C}_0, C_1, \hat{C}_1, C_2)$ and a shared key K.

Decapsulation(sk, $(C_0, \hat{C}_0, C_1, \hat{C}_1, C_2)$). Compute $t \leftarrow \mathsf{TCR}(C_0, \hat{C}_0)$. Check whether $C_1 = C_0^{xt+x'}, \hat{C}_1 = \hat{C}_0^{yt+y'}$ and $C_2 = C_0^{yt+y'} \hat{C}_0^{xt+x'}$ holds. If the equation does not hold, the decapsulate algorithm outputs $\perp$ and stop. Else compute $k_{1,i} \leftarrow f_{gl}(C_0^{z_i}, R); k_{2,i} \leftarrow f_{gl}(\hat{C}_0^{z_i}, R)$; for all i such that $1 \leq i \leq n/2$, and assign $K \leftarrow k_{1,1} \| k_{2,1} \| \ldots \| k_{1,n/2} \| k_{2,n/2}$, and return K.

Remark 2. We can construct other scheme by applying batch verification technique to other part of a ciphertext, e.g. its ciphertext is $C_0 \leftarrow g^{r_1}, \hat{C}_0 \leftarrow g^{r_2}, C_1 \leftarrow (X^t X')^{r_1}$, $\hat{C}_1 \leftarrow (X^t X')^{r_2}, C_2 \leftarrow (Y^t Y')^{r_1 + r_2}$, but we cannot construct corresponding trapdoor test. Therefore, we cannot prove its IND-CCA security under the CDH assumption even if we can prove its IND-CCA security under another modified twin DH assumption.

4.2 Security

Theorem 5. *Let* TCR *be a target collision-resistant hash function, and suppose that the extended strong hashed twin DH assumption holds on* $\mathbb{G}$. *Then* KEM_{e2dh} *is IND-CCA secure.*   □

Proof. We give the security proof as sequences of games[14]. We treat Setup, Challenge, and Decrypt (Sec.2.2) as a key generation oracle KG, a challenge oracle E, and a decryption oracle D, respectively. Let S_i be an event such that $\mathcal{A}$ did not query the challenge ciphertext to D and $b^* = b$ in the game i.

Game 0. Game 0 is the original attack game of KEM_{e2dh} by IND-CCA adversary $\mathcal{A}$. The adversary $\mathcal{A}$ is allowed to access the key generation oracle KG, the challenge oracle E, and the decryption oracle D. KG runs KeyGen of KEM_{e2dh}, and generates the public key pk and the secret key sk, and gives pk to $\mathcal{A}$. E chooses random $b \overset{R}{\leftarrow} \{0, 1\}$ and $K_1 \overset{R}{\leftarrow} \{0, 1\}^{nv}$, and computes $((C_0^*, \hat{C}_0^*, C_1^*, \hat{C}_1^*, C_2^*), K_0)$ by running Encapsulation(pk) of KEM_{e2dh}, and returns the challenge ciphertext $((C_0^*, \hat{C}_0^*, C_1^*, \hat{C}_1^*, C_2^*), K_b)$. D receives $(C_0, \hat{C}_0, C_1 \hat{C}_1, C_2)$ from $\mathcal{A}$, computes K by running Decapsulation(sk, ψ) of KEM_{e2dh}, and returns K. Finally $\mathcal{A}$ outputs $b^* \in \{0, 1\}$.

From the definition of IND-CCA game(Sec.2.2), the following equation holds.

$$\left| \Pr[S_0] - \frac{1}{2} \right| = \mathsf{AdvCCA}_{\mathsf{KEM}_{e2dh}, \mathcal{A}}.$$

Game 1. We transform D of the game 0 so that D returns $\perp$ when $(C_0, \hat{C}_0)$, which is a part of decryption query, and $(C_0^*, \hat{C}_0^*)$, which is a part of the challenge ciphertext, satisfy $C_0 = C_0^*$ and $\hat{C}_0 = \hat{C}_0^*$.

The probability that $\mathcal{A}$ sends a decryption query $(C_0, \hat{C}_0, C_1\hat{C}_1, C_2)$ satisfying $C_0 = C_0^* \wedge \hat{C}_0 = \hat{C}_0^*$ before receiving the challenge ciphertext is at most q_D/q^2. If $((C_0 = C_0^*) \wedge (\hat{C}_0 = \hat{C}_0^*))$ and $((C_1 \neq C_1^*) \vee (\hat{C}_1 \neq \hat{C}_1^*) \vee (C_2 \neq C_2^*))$, then $(C_0, \hat{C}_0, C_1\hat{C}_1, C_2)$ is an invalid ciphertext and the verification result of the decryption algorithm is false. When $C_0 = C_0^*$, $\hat{C}_0 = \hat{C}_0^*$, $C_1 = C_1^*$, $\hat{C}_1 = \hat{C}_1^*$, and $C_2 = C_2^*$, $\mathcal{A}$ loses the attack game from the definition of the IND-CCA game. Therefore,

$$|\Pr[S_1] - \Pr[S_0]| \leq \frac{q_D}{q^2}.$$

Game 2. We transform D of the game 1 so that D aborts when $t = t^* \wedge (C_0 \neq C_0^* \vee \hat{C}_0 \neq \hat{C}_0^*)$ where $t = \mathsf{TCR}(C_0, \hat{C}_0)$ and $t^* = \mathsf{TCR}(C_0^*, \hat{C}_0^*)$. The behaviors of the game 1 and the game 2 are only different when $\mathcal{A}$ sends $(C_0, \hat{C}_0, C_1\hat{C}_1, C_2)$ satisfying $((C_0 \neq C_0^*) \vee (\hat{C}_0 \neq \hat{C}_0^*))$ and $\mathsf{TCR}(C_0, \hat{C}_0) = \mathsf{TCR}(C_0^*, \hat{C}_0^*)$.

$\mathcal{A}'$ who sends such query breaks the target collision resistance of TCR. Thus, we can easily construct the adversary $\mathcal{B}_{tcr}$ for TCR by using $\mathcal{A}'$. Therefore,

$$|\Pr[S_2] - \Pr[S_1]| \leq \mathsf{AdvTCR}_{\mathsf{TCR}, \mathcal{B}_{tcr}}.$$

Game 3. We transform D of the game 2 so that D returns $\perp$ when $(C_0, \hat{C}_0)$ and $(C_0^*, \hat{C}_0^*)$ satisfy $C_0 = C_0^*$ and $\hat{C}_0 \neq \hat{C}_0^*$. Let F_3 be the event such that a decryption query $(C_0, \hat{C}_0, C_1\hat{C}_1, C_2)$ is $C_0 = C_0^* \wedge \hat{C}_0 \neq \hat{C}_0^*$, and the ciphertext passes all verification of D of the game 2. The game 2 and the game 3 are the same excluding occurrence of F_3. Therefore,

$$|\Pr[S_3] - \Pr[S_2]| \leq \Pr[F_3].$$

We can show that $\Pr[F_3]$ is negligible under the extended strong twin DH assumption by the following lemma. The proof is described in detail in appendix A. It is clear that if the extended hashed strong twin DH assumption holds then the strong twin DH assumption also holds.

Lemma 1. *If there exists the adversary who causes F_3 to occur with non-negligible probability, then there exists the algorithm that solves the extended strong twin DH assumption with non-negligible probability.* □

Game 4. We transform D of the game 3 so that D returns $\perp$ when $(C_0, \hat{C}_0)$ and $(C_0^*, \hat{C}_0^*)$ satisfy $C_0 \neq C_0^*$ and $\hat{C}_0 = \hat{C}_0^*$. Let F_4 be the event such that a decryption query $(C_0, \hat{C}_0, C_1\hat{C}_1, C_2)$ is $C_0 \neq C_0^* \wedge \hat{C}_0 = \hat{C}_0^*$, and the ciphertext passes all verification of D of the game 3. The game 3 and the game 4 are the same excluding occurrence of F_4. Therefore,

$$|\Pr[S_4] - \Pr[S_3]| \leq \Pr[F_4].$$

We can show that $\Pr[F_4]$ is negligible under the extended strong twin DH assumption by the following lemma. The proof is almost the same as the lemma 1. We can prove the following lemma by replacing $(C_0^*, \hat{C}_0^*)$ with $(C_1^*, \hat{C}_1^*)$ in the proof of the lemma 1.

Lemma 2. *If there exists the adversary who causes F_4 to occur with non-negligible probability, then there exists the algorithm that solves the extended strong twin DH assumption with non-negligible probability.* □

Game 5. We transform the operation of E of the game 4 (i.e. the game 1) from $K_0 \leftarrow k_{1,1}\|\dots\|k_{2,n/2}$ into $K_0 \overset{R}{\leftarrow} \{0,1\}^{nv}$. Then, in the game 5, K_b is a random value over $\{0,1\}^{nv}$ regardless of the value of b. We show that

$$|\Pr[S_5] - \Pr[S_4]| \le negl(k)$$

holds by using the hybrid argument. We construct hybrid games $H_0, \dots, H_n$ so that H_0 and the game 4 are the same, and H_n and the game 5 are the same. And, we show that H_i is indistinguishable from H_{i-1} under the CDH assumption for all $i = 1, \dots, n$.

The detail of the proof is as followsAD Let H_0 be the game 4, and let H_i be the same game as H_{i-1} excluding the first iv bits of K_0^* that is random bit string. Thus H_n and the game 5 are the same. Let E_i be the event such that $\mathcal{A}$ outputs 1 in H_i. If

$$|\Pr[E_0] - \Pr[E_n]| \le 1/poly(k) \tag{5}$$

holds, the difference between $\mathcal{A}$'s advantage in H_0 and $\mathcal{A}$'s advantage in H_n is non-negligible. In this case, there must exists i such that $|\Pr[E_{i-1}] - \Pr[E_i]| = 1/poly(k)$ [1]. We assume that there exists $\mathcal{A}$ who satisfies the equation (5). By using $\mathcal{A}$, we show the construction of the adversary $\mathcal{B}$ who has access to the $e2dhp$ oracle that computes $e2dhp(A_1, A_2, \cdot, \cdot, \cdot, \cdot, \cdot, \cdot)$ and distinguishes $\Delta_{dh} = (g, A_1, A_2, B, f_{gl}(dh(A_1, B), R))$ from $\Delta_{rand} = (g, A_1, A_2, B, U_v, R)$ with non-negligible advantage where $U_v \overset{R}{\leftarrow} \{0,1\}^v$. If we can show the construction of such $\mathcal{B}$, from the theorem 3, we can prove the IND-CCA security of KEM_{e2dh} under the CDH assumption on $\mathbb{G}$.

$\mathcal{B}$ receives the challenge problem (g, A_1, A_2, B, L, R), then guesses an index $i \in [1, n]$ at random, and operates as follows. In this case, the probability that the guessed i satisfies $|\Pr[E_{i-1}] - \Pr[E_i]| = \max_i |\Pr[E_{i-1}] - \Pr[E_i]|$ is at least $1/n$.

We show the construction of $\mathcal{B}$. $\mathcal{B}$ chooses $i_1 \overset{R}{\leftarrow} \{1, \dots, n/2\}$ and $i_2 \overset{R}{\leftarrow} \{1, 2\}$, that is $i = i_1 i_2$. If $i_2 = 1$, then $\mathcal{B}$ runs the attack game for $\mathcal{A}$ by using the oracles KG_0, E_0 and D, else if $i_2 = 2$ then $\mathcal{B}$ runs the attack game by using KG_1, E_1 and D. Construction of each oracle is as follows:

Key generation oracle KG_0

1. $d, e, f, r \overset{R}{\leftarrow} \mathbb{Z}_q$;
2. Choose TCR;
3. $t^* \leftarrow \mathsf{TCR}(B, g^r)$;
4. $X \leftarrow A_1^e; X' \leftarrow A_1^{-et^*} g^d$;
   $Y \leftarrow A_2; Y' \leftarrow A_2^{-t^*} g^f$;
5. $z_j \overset{R}{\leftarrow} \mathbb{Z}_q; Z_j \leftarrow g^{z_j}$;
   $((1 \le j \le n/2) \wedge (j \ne i_1))$
6. $Z_{i_1} \leftarrow A_1$;
7. $R \overset{R}{\leftarrow} \{0,1\}^u$.

Key generation oracle KG_1

1. $d, e, f, r \overset{R}{\leftarrow} \mathbb{Z}_q$;
2. Choose TCR;
3. $t^* \leftarrow \mathsf{TCR}(g^r, B)$
4. $X \leftarrow A_1^e; X' \leftarrow A_1^{-et^*} g^d$;
   $Y \leftarrow A_2; Y' \leftarrow A_2^{-t^*} g^f$;
5. $z_j \overset{R}{\leftarrow} \mathbb{Z}_q; Z_j \leftarrow g^{z_j}$;
   $((1 \le j \le n/2) \wedge (j \ne i_1))$
6. $Z_{i_1} \leftarrow A_1$;
7. $R \overset{R}{\leftarrow} \{0,1\}^u$.

---

[1] If $|\Pr[E_{i-1}] - \Pr[E_i]| \le negl(k)$ holds for all i, then $|\Pr[E_0] - \Pr[E_n]| \le negl(k)$ holds.

KG_0 and KG_1 send a public key $\mathsf{pk} = (g, X, X', Y, Y', \{Z_j\}_{j=1,...,n/2}, R, \mathsf{TCR})$ to $\mathcal{A}$.

Challenge oracle E_0

1. $b \xleftarrow{R} \{0, 1\}$;
2. $C_0^* \leftarrow B; \hat{C}_0^* \leftarrow g^r$;
3. $C_1^* \leftarrow B^d; \hat{C}_1^* \leftarrow g^{rf}$;
4. $C_2^* \leftarrow g^{rd} B^f$;
5. $k_{1,j}^* \leftarrow \{0, 1\}^\nu; k_{2,j}^* \leftarrow \{0, 1\}^\nu$;
   $(1 \le j \le i_1 - 1)$;
6. $k_{1,i_1}^* \leftarrow L; k_{2,i_1}^* \leftarrow f_{gl}(\hat{C}_0^{*z_{i_1}}, R)$;
7. $k_{1,j}^* \leftarrow f_{gl}(C_0^{*z_j}, R); k_{2,j}^* \leftarrow f_{gl}(\hat{C}_0^{*z_j}, R)$;
   $(i_1 + 1 \le j \le n/2)$;
8. $K_0 \leftarrow k_{1,1}^* \| k_{2,1}^* \| \ldots \| k_{1,n/2}^* \| k_{2,n/2}^*$;
9. $K_1 \leftarrow \{0, 1\}^{n\nu}$.

Challenge oracle E_1

1. $b \xleftarrow{R} \{0, 1\}$;
2. $C_0^* \leftarrow g^r; \hat{C}_0^* \leftarrow B$;
3. $C_1^* \leftarrow g^{rd}; \hat{C}_1^* \leftarrow B^f$;
4. $C_2^* \leftarrow B^d g^{rf}$;
5. $k_{1,j}^* \leftarrow \{0, 1\}^\nu; k_{2,j}^* \leftarrow \{0, 1\}^\nu$;
   $(1 \le j \le i - 1)$;
6. $k_{1,i_1}^* \leftarrow f_{gl}(\hat{C}_0^{*z_i}, R); k_{2,i_1}^* \leftarrow L$;
7. $k_{1,j}^* \leftarrow f_{gl}(C_0^{*z_j}, R); k_{2,j}^* \leftarrow f_{gl}(\hat{C}_0^{*z_j}, R)$;
   $(i_1 + 1 \le j \le n/2)$;
8. $K_0 \leftarrow k_{1,1}^* \| k_{2,1}^* \| \ldots \| k_{1,n/2}^* \| k_{2,n/2}^*$;
9. $K_1 \leftarrow \{0, 1\}^{n\nu}$.

E_0 and E_1 send a challenge ciphertext $((C_0^*, \hat{C}_0^*, C_1^*, \hat{C}_1^*, C_2^*), K_b)$ to $\mathcal{A}$.

Decryption oracle $D(C_0, \hat{C}_0, C_1, \hat{C}_1, C_2)$

1. If $C_0 = C_0^* \wedge \hat{C}_0 = \hat{C}_0^*$ then output $\bot$ and stop;
2. $t \leftarrow \mathsf{TCR}(C_0, \hat{C}_0)$;
3. If $(t = t^* \wedge (C_0 \ne C_0^* \vee \hat{C}_0 \ne \hat{C}_0^*))$ then stop;
4. If $(C_0 = C_0^* \wedge \hat{C}_0 \ne \hat{C}_0^*)$ then outputs $\bot$ and stop;
5. If $(C_0 \ne C_0^* \wedge \hat{C}_0 = \hat{C}_0^*)$ then outputs $\bot$ and stop;
6. $\tilde{X}_1 \leftarrow (C_1/C_0^d)^{1/e(t-t^*)}; \tilde{X}_2 \leftarrow (\hat{C}_1/\hat{C}_0^f)^{1/(t-t^*)}; \tilde{Y} \leftarrow (C_2/C_0^f \hat{C}_0^d)^{1/(t-t^*)}$;
7. If $(e2dhp(A_1, A_2, C_0, \hat{C}_0, \tilde{X}_1, \tilde{X}_2, \tilde{Y}, e) = 1)$ holds, then
   (a) $k_{1,j} \leftarrow f_{gl}(C_0^{z_j}, R); k_{2,j} \leftarrow f_{gl}(\hat{C}_0^{z_j}, R); (1 \le j \le n/2) \wedge j \ne i_1$;
   (b) $k_{1,i_1} \leftarrow f_{gl}(\tilde{X}_1, R); k_{2,i_1} \leftarrow f_{gl}(\tilde{X}_2, R)$;
   (c) $K \leftarrow k_{1,1} \| k_{2,1} \| \ldots \| k_{1,n/2} \| k_{2,n/2}$, outputs K and stop;
8. Else outputs $\bot$ and stop.

When $i_2 = 1$, we can show that the challenge ciphertext $(C_0^* = B, \hat{C}_0^* = g^r, C_1^* = B^d, \hat{C}_1^* = g^{rf}, C_2^* = g^{rd} B^f)$ is a valid ciphertext, in almost the same way as for the equation (6). When $i_2 = 2$,

$$(X^{t^*} X')^r = ((A_1^e)^{t^*} A_1^{-et^*} g^d)^r = g^{rd}$$

$$(Y^{t^*} Y')^{\log_g B} = (A_2^{t^*} A_2^{-t^*} g^f)^{\log_g B} = B^f$$

$$(X^{t^*} X')^{\log_g B} (Y^{t^*} Y')^r = ((A_1^e)^{t^*} A_1^{-et^*} g^d)^{\log_g B} (A_2^{t^*} A_2^{-t^*} g^f)^r = B^d g^{rf}$$

hold because X, X', Y, Y' are set in the above way. Thus the challenge ciphertext $(C_0^* = g^r, \hat{C}_0^* = B, C_1^* = g^{rd}, \hat{C}_1^* = B^f, C_2^* = B^d g^{rf})$ is valid.

On the other hand, if a decryption query $(C_0, \hat{C}_0, C_1, \hat{C}_1, C_2)$ is a valid ciphertext, then $t = \mathsf{TCR}(C_0, \hat{C}_0), C_0 = g^{r_1}, \hat{C}_0 = g^{r_2}, C_1 = (X^t X')^{r_1}, \hat{C}_1 = (Y^t Y')^{r_2}$ and $C_2 = (X^t X')^{r_2} (Y^t Y')^{r_1}$ hold. Therefore,

$$\tilde{X}_1 = dh(A_1, C_0), \tilde{X}_2 = dh(A_2, \hat{C}_0), \text{ and } \tilde{Y} = dh(A_1^e, \hat{C}_0) dh(A_2, C_0)$$

hold. $e2dhp(A_1, A_2, C_0, \hat{C}_0, \tilde{X}_1, \tilde{X}_2, \tilde{Y}, e)$ outputs 1 if $\tilde{X}_1 = dh(A_1, C_0) \wedge \tilde{X}_2 = dh(A_2, \hat{C}_0) \wedge$
$\tilde{Y} = dh(A_1^e, \hat{C}_0)dh(A_2, C_0)$ hold. Therefore, the valid ciphertext passes the verification
of the decryption oracle.

Next we consider whether an invalid ciphertext $(C_0', \hat{C}_0', C_1', \hat{C}_1', C_2')$ satisfies $\tilde{X}_1 =$
$dh(A_1, C_0') \wedge \tilde{X}_2 = dh(A_2, \hat{C}_0') \wedge \tilde{Y} = dh(A_1^e, \hat{C}_0')dh(A_2, C_0')$. Suppose $\log_g C_0' = r_1'$, if
$\tilde{X}_1 = dh(A_1, C_0')$ holds, then $(C_1'/g^{r_1'd})^{1/e(t-t^*)} = A_1^{r_1'}$ holds. Since

$$C_1' = A_1^{r_1'e(t-t^*)}g^{r_1'd} = (X^tX')^{r_1'}(g^{r_1'}/g^{r_1'})^d = (X^tX')^{r_1'}$$

holds, then C_1' is valid. Suppose $\log_g \hat{C}_0' = r_2'$, in the same way, we can confirm that

$$\hat{C}_1' = A_2^{r_2'(t-t^*)}g^{r_2'f} = (Y^tY')^{r_2'},$$
$$C_2' = A_1^{r_2'e(t-t^*)}A_2^{r_1'(t-t^*)}g^{r_1'f}g^{r_2'd} = (X^tX')^{r_2'}(Y^tY')^{r_1'}$$

hold, then $\hat{C}_1'$ and C_2' are also valid. Thus, only a valid ciphertext $(C_0', \hat{C}_0', C_1', \hat{C}_1', C_2')$
satisfies

$$\tilde{X}_1 = dh(A_1, C_0'), \tilde{X}_2 = dh(A_2, \hat{C}_0'), \text{ and } \tilde{Y} = dh(A_1^e, \hat{C}_0')dh(A_2, C_0').$$

Therefore, $\mathcal{B}$ can check the validity of ciphertext by using $e2dhp(A_1, A_2, \cdot, \cdot, \cdot, \cdot, \cdot, \cdot)$.

When $\delta \xleftarrow{R} \Delta_{dh}$, the information that $\mathcal{B}$ gives $\mathcal{A}$ is the same as the hybrid game
$H_{2i+(i_2-2)-1}$, because $L = f_{gl}(dh(B, Z_i), R)$. On the other hand, when $\delta \xleftarrow{R} \Delta_{rand}$, the
information that $\mathcal{B}$ gives $\mathcal{A}$ is the same as the hybrid game $H_{2i+(i_2-2)}$. Therefore, we
show that $\mathcal{B}$ can distinguish $\delta \in \Delta_{dh}$ from $\delta \in \Delta_{rand}$ by using $\mathcal{A}$.   ∎

5   Comparison

Table 1 shows comparison of our scheme with other IND-CCA secure CDH-based
schemes. Our scheme has mild trade-off relation between the key size and the ciphertext
overhead compare with other CDH-based schemes, because we reduce the ciphertext
overhead by using batch verification. On the other hand, our scheme increases the computational cost a little bit compared with [12] and [16].

Table 1. Comparison with other schemes

	Ciphertext Overhead	Key Size Public Key	Key Size Secret Key	Efficiency #exp Encryption	Efficiency #exp Decryption
CKS[6]	$(n+2)|G|$	$(2n+3)|G|$	$(2n+2)|G|$	$3n+1$	$2n+1$
HK[11]	$3|G|$	$(n+4)|G|$	$(n+3)|G|$	$3n+7$	$n+2$
HJKS[12]	$3|G|$	$(n+5)|G|$	$(n+4)|G|$	$n+5$	$n+2$
YKHK[16]	$3|G|$	$(n+4)|G|$	$(n+3)|G|$	$n+5$	$n+2$
Wee[15]	$3n|G|$	$5|G|$	$4|G|$	$4n+2$	$3n$
KEM$_{e2dh}$	$5|G|$	$(n/2+5)|G|$	$(n/2+4)|G|$	$n+8$	$n+4$

6   Conclusion

We give the compact public key encryption based on the CDH assumption. Our scheme reduces the secret and the public key sizes without the bilinear map. Moreover our scheme reduces the ciphertext size by applying the batch verification technique. We give the security proof by extending the twin DH framework.

Our reducing technique can easily be applied to other schemes such as [17,16,15].

Acknowledgments. We thank the anonymous ProvSec 2011 reviewers for many helpful and kindly comments.

References

1. Bellare, M., Garay, J.A., Rabin, T.: Fast batch verification for modular exponentiation and digital signatures. In: Nyberg, K. (ed.) EUROCRYPT 1998. LNCS, vol. 1403, pp. 236–250. Springer, Heidelberg (1998)
2. Bellare, M., Rogaway, P.: Random oracles are practical: A paradigm for designing efficient protocols. In: ACM Conference on Computer and Communications Security, pp. 62–73 (1993)
3. Boneh, D.: The decision Diffie-Hellman problem. In: Buhler, J.P. (ed.) ANTS 1998. LNCS, vol. 1423, pp. 48–63. Springer, Heidelberg (1998)
4. Boneh, D., Shparlinski, I.E.: On the unpredictability of bits of the elliptic curve Diffie–Hellman scheme. In: Kilian, J. (ed.) CRYPTO 2001. LNCS, vol. 2139, pp. 201–212. Springer, Heidelberg (2001)
5. Boneh, D., Venkatesan, R.: Hardness of computing the most significant bits of secret keys in Diffie-Hellman and related schemes. In: Koblitz, N. (ed.) CRYPTO 1996. LNCS, vol. 1109, pp. 129–142. Springer, Heidelberg (1996)
6. Cash, D., Kiltz, E., Shoup, V.: The twin Diffie-Hellman problem and applications. In: Smart, N.P. (ed.) EUROCRYPT 2008. LNCS, vol. 4965, pp. 127–145. Springer, Heidelberg (2008)
7. Cramer, R., Shoup, V.: A practical public key cryptosystem provably secure against adaptive chosen ciphertext attack. In: Krawczyk, H. (ed.) CRYPTO 1998. LNCS, vol. 1462, pp. 13–25. Springer, Heidelberg (1998)
8. Cramer, R., Shoup, V.: Universal hash proofs and a paradigm for adaptive chosen ciphertext secure public-key encryption. In: Knudsen, L.R. (ed.) EUROCRYPT 2002. LNCS, vol. 2332, pp. 45–64. Springer, Heidelberg (2002)
9. Fiat, A.: Batch RSA. In: Brassard, G. (ed.) CRYPTO 1989. LNCS, vol. 435, pp. 175–185. Springer, Heidelberg (1990)
10. Goldreich, O., Levin, L.A.: A hard-core predicate for all one-way functions. In: STOC, pp. 25–32 (1989)
11. Hanaoka, G., Kurosawa, K.: Efficient chosen ciphertext secure public key encryption under the computational Diffie-Hellman assumption. In: Pieprzyk, J. (ed.) ASIACRYPT 2008. LNCS, vol. 5350, pp. 308–325. Springer, Heidelberg (2008)
12. Haralambiev, K., Jager, T., Kiltz, E., Shoup, V.: Simple and efficient public-key encryption from computational Diffie-Hellman in the standard model. In: Nguyen, P.Q., Pointcheval, D. (eds.) PKC 2010. LNCS, vol. 6056, pp. 1–18. Springer, Heidelberg (2010)
13. Shoup, V.: Lower bounds for discrete logarithms and related problems. In: Fumy, W. (ed.) EUROCRYPT 1997. LNCS, vol. 1233, pp. 256–266. Springer, Heidelberg (1997)
14. Shoup, V.: Sequences of games: a tool for taming complexity in security proofs. Cryptology ePrint Archive, Report 2004/332 (2004), http://eprint.iacr.org/

15. Wee, H.: Efficient chosen-ciphertext security via extractable hash proofs. In: Rabin, T. (ed.) CRYPTO 2010. LNCS, vol. 6223, pp. 314–332. Springer, Heidelberg (2010)
16. Yamada, S., Kawai, Y., Hanaoka, G., Kunihiro, N.: Public key encryption schemes from the (B)CDH assumption with better efficiency. IEICE Transactions 93-A(11), 1984–1993 (2010)
17. Yamada, S., Kawai, Y., Hanaoka, G., Kunihiro, N.: Public key encryption schemes from the (B)CDH assumption with shorter keys. In: SCIS 2010, 1A1-5 (2010) (in Japanese)

A Proof of Lemma 1

We show the construction of the extended twin DH adversary $\mathcal{B}$ by using the IND-CCA adversary $\mathcal{A}$ who makes a decryption query $(C_0', \hat{C}_0', C_1', \hat{C}_1', C_2')$ which satisfies $C_0' = C_0^* \wedge \hat{C}_0' \neq \hat{C}_0^*$ and the decryption query is valid (i.e. $C_1' = C_0^{'xt+x'} \wedge \hat{C}_1' = \hat{C}_0^{'yt+y'} \wedge C_2' = C_0^{'yt+y'}\hat{C}_0^{'xt+x'}$ hold). When $\mathcal{B}$ is given the extended strong twin DH tuple (g, A_1, A_2, B), $\mathcal{B}$ runs the attack game for $\mathcal{A}$ by using KG, E, and D. Construction of each oracle is as follows:

Key Generation Oracle KG

1. $d, e, f, r \xleftarrow{R} \mathbb{Z}_q$;
2. $R \xleftarrow{R} \{0, 1\}^u$ and choose TCR;
3. $t^* \leftarrow \text{TCR}(B, g^r)$
4. $X \leftarrow A_1^e; X' \leftarrow A_1^{-et^*} g^d; Y \leftarrow A_2; Y' \leftarrow A_2^{-t^*} g^f$;
5. $z_i \xleftarrow{R} \mathbb{Z}_q; Z_i \leftarrow g^{z_i}$; for all i such that $1 \leq i \leq n/2$

KG returns a public key $(g, X, X', Y, Y', \{Z_i\}_{i=1,\ldots,n/2}, R, \text{TCR})$ to $\mathcal{A}$.

Challenge Oracle E

1. $b \xleftarrow{R} \{0, 1\}$;
2. $C_0^* \leftarrow B; \hat{C}_0^* \leftarrow g^r$;
3. $C_1^* \leftarrow B^d; \hat{C}_1^* \leftarrow g^{rf}$;
4. $C_2^* \leftarrow B^{rd} g^f$;
5. $k_{1,i} \leftarrow f_{gl}(C_0^{*z_i}, R); k_{2,i} \leftarrow f_{gl}(\hat{C}_0^{*z_i}, R)$; for all i such that $1 \leq i \leq n/2$
6. $K_0 \leftarrow k_{1,1}\|k_{2,1}\|\ldots\|k_{1,n}\|k_{2,n}$;
7. $K_1 \leftarrow \{0, 1\}^{nv}$.

E returns a challenge ciphertext $((C_0^*, \hat{C}_0^*, C_1^*, \hat{C}_1^*, C_2^*), K_b)$ to $\mathcal{A}$.

Decryption Oracle $D(C_0, \hat{C}_0, C_1, \hat{C}_1, C_2)$

1. If $(C_0 = C_0^* \wedge \hat{C}_0 = \hat{C}_0^*)$ then outputs $\perp$ and stop;
2. $t \leftarrow \text{TCR}(C_0, \hat{C}_0)$;
3. If $(t = t^* \wedge (C_0 \neq C_0^* \vee \hat{C}_0 \neq \hat{C}_0^*))$ then stop;
4. $\tilde{X}_1 \leftarrow (C_1/C_0^d)^{1/e(t-t^*)}; \tilde{X}_2 \leftarrow (\hat{C}_1/\hat{C}_0^f)^{1/t-t^*}; \tilde{Y} \leftarrow (C_2/C_0^f \hat{C}_0^d)^{1/t-t^*}$;
5. If $(e2dhp(A_1, A_2, C_0, \hat{C}_0, \tilde{X}_1, \tilde{X}_2, \tilde{Y}, e) = 1)$ holds, then

(a) If $(C_0 = C_0^* \wedge \hat{C}_0 \neq \hat{C}_0^*)$ then stop;
(b) $k_{1,i} \leftarrow f_{gl}(C_0^{z_i}, R)$; $k_{2,i} \leftarrow f_{gl}(\hat{C}_0^{z_i}, R)$; for all i such that $1 \leq i \leq n/2$;
(c) $K \leftarrow k_{1,i}\|k_{2,i}\|\dots\|k_{1,n}\|k_{2,n}$, outputs K and stop;
6. Else outputs $\perp$ and stop.

$$(X^{t^*}X')^{\log_g C_0^*} = (A_1^{et^*}A_1^{-et^*}g^d)^{\log_g B} = B^d$$
$$(Y^{t^*}Y')^{\log_g \hat{C}_0^*} = (A_2^t A_2^{-t^*}g^f)^r = g^{rf} \tag{6}$$
$$(X^{t^*}X')^{\log_g \hat{C}_0^*}(Y^{t^*}Y')^{\log_g C_0^*} = (g^d)^r(g^f)^{\log_g B} = g^{rd}B^f$$

hold because X, X', Y, Y' are set in the above way. Thus the challenge ciphertext $(C_0^* = B, \hat{C}_0^* = g^r, C_1^* = B^d, \hat{C}_1^* = g^{rf}, C_2^* = g^{rd}B^f)$ is valid.

On the other hand, if a decryption query $(C_0, \hat{C}_0, C_1, \hat{C}_1, C_2)$ is a valid ciphertext, then $t = \mathsf{TCR}(C_0, \hat{C}_0)$, $C_0 = g^{r_1}$, $\hat{C}_0 = g^{r_2}$, $C_1 = (X^tX')^{r_1}$, $\hat{C}_1 = (Y^tY')^{r_2}$, $C_2 = (X^tX')^{r_2}(Y^tY')^{r_1}$ hold. Therefore

$$\tilde{X}_1 = \left(\frac{(X^tX')^{r_1}}{(g^{r_1})^d}\right)^{\frac{1}{e(t-t^*)}} = \left(\frac{A_1^{er_1(t-t^*)}g^{r_1d}}{g^{r_1d}}\right)^{\frac{1}{e(t-t^*)}} = A_1^{r_1} = dh(A_1, C_0)$$

$$\tilde{X}_2 = \left(\frac{(Y^tY')^{r_2}}{(g^{r_2})^f}\right)^{\frac{1}{t-t^*}} = \left(\frac{A_2^{r_2(t-t^*)}g^{r_2f}}{g^{r_2f}}\right)^{\frac{1}{t-t^*}} = A_2^{r_2} = dh(A_2, \hat{C}_0) \tag{7}$$

$$\tilde{Y} = \left(\frac{(X^tX')^{r_2}(Y^tY')^{r_1}}{(g^{r_1})^f(g^{r_2})^d}\right)^{\frac{1}{t-t^*}} = \left(\frac{A_1^{r_2e(t-t^*)}g^{r_2d}A_2^{r_1(t-t^*)}g^{r_1f}}{g^{r_1f}g^{r_2d}}\right)^{\frac{1}{t-t^*}}$$
$$= A_1^{er_2}A_2^{r_1} = dh(A_1^e, \hat{C}_0)dh(A_2, C_0)$$

hold.

$e2dhp(A_1, A_2, C_0, \hat{C}_0, \tilde{X}_1, \tilde{X}_2, \tilde{Y}, e)$ outputs 1 if $\tilde{X}_1 = dh(A_1, C_0) \wedge \tilde{X}_2 = dh(A_2, \hat{C}_0) \wedge \tilde{Y} = dh(A_1^e, \hat{C}_0)dh(A_2, C_0)$ hold. Therefore, the valid ciphertext passes the verification of the decryption oracle.

Next we consider whether an invalid ciphertext $(C_0', \hat{C}_0', C_1', \hat{C}_1', C_2')$ satisfies $\tilde{X}_1 = dh(A_1, C_0') \wedge \tilde{X}_2 = dh(A_2, \hat{C}_0') \wedge \tilde{Y} = dh(A_1^e, \hat{C}_0')dh(A_2, C_0')$. Suppose $\log_g C_0' = r_1'$, if $\tilde{X}_1 = dh(A_1, C_0')$ holds, then $(C_1'/g^{r_1'd})^{1/e(t-t^*)} = A_1^{r_1'}$ holds. Since

$$C_1' = A_1^{r_1'e(t-t^*)}g^{r_1'd} = (X^tX')^{r_1'}(g^{r_1'}/g^{r_1'})^d = (X^tX')^{r_1'}$$

holds, then C_1' is valid. Suppose $\log_g \hat{C}_0' = r_2'$, in the same way, we can confirm that

$$\hat{C}_1' = A_2^{r_2'(t-t^*)}g^{r_2'f} = (Y^tY')^{r_2'},$$
$$C_2' = A_1^{r_2'e(t-t^*)}A_2^{r_1'(t-t^*)}g^{r_1'f}g^{r_2'd} = (X^tX')^{r_2'}(Y^tY')^{r_1'}$$

hold, then $\hat{C}_1'$ and C_2' are also valid. Thus, only a valid ciphertext $(C_0', \hat{C}_0', C_1', \hat{C}_1', C_2')$ satisfies

$$\tilde{X}_1 = dh(A_1, C_0'), \tilde{X}_2 = dh(A_2, \hat{C}_0'), \text{ and } \tilde{Y} = dh(A_1^e, \hat{C}_0')dh(A_2, C_0').$$

Therefore, $\mathcal{B}$ can check the validity of ciphertext by using $e2dhp(A_1, A_2, \cdot, \cdot, \cdot, \cdot, \cdot, \cdot)$. If $\mathcal{A}$ makes a decryption query $(C'_0, \hat{C}'_0, C'_1, \hat{C}'_1, C'_2)$ which satisfies $C'_0 = C^*_0 \wedge \hat{C}'_0 \neq \hat{C}^*_0$ and it is valid, then D passes step. 5 and stops at step. 5-(a). Let $t' \leftarrow \mathsf{TCR}(C'_0, \hat{C}'_0)$, then, $C^*_1 = (X^{t^*} X')^{\log_g C^*_0}$, $C'_1 = (X^{t'} X')^{\log_g C^*_0}$, and $t' \neq t^*$ hold, because $C_0 = C^*_0$ hold. Therefore, $\mathcal{B}$ can obtain $dh(A_1, B)$ which is the solution of the extended strong twin DH tuple (g, A_1, A_2, B) by computing

$$(C'_1 / C^*_1)^{1/e(t'-t^*)} = A_1^{\log_g C^*_0} = A_1^{\log_g B} = dh(A_1, B).$$

∎

Anonymous Encryption with Partial-Order Subset Delegation Functionality

Mingwu Zhang[1,3], Takashi Nishide[2], Bo Yang[1], and Tsuyoshi Takagi[3]

[1] College of Informatics, South China Agricultural University,
Guangzhou 510642, China
[2] Information Technology and Security Laboratory, Kyushu University,
Fukuoka 819-0395, Japan
[3] Institute of Mathematics for Industry, Kyushu University, Fukuoka 819-0395, Japan

Abstract. We present a general encryption model with partial order delegation ability, which is a generalized extension for hierarchical identity-based encryption, broadcast encryption and delegatable functional encryption, etc. We also construct a concrete anonymous encryption scheme with constant-size ciphertext which may perform key derivation with partial-order subset delegation functionality, and prove its security in the standard model including semantic security, anonymity, and delegation indistinguishability. We give some practical application scenarios and deployments for our scheme.

Keywords: Partial order, Delegation, Functional encryption, Anonymity.

1 Introduction

In public key encryption systems, public keys (encryption keys) can be considered as encryption policies which describe who can decrypt the ciphertext, and private keys (decryption keys) can be regarded as decryption roles. If someone's decryption role satisfies the encryption policy, then he can extract the plaintext from the ciphertext legally. In traditional public keys framework, the encryption policy and decryption role are the same such that a public key corresponds to only one private key. In attribute based encryption (ABE) systems, ciphertexts are not necessarily encrypted to one particular user as in traditional public key cryptography. Users' private keys and ciphertexts will be associated with a set of attributes or a policy over attributes set. A user is able to decrypt a ciphertext if his private key matches the encryption policy. This can be flexibly extended to multiple level encryption systems such as hierarchical IBE (HIBE) [5,12,14,19], broadcast encryption [8], delegatable attribute-based encryption [13], predicate encryption [16,20], functional encryption [8,13], etc.

In identity-based encryption (IBE) system, the encryption policies are simply identities and the decryption roles are corresponding identities [4]. A message encrypted to an identity can be decrypted only if one has the corresponding private key. In order to implement the delegation ability, hierarchical

X. Boyen and X. Chen (Eds.): ProvSec 2011, LNCS 6980, pp. 154–169, 2011.

IBE schemes [5, 12, 19] are constructed to expand the functionality of identity to include a hierarchical structure on identities, where identities can delegate private keys to their subordinates. A user at level k can delegate private key to descendant identities at lower levels $k+1$, but can not decrypt message intended for a recipient that is not among his descendants.

To present a general delegation ability, Boneh and Hamburg [6] first introduced a generalized framework for constructing broadcast encryption scheme, and they constructed a spatial encryption scheme to perform delegation relation on a partial order space. In spatial encryption system, policies are defined as points in $\mathbb{F}_p^n$ and roles are defined as affine subspaces of $\mathbb{F}_p$.

1.1 Motivation

In roles delegation procedure, delegation may not be in a tree-based hierarchical way. This feature was referred to before as limited delegation by Boneh et al. [5], who show a tweak to their HIBE scheme. We take a polygon area delegation as an example. A user role is associate with a polygon area. The private key of a user can be derived from the delegation procedure by his super-polygon area key carriers. We consider a pentagon in Fig.1(a) as an instance. The level-1 user (root role) has the role polygon $ABCDE$, and he can delegation his subarea (quadrangle) to his level-2 delegatee. That is, level-1 user produces the private key of quadrangle $\square ABCD$, $\square ABCE$, $\square ACDE$ or $\square BCDE$ role as his delegatee's decryption key. Every quadrangle carrier can also perform the same role delegation procedure for his subordinate. In HIBE delegation procedure for this scenario, level-3 users (triangle roles) will import a funny scene: the same roles have different private keys. In Fig.1(b), the first and the third users have the same decryption roles $\triangle ABC$ in level-3. The reason is in that the intersection of two level-2 roles are not empty which may produce the same subordinate role, i.e., $\square ABCD \cap \square ABCE = \triangle ABC$.

To overcome this problem, we propose a partial-order subset delegation model. Distinguished to a tree-based hierarchical delegation model in HIBE, our model is subset delegation which satisfies general delegation properties such as reflexivity, transitivity and asymmetry. In Fig.1(c), level-1 user can implement delegation for level-3 user directly. This property is because of the transitivity of partial-order relation.

1.2 Related Works

HIBE Hierarchical IBE provides a private key from the superior and can delegate this key to his subordinate. This delegation is one-way such that a subordinate cannot use his private key to recover the key of his superior or siblings. Boneh and Boyen [4] constructed a selectively secure HIBE scheme, and Boneh et al. [5] presented a selectively secure HIBE scheme with constant size ciphertext. Gentry and Halevi [12] proposed a fully secure HIBE scheme under q-type assumptions. Waters [21] leveraged the dual system encryption methodology to obtain fully secure IBE and HIBE systems from simple assumptions. Lewko and Waters

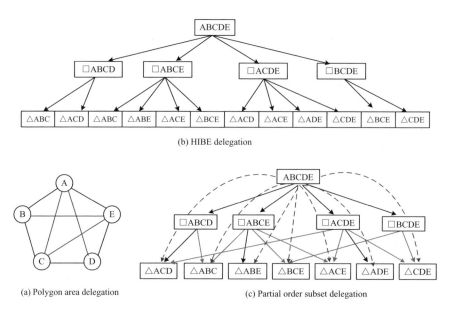

(b) HIBE delegation

(a) Polygon area delegation

(c) Partial order subset delegation

Fig. 1. Instance of partial-order delegation

[14] extended the dual system encryption technique to anticipate a fully secure HIBE scheme with constant size ciphertext. In HIBE system, the delegation hierarchical roles are a tree-based structure in such a way that a delegatee has only one delegator. Abdalla et al. [1] introduced a key delegation technique in HIBE scheme. Recently, lattice-based HIBE schemes have been constructed [2, 10].

An encryption scheme is recipient anonymous if the ciphertext leaks no information about the recipient's public key or identity [9, 19, 11]. Roughly speaking, if it hard for an eavesdropper to distinguish which identity was used to generate a given cipher- text. Informally, recipient anonymity is the property that the adversary be unable to distinguish the ciphertext of a chosen message for a first chosen identity from the ciphertext of the same message for a second chosen identity. Equivalently, the adversary must be unable to decide whether a ciphertext was encrypted for a chosen identity, or for a random identity.

ABE Attribute-based encryption was first introduced by Sahai and Waters [18], which deploys a complex control structure for encryption policies and decryption roles. ABE schemes have desirable functionality, but have one limitation in that the structure of the ciphertext is revealed to users [17, 13]. For example, in a CP-ABE system, a user who cannot decrypt the ciphertext can still learn the encryption policy associated with the ciphertext. For applications where the access policy must also be kept secret, this is unacceptable.

PREDICATE ENCRYPTION AND FUNCTIONAL ENCRYPTION. Predicate encryption (PE) can overcome the limitation of ABE to keep the secret of encryption policy. Informally, private keys in a PE scheme corresponds to predicates in some class $\mathcal{F}$, and a sender associates a ciphertext with attribute in set Σ; a ciphertext associated with attribute $I \in \Sigma$ can be decrypted using a private key SK_f corresponding to predicate $f \in \mathcal{F}$ if and only if $f(I) = 1$. Roughly speaking, attribute-hiding requires that a ciphertext conceals the associated attribute as well as the plaintext, while payload-hiding only requires that a ciphertext conceals the plaintext. If attributes are identities, i.e., PE is IBE, attribute-hiding PE implies anonymous IBE.

An important research direction is to construct functional encryption schemes for function classes $\mathcal{F}$ that are as expressive as possible, with the ultimate goal being to handle all polynomial-time predicates [20, 15, 16]. Shi and Waters [20] presented a delegation mechanism for a class of PE, but the admissible predicates is a class of equality tests for HVE, are more limited than inner-product predicates. Moreover, the security proof is selective security in [20]. Okamoto and Takashima [16] proposed a hierarchical delegation mechanism for a PE scheme, i.e., a hierarchical PE scheme supporting inner-product predicate. Dual pairing vector spaces (DPVS) were introduced in [15, 16], who presented a selectively secure PE scheme based on DPVS. Attrapadung and Libert [3] constructed a non-anonymous IPE system with constant-size ciphertexts for the zero and non-zero evaluations, which is adaptively secure.

SPATIAL ENCRYPTION In functional encryption systems such as ABE, PE, and FE, they consider that encryption policies comply with decryption roles. But they make fewer consideration on their delegation abilities. Boneh, Sahai and Waters [8] defined a general functional encryption, and they pointed out that it is a great challenge to construct a secure functional encryption for all polynomial-time functionalities. Spatial encryption (SE) was first proposed by Boneh and Hamburg [6], which is a new instance of generalized IBE (GIBE) to construct IBE systems with different properties. GIBE is close to PE scheme excepting that incorporates delegation property in PE. In spatial encryption, given a key $SK_{\rho 1}$ that ρ_1 affine space contains ρ_2's space, then there is a delegation algorithm that can produce the key $SK_{\rho 2}$, as long as $SK_{\rho_2} \preceq SK_{\rho_1}$. Zhou and Cao [22] improved the spatial encryption in simpler assumption under the bilinear Diffie-Hellman assumption, where they proposed two variants of SE constructions, but their schemes have larger ciphertext size (without constant-size) and private key.

1.3   Our Contribution

We construct an anonymous partial-order subset delegation encryption scheme with constant-size ciphertext which is a generalized extension for anonymous HIBE. To support role delegation, we introduce a partial order $\preceq$ over a set Λ of roles $\mathcal{R}$, and define the partial order as a strict order under the set Λ with inclusion operator. Informally, our contribution is described as follows

1. In our scheme, the partial order delegation supports arbitrary subset delegation, which is an extension of HIBE. In particular, if operator $\preceq$ is defined as set extension operator *concatenation* such that $I^{n+1} := I^n || I^{n+1}$, then our partial order delegation scheme is a HIBE scheme. In Fig.1(a), the hierarchy is fixed as a tree structure in HIBE scheme, and each node has only one

delegator. In the partial order delegation in Fig.1(c), the delegation is flexible that a delegatee may have several delegators. For instance, left node has three delegators (i.e., root node, 1st, and 3rd nodes in level-2, respectively).

2. The delegation is independent to the path. The delegation invertability[1] of our scheme is supported by the asymmetric property of partial order. In our scheme, a subordinate may have multiple superiors. Any of superiors may generate a private key for a subrole ρ if ρ is the common subrole of these superiors. The private keys of ρ generated by multiple superiors is independent to the delegation path. That is, it is indistinguishable in probabilistic evaluation for these private keys of ρ.

3. Our proposed scheme is an anonymous encryption scheme that leaks no information about the recipient's identity, i.e., any other party can neither obtain the encrypted cleartext nor guess who is the valid ciphertext decryptor if he/she does not carry valid decryption key.

1.4   Organization

In Section 2, we give some notations and preliminaries. In Section 3, we formal an anonymous encryption scheme which supports partial order subset delegation, and give its security definitions. In Section 4, we give the concrete construction and describe its proofs, and describe our discussion in Section 5. Finally, we draw our conclusion in Section 6.

2   Notations and Backgrounds

2.1   Notations

Let $\mathbb{F}_N := \{0,1,2,\ldots,N\text{-}1\}$. We denote the finite field of order p by $\mathbb{F}_p$, and $\mathbb{F}_p \setminus \{0\}$ by $\mathbb{F}_p^\times$. When $\mathbb{G}$ is a group, $g \xleftarrow{\$} \mathbb{G}$ denotes that g is randomly picked from $\mathbb{G}$.

Let $\boldsymbol{S} := \{s_1, s_2, \ldots, s_n\}$ with capital bold-case letter be a set and $\mathbf{u}$ with lower-case letter be a vector, we denote Λ be a full-set and ϕ be an empty set. $\boldsymbol{X}, \boldsymbol{Y}$ be subsets of Λ such that $\boldsymbol{X}, \boldsymbol{Y} \subseteq \Lambda$. $|X|, |Y|$ be the cardinality of $\boldsymbol{X}$ and $\boldsymbol{Y}$, respectively. $\boldsymbol{X} - \boldsymbol{Y}$ or $\boldsymbol{X} \backslash \boldsymbol{Y}$ be the set that all elements in $\boldsymbol{X}$ but not in $\boldsymbol{Y}$, i.e., $\boldsymbol{X} \backslash \boldsymbol{Y} = \boldsymbol{X} \cap (\overline{\boldsymbol{X}} \cup \overline{\boldsymbol{Y}})$. We denote vector $(h_1, h_2, \ldots, h_{|\Lambda|})$ over the full set Λ as $\mathbf{h}$ (similar, $(h_1, h_2, \ldots, h_{|X|})$ over subset $\boldsymbol{X}$ as $\mathbf{h}^X$). We use the notation $\mathbf{u}^{<\mathbf{a},r>}$ to indicate the vector $((u_1^{a_1})^r, (u_2^{a_2})^r, \ldots, (u_n^{a_n})^r)$.

2.2   Partial Order and Conditional PO Graph

A partial order (PO) $P(\boldsymbol{S}, \preceq)$ is a binary relation $\preceq$ over a set of elements $\boldsymbol{S}$ which satisfies the following conditions

---

[1] Delegation invertability means that a superior can produce a subrole key for his subordinate, but a subordinate can not obtain his superior's private key.

- *Reflexivity*: $\forall a \in \boldsymbol{S}, a \preceq a$;
- *Asymmetry*: $\forall a, b \in \boldsymbol{S}, (a \preceq b) \Rightarrow \neg(b \preceq a)$;
- *Transitivity*: $\forall a, b, c \in \boldsymbol{S}, (a \preceq b) \wedge (b \preceq c) \Rightarrow (a \preceq c)$.

A partial order set is also called *poset*. The size of the longest chain is called the partial order length.

A partial order is a strict (partial) order if it satisfies the irreflexivity property in place of the reflexivity.

- *Irreflexivity*: $\forall a \in \boldsymbol{S}, \neg(a \preceq a)$;

We can see that every partial order $(\boldsymbol{S}, \subseteq)$ can induce a strict partial order, i.e., $\forall \boldsymbol{X}, \boldsymbol{Y} \subseteq \boldsymbol{S}, \boldsymbol{X} \subseteq \boldsymbol{Y} \Leftrightarrow \boldsymbol{X} \subset \boldsymbol{Y} \vee \boldsymbol{X} = \boldsymbol{Y}$.

A conditional partial order graph is a tuple $H(V, E, X, \psi)$ where V is the set of vertices (or nodes), $E \subseteq V \times V$ is the set of ordered pairs of vertices, called arcs. X is the set of Boolean variables, and function $\psi : V \cup E \rightarrow F(x)$ assigns a condition to every vertex and arc.

If a user A who carries subset private key $\boldsymbol{S}_A$ can delegate his all decryption ability to B, i.e., $Open(\rho_B, \pi) = Open(\rho_A, \pi)$ for all $\pi \in \mathcal{P}$, then we consider it is a full delegatable encryption. A full delegatable encryption scheme supports a general partial order delegation.

2.3 Admissible Bilinear Maps in Composite Order Groups

Let $\mathbb{G} = < g >$ and $\mathbb{G}_T$ be two cyclic multiplicative groups of prime order p, i.e., $|\mathbb{G}| = |\mathbb{G}_T| = p$. $\hat{e}$ be an admissible bilinear map from $\mathbb{G}^2$ to $\mathbb{G}_T$. We extend the general prime groups to composite order bilinear groups [7], i.e., the orders of $\mathbb{G}$ and $\mathbb{G}_T$ are $N = pq$ where p, q are distinct primes such that $gcd(p, q) = 1$. We also assume that it is a hard problem to factor p, q on N. Note that N should be at least 1024-bit under the same security level of AES-128. Let $\mathbb{G}_p$ and $\mathbb{G}_q$ denote the subgroups of order p, q of $\mathbb{G}$, and $\mathbb{G}_{T,p}$ and $\mathbb{G}_{T,q}$ denote as the subgroups of $\mathbb{G}_T$, respectively. Then $\mathbb{G} = \mathbb{G}_p \times \mathbb{G}_q$, and $\mathbb{G}_T = \mathbb{G}_{T,p} \times \mathbb{G}_{T,q}$.

Note that $\hat{e}(h_p, h_q) = 1_{\mathbb{G}_T}$ for all random elements $h_p \in \mathbb{G}_p, h_q \in \mathbb{G}_q$ since $\hat{e}(h_p, h_q) = \hat{e}(g_p^r, g_q^s)$ for some $r, s \in \mathbb{F}_N$, and $\hat{e}(g^{qr}, g^{ps}) = \hat{e}(g, g)^{pqrs} = 1_{\mathbb{G}_T}$ for some generator $g \in \mathbb{G}$.

2.4 Security Assumption

ℓ-wBDHI ASSUMPTION. The ℓ-wBDHI assumption has been for constructing HIBE with constant ciphertext in [5,19]. For given bilinear groups with composite order $N = pq$, let the following distribute be $P(\lambda)$.

$$
\begin{aligned}
& (N = pq, \mathbb{G}, \mathbb{G}_T, \hat{e}) \xleftarrow{\$} \mathcal{G}(\lambda) \\
& g_1, g_p \xleftarrow{\$} \mathbb{G}_p, g_q \xleftarrow{\$} \mathbb{G}_q, a \xleftarrow{\$} \mathbb{F}_N \\
& \Phi \leftarrow (g_q, g_p^a, g_p^{a^2}, \ldots, g_p^{a^\ell}, \Omega \leftarrow \hat{e}(g_p, g_1); N, \mathbb{G}, \mathbb{G}_T, \hat{e}) \\
& T_1 \leftarrow \Omega^{a^{\ell+1}}, T_2 \xleftarrow{\$} \mathbb{G}_T, \eta \xleftarrow{\$} \{0, 1\} \\
& T' \leftarrow \eta T_1 + (1 - \eta) T_2
\end{aligned}
$$

160 M. Zhang et al.

We call $(\varPhi, T')$ the challenge pair of ℓ-wBDHI problem where $\varPhi \xleftarrow{\$} P(\lambda)$. After given the challenge pair to adversary $\mathcal{A}$, $\mathcal{A}$ outputs η' and succeeds if $\eta = \eta'$ in ℓ-wBDHI assumption. The advantage of $\mathcal{A}$ in solving ℓ-wBDHI assumption is

$$Adv_{\mathcal{G},\mathcal{A}}^{\ell-wBDHI}(\lambda) := |Pr[\mathcal{A}(\varPhi, T_1) = 1] - Pr[\mathcal{A}(\varPhi, T_2) = 1]|$$

ℓ-cDH ASSUMPTION. For a given composite order group generating $\mathcal{G}$, let the following distribute be $P(\lambda)$.

$$(N = pq, \mathbb{G}, \mathbb{G}_T, \hat{e}) \xleftarrow{\$} \mathcal{G}(\lambda)$$
$$g_p \xleftarrow{\$} \mathbb{G}_p, g_q \xleftarrow{\$} \mathbb{G}_q, a, b, z_1, z_2, z_3 \xleftarrow{\$} \mathbb{F}_N$$
$$\varPhi \leftarrow (g_q, g_p^a, g_p^{a^2}, \dots, g_p^{a^\ell}, g_p^{a^{\ell+1}} \cdot g_q^{z_1}, g_p^{a^{\ell+1}b} \cdot g_q^{z_2}; N, \mathbb{G}, \mathbb{G}_T, \hat{e})$$
$$T_1 \leftarrow g_p^b g_q^{z_3}, \ T_2 \xleftarrow{\$} \mathbb{G}, \ \eta \xleftarrow{\$} \{0,1\}$$
$$T' \leftarrow \eta T_1 + (1-\eta)T_2$$

We call $(\varPhi, T')$ the challenge pair of ℓ-cDH problem where $\varPhi \xleftarrow{\$} P(\lambda)$. After given the challenge pair to adversary $\mathcal{A}$, $\mathcal{A}$ outputs η' and succeeds if $\eta = \eta'$ in ℓ-cDH assumption. The advantage of $\mathcal{A}$ in solving ℓ-cDH assumption in groups generated by $\mathcal{G}$ is

$$Adv_{\mathcal{G},\mathcal{A}}^{\ell-cDH}(\lambda) := |Pr[\mathcal{A}(\varPhi, T_1) = 1] - Pr[\mathcal{A}(\varPhi, T_2) = 1]|$$

3 Anonymous Encryption with Partial Order Subset Delegation

3.1 Framework of Encryption with Partial Order Subset Delegation

The anonymous encryption scheme with partial order subset delegation is comprised of the following four randomized PPT algorithms

- *SysSetup*(λ, Λ). Takes as input a security parameter λ and a set Λ, this algorithm generates system public parameters *params*, master key *msk* and top private key PosKey$^\Lambda$ for set Λ. This algorithm is performed by trusted authority (TA).
- *PosDelegate*$(params, PosKey^X, X, Y)$. Takes the private key PosKey^X, this algorithm outputs the partial order delegation key for Y if $Y \preceq X$;
- *Encrypt*$(params, Y, M)$. To encrypt a message M to a recipient who carries a partial order subset $Y \preceq \Lambda$, this algorithm outputs a ciphertext CT^Y;
- *Decrypt*$(params, PosKey^V, CT^Y)$. Takes as input a ciphertext CT^Y, decryption key PosKey^V and public parameters *params*, this algorithm outputs the plaintext M if $Y \preceq V$.

Formally, if $V, X, Y, Z \preceq \Lambda$ and $Y \preceq V, Y \preceq X$, then the following consistent equations will hold

$$\begin{cases} Decrypt(params, PosKey^\Lambda, Encrypt(params, Z, M)) = M \\ Decrypt(params, PosKey^V \leftarrow PosKey^\Lambda, Encrypt(params, Y, M)) = M \\ Decrypt(params, PosKey^Y \leftarrow PosKey^V, Encrypt(params, Y, M)) = M \\ Pr[Poskey^Y \leftarrow PosKey^V - Poskey^Y \leftarrow PosKey^X] \approx 0 \end{cases}$$

3.2   Security Models

The security of the partial order delegation based anonymous encryption scheme includes the *message confidentiality, recipient anonymity*, and *delegation indistinguishability*.

Definition 1. *Message confidentiality This is the usual security notion of semantic security for encryption scheme. Semantic security states that no computationally bounded adversary given the ciphertext can predict anything about the plaintext any better than it can when it is not given the ciphertext. Formally, confidentiality means that adversary cannot distinguish two different message ciphertexts after he performs a lot of partial order subset key extraction queries, which is formally defined as the IND-sSET-CSA game as follows*

- *Init.* The adversary $\mathcal{A}$ commits a target subset Z to the challenger $\mathcal{C}$;
- *SysSetup.* The challenger $\mathcal{C}$ runs the SysSetup algorithm to generate the system parameters *params* and master key *msk*, and produces the top private PosKey$^{\Lambda}$ for full set Λ. $\mathcal{C}$ then sends the public *params* to $\mathcal{A}$;
- *Query*-I. $\mathcal{A}$ makes a bounded number of key extraction queries for subsets $Y_i(i = 1, \ldots, q_1)$ with the restriction that $Z \not\preceq Y_i$ holds. $\mathcal{C}$ returns the private key PosKey^{Y_i} to $\mathcal{A}$ by performing PosDelegate algorithm;
- *Challenge.* $\mathcal{A}$ chooses two message M_0, M_1 with equal size and sends them to $\mathcal{C}$. Then, $\mathcal{C}$ flips a random coin η and produces the challenged ciphertext $CT^Z \leftarrow \text{Encrypt}(params, Z, M_b)$ and sends to $\mathcal{A}$;
- *Query*-II. $\mathcal{A}$ may continue to perform *Query-I* queries for $i = q_1, \ldots, q_s$;
- *Guess.* Finally, $\mathcal{A}$ outputs a guess η' as the answer for confidentiality game, and wins the game if $\eta' = \eta$.

An encryption scheme is said to be IND-sSET-CSA secure if we can prove that no polynomial-time-bounded adversary can win the above game with probability that is non-negligibly greater than $1/2$ in the parameter λ. The advantage for adversary $\mathcal{A}$ in IND-sSET-CSA game is defined as

$$\epsilon_{IND} := |Pr[(\eta = \eta')] - \frac{1}{2}|$$

Definition 2. *Recipient anonymity Recipient anonymity encryption means that the adversary be unable to distinguish the ciphertext of a chosen message for a first chosen partial order subset from the ciphertext of the same message for a second chosen subset. Formally, the adversary must be unable to decide whether a ciphertext was encrypted for a chosen subset, or for a random subset. Anonymity game ANON-sSET-CSA is formally defined as confidentiality except that the challenge phase is changed as below*

Challenge. The adversary $\mathcal{A}$ outputs a message M by his choice, then $\mathcal{C}$ flips a random coin η. If $\eta = 1$ then $\mathcal{C}$ encrypts M with subset Z chosen by $\mathcal{A}$ in *Init* phase, otherwise if $\eta = 0$ he encrypts a random subset Z' such that $Z' \not\preceq Y_i$.

Definition 3. ***Delegation indistinguishability*** *Delegation indistinguishability requires that a partial order private key is independent to the delegation path. Formally, let partial order subsets* $Z \preceq Y_0, Z \preceq Y_1$, *partial order delegation key* $PosKey^Z$ *may be derived from* $PosKey^{Y_0}$ *or* $PosKey^{Y_1}$, *then* $PosKey^Z$ *is probabilistically indistinguishable between* $PosKey^Z \leftarrow PosKey^{Y_0}$ *and* $PosKey^Z \leftarrow PosKey^{Y_1}$ *under chosen subset attack (CSA) model. The delegation indistinguishability game IND-sSET-CSA is formally defined as the confidentiality game except that the challenge phase is changed as the below*

> **Challenge.** Adversary $\mathcal{A}$ outputs three chosen subsets Y_0, Y_1, Z with the restriction that: (1)these subsets must not be performed in the key extraction queries in Query-I phase and, (2)$Z \preceq Y_0$, and $Z \preceq Y_1$. $\mathcal{C}$ generate the $PosKey^{Y_0}$ and $PosKey^{Y_1}$ first. Then he flips a random coin $\eta \xleftarrow{\$} \{0,1\}$ and produces the challenged delegation private key $PosKey^Z \leftarrow PosDelegate$ $(params, Y_\eta, Z)$ and sends the $PosKey^Z$ to $\mathcal{A}$.

The advantage for $\mathcal{A}$ in ANON-sSET-CSA game is defined as

$$\epsilon_{ANON} := |Pr[(\eta = \eta')] - \frac{1}{2}|$$

Delegation indistinguishability concept is identical to the HIBE schemes [5, 9, 12], since the HIBE delegation structure is previous fixed and the identity is linear increasing with 1. In our partial order delegation model, delegation is implemented by partial order $\preceq$. Especially, if the partial order operator $\preceq$ is defined as set extension *concatenation* in such a way that $I^{n+1} := I^n || I^{n+1}$, then our scheme is simplified as a HIBE.

4   Construction and Analysis

In this section, we will present the concrete construction of our scheme. Let λ be the system security parameter. We assume that the elements in set Λ are marked with label $1, \ldots, \Delta$, where $|\Lambda| = \Delta$.

4.1   Construction

The anonymous encryption scheme with partial order subset delegation, which uses two prime composite order groups, is described as follows.

> **SysSetup**(λ, Λ): First, TA generates $(N, p, q, \mathbb{G}, \mathbb{G}_T, \hat{e}) \xleftarrow{\$} \mathcal{G}(\lambda)$ where $N = pq$. Selects random elements $g, g_p, g_1, v, w, u_1, \ldots, u_\Delta \in \mathbb{G}_p$, $g_q \in \mathbb{G}_q$, and $b_0, b_1, b_2, c_1, \ldots, c_\Delta \in \mathbb{F}_N^\times$. TA then computes $G = gg_q^{b_0}, V = vg_q^{b_1}, W = wg_q^{b_2}, U_i = u_ig_q^{c_i}$ and $\Omega = \hat{e}(g, g_1)$, and publishes *params* together with the description of group $\mathbb{G}$ and $\mathbb{G}_T$ as
>
> $$params := [N, \mathbb{G}, \mathbb{G}_T, \hat{e}; g_q, G, V, W, U_1, \ldots, U_\Delta, \Omega]$$

Note that the *params* contains N but not p, q. TA retains *msk* as the private key

$$msk := [p, q, g, g_p, v, w, u_1, \ldots, u_\Delta, g_1]$$

Let full set $\Lambda = \{a_1, \ldots, a_\Delta\} \in \mathbb{F}_N^\Delta$ be an ordered set and corresponding element a_i is associated with public key $U_i^{a_i}$. TA also produces the system top private key for Λ as:

First picks random integers $r_1, r_2, s_1, s_2 \in \mathbb{F}_N^\times$, and produces the private key PosKey$^\Lambda$ consisting of two subkeys, i.e., PosKey$_d^\Lambda$ for decryption and PosKey$_r^\Lambda$ for partial order subset delegation and re-randomization, where

$$
\begin{aligned}
PosKey_d^\Lambda &:= [k_0^\Lambda, k_1^\Lambda, k_2^\Lambda, (\mathbf{h})^\Lambda] \\
&= [g^{r_1}, g^{r_2}, g_1 v^{r_1} w^{r_2}, \mathbf{u}^{<\mathbf{a}, r_1>}] \\
PosKey_r^\Lambda &:= [\tilde{k}_0^\Lambda, \tilde{k}_1^\Lambda, \tilde{k}_2^\Lambda, (\tilde{\mathbf{h}})] \\
&= [g^{s_1}, g^{s_2}, v^{s_1} w^{s_2}, \mathbf{u}^{<\mathbf{a}, s_1>}]
\end{aligned}
$$

PosDelegate($PosKey^X, \mathbf{X}, \mathbf{Y} = \{b_1, \ldots, b_k\}$: Let the PosKey$^X = [[k_0^X, k_1^X, k_2^X, (\mathbf{h})^X], [\tilde{k}_0^X, \tilde{k}_1^X, \tilde{k}_2^X, (\tilde{\mathbf{h}})^X]]$ be the parent set private key. To generate the delegation PosKey^Y where $\mathbf{Y} \preceq \mathbf{X}$, which means that $\mathbf{Y}$ is the partial order subset of $\mathbf{X}$. Let $\mathcal{U}_{X-Y} \subseteq \{1, 2, \ldots, \Delta\}$ be the set of indices i such that $b[i] \notin \mathbf{X}$. It then outputs the PosKey$_d^Y$ and PosKey$_r^Y$ as follows

S1: *Key delegation.*

$$[\zeta_0, \zeta_1, \zeta_2, \{\eta_i | i \in \mathcal{U}_Y\}] := [k_0^X, k_1^X, k_2^X \prod_{i \in \mathcal{U}_{X-Y}} h_i^X, (\mathbf{h})^X - (\mathbf{h})^{X-Y}] \quad (1)$$

$$[\theta_0, \theta_1, \theta_2, \{\phi_i | i \in \mathcal{U}_Y\}] := [\tilde{k}_0^X, \tilde{k}_1^X, \tilde{k}_2^X \prod_{i \in \mathcal{U}_{X-Y}} \tilde{h}_i^X, (\tilde{\mathbf{h}})^X - (\tilde{\mathbf{h}})^{X-Y}] \quad (2)$$

S2: *Key re-randomization.*

It first random picks $\gamma, \delta \in \mathbb{F}_N^\times$, and computes the randomized partial order delegation private key as

$$
\begin{aligned}
PosKey_d^Y &:= [k_0^Y = g^{r_1'}, k_1^Y = g^{r_2'}, k_2^Y = g_1 (v \prod_{i \in \Lambda - \mathcal{U}_Y} u_i^{a_i})^{r_1'} w^{r_2'}, \\
&\quad (\mathbf{h})^Y = \{h_i^Y = (u_i^{a_i})^{r_1'} | i \in \mathcal{U}_Y\}] \\
&= [\zeta_0 \theta_0^\gamma, \ \zeta_1 \theta_1^\gamma, \ \zeta_2 \theta_2^\gamma, \ (\mathbf{h})^Y = \{\eta_i \phi_i^\gamma | i \in \mathcal{U}_Y\}] \quad (3) \\
PosKey_r^Y &:= [\tilde{k}_0^Y = g^{s_1'}, \tilde{k}_1^Y = g^{s_2'}, \tilde{k}_2^Y = (v \prod_{i \in \Lambda - \mathcal{U}_Y} u_i^{a_i})^{s_1'} w^{s_2'}, \\
&\quad (\tilde{\mathbf{h}})^Y = \{\tilde{h}_i^Y = (u_i^{a_i})^{s_1'} | i \in \mathcal{U}_Y\}] \\
&= [\theta_0^\delta, \ \theta_1^\delta, \ \theta_2^\delta, \ (\tilde{\mathbf{h}})^Y = \{\phi_i^\delta | i \in \mathcal{U}_Y\}] \quad (4)
\end{aligned}
$$

As $\boldsymbol{Y} \preceq \boldsymbol{X}$ which means that $\boldsymbol{Y}$ is a partial order subset of $\boldsymbol{X}$, then it has $\{h_1^X, \ldots, h_{|X|}^X\} \backslash \{h_i^X | i \in \mathcal{U}_{X-Y}\} = \{h_i^Y | i \in \mathcal{U}_Y\} = (\mathbf{h})^Y$.

We observe that the new delegation key PosKey^Y has the same distribution as the superset key with PosKey^X on $\boldsymbol{Y} \preceq \boldsymbol{X}$. Four random integers r_1', r_2', s_1', s_2' of $PosKey^Y$ are re-randomized as follows

$$\begin{pmatrix} r_1' \\ r_2' \\ s_1' \\ s_2' \end{pmatrix} = \begin{pmatrix} r_1 \\ r_2 \\ 0 \\ 0 \end{pmatrix} + \begin{pmatrix} s_1 \\ s_2 \\ s_1 \\ s_2 \end{pmatrix} \times \begin{pmatrix} \gamma \\ \gamma \\ \delta \\ \delta \end{pmatrix} \quad \mod \ N \tag{5}$$

Since $\gamma, r_1, r_2, s_1, s_2$ are picked uniformly and independently from $\mathbb{F}_N$, then r_1' and r_2' are also distributed uniformly in $\mathbb{F}_N$. Therefore, $PosKey_d^Y$ has the same distribution as that of the private key of PosKey_d^X. At the same time, s_1, s_2 and δ are randomly picked from $\mathbb{F}_N$, then s_1', s_2' are also uniformly distributed in $\mathbb{F}_N$ in $PosKey_r^Y$ key. Therefore, the partial order delegation key generated by the *PosDelegate* algorithm has the same distribution as that of the private key of PosKey_r^X.

After received the private key, user can verify the validate of the private key PosKey^Y by

$$\begin{cases} \hat{e}(k_2^Y, G) = \Omega \cdot \hat{e}(V, k_0^Y)\hat{e}(W, k_1^Y)\hat{e}(\prod_{i \in \Lambda - \mathcal{U}_Y} U_i^{a_i}, k_0^Y) \\ \hat{e}(k_2^Y \prod \mathbf{h}^Y, G) = \Omega \cdot \hat{e}(V, k_0^Y)\hat{e}(W, k_1^Y)\hat{e}(\prod_{i \in \Lambda} U_i^{a_i}, k_0^Y) \\ \hat{e}(\tilde{k}_2^Y, G) = \hat{e}(V, \tilde{k}_0^Y)\hat{e}(W, \tilde{k}_1^Y)\hat{e}(\prod_{i \in \Lambda - \mathcal{U}_Y} U_i^{a_i}, \tilde{k}_0^Y) \\ \hat{e}(\tilde{k}_2^Y \prod \tilde{\mathbf{h}}^Y, G) = \hat{e}(V, \tilde{k}_0^Y)\hat{e}(W, \tilde{k}_1^Y)\hat{e}(\prod_{i \in \Lambda} U_i^{a_i}, \tilde{k}_0^Y) \end{cases}$$

Encrypt(*params, Y, M*): To encrypt a message $M \in \mathbb{G}_T$ to roles who carry the subset $Y = \{y_i | i \in \mathcal{U}_Y, y_i \in \Lambda\}$, sender picks $s, t_1, t_2, t_3 \in \mathbb{F}_N^\times$ randomly, and produces the ciphertext $\text{CT}^Y = [C_1, C_2, C_3, C_4] \in \mathbb{G}_T \times \mathbb{G}^3$ as

$$C_1 \leftarrow M \cdot \Omega^s, \ C_2 \leftarrow G^s g_q^{t_1}, \ C_3 \leftarrow W^s g_q^{t_2}, \ C_4 \leftarrow (V \prod_{i \in \Lambda - \mathcal{U}_Y} U_i^{y_i})^s g_q^{t_3}$$

Decrypt(*params, PosKey^V, CT^Y*): User decrypts the ciphertext $\text{CT}^Y = [C_1 C_2, C_3, C_4]$ using his first three elements k_0, k_1, k_2 of subkey PosKey_d^Y, and extracts the plaintext M from the ciphertext CT^Y by computing

$$M \leftarrow C_1 \cdot \hat{e}(k_0, C_4)\hat{e}(k_1, C_3)\hat{e}(k_2, C_2)^{-1}$$

4.2 Decryption Consistency

As we consider the partial order as subset inclusion, it is obvious that $y_i = a_j$ for all $i \in \mathcal{U}_Y$ and some $j \in \mathcal{U}_X$ since $Y \subseteq X$. The blinding factor for decryption algorithm is computed as

$$\frac{\hat{e}(k_0, C_4)\hat{e}(k_1, C_3)}{\hat{e}(k_2, C_2)} = \frac{\hat{e}(g^{r_1}, (V\prod_{i\in\Lambda-\mathcal{U}_Y} U_i^{a_i})^s g_q^{t_3})\hat{e}(g^{r_2}, W^s g_q^{t_2})}{\hat{e}(g_1(v\prod_{i\in\Lambda-\mathcal{U}_Y} u_i^{a_i})^{r_1} w^{r_2}, G^s g_q^{t_1})}$$

$$= \frac{\hat{e}(g^{r_1}, (V\prod_{i\in\Lambda-\mathcal{U}_Y} U_i^{a_i})^s)\hat{e}(g^{r_2}, W^s)}{\hat{e}(g_1(v\prod_{i\in\mathcal{U}_Y} u_i^{a_i})^{r_1} w^{r_2}), G^s)}$$

$$= \frac{\hat{e}(g^s, (v\prod_{i\in\Lambda-\mathcal{U}_Y} u_i^{a_i})^{r_1})\hat{e}(g^s, w^{r_2})}{\hat{e}(g_1(v\prod_{i\in\Lambda-\mathcal{U}_Y} u_i^{a_i})^{r_1} w^{r_2}, g^s)}$$

$$= \frac{1}{\hat{e}(g^s, g_1)} = \frac{1}{\Omega^s}$$

4.3 Security Analysis

We prove the security of confidentiality and anonymity under the structure as a hybrid experiment over a sequence of games which is defined as follows:

- $Game_0$: $CT_0 = [C_1, C_2, C_3, C_4]$;
- $Game_1$: $CT_1 = [C_1 R' = R_1, C_2, C_3, C_4]$;
- $Game_2$: $CT_2 = [R_1, R_2, C_3, C_4]$;
- $Game_3$: $CT_3 = [R_1, R_2, R_3, R_4]$;

where $R' \in \mathbb{G}_T$ and $R_2, R_3, R_4 \in \mathbb{G}$ with random picked.

The first game $Game_0$ is the game of real anonymous partial order delegation ciphertext, and CT_3 is random components with same structure.

We show that under the ℓ-wBDHI assumption and ℓ-cDH assumption hold, there are no algorithm that can distinguish between $Game_i$ and $Game_{i+1}(i = 0, 1, 2)$. Furthermore, in CT_3 of $Game_3$, four components are randomly picked from $\mathbb{G}_T$ or $\mathbb{G}$, so it is indistinguishable between the real ciphertext CT_0 and random group elements of CT_3. We give the detail proofs in Lemma 1, Lemma 2, and Lemma 3 for indistinguishability between $Game_i$ and $Game_{i+1}$ ($i=0,1,2$) in the full version of this paper.

Lemma 1. *If an adversary can distinguish the $Game_0$ and $Game_1$ with ϵ_1 advantage in time t after he performs at most q_s PosDelegate extraction queries, then there exist an algorithm can solve the ℓ-wBDHI problem with the advantage $(\Theta(t), \epsilon_1)$.*

Lemma 2. *If an adversary can distinguish the $Game_1$ and $Game_2$ with ϵ_2 advantage in time t after he performs at most q_s PosDelegate key extraction queries, then there exist an algorithm can solve the ℓ-cDH problem with the advantage $(\Theta(t), \epsilon_2)$.*

Lemma 3. *If an adversary can distinguish the $Game_2$ and $Game_3$ with ϵ_3 advantage in time t after he performs at most q_s PosDelegate key extraction queries, then there exist an algorithm can solve the ℓ-cDH problem with the advantage $(\Theta(t), \epsilon_3)$.*

Theorem 1. *[**Confidentiality**]. If group generator $\mathcal{G}$ satisfies the (t, ϵ_1) ℓ-wBDHI assumption, then the proposed scheme is $(\Theta(t), \epsilon_1)$-IND-sSET-CSA secure.*

proof. If the group algorithm $\mathcal{G}$ exists and ℓ-wBDHI assumption holds in $\mathcal{G}$, then Lemma 1 shows that there is no adversary with non-negligible advantage ϵ_1 to distinguish Game_0 and Game_1. In particular, it is indistinguishable between C_1 in CT_0 and R_1 in CT_1. As the adversary's view R_1 is randomly picked from $\mathbb{G}_T$ because $R_1 = C_1 R'$ and R' is randomly picked from $\mathbb{G}_T$. The proposed scheme is semantic secure since only component C_1 consists of the plaintext M in CT_1.

Theorem 2. *[Anonymity].* *If group generator $\mathcal{G}$ makes the (t, ϵ_2)-ℓ-cDH assumption hold in Lemma 2 and (t, ϵ_3)-ℓ-cDH assumption hold in Lemma 3, then the proposed scheme is $(\Theta(t), \epsilon_2 + \epsilon_3)$-ANON-sSET-CSA secure.*

proof. In according to Lemma 2 and Lemma 3, we show that there is no adversary with non-negligible advantage $\epsilon_2 + \epsilon_3$ to distinguish CT_1 and CT_3 under the ℓ-cDH assumption holds. Informally, R_2, R_3, R_4 in CT_3 are randomly picked from $\mathbb{G}$ where they leak no information about decryptor information. Then, CT_0 may keep the anonymity since CT_1 also leaks no information about the recipient.

Theorem 3. *[Delegation indistinguishability].* *The proposed scheme is probabilistic delegation indistinguishable for two delegation paths. That is, the delegation key is independent to delegation paths.*

proof. In order to prove the delegation indistinguishability, first we consider two basic delegation model: vertical delegation(Fig.2(a)) and horizonal delegation(Fig.2(b)). We prove these basic partial order delegations are independent to the delegation paths. Then we use these two atoms delegation to demonstrate that arbitrary hybrid delegation(Fig.2(c)) is indistinguishable.

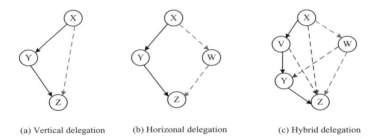

(a) Vertical delegation   (b) Horizonal delegation   (c) Hybrid delegation

Fig. 2. Delegation indistinguishability

In Fig.2(a), as $Z \preceq Y \preceq X$, it is easy to see that $Z \preceq X$ because of the transitivity property of partial order relationship. The PosKey_d^Y is delegated and randomized from PosKey^X by PosDelegate algorithm as $\text{PosKey}_d^Y = [k_0^X, k_1^X, k_2^X \prod_{i \in \mathcal{U}_{X-Y}} h_i^X, (\mathbf{h})^X - (\mathbf{h})^{X-Y}]$, and PosKey_d^Z is also partial order delegated from PosKey^X by PosDelegate algorithm such that $\text{PosKey}_d^Z = [k_0^X, k_1^X, k_2^X \prod_{i \in \mathcal{U}_{X-Z}} h_i^X, (\mathbf{h})^X - (\mathbf{h})^{X-Z}]$ without randomization. Meanwhile, PosKey_d^Z can be delegated from PosKey_d^Y as $\text{PosKey}_{d_2}^Z = [k_0^Y, k_1^Y, k_2^Y \prod_{i \in \mathcal{U}_{Y-Z}} h_i^Y, (\mathbf{h})^Y - (\mathbf{h})^{Y-Z}]$.

It is easy to see that k_0^X (*resp.* k_1^X) in $\text{PosKey}_{d_1}^Z$ and k_0^Y (*resp.* k_1^Y) in $\text{PosKey}_{d_1}^Z$ is indistinguishable since delegation key PosKey^Y has the same distribution with PosKey^X by evolution randomization variate in eqn. (1). Furthermore, we have $(\mathbf{h})^X - (\mathbf{h})^{X-Z} = (\mathbf{h})^Z = (\mathbf{h})^Y - (\mathbf{h})^{X-Z}$. As the randomization derivation key in the PosDelegate algorithm has the same distribution with delegation procedure, then $\text{PosKey}_{d_1}^Z$ and $\text{PosKey}_{d_2}^Z$ is indistinguishable. It is easy to prove that the delegation key PosKey_r^Z is also indistinguishable since it only excludes the g_1 in k_2^Z. Thus, the two delegation chains $X \to Y \to Z$ and $X \to Z$ are indistinguishable.

In Fig.2(b), as delegation chain $X \to Y \to Z$ is indistinguishable to chain $X \to Z$, and $X \to W \to Z$ is also indistinguishable to chain $X \to Z$, then the chain $X \to Y \to Z$ and the chain $X \to W \to Z$ are indistinguishable. By the combination of vertical delegation and horizonal delegation, we can prove a hybrid partial order delegation is indistinguishable in Fig.2(c).

5   Discussion

5.1   Key Derivation

In hierarchical delegation schemes [5, 6, 9, 12, 19], ciphertext CT^Y can be decrypted with decryption key PosKey^Y directly. However, the superior role V has to perform the key delegation procedure to obtain the decryption key PosKey^Y if $Y \preceq V$ since V's decryption key cannot decrypt CT^Y immediately. Our scheme has the same problem. Decryptor V tries the subrole combinations to generate an appropriate key of Y by the delegation algorithm if he does not know the decryption role distinctly. This is an open problem for a superior to decrypt the ciphertext (someone encrypts a message to his delegatee) without key derivation procedure in hierarchical delegation scheme. In our scheme, the ciphertext CT^Y can be decrypted by the decryption key owner Y or his partial order superset V. Thus, we define the anonymity against the adversary $\mathcal{A}$ whose role restricts that Y is not the partial order subset of $\mathcal{A}$.

HIBE is a tree-based sequential delegation scheme. It will generate different private keys if two hierarchical identities were exchanged, i.e. $\text{sk}^{a_1 a_2} \neq \text{sk}^{a_2 a_1}$. Our scheme is based on partial order subset delegation, and then it is independent of the delegation path, that is, $\text{sk}^{a_1 a_2} = \text{sk}^{a_2 a_1}$. Let Y be the encryption policy, and then role V can decrypt the ciphertext CT^Y if $Y \preceq V$ holds. In particular, role Y itself can also decrypt the ciphertext since $Y \preceq Y$.

5.2   Application in Broadcasting Message with Confidentiality

We can deploy the proposed scheme into broadcast encryption [23] with slight modification. First, we re-define the partial order as $\in$ (belong to) over set Λ, and use broadcast recipient public keys set S as an encryption policy to encrypt a message. Intuitively, role v_ρ can decrypt the ciphertext if his role satisfies the encryption policy, i.e., $\rho \in S$.

6   Concluding Remarks

In this paper, we proposed a general encryption scheme with partial order dele-gation, and presented its security models. Especially, except the confidentiality and anonymity, we introduced a new security conception called delegation in-distinguishability for partial-order delegation functionality. Meanwhile, we also constructed a concrete scheme with anonymous partial-order subset delegation encryption scheme that holds the constant-size ciphertext, and presented its se-lective security analysis in the standard model. The proposed scheme can be considered as a generalized extension for anonymous HIBE, broadcast encryp-tion, and delegatable function encryptions such as delegatable ABE, predicate encryption, hidden-vector encryption, etc.

To construct a general function encryption for all polynomial-time function-alities is an open problem [8], so we consider that it is an interesting issue in implementing a partial-order delegation relationship based on general polynomial-time functionalities that is a practical delegation model. We also consider the conditional partial-order delegation scheme in the future.

Acknowledgment. The authors grateful thank the anonymous reviewers for their valuable comments. We also thank Dr. Fagen Li for his helpful discussion in security proof. This work is supported by National Science Foundation of China under Grant 60973134, National Science Foundation of Guangdong Under Grant 10151064201 000028 and 10351806001000000, the Foundation for Distinguished Young Talents in Higher Education of Guangdong under Grant wym09066, and supported by Grant-in-Aid for JSPS Fellows of Japan under Grant 22·00045.

References

1. Abdalla, M., Kiltz, E., Neven, G.: Generalized key delegation for hierarchical identity-based encryption. IET Information Security 2(3), 67–78 (2008)
2. Agrawal, S., Boneh, D., Boyen, X.: Lattice basis delegation in fixed dimension and shorter-ciphertext hierarchical IBE. In: Rabin, T. (ed.) CRYPTO 2010. LNCS, vol. 6223, pp. 98–115. Springer, Heidelberg (2010)
3. Attrapadung, N., Libert, B.: Functional encryption for inner product: Achiev-ing constant-size ciphertexts with adaptive security or support for negation. In: Nguyen, P.Q., Pointcheval, D. (eds.) PKC 2010. LNCS, vol. 6056, pp. 384–402. Springer, Heidelberg (2010)
4. Boneh, D., Boyen, X.: Efficient selective-ID secure identity-based encryption with-out random oracles. In: Cachin, C., Camenisch, J.L. (eds.) EUROCRYPT 2004. LNCS, vol. 3027, pp. 223–238. Springer, Heidelberg (2004)
5. Boneh, D., Boyen, X., Goh, E.-J.: Hierarchical identity based encryption with con-stant size ciphertext. In: Cramer, R. (ed.) EUROCRYPT 2005. LNCS, vol. 3494, pp. 440–456. Springer, Heidelberg (2005)
6. Boneh, D., Hamburg, M.: Generalized identity based and broadcast encryption schemes. In: Pieprzyk, J. (ed.) ASIACRYPT 2008. LNCS, vol. 5350, pp. 455–470. Springer, Heidelberg (2008)

7. Boneh, D., Goh, E.-J., Nissim, K.: Evaluating 2-DNF formulas on ciphertexts. In: Kilian, J. (ed.) TCC 2005. LNCS, vol. 3378, pp. 325–341. Springer, Heidelberg (2005)
8. Boneh, D., Sahai, A., Waters, B.: Functional encryption: Definitions and challenges. In: Ishai, Y. (ed.) TCC 2011. LNCS, vol. 6597, pp. 253–273. Springer, Heidelberg (2011)
9. Boyen, X., Waters, B.: Anonymous hierarchical identity-based encryption (Without random oracles). In: Dwork, C. (ed.) CRYPTO 2006. LNCS, vol. 4117, pp. 290–307. Springer, Heidelberg (2006)
10. Cash, D., Hofheinz, D., Kiltz, E., Peikert, C.: Bonsai trees, or how to delegate a lattice basis. In: Gilbert, H. (ed.) EUROCRYPT 2010. LNCS, vol. 6110, pp. 523–552. Springer, Heidelberg (2010)
11. Ducas, L.: Anonymity from asymmetry: New constructions for anonymous HIBE. In: Pieprzyk, J. (ed.) CT-RSA 2010. LNCS, vol. 5985, pp. 148–164. Springer, Heidelberg (2010)
12. Gentry, C., Halevi, S.: Hierarchical identity based encryption with polynomially many levels. In: Reingold, O. (ed.) TCC 2009. LNCS, vol. 5444, pp. 437–456. Springer, Heidelberg (2009)
13. Lewko, A., Okamoto, T., Sahai, A., Takashima, K., Waters, B.: Fully secure functional encryption: Attribute-based encryption and (Hierarchical) inner product encryption. In: Gilbert, H. (ed.) EUROCRYPT 2010. LNCS, vol. 6110, pp. 62–91. Springer, Heidelberg (2010)
14. Lewko, A., Waters, B.: New techniques for dual system encryption and fully secure HIBE with short ciphertexts. In: Micciancio, D. (ed.) TCC 2010. LNCS, vol. 5978, pp. 455–479. Springer, Heidelberg (2010)
15. Okamoto, T., Takashima, K.: Homomorphic encryption and signatures from vector decomposition. In: Galbraith, S.D., Paterson, K.G. (eds.) Pairing 2008. LNCS, vol. 5209, pp. 57–74. Springer, Heidelberg (2008)
16. Okamoto, T., Takashima, K.: Hierarchical predicate encryption for inner-products. In: Matsui, M. (ed.) ASIACRYPT 2009. LNCS, vol. 5912, pp. 214–231. Springer, Heidelberg (2009)
17. Ostrovsky, R., Sahai, A., Waters, B.: Attribute-based encryption with nonmonotonic access structures. In: CCS 2007, pp. 195–203 (2007)
18. Sahai, A., Waters, B.: Fuzzy identity-based encryption. In: Cramer, R. (ed.) EUROCRYPT 2005. LNCS, vol. 3494, pp. 457–473. Springer, Heidelberg (2005)
19. Seo, J.H., Kobayashi, T., Ohkubo, M., Suzuki, K.: Anonymous hierarchical identity-based encryption with constant size ciphertexts. In: Jarecki, S., Tsudik, G. (eds.) PKC 2009. LNCS, vol. 5443, pp. 215–234. Springer, Heidelberg (2009)
20. Shi, E., Waters, B.: Delegating capabilities in predicate encryption systems. In: Aceto, L., Damgård, I., Goldberg, L.A., Halldórsson, M.M., Ingólfsdóttir, A., Walukiewicz, I. (eds.) ICALP 2008, Part II. LNCS, vol. 5126, pp. 560–578. Springer, Heidelberg (2008)
21. Waters, B.: Dual system encryption: Realizing fully secure IBE and HIBE under simple assumptions. In: Halevi, S. (ed.) CRYPTO 2009. LNCS, vol. 5677, pp. 619–636. Springer, Heidelberg (2009)
22. Zhou, M., Cao, Z.: Spatial encryption under simpler assumption. In: Pieprzyk, J., Zhang, F. (eds.) ProvSec 2009. LNCS, vol. 5848, pp. 19–31. Springer, Heidelberg (2009)
23. Zhou, Z., Huang, D.: On efficient ciphertext-policy attribute based encryption and broadcast encryption (extend abstract). In: CCS 2010, pp. 753–755. ACM, New York (2010)

Concurrent Signatures with Fully Negotiable Binding Control

Tsz Hon Yuen[1], Duncan S. Wong[2], Willy Susilo[3], and Qiong Huang[4]

[1] University of Hong Kong, Hong Kong
thyuen@cs.hku.hk
[2] City University of Hong Kong, Hong Kong
duncan@cityu.edu.hk
[3] University of Wollongong, Australia
wsusilo@uow.edu.au
[4] South China Agricultural University, China
csqhuang@alumni.cityu.edu.hk

Abstract. Since the introduction of concurrent signatures, the authorship binding of concurrent signatures has always been initiator-controlled, that is, only the initiator of a concurrent signature exchange can control "whether" and "when" to convert the exchanging ambiguous signatures to publicly verifiable ones concurrently. This binding control is not negotiable. In some applications however, this limitation is undesirable, and instead, as of optimistic fair exchange does, letting the responder control "whether" and "when" to have exchanged ambiguous signatures bound is needed. This motivates us towards constructing a new concurrent signature variant which supports negotiation between the original initiator-controlled binding and a new responder-controlled binding. In this paper, we formalize the notion and propose the first construction, which allows either the initiator or the responder to control "whether" and "when" the binding of the exchanging ambiguous signatures will take place concurrently. The scheme is backward compatible to the original concurrent signature and is also comparable in performance to the existing ones.

Keywords: Concurrent Signature, Fair Exchange, Authorship Binding.

1   Introduction

Fair exchange of digital signatures is a useful cryptographic protocol which enables e-commerce applications to exchange digital signatures for legal contracts or agreements in a fair manner. In daily commercial operations, it usually involves the exchange of an item for another. In ancient world, the bartering system allows goods or services to be exchanged directly for other goods or services. Today, goods and services are exchanged electronically on the Internet. No matter which system we are in, we want our exchanges to be *fair*, that is, at end of an exchange between two parties, either both parties receive the complete items they expect, or none of them gets anything, in an all-or-nothing manner.

X. Boyen and X. Chen (Eds.): ProvSec 2011, LNCS 6980, pp. 170–187, 2011.
© Springer-Verlag Berlin Heidelberg 2011

Optimistic fair exchange [6,1,8,7] is a type of fair exchange protocols which require a trusted third party, Arbitrator, to get involved between two communicating parties when there is a dispute to be resolved between them. In an optimistic fair exchange protocol, an initiator A first sends an ambiguous signature σ_A to a responder B who verifies the signature, then generates and sends back a publicly verifiable signature S_B to A. A verifies S_B, then generates and sends a publicly verifiable signature S_A to B. The exchange is completed if B finds that S_A is valid. When there is a dispute, namely after B sends back S_B, A does not send out S_A, or S_A is invalid, B can ask the Arbitrator for resolving the dispute by sending σ_A and S_B to the Arbitrator. The Arbitrator verifies σ_A and S_B, then converts σ_A to S_A, and sends it back to B.

In [4], Chen, Kudla and Paterson introduced a notion called *Concurrent Signature*. It is another approach to achieving fair exchange of digital signatures. Unlike optimistic fair exchange, a concurrent signature scheme does not have the Arbitrator. Instead, the two parties interact in the following three phases:

1. **Keystone Generation Phase:** An initiator A generates a *keystone ks* and a *keystone fix KF*, and sends KF to a responder B.
2. **Ambiguous Signature Generation Phase:** A generates and sends an ambiguous signature σ_A to B. Then B generates and sends an ambiguous signature σ_B back to A after verifying the validity of σ_A.
3. **Signature Authorship Binding Phase:** After verifying the validity of σ_B, A sends the keystone ks to B.

The keystone binds the authorship of σ_A and σ_B to A and B, respectively, that is, σ_A and σ_B are becoming publicly verifiable to A and B, respectively, once ks is given. The binding of σ_A to A and that of σ_B to B happen *concurrently*. If ks is not released, none of σ_A or σ_B will bind to any signer.

Signature Authorship Binding Control. A concurrent signature gives the initiator A the full control on "whether" and "when" the binding of the authorship of ambiguous signatures σ_A and σ_B will take place through releasing the keystone ks, which converts σ_A and σ_B to publicly verifiable ones concurrently. This binding process of signers' authorship is not negotiable, and the responder B has no control once σ_B is sent out. We call this property as *initiator-controlled*. On the contrary, optimistic fair exchange has always been *responder-controlled*. Once after the initiator A sends out an ambiguous signature σ_A, A can no longer control "whether" or "when" σ_A will be converted to S_A, which is publicly verifiable. Instead, the control is under the responder B through sending out a publicly verifiable signature S_B which makes A to compel and complete the exchange by sending out a valid S_A. Even if A does not compel, B can always solicit the Arbitrator and get S_A.

For all the current concurrent signature schemes [4,11,5,9,13,12], the binding has always been initiator-controlled. In some applications, this limitation is undesirable. Instead, as of optimistic fair exchange, letting the responder control "whether" and "when" to have both exchanged ambiguous signatures bound may be needed. Consider that an initiator Alice is making a fair exchange of signatures with a responder Bob using concurrent signature. At the same time, Alice is making another fair exchange of signatures with a responder Carol. One concrete example is that Alice is a consumer, and Bob and Carol are two merchants. Alice is about to make a deal with one of the merchants. After getting the responses (i.e. the ambiguous signatures) from Bob and Carol, Alice will decide which keystone to throw out, that is, which responder's signature to bind to, for example, depending on which responder's offer is better. The fairness is still maintained, however, Alice may have a fair exchange completed with Bob only but not with Carol, maybe because Bob's offer is better.

In the application above, although concurrent signature ensures fairness between Alice and each of the two merchants, initiator-controlled concurrent signature is not desirable from the merchants' perspective because the merchants have no control on "whether" the initiator will finally release the keystone and complete the exchange. A responder-controlled concurrent signature scheme might be more suitable as once the consumer Alice has committed to a price that she is willing to pay for a service offered by a merchant, say Bob, Alice can no longer commits herself to a similar service offered by another merchant, Carol, while later can withdraw one of her commitments by simply not releasing the corresponding keystone.

Consider another scenario where concurrent signature scheme is used for fairly exchanging signatures between two parties, A and B, for example, for fairly exchanging two electronic items via the Internet on some electronic auction site. As concurrent signature is initiator-controlled, the initiator A has full control on "when" to complete the fair exchange with the responder B. Unless making B as the initiator of the concurrent signature, B cannot be sure when the fair exchange will end. If A is the auctioneer and B is a bidder, then B cannot be sure "when" the exchanging signature from the auctioneer will finally be actualized unless the system explicitly reverts the protocol run and sets B as the initiator of the concurrent signature.

These applications and scenarios motivate us towards formalizing and constructing a new concurrent signature variant called Concurrent Signature with Fully Negotiable Binding Control (CS-FNBC) which supports negotiation between initiator-controlled binding and responder-controlled binding.

1.1   Concurrent Signature with Fully Negotiable Binding Control

We propose a new notion called *Concurrent Signature with Fully Negotiable Binding Control (CS-FNBC)*. In a CS-FNBC scheme, initiator A and responder B generate their own keystone and keystone fix pairs, say (ks_A, KF_A) and (ks_B, KF_B), respectively. In the Keystone Generation Phase (i.e. phase 1), A and B releases their keystone fixes KF_A and KF_B. In the Ambiguous Signature Generation Phase (i.e. phase 2), A sends out an ambiguous signature σ_A and then B sends out another ambiguous signature σ_B after checking the validity of σ_A. In the Signature Authorship Binding Phase (i.e. phase 3 above), A and B can negotiate on who will be the last one to release its keystone, and this party will be the one who controls "whether" and "when" the binding of their ambiguous signatures (σ_A and σ_B) will finally take place. For example, if ks_A (resp. ks_B) is released before ks_B (resp. ks_A) in phase 3, B (resp. A) will have the binding control. The order of releasing the keystones by A and B can be freely negotiated by A and B, and easily implemented in phase 3. The fairness of the concurrent signature will not be affected. Once both ks_A and ks_B are released, the authorship binding of σ_A to A and σ_B to B will take place concurrently, while none of the ambiguous signatures will bind to any signer if one of the keystones is not released.

CS-FNBC is backward compatible to the original concurrent signature. In the Keystone Generation Phase (i.e. phase 1), we may set $ks := ks_A$ and $KF := \langle KF_A, ks_B, KF_B \rangle$. The Ambiguous Signature Generation Phase (i.e. phase 2) is identical to that of the original concurrent signature, namely A sends out σ_A, and then B sends out σ_B. In the Signature Authorship Binding Phase (i.e. phase 3), A releases ks_A which, together with ks_B (already released in phase 1), concurrently binds the authorship of σ_A to A and σ_B to B.

To realize responder-controlled binding, the CS-FNBC can be run in the following steps. In the Keystone Generation Phase (phase 1), the keystone fix is set to $\langle KF_A, KF_B \rangle$. In the Ambiguous Signature Generation Phase (phase 2), initiator A sends out σ_A, and then responder B sends out σ_B. In the Signature Authorship Binding Phase (phase 3), A releases ks_A then B determines "whether" and "when" the authorship binding will take place through controlling "whether" and "when" to release ks_B.

In this paper, we formalize CS-FNBC, define a new security model, and propose the first construction of CS-FNBC. The more stringent ambiguous requirement of perfect concurrent signature [11,5,13] is also captured in the model. The construction is proven secure under the security models we defined in the random oracle model. The performance of the construction is also comparable to that of the most efficient concurrent signature scheme currently available.

1.2   Related Work

A concurrent signature [4,11,5,9,13,12] ensures the *ambiguity* of the signatures σ_A and σ_B exchanged between an initiator A and a responder B provided that the corresponding keystone ks of a released keystone fix KF is not known, that is, the public should not be able to tell if σ_A (resp. σ_B) was generated by A or B (resp. B or A) before ks is released. In addition, no one including B (resp. A) should be able to convince anyone else that σ_A (resp. σ_B) was generated by A (resp. B). While at the same time, when B receives σ_A, B can be sure that σ_A must be generated by A (i.e. *unforgeability*). In addition, a concurrent signature should be *fair*, that is, once ks is released, the authorship of σ_A to A and that of σ_B to B should be bound concurrently.

In [11], Susilo, Mu and Zhang proposed an enhanced ambiguity requirement for concurrent signature and called a scheme satisfying this enhanced requirement as *perfect concurrent signature*. It requires that before releasing ks, the public cannot tell if σ_A and σ_B are generated by A and B, respectively. In the original ambiguity requirement, the adversary is given only one ambiguous signature, say σ_A and the adversary is trying to find out whether σ_A is generated by A or B. In this enhanced ambiguity requirement, the adversary is given a pair of ambiguous signatures σ_A and σ_B, and the adversary is trying to distinguish the following four disjointed scenarios:

1. σ_A is generated by A and σ_B is generated by B;
2. σ_A is generated by B and σ_B is generated by A;
3. Both σ_A and σ_B are generated by A;
4. Both σ_A and σ_B are generated by B.

The first concurrent signature scheme [4] does not satisfy this enhanced ambiguity requirement. In [11] and [5], two perfect concurrent signature schemes were proposed while both of them were later found insecure and then improved in [13]. Some variants of concurrent signatures can also be found in the literature, for example, an asymmetric concurrent signature [9], an identity-based concurrent signature [5] and multi-party concurrent signature [12,10].

2   Definitions and Security Models

A Concurrent Signature with Fully Negotiable Binding Control (CS-FNBC) consists of the following probabilistic polynomial-time (PPT) algorithms.

- Setup(1^k). On input a security parameter $k \in \mathbb{N}$, it outputs a list params of system parameters, that include a keystone space $\mathcal{K}$, a keystone fix space $\mathcal{F}$ and a message space $\mathcal{M}$.
- KeyGen(params). On input params, it outputs a private/public key pair (x, y).
- KSGen(m_A, y_A, y_B). On input a message m_A, a sender public key y_A and a receiver public key y_B, it outputs a keystone $ks_A \in \mathcal{K}$ and a keystone fix $KF_A \in \mathcal{F}$.
- ASign($m_A, y_A, y_B, x_A, ks_A, KF_A, KF_B$). On input a message $m_A \in \mathcal{M}$, two public keys (y_A, y_B), a sender secret key x_A, a sender keystone ks_A, a sender keystone fix KF_A and a receiver keystone fix KF_B, it outputs an ambiguous signature σ_A.
- AVerify($\sigma_A, m_A, y_A, y_B, KF_A, KF_B, x_B, ks_B$). On input an ambiguous signature σ_A, message $m_A \in \mathcal{M}$, public keys (y_A, y_B), sender keystone fix KF_A, receiver keystone fix KF_B, receiver secret key x_B and receiver keystone ks_B, it outputs accept meaning that the receiver is convinced that σ_A is generated by the sender whose public key is y_A; otherwise, it outputs reject.
- Verify($\sigma_A, m_A, m_B, y_A, y_B, ks_A, ks_B, KF_A, KF_B$). On input an ambiguous signature σ_A, messages (m_A, m_B), public keys (y_A, y_B), sender and receiver keystones (ks_A, ks_B), and sender and receiver keystone fixes (KF_A, KF_B), it outputs accept meaning that σ_A is generated by the one whose public key is y_A; otherwise, it outputs reject.

Suppose that after Setup and KeyGen, A's public and private keys are y_A and x_A, and B's public and private keys are y_B and x_B. A will sign on a message m_A and Bob will sign on a message m_B. The CS-FNBC scheme will carry out the steps shown in Table 1.

Below is the flow of a normal run with respect to the steps shown in Table 1.

Table 1. The Steps of Running a CS-FNBC Scheme

Step	Operation	Output
1_A	$(ks_A, KF_A) \leftarrow \mathsf{KSGen}(m_A, y_A, y_B)$	Send KF_A to B
1_B	$(ks_B, KF_B) \leftarrow \mathsf{KSGen}(m_B, y_B, y_A)$	Send KF_B to A
2_A	$\sigma_A \leftarrow \mathsf{ASign}(m_A, y_A, y_B, x_A, ks_A, KF_A, KF_B)$	Send (m_A, σ_A) to B
2_B	$\sigma_B \leftarrow \mathsf{ASign}(m_B, y_B, y_A, x_B, ks_B, KF_B, KF_A)$	Send (m_B, σ_B) to A
3_A	Release ks_A	ks_A
3_B	Release ks_B	ks_B

1. Keystone Generation Phase
   (a) Step 1_A
   (b) Step 1_B
2. Ambiguous Signature Generation Phase
   (a) Step 2_A
   (b) B checks if accept $\leftarrow \mathsf{AVerify}(\sigma_A, m_A, y_A, y_B, KF_A, KF_B, x_B, ks_B)$. If so, proceed; otherwise, abort.
   (c) Step 2_B
   (d) A checks if accept $\leftarrow \mathsf{AVerify}(\sigma_B, m_B, y_B, y_A, KF_B, KF_A, x_A, ks_A)$. If so, proceed; otherwise, abort.
3. Signature Authorship Binding Phase
   (a) A and B negotiate on who will take the binding control. Suppose that B will take the binding control.
   (b) Step 3_A
   (c) Step 3_B
   (d) The public can verify that

$$\text{accept} \leftarrow \mathsf{Verify}(\sigma_A, m_A, m_B, y_A, y_B, ks_A, ks_B, KF_A, KF_B)$$
$$\text{accept} \leftarrow \mathsf{Verify}(\sigma_B, m_B, m_A, y_B, y_A, ks_B, ks_A, KF_B, KF_A).$$

The above gives the binding control to B, that is, responder-controlled binding. For backward compatibility, that is, initiator-controlled binding, we may swap Step 3_A and Step 3_B. An alternative way, which yields fewer number of message flows, is given in Sec. 1.1

The correctness requirement of a CS-FNBC can be defined in an obvious way and therefore is skipped over here. In the following, we define the security requirements of *unforgeability*, *ambiguity* and *fairness* for CS-FNBC.

2.1   Unforgeability

We define the existential unforgeability against chosen message attacks for CS-FNBC. An adversary is given a set of public keys. The adversary can interact with any one of them and ask him to generate keystone fix, compute partial signatures, or reveal keystone. The adversary can also corrupt some users by obtaining their secret keys. The adversary should not be able to output a signature of an uncorrupted user, such that the corresponding keystone is not revealed before. We use the following game which is run by a challenger $\mathcal{C}$ against an adversary $\mathcal{A}$:

1. **Setup Phase.** On input a security parameter $k \in \mathbb{N}$, $\mathcal{C}$ runs params $\leftarrow$ Setup(1^k), then $(x_i, y_i) \leftarrow$ KeyGen(params) for $i = 1, \ldots, n$, where n is bounded polynomially in k. Denote $\mathcal{U} = \{y_1, \ldots, y_n\}$ as the set of public keys. $\mathcal{C}$ gives params and $\mathcal{U}$ to $\mathcal{A}$.

2. **Query Phase.** $\mathcal{A}$ queries the following oracles adaptively:
   - KSGenOracle: On input (m_A, y_A, y_B), where $y_A, y_B \in \mathcal{U}$, the oracle computes $(ks_A, KF_A) \leftarrow$ KSGen(m_A, y_A, y_B) and returns KF_A.
   - ASignOracle: On input $(m_A, y_A, y_B, KF_A, KF_B)$ where $y_A, y_B \in \mathcal{U}$, KF_A is the output of KSGenOracle(m_A, y_A, y_B) and $KF_B \in \mathcal{F}$ is chosen by $\mathcal{A}$, the oracle retrieves ks_A computed in KSGenOracle and returns an ambiguous signature $\sigma_A \leftarrow$ ASign($m_A, y_A, y_B, x_A, ks_A, KF_A, KF_B$).
   - KSRevealOracle: On input KF_A, the oracle retrieves ks_A from the answer of KSGenOracle(m_A, y_A, y_B) and outputs it. If KF_A is not the output of KSGenOracle(m_A, y_A, y_B), it returns nothing.
   - ExtractOracle: On input a public key $y_i \in \mathcal{U}$, the oracle returns the corresponding private key x_i.

3. **Output Phase.** $\mathcal{A}$ outputs a tuple $(\sigma_A^*, m_A^*, m_B^*, y_A^*, y_B^*, ks_A^*, ks_B^*, KF_A^*, KF_B^*)$, where $y_A^*, y_B^* \in \mathcal{U}$.

Adversary $\mathcal{A}$ wins if

1. accept $\leftarrow$ Verify($\sigma_A^*, m_A^*, m_B^*, y_A^*, y_B^*, ks_A^*, ks_B^*, KF_A^*, KF_B^*$);
2. y_A^* has never been queried to ExtractOracle; and
3. the output of KSGenOracle(m_A^*, y_A^*, y_B^*) has never been queried to KSRevealOracle such that the oracle returns the keystone ks_A^*.

The advantage of $\mathcal{A}$ is its probability of winning the game above.

Definition 1. *A CS-FNBC is* $(\epsilon, t, q_g, q_s, q_r, q_e)$-*EU-CMA secure if there is no adversary that runs in time* t, *issues at most* q_g, q_s, q_r, *and* q_e *queries to* KSGenOracle, ASignOracle, KSRevealOracle *and* ExtractOracle, *respectively, and has advantage at least* ϵ, *provided that* $q_e < n$, *where* n *is the number of public keys in the game above.*

2.2 Ambiguity

We now formalize the perfect ambiguity requirement for CS-FNBC under a chosen message attack model. The term *perfect ambiguity* is referred to the enhanced ambiguity requirement given in [11]. The game below is run by a challenger $\mathcal{C}$ against an adversary $\mathcal{A}$. We start with an overview of the game. Firstly, $\mathcal{A}$ receives two key pairs for parties A and B. Then $\mathcal{A}$ adaptively queries KSGenOracle and KSRevealOracle. After that, $\mathcal{C}$ generates two ambiguous signatures σ_A and σ_B in one of the following four ways:

   - σ_A and σ_B are generated by A and B, respectively;
   - σ_A and σ_B are generated by B and A, respectively;
   - σ_A and σ_B are generated by A;
   - σ_A and σ_B are generated by B;

Finally, $\mathcal{A}$ is to determine which of the four cases above is true. Note that $\mathcal{A}$ has the private keys of both A and B. Below is the game:

1. **Setup Phase.** On input $k \in \mathbb{N}$, $\mathcal{C}$ runs params $\leftarrow$ Setup(1^k), then generates two key pairs (y_A^*, x_A^*), (y_B^*, x_B^*) by running KeyGen(params) twice. $\mathcal{C}$ sends params, (y_A^*, x_A^*), and (y_B^*, x_B^*) to $\mathcal{A}$.
2. **Phase 1.** $\mathcal{A}$ queries KSGenOracle and KSRevealOracle, where the input public keys must be y_A^* and/or y_B^*.
3. **Challenge Phase.** $\mathcal{A}$ sends two messages m_A^*, m_B^* to $\mathcal{C}$. $\mathcal{C}$ queries KSGenOracle for $(ks_A^*, KF_A^*) \leftarrow$ KSGen(m_A^*, y_A^*, y_B^*) and $(ks_B^*, KF_B^*) \leftarrow$ KSGen(m_B^*, y_A^*, y_B^*), randomly picks $b \in \{1, 2, 3, 4\}$ and performs one of the following cases:
   - If $b = 1$, $\mathcal{C}$ calculates $\sigma_A^* \leftarrow$ ASign$(m_A^*, y_A^*, y_B^*, x_A^*, ks_A^*, KF_A^*, KF_B^*)$ and $\sigma_B^* \leftarrow$ ASign$(m_B^*, y_B^*, y_A^*, x_B^*, ks_B^*, KF_B^*, KF_A^*)$.
   - If $b = 2$, $\mathcal{C}$ calculates $\sigma_A^* \leftarrow$ ASign$(m_A^*, y_B^*, y_A^*, x_A^*, ks_A^*, KF_A^*, KF_B^*)$ and $\sigma_B^* \leftarrow$ ASign$(m_B^*, y_A^*, y_B^*, x_A^*, ks_B^*, KF_B^*, KF_A^*)$.
   - If $b = 3$, $\mathcal{C}$ calculates $\sigma_A^* \leftarrow$ ASign$(m_A^*, y_A^*, y_B^*, x_A^*, ks_A^*, KF_A^*, KF_B^*)$ and $\sigma_B^* \leftarrow$ ASign$(m_B^*, y_A^*, y_B^*, x_A^*, ks_B^*, KF_B^*, KF_A^*)$.
   - If $b = 4$, $\mathcal{C}$ calculates $\sigma_A^* \leftarrow$ ASign$(m_A^*, y_B^*, y_A^*, x_B^*, ks_A^*, KF_A^*, KF_B^*)$ and $\sigma_B^* \leftarrow$ ASign$(m_B^*, y_B^*, y_A^*, x_B^*, ks_B^*, KF_B^*, KF_A^*)$.
   $\mathcal{C}$ sends $(\sigma_A^*, \sigma_B^*, KF_A^*, KF_B^*)$ to $\mathcal{A}$.
4. **Phase 2.** $\mathcal{A}$ makes queries to KSGenOracle and KSRevealOracle but cannot query KSRevealOracle with any of KF_A^* and KF_B^* for ks_A^* or ks_B^*.
5. **Output Phase.** $\mathcal{A}$ returns a value $b' \in \{1, 2, 3, 4\}$ as its guess for b.

Adversary $\mathcal{A}$ wins the game above if $b = b'$. The advantage of $\mathcal{A}$ is defined as $|\Pr[b = b'] - 1/4|$.

Definition 2. *A CS-FNBC is (ϵ, t, q_g, q_r)-ambiguous if there is no adversary that runs in time t, issues at most q_g and q_r queries to* KSGenOracle *and* KSRevealOracle, *respectively, and has advantage at least ϵ in the game above.*

2.3   Fairness

The fairness of CS-FNBC is defined under a chosen message attack model using the following game played between an adversary $\mathcal{A}$ and a challenger $\mathcal{C}$. As of ambiguity, we start with an overview of the game. $\mathcal{A}$ receives two key pairs for parties A and B. Then $\mathcal{A}$ carries out the game with $\mathcal{C}$ by acting as A while having $\mathcal{C}$ act as B. $\mathcal{A}$ wins if:

- $\mathcal{C}$ outputs σ_B and a keystone fix KF_B as generated by B, while $\mathcal{A}$ can output the corresponding keystone ks_B without querying KSRevealOracle; or
- $\mathcal{C}$ outputs σ_B, KF_B and ks_B as generated by B, while $\mathcal{A}$ can output σ_A, KF_A and ks_A such that

$$\text{reject} \leftarrow \text{Verify}(\sigma_A, m_A, m_B, y_A, y_B, ks_A, ks_B, KF_A, KF_B)$$
$$\text{accept} \leftarrow \text{Verify}(\sigma_B, m_B, m_A, y_B, y_A, ks_B, ks_A, KF_B, KF_A).$$

Below is the fairness game.

1. **Setup Phase.** On input $k \in \mathbb{N}$, $\mathcal{C}$ runs params $\leftarrow$ Setup(1^k), then generates two key pairs (y_A^*, x_A^*), (y_B^*, x_B^*) by running KeyGen(params) twice. $\mathcal{C}$ sends params, (y_A^*, x_A^*), and (y_B^*, x_B^*) to $\mathcal{A}$.
2. **Query Phase.** $\mathcal{A}$ makes queries to KSGenOracle and KSRevealOracle, where the input public keys must be y_A^* and/or y_B^*.
3. **Keystone Fix Generation Phase.** $\mathcal{A}$ sends a message m_B^* to $\mathcal{C}$, in return a keystone fix KF_B^* from $\mathcal{C}$, where $(ks_B^*, KF_B^*) \leftarrow$ KSGen(m_B^*, y_B^*, y_A^*). $\mathcal{A}$ then sends a keystone fix KF_A^* to $\mathcal{C}$.
4. **Output Phase.** $\mathcal{C}$ sends $\sigma_B^* \leftarrow$ ASign($m_B^*, y_A^*, y_B^*, x_B^*, ks_B^*, KF_B^*, KF_A^*$) to $\mathcal{A}$. $\mathcal{A}$ wins by one of the following ways:
   (a) $\mathcal{A}$ outputs a tuple $(m_A^*, ks_A^*, \tilde{K})$ such that

$$\text{accept} \leftarrow \text{Verify}(\sigma_B^*, m_B^*, m_A^*, y_B^*, y_A^*, \tilde{K}, ks_A^*, KF_B^*, KF_A^*).$$

   (b) $\mathcal{A}$ outputs an ambiguous signature σ_A^* and a message m_A^*. $\mathcal{C}$ then outputs ks_B^*. Finally $\mathcal{A}$ outputs a keystone ks_A^* and wins if

$$\text{accept} \leftarrow \text{AVerify}(\sigma_A^*, m_A^*, y_A^*, y_B^*, KF_A^*, KF_B^*, x_B^*, ks_B^*),$$
$$\text{reject} \leftarrow \text{Verify}(\sigma_A^*, m_A^*, m_B^*, y_A^*, y_B^*, ks_A^*, ks_B^*, KF_A^*, KF_B^*), \text{ and}$$
$$\text{accept} \leftarrow \text{Verify}(\sigma_B^*, m_B^*, m_A^*, y_B^*, y_A^*, ks_B^*, ks_A^*, KF_B^*, KF_A^*).$$

The advantage of $\mathcal{A}$ is its probability of winning the game above.

Definition 3. *A CS-FNBC is* (ϵ, t, q_g, q_r)*-fair if there is no adversary that runs in time* t*, issues at most* q_g *and* q_r *queries to the* KSGenOracle*, and* KSRevealOracle*, respectively, and has advantage at least* ϵ *in the game above.*

3   A CS-FNBC Construction

The idea of our construction is to identify the core cryptographic primitive of a conventional concurrent signature scheme (iPCS1 [13]), then run it in parallel, one initiated by A and the other one by B. We utilize a Diffie-Hellman tuple to prevent anyone (even after compromising the private keys of initiator A and responder B) from telling if a combined keystone fix from KF_A and KF_B is generated by A or B, hence achieving the perfect ambiguity requirement. The (strong) unforgeability (i.e. the security model of unforgeability defined in Sec. 2.1) will be achieved by applying the conventional non-interactive Fair-Shamir transformation of the witness indistinguishability proof of the knowledge of the private key of A or B. Below are details.

- **Setup.** Let $k \in \mathbb{N}$ be a security parameter. Let $\mathbb{G}$ be a cyclic group of prime order p, where $p \geq 2^k$, and let g be a generator of $\mathbb{G}$. Set the keystone space to $\mathcal{K} := \mathbb{Z}_p \times \mathbb{Z}_p$, keystone fix space to $\mathcal{F} := \mathbb{Z}_p \times \mathbb{G}$, and message space to $\mathcal{M} := \{0,1\}^*$. Let $H : \{0,1\}^* \to \mathbb{Z}_p$, $H_1 : \{0,1\}^* \to \mathbb{Z}_p$ and $H_2 : \{0,1\}^* \to \mathbb{Z}_p$ be hash functions. Set params $:= \{\mathcal{K}, \mathcal{F}, \mathcal{M}, p, \mathbb{G}, g, H, H_1, H_2\}$.

- KeyGen. On input params, randomly pick a private key $x \in_R \mathbb{Z}_p$ and set the public key to $y = g^x$.

- KSGen. On input $m_A \in \mathcal{M}$, sender public key y_A and receiver public key y_B, randomly pick $k_A \in_R \mathbb{Z}_p$ and $r_A \in_R \mathbb{Z}_p$, then set the keystone as $ks_A = (k_A, r_A)$ and keystone fix as $KF_A = (s_A, R_A)$, where

$$s_A = H_1(k_A, R_A, m_A, y_A, y_B) \quad \text{and} \quad R_A = g^{r_A}.$$

- ASign. On input $m_A \in \mathcal{M}$, public keys (y_A, y_B), sender secret key x_A, sender keystone $ks_A = (k_A, r_A)$, sender keystone fix $KF_A = (s_A, R_A)$ and receiver keystone fix $KF_B = (s_B, R_B)$, randomly pick $\alpha_A \in_R \mathbb{Z}_p$ and compute:

$$t_A = H_2(R_B^{r_A}, m_A, y_A, y_B, KF_A, KF_B) + s_A + s_B \bmod p,$$
$$c_A = H(m_A, g^{\alpha_A} y_B^{t_A}, KF_A, KF_B),$$
$$z_A = (\alpha_A - c_A)x_A^{-1} \bmod p.$$

The ambiguous signature is $\sigma_A = (c_A, z_A, t_A)$.

- AVerify. On input $\sigma_A = (c_A, z_A, t_A)$, $m_A \in \mathcal{M}$, (y_A, y_B), $KF_A = (s_A, R_A)$, $KF_B = (s_B, R_B)$, x_B, and $ks_B = (k_B, r_B)$, output accept if

$$t_A = H_2(R_A^{r_B}, m_A, y_A, y_B, KF_A, KF_B) + s_A + s_B \bmod p,$$
$$c_A = H(m_A, g^{c_A} y_A^{z_A} y_B^{t_A}, KF_A, KF_B).$$

Otherwise, output reject.

- Verify. On input $\sigma_A = (c_A, z_A, t_A)$, $m_A, m_B \in \mathcal{M}$, (y_A, y_B), $ks_A = (k_A, r_A)$, $ks_B = (k_B, r_B)$, $KF_A = (s_A, R_A)$, and $KF_B = (s_B, R_B)$, output accept if all of the following hold:

$$s_A = H_1(k_A, R_A, m_A, y_A, y_B),$$
$$s_B = H_1(k_B, R_B, m_B, y_B, y_A),$$
$$t_A = H_2(g^{r_A r_B}, m_A, y_A, y_B, KF_A, KF_B) + s_A + s_B \bmod p,$$
$$c_A = H(m_A, g^{c_A} y_A^{z_A} y_B^{t_A}, KF_A, KF_B),$$
$$R_A = g^{r_A},$$
$$R_B = g^{r_B}.$$

Otherwise, output reject.

3.1   Security

The correctness of the scheme is obvious. The security relies on the conventional discrete logarithm assumption and the Computational Diffie-Hellman assumption. Let $\mathbb{G}$ be a cyclic group of prime order p and g a generator of $\mathbb{G}$.

Discrete Logarithm (DL) Problem. Given $g, y \in \mathbb{G}$, output $\alpha \in \mathbb{Z}_p$ such that $y = g^\alpha$. We say that the (ϵ, t)-DL assumption holds if there is no algorithm which runs in time t having the probability at least ϵ in solving the DL problem.

Computational Diffie-Hellman (CDH) Problem. Given $g, g^\alpha, g^\beta \in \mathbb{G}$ for some randomly chosen $\alpha, \beta \in_R \mathbb{Z}_p$, output $g^{\alpha\beta}$. We say that the (ϵ, t)-CDH assumption holds if there is no algorithm which runs in time t having probability at least ϵ in solving the CDH problem.

Theorem 1. *The CS-FNBC above is $(\epsilon, t, q_g, q_s, q_r, q_e)$-unforgeable if the (ϵ', t')-DL assumption holds in the random oracle model, where*

$$\epsilon' \geq (\frac{\epsilon}{n} - 2^{-k})^2 (1 - \frac{q_H}{2^k - q_H} - 2^{-k}), \qquad t' = t + O\Big((q_s + q_g + n)\rho\Big),$$

q_H *is the number of queries to the random oracle of H. ρ is the time for one exponentiation in $\mathbb{Z}_p$ and n is the number of public keys generated in the unforgeability game defined in Sec. 2.*

Proof. For contradiction, suppose that there exists an adversary $\mathcal{A}$ which wins the unforgeability game, we construct an algorithm $\mathcal{B}$ which solves a DL problem instance (g, g^α), where the unknown α is chosen uniformly at random from $\mathbb{Z}_p$. $\mathcal{B}$ simulates the unforgeability game by setting params = $\{\mathcal{K}, \mathcal{F}, \mathcal{M}, p, \mathbb{G}, g, H, H_1, H_2\}$, then it picks an index $j \in_R \{1, \ldots, n\}$ randomly. Without loss of generality, assume that $\mathcal{B}$ picks $j = n$. For $i = 1, \cdots, n-1$, $\mathcal{B}$ randomly picks $x_i \in_R \mathbb{Z}_p$ and sets $y_i = g^{x_i}$, then it sets y_n to the DL problem instance, that is, setting $y_n := g^\alpha$. $\mathcal{B}$ gives params and $\mathcal{U} = \{y_1, \ldots, y_n\}$ to $\mathcal{A}$. In the Query Phase, $\mathcal{B}$ simulates the oracles as follows.

- H-Oracle, H_1-Oracle and H_2-Oracle : They are simulated as random oracles, namely, for the H-Oracle, $\mathcal{B}$ maintains a H-list which is initially empty. When there is an $H(m_A, T_A, KF_A, KF_B)$ query, $\mathcal{B}$ sets its output to a random value, for example, $h \in_R \mathbb{Z}_p$ and adds $(m_A, T_A, KF_A, KF_B, h)$ into the H-list. If the same query $H(m_A, T_A, KF_A, KF_B)$ is made again, $\mathcal{B}$ looks up the H-list and returns with h. H_1-Oracle and H_2-Oracle are simulated similarly.
- KSGenOracle. On query (m, y_A, y_B), $\mathcal{B}$ follows the CS-FNBC scheme by running $(ks, KF) \leftarrow$ KSGen(m, y_A, y_B). The keystone fix $KF = (s, R)$ is returned. $\mathcal{B}$ stores (ks, KF, m, y_A, y_B) in a list $\mathcal{L}$ which is initially empty.
- ASignOracle. On query $(m_A, y_A, y_B, KF_A, KF_B)$, $\mathcal{B}$ searches the list $\mathcal{L}$ for an entry $(ks_A, KF_A, m_A, y_A, y_B)$. As specified in the unforgeability game, KF_A has to be the output of KSGenOracle(m_A, y_A, y_B), hence if it is not found, the oracle will return nothing. If it is found, then $\mathcal{B}$ runs ASign according to the CS-FNBC scheme if $y_A \neq y_n$. If $y_A = y_n$, $\mathcal{B}$ parses ks_A, KF_A, and KF_B as $ks_A = (k_A, r_A)$, $KF_A = (s_A, R_A)$ and $KF_B = (s_B, R_B)$, then queries H_2-Oracle for $H_2(R_B^{r_A}, m_A, y_A, y_B, KF_A, KF_B)$, and computes $t_A = s_A + s_B + H_2(R_B^{r_A}, m_A, y_A, y_B, KF_A, KF_B) \mod p$. It then randomly picks $z_A, c_A \in_R \mathbb{Z}_p$, computes $T_A = g^{c_A} y_A^{z_A} y_B^{t_A}$, and adds the tuple $(m_A, T_A, KF_A, KF_B, c_A)$ into the H-list ($\mathcal{B}$ declares failure and exits if

$(m_A, T_A, KF_A, KF_B, \cdot)$ is already in the H-list). Finally it returns (c_A, z_A, t_A) to $\mathcal{A}$ as an ambiguous signature.

- KSRevealOracle. On query KF_A, $\mathcal{B}$ looks up the list $\mathcal{L}$ for an entry $(ks_A, KF_A, m_A, y_A, y_B)$. If it is found, ks_A is returned. Otherwise, nothing is returned.
- ExtractOracle. On input $y_i \in \mathcal{U}$, $\mathcal{B}$ returns x_i if $i \neq n$. Otherwise, $\mathcal{B}$ aborts.

At the Output Phase, $\mathcal{A}$ outputs $(\sigma_A^*, m_A^*, m_B^*, y_A^*, y_B^*, ks_A^*, ks_B^*, KF_A^*, KF_B^*)$. If $y_A^* \neq y_n$, $\mathcal{B}$ aborts. Suppose that $\sigma_A^* = (c_A^*, t_A^*, z_A^*)$, $KF_A^* = (s_A^*, R_A^*)$, $ks_A^* = (k_A^*, r_A^*)$, $ks_B^* = (k_B^*, r_B^*)$, we have the following equations hold if the tuple output by $\mathcal{A}$ can pass the checking of Verify.

$$s_A^* = H_1(k_A^*, R_A^*, m_A^*, y_A^*, y_B^*),$$
$$s_B^* = H_1(k_B^*, R_B^*, m_B^*, y_B^*, y_A^*),$$
$$t_A^* = s_A^* + s_B^* + H_2(g^{r_A^* r_B^*}, m_A^*, y_A^*, y_B^*, KF_A^*, KF_B^*) \bmod p,$$
$$c_A^* = H(m_A^*, g^{c_A^*} y_A^{* z_A^*} y_B^{* t_A^*}, KF_A^*, KF_B^*),$$
$$R_A^* = g^{r_A^*},$$
$$R_B^* = g^{r_B^*}.$$

We consider the following events:

E1. σ_A^* is the output of ASignOracle:
- If s_A^* is equal to the s_A in the same ASignOracle query, this implies that $\mathcal{A}$ finds k_A^* of the query $(k_A^*, R_A^*, t_A^*, m_A^*, y_A^*, y_B^*)$ to H_1-Oracle while $\mathcal{A}$ is restricted from obtaining k_A^* in ks_A^* via making a query to KSRevealOracle, due to the corresponding restriction in the unforgeability game. The probability that $\mathcal{A}$ guesses k_A^* correctly is at most $\frac{q_H}{p - q_H} \leq \frac{q_H}{2^k - q_H}$, where q_H is the number of queries to H-Oracle.
- If $s_A^* \neq s_A$, then we have $KF_A^* \neq KF_A$ where KF_A is the keystone fix in the ASignOracle query which outputs σ_A^*. In other words, we have an event that two distinct queries of H-Oracle (one containing KF_A, the other one containing KF_A^*) outputting the same value c_A^*. The probability of this event is $\frac{1}{p} \leq 2^{-k}$.

E2. σ_A^* is not the output of ASignOracle:
In this event, $\mathcal{B}$ rewinds $\mathcal{A}$ to the point where the query $(m_A^*, g^{c_A^*} y_A^{* z_A^*} y_B^{* t_A^*}, KF^*A, KF_B^*)$ was made to the H-Oracle. This time the H-Oracle answers with a different value. Suppose that the value is c_A' and $\mathcal{A}$ outputs (c_A', t_A', z_A') as the new ambiguous signature at the end of the simulation. We have

$$g^{c_A^*} y_A^{* z_A^*} y_B^{* t_A^*} = g^{c_A'} y_A^{* z_A'} y_B^{* t_A'} \bmod p.$$

This implies that $c_A^* - c_A' = (z_A' - z_A^*) x_A^* + (t_A' - t_A^*) x_B^* \bmod p$. We consider two cases:

(a) $z'_A \neq z^*_A$. Since $y^*_A = y_n$, $\mathcal{B}$ can compute

$$\alpha = x^*_A = [(c^*_A - c'_A) + (t^*_A - t'_A)x^*_B]/(z'_A - z^*_A) \bmod p$$

as the solution to the DL problem instance.

(b) $z'_A = z^*_A$. Since $c^*_A \neq c'_A$, it implies that $t'_A \neq t^*_A$ where

$$t'_A = s'_A + s'_B + H_2(g^{r'_A r'_B}, m^*_A, y^*_A, y^*_B, KF^*_A, KF^*_B) \bmod p.$$

Since KF^*_A and KF^*_B have been fixed before the rewinding point where H-Oracle is queried with $(m^*_A, g^{c^*_A} y^{*z^*_A}_A y^{*t^*_A}_B \ KF^*A, KF^*_B)$, we have $g^{r'_A r'_B} = g^{r^*_A r^*_B}$ and $s'_A = s^*_A$, $s'_B = s^*_B$. Therefore, we have

$$t'_A = s^*_A + s^*_B + H_2(g^{r^*_A r^*_B}, m^*_A, y^*_A, y^*_B, KF^*_A, KF^*_B) \bmod p = t^*_A.$$

Contradiction occurs.

By the Reset Lemma [3], and that the chance of picking y^*_A as y_n as $\frac{1}{n}$, the rewind in the simulation above will succeed with probability at least $(\frac{\epsilon}{n} - \frac{1}{p})^2$. Note that $\Pr[\mathbf{E}2] = 1 - \Pr[\mathbf{E}1]$. We have

$$\Pr[\mathcal{B} \text{ wins}] = \Pr[\mathcal{B} \text{ wins} \wedge \mathbf{E}2]$$
$$= \Pr[\mathcal{B} \text{ wins} \mid \mathbf{E}2](1 - \Pr[\mathbf{E}1])$$
$$\geq (\frac{\epsilon}{n} - 2^{-k})^2 (1 - \frac{q_H}{2^k - q_H} - 2^{-k})$$

The time complexity of $\mathcal{B}$ is determined as follows. There are $O(1)$ exponentiations for simulating each query to ASignOracle and KSGenOracle. There are n exponentiations in the Setup Phase. Hence the time complexity of $\mathcal{B}$ is $t + O\big((q_s + q_g + n)\rho\big)$.   □

Theorem 2. *The CS-FNBC above is (ϵ, t, q_g, q_r)-ambiguous if the (ϵ', t')-CDH assumption holds in the random oracle model, where*

$$\epsilon' \geq \frac{\epsilon}{q_{H_2}}, \qquad t' = t + O(q_g \rho),$$

q_{H_2} is the number of queries to the random oracle of H_2. ρ is the time for doing one exponentiation in $\mathbb{Z}_p$.

Proof. For contradiction, suppose that there exists an adversary $\mathcal{A}$ which wins the ambiguity game, we construct an algorithm $\mathcal{B}$ which solves a CDH problem instance (g, g^α, g^β) by returning $g^{\alpha\beta}$. $\mathcal{B}$ simulates the ambiguity game by setting params $= \{\mathcal{K}, \mathcal{F}, \mathcal{M}, p, \mathbb{G}, g, H, H_1, H_2\}$, then randomly picks $x^*_A, x^*_B \in_R \mathbb{Z}_p$ and sets $y^*_A = g^{x^*_A}$ and $y^*_B = g^{x^*_B}$. $\mathcal{B}$ gives params, (y^*_A, x^*_A) and (y^*_B, x^*_B) to $\mathcal{A}$. In Phase 1 and Phase 2, $\mathcal{B}$ simulates KSGenOracle and KSRevealOracle in the same way as that in the proof of Theorem 1. H-Oracle, H_1-Oracle and H_2-Oracle are also simulated similarly.

In the **Challenge Phase**, $\mathcal{A}$ sends two messages m_A^*, m_B^* to $\mathcal{B}$. $\mathcal{B}$ then randomly picks $k_A^*, k_B^* \in_R \mathbb{Z}_p$ and sets

$$R_A^* = g^\alpha, \qquad\qquad s_A^* = H_1(k_A^*, g^\alpha, m_A^*, y_A^*, y_B^*),$$
$$R_B^* = g^\beta, \qquad\qquad s_B^* = H_1(k_B^*, g^\beta, m_B^*, y_B^*, y_A^*).$$

Also set $KF_A^* = (s_A^*, R_A^*)$ and $KF_B^* = (s_B^*, R_B^*)$. H_1-list is also updated during the two queries to H_1-Oracle. Then, $\mathcal{B}$ simulates the random oracle H_2-Oracle for the following four queries.

- $H_2(\perp, m_A^*, y_A^*, y_B^*, KF_A^*, KF_B^*)$: $\mathcal{B}$ randomly picks $t_{A,1}^* \in_R \mathbb{Z}_p$ and sets it as the answer. The symbol $\perp$ represents the value of $g^{\alpha\beta}$ which is not available yet. The list H_2-list is updated accordingly.
- $H_2(\perp, m_B^*, y_B^*, y_A^*, KF_B^*, KF_A^*)$: $\mathcal{B}$ randomly picks $t_{B,1}^* \in_R \mathbb{Z}_p$ and sets it as the answer. The list H_2-list is updated accordingly.
- $H_2(\perp, m_A^*, y_B^*, y_A^*, KF_A^*, KF_B^*)$: $\mathcal{B}$ randomly picks $t_{A,2}^* \in_R \mathbb{Z}_p$ and sets it as the answer. The list H_2-list is updated accordingly.
- $H_2(\perp, m_B^*, y_A^*, y_B^*, KF_B^*, KF_A^*)$: $\mathcal{B}$ randomly picks $t_{B,2}^* \in_R \mathbb{Z}_p$ and sets it as the answer. The list H_2-list is updated accordingly.

$\mathcal{B}$ randomly picks $b \in_R \{1, 2, 3, 4\}$ and carries out the following according to the value of b:

- If $b = 1$, $\mathcal{B}$ uses $t_{A,1}^*$ and $t_{B,1}^*$, and continue carrying out the ambiguous signature generation algorithm ASign to generate $\sigma_A^* = (c_A^*, z_A^*, t_{A,1}^*)$ and $\sigma_B^* = (c_B^*, z_B^*, t_{B,1}^*)$ where $c_A^* = H(m_A^*, g^{c_A^*} y_A^{*z_A^*} y_B^{*t_{A,1}^*}, KF_A^*, KF_B^*)$ and $c_B^* = H(m_B^*, g^{c_B^*} y_B^{*z_B^*} y_A^{*t_{B,1}^*}, KF_B^*, KF_A^*)$.
- If $b = 2$, $\mathcal{B}$ uses $t_{A,2}^*$ and $t_{B,2}^*$, and continue carrying out the ambiguous signature generation algorithm ASign to generate $\sigma_A^* = (c_A^*, t_{A,2}^*, z_A^*)$ and $\sigma_B^* = (c_B^*, t_{B,2}^*, z_B^*)$ where $c_A^* = H(m_A^*, g^{c_A^*} y_B^{*z_A^*} y_A^{*t_{A,2}^*}, KF_A^*, KF_B^*)$ and $c_B^* = H(m_B^*, g^{c_B^*} y_A^{*z_B^*} y_B^{*t_{B,2}^*}, KF_B^*, KF_A^*)$.
- If $b = 3$, $\mathcal{B}$ uses $t_{A,1}^*$ and $t_{B,2}^*$, and continue carrying out the ambiguous signature generation algorithm ASign to generate $\sigma_A^* = (c_A^*, z_A^*, t_{A,1}^*)$ and $\sigma_B^* = (c_B^*, t_{B,2}^*, z_B^*)$ where $c_A^* = H(m_A^*, g^{c_A^*} y_A^{*z_A^*} y_B^{*t_{A,1}^*}, KF_A^*, KF_B^*)$ and $c_B^* = H(m_B^*, g^{c_B^*} y_A^{*z_B^*} y_B^{*t_{B,2}^*}, KF_B^*, KF_A^*)$.
- If $b = 4$, $\mathcal{B}$ uses $t_{A,2}^*$ and $t_{B,1}^*$, and continue carrying out the ambiguous signature generation algorithm ASign to generate $\sigma_A^* = (c_A^*, t_{A,2}^*, z_A^*)$ and $\sigma_B^* = (c_B^*, z_B^*, t_{B,1}^*)$ where $c_A^* = H(m_A^*, g^{c_A^*} y_B^{*z_A^*} y_A^{*t_{A,2}^*}, KF_A^*, KF_B^*)$ and $c_B^* = H(m_B^*, g^{c_B^*} y_B^{*z_B^*} y_A^{*t_{B,1}^*}, KF_B^*, KF_A^*)$.

$\mathcal{B}$ continues simulating the ambiguity game. As KSRevealOracle cannot be queried with KF_A^* or KF_B^*, the simulation does not abort. We can see that the ambiguity game is perfectly simulated.

Let **E** be the event that $\mathcal{A}$ has queried H_2-Oracle with at least one of the four queries above, namely

$$H_2(\perp, m_A^*, y_A^*, y_B^*, KF_A^*, KF_B^*)$$
$$H_2(\perp, m_B^*, y_B^*, y_A^*, KF_B^*, KF_A^*)$$
$$H_2(\perp, m_A^*, y_B^*, y_A^*, KF_A^*, KF_B^*)$$
$$H_2(\perp, m_B^*, y_A^*, y_B^*, KF_B^*, KF_A^*)$$

In all the four cases of b above, c_A^*, and c_B^* are always randomly and independently chosen in the simulation of H-Oracle, while z_A^* and z_B^* are always uniquely determined in ASign. Hence the four cases differ only in the use of $t_{A,1}^*$, $t_{A,2}^*$, $t_{B,1}^*$ and $t_{B,2}^*$. In event $\overline{\mathbf{E}}$, given a pair $(t_{A,\gamma}^*, t_{B,\lambda}^*)$, where $\gamma, \lambda \in \{1,2\}$, the probability of determining the values of γ and λ correctly is $1/4$ due to the idealness of random oracle. Hence the probability that $\mathcal{A}$ outputs b in event $\overline{\mathbf{E}}$ is $1/4$.

Suppose event **E** occurs. Then $\mathcal{A}$ queried H_2-Oracle with $(g^{\alpha\beta}, m_P^*, y_Q^*, y_W^*, KF_P^*, KF_{\bar{P}}^*)$ where $P, Q, W \in \{A, B\}$ and $\bar{P} = \{A, B\} \backslash \{P\}$. Hence in this event, $\mathcal{B}$ solves the CDH problem instance. Suppose $\mathcal{A}$ makes q_{H_2} queries to H_2-Oracle. We have

$$\Pr[\mathcal{B} \text{ wins}] \geq \frac{1}{q_{H_2}} \Pr[\mathcal{A} \text{ outputs } b \wedge \mathbf{E}]$$

and

$$\Pr[\mathcal{A} \text{ outputs } b] = \Pr[\mathcal{A} \text{ outputs } b \wedge \mathbf{E}] + \Pr[\mathcal{A} \text{ outputs } b \wedge \overline{\mathbf{E}}]$$
$$\epsilon + \frac{1}{4} \leq \Pr[\mathcal{A} \text{ outputs } b \wedge \mathbf{E}] + \Pr[\mathcal{A} \text{ outputs } b \mid \overline{\mathbf{E}}]\Pr[\overline{\mathbf{E}}]$$
$$\epsilon + \frac{1}{4} \leq \Pr[\mathcal{A} \text{ outputs } b \wedge \mathbf{E}] + \Pr[\mathcal{A} \text{ outputs } b \mid \overline{\mathbf{E}}]$$
$$\epsilon \leq \Pr[\mathcal{A} \text{ outputs } b \wedge \mathbf{E}]$$

Hence

$$\Pr[\mathcal{B} \text{ wins}] \geq \frac{\epsilon}{q_{H_2}}$$

There are $O(1)$ exponentiations for simulating each query to KSGenOracle. Hence the time complexity of $\mathcal{B}$ is $t + O(q_g \rho)$.   □

Theorem 3. *Let k be a security parameter. The CS-FNBC above is $(q_{H_1} 2^{-k}, t, q_g, q_r)$-fair in the random oracle model.*

Proof. Let $\mathcal{A}$ be an adversary in the fairness game. We construct a simulator $\mathcal{B}$ as follows. $\mathcal{B}$ sets params $= \{\mathcal{K}, \mathcal{F}, \mathcal{M}, p, \mathbb{G}, \mathbb{G}_T, g, H, H_1, H_2\}$ according to the scheme description. $\mathcal{B}$ generates two key pairs (y_A^*, x_A^*) and (y_B^*, x_B^*) and sends to $\mathcal{A}$. $\mathcal{B}$ simulates KSGenOracle and KSRevealOracle accordingly as described in the proof of Theorem 1. When $\mathcal{A}$ sends a message m_B^* to $\mathcal{B}$ in the Keystone Fix Generation Phase, $\mathcal{B}$ randomly picks $k_B^*, r_B^* \in \mathbb{Z}_p$, sets $R_B^* = g^{r_B^*}$ and calculates

$s_B^* = H_1(k_B^*, R_B^*, m_B^*, y_B^*, y_A^*)$. It then returns $KF_B^* = (s_B^*, R_B^*)$ to $\mathcal{A}$, which gives back a keystone fix $KF_A^* = (s_A^*, R_A^*)$.

In the Output Phase, $\mathcal{B}$ computes an ambiguous signature on m_B^* as $\sigma_B^* = (c_B^*, z_B^*, t_B^*) \leftarrow \mathsf{ASign}(m_B^*, y_B^*, y_A^*, x_B^*, (k_B^*, r_B^*), KF_B^*, KF_A^*)$. According to the fairness game, at this point, $\mathcal{A}$ wins in either of the following ways:

- $\mathcal{A}$ outputs a tuple $(m_A^*, (k_A^*, r_A^*), (k_B', r_B'))$ such that

$$\mathsf{accept} \leftarrow \mathsf{Verify}(\sigma_B^*, m_B^*, m_A^*, y_B^*, y_A^*, (k_B', r_B'), (k_A^*, r_A^*), KF_B^*, KF_A^*).$$

It implies that

$$s_A^* = H_1(k_A^*, R_A^*, m_A^*, y_A^*, y_B^*),$$
$$s_B^* = H_1(k_B', R_B^*, m_B^*, y_B^*, y_A^*),$$
$$t_B^* = s_B^* + s_A^* + H_2(g^{r_B' r_A^*}, m_B^*, y_B^*, y_A^*, KF_B^*, KF_A^*) \bmod p,$$
$$c_B^* = H(m_B^*, g^{c_B^*} y_B^{* z_B^*} y_A^{* t_B^*}, KF_B^*, KF_A^*),$$
$$R_B^* = g^{r_B'},$$
$$R_A^* = g^{r_A^*}.$$

Due to the idealness of the random oracle H_1-Oracle, the probability of finding k_B' such that $H_1(k_B', R_B^*, m_B^*, y_B^*, y_A^*) = s_B^*$ is

$$1 - (1 - \frac{1}{p})^{q_{H_1}} \leq 1 - (1 - q_{H_1}/p)$$
$$\leq q_{H_1} 2^{-k}$$

where q_{H_1} is the number of queries to the random oracle of H_1.

- $\mathcal{A}$ outputs $(m_A^*, \sigma_A^* = (c_A^*, z_A^*, t_A^*))$, and after $\mathcal{B}$ sends back the keystone (k_B^*, r_B^*), $\mathcal{A}$ output the keystone (k_A', r_A') such that

$$c_A^* = H(m_A^*, g^{c_A^*} y_A^{* z_A^*} y_B^{* t_A^*}, KF_A^*, KF_B^*),$$
$$t_A^* = H_2(R_A^{* r_B^*}, m_A^*, y_A^*, y_B^*, KF_A^*, KF_B^*) + s_A^* + s_B^* \bmod p,$$
$$s_A^* = H_1(k_A', R_A^*, m_A^*, y_A^*, y_B^*),$$
$$s_B^* = H_1(k_B^*, R_B^*, m_B^*, y_B^*, y_A^*),$$
$$c_B^* = H(m_B^*, g^{c_B^*} y_B^{* z_B^*} y_A^{* t_B^*}, KF_B^*, KF_A^*),$$
$$t_B^* = s_B^* + s_A^* + H_2(g^{r_A' r_B^*}, m_B^*, y_B^*, y_A^*, KF_A^*, KF_B^*) \bmod p,$$
$$R_B^* = g^{r_B^*},$$
$$R_A^* = g^{r_A'}.$$

while

$$\mathsf{reject} \leftarrow \mathsf{Verify}(\sigma_A^*, m_A^*, m_B^*, (y_A^*, y_B^*), (k_A', r_A'), (k_B^*, r_B^*), (s_A^*, R_A^*), (s_B^*, R_B^*)).$$

However, this is impossible because all the equations in the verification already hold as shown above. Hence this case will not happen.

$\square$

Table 2. Comparison of concurrent signature schemes

Scheme	Initiator Cost	Responder Cost	Verification Cost	Signature Size	Keystone Size	Binding Control
iPCS1 [13]	3.41E	4.41E	2.5E	$3\lvert p\rvert$	$2\lvert p\rvert$	Initiator-Controlled
iPCS2 [13]	6B+3.41E	6B+3.41E+1M	6B+2.5E	$3\lvert p\rvert$	$2\lvert p\rvert$	Initiator-Controlled
This paper	5.41E	5.41E	3.66E	$3\lvert p\rvert$	$2\lvert p\rvert$	FNBC

3.2   Comparison

Table 2 shows the comparison of our CS-FNBC construction and two conventional concurrent signature schemes satisfying perfect ambiguity requirement. In the table, 'E' denotes multi-exponentiation, 'M' denotes elliptic curve scalar multiplication, and 'B' denotes bilinear pairing. As simultaneous exponentiation operations may be carried out more efficiently than the conventional method, for example, through the method of an exponent array [2], the cost for computing $g_1^{x_1} g_2^{x_2}$ and $g_1^{x_1} g_2^{x_2} g_3^{x_3}$ are estimated as about 1.16 and 1.25 single exponentiation operations, respectively.

As we can see, the signature size and keystone size of all the schemes are comparable. The computational complexity of this CS-FNBC scheme is slightly higher than iCPS1 [13], while it is much more efficient than iCPS2 as no bilinear pairing is needed in the CS-FNBC scheme.

Note that in our construction, the value t_A and t_B is determined by both user A and B. Therefore, it does not suffer from the attack on fairness [13] for some concurrent signature schemes. In fact, the iPCS1 [13] also uses similar method to avoid this kind of attack.

4   Conclusion

In this paper, we introduced a new notion called *Fully Negotiable Binding Control* for concurrent signature. The notion captures the advantages of both conventional concurrent signature and optimistic fair exchange in terms of signature authorship binding control. It allows the initiator and responder to negotiate on who will be the one to control "whether" and "when" the signature authorship binding will take place. We formalized the notion and called it as Concurrent Signature with Fully Negotiable Binding Control (CS-FNBC) and proposed a concrete CS-FNBC scheme. The scheme is proven secure under the game we defined which captures the strong security requirements of conventional concurrent signature including the perfect ambiguity requirement. One open problem remains in general for concurrent signature is the construction of a scheme with security in the standard model.

References

1. Asokan, N., Shoup, V., Waidner, M.: Optimistic fair exchange of digital signatures. In: Nyberg, K. (ed.) EUROCRYPT 1998. LNCS, vol. 1403, pp. 591–606. Springer, Heidelberg (1998)
2. Ateniese, G.: Efficient verifiable encryption (and fair exchange) of digital signatures. In: ACM CCS 1999, pp. 138–146 (1999)
3. Bellare, M., Palacio, A.: GQ and schnorr identification schemes: Proofs of security against impersonation under active and concurrent attacks. In: Yung, M. (ed.) CRYPTO 2002. LNCS, vol. 2442, pp. 162–177. Springer, Heidelberg (2002)
4. Chen, L., Kudla, C., Paterson, K.G.: Concurrent signatures. In: Cachin, C., Camenisch, J.L. (eds.) EUROCRYPT 2004. LNCS, vol. 3027, pp. 287–305. Springer, Heidelberg (2004)
5. Chow, S.S.M., Susilo, W.: Generic construction of (Identity-based) perfect concurrent signatures. In: Qing, S., Mao, W., López, J., Wang, G. (eds.) ICICS 2005. LNCS, vol. 3783, pp. 194–206. Springer, Heidelberg (2005)
6. Franklin, M.K., Reiter, M.K.: Fair exchange with a semi-trusted third party (extended abstract). In: CCS 1997, pp. 1–5. ACM, New York (1997)
7. Huang, Q., Yang, G., Wong, D.S., Susilo, W.: Ambiguous optimistic fair exchange. In: Pieprzyk, J. (ed.) ASIACRYPT 2008. LNCS, vol. 5350, pp. 74–89. Springer, Heidelberg (2008)
8. Huang, Q., Yang, G., Wong, D.S., Susilo, W.: Efficient optimistic fair exchange secure in the multi-user setting and chosen-key model without random oracles. In: Malkin, T. (ed.) CT-RSA 2008. LNCS, vol. 4964, pp. 106–120. Springer, Heidelberg (2008)
9. Nguyen, K.: Asymmetric concurrent signatures. In: Qing, S., Mao, W., López, J., Wang, G. (eds.) ICICS 2005. LNCS, vol. 3783, pp. 181–193. Springer, Heidelberg (2005)
10. Shieh, C., Lin, H., Yen, S.: Fair Multi-party Concurrent Signatures. In: Proc. of 18th Cryptology and Information Security Conference, CISC 2008, pp. 108–118 (2008)
11. Susilo, W., Mu, Y., Zhang, F.: Perfect concurrent signature schemes. In: López, J., Qing, S., Okamoto, E. (eds.) ICICS 2004. LNCS, vol. 3269, pp. 14–26. Springer, Heidelberg (2004)
12. Tonien, D., Susilo, W., Safavi-Naini, R.: Multi-party concurrent signatures. In: Katsikas, S.K., López, J., Backes, M., Gritzalis, S., Preneel, B. (eds.) ISC 2006. LNCS, vol. 4176, pp. 131–145. Springer, Heidelberg (2006)
13. Wang, G., Bao, F., Zhou, J.: The fairness of perfect concurrent signatures. In: Ning, P., Qing, S., Li, N. (eds.) ICICS 2006. LNCS, vol. 4307, pp. 435–451. Springer, Heidelberg (2006)

Secure Obfuscation of Encrypted Verifiable Encrypted Signatures

Rong Cheng, Bo Zhang, and Fangguo Zhang

School of Information Science and Technology,
Sun Yat-sen University, Guangzhou 510006, China
chengrongada@163.com, ldzhbo@hotmail.com, isszhfg@mail.sysu.edu.cn

Abstract. Since obfuscation was brought into the field of cryptography, it has become one of the most difficult and hottest problems. Because a general secure obfuscating method, if exists, will lead to the solution of many open problems in cryptography. However, after Bark *et al.*'s negative impossibility result for general obfuscation became well-known, only a few positive results was brought out. In *EUROCRYPT 2010*, Hada proposed a secure obfuscator of encrypted signatures (ES), which signs a message under Alice's secret signing key and then encrypts the signature using Bob's public encryption key. This result is the only few secure obfuscation of complicated cryptographic primitives. In this paper, we consider the obfuscation of encrypted verifiable encrypted signatures (EVES). There is a trusted third party (TTP) in our protocol, and EVES first generates a verifiable encrypted signature (VES) under Alice's secret signing key and the TTP's public encryption key and then the VES is encrypted using Bob's public encryption key. We give out the detailed EVES protocol and securely obfuscate it. We prove the security requirement of virtual black box property under standard assumptions and the secure obfuscation result will have many practical applications as we issue.

Keywords: obfuscation, virtual black box property, encrypted verifiable encrypted signature.

1 Introduction

The concept of obfuscation was first proposed in the computer programming field, which makes computer codes unintelligible while preserves the original functionality. After Barak *et al.* [4] brought the concept of obfuscation into the field of cryptography, it has become one of the most intriguing and interesting problems that whether there exists secure obfuscator for cryptographic functions. If there exists a general secure obfuscator in cryptography, many open problems will be solved such as solving the long-standing problem of homomorphic encryption, transforming private key encryption into public key encryption, removing random oracles, etc [13]. Researchers have proposed several definitions and security requirements of obfuscation in cryptography. Informally, an obfuscator is an efficient compiler that converts a program P into a new program

X. Boyen and X. Chen (Eds.): ProvSec 2011, LNCS 6980, pp. 188–203, 2011.

$\mathcal{O}(P)$ with the same functionality as P, while the new program doesn't leak any secret information about the original one. In conclusion, a secure obfuscator should satisfy the following three requirements: (1)functionality: the obfuscated program should preserve the functionality as the original one; (2)secrecy, which can also be called "virtual black box property": anything one can efficiently compute from the obfuscated program can also be efficiently computed given oracle access to the original program; (3)polynomial slow-down: the execution time of the obfuscated program should not exceed the polynomial of the execution time of the original program.

However, in *CRYPTO'01* Barak *et al.* [4] proposed the well-known impossibility result for general obfuscation of programs. Under the security definition of theirs, they constructed a particular family of functions that inherently can't be securely obfuscated, hence excluded the possibility of general obfuscation of all families of functions. Though general obfuscation is impossible under their definition, there still exists hope for secure obfuscation for some special family of functions. Or the requirements of secure obfuscation can be relaxed to some extent in order to find the general obfuscator for all kinds of functions. Following that, researchers have explored several different relaxed definitions of secure obfuscation and obtained some positive results. Canetti *et al.* [6] have given out the first secure obfuscation of point functions under a very strong Diffie-Hellman assumption. After that, in [15,16,7,8,3,13] several new relaxed definitions have been proposed and under these definitions the point function and some related functions were securely obfuscated both in random oracle model and standard model. To be worth raising, besides these simple functionalities, Hohenberger *et al.* [14] proposed the first positive result for complicated cryptographic functionality. They constructed a special re-encryption function and securely obfuscated it. More importantly, they gave out a new security requirement that is more applicable to cryptographic systems, that is [14] "*If a cryptographic scheme is secure when the adversary is given black-box access to a program, then it remains secure when the adversary is given the obfuscated program.*" This definition is more secure when the obfuscated program is used as a part of a larger system as they stated. Following the result of [14], Hada [12] considered the obfuscation for encrypted signature (ES) functionalities in *EUROCRYPT 2010* . An ES functionality generates a signature under Alice's secret signing key and then encrypts the signature under Bob's public encryption key. The detailed ES function is the simple sequential of Waters's signature scheme [5] and the linear encryption scheme proposed by Boneh *et al.* [2]. In their paper, they adopted the security definition of Hohenberger *et al.* and made a little change to it. Under their definition, the obfuscation was proved to be secure and the encrypted signature was existentially unforgeable even when the adversary was given the obfuscated program under the Decisional Linear (DL) and Decisional Bilinear Diffie-Hellman (DBDH) assumptions.

In this paper we consider the special functionality of encrypted verifiable encrypted signatures (EVES). As we know, verifiable encryption of digital signatures is widely used in fair exchange, contact signing, certified email, etc.

Verifiable encrypted signatures (VES) enable Alice to generate a signature signed using her secret signing key and encrypted under the trusted third party (TTP)'s public key. Then the verifier Bob can verify the encrypted signature is valid but has no knowledge of the real signature. The trusted third party doesn't participate in the protocol until there exist disputes. In cases of dispute, the TTP can recover the actual signature for fairness. Considering this scenario, Alice is a manager of the company who always has some contacts to sign. When signing a contact, Alice first signs a signature and encrypts it under the TTP's public key, then the VES is encrypted using the receiver's public key and the EVES is sent to the receiver. When Alice is out of business, she wants to have somebody signing these contacts for her. The secure obfuscation of EVES can achieve this, any proxy can generate valid encrypted verifiable encrypted signatures with the obfuscated program. Following Hada's protocol, we give out a special EVES functionality and securely obfuscate it. Similarly, we adopt a special EVES which has this property *"The encryption of signature is equivalent to generating a signature using the encrypted key."* However, our encrypted signature is to be verified by the receiver while reveals no knowledge of the real signature, which is the main difference to obfuscation of ES. So the key point to obfuscate EVES is to generate a public verifying key and a zero knowledge corresponding to the signature which enable the receiver to verify the encrypted signature. We detailedly describe the construction in section 3. We can prove its security under the similar security definition as Hada's, and this secure obfuscation result may have wide applications in those fair deals over the Internet.

The remainder of this paper is organized as follows. In section 2 we briefly introduce the VES and zero-knowledge proof, and give out the security assumptions. Then our security definition of obfuscation is presented in section 3. In section 4 we describe the detailed construction of EVES and the obfuscation of it. Then the security of the obfuscation is analyzed in section 5. Lastly we compare and give the conclusion in section 6.

2   Preliminaries

2.1   Verifiable Encrypted Signature

As nowadays network computers are increasingly being used to exchange messages between distrusted parties, so fair exchange is becoming more and more important. Verifiable encrypted signature (VES) is a special extension of digital signatures and it can be used to build many practical fair applications. A trusted third party (TTP) is issued in the protocol but doesn't participate until there are cases of dispute. For example, Alice signs a message and encrypts the signature under the TTP's public key. Then the encrypted signature is sent to Bob, and Bob can verify that the signature is valid while has no knowledge of the real signature. However, if there is a dispute that when Bob has given Alice his signature but Alice refuses to reveal her signature, then Bob can require the TTP to reveal the real signature for fairness.

Several constructions of VES have been proposed [1,11,17] and it has been widely used in practical fair exchange protocols, such as fair signature exchange, certified email, certified delivery of e-goods, etc.

2.2 Zero Knowledge Proof

Zero knowledge proof system is usually used by a party to prove that he knows some secrets to another party, while the verifier has no knowledge of the proved secret after interactions. Earlier zero knowledge proofs are always implemented with interactions between prover and verifier, while sometimes non-interactive zero knowledge proof is needed in some cases. Interactive zero knowledge proof system can be transformed into non-interactive ones using the generic transforming proposed by Fiat and Shamir [10].

Proof of $\log_{g_1} y_1 = \log_{g_2} y_2$. Zero knowledge proof of equivalence of two discrete logarithms is frequently used in cryptographic protocols, and several methods have been raised. Here we briefly introduce a non-interactive zero knowledge proof of $\log_{g_1} y_1 = \log_{g_2} y_2 = x$ which is raised in [9]. g_1, g_2, y_1, y_2 are elements in group $\mathbb{G}$ with order q, and $h(\cdot, \cdot)$ is a cryptographic hash function from $\mathbb{G}$ to $\mathbb{Z}_q$.

1. Randomly select $R \in \mathbb{Z}_q$, compute $w_1 = y_1^r$, $w_2 = y_2^r$, $C = h(w_1, w_2)$ and $Z = (x - CR) \bmod q$.
2. The zero knowledge proof is (Z, C).
3. Verify the zero knowledge by $C \stackrel{?}{=} h(g_1^Z y_1^C, g_2^Z y_2^C)$.

Proof of $\log_{g_1} y_1 + \log_{g_2} y_2 = \log_{g_3} y_3$. This zero knowledge proof is needed in our construction, and we give out an easy realization using the above zero knowledge of equivalence of two discrete logarithms. The parameters are set similarly to the above, and we denote $\log_{g_1} y_1 = x_1$, $\log_{g_2} y_2 = x_2$, $\log_{g_3} y_3 = x_3$. Randomly choose another element $h \in \mathbb{G}$ and compute $h_1 = h^{x_1}$, $h_2 = h^{x_2}$, $h_3 = h^{x_3}$. Then

$$ZKP(\log_{g_1} y_1 + \log_{g_2} y_2 = \log_{g_3} y_3) = \{ZKP(\log_{g_1} y_1 = \log_h h_1) \parallel$$

$$ZKP(\log_{g_2} y_2 = \log_h h_2) \parallel ZKP(\log_{g_3} y_3 = \log_h h_3) \parallel h_1 h_2 = h_3\}.$$

2.3 Security Assumptions

Definition 1 (DBDH Assumption). *[12] For every PPT distinguisher D, every polynomial $P(\cdot)$, all sufficiently large $n \in \mathbb{N}$, and every $z \in \{0,1\}^{poly(n)}$,*

$$\left| Pr \left[\begin{array}{l} p = (\mathbb{G}, \mathbb{G}_T, q, g, e) \leftarrow Setup(1^n); \\ a \in \mathbb{Z}_q; b \in \mathbb{Z}_q; c \in \mathbb{Z}_q; \\ decision \leftarrow D(p, g^a, g^b, g^c, e(g,g)^{abc}, z) \end{array} : decision = 1 \right] - \right.$$

$$Pr \left[\begin{array}{l} p = (\mathbb{G}, \mathbb{G}_T, q, g, \boldsymbol{e}) \leftarrow Setup(1^n); \\ a \in \mathbb{Z}_q; b \in \mathbb{Z}_q; c \in \mathbb{Z}_q; d \in \mathbb{Z}_q; \\ decision \leftarrow D(p, g^a, g^b, g^c, e(g,g)^d, z) \end{array} : decision = 1 \right] \bigg| < \frac{1}{p(n)}.$$

Definition 2 (DL Assumption). *[12] For every PPT distinguisher D, every polynomial $P(\cdot)$, all sufficiently large $n \in \mathbb{N}$, and every $z \in \{0,1\}^{poly(n)}$,*

$$\left| Pr \left[\begin{array}{l} p = (\mathbb{G}, \mathbb{G}_T, q, g, \boldsymbol{e}) \leftarrow Setup(1^n); \\ a \in \mathbb{Z}_q; b \in \mathbb{Z}_q; r \in \mathbb{Z}_q; s \in \mathbb{Z}_q; \\ decision \leftarrow D(p, (g^a, g^b), ((g^a)^r, (g^b)^s, g^{r+s}), z) \end{array} : decision = 1 \right] - \right.$$

$$Pr \left[\begin{array}{l} p = (\mathbb{G}, \mathbb{G}_T, q, g, \boldsymbol{e}) \leftarrow Setup(1^n); \\ a \in \mathbb{Z}_q; b \in \mathbb{Z}_q; r \in \mathbb{Z}_q; s \in \mathbb{Z}_q; t \in \mathbb{Z}_q; \\ decision \leftarrow D(p, (g^a, g^b), ((g^a)^r, (g^b)^s, g^t), z) \end{array} : decision = 1 \right] \bigg| < \frac{1}{p(n)}.$$

Definition 3 (Exponent l-weak Diffie-Hellman Problem). *[18] For a randomly chosen element $x \in \mathbb{Z}_q$ and a random generator $g \in \mathbb{G}_1$, the Exponent l-weak Diffie-Hellman Problem is, given $(g, g^x, g^{x^2}, \ldots, g^{x^l}) \in \mathbb{G}_1^{l+1}$, to compute an element $g^{x^{l+1}} \in \mathbb{G}_1$*

3   Definition of Secure Obfuscation

There are various relaxed definitions of secure obfuscation. In our protocol, we follow the security definition of Hada's construction which considers average-case virtual black-box property (ACVBP). For cryptographic functions, it's meaningful to consider average security. Samely we make the distinguisher D have access to signing oracle dependent on the circuit C(we don't make D have access to the EVESVerify oracle as we only want the verifier to verify EVES). Here we review the security definition of theirs.

Definition 4 (ACVBP with Dependent Oracles). *[12] Let $T(C)$ be a set of oracles dependent on the circuit C. An obfuscator Obf for C satisfies ACVBP with dependent oracle set T if the following condition holds: There exists a PPT simulator S such that, for every PPT distinguisher D, every polynomial $p(\cdot)$, all sufficiently large $n \in \mathbb{N}$, and every $z \in \{0,1\}^{poly(n)}$,*

$$\left| Pr \left[\begin{array}{l} C \leftarrow \mathcal{C}_n; \\ C' \leftarrow Obf(C); \\ b \leftarrow D^{\ll C, T(C) \gg}(C', z) \end{array} : b = 1 \right] - Pr \left[\begin{array}{l} C \leftarrow \mathcal{C}_n; \\ C'' \leftarrow S^{\ll C \gg}(1^n, z); \\ b \leftarrow D^{\ll C, T(C) \gg}(C'', z) \end{array} : b = 1 \right] \right| < \frac{1}{p(n)}.$$

where $D^{\ll C, T(C) \gg}$ means that D has sampling access to all the dependent oracles contained in $T(C)$ besides C.

4   Obfuscation of Encrypted Verifiable Encrypted Signatures

In this section, we construct a special EVES functionality with Waters's signature and Boneh *et al.*'s linear encryption scheme as building blocks. Then we propose the obfuscation result of the EVES functionality.

4.1   A Special EVES Construction

The main building blocks of our EVES functionality are Waters's signature scheme and Boneh *et al.*'s encryption scheme. We first simply describe these two building blocks and then give out the detailed construction of our EVES functionality.

The system parameters setting is same for both of Waters's signature and Boneh's encryption scheme, and it's also the system parameters throughout the EVES functionality. For security parameter 1^n, system parameter generator randomly generates the parameters for a bilinear map $(\mathbb{G}, \mathbb{G}_T, q, g, \mathbf{e})$. Here q is a large prime of length n, both $\mathbb{G}$ and $\mathbb{G}_T$ are groups of order q, g is a generator of group $\mathbb{G}$, $\mathbf{e}$ is an efficient bilinear mapping $\mathbf{e} : \mathbb{G} \times \mathbb{G} \rightarrow \mathbb{G}_T$. The bilinear mapping $\mathbf{e}$ is a non-degenerate mapping which satisfies bilinearity and non-degenerate property.

Waters's Signature Scheme. We simply review Waters's signature scheme [16]. The scheme includes key generation algorithm (SKG), signing algorithm (Sign) and signature verifying algorithm (Verify), and the message space is $\{0, 1\}^n$.

- $SKG(params)$:
    1. Parse system parameter $params = (\mathbb{G}, \mathbb{G}_T, q, g, \mathbf{e})$.
    2. Randomly choose $\alpha \in \mathbb{Z}_q$ and compute $g_1 = g^\alpha$, then randomly select $g_2 \in \mathbb{G}$ and $u' \in \mathbb{G}$.
    3. For every $i \in \{1, \ldots, n\}$, randomly select $u_i \in \mathbb{G}$ and set $U = \{u_i\}$.
    4. Output the system's public and private keys $pk_s = (g_1, g_2, u', U)$, $sk_s = (g_2^\alpha, u', U)$.
- $Sign(sk_s, m)$:
    1. For an n bit length message $m = (m_1, m_2, \cdots, m_n)$, where m_i denotes the ith bit of m, let M be the set of all i such that $m_i = 1$.
    2. Randomly choose $x \in \mathbb{Z}_q$ and compute $\sigma_1 = g_2^\alpha (u' \prod_{i \in M} u_i)^x$, $\sigma_2 = g^x$.
    3. Output signature $\sigma = (\sigma_1, \sigma_2)$.
- $Verify(pk_s, m, \sigma)$:
    1. Parse $pk_s = (g_1, g_2, u', U)$, $m = (m_1, m_2, \cdots, m_n)$ and $\sigma = (\sigma_1, \sigma_2)$.
    2. If $\mathbf{e}(\sigma_1, g)/\mathbf{e}(\sigma_2, u' \prod_{i \in M} u_i) = \mathbf{e}(g_1, g_2)$, output Accept. Otherwise output Reject.

Boneh's Linear Encryption Scheme. Boneh *et al.*'s linear encryption scheme
[2] is composed of key generation algorithm (EKG), encryption algorithm (Enc)
and decryption algorithm (Dec). The message space is $\mathbb{G}$.

- *EKG(params)*:
    1. Parse system parameter $params = (\mathbb{G}, \mathbb{G}_T, q, g, \mathbf{e})$.
    2. Randomly choose $a \in \mathbb{Z}_q$ and $b \in \mathbb{Z}_q$, then the public and private keys
       are $pk_r = (g^a, g^b)$, $sk_r = (a, b)$.
- *Enc(pk_r, m)*:
    1. Randomly choose $r \in \mathbb{Z}_q$ and $s \in \mathbb{Z}_q$.
    2. Compute $c_1 = (g^a)^r$, $c_2 = (g^b)^s$, $c_3 = g^{r+s}m$.
    3. Output ciphertext $c = (c_1, c_2, c_3)$.
- *Dec(sk_r, c)*:
    1. Parse ciphertext $c = (c_1, c_2, c_3)$.
    2. Output plaintext $m = c_3/(c_1^{1/a} \cdot c_2^{1/b})$.

EVES Functionality. Our special EVES functionality can be built with these
two building blocks. A trusted third party (TTP) is involved in our construction,
with its public encryption key published to the outside. First, signer generates a
signature for a message under her secret signing key (sk_s) and encrypts it using
the TTP's public encryption key (pk_T). When being sent to receiver(verifier),
the encrypted signature is again encrypted under the receiver's public encryption
key (pk_r). Besides the encrypted verifiable encrypted signature, a public verifying
key and a respective zero-knowledge proof also should be sent to the receiver,
which can be used to verify the EVES. The EVES functionality is composed
of system key generation algorithm (EVESKG), signature generation algorithm
(EVESSign), signature verifying algorithm (EVESVerify).

- *EVESKG(params)*:
    1. Parse system parameter $params = (\mathbb{G}, \mathbb{G}_T, q, g, \mathbf{e})$.
    2. For signer, randomly choose $\alpha, \beta \in \mathbb{Z}_q$ and compute $g_1 = g^\alpha, g_2 = g^\beta$,
       then randomly select $u' \in \mathbb{G}$. For every $i \in \{1, \dots, n\}$, randomly select
       $u_i \in \mathbb{G}$ and set $U = \{u_i\}$.
    3. For the TTP, randomly choose $a \in \mathbb{Z}_q$ and $b \in \mathbb{Z}_q$, compute g^a and g^b.
    4. For receiver(verifier), randomly choose $c \in \mathbb{Z}_q$ and $d \in \mathbb{Z}_q$, compute g^c
       and g^d.
    5. Signer's public and private keys are $pk_s = (g_1, g_2, u', U)$ and $sk_s = (g_2^\alpha, \beta, u', U)$. The TTP's public and private keys are $pk_T = (g^a, g^b)$
       and $sk_T = (a, b)$. Receiver's public and private keys are $pk_r = (g^c, g^d)$
       and $sk_r = (c, d)$.
- *EVESSign(sk_s, pk_T, pk_r, m)*:
    1. For an n bit length message $m = (m_1, m_2, \cdots, m_n)$, where m_i denote the
       ith bit of m, let M be the set of all i such that $m_i = 1$.

2. Randomly choose $x \in \mathbb{Z}_q$ and compute

$$\sigma_1 = g_2^\alpha (u' \prod_{i \in M} u_i)^x, \sigma_2 = g^x.$$

3. Randomly choose $r \in \mathbb{Z}_q$ and $s \in \mathbb{Z}_q$, then compute

$$c_1 = (g^a)^r, c_2 = (g^b)^s, c_3 = g^{r+s}\sigma_1.$$

4. Randomly choose $r' \in \mathbb{Z}_q$ and $s' \in \mathbb{Z}_q$, then compute

$$c_4 = (g^c)^{r'}, c_5 = (g^d)^{s'}, c_6 = g^{r'+s'}c_3.$$

5. Encrypt $PK = g^{\frac{r+s}{\beta}}$ under the receiver's public encryption key, that is

$$(c_4, c_5, c_7) = ((g^c)^{r'}, (g^d)^{s'}, g^{r'+s'}g^{\frac{r+s}{\beta}}).$$

Here we use the same random number as the encryption of c_3.

6. Set public verifying key $PK' = (c_4, c_5, c_7)$.

7. Compute $v_1 = g^{\frac{1}{\beta}}$ and encrypt it under the receiver's public encryption key, that is

$$(c_4, c_5, c_8) = ((g^c)^{r'}, (g^d)^{s'}, g^{r'+s'}g^{\frac{1}{\beta}}).$$

Here we use the same random number as the encryption of c_3. Besides, compute zero knowledge proof

$$ZKP = ZKP(\log_{g^a} c_1 + \log_{g^b} c_2 = \log_{g^{\frac{1}{\beta}}} PK).$$

Here we omit the detailed expression of zero knowledge proof.

8. Set zero knowledge proof $ZKP' = (c_4, c_5, c_8, ZKP, c_1, c_2)$

9. Output encrypted verifiable encrypted signature $\sigma = (c_4, c_5, c_6, \sigma_2)$, public verifying key $PK' = (c_4, c_5, c_7)$, and zero-knowledge $ZKP' = (c_4, c_5, c_8, ZKP, c_1, c_2)$.

Note: When sending to the receiver, we only encrypt those parts which involve the signer's secret information. And we use the same random numbers in order to decrease the communication traffic. We will show that the security will not be influenced when using the same random numbers.

- $EVESVerify(sk_r, pk_s, PK', \sigma, m, ZKP')$:
  1. Parse $pk_s = (g_1, g_2, u', U)$, $PK' = (c_4, c_5, c_7)$, $\sigma = (c_4, c_5, c_6, \sigma_2)$, $m = (m_1, m_2, \cdots, m_n)$ and $ZKP' = (c_4, c_5, c_8, ZKP, c_1, c_2)$.
  2. Decrypt the encrypted verifiable encrypted signature

$$c_3 = c_6 / (c_4^{1/c} \cdot c_5^{1/d}) = g^{r+s}g_2^\alpha (u' \prod_{i \in M} u_i)^x.$$

Decrypt the public verifying key

$$PK = c_7 / (c_4^{1/c} \cdot c_5^{1/d}) = g^{\frac{r+s}{\beta}}.$$

Decrypt the zero knowledge proof

$$v_1 = c_8 / (c_4^{1/c} \cdot c_5^{1/d}) = g^{\frac{1}{\beta}}.$$

3. Verify the encrypted signature by

$$\mathbf{e}(v_1, g_2) \stackrel{?}{=} \mathbf{e}(g, g),$$

$$\mathbf{e}(c_3, g)/\mathbf{e}(\sigma_2, u' \prod_{i \in M} u_i) \stackrel{?}{=} \mathbf{e}(g_1, g_2)\mathbf{e}(PK, g_2).$$

4. Verify the validity of zero knowledge proof ZKP.
5. If both the encrypted signature and the zero knowledge is verified, then output Accept. Otherwise output Reject.

The public verifying key $PK = g^{\frac{r+s}{\beta}}$ and zero knowledge proof of $\log_{g^a} c_1 + \log_{g^b} c_2 = \log_{g^{\frac{1}{\beta}}} PK$ can assure that the signature is indeed generated by the signer and encrypted using the TTP's public encryption key. So when there are cases of disputes, receiver can give the verifiable encrypted signature (c_1, c_2, c_3) to the TTP, then the TTP can open the real signature by $\sigma_1 = c_3/(c_1^{1/a} \cdot c_2^{1/b})$.

Theorem 1. *The encrypted verifiable encrypted signature scheme EVES is existentially unforgeable if exponent 3-weak Diffie-Hellman problem is hard.*

The proof sketch is given in Appendix A.

4.2   The Obfuscation of the EVES Functionality

From the description of the EVES functionality in above section, we define a family of circuits $\mathcal{C}_{EVES} = \{\mathcal{C}_n\}_{n \in \mathbb{N}}$ for the EVES functionality, which we want to obfuscate. $\mathcal{C}_n$ is a set of circuits $C_{params, sk_s, pk_T, pk_r}$ related to the security parameter n. We can extract system parameters $(params, sk_s, pk_T, pk_r)$ from the description of the circuit. When having oracle access to the circuit, if input security parameter 1^n, the circuit outputs system parameters $(params, pk_T, pk_r)$. While if input a message m, the circuit outputs the corresponding encrypted verifiable encrypted signature, public verifying key and zero knowledge proof.

Then we give out the obfuscation Obf_{EVES} for $\mathcal{C}_{EVES}$ below. The main idea of the obfuscation is to encrypt the signing key twice under the TTP's public key and the receiver's public key, then anyone having the obfuscated program can generate a EVES by signing a signature with the new signing key. In order to preserve the probabilistic property of the EVES, we need to rerandomize it. It can be easily realized by encrypting it once again using the receiver's public key. Besides, the public verifying key and zero knowledge proof remain the same, and they don't need to be rerandomized as different signatures can share the same verifying key and zero knowledge proof.

Given a circuit $C_{params, sk_s, pk_T, pk_r}$, the obfuscation Obf_{EVES} is as following:

– $OBF(C_{params, sk_s, pk_T, pk_r})$:
   1. Extract system parameters $(params, sk_s, pk_T, pk_r)$.
   2. Parse $params = (\mathbb{G}, \mathbb{G}_T, q, g, \mathbf{e})$ and $sk_s = (g_2^\alpha, \beta, u', U)$.

3. Encrypt g_2^α under the TTP's public key $(c_1, c_2, c_3) \leftarrow Enc(pk_T, g_2^\alpha)$, that is

$$(c_1, c_2, c_3) = ((g^a)^r, (g^b)^s, g^{r+s} g_2^\alpha).$$

Then encrypt c_3 under the receiver's public key $(c_4, c_5, c_6) \leftarrow Enc(pk_r, c_3)$, that is

$$(c_4, c_5, c_6) = ((g^c)^{r'}, (g^d)^{s'}, g^{r+s+r'+s'} g_2^\alpha).$$

4. Set $sk'_s = (c_6, u', U)$, which is an encrypted form of the original signing key.
5. Encrypt $PK = g^{\frac{r+s}{\beta}}$ under the receiver's public encryption key, that is

$$(c_4, c_5, c_7) = ((g^c)^{r'}, (g^d)^{s'}, g^{r'+s'} g^{\frac{r+s}{\beta}}).$$

Here we use the same random number as the encryption of c_3.
6. Set public verifying key $PK' = (c_4, c_5, c_7)$.
7. Compute $v_1 = g^{\frac{1}{\beta}}$ and encrypt it under the receiver's public encryption key, that is

$$(c_4, c_5, c_8) = ((g^c)^{r'}, (g^d)^{s'}, g^{r'+s'} g^{\frac{1}{\beta}}).$$

Here we use the same random number as the encryption of c_3. Besides, compute zero knowledge proof

$$ZKP = ZKP(\log_{g^a} c_1 + \log_{g^b} c_2 = \log_{g^{\frac{1}{\beta}}} PK).$$

Here we omit the detailed expression of zero knowledge proof.
8. Set zero knowledge proof $ZKP' = (c_4, c_5, c_8, ZKP, c_1, c_2)$.

- $OBFCIR(params, pk_r, pk_T, sk'_s, ZKP', PK')$:

1. Construct an obfuscated circuit that contains the values $(params, pk_r, pk_T, sk'_s, ZKP', PK')$.
2. When input security parameter 1^n, the circuit outputs $(params, pk_T, pk_r)$.
3. When input an n bit long message m, it does as following:
   (1) Run $(\sigma_1, \sigma_2) \leftarrow Sign(sk'_s, m)$, that is

$$(\sigma_1, \sigma_2) = (g^{r+s+r'+s'} g_2^\alpha (u' \prod_{i \in M} u_i)^x, g^x).$$

We observe that (c_4, c_5, σ_1) is an encryption of the verifiable encrypted signature c_3, that is

$$(c_4, c_5, \sigma_1) = ((g^c)^{r'}, (g^d)^{s'}, g^{r'+s'} g^{r+s} g_2^\alpha (u' \prod_{i \in M} u_i)^x).$$

   (2) Randomly choose $i, j \in \mathbb{Z}_q$. Rerandomize the generated signature σ_1 using the receiver's public key $(c'_4, c'_5, \sigma'_1) \leftarrow ReRandom(pk_r, \sigma_1)$, that is

$$(c'_4, c'_5, \sigma'_1) = ((g^c)^{r'+i}, (g^d)^{s'+j}, g^{r'+s'+i+j} g^{r+s} g_2^\alpha (u' \prod_{i \in M} u_i)^x).$$

(3) Output encrypted verifiable encrypted signature $\sigma = (c'_4, c'_5, \sigma'_1, \sigma_2)$, the public verifying key $PK' = (c_4, c_5, c_7)$ and zero-knowledge proof $ZKP' = (c_4, c_5, c_8, ZKP, c_1, c_2)$.

It is easily to verify that the obfuscated program preserves the functionality of the original EVES.

1. On receiving (m, σ, PK', ZKP'), receiver parses $m = (m_1, m_2, \cdots, m_n)$, $\sigma = (c'_4, c'_5, \sigma'_1, \sigma_2)$, $PK' = (c_4, c_5, c_7)$ and $ZKP' = (c_4, c_5, c_8, ZKP, c_1, c_2)$.
2. Receiver decrypts the encrypted signature σ'_1, the public verifying key PK', the zero knowledge proof ZKP' using his secret key:

$$\sigma_1 = \frac{\sigma'_1}{(c'_4)^{1/c}(c'_5)^{1/d}} = g^{r+s}g_2^{\alpha}(u' \prod_{i \in M} u_i)^x),$$

$$PK = \frac{c_7}{c_4^{1/c}c_5^{1/d}} = g^{\frac{r+s}{\beta}}, v_1 = \frac{c_8}{c_4^{1/c}c_5^{1/d}} = g^{\frac{1}{\beta}}.$$

3. Then the receiver can verify the encrypted signature by

$$\mathbf{e}(v_1, g_2) \stackrel{?}{=} \mathbf{e}(g, g),$$

$$\mathbf{e}(\sigma_1, g)/\mathbf{e}(\sigma_2, u' \prod_{i \in M} u_i) \stackrel{?}{=} \mathbf{e}(g_1, g_2)\mathbf{e}(PK, g_2).$$

4. Verify the validity of zero knowledge proof ZKP.

Also, the TTP can open the real signature when there exist disputes.

Besides, the polynomial time property is obvious as all the computation here is efficient in polynomial time. We proof security of the obfuscation in the next section.

5 Security Analysis

Based on DBDH assumption and DL assumption, we show that the obfuscator Obf_{EVES} satisfies the security requirements in definition 4.

Theorem 2. *Let $T(C_{params,sk_s,pk_T,pk_r})$ be $\{Sign_{params,sk_s}\}$. Under the DBDH assumption and DL assumption, Obf_{EVES} satisfies ACVBP with dependent oracle set T.*

Proof. Since the obfuscated program Obf_{EVES} is identified with the values $(params, pk_r, pk_T, sk'_s, ZKP', PK')$ where $sk'_s = (c_6, u', U)$, $PK' = (c_4, c_5, c_7)$ and $ZKP' = (c_4, c_5, c_8, ZKP, c_1, c_2)$. So we can construct a simulator which simulates these values with sampling access to the original circuit $C_{params,sk_s,pk_T,pk_r}$. The values $(params, pk_r, pk_T)$ can be easily extract from the circuit. Besides, we observe that, without the decryption of PK and $g^{\frac{1}{\beta}}$, element ZKP are just random numbers to the adversary because it can't be verified. So it has no help on the ability of adversary. So the key point is to simulate the values $(c_4, c_5, c_6, c_7, c_8)$, where (c_4, c_5, c_6), (c_4, c_5, c_7), (c_4, c_5, c_8) are respectively the ciphertexts of encrypting $g^{r+s}g_2^\alpha$, $g^{\frac{r+s}{\beta}}$, $g^{\frac{1}{\beta}}$ under the receiver's public key. Then the simulator can just choose three junk values and encrypt them using the receiver's public encryption key pk_r.

The detailed procedure of simulator S is as below.

1. Input the security parameter 1^n, Extract system parameters $(params, pk_s, pk_T, pk_r)$.
2. Parse $params = (\mathbb{G}, \mathbb{G}_T, q, g, \mathbf{e})$ and $pk_s = (g_1, g_2, u', U)$.
3. Randomly choose $Junk_1, Junk_2, Junk_3 \in \mathbb{G}$. Randomly select $Junk_4 \in \mathbb{Z}_q$.
4. Encrypt $Junk_1$ using the TTP's public key

$$(c_1, c_2, c_3) = ((g^a)^r, (g^b)^s, g^{r+s}Junk_1),$$

then encrypt $c_3, Junk_2, Junk_3$ using the receiver's public key

$$(c_4, c_5, c_6, c_7, c_8) \leftarrow Enc(p, pk_r, c_3, Junk_2, Junk_3).$$

5. Set $sk_s' = (c_6, u', U)$, $PK' = (c_4, c_5, c_7)$ and $ZKP' = (c_4, c_5, c_8, Junk_4, c_1, c_2)$.
6. Output $(params, pk_r, pk_T, sk_s', ZKP', PK')$.

Following we need to show that, for any distinguisher (except the receiver) with sampling access to oracles $\{C_{params, sk_s, pk_T, pk_r}, Sign_{params, sk_s}\}$, the output distribution of simulator is indistinguishable from the real output distribution of the obfuscator. As we see, the fourth element of ZKP' in both output distributions are actually random numbers to the adversary without the decryption key, so it has no help on the ability of distinguisher to distinguish these two. Moreover, for distinguisher without the decryption key sk_r, (c_4, c_5, c_6), (c_4, c_5, c_7), (c_4, c_5, c_8) are just three independent ciphertexts because the encryption scheme satisfies indistinguishable CPA security. Assume there exists a distinguisher which can distinguish these two distributions given three tuples of ciphertexts with advantage at least ε, then for distinguisher given only one tuple of ciphertexts, the advantage to distinguish these two is at least $\frac{\varepsilon}{3}$. So it's sufficient for us to prove the security of the obfuscator when obtaining one tuple of the encryption. Here we prove the situation of giving (c_4, c_5, c_6) to the distinguisher, which is similar to the security proof in [12]. We need to prove that:

$$\left| Pr \left[\begin{array}{l} params = (\mathbb{G}, \mathbb{G}_T, q, g, \mathbf{e}) \leftarrow Setup(1^n); \\ (pk_s, sk_s, pk_r, sk_r, pk_T, sk_T) \leftarrow EVESKG(params); \\ (c_1, c_2, c_3) \leftarrow Enc(params, pk_T, g_2^\alpha), c_3 = g^{r+s}g_2^\alpha; \\ (c_4, c_5, c_6) \leftarrow Enc(params, pk_r, g^{r+s}g_2^\alpha); \\ b \leftarrow D^{\ll C, S \gg}(params, pk_r, pk_T, pk_s, (c_4, c_5, c_6), z) \end{array} : b = 1 \right] - \right.$$

$$\left. Pr \left[\begin{array}{l} params = (\mathbb{G}, \mathbb{G}_T, q, g, \mathbf{e}) \leftarrow Setup(1^n); \\ (pk_s, sk_s, pk_r, sk_r, pk_T, sk_T) \leftarrow EVESKG(params); \\ Junk \in \mathbb{G}; \\ (c_4, c_5, c_6) \leftarrow Enc(params, pk_r, Junk); \\ b \leftarrow D^{\ll C, S \gg}(params, pk_r, pk_T, pk_s, (c_4, c_5, c_6), z) \end{array} : b = 1 \right] \right| < \frac{1}{p(n)}.$$

We prove this by contradiction. Assume that the probability of distinguisher to win is not negligible, then we can construct an adversary (A_1, A_2) to break the linear encryption scheme. First, A_1 dose as below:

1. Take as input $(params, pk_r, pk_T, z)$.
2. Parse $params = (\mathbb{G}, \mathbb{G}_T, q, g, \mathbf{e})$.
3. Randomly generate key pairs $(pk_s, sk_s) \leftarrow SKG(params)$, that is

$$(pk_s, sk_s) = ((g_1, g_2, u', U), (g_2^\alpha, \beta, u', U)).$$

4. Encrypt the secret signing key using the TTP's public key $(c_1, c_2, c_3) \leftarrow Enc(params, pk_T, g_2^\alpha)$, that is $c_3 = g^{r+s}g_2^\alpha$.
5. Randomly select $Junk \in \mathbb{G}$.
6. Set $m_1 = g^{r+s}g_2^\alpha$, $m_2 = Junk$.
7. Output m_1, m_2, pk_s.

Given a challenge ciphertext c of m_i, adversary A_2 can distinguish between m_1 and m_2 with the help of distinguisher D.

1. Take as input $(params, pk_r, pk_T, pk_s, m_1, m_2, c, z)$,
2. Parse $params = (\mathbb{G}, \mathbb{G}_T, q, g, \mathbf{e})$, $pk_s = (g_1, g_2, u', U)$ and $c = (c_4, c_5, c_6)$.
3. Run $D \ll C, S \gg (params, pk_r, pk_T, pk_s, (c_4, c_5, c_6), z)$, the oracles can be simulated with $params, sk = (m_1, u', U), pk_r, pk_T$.
4. Output whatever D outputs.

The probability of adversary (A_1, A_2) to win is same to the advantage of D to distinguish the output distribution of obfuscator and simulator. So if it's not negligible, then it contradicts the DL assumption. Thus the advantage of D is negligible when given one tuple of ciphertexts, then the advantage when given three tuples is also negligible. So we conclude that the obfuscator satisfies ACVBP with dependent oracle set T, and the signature scheme is existentially unforgeable even given the obfuscated program under the DL and DBDH assumption. Besides, even if the receiver colludes with the proxy executing the obfuscated program, the secret signing key is still secure as it's encrypted under the TTP's public key.

6   Conclusion and Comparison

In this paper we give out a special EVES functionality and obfuscate it. We prove its security under the DBDH and DL assumption. The obfuscator enables anyone to generate a valid encrypted verifiable encrypted signature of the signer using the obfuscated program, while any secret information about the signer computed from the obfuscated program can also be obtained from oracle access to the original program. On the receiver's side, he can verify the encrypted signature using the public verifying key and the zero knowledge proof but has no knowledge of the real signature. When there is a dispute, the receiver can request the TTP to open the real signature. Compared to Hada's obfuscator of ES [12], our construction can fulfill the fair exchange functionality, which is our main motivation. Besides, in their construction, the signer's signing key will be leaked if the malicious operator colludes with the receiver. While in our construction, this problem doesn't exist as the signer's secret key is first encrypted using the TTP's public encryption key.

Acknowledgement. We would like to thank the anonymous reviewers of Provsec 2011 for their valuable suggestions. This work is supported by the National Natural Science Foundation of China (No. 61070168).

References

1. Ateniese, G.: Verifiable Encryption of Digital Signatures and Applications. ACM Transactions on Information and System Security 7(1), 1–20 (2004)
2. Boneh, D., Boyen, X., Shacham, H.: Short Group Signatures. In: Franklin, M. (ed.) CRYPTO 2004. LNCS, vol. 3152, pp. 41–55. Springer, Heidelberg (2004)
3. Bitansky, N., Canetti, R.: On Strong Simulation and Composable Point Obfuscation. In: Rabin, T. (ed.) CRYPTO 2010. LNCS, vol. 6223, pp. 520–537. Springer, Heidelberg (2010)
4. Barak, B., Goldreich, O., Impagliazzo, R., Rudich, S., Sahai, A., Vadhan, S.P., Yang, K.: On the (Im)possibility of Obfuscating Programs. In: Kilian, J. (ed.) CRYPTO 2001. LNCS, vol. 2139, pp. 1–18. Springer, Heidelberg (2001)
5. Waters, B.: Efficient Identity-Based Encryption Without Random Oracles. In: Cramer, R. (ed.) EUROCRYPT 2005. LNCS, vol. 3494, pp. 114–127. Springer, Heidelberg (2005)
6. Canetti, R.: Towards Realizing Random Oracles: Hash Functions that Hide All Partial Information. In: Kaliski Jr., B.S. (ed.) CRYPTO 1997. LNCS, vol. 1294, pp. 455–469. Springer, Heidelberg (1997)
7. Canetti, R., Dakdouk, R.R.: Obfuscating Point Functions with Multibit Output. In: Smart, N.P. (ed.) EUROCRYPT 2008. LNCS, vol. 4965, pp. 489–508. Springer, Heidelberg (2008)
8. Canetti, R., Tauman Kalai, Y., Varia, M., Wichs, D.: On Symmetric Encryption and Point Obfuscation. In: Micciancio, D. (ed.) TCC 2010. LNCS, vol. 5978, pp. 52–71. Springer, Heidelberg (2010)
9. Chaum, D., Pedersen, T.P.: Wallet databases with observers. In: Brickell, E.F. (ed.) CRYPTO 1992. LNCS, vol. 740, pp. 89–105. Springer, Heidelberg (1993)
10. Fiat, A., Shamir, A.: How to prove yourself: Practical solutions to identification and signature problems. In: Odlyzko, A.M. (ed.) CRYPTO 1986. LNCS, vol. 263, pp. 186–194. Springer, Heidelberg (1987)
11. Gu, C., Zhu, Y.: An ID-Based Verifiable Encrypted Signature Scheme Based on Hess's Scheme. In: Feng, D., Lin, D., Yung, M. (eds.) CISC 2005. LNCS, vol. 3822, pp. 42–52. Springer, Heidelberg (2005)
12. Hada, S.: Secure Obfuscation for Encrypted Signatures. In: Gilbert, H. (ed.) EUROCRYPT 2010. LNCS, vol. 6110, pp. 92–112. Springer, Heidelberg (2010)
13. Hofheinz, D., Malone-Lee, J., Stam, M.: Obfuscation for Cryptographic Purposes. In: Vadhan, S.P. (ed.) TCC 2007. LNCS, vol. 4392, pp. 214–232. Springer, Heidelberg (2007)

14. Hohenberger, S., Rothblum, G.N., Shelat, A., Vaikuntanathan, V.: Securely Obfuscating Re-encryption. In: Vadhan, S.P. (ed.) TCC 2007. LNCS, vol. 4392, pp. 233–252. Springer, Heidelberg (2007)
15. Lynn, B.Y.S., Prabhakaran, M., Sahai, A.: Positive Results and Techniques for Obfuscation. In: Cachin, C., Camenisch, J.L. (eds.) EUROCRYPT 2004. LNCS, vol. 3027, pp. 20–39. Springer, Heidelberg (2004)
16. Wee, H.: On Obfuscation Point Funtions. In: Proceedings of the 37th ACM Symposium on Theory of Computing, pp. 523–532 (2005)
17. Zhang, F., Safavi-Naini, R., Susilo, W.: Efficient Verifiably Encrypted Signature and Partially Blind Signature from Bilinear Pairings. In: Johansson, T., Maitra, S. (eds.) INDOCRYPT 2003. LNCS, vol. 2904, pp. 191–204. Springer, Heidelberg (2003)
18. Zhang, F., Safavi-Naini, R., Susilo, W.: An Efficient Signature Scheme from Bilinear Pairings and Its Applications. In: Bao, F., Deng, R., Zhou, J. (eds.) PKC 2004. LNCS, vol. 2947, pp. 277–290. Springer, Heidelberg (2004)

A   Proof of Security for EVES Scheme

Proof sketch.[of Thm.1] First, we argue that if exponent 3-weak problem is hard, then it is also a hard problem that given $(g, g^{a'}, g^{b'}, g^{\frac{1}{b'}})$, find $g^{a'b'}$. We can see that if $(g, g^{a'}, g^{b'}, g^{\frac{1}{b'}}) \to g^{a'b'}$ is easy, then $(h, h^x, h^{x^2}, h^{x^3}) \to h^{x^4}$ is solvable. It can be proved by set $h = g^{\frac{1}{b'}}$, then $g = h^x$, $g^{b'} = h^{x^2}$, $g^{a'} = h^{x^3}$. So if given $(g, g^{a'}, g^{b'}, g^{\frac{1}{b'}})$, $g^{a'b'}$ can be obtained. Then given $(h, h^x, h^{x^2}, h^{x^3})$, h^{x^4} can be solved as $g^{a'b'} = h^{x^4}$.

Following, we prove that EVES is existentially unforgeable if $(g, g^{a'}, g^{b'}, g^{\frac{1}{b'}}) \to g^{a'b'}$ problem is hard. Specially, in our EVES scheme, only the receiver can verify the EVES because only he can decrypt to get the c_3, PK and v_1. For outsider adversaries, they can't even verify the validity of EVES. So the strongest adversary is the receiver. Besides, forgery of EVES actually equals to forgery of VES as EVES can be obtained by encrypting VES using the receiver's public key. So it makes more sense to prove that VES is unforgeable to the strongest adversaries. Suppose there exists an adversary $\mathcal{A}$ can forge a valid VES with advantage ϵ, then we can construct a simulator $\mathcal{B}$, under the help of TTP whose public key is (g^a, g^b), to solve $(g, g^{a'}, g^{b'}, g^{\frac{1}{b'}}) \to g^{a'b'}$ problem with advantage $\frac{1}{8(n+1)p}\epsilon$, where p is the number of adversary $\mathcal{A}$'s queries. The simulator will take challenge group $(g, g^{a'}, g^{b'}, g^{\frac{1}{b'}})$ and outputs $g^{a'b'}$. The simulator runs $\mathcal{A}$ executing the following steps. As our EVES scheme is composed by Waters's signature scheme and Boneh's linear encryption scheme, so our proof is similar to the security proof of Waters's signature[5].

Setup. The simulator sets an integer $v = 4p$ (assume $q > vn$), then uniformly and randomly chooses an integer k between 0 and n. It then chooses a random x' and an n-length vector, $\overrightarrow{x} = (x_i)$, where x' and x_i are chosen at random between 0 and $v - 1$. Additionally, the simulator chooses a random y' and an n-length vector, $\overrightarrow{y} = (y_i)$, where all these elements are chosen randomly in $\mathbb{Z}_q$. All these values are kept internal to the simulator. Besides, we define $F(m) = (q - vk) + x' + \sum_{i \in m} x_i$, and $J(m) = y' + \sum_{i \in m} y_i$.

The simulator assigns $g_1 = g^{a'}$, $g_2 = g^{b'}$ and $v_1 = g^{\frac{1}{b'}}$. It then assigns the public parameters $u' = g_2^{q-vk+x'} g^{y'}$ and $u_i = g_2^{x_i} g^{y_i}$. So adversaries can't distinguish the distribution of the public parameters from the real construction.

Phase 1. When adversary $\mathcal{A}$ issues a signing query for a message m. If $F(m) = 0$ mod q, the simulator aborts.

Otherwise, the simulator randomly chooses $x \in \mathbb{Z}_q$, it constructs the signature as below:

$$\sigma = (\sigma_1, \sigma_2) = (g_1^{\frac{-J(m)}{F(m)}} (u' \prod_{i \in m} u_i)^x, g_1^{\frac{-1}{F(m)}} g^x).$$

Let $\tilde{x} = x - \frac{a}{F(m)}$. Then we have

$$\sigma_1 = g_1^{\frac{-J(m)}{F(m)}} (g_2^{F(m)} g^{J(m)})^x = g_2^{a'} (g_2^{F(m)} g^{J(m)})^{-\frac{a'}{F(m)}} (g_2^{F(m)} g^{J(m)})^x = g_2^{a'} (u' \prod_{i \in m} u_i)^{\tilde{x}},$$

$$\sigma_2 = g_1^{\frac{-1}{F(m)}} g^x = g^{x - \frac{a}{F(m)}} = g^{\tilde{x}}.$$

Then the simulator randomly chooses $r, s \in \mathbb{Z}_q$, and encrypts the signature under the TTP's public key, that is:

$$c_1 = (g^a)^r, c_2 = (g^b)^s, c_3 = g^{r+s} \sigma_1.$$

Lastly, the simulator computes $PK = v_1^{r+s}$ and correctly constructs the zero knowledge proof of $ZKP = ZKP(\log_{g^a} c_1 + \log_{g^b} c_2 = \log_{v_1} PK)$. The simulator returns the VES $(c_1, c_2, c_3, \sigma_2, v_1, PK, ZKP)$ to the adversary.

Phase 2. After the adversary $\mathcal{A}$ issues p signing queries, it outputs a forgery of VES $(m', c_1', c_2', c_3', \sigma_2', v_1', PK', ZKP')$. If $x' + \sum_{i \in m'} x_i \neq kv$, the simulator aborts. Otherwise, $F(m') = 0$ mod q so that $u' \prod_{i \in m'} u_i = g_2^{F(m')} g^{J(m')} = g^{J(m')}$. Then the simulator can request the TTP to decrypt (c_1', c_2', c_3') to get σ_1'. From this, the simulator can output

$$\sigma_1' / \sigma_2'^{J(m')} = g_2^{a'} = g^{a'b'}.$$

We see that if adversary $\mathcal{A}$ can successfully forge the VES at advantage ϵ, then the simulator $\mathcal{B}$ can solve the $(g, g^{a'}, g^{b'}, g^{\frac{1}{b'}}) \to g^{a'b'}$ problem with advantage:

$$\epsilon' = Pr[(\bigwedge_{i=1}^{p} F(m_i \neq 0 \bmod q)) \bigwedge \sum_{i \in m'} x_i = kv]\epsilon \geq \frac{1}{(n+1)v}(1 - 2\frac{p}{v})\epsilon = \frac{1}{8(n+1)p}\epsilon.$$

This probability computation is same to [5], so we omit it here.

Identity-Based Trace and Revoke Schemes

Duong Hieu Phan[1,2] and Viet Cuong Trinh[1]

[1] LAGA, UMR 7539, CNRS, Université Paris 8, Université Paris 13
[2] Ecole normale supérieure, Paris, France

Abstract. Trace and revoke systems allow for the secure distribution of digital content in such a way that malicious users, who collude to produce pirate decoders, can be traced back and revoked from the system. In this paper, we consider such schemes in the identity-based setting, by extending the model of identity-based traitor tracing scheme by Abdalla et al. to support revocation.

The proposed constructions rely on the subset cover framework. We first propose a generic construction which transforms an identity-based encryption with wildcard (WIBE) of depth $\log(N)$ (N being the number of users) into an identity-based trace and revoke scheme by relying on the complete subtree framework (of depth $\log(N)$). This leads, however, to a scheme with $\log(N)$ private key size (as in a complete subtree scheme). We improve this scheme by introducing generalized WIBE (GWIBE) and propose a second construction based on GWIBE of two levels. The latter scheme provides the nice feature of having constant private key size (3 group elements).

In our schemes, we also deal with advanced attacks in the subset cover framework, namely pirate evolution attacks (PEvoA) and pirates 2.0. The only known strategy to protect schemes in the subset cover framework against pirate evolution attacks was proposed by Jin and Lotspiech but decreases seriously the efficiency of the original schemes: each subset is expanded to many others subsets; the total number of subsets to be used in the encryption could thus be $O(N^{1/b})$ to prevent a traitor from creating more than b generations. Our GWIBE based scheme, resisting PEvoA better than the Jin and Lotspiech's method. Moreover, our method does not need to change the partitioning procedure in the original complete subtree scheme and therefore, the resulted schemes are very competitive compared to the original scheme, with $r \log(N/r) \log N-$size ciphertext and constant size private key.

Keywords: Traitor Tracing, Broadcast Encryption, Subset-cover Framework, Pirate Evolution Attacks, Pirates 2.0.

1 Introduction

In a system of secure distribution of digital content, a center broadcasts encrypted content to legitimate recipients. Most solutions to this problem can be categorized into broadcast encryption or traitor tracing.

X. Boyen and X. Chen (Eds.): ProvSec 2011, LNCS 6980, pp. 204–221, 2011.
© Springer-Verlag Berlin Heidelberg 2011

Broadcast encryption systems, independently introduced by Berkovits [Ber91] and Fiat-Naor [FN94], enable a center to encrypt a message for any subset of legitimate users and to prevent any set of revoked users from recovering the broadcasted information. Moreover, even if all revoked users collude, they don't obtain any information about the content sent by the center.

Traitor tracing schemes, introduced in [CFN94], enable the center to trace users who collude to produce pirate decoders. The center broadcasts encrypted content so that all users can decrypt this content. The risk here is that different users successfully collude (they are then called traitors) by contributing their private keys to build a pirate decoder and distribute this decoder to illegitimate users. The goal of a traitor tracing system is to allow, when a pirate decoder is found, the authority to run a tracing procedure to identify the traitors.

Trace and Revoke systems [NP00, NNL01] provide the functionalities of both broadcast encryption and traitor tracing. The most famous trace and revoke schemes are those from the subset-cover framework [NNL01], namely complete subtree scheme and subset difference scheme. They have been used as a basis to design the widely spread content protection system for HD-DVDs and Blu-ray disks called AACS [AAC].

Identity-based cryptography was introduced by Shamir in 1984 [Sha85]. However, it's only very recently that identity-based schemes in "one-to-many" settings were introduced, namely identity-based traitor tracing [ADML+07] and identity-based broadcast encryption [Del07, SF07]. In the first identity-based traitor tracing scheme, proposed by Abdalla *et al.* [ADML+07], each group of users has an identity and the encryption is based on Waters' WIBE [ACD+06] and on collusion secure codes [BS95]. The use of collusion secure codes results in unfeasibly large public key and ciphertext sizes. The authors left as an open question the problem of constructing "efficient identity-based traitor tracing scheme, even in the random oracle model". We consider the more general problem of constructing efficient identity-based trace and revoke systems in the standard model.

Recently, two new types of attack have been proposed which point out some weakness of schemes in the subset-cover framework, namely pirate evolution attacks [KP07] and pirates 2.0 [BP09].

Pirate evolution [KP07] is an attack concept against a trace and revoke scheme that exploits the properties of the combined functionality of tracing and revocation in a tree based scheme. Using a set of users' keys, the pirate produces an initial pirate decoder. When this pirate decoder is seized, the pirate evolves the first pirate decoder by issuing a second version that succeeds in decrypting ciphertexts. The same step can be repeated again and again and the pirate continues to evolve a new version of the previous decoder.

Pirates 2.0 attacks [BP09] result from traitors collaborating in a public way. In other words, traitors do not secretly collude but display part of their secret keys in a public place; pirate decoders are then built from this public information. The distinguishing property of pirates 2.0 attacks is that traitors only contribute partial information about their secret key material which suffices to produce (possibly imperfect) pirate decoders while allowing them to remain anonymous. This type of attacks has been shown to be a real threat for tree based and code based schemes [BP09].

Since schemes from the subset-cover framework have been widely implemented in practice, it's a challenge to build new schemes in this framework that can resist these two type of attacks.

1.1   Our Contribution

We propose the first Identity-based Trace and Revoke system, along with an efficient method for fighting pirates 2.0 and pirate evolution attacks. Our constructions can be considered as variants of the complete subtree scheme. The first scheme makes use of an identity-based encryption with wildcards [ACD$^+$06] (WIBE for short) scheme with linear pirate key size in the depth of the tree. In order to improve this, we first propose a generalized WIBE (GWIBE for short) and then propose a second scheme that relies on 2-level GWIBE. Our second scheme have the following properties:

- It outperforms, in term of efficiency, the identity based traitor tracing scheme in [ADML$^+$07] as it does not need to use a collusion secure code. Note that the scheme in [ADML$^+$07] does not support revocability.
- It resists known pirate evolution attacks [KP07] and pirates 2.0 attacks [BP09].
- It is, asymptotically, very competitive with the original scheme, namely the complete subtree and subset difference schemes (detailed comparisons is given in the full version [PT11].). Moreover, in our scheme, private keys of users are of constant sizes.

1.2   Related Works

Recently, [JL09] proposed a new method to defend against pirate evolution attacks in the subset difference framework. However, their method decreases seriously the efficiency of the original schemes because each subset need to be expanded to many others subsets; the total number of subsets to be used in the encryption becomes sub-linear in the total number of users in the system.

A new method has recently proposed in [DdP11] to defend against pirates 2.0 in the subset-cover framework by integrating the Naor-Pinkas scheme[NP00] into complete subtree scheme (CS) or subset difference scheme (SD). However, because of integrating polynomial interpolation method of Naor-Pinkas [NP00], their method decreases the efficiency of the original schemes and cannot support unbounded number of traitors as in subset-cover schemes.

Finally, in a recently proposed work [ZZ11], the authors also proposed a method to deal with pirates 2.0 in code-based schemes. In fact, their method is essentially similar to the method in [ADML$^+$07] except that they split the second level in [ADML$^+$07] into L levels (L is the length of code). This work shows an interesting result that the scheme [ADML$^+$07] can made to be resistant against pirates 2.0 with almost no additional cost. Note however that code-based schemes actually do not support revocation, they are thus not a trace and revoke system. Our schemes are by far more efficient than the above mentioned schemes (detailed comparisons is given in the full version [PT11]). In fact, our scheme are, asymptotically, very competitive with the original schemes in [NNL01], namely the complete subtree scheme and the subset difference scheme. Because these schemes are widely implemented in practice, our results could also give a significant impact in practice.

We now figure out the general literature about broadcast encryption and traitor tracing. Tree based schemes were proposed by Wallner *et al.* [WHA99] and Wong *et al.* [WGL98] and [NNL01]. Some methods for combining key tree structure with other techniques have been proposed: Sherman-McGrew [SM03] used a one-way function, Canetti et al. [CMN99] used a pseudo-random generator, and Kim et al. [KPT00] used a Diffie-Hellman key exchange scheme.

Dodis and Fazio [DF02] introduced a way to transform NNL schemes from a secret setting to a public-key setting by using IBE and HIBE. Though based on the same primitive, namely HIBE, each user's private key is still composed by a set of sub-keys and therefore, these schemes suffer from pirates 2.0 and pirate evolution attacks.

In addition to combinatoric schemes, many algebraic schemes with very nice features have been introduced. Kurosawa-Desmedt [KD98] and Boneh-Franklin [BF99] proposed the first elegant algebraic constructions with a deterministic tracing procedure. Boneh and Waters designed a fully collusion resistant trace and revoke scheme [BW06]. This last scheme is very interesting from a theoretical point of view as it is the first scheme that supports full collusion with sub-linear ciphertext size. It is, however, hard to implement in practice because the size of ciphertext is always $O(\sqrt{N})$ whatever the size of collusion, *i.e.* even if there are very few traitors.

Public-key broadcast schemes with constant-size ciphertexts have been proposed in [BGW05] and in [DPP07]. These schemes require decryption keys of size linear in the number of users (a receiver has a constant-size private key, but needs the encryption key to perform a decryption). This storage may be excessive for low-cost devices.

Adaptive security has been investigated in [DF03, GW09]. Attribute based broadcast encryption scheme has recently been proposed in [LS08]

Traitor tracing schemes based on codes have been much investigated since the seminal work of Boneh and Shaw [BS95] on collusion secure codes: Kiayias and Yung [KY02] proposed a scheme with constant rate. [BP08, BN08] recently achieved constant size ciphertexts. One of the main shortcoming of the code based schemes remains that the user's key is very large (linear in the length of codewords).

1.3   About the Model of PEvoA and Pirates 2.0

We remark that the considerer model of PEvoA and Pirates 2.0 in our paper is not the most general one. However, this model covers the main idea of the attacks presented in [KP07] and [BP09], it also covers the proposed attacks in these original papers. Moreover, the countermeasures mentioned above [JL09], [DdP11] and [ZZ11] are all under our model. Formal definitions of our model of PEvoA and Pirates 2.0 will be given in the paper. Informally speaking, this model requires that the pirate needs to have a sub-key to be able to decrypt a sub-ciphertext. We recall that in combinatoric schemes, a ciphertext is composed by a set of sub-ciphertext each of them is encrypted by a sub-key. The known PEvoA and Pirates 2.0 exploit the fact that a pirate can combine some sub-keys to break the system. The most general model for PEvoA and Pirates 2.0 would be the case that a pirate can combine partial information about sub-keys to break the whole scheme. This model is not considered in this paper neither in previous papers and it is still an open question to find out a countermeasures for the most general form of PEvoA and Pirates 2.0. It appears that this closely relates to the subject of key-leakage resilient cryptography .

2   Fighting Pirates 2.0 and Pirate Evolution Attacks in Tree Based Systems

In this section we present the ideas behind our constructions. The main problem of schemes in the tree-based framework (or more generally, in the combinatoric setting) is that the users' keys contain many sub-keys. Each sub-key corresponds to an internal node of the tree. Consequently, each sub-key can be shared between many users. Thus, if a user only publish sub-keys of a certain level (to ensure that there are many users that share that sub-key), this user cannot be traced but pirates can efficiently collect different sub-keys to build a practical decoder.

Our method for fighting pirates 2.0 and pirate evolution attacks consists of two steps: making private keys indecomposable (the private keys are not composed of sub-keys) and avoiding the derivation of sub-keys of any internal node from the private keys.

2.1   Framework

First Step: Making Private Keys Indecomposable. Since the core of pirates 2.0 attacks is the public contribution of partial private key, a natural idea is to render private keys indecomposable. But this condition is not sufficient.

Asano [Asa02] and [AK05] proposed very interesting schemes with constant size private keys. Because private keys in these scheme are of constant size, one might think traitors cannot contribute a partial key information to the public and that pirates 2.0 can then be excluded. However, this is not the case. Indeed, in order for a user U to be able to decrypt a ciphertext at a node in the path from U to the root, U has to be able to derive the corresponding key at that node. This is the reason why these schemes are still vulnerable to pirates 2.0 and pirate evolution attacks. The user U does not need to contribute his key but can compute and contribute any key corresponding to the nodes on the path from U to the root.

Second Step: No Intermediate Key Should be Derived from a Private Key. The goal in this step is to construct a scheme that, along with the undecomposability of private keys, enjoying the following additional property: no key at internal nodes can be derived from a private key. This property ensures preventing a traitor to derive and then publish keys at internal nodes and therefore it can only contribute its own key which leaks its identity.

Main Idea: Delegation of Ciphertexts. Our main idea is to allow a sub-ciphertext at a node being publicly modifiable to be another sub-ciphertext at any descendant node. This way, by possessing a private key at a leaf, a user can decrypt any sub-ciphertext at its ancestor node. We illustrate the idea in the figure 1. The sub-ciphertext C could be publicly modified to be a ciphertext C_U that can be decryptable by any user U lying in the sub-tree rooted at the corresponding node C. At this stage, we see that the user U could have just one key, this key cannot be used to derive sub-keys for other nodes but it can decrypt ciphertexts at any node in the path from U to the root.

The construction of WIBE in [ACD$^+$06] implicitly gives a delegation of ciphertexts as we need. This is indeed our first solution which is quite inefficient. We then introduce a generalized notion of WIBE and propose a much more efficient solution.

Fig. 1. Compairison between Asano's method and our method

2.2   Solutions

First Solution: Integration of WIBE Into a Complete Subtree Scheme
In our framework 2, the first step is to propose a scheme so that a user is unable to derive any key corresponding to its ancestor node. This requirement fits perfectly hierarchical identity based encryption systems (HIBE for short). However, an HIBE system cannot be directly employed for dealing with the second step because a user at a lower level cannot decrypt a ciphertext at a higher level. Fortunately, identity-based encryption with wildcards [ACD$^+$06] (WIBE for short) can be used to solve this issue. The main idea in constructions of current WIBE is to be able to modify the ciphertext so that a legitimate user can put information on the ciphertext to obtain a new ciphertext specifically crafted for him and then can decrypt this modified ciphertext as in HIBE system. This completes the second step. We discuss this with a concrete construction later on.

Main Solution: Introduction of Generalized WIBE Primitive A short-coming in our first scheme is that the private key size is linearly in the depth of the tree. To overcome this issue, we propose a new primitive, called generalized WIBE (GWIBE for short) where the wildcard does not need to replace the whole identity at a given level but can be part of the identity at each level. We can thus regroup all levels below the root into a single level and put the wildcard as part of the identity. Therefore, we only need a 2-level GWIBE for encryption.

2.3 Efficiency Comparison

Besides the property of resisting pirates 2.0 and pirate evolution attacks, our schemes are also very competitive in terms of efficiency. The only previous traitor tracing scheme in the identity based setting is much less efficient than ours, especially when the number of traitors is large.

Compared to the complete subtree and subset difference schemes, the ciphertext in ours schemes is larger (more a factor of $\log(N)$) but our second scheme has constant size private keys.

Dodis and Fazio [DF02] showed a way to transform NNL schemes from a secret setting to a public-key setting by using IBE and HIBE. Their best schemes are denoted by DF-CS (transforming complete subtree scheme to public-key setting by using the Waters IBE in [Wat05]) and DF-SD (transforming subset difference scheme to public-key setting by using the BBG scheme [BBG05]).

A more detailed comparison is given in the full version [PT11].

3   Construction of Identity-Based Trace and Revoke from WIBE (WIBE-IDTR)

3.1   Background

The definition of an identity-based trace and revoke scheme IDTR, as well as the adaptive security model for IDTR systems, can be found in the full version of this paper [PT11]. Our model follows the model of identity-based traitor tracing [ADML+07] in which each group of users has an identity and the broadcaster encrypts messages to a group by using the group's identity. We also deal with revocation, the encryption depends thus on the group's identity and the set of revoked users in that group.We first recall the basic definitions of WIBE, and its security model.

Identity-Based Encryption with Wildcards. schemes are essentially a generalization of HIBE schemes where at the time of encryption, the sender can decide to make the ciphertext decryptable by a whole range of users whose identities match a certain pattern. Such a pattern is described by a vector $P = (P_1, ..., P_l) \in (\{0,1\}^* \cup \{*\})^l$, where $*$ is a special wildcard symbol. We say that identity $ID = (ID_1, ..., ID_{l'})$ *matches* P, denoted $ID \in_* P$, if and only if $l' \leq l$ and $\forall i = 1...l': ID_i = P_i$ or $P_i = *$. Note that under this definition, any ancestor of a matching identity is also a matching identity. This is reasonable for our purposes because any ancestor can derive the secret key of a matching descendant identity anyway.

More formally, a WIBE scheme is a tuple of algorithms WIBE = (**Setup**, **KeyDer**, **Enc**, **Dec**) providing the following functionality. The **Setup** and **KeyDer** algorithms behave exactly as those of an HIBE scheme. To create a ciphertext of message $m \in \{0,1\}^*$ intended for all identities matching pattern P, the sender computes $C \overset{\$}{\leftarrow} \mathbf{Enc}(\mathsf{mpk}, P, m)$. Any of the intended recipients $ID \in_* P$ can decrypt the ciphertext using its own decryption key as $m \leftarrow \mathbf{Dec}(d_{ID}, C)$. Correctness requires that for all key pairs (mpk, msk) output by **Setup**, all messages $m \in \{0,1\}^*$, all $0 \le l \le L$, all patterns $P \in (\{0,1\}^* \cup \{*\})^l$, and all identities $ID \in_* P$, $\mathbf{Dec}(\mathbf{Keyder}(msk, ID), \mathbf{Enc}(\mathsf{mpk}, P, m)) = m$ with probability one.

Security Model for WIBE. We recall the define of the security of WIBE schemes in [ACD+06]. In the first phase the adversary is run on input the master public key of a freshly generated key pair $(mpk, msk) \overset{\$}{\leftarrow} \mathbf{Setup}(1^k)$. In a chosen-plaintext attack (IND-WID-CPA), the adversary is given access to a key derivation oracle that on input $ID = (ID_1, \cdots, ID_k)$ returns $d_{ID} \overset{\$}{\leftarrow} \mathbf{Keyder}(msk, ID)$. At the end of the first phase, the adversary outputs two equal length challenge messages m_0, m_1 and a challenge pattern $P^* = (P_1^*, \cdots, P_{k^*}^*)$ where $0 \le k^* \le L$, L is the depth of the root tree. The adversary is given a challenge ciphertext $C^* \overset{\$}{\leftarrow} \mathbf{Enc}(mpk, P^*, m_b)$ for a randomly chosen bit b, and is given access to the same oracles as during the first phase of the attack. The second phase ends when the adversary outputs a bit b'. The adversary is said to win the IND-WID-CPA game if $b = b'$ and if it never queried the key derivation oracle for the keys of any identity that matches the target pattern (i.e., any ID such that $ID \in_* P^*$).

Definition 1. *A WIBE scheme is (t, q_K, ϵ) IND-WID-CPA-secure if all t-time adversaries making at most q_K queries to the key derivation oracle have at most advantage ϵ in winning the IND-WID-CPA game described above. It is said to be (t, q_K, q_D, ϵ) IND-WID-CCA-secure if all such adversaries that additionally make at most q_D queries to the decryption oracle have advantage at most ϵ in winning the IND-WID-CCA game described above.*

3.2 Generic Construction

We combine WIBE with the complete subtree method: each group $ID \in \{0,1\}^*$ represents a binary tree and each user $id \in \{0,1\}^l$ (we write $id = id_1 id_2 \cdots id_l$,

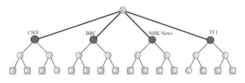

Fig. 2. Identity based Trace and Revoke in Complete Subtree structure

$id_i \in \{0, 1\}$) in a group ID is assigned to be a leaf of the binary tree rooted at ID. For encryption, we will use a WIBE of depth $l + 1$, each user is associated with a vector $(ID, id_1, \cdots, id_l)$. This is illustrated in Figure 2.

Concretely, the WIBE-IDTR system works as follows:

Setup($1^k, N$): Take a security parameter k and the maximum number of user in each group N (thus $l = \lceil \log_2 N \rceil$). Run the setup algorithm of WIBE with the security parameter k and the hierarchical depth $L = l + 1$ which returns (mpk, msk). The setup then outputs (mpk, msk). As in the complete subtree method, the setup also defines a data encapsulation method $E_K : \{0, 1\}^* \rightarrow \{0, 1\}^*$ and its corresponding decapsulation D_K.

Keyder(msk, ID, id): Run the key derivation of WIBE for $l + 1$ level identity $WID = (ID, id_1, id_2, \ldots, id_l)$ (the j-th component corresponds to the j-th bit of the identity id) and get the decryption key d_{WID}. Output $d_{ID,id} = d_{WID}$.

Enc(mpk, $ID, \mathcal{R}_{ID}, M$): A sender wants to send a message M to a group ID with the revocation list $\mathcal{R}_{ID}$. The revocation works as in the complete subtree scheme. Considering a group ID with its revocation list $\mathcal{R}_{ID}$, the users in $\mathcal{N}_{ID} \backslash \mathcal{R}_{ID}$ are partitioned into disjoint subsets $S_{i_1}, \ldots, S_{i_w}$ which are all the subtrees of the original tree (rooted at ID) that hang off the Steiner tree defined by the set $\mathcal{R}_{ID}$.

Each subset $S_{i_j}, 1 \le j \le w$, is associated to an $l+1$ vector identity $ID_{S_{i_j}} = (ID, id_{i_j,1}, \ldots, id_{i_j,k}, *, *.., *)$ where $id_{i_j,1}, \ldots, id_{i_j,k}$ is the path from the root ID to the node S_{i_j} and the number of wildcards $*$ is $l - k$.

The encryption algorithm randomly chooses a session key K, encrypts M under the key K by using an symetric encryption, and outputs as a header the encryption of WIBE for each $ID_{S_{i_1}}, \ldots, ID_{S_{i_w}}$.

$$C = \langle [i_1, \ldots, i_w][\text{WIBE.}\mathbf{Enc}(\text{mpk}, ID_{S_{i_1}}, K), \ldots, \text{WIBE.}\mathbf{Enc}(\text{mpk}, ID_{S_{i_w}}, K)], E_K(M) \rangle$$

Dec($d_{ID,id}, C$): The user received the ciphertext C as above. First, find j such that $id \in S_{i_j}$ (in case $id \in \mathcal{R}_{ID}$ the result is null). Second, use private key $d_{ID,id}$ to decrypt WIBE.$\mathbf{Enc}$(mpk, $ID_{S_{i_j}}, K$) to obtain K. Finally, compute $D_K(E_K(M))$ to recover the message M.

Trace$^{\mathbb{D}}$(msk, ID): Our tracing algorithm is similar to the one in [NNL01]. It takes as input msk, ID, an illegal decryption box $\mathbb{D}$, returns either a subset consisting at least one traitor or a new partition of $\mathcal{N}_{ID} \backslash \mathcal{R}_{ID}$ that renders the illegal decryption box useless. We note that this is not the strongest notion of traceability. In a black-box traitor tracing, one can identify at least one traitor. Our tracing algorithm relies on the tracing algorithms in NNL framework and target the same notion of traceability. However, unlike the tracing algorithms in NNL, our tracing algorithm can deal with PEvoA and Pirates 2.0, as will be shown in the next sections.

3.3 Security of WIBE-IDTR

Theorem 2. *If the* WIBE *of depth* l *is* (t', q'_K, ϵ') IND-WID-CPA-*secure, then the* WIBE-IDTR *is* (t^*, q^*_K, ϵ^*) IND-CPA-*secure with*

$$t^* \leq t' / (r \log(\frac{N}{r})), \quad q^*_K \leq q'_K, \quad \epsilon^* \leq r \log(\frac{N}{r}) \times \epsilon'$$

where N *is the bound on the number of users and* r *is the number of revoked users.*

The proof is provided in the full version of this paper [PT11]. We note that $r \log(\frac{N}{r})$ is the upper-bound on the number of subsets in the partition of non-revoked users. Like in NNL schemes, we should also pay a factor of $r \log(\frac{N}{r})$ in the reduction cost to the security of the chosen primitive for encryption, here is the security of WIBE.

We also present an Instantiation as well as the security analysis of our identity-based trace and revoke from Waters' WIBE in the full version of this paper [PT11]. We briefly remark here that, for a general construction of WIBE, the security can be reduced to the security of the underlying primitive HIBE with a lost of an exponential factor (in the hierarchical depth) in the security reduction [ACD+06]. This is due to the fact the simulator has to guess the positions of the wildcards. Fortunately, in our scheme, all the wildcards are regrouped at the end and therefore, the simulator only needs to guess the position of the first wildcard: the lost becomes linear in the hierarchical depth, which is acceptable.

3.4 Resistance to Pirate Evolution Attacks - PEvoA

Formalization of PEvoA. Before proving that our scheme resists to this type of attack, we propose a formalization of pirate evolution attack that covers all known attacks of this type.

Definition 3 (PEvoA **in Subset-Cover Systems**). *In a subset-cover system with* N *users, each user* u_i, $i = 1, \ldots, N$, *possesses a set of decryption keys* $K_{u_i} = (K_{u_{i,1}}, \ldots, K_{u_{i,h_i}})$. *A master pirate box* B *is built from* t *traitors* $(u_1, \ldots, u_t)$ *should possess a set of decryption keys* $(K_{u_1}, \ldots, K_{u_t})$.
A pirate evolution attack is an attack in which B *spawns successively a sequence of pirate boxes decoders* $B_1, B_2, \ldots$ *corresponding to each iterations* $1, 2, \ldots$. *The evolution from the iteration* i *to the iteration* $i + 1$ *is defined as follows:*

- *At each iteration* i, *after the tracing algorithm creates a new partition* S_{i+1} *which renders the pirate box* B_i *useless or which revokes some set of users.* B *spawns a new version* B_{i+1} *of pirate box, where* B_{i+1} *must contain at least a decryption key* d_{i+1} *such that, by using this decryption key* d_{i+1}, B_{i+1} *can decrypt the ciphertext encrypted based on the new partition* S_{i+1} *with probability higher than a given threshold* q.
- *The iteration repeats until* B *cannot spawn a new version of the pirate box decoder.*

Definition 4 (Resistance to PEvoA). *A system is susceptible to* PEvoA *if the maximum number of pirate box decoders that B can spawn is greater than the number of traitors t. The system is immune from* PEvoA *if the maximum number of pirate box decoders is less than or equal to t.*

In our definition, we closely follow the formalization of [KP07] but we refine the user's private key and evolution step: each user possesses a set of decryption keys, and at each iteration i a pirate box B_i must contain at least a decryption key which is used to decrypt the ciphertext encrypted at that iteration. This consideration might fail to cover attacks who can derive some partial decryption keys from a set of its key and then could use the partial key to break the security. In any case, our formalization covers the idea of the type of attacks described in [KP07]: each user in [NNL01] possesses a set of decryption keys (a set of long lived keys), and at each iteration master pirate box B spawns a new version of pirate box B_i, where B_i contains at least a decryption key (a long lived key) at some node in the tree.

We also note that the previous schemes in the subset-cover framework are susceptible to pirate evolution attacks because each user can always possess (or derive, in Asano *et. al*'s schemes [Asa02, AK05]) keys corresponding to intermediate nodes in the tree. Therefore, the traitors can easily produce many pirate boxes. This way of attacks are covered in our formalization.

We now show that our WIBE-IDTR scheme resist pirate evolution attacks.

Theorem 5 (Resistance of WIBE-IDTR to Pirate Evolution Attacks). *If there exists a pirate evolution adversary B on* WIBE-IDTR *of depth L, then there exists an adversary B' that breaks the security of* HIBE.

Proof. The main idea how our scheme can resist to this type of attacks is come from the property of the underlying HIBE. In our scheme, each user has only a private key corresponding to its identity at depth L. By the property of HIBE, no key at any intermediate node can be derived from the users' key. Therefore, the traitors can only produce pirate box by putting in it their collected keys and the number of pirate box is thus the number of traitors.

The proof is given in the full version of this paper [PT11].

3.5 Resistance to Pirates 2.0

Pirates 2.0 is a new type of attack against traitor tracing schemes. This type of attack results from traitors collaborating together *in a public way* and display part of their secret keys in a public place, allowing pirate decoders to be built from this public information. Traitors contribute part of their secret keys in an appropriate way in order to remain anonymous. Moreover, the traitors can contribute information at their discretion and they can publicly collude in groups of very large size.

Pirates 2.0. We consider the Pirates 2.0 model for subset-cover framework. Recall that, in this framework, a traitor is a legitimate user u_i who possesses a set of decryption keys $K_{u_i} = (K_{u_{i,1}}, \cdots , K_{u_{i,h_i}})$. We suppose that traitors leaks a subset of their decryption keys to the public domain in a discrete process. When pirates want to decrypt a ciphertext C, they should collect relevant decryption keys from their public environment in order to produce a pirate decoder. We consider that a pirate decoder should contain at least a decryption key that can be based on it to decrypt C. Our consideration, though not in the most general form, exactly reflects the attacks described in [BP09] against subset-cover schemes. We also note that the previous schemes in the subset-cover framework are susceptible to pirates 2.0 attacks because each user can always possess (or derive, in Asano *et. al*'s schemes [Asa02, AK05]) keys corresponding to intermediate nodes in the tree. Therefore, the traitors can easily contribute to the public domain a subset of their decryption keys leading to the production of a pirate decoder. These attack are covered by our considered formalization.

Following the same argument as in the case of pirate evolution attacks, we can show that our WIBE-IDTR scheme resists pirates 2.0.

Theorem 6 (Resistance of WIBE-IDTR to Pirates 2.0). *For any pirates 2.0 adversary B against WIBE-IDTR of depth L, there exists an efficient algorithm to output at least a traitor in the collusion that produced B.*

Proof. The proof is given in the full version of this paper [PT11]. $\qquad \blacksquare$

3.6   Instantiation

We give a concrete construction of IDTR From Waters' WIBE-2 as well as the security analysis of the scheme in the full version of this paper [PT11].

4   Identity-Based Encryption with Generalized Wildcards - GWIBE

Identity-based encryption with generalized wildcards schemes are essentially generalizations of WIBE schemes. The difference is that, in WIBE, at each level, the wildcard is added to replace the whole identity at that level, while in GWIBE, the wildcard might be employed to replace a part of the identity.

More formally, at the time of encryption, the sender can decide to make the ciphertext decryptable by a whole range of users whose identities match a certain pattern. For an l-level GWIBE, such a pattern is described by a vector $P = (P_1, ..., P_l)$. Each P_i, $1 \leq i \leq l$, is a bit string of length n, and can contain a wildcard. The wildcard is determined by its starting position and its final position. For example, for an identity "univ*math" of size 16, the starting position of the wildcard is 5 and the final position is 12, the size of the wildcard is 8. When encrypting with the identity "univ*math", any user who has a key corresponding to identities "univ-paris6.math" or "univ-paris9.math", ... should be able to decrypt.

The starting position is in $\{1, 2, .., n, n+1\}$ with the convention that the value $n+1$ implies no wildcard in P_i. If P_i contains a wildcard (that means a starting position is between 1 and n) we call P_i a generalized wildcard.

At this point, each P_i can be rewritten as $P_i = P_{ip}|| * ||P_{is}$ where P_{ip}, P_{is} are the bit strings of length ip, is; $0 \leq ip, is \leq n$. The size of the wildcard is $n - ip - is$, its starting position is $ip + 1$ and its final position is $n - is$.

We say that an identity $ID = (ID_1, \cdots, ID_{l'})$ *matches* P, denote $ID \in_* P$, if and only if $l' \leq l$ and $\forall i = 1, ..., l' : ID_i = P_i$ or ID_i and P_i have the form $P_i = P_{ip}|| * ||P_{is}$ and $ID_i = P_{ip}||ID_*||P_{is}$ where ID_* is some bit string of length $n - ip - is$.

From the above generalized notions of pattern and matching, the definition and the security model of GWIBE follows exactly the one of WIBE.

The generic construction of IDTR from 2-Level GWIBE is similar to the generic construction of IDTR from WIBE in Section 3.2. The only difference is that, instead of encrypting with WIBE, we will encrypt with 2-level GWIBE. The Theorem 2 can be adapted as follows.

Theorem 7. *If the* GWIBE *of depth 2 is* (t', q'_K, ϵ') IND-WID-CPA-*secure, then the 2level-*GWIBE-IDTR *is* (t^*, q^*_K, ϵ^*) IND-CPA-*secure with*

$$ t^* \leq t'/(r\log(\frac{N}{r})), \quad q^*_K \leq q'_K, \quad \epsilon^* \leq r\log(\frac{N}{r}) \times \epsilon' $$

where N is the upper bound on the number of users in the system and r is the number of revoked users.

The main contributions in this section are about constructing a GWIBE scheme and then applying it to obtain an efficient trace and revoke system. We now detail these parts.

4.1   Concrete Construction of GWIBE Based on Waters' HIBE (Wa-GWIBE)

We first explain some notation and the high level of the construction. A user's identity is given by a vector $ID = (ID_1, ID_2, \cdots, ID_l)$ where each ID_i is an $n - bit$ string, applying a collision resistant hash function if neccesary. When we write $j \in ID_i$, we mean that the variable j iterates over all bit positions of string of ID_i where the j-th bit of ID_i is one. Using this notation, for $i = 1, \ldots, l$, the Waters' hash function F_i is defined as

$$ F_i(ID_i) := u_{i,0} \prod_{j \in ID_i} u_{i,j} $$

where the $u_{i,j}$ are the elements in the master public key.

Now, for a generalized wildcard $ID_{ip}|| * ||ID_{is}$, we define $F_i(ID_{ip}|| * ||ID_{is}) := F_i(ID_{ip}||0 \ldots 0||ID_{is})$ with the number of added bit 0 is the size of the wildcard $*$. The main remark is that if we have the values $u^t_{i,j}$ for all $j = ip+1, ..., n-is$ and $t \xleftarrow{\$}$, we can compute the values of $F_i(ID_{ip}||ID^*||ID_{is})^t$ from $F_i(ID_{ip}|| * ||ID_{is})^t$ for any bit string ID^* of length $n - ip - is$.

Making use of this property, the main idea is that, if we postpone the computation of elements of wildcard to decryption time by including the separate elements $u_{i,j}^t$ corresponding to wildcards in the ciphertext, each recipient can combine the factors corresponding to his own identity in the decryption.

We extend some notations from WIBE [ACD$^+$06]. Let $P = (P_1, \cdots, P_l)$ is a pattern where P_i is a string of length n, define $W(P)$ be the set containing all generalized wildcard indices in P, i.e. the indices $1 \leq i \leq l$ such that $P_{ip} || * || P_{is}$, $1 \leq ip \leq n$. Let $\overline{W}(P)$ be the complementary set containing all non-generalized wildcard indices in P. Clearly $W(P) \cap \overline{W}(P)) = \phi$ and $W(P) \cup \overline{W}(P) = \{1, ..., l\}$.

Let $\mathbb{G}, \mathbb{G}_T$ be multiplicative groups of prime order p with an admissible map $\hat{e}: \mathbb{G} \times \mathbb{G} \leftarrow \mathbb{G}_T$.

Setup: The trusted authority chooses randomly generators $g_1, g_2, u_{1,0}, \cdots, u_{L,n}$ $\xleftarrow{\$} \mathbb{G}^*$, and a random value $\alpha \xleftarrow{\$} \mathbb{Z}_p$, where L is the maximum hierachy depth. Next, it computes $h_1 \leftarrow g_1^\alpha$ and $h_2 \leftarrow g_2^\alpha$. The master public key is $mpk = (g_1, g_2, h_1, u_{1,0}, \cdots, u_{L,n})$, and the master secret key is $msk = h_2$.

Keyder: An identity of a user is given by a vector $ID = (ID_1, \cdots, ID_l)$, where ID_i is a bit string of length n (applying a collision-resistant hash function if necessary). First, random values $r_1, \cdots, r_l \xleftarrow{\$} \mathbb{Z}_p$ are chosen, then the private key d_{ID} is computed as

$$(a_0, a_1, \cdots, a_l) = \left(h_2 \prod_{i=1}^{l} F_i(ID_i)^{r_i}, g_1^{r_1}, \cdots, g_1^{r_l} \right)$$

A secret key for identity $ID = (ID_1, ID_2, \cdots, ID_l)$ can be computed by its parent with identity $ID = (ID_1, ID_2, \cdots, ID_{l-1})$ as follows. Let $(a_0, a_1, \cdots, a_{l-1})$ be the parent's secret key. It chooses $r_l \xleftarrow{\$} \mathbb{Z}_p$ and outputs

$$d_{ID} = (a_0 \times F_l(ID_l)^{r_l}, a_1, \cdots, a_{l-1}, g_1^{r_l})$$

Enc: To encrypt a message $m \rightarrow \mathbb{G}_T$ to all identities matching pattern $P = (P_1, \cdots, P_l)$, the sender chooses $t \xleftarrow{\$} \mathbb{Z}_p$ and outputs the ciphertext $C = (P, C_1, C_2, C_3, C_4)$, where

$$C_1 \leftarrow g_1^t \qquad C_2 \leftarrow (C_{2,i} = F_i(P_i)^t)_{i \in \overline{W}(P)} \qquad C_3 \leftarrow m \cdot \hat{e}(h_1, g_2)^t$$

$$C_4 \leftarrow (C_{4,ip,is} = F_i(P_{ip} || 0...0 || P_{is})^t, (C_{4,i,j} = u_{i,j}^t)_{j=ip+1,...,n-is})_{i \in W(P)}$$

Where $P_{ip} || 0...0 || P_{is}$ is a string of length n, or the number of bit 0 is $n - ip - is$. That means we replace the elements of wildcard in identity P_i by bit 0.

Dec: If the receiver is the root authority holding the master key $msk = h_2$, then it can recover the message by computing $C_3 / \hat{e}(C_1, h_2)$. Any other receiver with identity $ID = (ID_1, \cdots, ID_l)$ matching the pattern P to which the ciphertext was created (i.e., $ID \in_* P$) can decrypt the ciphertext $C = (P, C_1, C_2, C_3, C_4)$ by computing $C_2' = (C_{2,i}')_{i=1,...,l}$ as

$$C_{2,i}' = F_i(ID_i)^t \leftarrow \begin{cases} C_{2,i} & \text{if } i \in \overline{W}(ID) \\ C_{4,ip,is} \times \prod_{j=ip+1,...,n-is}^{j \in ID_i} C_{4,i,j} & \text{if } i \in W(ID) \end{cases}$$

then computes

$$C_3 \cdot \frac{\prod_{i=1}^{l} \hat{e}(a_i, C'_{2,i})}{\hat{e}(C_1, a_0)} \quad = \quad m$$

4.2 Security Analysis

The proof of the following theorem can be found in the full version of this paper [PT11].

Theorem 8. *If the* Wa-HIBE *of depth* L *is* (t, q_K, ϵ) IND-ID-CPA-*secure, then the* Wa-GWIBE *scheme of depth* L *is* (t', q'_K, ϵ') IND-GWID-CPA-*secure*

$$t' \leq t - L \cdot n(1 + q_K) \times t_{exp}, \quad q'_K \leq q_K, \quad \epsilon' \leq \epsilon \times n^{2 \times L}$$

where t_{exp} *is the time taken to perform an exponentiation in* $\mathbb{G}$.

The Wa-GWIBE *used in our Trace and Revoke system.* We first remark that the above reduction of a general construction of GWIBE is extremely costly. Fortunately, in our construction of a trace and revoke system, we only need to a 2-level Wa-GWIBE and we can get a much more efficient reduction. Let us briefly explain the presence of the factor $n^{2 \times L}$ in the reduction of the above theorem. In fact, at each level the simulator has to guess the start position and the final position of wildcard (note that if the start position is $n + 1$ then it means there is no wildcard at this level). The probability of a good guess at a level is $1/n^2$. Because there are L levels, therefore the probability that A guesses $W(P^*)$ correctly is $1/n^{2 \times L}$. We now see how we can reduce this reduction cost for the purpose of a trace and revoke system. Indeed, we only need to a 2-level Wa-GWIBE and moreover, the first layer (the group identity) does not contain wildcard. The used pattern P used in encryption always has the form $P = (P_1, P_{2p}||*)$. Therefore, in the proof of the above theorem, the simulator does not need to guess the position of wildcard in the first layer, and at the second level, $\mathcal{B}$ needs only to guess the starting position of the wildcard. Therefore, the factor $1/n^{2 \times L}$ becomes $1/n$ in this case. This is acceptable because $n = \log(N)$ where N is the number of users in the system. We conclude that the (t', q'_K, ϵ') IND-GWID-CPA security of 2-level Wa-GWIBE can thus be reduced to a (t, q_K, ϵ) IND-ID-CPA-security of a 2-level Wa-HIBE with:

$$t' \leq t - \log(N)(1 + q_K) \times t_{exp}, \quad q'_K \leq q_K, \quad \epsilon' \leq \epsilon \times \log(N). \qquad (1)$$

4.3 Construction of IDTR from 2-Level Wa-GWIBE (2level-Wa-GWIBE-IDTR)

Applying the above construction of 2-level-Wa-GWIBE to the generic construction of IDTR from 2-level-GWIBE, we obtain a 2level-Wa-GWIBE-IDTR. We give the construction in the full version of this paper [PT11].

Concerning the security of the scheme, from Theorem 8 and the equation 1 which precisely states the security of the 2-level Wa-GWIBE used in our construction of trace and revoke system, and from Theorem 7, we directly obtain the following result:

Theorem 9. *If Waters'* HIBE *of depth 2 is* (t, q_K, ϵ) IND-WID-CPA-*secure, then the 2level-*Wa*-GWIBE-IDTR is* (t^*, q_K^*, ϵ^*) IND-CPA-*secure with*

$$t^* \leq (t - \log(N)(1 + q_K)/(r \log(\frac{N}{r})), \quad q_K^* \leq q_K, \quad \epsilon^* \leq r \log(\frac{N}{r}) \times \epsilon \times \log(N)$$

In addition, it is proved in [ACD+06] that: if there exists a (t, q_K, ϵ) adversary against Waters' HIBE of depth L, then there exists an algorithm solving the BDDH problem with advantage $\epsilon_{\mathsf{BDDH}} = O(\epsilon/(n q_K)^L)$. In our scheme, we only use 2-level Waters' HIBE, and since $n \leq \log(N)$, we have $\epsilon_{\mathsf{BDDH}} = O(\epsilon/\log^2(N) q_K^2)$.

In conclusion, the security of our scheme can be based on the hardness of the BDDH problem:

Theorem 10. *If the* BDDH *is* $(\epsilon_{\mathsf{BDDH}})$ *secure, then the 2level-*Wa*-GWIBE-IDTR is* (q_K^*, ϵ^*) IND-CPA-*secure with*

$$\epsilon^* = O(r \log(\frac{N}{r}) \times \epsilon_{\mathsf{BDDH}} \times (q_K^*)^2 \times \log^3(N)).$$

Resistance to PEvoA *and Pirates 2.0.* Under similar arguments for the WIBE-IDTR scheme, our construction of 2level-GWIBE-IDTR resists to PEvoA and pirates 2.0. Detailed explanations are given in the full version of this paper [PT11].

Acknowledgments. This work was supported in part by the French ANR-09-VERS-016 BEST Project.

References

[AAC] AACS LA. AACS Specifications,
http://www.aacsla.com/specifications/

[ACD+06] Abdalla, M., Catalano, D., Dent, A.W., Malone-Lee, J., Neven, G., Smart, N.P.: Identity-based encryption gone wild. In: Bugliesi, M., Preneel, B., Sassone, V., Wegener, I. (eds.) ICALP 2006. LNCS, vol. 4052, pp. 300–311. Springer, Heidelberg (2006)

[ADML+07] Abdalla, M., Dent, A.W., Malone-Lee, J., Neven, G., Phan, D.H., Smart, N.P.: Identity-based traitor tracing. In: Okamoto, T., Wang, X. (eds.) PKC 2007. LNCS, vol. 4450, pp. 361–376. Springer, Heidelberg (2007)

[Asa02] Asano, T.: A revocation scheme with minimal storage at receivers. In: Zheng, Y. (ed.) ASIACRYPT 2002. LNCS, vol. 2501, pp. 433–450. Springer, Heidelberg (2002)

[AK05] Asano, T., Kamio, K.: A tree based one-key broadcast encryption scheme with low computational overhead. In: Boyd, C., González Nieto, J.M. (eds.) ACISP 2005. LNCS, vol. 3574, pp. 89–100. Springer, Heidelberg (2005)

[Ber91] Berkovits, S.: How to broadcast a secret (rump session). In: Davies, D.W. (ed.) EUROCRYPT 1991. LNCS, vol. 547, pp. 535–541. Springer, Heidelberg (1991)

[BP08]   Billet, O., Phan, D.H.: Efficient traitor tracing from collusion secure codes. In: Safavi-Naini, R. (ed.) ICITS 2008. LNCS, vol. 5155, pp. 171–182. Springer, Heidelberg (2008)

[BP09]   Billet, O., Phan, D.H.: Traitors collaborating in public: Pirates 2.0. In: Joux, A. (ed.) EUROCRYPT 2009. LNCS, vol. 5479, pp. 189–205. Springer, Heidelberg (2009)

[BBG05]   Boneh, D., Boyen, X., Goh, E.-J.: Hierarchical identity based encryption with constant size ciphertext. In: Cramer, R. (ed.) EUROCRYPT 2005. LNCS, vol. 3494, pp. 440–456. Springer, Heidelberg (2005)

[BF99]   Boneh, D., Franklin, M.K.: An efficient public key traitor scheme (Extended abstract). In: Wiener, M. (ed.) CRYPTO 1999. LNCS, vol. 1666, pp. 338–353. Springer, Heidelberg (1999)

[BGW05]   Boneh, D., Gentry, C., Waters, B.: Collusion resistant broadcast encryption with short ciphertexts and private keys. In: Shoup, V. (ed.) CRYPTO 2005. LNCS, vol. 3621, pp. 258–275. Springer, Heidelberg (2005)

[BN08]   Boneh, D., Naor, M.: Traitor tracing with constant size ciphertext. In: ACM CCS 2008, pp. 501–510. ACM Press, New York (2008)

[BS95]   Boneh, D., Shaw, J.: Collusion-secure fingerprinting for digital data (extended abstract). In: Coppersmith, D. (ed.) CRYPTO 1995. LNCS, vol. 963, pp. 452–465. Springer, Heidelberg (1995)

[BW06]   Boneh, D., Waters, B.: A fully collusion resistant broadcast, trace, and revoke system. In: ACM CCS 2006, pp. 211–220. ACM Press, New York (2006)

[CMN99]   Canetti, R., Malkin, T., Nissim, K.: Efficient communication-storage tradeoffs for multicast encryption. In: Stern, J. (ed.) EUROCRYPT 1999. LNCS, vol. 1592, pp. 459–474. Springer, Heidelberg (1999)

[CFN94]   Chor, B., Fiat, A., Naor, M.: Tracing traitors. In: Desmedt, Y.G. (ed.) CRYPTO 1994. LNCS, vol. 839, pp. 257–270. Springer, Heidelberg (1994)

[DdP11]   D'Arco, P., Perez del Pozo, A.L.: Fighting Pirates 2.0. In: Lopez, J., Tsudik, G. (eds.) ACNS 2011. LNCS, vol. 6715, pp. 359–376. Springer, Heidelberg (2011)

[Del07]   Delerablée, C.: Identity-based broadcast encryption with constant size ciphertexts and private keys. In: Kurosawa, K. (ed.) ASIACRYPT 2007. LNCS, vol. 4833, pp. 200–215. Springer, Heidelberg (2007)

[DPP07]   Delerablée, C., Paillier, P., Pointcheval, D.: Fully collusion secure dynamic broadcast encryption with constant-size ciphertexts or decryption keys. In: Takagi, T., Okamoto, T., Okamoto, E., Okamoto, T. (eds.) Pairing 2007. LNCS, vol. 4575, pp. 39–59. Springer, Heidelberg (2007)

[DF02]   Dodis, Y., Fazio, N.: Public Key Broadcast Encryption for Stateless Receivers. In: Feigenbaum, J. (ed.) DRM 2002. LNCS, vol. 2696, pp. 61–80. Springer, Heidelberg (2003)

[DF03]   Dodis, Y., Fazio, N.: Public key trace and revoke scheme secure against adaptive chosen ciphertext attack. In: Desmedt, Y.G. (ed.) PKC 2003. LNCS, vol. 2567, pp. 100–115. Springer, Heidelberg (2002)

[FN94]   Fiat, A., Naor, M.: Broadcast encryption. In: Stinson, D.R. (ed.) CRYPTO 1993. LNCS, vol. 773, pp. 480–491. Springer, Heidelberg (1994)

[GW09]   Gentry, C., Waters, B.: Adaptive security in broadcast encryption systems (with short ciphertexts). In: Joux, A. (ed.) EUROCRYPT 2009. LNCS, vol. 5479, pp. 171–188. Springer, Heidelberg (2009)

Identity-Based Trace and Revoke Schemes   221

[JL09]   Jin, H., Lotspiech, J.: Defending against the pirate evolution attack. In: Bao, F., Li, H., Wang, G. (eds.) ISPEC 2009. LNCS, vol. 5451, pp. 147–158. Springer, Heidelberg (2009)

[KP07]   Kiayias, A., Pehlivanoglu, S.: Pirate evolution: How to make the most of your traitor keys. In: Menezes, A. (ed.) CRYPTO 2007. LNCS, vol. 4622, pp. 448–465. Springer, Heidelberg (2007)

[KY02]   Kiayias, A., Yung, M.: Traitor tracing with constant transmission rate. In: Knudsen, L.R. (ed.) EUROCRYPT 2002. LNCS, vol. 2332, pp. 450–465. Springer, Heidelberg (2002)

[KPT00]   Kim, Y., Perrig, A., Tsudik, G.: Simple and fault-tolerant key agreement for dynamic collaborative groups. In: ACM CCS 2000, pp. 235–244. ACM Press, New York (2000)

[KD98]   Kurosawa, K., Desmedt, Y.G.: Optimum traitor tracing and asymmetric schemes. In: Nyberg, K. (ed.) EUROCRYPT 1998. LNCS, vol. 1403, pp. 145–157. Springer, Heidelberg (1998)

[LS08]   Lubicz, D., Sirvent, T.: Attribute-based broadcast encryption scheme made efficient. In: Vaudenay, S. (ed.) AFRICACRYPT 2008. LNCS, vol. 5023, pp. 325–342. Springer, Heidelberg (2008)

[NNL01]   Naor, D., Naor, M., Lotspiech, J.: Revocation and tracing schemes for stateless receivers. In: Kilian, J. (ed.) CRYPTO 2001. LNCS, vol. 2139, pp. 41–62. Springer, Heidelberg (2001)

[NP00]   Naor, M., Pinkas, B.: Efficient trace and revoke schemes. In: Frankel, Y. (ed.) FC 2000. LNCS, vol. 1962, pp. 1–20. Springer, Heidelberg (2001)

[PT11]   Phan, D.H., Trinh, V.C.: Identity-based trace and revoke schemes. In: Boyen, X., Chen, X. (eds.) Provsec 2011. LNCS, vol. 6980, pp. 208–225. Springer, Heidelberg (2011)

[SF07]   Sakai, R., Furukawa, J.: Identity-based broadcast encryption. Cryptology ePrint Archive, Report 2007/217 (2007)

[Sha85]   Shamir, A.: Identity-based cryptosystems and signature schemes. In: Blakely, G.R., Chaum, D. (eds.) CRYPTO 1984. LNCS, vol. 196, pp. 47–53. Springer, Heidelberg (1985)

[SM03]   Sherman, A.T., McGrew, D.A.: Key establishment in large dynamic groups using one-way function trees. IEEE Trans. Softw. Eng. 29(5), 444–458 (2003)

[WHA99]   Wallner, D.M., Harder, E.J., Agee, R.C.: Key management for multicast: Issues and architectures. In: RFC 2627 (1999)

[Wat05]   Waters, B.: Efficient identity-based encryption without random oracles. In: Cramer, R. (ed.) EUROCRYPT 2005. LNCS, vol. 3494, pp. 114–127. Springer, Heidelberg (2005)

[WGL98]   Wong, C.K., Gouda, M.G., Lam, S.S.: Secure group communications using key graphs. In: Proceedings of ACM SIGCOMM, Vancouver, BC, Canada, August 31 - September 4, pp. 68–79 (1998)

[ZZ11]   Zhao, X., Zhang, F.: Traitor tracing against public collaboration. In: Bao, F., Weng, J. (eds.) ISPEC 2011. LNCS, vol. 6672, pp. 302–316. Springer, Heidelberg (2011)

Universally Composable Private Proximity Testing

Rafael Tonicelli, Bernardo Machado David, and Vinícius de Morais Alves

Department of Electrical Engineering, University of Brasilia
Campus Darcy Ribeiro, 70910-900, Brasilia, DF, Brazil
{tonicelli,bernardo.david,vmalves}@redes.unb.br

Abstract. This paper aims at studying privacy-preserving tests for proximity. In a *private proximity test*, Alice can verify if she is close to Bob without either party revealing any other information about their location. We propose a system for private proximity testing based on the pre-distribution of data: the so-called *commodity-based model*. Our system is proven secure in the *Universal Composability* (UC) framework and uses as the core building block an efficient UC-secure equality testing protocol. To our knowledge this is the first work in the literature that contemplates this problem in the UC framework.

Keywords: Universal Composability, commodity-based cryptography, private proximity tests.

1 Introduction

The emergence of wireless networking technologies (3G, Wi-MAX, Wi-Fi, Bluetooth, among others) has allowed the increasing adoption of location-sensing technologies. Moreover, the recent development of ubiquitous computing has led mobile phones to become a powerful computing platform capable of downloading and executing location-aware applications. As a result, many devices are equipped with radio frequency hardware that can be used for location-sensing applications, and there are numerous location-aware services available in the Internet, such as Google Latitude® and Foursquare®. Since its introduction, location-sensing technology has been used to find kidnap victims, let parents to keep track on their children, and rescue lost drivers.

Despite the large offer of location-based services and their benefits, there is a major concern that prevents more people of adhering to those services: *users' privacy*. Information associated to location tells a lot about the individuals' habits and activities and can unveil personal and corporate secrets. In current location-based services, users are required to send their location data to a third party server. This location data may be inappropriately stored by service providers and be potentially leaked. In other situations, such as a soldier on a battlefield, his/her location data are of vital importance. Thus, since location data carries sensitive information about a given individual, it is preferable to keep them private and not to rely on service providers.

X. Boyen and X. Chen (Eds.): ProvSec 2011, LNCS 6980, pp. 222–239, 2011.

This paper is focused on the problem of *proximity testing with privacy*. Private proximity testing allows two parties to be notified when they are within a threshold distance of each other without revealing any information about their location. The use of private proximity tests presents a wide range of applications. It can be used as a proximity detection mechanism for group meeting or can be deployed in ground combat, where military units may wish to verify their proximity in a private way. Some practical examples of the utility of private proximity testing are described in the following lines:

- Alice manages an ample industrial park and she wishes to automatically record the presence of her employees in the industrial campus. Nevertheless, they do not want to have their location tracked. Private proximity tests fulfill both aspirations.
- Alice and Bob are friends. A private proximity test allows Alice to check if Bob is in the same neighborhood as her, so they can meet and have lunch together.
- Alice is a soldier and she wants to verify if her colleague Bob is within a given threshold distance without revealing the parties' exact location. In this way, even if Alice's device is seized by an enemy, and this enemy runs the protocol on behalf of Alice, he will be unable to determine Bob's exact location.
- Unmanned aerial vehicles (UAVs) are often used in many critical military missions. Sometimes, it is needed to simply verify if a given UAV is in the same area of other allied military units. It is desirable to accomplish this task in a private manner. It means that the parties' location should not be revealed in the process. As a consequence, if the UAV is captured, the enemy forces will be incapable of determining the precise location of the UAV owner.

As one can see, the proximity detection mechanism has various commercial and military applications and may be adjusted to different levels of granularity: a room, a building, a town, etc.

The problem of private proximity testing was first formalized and solved in [22]. They studied the problem in the context of social networks and proposed three different protocols to solve it: (I) a synchronous protocol based on the Decisional Diffie-Hellman (DDH) assumption that only relied on a message-passing server; (II) an asynchronous and more efficient protocol that relied on a sever with active participation in the protocol; and (III) a protocol that combined the use of oblivious polynomial evaluation (OPE) and *location tags*[1]. Each solution proposed in [22] has advantages and drawbacks and their adoption depends on the clients' computing capabilities and the level of trust placed on service providers. For instance, the solution in (I) does not use an active server, but is

---

[1] Location tags [27] are secrets related to a point in time and space. They comprise a collection of location characteristics resultant from measuring signals in the physical environment. Possible location tags include: WiFi access point IDs, Bluetooth IDs, etc. Location tags are used to prevent one of the parties to lie about his/her location during a private proximity test.

computationally expensive and requires synchronous communications (the two parties must be online during the protocol). On the other hand, the solution depicted in (II) is more efficient, requires asynchronous communications (the parties need not to be simultaneously online), but demands a server that has active participation in the protocol.

In this paper, we benefit from the ingenious approach developed by Naraynan *et al.* [22] and take a step further. We study the private proximity testing problem under a more rigorous security definition (the Universal Composability framework) without the reliance on active service providers. We advocate that, in hostile environments such as battlefields, there is a need for efficient and low bandwidth proximity detection mechanisms that do not depend on servers to perform the desired computation. We are focused on solving this cumbersome problem and fulfilling the requirements of low computational overhead and low bandwidth consumption.

Contributions. We solve the practical problem of private proximity testing on a theoretical formal ground by proposing a system secure in the *Universal Composability* framework. It means that our system is guaranteed to remain secure even when composed with an arbitrary set of protocols or, more generally, when it is used as a component of an arbitrary system. Our solution is based on the commodity-based model. In this model, the service providers do not have any access to the parties's private data or take any active role in the process. These features make our solution particularly attractive. Our approach uses as the main building blocks a UC-secure equality testing protocol, which is based on reasonable assumptions and achieves UC-security.

Organization. This paper is organized as follows. In section 2, we formalize the problem and outline the main concepts involved in our paper, namely the formalization of the problem, the commodity-based model and the Universal Composability framework. Section 3 presents our building blocks and their respective proof of security. Finally, in section 4, as an application of our approach, we provide a solution to the private proximity testing problem that is UC-secure.

2   Preliminaries

2.1   Formalization of the Problem

The first step towards the proposed system is to define how to represent a location over the Earth's surface. We adopt the same approach developed in [22]: we divide the Earth's surface into a tessellation (grid) of the plane, and we use *quantized locations* (expressed as the *center* of the underlying grid cells).

Let Alice and Bob be two user of a location system with quantized locations C_a and C_b, respectively. Now suppose that Bob wants to detect if Alice is nearby. As stated in [22], private proximity testing can be reduced to the *private equality testing problem*[2]. This reduction is very useful, since private equality testing is a well-known and studied problem.

A desirable equality testing function between Bob and Alice, denoted by $EQ_{b,a}$, must satisfy the following:

$$\begin{cases} \text{If } C_b = C_a, & \text{then } B \text{ learns } C_a. \\ \text{If } C_b \neq C_a, & \text{then } B \text{ learns nothing (what we will represent as } \perp \text{).} \end{cases}$$

Let G_1, G_2, G_3 represent three hexagonal grids that are mutually offset of each other (see figure 1). Let $Q_{u,i}$ denote the quantized location of user u in grid i, and P_u denote the exact position in space of user u. Assume that each hexagonal cell has side measuring s, applying the algorithm $EQ_{b,a}$ on the three grids yields us to the protocol $\overline{EQ}_{b,a}$, such that:

$$\begin{cases} \text{If } \|P_b - P_a\| < \left(\sqrt{3}s\right)/2, & \text{then } B \text{ learns at least one of } C_{a,1}, \ C_{a,2}, \text{ and } C_{a,3}. \\ \text{If } \|P_b - P_a\| \geq 2s & \text{then } B \text{ only learns that } \|P_b - P_a\| > \left(\sqrt{3}s\right)/2. \end{cases}$$

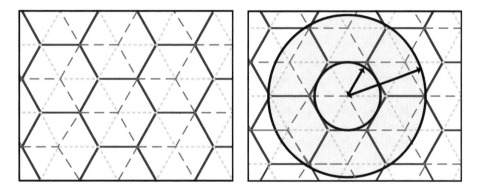

Fig. 1. The first figure illustrates a tessellation of the plane comprised of 3 hexagonal grids. The second figure illustrates two circles with radii $\left(\sqrt{3}s\right)/2$ and $2s$ (where s is the side of the hexagon).

Consequently, the protocol $\overline{EQ}_{b,a}$ will only disclose quantized locations. Bob will detect Alice as nearby if she is within a distance of $\left(\sqrt{3}s\right)/2$ and will detect she as far apart if she is at a distance equal or superior to $2s$. It is worth saying that no security is lost by using the aforementioned method.

It is worth noticing that we consider *asymmetric private equality testing*, meaning that only one of the parties will learn the outcome of the protocol (i.e. if they are within a given threshold distance of each other). Asymmetry is

---

[2] The problem can also be referred as oblivious equality testing [26].

sufficient for many applications. For instance, if Alice is a industrial manager, she might be interested to know if her employees are present in the industrial campus. On the other hand, the employees are indifferent about Alice's location. If symmetry is required, then it can be trivially achieved by executing the protocol twice in either direction.

It is also worth to emphasize that, depending on the technology used and the requirements of the application, the granularity level of the protocol can be adjusted. Thus, the quantization strategy proposed by Narayanan *et al.* [22] provides high flexibility, one of the reasons why we also adopted it.

2.2   Commodity-Based Model

The *commodity-based model*, inspired in the client-server architecture, was proposed by Beaver [2,3] as an alternative approach to construct secure distributed computation protocols.

In this model, the parties, who wish to perform a secure computation, receive pre-distributed and correlated data (*commodities*) from one or more service providers (called *trusted initializers*). After the pre-distribution of data, the parties directly interact between themselves without the intermediation of the trusted initializers (TIs).

Among the several appealing properties of this model, we outline the following ones:

- The information flow is unidirectional, occurs from servers to clients, and the servers do not take any active role in the secure computation. Therefore, it reduces the level of trust placed in third parties.
- The TIs do not have access to the parties' private inputs. Their participation is restricted to the pre-distribution of data.
- It presents high scalability, meaning that it can be amplified to accommodate multiple servers. Additionally, resources distributed by distinct TIs can be combined by the parties (without involvement of the TIs) to reduce weakness.

Applications of commodity-based cryptography can be found in a wide range of computational tasks, including commitment schemes [5,25] and oblivious transfer [2].

2.3   Universal Composability Framework

The Universal Composability (UC) framework, introduced by Canetti [10], consists of a model suitable for analyzing the security of protocols in complex network scenarios, such as the Internet. Since this framework defines the security of a cryptographic protocol under general composition operations, it allows the truly modular design of secure systems. A cryptographic protocol proven secure under this paradigm has its security preserved even when arbitrarily composed with other protocols or with copies of itself.

The UC framework is built upon the *simulation paradigm* [18]. According to this paradigm, proving the security of a given cryptographic protocol comprises two main tasks: (I) defining an *ideal* and a *real* models of computation and (II) demonstrating that any *real-world adversary* can be emulated by an *ideal-world adversary*. The process is briefly presented in the following lines.

- **Overview.** When dealing with the UC framework, we consider ideal and real-world executions. The ideal model translates the security requirements that a given cryptographic task must achieve. In an *ideal-world execution*, the parties have access to a trusted third party called the *ideal functionality*. When the parties wish to engage in secure computation, they simply forward their inputs to the ideal functionality who performs all the computation and sends them the stipulated outputs. The adversarial entity in this model, called *simulator* (denoted by $\mathcal{S}$), is able to control the communication channels and to potentially corrupt any party (which allows access to the party's internal information as well as full control over its future actions). Contrastingly, in a *real-world execution*, no trusted entity is available and the parties have to directly interact between themselves. Similarly to the simulator, the *real-world adversary* (denoted by $\mathcal{A}$) also has the ability of controlling the communication channels and corrupting any party.

We also introduce an entity called the environment (denoted by $\mathcal{E}$). The environment denotes all the activity external to the protocol execution, meaning that it provides inputs to the parties, observes all the generated outputs, and arbitrarily interacts with the adversary. Furthermore, $\mathcal{E}$ plays the role of an interactive distinguisher and its goal is to distinguish between an execution of the real protocol and an execution that occurs in the ideal model. Roughly speaking, a protocol Π is said to securely realize a given ideal functionality $\mathcal{F}$ if for every real-world adversary $\mathcal{A}$ that interacts with the protocol, there exists a simulator $\mathcal{S}$, such that no environment $\mathcal{E}$ can distinguish whether it is interacting with $\mathcal{A}$ and parties running the protocol Π, or with $\mathcal{S}$ and parties that access the functionality $\mathcal{F}$. More formally:

- **Ideal Process.** An ideal-world execution consists of two dummy parties P_A and P_B, the ideal-process adversary $\mathcal{S}$, the ideal functionality $\mathcal{F}$, and the environment $\mathcal{E}$. The distribution ensemble that describes the environment's output when the ideal process takes place is denoted by:

$$\text{IDEAL}_{\mathcal{F}, \mathcal{S}, \mathcal{E}}$$

- **Real Process.** A real-world execution consists of the two parties P_A and P_B, the environment $\mathcal{E}$ and the adversary $\mathcal{A}$. The distribution ensemble that represents the environment's output when a protocol Π is run with adversary $\mathcal{A}$ is denoted by:

$$\text{REAL}_{\Pi, \mathcal{A}, \mathcal{E}}.$$

Definition 1 *Perfect UC-Security.* *A protocol Π perfectly UC-realizes $\mathcal{F}$ if, for every real-world adversary $\mathcal{A}$ there exists an ideal-world adversary $\mathcal{S}$ such that, for all environments $\mathcal{E}$, the distribution ensembles $\mathrm{REAL}_{\Pi,\mathcal{A},\mathcal{E}}$ and $\mathrm{IDEAL}_{\mathcal{F},\mathcal{S},\mathcal{E}}$ are perfect indistinguishable.*

$$\forall \mathcal{A} \exists \mathcal{S} \forall \mathcal{E} \; : \; \mathrm{REAL}_{\Pi,\mathcal{A},\mathcal{E}} \equiv \mathrm{IDEAL}_{\mathcal{F},\mathcal{S},\mathcal{E}}$$

When analyzing the security of complex protocols, it is a useful technique to divide the subject protocol into modules (or fragments) and, then, analyze the security of each fragment. Consonant with this approach, the *hybrid model* was introduced. The hybrid model is alike the real model, except that the parties and the adversary $\mathcal{A}$ have access to some ideal functionality. The distribution ensemble that describes $\mathcal{E}$'s output when interacting in the hybrid model with adversary $\mathcal{A}$ and parties running a protocol Π with access to some ideal functionality $\mathcal{G}$ is denoted by:

$$\mathrm{HYBRID}^{\mathcal{G}}_{\Pi,\mathcal{A},\mathcal{E}}$$

Now, we enunciate the *Composability Theorem*, which allows the modular design of UC-secure cryptographic protocols. The main idea behind our scheme is to use UC-secure building blocks in order to achieve a system that UC-realizes the required task of proximity testing.

Theorem 1. *(Composability Theorem from [10]) Let Π be a protocol that operates in the $\mathcal{G}$-hybrid model, where the parties are given access to an ideal functionality $\mathcal{G}$. Let ρ be a protocol that UC-realizes $\mathcal{G}$ and let Π^{ρ} be a protocol that is identical to Π, except for the fact that it replaces each interaction with $\mathcal{G}$ for an interaction with ρ. It follows that, if Π securely realizes some functionality $\mathcal{F}$ in the $\mathcal{G}$-hybrid model, then Π^{ρ} securely realizes $\mathcal{F}$ in the standard model (without access to any ideal functionality).*

3   Building Blocks

3.1   Universally Composable Secure Channels

Our proximity testing protocol requires private authenticated communication as a means to ensure the secure exchange of messages between the parties and the secure delivery of data by the trusted initializer (TI). In a battlefield scenario, the parties may simply contact the TI while still in their base, where private authenticated communication is given for free. However, should the necessity arise for contacting the TI after they leave the base, it is then necessary to ensure that the communication channels are secure[3]. Moreover, in realistic scenarios,

---

[3] We could consider that the parties and the TI possess pre-shared keys, which are pre-configured before the parties leave the base. Nevertheless, for sake of generality, we will only assume the availability of a Public-Key Infrastructure (PKI).

authentication is required to thwart man-in-the-middle attacks. So, our first building block is a universally composable secure channel scheme.

We consider that the parties communicate through wireless links, which are public and without guaranteed delivery of messages. The security of these channels is captured by a model proposed by Canetti *et al.* [9], the *unauthenticated-links model* (denoted by UM). In this model, the adversaries have the power to adaptively corrupt the parties and completely control the communication, as well as to arbitrarily modify the messages before delivery.

The ideal functionality that captures the security requirements of a secure channel is given below.

Functionality $\mathcal{F}_{SC}$

- Upon receiving a message (INITIATE-SESSION, P_j, *initiator*, *sid*) from a party P_i, send (sid, P_i, P_j) to the adversary and wait to receive a message (INITIATESESSION, P_i, *responder*, *sid*) from P_j. Upon receipt of this message, set a boolean variable ACTIVE. We call P_i and P_j are called partners of the session.

- Upon receiving a message (SEND, sid, m) from a party P_e, $e \in \{0, 1\}$, and if ACTIVE is set, send (RECEIVED, sid, m) to the other party and $(sid, P_i, |m|)$ to the adversary.

- Upon receiving a message (TERMINATE-SESSION, sid) from either party and unset the variable *textscactive*.

Our goal is to instantiate a real-world protocol (that we will call SC) that realizes the functionality $\mathcal{F}_{SC}$. We invoke the following theorem, which establishes the possibility of achieving UC-secure protocols that realize secure channels:

Theorem 2. *(**UC secure channels** from [12]) Let MAC be a secure Message Authentication Code function, and let Γ be a weakly UC-secure key exchange protocol. Then there exist symmetric encryption schemes $E = (Enc, Dec)$ such that a protocol SC, based on Γ, MAC, and E, securely realizes $\mathcal{F}_{SC}$ in the UM.*

Thus, a UC-secure channel protocol can be built given a secure MAC and a weakly UC-secure key exchange protocol. It is possible to obtain a practical fully UC-secure key exchange protocol from standard assumptions (DDH and RSA) [12]. The Hashed Message Authentication Code (HMAC) [4] can be used as a secure MAC and standard symmetric ciphers, such as AES 128, can be applied.

Let λ denote a set of pre-agreed parameters between the parties.

$\lambda = \{Enc; Dec;$ key length; cyclic group $\mathbb{G}$ of order q; generator number g of $\mathbb{G}\}$.

Based on the previous classical results, the following practical protocol UC-realizes the secure channel functionality.

Protocol $SC(\lambda)$

$\{$Parties' input: A set λ of agreed parameters, e.g., the key length.

• **Key Exchange:**

The two parties run the ISO 9798-3 Diffie-Hellman key exchange authenticated through UC signature scheme based on the RSA assumptions [8]. The secret key obtained is further divided into an encryption key sk_E and an authentication key sk_A

• **Send message:**

For each message m sent, the sender encrypts the message under key sk_E using the AES ecnryption algorithm: $Enc(sk_E, m) := c$. It then computes the HMAC of the ciphertext under key sk_A: $HMAC(sk_A, c) := auth$. It sends both the ciphertext and the HMAC: $(c, auth)$.

• **Receive message:**

For each message received, the receiver first verifies the HMAC under key sk_A, *i.e.* checks if $HMAC(sk_A, c) = auth$. It decrypts the message using the AES decryption algorithm with key sk_E if the verification succeeds: $Dec(sk_E, c)$. Otherwise, it drops the message.

3.2 UC Private Equality Testing

The core part of our construction is a universally composable equality testing protocol. As we previously outlined, proximity testing can be reduced to private equality testing, which constitutes a classical problem in Cryptography. This problem has been studied in several different settings [6,7,20,26], each one suitable for a given purpose.

We chose to use an unconditionally secure protocol proposed by Tonicelli *et al.* [26] due to some crucial benefits. The protocol only requires simple computations that can be efficiently implemented, it requires low bandwidth, it relies on a reasonable assumption (the availability of a passive server that pre-distributes data), and it satisfies strong security requirements. All of these features makes the protocol of [26] suitable for resource constrained devices, where energy consumption, processing capabilities, and memory availability are of vital importance. We also advocate that the commodity-based model is an interesting assumption for our problem. It seems to be viable in commercial and military scenarios. For instance, in a military scenario, Alice and Bob could charge their devices with pre-distributed data (commodities) before leaving the base and later, in case of exhaustion of all their commodities, they could contact the TI server to get some more.

Let $EQ : \mathbb{F}_q \times \mathbb{F}_q \to \{\text{TRUE}, \text{FALSE}\}$ denote the equality testing function. $EQ(x_a, x_b)$ returns TRUE if $x_a = x_b$ or FALSE otherwise. First, we define the functionality $\mathcal{F}_{EQ}$, that represents the process of performing an EQ protocol in the ideal-world.

Functionality $\mathcal{F}_{EQ}$

- Upon receiving an (ASENDSINPUT, x_a, sid) message from Alice:

Ignore any subsequent ASENDSINPUT messages. If $x_a \notin \mathbb{F}_q$, then send an INVALIDINPUT message to Alice and Bob and halt. If no BSENDSINPUT message has been received from Bob, then store x_a and sid, and send the public delayed message (AINPUTRECEIVED, sid) to Bob, else computes $v := EQ(x_a, x_b)$ and send the public delayed output (BGETSOUTPUT, v, sid) to Bob.

- Upon receiving an (BSENDSINPUT, x_b, sid) message from Bob:

Ignore any subsequent BSENDSINPUT messages. If $x_b \notin \mathbb{F}_q$, then send an INVALIDINPUT message to Alice and Bob and halt. If no ASENDSINPUT message has been received from Alice, then store x_b and sid, and send the public delayed message (BINPUTRECEIVED, sid) to Alice, else compute $v := EQ(x_a, x_b)$ and send the public delayed output (BGETSOUTPUT, v, sid) to Bob.

Now we proceed by describing our UC-secure equality testing protocol.

The idea of the equality testing procedure is simple: let $l(x)$ be a linear polynomial with root x_a, to perform the equality test, Bob obliviously evaluates $l(x)$ on his location x_b. If $l(x_b) = 0$, then Bob knows that he is in the same quantized location as Alice.

Assume that the TI and the parties are connected by means of confidential and authenticated channels. Assume also that the parties can communicate through authenticated channels. Here, we call by "valid" a linear polynomial of the form $l(x) = \alpha x + \beta$, with $\alpha \neq 0$.

The protocol is as follows.

Protocol $EQ(x_a, x_b)$

$$\begin{cases} \text{Alice's input: } x_a \in \mathbb{F}_q. \\ \text{Bob's input: } x_b \in \mathbb{F}_q. \end{cases}$$

Setup Phase:

• The TI selects with uniform randomness a linear polynomial $r(x)$ and a point d belonging to $\mathbb{F}_q$.

• The TI sends $\mu_A := r(x)$ to Alice and $\mu_B := \{d; g = r(d)\}$ to Bob.

Computing Phase:

• Bob computes $t := x_b - d$ and sends $\mu_1 := t$ to Alice.

• Alice picks up a random linear function $l(x) \in_R \mathbb{F}_q[X]$ such that $l(x_a) = 0$.

• Upon receiving the message μ_1, Alice verifies its validity. If μ_1 is invalid Alice halts, else she computes $f(x) := l(x + t) + r(x)$ and sends $\mu_2 := f(x)$ to Bob.

• Upon receiving the message μ_2, Bob verifies its validity. If μ_2 is invalid Bob halts, else he computes $f(d) - g = l(d + t) + r(d) - r(d) = l(x_b)$, the desired output. As one can see, if the result is zero, Bob knows that the inputs are the same.

The next step consists of showing that the protocol EQ UC-realizes $\mathcal{F}_{EQ}$ in the $\mathcal{F}_{SC}, \mathcal{F}_{TI}$-Hybrid model, where an ideal functionalities $\mathcal{F}_{SC}$ and $\mathcal{F}_{TI}$ are available. The functionality $\mathcal{F}_{SC}$, that provides secure channels, was already defined.Thus, we must define the functionality $\mathcal{F}_{TI}$ that represents our setup assumption, i.e., the trusted initializer server.

The functionality $\mathcal{F}_{TI}$ is as follows.

Functionality $\mathcal{F}_{TI}$

• When first activated, select with uniform randomness a linear polynomial $r(x)$ and a point $d \in_R \mathbb{F}_q$.

• Send $r(x)$ to Alice and $\{d; g = r(d)\}$ to Bob.

The final step is to show by simulation that, for each situation, our practical scheme emulates the idealized protocol. Henceforth, the variables in the simulated scenario will be written with a prime symbol ('). The simulation experiments are described in the following lines.

• A - Simulation: Alice Corrupted and Bob Honest

Since Alice is corrupted, $\mathcal{S}$ can read her input x_a. Assume that the simulator $\mathcal{S}$ runs an internal copy of the hybrid-world adversary $\mathcal{A}$ denoted by A'. The interactions between A' and $\mathcal{S}$ are those of Alice with the other parties (TI, Bob and $\mathcal{E}$). The simulation experiment is described next.

1. The environment $\mathcal{E}$ activates the simulator $\mathcal{S}$ by sending it the input $x_a \in \mathbb{F}_q$.

2. Upon its activation, the simulator $\mathcal{S}$ sets $x'_a := x_a$, i.e., it feeds its internal adversarial copy A' with x_a. Subsequently, $\mathcal{S}$ plays the role of the trusted initializer:
   (a) It chooses with uniform randomness a linear polynomial $r'(x)$ and forwards $\mu'_A := r'(x)$ to A'.

3. Upon receiving the message (BINPUTRECEIVED, sid), the simulator sends $\mu'_1 := t' \in_R \mathbb{F}_q$ to A'.

4. When an INVALIDINPUT message is received from $\mathcal{F}_{EQ}$, then $\mathcal{S}$ simply forwards it to the environment $\mathcal{E}$.

5. Upon receiving a message $\mu'_2 := f'(x)$ from its internal adversarial copy A', the simulator verifies its validity.

6. If A' sent something invalid, then $\mathcal{S}$ forwards an invalid input to $\mathcal{F}_{EQ}$.

7. If $\mathcal{A}'$ sent a valid message, then $\mathcal{S}$ performs the following actions:
   (a) If μ'_2 is not consistent with $\{x_a, \mu'_1, r'(x)\}$, then $\mathcal{S}$ forwards a message (ASENDSINPUT, $\overline{x}_a$, sid) to $\mathcal{F}_{EQ}$, where $\overline{x}_a$ is a value in $\mathbb{F}_q$ is different from x_a.
   (b) If μ'_2 is consistent with $\{x_a, \mu'_1, r'(x)\}$, then $\mathcal{S}$ forwards a message given by (ASENDSINPUT, x_a, sid) to $\mathcal{F}_{EQ}$.

8. Once $\mathcal{S}$ sent a message to the functionality, it waits the functionality $\mathcal{F}_{EQ}$ to produce the prescribed output and it lets $\mathcal{F}_{EQ}$ to deliver the appropriate message (BGETSOUTPUT, v, sid) to the honest Bob.

Indistinguishability

In order to prove the indistinguishability, we need to show that the views acquired by the environment in the hybrid and in the ideal executions are identical.

<u>Remarks about the simulation</u>

• The environment can make Bob to send an invalid input or to send no input. The actions performed by $\mathcal{S}$, after sending its input to $\mathcal{F}_{EQ}$, completely reproduces this situation.

- The adversary A' has the alternative to send a valid or invalid message μ_2'. In both protocols, if an invalid message is sent by the adversary, there will be delivered an INVALIDINPUT message to the parties, which will be, subsequently, received by the environment $\mathcal{E}$.

- $\mathcal{S}$ can easily verify if the internal adversary A' cheated or not by checking the consistency of the message μ_2' with $\{x_a, \mu_1', r'(x)\}$. If A' did follow the protocol, $\mathcal{S}$ supplies $\mathcal{F}_{EQ}$ with the correct input x_a; otherwise, it supplies $\mathcal{F}_{EQ}$ with a wrong input $\overline{x}_a$.

Remarks about the probability distributions

- The first step to prove the indistinguishability between the two models is to show that the data pre-distributed by the TI in the real protocol μ_A and the message μ_A' produced by $\mathcal{S}$ have the same probability distribution. This is easily verifiable since both are generated by the uniform distribution on the set of linear polynomials defined over $\mathbb{F}_q[X]$.
- The remaining step is to show that the message μ_1, produced by Bob in a real execution, and the message μ_1', produced by $\mathcal{S}$ in the simulation, have the same distribution. The message μ_1 is uniformly distributed since $\mu_1 := x_b - d$, where $d \in_R \mathbb{F}_q$. Hence, it follows that both messages μ_1 and μ_1' have the same distribution.

Consequently, no environment is capable of telling the difference between the hybrid and the ideal executions, what finishes the proof for the case "Alice corrupted and Bob honest".

B - Simulation: Alice Honest and Bob Corrupted

Assume that the simulator $\mathcal{S}$ runs an internal copy of the hybrid-world adversary $\mathcal{A}$ denoted by B'. The interactions between B' and $\mathcal{S}$ are those of Bob with the other parties (TI, Alice and $\mathcal{E}$). The simulation experiment is as follows.

1. The environment $\mathcal{E}$ activates the simulator $\mathcal{S}$ by sending it the input x_b.

2. Upon its activation, the simulator feeds B' with $x_b' := x_b$ and plays the role of the trusted initializer:
   (a) It chooses with uniform randomness a linear polynomial $r'(x)$ and a value $d' \in_R \mathbb{F}_q$.
   (b) It forwards $\mu_B' := \{d'; s'(d')\}$ to its internal adversarial copy B'.

3. Upon receiving a message $\mu_1' := t'$ from its internal adversarial copy B', the simulator verifies its validity.

4. If B' sent something invalid, then $\mathcal{S}$ forwards an invalid input to the functionality $\mathcal{F}_{EQ}$.

5. If B' sent a valid message then $\mathcal{S}$ performs the following actions:
   (a) If μ_1' is not consistent with $\{x_b, \mu_B'\}$, then $\mathcal{S}$ forwards a message given by (BSENDSINPUT, $\overline{x}_b$, sid) to $\mathcal{F}_{EQ}$, where $\overline{x}_b$ is a point in $\mathbb{F}_q$ different from x_b.

(b) If μ_2' is consistent with $\{x_b, \mu_B'\}$, then $\mathcal{S}$ forwards a message given by (BSENDSINPUT, x_b, sid) to $\mathcal{F}_{EQ}$.

6. Once $\mathcal{S}$ sent a message to the functionality, it waits the functionality $\mathcal{F}_{EQ}$ to produce the prescribed output and it lets $\mathcal{F}_{EQ}$ to deliver the appropriate message with the form (BGETSOUTPUT, v, sid). When this message is received, $\mathcal{S}$ simply copies it through Bob's output interface, where $\mathcal{E}$ is going to read.

The proof of indistinguishability for this case is analogous to the one previously presented, therefore it will be omitted here.

C - Simulation: Alice and Bob Honest

Assume that both parties behave honestly. Internally, $\mathcal{S}$ simulates the transcript of messages between the hybrid parties by using arbitrary inputs. Externally, $\mathcal{S}$ lets the ideal functionality deliver the prescribed output to the honest Bob. The simulated and the hybrid transcripts will be perfectly indistinguishable in the presence of an eavesdropper, i.e., in the presence of an adversary that only observes the messages exchanged through the channels.

D - Simulation: Alice and Bob Corrupted

In the case where both participants are corrupted, the simulator $\mathcal{S}$ will have unrestrictive access to their internal states, what includes their inputs and local randomness. As the participants behavior is a deterministic function of their internal state, $\mathcal{S}$ can completely simulate the protocol and the environment will be unable to distinguish the hybrid and the ideal models.

We proved that our scheme successfully emulates the ideal model for all the existent scenarios. Thus, one may conclude that the protocol EQ UC-realizes $\mathcal{F}_{EQ}$ in the $\mathcal{F}_{SC}, \mathcal{F}_{TI}$-Hybrid model.

4   Private Proximity Testing Protocol

As previously explained, according to the location quantization technique, the parties have a triple of quantized locations, one for each grid ($G_i, i \in [1,3]$). Then, the protocol must be executed three times, one for each grid.

Let q be a large prime so that all possible locations are in the range $[1, q]$. If location data is 32 bits then an appropriate setting is $q = 2^{32} + 15$. We assume that the clients in the system share the same q. Let λ be a set of pre-agreed parameters, such that

$$\lambda = \{Enc; Dec; \text{key length}; \text{cyclic group } \mathbb{G} \text{ of order } q; \text{generator number } g \text{ of } \mathbb{G}\}.$$

The private proximity testing protocol is described next. For sake of simplicity, the protocol description only includes one iteration (the reader must remember that three iterations are needed).

$\mathbf{PT}(x_a, x_b, \lambda)$ **Protocol**

$\begin{cases} \text{Alice's inputs:} & \text{Alice's quantized location } x_a \in \mathbb{F}_q \text{ and the parameters } \lambda. \\ \text{Bob's inputs:} & \text{Bob's quantized location } x_b \in \mathbb{F}_q \text{ and the parameters } \lambda. \end{cases}$

Setup Phase:

• Each party (Alice and Bob) run with the TI a Diffie-Hellman protocol to agree on symmetric keys $sk_{a,TI}$ and $sk_{b,TI}$, respectively.

• The TI computes $c_A := Enc(sk_{a,TI}, r(x))$, where $r(x)$ is a randomly chosen linear polynomial in $\mathbb{F}_q$ and computes $c_b := Enc(sk_{b,TI}, \{d, r(d)\})$, such that $d \in_R \mathbb{F}_q$. The TI sends to Alice $\mu_A := c_a||Hmac(c_a, sk_{a,TI})$ and sends to Bob $\mu_B := c_b||Hmac(c_b, sk_{a,TI})$.

• Alice and Bob run the Diffie-Hellman protocol, obtaining the symmetric key $sk_{a,b}$.

Computing Phase:

• Bob computes $t := x_b - d$ and $c_1 := Enc(sk_{a,b}, t)$. Bob sends to Alice $\mu_1 := c_1||Hmac(c_1, sk_{a,b})$.

• Alice picks up a linear function $l(x)$ at random such that $l(x_a) = 0$.

• Alice performs the decryption and verification procedures on μ_1. If the message passes through the test, Alice computes the function $f(x)$, such that $f(x) := l(x + t) + r(x)$ and computes $c_2 := Enc(sk_{a,b}, f(x))$. Then, Alice sends to Bob $\mu_2 := c_2||Hmac(c_2, sk_{a,b})$ to Bob. Otherwise, Alice aborts the protocol.

• Bob checks the validity of μ_2. If the message is valid, Bob computes $f(d) - r(d) = l(d + x_b - d) + r(d) - r(d) = l(x_b)$. Otherwise, he aborts the protocol. As one can see, if the result is zero, Bob knows that the inputs are the same, meaning that he is in the same quantized position as Alice. Otherwise, he is not.

Let $ticket_A = \{\mu_{A,G_i}\}_{i=1}^{3}$ and $ticket_B = \{\mu_{B,G_i}\}_{i=1}^{3}$ denote the data predistributed to Alice and Bob, respectively, for the realization of a proximity testing procedure. The scheme we describe presents several attractive features, such as low computational overhead, flexibility, low storage requirement and low communication cost.

Nevertheless, the simplicity of the system comes with one cost: the requirement of fresh randomness for each proximity test. One could also point out that the requirement of a server interaction for each proximity test also constitutes a problem. However, one can easily overcome this problem by simply adapting the protocol to support various proximity tests for each server interaction. In this case, the TI would distribute multiple commodities $ticket_{A,j}$ and $ticket_{B,j}$, with $j \in [1, k]$, that would allow Alice and Bob to execute k proximity tests for a single server interaction. I.e., each pair of commodities ($ticket_{A,j}$ and $ticket_{B,j}$) could be used in the i-th proximity test. This demonstrates the flexibility of the overall system. In battlefield scenarios, before leaving the base, the parties can charge their devices with k commodities each and then later perform the protocol. In another possible scenario the parties could previously buy the k commodities on-line in their respective homes (as was envisioned by Beaver [2]).

4.1   Security of the Overall System

The *Universal Composability theorem* [10] is a well-known result that helps us in the task of defining the security of a cryptosystem in a modular way. The proof of security of the overall system is a simple consequence of this theorem.

In the first part, we presented a classical UC-secure protocol (SC) that provided confidential and authenticated channels for the parties. Then, we used the fact that proximity testing can be reduced to the private equality testing problem. Finally, we presented a UC-secure equality testing protocol (EQ) that realized the ideal functionality $\mathcal{F}_{EQ}$ in the $\mathcal{F}_{SC}, \mathcal{F}_{TI}$-Hybrid model.

The complete proximity testing protocol (PT) uses a (I) TI server that realizes $\mathcal{F}_{TI}$; (II) a secure channel scheme that UC-realizes $\mathcal{F}_{SC}$; and an (III) equality testing protocol that is UC-secure in the $\mathcal{F}_{SC}, \mathcal{F}_{TI}$-Hybrid model. Consequently, it is straightforward to see that the *overall composite system is indeed universally composable*. This brief analysis completes the proof, and illustrates the practical usefulness of the universally composable framework and the UC theorem.

5   Conclusions

The purpose of this work was to harmonize the best of two worlds: the real-world, where simplicity, practicality, and efficiency are of fundamental importance; and the theoretical-world, where formal and rigorous security proofs are required. In this work, we solved the problem of private proximity testing under considerably strong security requirements (the UC framework) by proposing a practical protocol for performing this task.

We demonstrated a practical application of the UC theorem by combining two UC-secure protocols (a secure channel mechanism and a UC equality testing protocol) to form a secure composite system.

We advocate that the use of formal techniques from provable security can enrich the design and development of practice-oriented applications. Other works share the same flavor of ours, as the work of Gajek *et al.* [17], where the authors analyzed the UC security of TLS. We believe that future incursions of provable security techniques into the implementation-world will dramatically contribute to the security and design of a wide range of critical applications.

References

1. Backes, M., Hofheinz, D.: How to Break and Repair a Universally Composable Signature Functionality. In: Zhang, K., Zheng, Y. (eds.) ISC 2004. LNCS, vol. 3225, pp. 61–72. Springer, Heidelberg (2004)
2. Beaver, D.: Commodity-Based Cryptography (Extended Abstract). In: STOC 1997, pp. 446–455 (1997)
3. Beaver, D.: Server-Assisted Cryptography. In: New Security Paradigms Workshop 1998, pp. 92–106 (1998)
4. Bellare, M., Canetti, R., Krawczyk, H.: Keying Hash Functions for Message Authentication. In: Koblitz, N. (ed.) CRYPTO 1996. LNCS, vol. 1109, pp. 1–15. Springer, Heidelberg (1996)
5. Blundo, C., Masucci, B., Stinson, D.R., Wei, R.: Constructions and Bounds for Unconditionally Secure Non-Interactive Commitment Schemes. Designs, Codes, and Cryptography 26(1-3), 97–110 (2002)
6. Boudot, F., Schoenmakers, B., Traore, J.: A fair and efficient solution to the socialist millionaires problem. Discrete Applied Mathematics 111, 23–36 (2001)
7. Fagin, R., Naor, M., Winkler, P.: Comparing information without leaking it. Communications of the ACM 39, 77–85 (1996)
8. Brakerski, Z., Kalai, Y.T.: A Framework for Efficient Signatures, Ring signatures and Identity based Encryption in the Standard Model. Cryptology ePrint Archive, Report 2010/086 (2010), http://eprint.iacr.org/2010/086.pdf
9. Canetti, R., Krawczyk, H.: Analysis of Key-Exchange Protocols and Their Use for Building Secure Channels. In: Pfitzmann, B. (ed.) EUROCRYPT 2001. LNCS, vol. 2045, pp. 453–474. Springer, Heidelberg (2001)
10. Canetti, R.: Universally Composable Security: A New Paradigm for Cryptographic Protocols. In: 42nd Symposium on Foundations of Computer Science (FOCS) (2001)
11. Canetti, R., Fischlin, M.: Universally Composable Commitments. In: Kilian, J. (ed.) CRYPTO 2001. LNCS, vol. 2139, pp. 19–40. Springer, Heidelberg (2001)
12. Canetti, R., Krawczyk, H.: Universally Composable Notions of Key Exchange and Secure Channels. In: Knudsen, L.R. (ed.) EUROCRYPT 2002. LNCS, vol. 2332, pp. 337–351. Springer, Heidelberg (2002)
13. Canetti, R., Lindell, Y., Ostrovsky, R., Sahai, A.: Universally Composable Two-Party and Multi-party Secure Computation. In: 34th STOC, pp. 494–503 (2002)
14. Chandran, N., Goyal, V., Sahai, A.: New Constructions for UC Secure Computation Using Tamper-Proof Hardware. In: Smart, N.P. (ed.) EUROCRYPT 2008. LNCS, vol. 4965, pp. 289–306. Springer, Heidelberg (2008)
15. Dowsley, R., Nascimento, A.C.A., Müller-Quade, J., Otsuka, A., Hanaoka, G., Imai, H.: Universally Composable and Statistically Secure Verifiable Secret Sharing Scheme Based on Pre-Distributed Data. IEICE Transactions 94(2), 725–734 (2011)
16. Damgård, I., Nielsen, J.B., Orlandi, C.: On the Necessary and Sufficient Assumptions for UC Computation. In: Micciancio, D. (ed.) TCC 2010. LNCS, vol. 5978, pp. 109–127. Springer, Heidelberg (2010)

17. Gajek, S., Manulis, M., Pereira, O., Sadeghi, A.-R., Schwenk, J.: Universally Composable Security Analysis of TLS. In: Baek, J., Bao, F., Chen, K., Lai, X. (eds.) ProvSec 2008. LNCS, vol. 5324, pp. 313–327. Springer, Heidelberg (2008)
18. Goldreich, O.: Foundations of Cryptography, Basic Applications, vol. II. Cambridge University Press, Cambridge (2004)
19. Hanaoka, G., Shikata, J., Zheng, Y., Imai, H.: Unconditionally Secure Digital Signature Schemes Admitting Transferability. In: Okamoto, T. (ed.) ASIACRYPT 2000. LNCS, vol. 1976, pp. 130–142. Springer, Heidelberg (2000)
20. Lipmaa, H.: Verifiable homomorphic oblivious transfer and private equality test. In: Laih, C.-S. (ed.) ASIACRYPT 2003. LNCS, vol. 2894, pp. 416–433. Springer, Heidelberg (2003)
21. Matsumoto, T., Imai, H.: On the Key Predistribution System: A Practical Solution to the Key Distribution Problem. In: Pomerance, C. (ed.) CRYPTO 1987. LNCS, vol. 293, pp. 185–193. Springer, Heidelberg (1988)
22. Narayanan, A., Thiagarajan, N., Lakhani, M., Hamburg, M., Boneh, D.: Location Privacy via Private Proximity Testing. In: NDSS (2011)
23. Orlandi, C.: Oblivious Transfer in the Universally Composable Security Model. MSc Thesis in Computer Engineering, Universita degli Studi di Firenze (2007)
24. Pass, R.: Bounded-Concurrent Secure Multi-Party Computation with a Dishonest Majority. In: 36th STOC, pp. 232–241 (2004)
25. Rivest, R.: Unconditionally Secure Commitment and Oblivious Transfer Schemes Using Concealing Channels and a Trusted Initializer (1999) (preprint), http://people.csail.mit.edu/rivest/Rivest-commitment.pdf
26. Tonicelli, R., Nascimento, A.C.A., Dowsley, R., Müller-Quade, J., Imai, H., Hanaoka, G., Otsuka, A.: Information-Theoretically Secure Oblivious Polynomial Evaluation in the Commodity-Based Model.Cryptology ePrint Archive, Report 2009/270 (2009), http://eprint.iacr.org/2009/270
27. Qiu, D., Boneh, D., Lo, S., Enge, P.: Robust location tag generation from Noisy Location Data for Security Applications. The Institute of Navigation International Technical Meeting (2009)
28. Yao, A.C.: Protocols for Secure Computations. In: FOCS 1982, pp. 160–164 (1982)

Generic Constant-Round Oblivious Sorting Algorithm for MPC

Bingsheng Zhang

University of Tartu, Estonia
zhang@ut.ee

Abstract. Various information-theoretically secure Multi-Party Computation (MPC) schemes have been proposed over some finite field $\mathbb{F}$ or some finite ring $\mathbb{R}$. A function f that can be evaluated on MPC is usually represented by boolean or arithmetic circuits. In general, the function class that have constant-depth arithmetic circuit is studied. Additionally, some literatures show that one can represent any formulas and branching program by low-degree randomizing polynomials, which can be evaluated in constant rounds. However, these approaches have their limitations, and it is not easy to construct the optimal branching program for a complex function. Therefore, it is not obvious how to efficiently perform oblivious sort in constant rounds, but oblivious sort is one of the most important primitive protocols for MPC in practice. In this paper, we are going to show several constant-round 0-error oblivious sorting algorithms, together with some useful applications.

Keywords: Secure Multi-party Computation, Constant-round, Oblivious Sort, Information-theoretic Security.

1 Introduction

In a secure Multi-Party Computation (MPC), n players want to compute an agreed function of their inputs in a secure way such that it guarantees the correctness of the output and the privacy of the players' inputs. Some players (parties) are dishonest or malicious. Let $x_1, x_2, \cdots, x_n$ and $y_1, y_2, \cdots, y_n$ to be the corresponding inputs and outputs of parties $\mathcal{P}_1, \mathcal{P}_2, \cdots, \mathcal{P}_n$, respectively. A (randomized) function is defined as $f(x_1, x_2, \cdots, x_n; [r]) = (y_1, y_2, \cdots, y_n)$, where r is a uniformly random value unknown to all parties. Yao's millionaires' problem [Yao82] is a famous problem that used to introduce secure two- or multi-party computation and Secure Function Evaluation (SFE). Many kinds of solutions are proposed to solve these problems, such as Yao's garble circuit [Yao82]. A wide range of literatures offered solutions based on homomorphic encryption schemes, and a new type of crypto-computing method that based on Branching Program (BP) is introduced in 2007 [IP07]. Recently, Fully-Homomorphic Encryption (FHE) schemes enjoy their popularities, such as Gentry's FHE based on lattice [Gen09]. However, they are rarely used in practice due to efficiency reasons. On the other hand, practical implementations of secure MPC have been developing recently [DGKN09, BLW08].

    A typical MPC scheme, e.g.[RBO89], is based on (verifiable) linear secret sharing, and n parties have shared values $x_1, x_2, \cdots, x_n$ over some finite field $\mathbb{F}$ or some finite

X. Boyen and X. Chen (Eds.): ProvSec 2011, LNCS 6980, pp. 240–256, 2011.

ring $\mathbb{R}$. Without loss of generality, denote $\mathbb{K} = \mathbb{Z}_N$, then $f : \mathbb{K}^n \to \mathbb{K}^n$. The function f can be computed securely on the shares via a network with pairwise secure channels. Particularly, we are interested in constant-round information-theoretically secure MPC. In terms of efficiency, round complexity [1] is widely used for MPC performance evaluation, because the main costs for MPC algorithms are network delays, especially via asynchronous Internet. It is an open question to determine which functions can be efficiently computed with information-theoretic security on shares, using constant-round protocols. In general, the function class that have constant-depth arithmetic circuit is studied. In paper [CFIK03, IK02], the authors showed that one can represent any formulas and branching program by low-degree randomizing polynomials over some finite field $\mathbb{F}$ or some finite ring $\mathbb{R}$, which can be evaluated in constant rounds. However, these approaches have their limitations and it is not easy to construct the optimal branching program for a complex function. On the other hand, papers [DFNT05, DFK$^+$06] show how to do equality-check, comparison, bit-decomposition and unbounded fan-In symmetric functions in constant-round over finite field $\mathbb{F}$. But it is not obvious how to efficiently perform oblivious sort in constant rounds by using these elementary protocols. Nowadays, most oblivious sorting protocols use compare-swap block together with oblivious sorting networks, such as AKS sorting network [AKS83]. Very few literatures [CKMH07] proposed specifically designed oblivious sorting algorithm or comparator network for MPC. In this paper, we are going to propose several information-theoretically secure constant-round oblivious sorting algorithms for MPC, together with their applications in secure $(M + 1)$st-price sealed-bid auction and obfuscated shuffle.

Sealed-bid auction is getting increasingly popular recently, for it preserves the privacy of losing bids after auction closes. It is proved that $(M + 1)$st-price sealed-bid auction satisfies incentive compatibility, i.e. the dominant strategy is for a bidder to bid his/her true valuation [WWW98]. Assume there is a set of L single-unit bids, in which M are sell offers and $N = L - M$ are buy offers. $(M + 1)$st-price auction rule says that the winner pays the $(M + 1)$-th bid. Note that the $(M + 1)$-th price is undefined if there is no buyer. For the case that $M = 1$, it is the same as the second-price auction. $(M + 1)$st-price sealed-bid auction problem is essentially finding the highest and the $(M + 1)$-th highest value, which can be simply solved by oblivious sort.

Obfuscated shuffle problem has been thoroughly studied in the context of e-voting with mix-nets [Cha81, Wik04] and onion-routing [CL05, MTHK09]. These solutions propagate encrypted messages through a network of servers to achieve unlinkability at the endpoint. In our context, we need multi-party computation protocols that shuffle secret shared values. A protocol that runs between a list of machines $\mathcal{P}_1, \cdots, \mathcal{P}_m$ perform a mix-net, and the parties $\mathcal{P}_1, \cdots, \mathcal{P}_m$ are referred as mix servers. Input is a list of messages $\mathcal{M}_1, \cdots, \mathcal{M}_n$, and output of the mix-net is a obfuscated permutation of the messages $\mathcal{M}_{\pi(1)}, \cdots, \mathcal{M}_{\pi(n)}$, where π is unknown to everyone. As another application, we can assign each input message a random number, and the obfuscated shuffle can be achieved in constant rounds by sorting the messages according to their associated random numbers.

---

[1] In general, the round complexity of MPC is proportional to the multiplicative depth of an arithmetic circuit to evaluate the function f.

Notations. Throughout the paper we use the following notations. The message space is denoted by $\mathbb{K}$ or depending on a context. Denote input array size by n and number of parties by m. $\mathcal{P}_i$ stands for the i-th party. Denote shares of value $\alpha \in \mathbb{K}$ as $[\![\alpha]\!]$ and a share held by $\mathcal{P}_i$ as $[\![\alpha]\!]_i$. In some protocols, R is the range of numbers to be sorted, and particularly, we assume that the numbers are from $[0, R]$. Let $\mathsf{COM}([\![x]\!], [\![y]\!])$ be the comparison circuit, s.t.

$$\mathsf{COM}([\![x]\!], [\![y]\!]) = \begin{cases} [\![1]\!] & x \geq y \\ [\![0]\!] & x < y \end{cases}$$

Denote Split as the bit-decomposition protocol that decomposes a share value into a vector of shared bits. Although comparison can be used for equality check in general, we only want to check whether a shared value is equal to a public value, which can be implemented by unbounded fan-in AND circuit. (c.f. Sect.5, below) Let $\mathsf{EQ}([\![x]\!], y)$ be equality-check circuit, s.t.

$$\mathsf{EQ}([\![x]\!], y) = \begin{cases} [\![1]\!] & x = y \\ [\![0]\!] & x \neq y \end{cases}$$

Let τ_{ad}, τ_{mul}, τ_{and}, τ_{or}, τ_{eq}, τ_{com} and τ_{bd} be the round complexity of addition, multiplication, unbounded fan-in AND, unbounded fan-in OR, equality-check, comparison and bit-decomposition protocol of the underlying secure MPC, respectively.

Our Contributions. We proposed several constant-round oblivious sorting algorithms for MPC with different properties. Table 1 illustrates the comparison bewteen some widely used oblivious sorting algorithms and our schemes, in terms of round complexity and communication & computation complexity. As applications, we also show how to use our sorting algorithms in secure $(M + 1)$st-price sealed-bid auction protocols and mix-net from obfuscated shuffle.

Table 1. Comparison of well-known oblivious sorting networks and our three new sorting algorithms for MPC. R is the range of numbers. COM is comparison, Split is bit-decomposition, EQ is equality-check and AND is unbounded fan-in AND gate.

Sorting Scheme	Rounds	Comm. Complexity	Comp. Complexity
AKS Sorting Network [AKS83]	$\mathcal{O}(\log n)$	$\mathcal{O}(n \log n)$	$\mathcal{O}(n \log n)$ COM
Balanced Sort [DPSR83]	$\mathcal{O}(\log^2 n)$	$\mathcal{O}(n \log^2 n)$	$\mathcal{O}(n \log^2 n)$ COM
Randomized Shellsort [Goo09]	$\mathcal{O}(\log n)$	$\mathcal{O}(n \log n)$	$\mathcal{O}(n \log n)$ COM
Oblivious Sort for MPC [JKU11]	$\mathcal{O}(\log^2 n)$	$\mathcal{O}(n \log^2 n)$	$\mathcal{O}(n \log^2 n)$ COM
Sect. 5	$\mathcal{O}(1)$	$\mathcal{O}(Rn)$	$\mathcal{O}(n + R)$ Split + $\mathcal{O}(Rn)$ AND
Sect. 6	$\mathcal{O}(1)$	$\mathcal{O}(Rn)$	$\mathcal{O}(Rn)$ COM
Sect. 7	$\mathcal{O}(1)$	$\mathcal{O}(n^2)$	$\mathcal{O}(n^2)$ COM + $\mathcal{O}(n^2)$ EQ

2   Related Works

A (multi-terminal) Binary Decision Diagram (BDD, also known as a branching program, [Weg00]) is a fanout-2 directed acyclic graph $(\mathcal{V}, \mathcal{E})$. A language has a polynomial-size branching program if and only if it belongs to the complexity class $\mathbf{L/poly}$ [Cob66], that is, if it can be decided by a nonuniform log-space Turing machine. In paper [IK02], the authors proposed a technique that representing any binary decision diagram by low-degree randomizing polynomials over field $\mathbb{F}$. And later, in paper [CFIK03], the authors generalized the randomizing polynomial approach to ring $\mathbb{R}$. For evaluating a binary decision diagram of size $\text{size}(P)$, the computation and communication complexities are around $\text{size}(P)^2$. However, this approach has its limitations, and it is not easy to construct the optimal branching program for a complex function.

As regarding to general oblivious sorting algorithms, research interests are focus on how to achieve asymptotically optimal complexity, i.e. $\mathcal{O}(n \log n)$. AKS [AKS83] sorting network is the first famous oblivious sorting network, whose computational complexity is $\mathcal{O}(n \log n)$ compare-swap blocks. However, its constant factor is more than 6000 and it is quite complicated to implement. In practice, a lot of well-known oblivious sorting algorithms with $\mathcal{O}(n \log^2 n)$ complexity are used in secure MPC systems, such as balanced sort [DPSR83] and Batcher's bitonic sort [Bat68]. One can easily build an oblivious compare-swap block based on comparison circuit COM in MPC. Assume $(\llbracket C \rrbracket, \llbracket D \rrbracket) \leftarrow \mathsf{ComSwap}(\llbracket A \rrbracket, \llbracket B \rrbracket)$, s.t. $C = min(A, B)$ and $D = max(A, B)$. One possible implementation could be as follows:

$$\llbracket C \rrbracket = \llbracket A \rrbracket \cdot (1 - \mathsf{COM}(\llbracket A \rrbracket, \llbracket B \rrbracket)) + \llbracket B \rrbracket \cdot \mathsf{COM}(\llbracket A \rrbracket, \llbracket B \rrbracket)$$
$$\llbracket D \rrbracket = \llbracket A \rrbracket \cdot \mathsf{COM}(\llbracket A \rrbracket, \llbracket B \rrbracket) + \llbracket B \rrbracket \cdot (1 - \mathsf{COM}(\llbracket A \rrbracket, \llbracket B \rrbracket))$$

So those algorithms require at least $\mathcal{O}(\log^2 n)$ rounds. In 2009, a new simple oblivious sort called randomized Shellsort is introduced by Goodrich [Goo09]. The sorting algorithm achieves $\mathcal{O}(n \log n)$ complexity, and it can finish with $\mathcal{O}(\log n)$ rounds. However, it is not guaranteed to sort, there is a small probability that the output array is not well sorted. The authors call it dirtiness, and we call it ε-error in this paper. Therefore, it is not very convincing to use randomized Shellsort for secure $(M + 1)$st-price sealed-bid auction, but it still can be used to generate random permutations. Very recently, Kristján Valur Jónsson *et al.* [JKU11] showed an oblivious sorting algorithm that is designed for MPC, and it uses $\mathcal{O}(n \log^2 n)$ comparisons in $\mathcal{O}(\log^2 n)$ rounds with practical constants.

3   Preliminaries

Share Computing. A typical MPC is based on a threshold linear secret sharing scheme, e.g. Shamir secret sharing scheme [Sha79]. Due to the linearity, parties can obliviously evaluate various linear combinations by doing local manipulations with shares. For all other operations, parties must execute secure multi-party protocols, which convert input shares to the shares of desired output without leaking any information about inputs. In particular, let $\llbracket x \rrbracket \cdot \llbracket y \rrbracket \equiv \llbracket x \cdot y \rrbracket$ denote output shares of a secure multiplication protocol. Then all other operations can be decomposed into multiplications and additions. The exact construction of a multiplication protocol uses the specifics of the underlying secret sharing scheme. For instance, the VIFF framework relies on properties of Shamir secret sharing [Sha79], whereas SHAREMIND uses tailor-suited solution for additive secret sharing [BLW08, BNTW10].

Adversarial Model. For clarity and brevity, we consider only the static corruption model where adversary specifies parties to be corrupted before the protocol starts. The adptive model could be sometimes more adequate in reality. However, the complexity of the formalism would carry us away from the core of our ideas. Although the list of tolerated adversarial coalitions can be arbitrary, share computing systems can achieve information theoretical security is only if the condition Q2 is satisfied in the semihonest model and the condition Q3 is satisfied in the malicious model [HM00]. Recall that the condition Q2 means that any union of two tolerated adversarial coalitions is not sufficient to corrupt all parties and the condition Q3 means that any union of three tolerated adversarial set are not sufficient. In the case of threshold corruption, the conditions Q2 and Q3 imply that the number corrupted parties is strictly below $\frac{m}{2}$ and $\frac{m}{3}$.

Universal Composability. As formal security proofs are rather technical, security proofs are often reduced to the security properties of sub-protocols. More specifically, one must assume that all sub-protocols are *universally composable* to automatically deduce security of a compound protocol. Although the formal definition of universal composability is rather complex, the intuition behind it is simple. Let $\varrho\langle\cdot\rangle$ be a global context that uses the functionality of a protocol π. Let π° be an idealized implementation, where all computations are done by trusted third party who privately gathers all inputs and distributes the resulting outputs. Then we can compare real and ideal world protocols $\varrho\langle\pi\rangle$ and $\varrho\langle\pi^\circ\rangle$. A protocol π is *universally composable* if for any real world adversary $\mathcal{A}$ there exist an adversary $\mathcal{A}^\circ$ against $\varrho\langle\pi^\circ\rangle$ with comparable complexity and success rate. That is, the joint distribution of all outputs in the real and ideal world must coincide for all input distributions. As a result, if a compound protocol consisting of several instances of π° preserves security if we replace π° by π. The latter means that we combine universally composable sub-protocols without any usage restrictions, e.g., execute them in parallel. See the standard treatments [Can00, PSW00] for further details.

Achieving universal composability in the semihonest model is rather straightforward, most share computing protocols satisfy this including the protocols used in SHAREMIND and VIFF [BLW08, vif]. Theoretical constructions for malicious model do exist [DGKN09], but these are not widely used in practical systems, yet.

Security against Active Adversaries. In this work, we explicitly assume that share-computing uses two-level secret sharing [CM00], where the shares $[\![x]\!]_i$ of shared values are shared again. Essentially, if $\mathcal{P}_i$ is honest then the malicious adversary is guaranteed to learn nothing during these proofs. The second level secret sharing scheme is commonly referred to as linear distributed commitment and it satisfies both perfect binding and hiding properties. As shown in [CM00], security against an active adversary can be achieved with three auxiliary protocols: commitment transfer protocol (CTP), commitment sharing protocol (CSP) and commitment multiplication protocol (CMP). CTP allows to transfer a commitment for a secret from one party to another, CSP allows to share a committed secret in a verifiable way such that the parties will be committed to their shares, and CMP allows to prove that three committed secrets a, b and c satisfy the relation $c = ab$.

Counting Sort and Bead Sort. Counting sort [Knu98] was created by Harold H. Seward in 1954. It is used to sort an array of numbers with discrete values, especially integers. Counting sort works with complexity $\mathcal{O}(n + R)$. During the counting sort, it first creates an array of counters. It then scans the input array once, increasing the corresponding counters one by one. At the end, it reconstructs the elements into output array, according to the counters.

Bead sort is a kind of natural sorting algorithm specifically for sorting natural numbers [ACD02]. The counting frame looks like an abacus that has rods and beads. Each numbers are represented as beads, e.g. 5 beads for number 5. For instance, the left matrix illustrates input numbers $4, 3, 5, 1, 3$, where 1 stands for bead and 0 stands for empty space. From top-down, there are 4 beads, 3 beads, 5 beads, 1 beads and 3 beads in each layer, respectively. Due to gravity, the beads fall down automatically, as the right matrix shows. Then if we read from top-down, the sorted numbers are $1, 3, 3, 4, 5$.

$$
\begin{Vmatrix}
1 & 1 & 1 & 1 & 0 \\
1 & 1 & 1 & 0 & 0 \\
1 & 1 & 1 & 1 & 1 \\
1 & 0 & 0 & 0 & 0 \\
1 & 1 & 1 & 0 & 0
\end{Vmatrix}
\implies
\begin{Vmatrix}
1 & 0 & 0 & 0 & 0 \\
1 & 1 & 1 & 0 & 0 \\
1 & 1 & 1 & 0 & 0 \\
1 & 1 & 1 & 1 & 0 \\
1 & 1 & 1 & 1 & 1
\end{Vmatrix}
$$

The authors constructed some special hardware to simulate such natural falling, while if we implement bead sort in software, its complexity is still around $\mathcal{O}(Rn)$. To sort numbers $a_0, \cdots, a_{n-1}$, the best complexity with software implementation is $\mathcal{O}(S)$, where $S = \sum_{i=0}^{n-1} a_i$.

4 Unbounded Fan-in AND Gate

It is possible to evaluate unbounded fan-in AND gate with constant rounds. As shown by Damgård *et al.* [DFNT05, DFK+06], there is a technique to evaluate unbounded fan-in multiplication in constant rounds. Assume we want to compute $[\![s]\!] = \prod_{i=1}^{k} [\![a_i]\!]$, where $a_i \in \mathbb{F}^*$. We can first generate random invertible pairs as follows: randomly pick $([\![b]\!], [\![c]\!]) \leftarrow \mathbb{F}^* \times \mathbb{F}^*$; Compute and open $d = [\![b]\!] \cdot [\![c]\!]$; Compute d^{-1}, then $[\![b]\!]$ and $[\![b^{-1}]\!] = d^{-1} \cdot [\![c]\!]$ give us a random invertible pair. To compute unbounded fan-in multiplication, we first generate random invertible pairs $([\![b_0]\!], [\![b_0^{-1}]\!]), \cdots, ([\![b_k]\!], [\![b_k^{-1}]\!])$. Compute and open $c_i = [\![b_{i-1}]\!] \cdot [\![a_i]\!] \cdot [\![b_i^{-1}]\!]$ for $i \in \{1, \cdots, k\}$. Comute $d = \prod_{i=1}^{k} c_i = b_0(\prod_{i=1}^{k} a_i)b_k^{-1}$, and then return $[\![s]\!] = [\![b_0^{-1}]\!] \cdot d \cdot [\![b_k]\!]$.

Armed with unbounded fan-in multiplication, one can evaluate unbounded fan-in AND gate, denoting as $\bigwedge_{i=1}^{m} [\![e_i]\!]$, where $e_i \in \{0, 1\}$. Because $e_i \in \{0, 1\}$, then $\sum_{i=1}^{m} [\![e_i]\!] \in [0, m]$. Thus, $[\![Y]\!] = (\sum_{i=1}^{m} [\![e_i]\!] + 1) \in [1, m+1] \subset \mathbb{F}^*$. It is possible to use Lagrange interpolation to construct a polynomial $P(X) = \sum_{i=0}^{m+1} \alpha_i X^i$, s.t.

$P(j) = 0$ *for* $j \in \{1, 2, \cdots, m\}$ and $P(m + 1) = 1$. Note that α_i are public, and we can use constant-round unbounded fan-in multiplication to compute $Y^2, \cdots, Y^{m+1}$. Therefore, we can evaluate polynomial $P(\llbracket Y \rrbracket)$ in constant rounds as well.

This technique can not be efficiently generalized to MPC over ring $\mathbb{R}$. However, for unbounded fan-in AND gate and OR gate, we can simply reduce them to equality-check.

Theorem 1. *There exists constants* $c_1, c_2 > 0$ *s.t.* $\tau_{\text{and}} = c_1 \cdot \tau_{\text{eq}}$ *and* $\tau_{\text{or}} = c_2 \cdot \tau_{\text{eq}}$ *for any MPC over linear secret sharing scheme.*

Proof. Let τ_{ad} be the round complexity for compute $\llbracket x \rrbracket + \llbracket y \rrbracket$. Due to linearity of the shares, we have $\tau_{\text{ad}} = 0$. τ_{and} is the round complexity of unbounded fan-in AND gate, i.e. $\alpha = \bigwedge_{i=1}^{m} \llbracket e_i \rrbracket$, where $e_i \in \{0, 1\}$. It is obvious that we have $\alpha = \text{EQ}(\sum_{i=1}^{m} \llbracket e_i \rrbracket, m)$. Similarly, τ_{or} is the round complexity of unbounded fan-in OR gate, i.e. $\beta = \bigvee_{i=1}^{m} \llbracket e_i \rrbracket$, where $e_i \in \{0, 1\}$. So we have $\beta = 1 - \text{EQ}(\sum_{i=1}^{m} \llbracket e_i \rrbracket, 0)$. Note that we assume $[0, m] \subseteq \mathbb{K}$, the same as Damgård *et al.* did in [DFNT05, DFK+06].   □

5   Constant-Round Oblivious Counting Sort

In a typical secure MPC, the underlying secret sharing scheme is over some finite field $\mathbb{F}$ or some finite ring $\mathbb{R}$. Thus, by its nature, the values are discrete and in limited range. It is a good scenario to use counting sort, but we have to make it oblivious. Alternatively, we can simulate bead sort in software and make it oblivious. It turns out that both methods converge to the same algorithm during our research. Assume that there is an input array A to be sorted, where $A[i] \in [0, R]$ for $i \in \{0, 1, \cdots, n - 1\}$. Alg. 1 depicts a constant-round oblivious counting sort that requires $(n + R)$ constant-round bit-decomposition sub-protocol(, e.g. [DFNT05],) calls and $2Rn$ constant-round unbounded fan-in AND gates. How to evaluate such unbounded fan-in AND gate in constant rounds is already shown in Sect. 4.

Analysis and Examples. In the first step, it compares each $A[i]$ with all the possible values in $[0, R]$. It first de-composites $A[i]$, and then it uses unbounded fan-in AND gate to evaluate equality-check gate $\text{EQ}(\llbracket x \rrbracket, y)$. We did not write equality-check gates explicitly in Alg. 1 in order to avoid unnecessary duplication of bit-decomposition sub-protocol calls. A stand alone equality-check gate $\text{EQ}(\llbracket x \rrbracket, y)$ can be evaluated by Alg. 2.

Theorem 2. $\tau_{\text{eq}} \leq \tau_{\text{bd}} + \tau_{\text{and}}$ *for any MPC over linear secret sharing scheme.*

Proof. There exists a construction to evaluate equality-check by using bit-decomposition and unbounded fan-in AND, such as Alg.2. Therefore, it is clear that τ_{eq} is upper-bounded by $\alpha = \tau_{\text{bd}} + \tau_{\text{and}}$.   □

Take input array $A[6] = \{3, 4, 1, 0, 2, 1\}$ as an example. After step 1, we have the following left matrix C, where each row has exactly one position to be 1. Each column stands for values $\{0, 1, \cdots, R\}$. After the inner sum of step 2, $S^* = \{1, 2, 1, 1, 1\}$. Here, $S^*[j]$ are the counters in counting sort. In order to make counting sort oblivious,

---

Algorithm 1. Constant-Round Oblivious Counting Sort

Data: Array $[\![A[0]]\!], \cdots, [\![A[n-1]]\!]$
Result: Sorted array $[\![A[0]]\!], \cdots, [\![A[n-1]]\!]$
1. **for** $i \in \{0, \cdots, n-1\}$ **do**
     Call bit-decomposition protocol $\{[\![A_0[i]]\!], \cdots, [\![A_t[i]]\!]\} \leftarrow \mathsf{Split}([\![A[i]]\!])$, where
     $t = \lfloor \log R \rfloor$.
     for $j \in \{0, \cdots, R\}$ **do**
         Let $b_0 b_1 \cdots b_t$ to be the binary expression of j.
         for $k \in \{0, \cdots, t\}$ **do**
             if $b_k = 0$ **then**
                 $|$ $[\![e_k]\!] = 1 - [\![A_k[i]]\!]$;
             end
             if $b_k = 1$ **then**
                 $|$ $[\![e_k]\!] = [\![A_k[i]]\!]$;
             end
         end
         $[\![C_{i,j}]\!] = \bigwedge_{k=0}^{t} [\![e_k]\!]$;
     end
end
2. **for** $j \in \{0, \cdots, R\}$ **do**
     $|$ $[\![S[j]]\!] = \sum_{w=j}^{R} \sum_{i=0}^{n-1} [\![C_{i,w}]\!]$;
end
3. **for** $j \in \{0, \cdots, R\}$ **do**
     Call bit-decomposition protocol $\{[\![S_0[j]]\!], \cdots, [\![S_m[j]]\!]\} \leftarrow \mathsf{Split}([\![S[j]]\!] - 1)$, where
     $m = \lfloor \log n \rfloor$.
     for $i \in \{0, \cdots, n-1\}$ **do**
         Let $b_0 b_1 \cdots b_m$ to be the binary expression of i.
         for $k \in \{0, \cdots, m\}$ **do**
             if $b_k = 0$ **then**
                 $|$ $[\![e_k]\!] = 1 - [\![S_k[j]]\!]$;
             end
             if $b_k = 1$ **then**
                 $|$ $[\![e_k]\!] = [\![S_k[j]]\!]$;
             end
         end
         $[\![E_{i,j}]\!] = \bigwedge_{k=0}^{m} [\![e_k]\!]$;
     end
     for $i \in \{0, \cdots, n-1\}$ **do**
         $|$ $[\![D_{i,j}]\!] = \sum_{w=i}^{n-1} [\![E_{i,w}]\!]$;
     end
end
4. **for** $i \in \{0, \cdots, n-1\}$ **do**
     $|$ $[\![A[n-i-1]]\!] = \sum_{j=0}^{R} [\![D_{i,j}]\!] - 1$;
end
5. **return** $[\![A[0]]\!], \cdots, [\![A[n-1]]\!]$;

Algorithm 2. Equality-Check

Data: $[\![x]\!]$ and public y ($x, y \in [0, R]$)
Result: $EQ([\![x]\!], y)$
1. Call bit-decomposition protocol $\{[\![x_0]\!], \cdots, [\![x_t]\!]\} \leftarrow \mathsf{Split}([\![x]\!])$, where $t = \lfloor \log R \rfloor$.
2. Let $b_0 b_1 \cdots b_t$ to be the binary expression of y.
for $k \in \{0, \cdots, t\}$ **do**
    if $b_k = 0$ **then**
        | $[\![e_k]\!] = 1 - [\![x_k]\!]$;
    end
    if $b_k = 1$ **then**
        | $[\![e_k]\!] = [\![x_k]\!]$;
    end
end
3. **return** $[\![C]\!] = \bigwedge_{k=0}^{t} [\![e_k]\!]$;

---

we computes $[\![S[j]]\!] = \sum_{w=j}^{R} S^*[w]$. After that, $S = \{6, 5, 3, 2, 1\}$. However, implicitly, we can have matrix C' during step 2, and it is equivalent to bead representation of the numbers.

$$
C = \begin{Vmatrix} 0\,0\,0\,1\,0 \\ 0\,0\,0\,0\,1 \\ 0\,1\,0\,0\,0 \\ 1\,0\,0\,0\,0 \\ 0\,0\,1\,0\,0 \\ 0\,1\,0\,0\,0 \end{Vmatrix}
\qquad
C' = \begin{Vmatrix} 1\,1\,1\,1\,0 \\ 1\,1\,1\,1\,1 \\ 1\,1\,0\,0\,0 \\ 1\,0\,0\,0\,0 \\ 1\,1\,1\,0\,0 \\ 1\,1\,0\,0\,0 \end{Vmatrix}
$$

During steps 3 and 4 in Alg. 1, it obliviously reconstructs the numbers back to array A, according to the modified counters. It first compare the modified counters $S[j] - 1$ with all the possible values $[0, n - 1]$. Consequently, we have the follow matrices E and D. In fact, we "visualize" the counters as bitmap D in step 3. After step 4, we got sorted array $A = \{0, 1, 1, 2, 3, 4\}$.

$$
E = \begin{Vmatrix} 0\,0\,0\,0\,1 \\ 0\,0\,0\,1\,0 \\ 0\,0\,1\,0\,0 \\ 0\,0\,0\,0\,0 \\ 0\,1\,0\,0\,0 \\ 1\,0\,0\,0\,0 \end{Vmatrix}
\qquad
D = \begin{Vmatrix} 1\,1\,1\,1\,1 \\ 1\,1\,1\,1\,0 \\ 1\,1\,1\,0\,0 \\ 1\,1\,0\,0\,0 \\ 1\,1\,0\,0\,0 \\ 1\,0\,0\,0\,0 \end{Vmatrix}
$$

Efficiency and Security. We have to make sure that $[0, max(n, R)] \subseteq \mathbb{K}$, where $\mathbb{K}$ is the message space of underlying secret sharing scheme. Although the sorting algorithm needs $\mathcal{O}(Rn)$ memory, it minimize the communication cost, for unbounded fan-in AND consumes much less communication than general comparison.

Theorem 3. *Sorting algorithm Alg. 1 achieves UC security, and it terminates after* $2(\tau_{bd} + \tau_{and})$ *rounds if the underlying MPC primitives are UC secure.*

Proof. For round complexity, evaluating share addition takes 0 rounds without communication cost in a typical secure MPC over linear secret sharing schemes. The sequentially dependent steps in Alg. 1 are only twice bit-decompositions and twice unbounded fan-in AND gates. Thus, it is clear that the sorting algorithm takes $2(\tau_{bd} + \tau_{and})$ rounds. Note that τ_{bd} and τ_{and} are constants that independent to input size n [DFNT05].

In terms of security, it follows standard hybrid model under UC theorem [Can01, Can00]. First, it is clear that this sorting algorithm is data-oblivious, because its behavior is always scanning the whole arrays and matrices. In our setting, if a tolerable subset of parties are corrupted, then each share computing protocol remains secure. Because of UC, we can replace them with ideal functionalities, where a trusted third party $\mathcal{T}$ carries over the computations. We only consider the malicious model here, and the security proof is analogous for the semihonest model. We replace each share computing protocol with an ideal functionality (i.e. $\mathcal{F}_{Add}$, $\mathcal{F}_{Split}$ and $\mathcal{F}_{AND}$), $\mathcal{T}$ privately collects input shares, reconstructs the inputs, computes the output, and sends the shares of the out- put back to the parties. In the resulting hybrid model, parties just use outputs as inputs of other protocols and corrupted parties can only alter the shares of intermediate results. However, the security of share computing protocols implies that the secret sharing scheme must be robust, i.e. the shared value can be still reliably reconstructed even if corrupted parties alter their shares. Consequently, the actions of a malicious coalition do not change the outcomes of sub-protocols in the hybrid model.

Hence, the resulting simulator construction $\mathcal{S}$ is straightforward. As $\mathcal{S}$ must simulate the remain parties to corrupted parties, it can reconstruct the corresponding input array from the shares sent from the parties and forward them to $\mathcal{T}$. To simulate the outcomes of sub-protocols for the parties, $\mathcal{S}$ can simply share 0 as many times as needed. This does not change the output distribution, as a tolerated malicious coalition cannot distinguish between shares of different values. For the simulation of the final result, $\mathcal{S}$ just forwards the shares of sorted output array generated by $\mathcal{T}$ to the corrupted parties. The simulation is perfect, because we have the same distribution in the ideal and hybrid world. As the simulator is non-rewinding, the oblivious sorting protocol is also universally composable, see the manuscript [Can00, p. 48–50] for further details.

□

6   Oblivious Arrayless Bead Sort

Since, sometimes, $\mathcal{O}(Rn)$ memory requirement is huge in Alg. 1. We are going to show how to get rid of the bitmap and simplify the sorting algorithm in this section. As depicted in Alg. 3, the pseudo-code looks very efficient at high level, and its minimum memory requirement is only $\mathcal{O}(R)$. Recall that $\mathsf{COM}(\llbracket x \rrbracket, y) = \llbracket 1 \rrbracket$ if $x \geq y$; $\mathsf{COM}(\llbracket x \rrbracket, y) = \llbracket 0 \rrbracket$, otherwise.

Analysis and Examples. Take the same input array $A[6] = \{3, 4, 1, 0, 2, 1\}$ as an example. $n = 6$ and $R = 4$. After step 1, we have the array of counters $\{S_j\}_{j=1}^{R} = \{5, 3, 2, 1\}$. S_j is used to count how many numbers in input array A is larger than or equal to j. Step 2 reconstructs the numbers obliviously according to the counters. After step 2, we get the sorted array $A = \{0, 1, 1, 2, 3, 4\}$.

Efficiency and Security. Again, we have to make sure that $[0, max(n, R)] \subseteq \mathbb{K}$, where $\mathbb{K}$ is the message space of underlying secret sharing scheme. The oblivious arrayless bead sort, Alg. 3, only needs R counters as minimum memory requirement. However, in order to evaluate the algorithm in parallel, the actual temporary memory usage is higher. The high level code looks very tidy, but the real communication is higher than Alg. 1 by a constant factor. On the other hand, since the sorting algorithm is very close to bead sort, we also can deal with negative numbers with anti-gravity bead sort, i.e. all the 1-s raise up to the ceiling for those columns corresponding to negative numbers.

Algorithm 3. Constant-Round Oblivious Arrayless Bead Sort

Data: Array $[\![A[0]]\!], \cdots, [\![A[n-1]]\!]$ $(A[i] \in [0, R])$
Result: Sorted array $[\![A[0]]\!], \cdots, [\![A[n-1]]\!]$
1. **for** $j \in \{1, \cdots, R\}$ **do**
  | $[\![S_j]\!] = \sum_{i=0}^{n-1} \mathrm{COM}([\![A[i]]\!], j)$;
end
2. **for** $i \in \{1, \cdots, n\}$ **do**
  | $[\![A[n-i]]\!] = \sum_{w=1}^{R} \mathrm{COM}([\![S_w]\!], i)$;
end
3. **return** $[\![A[0]]\!], \cdots, [\![A[n-1]]\!]$;

Theorem 4. *Sorting algorithm Alg. 3 achieves UC security, and it terminates after* $2\tau_{\mathrm{com}}$ *rounds if the underlying MPC primitives are UC secure.*

Proof (Sketch). For round complexity, evaluating share addition takes 0 rounds without communication cost. The sequentially dependent steps in Alg. 3 is only twice comparisons. Thus, it is clear that the sorting algorithm takes $2\tau_{\mathrm{com}}$ rounds. Here, τ_{com} is constant that independent to input size n [DFK+06]. In terms of security, it is clear that this sorting algorithm is data-oblivious, for it only scans the whole array and counters. The security proof is very similar as the proof of Theorem 3, and it follows standard hybrid model under universally composability [Can01, Can00]. Since all the share computing sub-protocols are UC secure, we can replace them with ideal functionalities. We skip straightforward simulator construction S for space limitation.

□

7   Sorting Key Indexed Data Structure

In this section, we are going to show how to construct a constant-round oblivious sort that is based on comparison. In some cases, we do not only want to sort an array of numbers, but also want to sort key indexed data structures. Denote $\hat{D}_i$ as an arbitrary shared data structure, e.g. a set of shared data. We want to sort $\hat{D}_i$ according to their associated keywords $[\![A_i]\!]$, for $i \in \{0, 1, \cdots, n-1\}$. The intuition of the oblivious sort is based on Observation 1.

Observation 1. *Given array A with size n to be sorted such that $\forall i, j$, if $i \neq j$ then $A[i] \neq A[j]$. The number of elements in A that are smaller than the element $A[i]$ indicates the exactly position that $A[i]$ should be after the sort.*

Therefore, we need a transformation scheme that guarantees no duplicated transformed keywords.

Theorem 5. *There exists a transformation map:* $\zeta : \{A_i\}_{i=0}^{n-1} \rightarrow \{A_i'\}_{i=0}^{n-1}$ *such that the following properties holds:*

1. $\forall i, j \quad i \neq j: \quad A_i' \neq A_j'$
2. $A_i' < A_j'$ *if* $A_i < A_j$
3. $A_i' < A_j'$ *if* $A_i = A_j$ *and* $i < j$
4. $A_i' > A_j'$ *otherwise*

Proof. Let $\beta \geq n$ be a constant. One possible transformation map ζ can be $A_i' \leftarrow A_i \cdot \beta + i$. It is obvious that this transformation scheme achieves these properties. $\square$

Algorithm 4. ExComp

Data: $(\llbracket A_i \rrbracket, i)$ and $(\llbracket A_j \rrbracket, j)$
Result: $\llbracket 1 \rrbracket$ if $A[i] \cdot n + i > A[j] \cdot n + j$; $\llbracket 0 \rrbracket$, otherwise
if $i > j$ **then**
   | return $\mathsf{COM}(\llbracket A_i \rrbracket, \llbracket A_j \rrbracket)$;
end
if $j > i$ **then**
   | return $(1 - \mathsf{COM}(\llbracket A_j \rrbracket, \llbracket A_i \rrbracket))$;
end

We are going to "use" the transformation ζ is our oblivious keyword sort. (c.f. Alg. 5, below) Note that the third property, i.e. $A_i' < A_j'$ if $A_i = A_j$ and $i < j$, is very important to keep our sort stable. However, in terms of efficiency, it is not necessary to require $[0, Rn] \subseteq \mathbb{K}$. Conceptually, we consider $A'[i] = A[i] \| i$ and extend the comparison as Alg. 4.

Algorithm 5. Constant-Round Oblivious Keyword Sort

Data: Array of pairs: $(\hat{D}_0, \llbracket A_0 \rrbracket), \cdots, (\hat{D}_{n-1}, \llbracket A_{n-1} \rrbracket)$
Result: Sorted array $\hat{D}$: $\hat{D}_0, \cdots, \hat{D}_{n-1}$
1. **for** $i \in \{0, \cdots, n-1\}$ **do**
   | $\llbracket C_i \rrbracket = \sum_{j=0, j \neq i}^{n-1} \mathsf{ExComp}((\llbracket A_i \rrbracket, i), (\llbracket A_j \rrbracket, j))$;
end
2. **for** $i \in \{0, \cdots, n-1\}$ **do**
   | $\hat{D}_i = \sum_{w=0}^{n-1} (\mathsf{EQ}(\llbracket C_w \rrbracket, i) \cdot \hat{D}_w)$;
end
3. **return** $\hat{D}_0, \cdots, \hat{D}_{n-1}$;

Efficiency and Correctness. Conceptually, the original keywords A_i is transformed to $A_i' \leftarrow A_i \cdot n + i$ to ensure that there is no duplicated value. After step 1, C_i stores the position that $\hat{D}_i$ is supposed to be in the sorted array. Step 2 puts $\hat{D}_i$ to their corresponding positions obliviously. This step is also called oblivious selection, which is very close to oblivious transfer. The complexity of this sorting algorithm is $\mathcal{O}(n^2)$, but it finishes in constant rounds. Note that we write EQ for simplicity. As mentioned in previous sections, n^2 EQ gates can share n bit-decomposition calls, and they can be evaluated with n^2 unbounded fan-in AND gates.

Theorem 6. *Sorting algorithm Alg. 5 is achieves UC security, and it terminates after* $\tau_{\mathrm{com}} + \tau_{\mathrm{eq}} + \tau_{\mathrm{mul}}$ *rounds if the underlying MPC primitives are UC secure.*

Proof (Sketch). Transformation $\zeta : [\![A_i]\!] \cdot n + i$ is virtual, and ExComp onlys cost τ_{com} rounds. Thus, it is clear that the sorting algorithm takes $\tau_{\mathrm{com}} + \tau_{\mathrm{eq}} + \tau_{\mathrm{mul}}$ rounds. In terms of security, it is clear that this sorting algorithm is data-oblivious, for it only scans the whole array and counters. The security proof is very similar as the proof of Theorem 3, and it follows standard hybrid model under universally composability [Can01, Can00]. Since all the share computing sub-protocols are UC secure, we can replace them with ideal functionalities. We skip the straightforward simulator construction $\mathcal{S}$ for space limitation.

$\square$

8 Dealing with Huge R

In some special cases, we want to sort huge numbers, where range $R \notin \mathbb{K}$. The numbers can be divided into several chunks and stored in several shares. Since the sorting algorithm Alg. 5 is stable, we can combine Alg. 5 with radix sort. We call it oblivious hybrid radix sort, as shown in Alg. 6, below. Assume $[0, 2^{\alpha}] \subseteq \mathbb{K}$ and $L = 2^{\alpha}$, where $L < R$ and $\alpha \geq 1$. The sorting algorithm takes $\mathcal{O}(\beta \cdot (\tau_{\mathrm{com}} + \tau_{\mathrm{eq}} + \tau_{\mathrm{mul}}))$ rounds, where $\beta = \lceil \lceil \log_2 R \rceil / \alpha \rceil$. We denote the number $A[i]$ as $A_{\beta-1}[i] \| \cdots \| A_0[i]$, where $A[i] = \sum_{j=0}^{\beta-1} A_j[i] \cdot 2^{j\alpha}$ and $A_j[i] \in [0, 2^{\alpha} - 1]$.

Algorithm 6. Oblivious Hybrid Radix Sort

Data: Array of splited numbers $([\![A_{\beta-1}[i]\!]\!], \cdots, [\![A_0[i]\!]\!])$, for $i \in [0, n-1]$
Result: Sorted array $([\![A_{\beta-1}[i]\!]\!], \cdots, [\![A_0[i]\!]\!])$, for $i \in [0, n-1]$
1. **for** $j \in \{0, \cdots, \beta - 1\}$ **do**
     Set $\hat{D}_i \leftarrow ([\![A_{\beta-1}[i]\!]\!], \cdots, [\![A_0[i]\!]\!])$;
     Call Alg. 5 to sort array $\hat{D}$ according to keywords $[\![A_j[i]\!]\!]$;
end
2. **return** $\hat{D}_i = ([\![A_{\beta-1}[i]\!]\!], \cdots, [\![A_0[i]\!]\!])$, for $i \in [0, n-1]$;

Theorem 7. *Sorting algorithm Alg. 6 achieves UC security, and it terminates after* $\mathcal{O}(\log R \cdot (\tau_{\mathrm{com}} + \tau_{\mathrm{eq}} + \tau_{\mathrm{mul}}))$ *rounds if the underlying MPC primitives are UC secure..*

Proof (Sketch). Since $\alpha = \lceil \log_2 L \rceil \geq 1$, the maximum number of sequential sorting algorithm Alg. 5 calls is $\beta = \Theta(\log R)$. As Alg. 5 terminates in $\tau_{\text{com}} + \tau_{\text{eq}} + \tau_{\text{mul}}$ rounds. The whole sort terminates in $\mathcal{O}(\log R \cdot (\tau_{\text{com}} + \tau_{\text{eq}} + \tau_{\text{mul}}))$ rounds. Since it is just a batch of Alg. 5, the security proof is similar as the proof for Alg. 5.

$\square$

9   Applications

9.1 $(M+1)$st-Price Auction

The first direct application is secure sealed-bid auction protocol. During a $(M+1)$st-price auction, each bidder i submits pairs $(\llbracket \text{name}_i \rrbracket, \llbracket \text{bid}_i \rrbracket)$. Set $\hat{D}_i \leftarrow (\llbracket \text{name}_i \rrbracket, \llbracket \text{bid}_i \rrbracket)$ and sort data structure $\hat{D}_i$ according to keywords $\llbracket \text{bid}_i \rrbracket$ by calling Alg. 5. After sort, open the winner's name $\llbracket \text{name}_0 \rrbracket$ and open the win price $\llbracket \text{bid}_M \rrbracket$, (the $(M+1)$-th price).

9.2   Constant-Round Obfuscated Shuffle

Naively, one can achieve obfuscated shuffle in by multiplying a $n \times n$ permutation matrix $\mathcal{A}_\pi$, because any permutation π can be represented as a permutation matrix $\mathcal{A}_\pi$. However, it is not trivial to prepare a $n \times n$ permutation matrix $\mathcal{A}_\pi$ in constant rounds. Alternatively, if each party $\mathcal{P}_i$ shares a permutation matrix $\mathcal{A}_{\pi_i}$. All parties check whether the sums of every column and row of matrix $\mathcal{A}_{\pi_i}$ are 1 by opening them for $i \in \{1, 2, \cdots, m\}$. Note there is no information leakage, for they are always 1 if the party is honest. Let $\mathcal{M}$ be the message vector, the obfuscated shuffle is computed by $\mathcal{M}' = \prod_{i=1}^{m} \mathcal{A}_{\pi_i} \cdot \mathcal{M}$. The resulting shuffle protocol contains $\mathcal{O}(mn^2)$ multiplications, which can be performed in $\mathcal{O}(m \cdot \tau_{\text{mul}})$ rounds. By computing $M_{\pi_1} \cdots M_{\pi_m}$ first, we can reduce the number of rounds to $\mathcal{O}(\log m \cdot \tau_{\text{mul}})$ with the cost of $\mathcal{O}(mn^3)$ multiplications.

On the other hand, obfuscated shuffle can be implemented by sorting random numbers. Assume we want to shuffle array $A[0], \cdots, A[n-1]$, we first generate a fresh random number with $k \log n$-bit long for each shared message, denoting as $R[i]$ for $i \in \{0, 1, \cdots, n-1\}$. Similarly, we can use out oblivious sorting algorithms to sort the shared messages according to associated random numbers. k is security parameter. If same random numbers are generated for two (or more) different documents, the relative order of them will be preserved after sort. The probability that we select n numbers out of $2^{(k \log n)} = n^k$ without collision is

$$P(n) = 1 \cdot (1 - \frac{1}{n^k})(1 - \frac{2}{n^k}) \dots (1 - \frac{n-1}{n^k})$$
$$\approx e^{-\frac{1}{n^k}} \cdot e^{-\frac{2}{n^k}} \cdot \dots \cdot e^{-\frac{n-1}{n^k}} \approx e^{-n^{2-k}}.$$

In practice, $k > 3$ is enough for large n. If $2^{k \log n} \notin \mathbb{K}$, we can divide the random numbers to several shares. (cf. Sect. 8) When m is big, it is clear that this approach is more round-efficient than the permutation matrix one.

10   Conclusions and Future Work

We proposed several constant-round oblivious sorting algorithms for secure MPC, which significantly improves current poly-logarithmic round complexity oblivious sorting network based solutions. We also showed some applications for our sorting algorithm is $(M + 1)$st-price auction protocol and obfuscated shuffle. The future work will be improving the efficiency and investigating constant-round oblivious sorting algorithms with poly-logarithmic complexity overhead, i.e. $\mathcal{O}(n \log^c n)$ computation & communication complexity.

Acknowledgments. The author is supported by Estonian Science Foundation, grant #8058, the European Regional Development Fund through the Estonian Center of Excellence in Computer Science (EXCS) and ICT doctoral school. Most of this work was done while the author was working at Cybernetica AS.

References

[ACD02]   Arulanandham, J.J., Calude, C., Dinneen, M.J.: Bead-sort: A natural sorting algorithm. Bulletin of the EATCS 76, 153–161 (2002) 3

[AKS83]   Ajtai, M., Komlós, J., Szemerédi, E.: Sorting in c log n parallel steps. Combinatorica 3, 1–19 (1983) 1, 1, 2

[Bat68]   Batcher, K.E.: Sorting networks and their applications. In: Proceedings of the Spring Joint Computer Conference, AFIPS 1968, April 30-May 2, pp. 307–314. ACM, New York (1968) 2

[BLW08]   Bogdanov, D., Laur, S., Willemson, J.: Sharemind: A Framework for Fast Privacy-Preserving Computations. In: Jajodia, S., Lopez, J. (eds.) ESORICS 2008. LNCS, vol. 5283, pp. 192–206. Springer, Heidelberg (2008) 1, 3, 3

[BNTW10]   Bogdanov, D., Niitsoo, M., Toft, T., Willemson, J.: . Improved protocols for the sharemind virtual machine. Research report T-4-10, Cybernetica (2010) http://research.cyber.ee 3

[Can00]   Canetti, R.: Universally composable security: A new paradigm for cryptographic protocols. Cryptology ePrint Archive, Report 2000/067 (2000), http://eprint.iacr.org/ 3, 5, 6, 7

[Can01]   Canetti, R.: Universally composable security: A new paradigm for cryptographic protocols. In: Annual IEEE Symposium on Foundations of Computer Science, p. 136 (2001) 5, 6, 7

[CFIK03]   Cramer, R., Fehr, S., Ishai, Y., Kushilevitz, E.: Efficient multi-party computation over rings. In: Biham, E. (ed.) EUROCRYPT 2003. LNCS, vol. 2656, p. 642. Springer, Heidelberg (2003) 1, 2

[Cha81]   Chaum, D.L.: Untraceable electronic mail, return addresses, and digital pseudonyms. Communications of the ACM 24(2), 84–90 (1981) 1

[CKMH07]   Chida, K., Kikuchi, H., Morohashi, G., Hirota, K.: Efficient multiparty computation for comparator networks. In: ARES, pp. 1183–1189 (2007) 1

[CL05]   Camenisch, J.L., Lysyanskaya, A.: A Formal Treatment of Onion Routing. In: Shoup, V. (ed.) CRYPTO 2005. LNCS, vol. 3621, pp. 169–187. Springer, Heidelberg (2005) 1

[CM00]   Cramer, R., Maurer, U.: General secure multi-party computation from any linear secret-sharing scheme, pp. 316–334. Springer, Heidelberg (2000) 3

[Cob66]   Cobham, A.: The recognition problem for the set of perfect squares. In: Proceedings of the 7th Annual Symposium on Switching and Automata Theory (Swat 1966), pp. 78–87. IEEE Computer Society, Washington, DC, USA (1966) 2

[DFK⁺06]   Damgård, I.B., Fitzi, M., Kiltz, E., Nielsen, J.B., Toft, T.: Unconditionally Secure Constant-Rounds Multi-party Computation for Equality, Comparison, Bits and Exponentiation. In: Halevi, S., Rabin, T. (eds.) TCC 2006. LNCS, vol. 3876, pp. 285–304. Springer, Heidelberg (2006) 1, 4, 4, 6

[DFNT05]   Damgård, I., Fitzi, M., Nielsen, J.B., Toft, T.: How to split a shared secret into shared bits in constant-round (2005), http://eprint.iacr.org/2005/140 1, 4, 4, 5, 5

[DGKN09]   Damgård, I., Geisler, M., Krøigaard, M., Nielsen, J.B.: Asynchronous Multiparty Computation: Theory and Implementation. In: Jarecki, S., Tsudik, G. (eds.) PKC 2009. LNCS, vol. 5443, pp. 160–179. Springer, Heidelberg (2009) 1, 3

[DPSR83]   Dowd, M., Perl, Y., Saks, M., Rudolph, L.: The balanced sorting network. In: Proceedings of the Second Annual ACM Symposium on Principles of Distributed Computing, PODC 1983, pp. 161–172. ACM, New York (1983) 1, 2

[Gen09]   Gentry, C.: Fully homomorphic encryption using ideal lattices. In: STOC 2009: Proceedings of the 41st Annual ACM Symposium on Theory of Computing, pp. 169–178. ACM, New York (2009) 1

[Goo09]   Goodrich, M.T.: Randomized shellsort: A simple oblivious sorting algorithm. CoRR, abs/0909.1037 (2009) 1, 2

[HM00]   Hirt, M., Maurer, U.M.: Player simulation and general adversary structures in perfect multiparty computation. Journal of Cryptology 13(1), 31–60 (2000) 3

[IK02]   Ishai, Y., Kushilevitz, E.: Perfect constant-round secure computation via perfect randomizing polynomials. In: Widmayer, P., Triguero, F., Morales, R., Hennessy, M., Eidenbenz, S., Conejo, R. (eds.) ICALP 2002. LNCS, vol. 2380, pp. 244–256. Springer, Heidelberg (2002) 1, 2

[IP07]   Ishai, Y., Paskin, A.: Evaluating Branching Programs on Encrypted Data. In: Vadhan, S.P. (ed.) TCC 2007. LNCS, vol. 4392, pp. 575–594. Springer, Heidelberg (2007) 1

[JKU11]   Jónsson, K.V., Kreitz, G., Uddin, M.: Secure multi-party sorting and applications. Cryptology ePrint Archive, Report 2011/122 (2011), http://eprint.iacr.org/ 1, 2

[Knu98]   Knuth, D.E.: Art of Computer Programming, Sorting and Searching, 2nd edn., vol. 3. Addison-Wesley Professional, Reading (1998) 3

[MTHK09]   McLachlan, J., Tran, A., Hopper, N., Kim, Y.: Scalable onion routing with torsk. In: Al-Shaer, E., Jha, S., Keromytis, A.D. (eds.) ACM Conference on Computer and Communications Security, pp. 590–599. ACM, New York (2009) 1

[PSW00]   Pfitzmann, B., Schunter, M., Waidner, M.: Secure reactive systems. RZ 3206 (#93252), IBM Research Division, Zrich (May 2000) 3

[RBO89]   Rabin, T., Ben-Or, M.: Verifiable secret sharing and multiparty protocols with honest majority. In: Proceedings of the Twenty-first Annual ACM Symposium on Theory of Computing, STOC 1989, pp. 73–85. ACM, New York (1989) 1

[Sha79]   Shamir, A.: How to share a secret. Commun. ACM 22, 612–613 (1979) 3

[vif]   Viff documentation, http://viff.dk/doc/index.html 3

[Weg00]   Wegener, I.: Branching programs and binary decision diagrams: theory and applica-
           tions. Society for Industrial and Applied Mathematics, Philadelphia (2000) 2
[Wik04]   Wikström, D.: A Universally Composable Mix-Net. In: Naor, M. (ed.) TCC 2004.
           LNCS, vol. 2951, pp. 317–335. Springer, Heidelberg (2004) 1
[WWW98]   Wurman, P.R., Walsh, W.E., Wellman, M.P.: Flexible double auctions for electronic
           commerce: theory and implementation. Decision Support Systems 24(1), 17–27
           (1998) 1
[Yao82]   Yao, A.C.: Protocols for secure computations. In: Proceedings of the 23rd Annual
           Symposium on Foundations of Computer Science, pp. 160–164. IEEE Computer
           Society, Los Alamitos (1982) 1

General Construction of Chameleon All-But-One Trapdoor Functions

Shengli Liu[1,2], Junzuo Lai[3,*], and Robert H. Deng[3]

[1] Department of Computer Science and Engineering
Shanghai Jiao Tong University, Shanghai 200240, China
slliu@sjtu.edu.cn
[2] State Key Laboratory of Information Security,
Institute of Software, Chinese Academy of Sciences
[3] School of Information Systems,
Singapore Management University, Singapore 178902
{junzuolai,robertdeng}@smu.edu.sg

Abstract. Lossy trapdoor functions enable black-box construction of public key encryption (PKE) schemes secure against chosen-ciphertext attack [18]. Recently, a more efficient black-box construction of public key encryption was given in [12] with the help of chameleon all-but-one trapdoor functions (ABO-TDFs).

In this paper, we propose a black-box construction for transforming any ABO-TDFs into chameleon ABO-TDFs with the help of chameleon hash functions. Instantiating the proposed general black-box construction of chameleon ABO-TDFs, we can obtain the first chameleon ABO-TDFs based on the Decisional Diffie-Hellman (DDH) assumption.

Keywords: Lossy Trapdoor Functions, Chameleon All-But-One Trapdoor Functions, Chameleon Hash Functions.

1   Introduction

Lossy trapdoor functions (LTDFs) were first introduced by Peikert and Waters [18] and further studied in [6,7,8,9,19,14]. LTDFs imply lots of fundamental cryptographic primitives, such as collision-resistant hash functions [18], oblivious transfer [17]. LTDFs can be used to construct many cryptographic schemes, such as deterministic public-key encryption [2], encryption and commitments secure against selective opening attacks [1], non-interactive string commitments [16]. Most important of all, LTDFs enable black-box construction of public key encryption (PKE) schemes secure against chosen-ciphertext attack (CCA-secure PKE in short) [18].

A lossy trapdoor function is a public function f which works in two computationally indistinguishable modes, i.e., there is no efficient adversary who can tell which working mode f is in, given only the function description. In the first

---

[*] Corresponding author.

X. Boyen and X. Chen (Eds.): ProvSec 2011, LNCS 6980, pp. 257–265, 2011.

mode, it behaves like an injective trapdoor function and the input x can be recovered from $f(x)$ with the help of a trapdoor. In the second mode, f turns into a many-to-one function and it loses a significant amount of information about the input x. Hence, f in the latter mode is called a lossy function.

LTDFs were further extended to a richer abstraction called all-but-one trapdoor functions (ABO-TDFs), which can be constructed from LTDFs [18]. A collection of ABO-TDFs is associated with a branch set $\mathcal{B}$, and an ABO trapdoor function $g_b(\cdot)$ is uniquely determined by a function index g and a branch $b \in \mathcal{B}$. There exists a unique branch $b^* \in \mathcal{B}$ such that $g_{b^*}(\cdot)$ is a lossy function, while all $g_b(\cdot)$, $b \neq b^*$, are injective ones. However, the lossy branch b^* is computationally hidden by description of the function g. Freeman et al. [6] generalized the definition of ABO trapdoor functions by allowing possibly many lossy branches instead of one. Let $\mathcal{B}^*$ be the set of lossy branches. Then, an ABO trapdoor function $g_b(\cdot)$ is injective if $b \in \mathcal{B}^*$ and lossy if $b \in \mathcal{B} \setminus \mathcal{B}^*$.

The black-box construction of CCA-secure PKE from LTDFs in [18] needs a collection of LTDFs, a collection of ABO-TDFs, a pair-wise independent family of hash functions, and a strongly unforgeable one-time signature scheme, where the set of verification keys is a subset of the branch set of the ABO collection.

The black-box construction of CCA-secure PKE from LTDFs was further improved in [12]. The improved construction is free of the strongly unforgeable one-time signature scheme, and employs a collision-resistant hash function instead. This results in ciphertexts of shorter length and encryption/decryption of greater efficiency. The price is that the collection of ABO-TDFs is replaced by a special kind of ABO-TDFs, namely chameleon ABO-TDFs. The notion of chameleon ABO-TDFs was first proposed in [12]. Chameleon ABO-TDFs behave just like ABO-TDFs except the following specific properties. Chameleon ABO-TDFs have two variables (u, v) to represent a branch. The chameleon property requires that given any half branch u, there exists an efficient algorithm to compute the other half branch v with a trapdoor such that (u, v) is a lossy branch.

Lai et al. [12] proposed a general construction of chameleon ABO-TDFs based on any CPA-secure homomorphic PKE scheme with some additional property, like the Damgård-Jurik encryption scheme [5]. This paper will further explore a more general construction of chameleon ABO-TDFs, which combines ABO-TDFs with chameleon hash functions.

1.1   Related Works

Since this paper focuses on the general construction of chameleon ABO-TDFs, we review here the existing constructions of LTDFs in the literature.

Peikert and Waters [18] showed how to construct LTDFs and ABO-TDFs based on the Decisional Diffie-Hellman (DDH) assumption and the worst-case hardness of lattice problem. Freeman et al. [6] presented LTDFs and ABO-TDFs based on the Quadratic Residuosity (QR) assumption, the Decisional Composite Residuosity (DCR) assumption and the d-Linear assumption. Hemenway and Ostrovsky [7] showed that smooth homomorphic hash proof systems imply LTDFs, and homomorphic encryption over cyclic groups also imply LTDFs [8]. Kiltz et al. [10] showed that the RSA trapdoor function is lossy under the ϕ-Hiding assumption of Cachin et al. [4]. Recently, Boyen and Waters [3] proposed two new discrete-log-type LTDFs based on the Decisional Bilinear Diffie-Hellman (DBDH) assumption.

Rosen and Segev [19] showed that any collection of injective trapdoor functions that is secure under very natural correlated products can be used to construct a CCA-secure PKE scheme, and demonstrated that any collection of LTDFs with sufficient lossiness yields a collection of injective trapdoor functions that is secure under natural correlated products.

Mol and Yilek [14] extended the results of [18] and [19] and showed that only a non-negligible fraction of a single bit of lossiness is sufficient for building CCA-secure PKE schemes.

Recently, Kiltz et al. [9] introduced the notion of adaptive trapdoor functions (ATDFs) and tag-based adaptive trapdoor functions (TB-ATDFs). They showed that ATDFs and TB-ATDFs can be constructed directly by combining LTDFs and ABO-TDFs.

Lai et al. [12] introduced the notion of chameleon ABO-TDFs, presented a construction using CPA-secure homomorphic PKE schemes with some additional property and instantiated it with the Damgård-Jurik encryption scheme [5].

Our work is also related to chameleon hash functions, which are randomized collision-resistant hash functions with the additional property that given a trapdoor, one can efficiently generate collisions. Chameleon hash functions found various applications in chameleon signatures [11], online/offline signatures [20], transformations for strongly unforgeable signatures [21], etc. Recently, Mohassel presented a general construction of one-time signatures from chameleon hash functions [13].

1.2   Our Contribution

We propose a black-box construction of chameleon ABO-TDFs by combining chameleon hash functions with ABO-TDFs with the help of a collision-resistant hash function family [15]. Let $\mathcal{Y}$ be the range of a collection of chameleon ABO-TDFs and $\mathcal{B}$ be the branch set of a collection of ABO-TDFs. With the help of a family $\mathcal{T}$ of collision-resistant hash functions from $\mathcal{Y}$ to $\mathcal{B}$, a collection of chameleon hash functions can be integrated into a collection of ABO-TDFs to result in a collection of chameleon ABO-TDFs.

Following our black-box construction of chameleon ABO-TDFs, we can obtain the first chameleon ABO-TDFs based on the DDH assumption, which is the integration of the DL-based chameleon hash function [11] proposed by Krawczyk and Rabin and the ABO-TDFs [6] based on the DDH assumption.

1.3   Organization of the Paper

The paper is organized as follows. In Section 2, we review the notion of chameleon hash functions. In Section 3, we review the notion of chameleon ABO-TDFs. In Section 4, we present a black-box construction of chameleon ABO-TDFs by combining any chameleon hash function with ABO-TDFs with the help of a collision-resistant hash function family. Finally, Section 5 concludes the paper.

1.4   Notation

Let $\mathcal{H}$ denote a set, $|\mathcal{H}|$ denote the cardinality of the set $\mathcal{H}$, and $h \xleftarrow{\$} \mathcal{H}$ denote sampling uniformly from the uniform distribution on set $\mathcal{H}$. If $A(\cdot)$ is an algorithm, then $a \xleftarrow{\$} A(\cdot)$ denotes running the algorithm and obtaining a as an output, which is distributed according to the internal randomness of $A(\cdot)$. A function $f(\lambda)$ is *negligible* if for every $c > 0$ there exists an λ_c such that $f(\lambda) < 1/\lambda^c$ for all $\lambda > \lambda_c$.

2   Chameleon Hash Functions

A family of chameleon hash functions is a set of randomized collision-resistant (CR) hash functions with an additional property that one can efficiently generate collisions with the help of a trapdoor.

Let $\mathcal{H}$ be a set of hash functions, with each function mapping $\mathcal{X}$ to $\mathcal{Y}$. Let $k \xleftarrow{\$} \textbf{Hindex}(1^\kappa)$ denote the index generation algorithm. Each index $k \in \{1, 2, \cdots, |\mathcal{H}|\}$ determines a hash function $H_k \in \mathcal{H}$. Then, $\mathcal{H}$ is collision-resistant if for any polynomial-time adversary $\mathcal{A}$, its advantage $\textbf{Adv}_{\mathcal{H},\mathcal{A}}^{CR}(1^\kappa)$, defined as

$$\textbf{Adv}_{\mathcal{H},\mathcal{A}}^{CR}(1^\kappa) = \Pr\left[H_k(x_1) = H_k(x_2) : k \xleftarrow{\$} \textbf{Hindex}(1^\kappa); x_1, x_2 \xleftarrow{\$} \mathcal{A}(H_k)\right],$$

is negligible.

A family $\mathcal{H}$ of chameleon hash functions [13], mapping $\mathcal{U} \times \mathcal{V}$ to $\mathcal{Y}$ consists of three (probabilistic) polynomial-time algorithms: the index generating algorithm, the evaluation algorithm and the inversion algorithm, satisfying *chameleon*, *uniformity* and *collision resistance* properties.

Index Generation Hgen(1^κ): On input a security parameter 1^κ, the key generation algorithm outputs an index k of $\mathcal{H}$ and a trapdoor td. The index k determines a specific hash function $H_k : \mathcal{U} \times \mathcal{V} \to \mathcal{Y}$.

Evaluation $H_k(u, v)$: Each hash function $H_k \in \mathcal{H}$, takes $u \in \mathcal{U}$ and $v \in \mathcal{V}$ as inputs, and outputs a hash value in $\mathcal{Y}$.

Inversion $H_k^{-1}(u, v, td, u')$: On input $(u, v) \in \mathcal{U} \times \mathcal{V}$, the trapdoor td and $u' \in \mathcal{U}$, where $(k, td) \xleftarrow{\$} \textbf{Hgen}(1^\kappa)$, the algorithm H_k^{-1} outputs $v' \in \mathcal{V}$.

Chameleon Property: Given a hash input (u, v) of H_k, the trapdoor td of H_k, and $u' \in \mathcal{U}$, the algorithm H_k^{-1} computes $v' \in \mathcal{V}$ such that $H_k(u, v) = H_k(u', v')$. More precisely,

$$\Pr[H_k(u, v) = H_k(u', v') : (k, td) \xleftarrow{\$} \textbf{Hgen}(1^\kappa), u, u' \in \mathcal{U},$$
$$v \in \mathcal{V}, v' \xleftarrow{\$} H_k^{-1}(u, v, td, u')] = 1. \tag{1}$$

Uniformity Property: There exists a distribution $\mathcal{D}_v$ over $\mathcal{V}$, such that for all $u \in \mathcal{U}$, the distributions $(k, H_k(u, v))$ and (k, b) are computationally indistinguishable, where $(k, td) \xleftarrow{\$} \mathbf{Hgen}(1^\kappa)$, v is chosen from $\mathcal{V}$ according to distribution $\mathcal{D}_v$, and $b \xleftarrow{\$} \mathcal{Y}$.

Collision Resistance Property: For all $H_k \in \mathcal{H}$, without the knowledge of the corresponding trapdoor, it is hard to find a collision, i.e., it is hard to compute two different pairs (u, v) and (u', v') such that $H_k(u, v) = H_k(u', v')$. More precisely, for any polynomial-time adversary $\mathcal{A}$, its advantage $\mathbf{Adv}_{\mathcal{A},\mathcal{H}}^{CR}(1^\kappa)$, defined as

$$\mathbf{Adv}_{\mathcal{A},\mathcal{H}}^{CR}(1^\kappa) = \Pr[H_k(u, v) = H_k(u', v') : (k, td) \xleftarrow{\$} \mathbf{Hgen}(1^\kappa);$$
$$(u, v, u', v') \xleftarrow{\$} \mathcal{A}(H_k)],$$

is negligible.

We generalize the definition of chameleon hash functions by allowing that Eq.(1) holds with overwhelming probability. Then, $\mathcal{H}$ is called a family of *almost-always* chameleon hash functions.

3   Chameleon ABO-TDFs

Chameleon ABO-TDFs is a specific kind of ABO-TDFs with two variable (u, v) as a branch [12]. The chameleon property requires that given any u, it is easy to compute a unique lossy branch (u, v) with the help of a trapdoor. The security requires that without the trapdoor, any lossy branch (u, v_0) and any branch (u, v_1) from the injective branch set are computationally indistinguishable. Meanwhile, given a lossy branch (u, v), it is impossible to generate another lossy branch (u', v') without the trapdoor.

Let $\mathbb{U} \times \mathbb{V} = \{\mathcal{U}_\kappa \times \mathcal{V}_\kappa\}_{\kappa \in \mathbb{N}}$ be a collection of sets whose elements represent the branches.

Definition 4 (Chameleon All-But-One Trapdoor Functions). A collection of (n, k)-chameleon all-but-one trapdoor functions is a 4-tuple of (possibly probabilistic) polynomial-time algorithms $(\mathsf{G}_{ch}, \mathsf{F}_{ch}, \mathsf{F}_{ch}^{-1}, \mathsf{CLB}_{ch})$ such that:

1. **Sampling a Function:** For any $\kappa \in \mathbb{N}$, $\mathsf{G}_{ch}(1^\kappa)$ outputs (i, td, S) where i is a function index, td is the trapdoor and $S \subset \mathcal{U}_\kappa \times \mathcal{V}_\kappa$ is a set of lossy branches. Hereafter we will use $\mathcal{U} \times \mathcal{V}$ instead of $\mathcal{U}_\kappa \times \mathcal{V}_\kappa$ for simplicity.

2. **Evaluation of Injective Functions:** For any $(u, v) \in \mathcal{U} \times \mathcal{V}$, if $(u, v) \notin S$, where $(i, td, S) \leftarrow \mathsf{G}_{ch}(1^\kappa)$, then $\mathsf{F}_{ch}(i, u, v, \cdot)$ computes a (deterministic) injective function $g_{i,u,v}(\cdot)$ over the domain $\{0, 1\}^n$, and $\mathsf{F}_{ch}^{-1}(i, u, v, td, \cdot)$ computes $g_{i,u,v}^{-1}(\cdot)$.

3. **Evaluation of Lossy Functions:** For any $(u, v) \in \mathcal{U} \times \mathcal{V}$, if $(u, v) \in S$, where $(i, td, S) \leftarrow \mathsf{G}_{ch}(1^\kappa)$, then $\mathsf{F}_{ch}(i, u, v, \cdot)$ computes a (deterministic) function $g_{i,u,v}(\cdot)$ over the domain $\{0, 1\}^n$ whose image has size at most 2^{n-k}.

4. **Chameleon Property:** there exists an algorithm CLB_{ch} which, on input the function index i, the trapdoor td and any $u \in \mathcal{U}$, computes a unique $v \in \mathcal{V}$ to result in a lossy branch (u, v). In formula, $v \leftarrow \mathsf{CLB}_{ch}(i, td, u)$ such that $(u, v) \in \mathcal{B}^*$.

5. **Security (1): Indistinguishability between Lossy Branches and Injective Branches.** It is hard to distinguish a lossy branch from an injective branch. Any probabilistic polynomial-time algorithm $\mathcal{A}$ that receives i as input, where $(i, td, S) \leftarrow \mathsf{G}_{ch}(1^\kappa)$, has only a negligible probability of distinguishing a pair $(u, v_0) \in S$ from $(u, v_1) \notin S$, even u is chosen by $\mathcal{A}$. Formally, Let $\mathcal{A}$ be a $\mathsf{CH\text{-}LI}$ distinguisher and define its advantage as

$$\mathsf{Adv}_{\mathcal{A}}^{\mathsf{CH\text{-}LI}}(1^\kappa) = \left| \Pr \left[\beta = \beta' : \begin{array}{c} (i, td, S) \leftarrow \mathsf{G}_{ch}(1^\kappa); u \leftarrow \mathcal{A}(i); \\ v_0 = \mathsf{CLB}_{ch}(i, td, u); v_1 \xleftarrow{\$} \mathcal{V}; \\ \beta \xleftarrow{\$} \{0, 1\}; \beta' \leftarrow \mathcal{A}(i, u, v_\beta) \end{array} \right] - \frac{1}{2} \right|.$$

Given a collection of chameleon all-but-one trapdoor functions, it is hard to distinguish a lossy branch from an injective branch, if $\mathsf{Adv}_{\mathcal{A}}^{\mathsf{CH\text{-}LI}}(\cdot)$ is negligible for every PPT distinguisher $\mathcal{A}$.

6. **Security (2): Hidden Lossy Branches.** It is hard to find one-more lossy branch. Any probabilistic polynomial-time algorithm $\mathcal{A}$ that receives (i, u, v) as input, where $(i, td, S) \leftarrow \mathsf{G}_{ch}(1^\kappa)$ and $(u, v) \xleftarrow{\$} S$, has only a negligible probability of outputting a pair $(u', v') \in S \setminus \{(u, v)\}$.

In the above definition, if $\mathsf{F}_{ch}^{-1}(s, td, u, v, \cdot)$ inverts correctly on all values in the image of $g_{s,u,v}(\cdot)$ with $(u, v) \notin S$, and $\mathsf{CLB}_{ch}(s, td, u)$ outputs v such that $(u, v) \in S$, both *with overwhelming probability*, the collection is called *almost-always* chameleon ABO-TDFs.

4   General Construction of Chameleon ABO-TDFs

Given a family of ABO-TDFs $(\mathsf{G}_{abo}, \mathsf{F}_{abo}, \mathsf{F}_{abo}^{-1})$, we show how to transform it into a family of chameleon ABO-TDFs $(\mathsf{G}_{ch}, \mathsf{F}_{ch}, \mathsf{F}_{ch}^{-1}, \mathsf{CLB}_{ch})$ with the help of a family of chameleon hash functions $(\mathsf{HGen}, H_k, H_k^{-1})$ and possibly a family $\mathcal{T}$ of collision-resistant hash functions. The idea is the integration of the chameleon hash functions into the ABO-TDFs by replacing each branch of an ABO-TDFs with the branch's pre-image in the chameleon hash function. Let $\mathcal{Y}$ be the range of the chameleon hash functions, and $\mathcal{B}$ the branch set of the family of ABO-TDFs. When $\mathcal{Y} \not\subseteq \mathcal{B}$ we still need a family $\mathcal{T}$ of collision-resistant hash functions to map $\mathcal{Y}$ to $\mathcal{B}$.

In the construction of chameleon ABO-TDFs from ABO-TDFs, a family of chameleon hash functions is needed and their input (u, v) serves as the branches of the chameleon ABO-TDFs. With the help of a family of chameleon hash functions $\mathcal{H}$ and a family $\mathcal{T}$ of collision-resistant hash functions, all (u, v) are mapped into branches of an ABO-TDF i.e., $b = T(H_k(u, v)) \in \mathcal{B}$ and $H_k \in \mathcal{H}, T \xleftarrow{\$} \mathcal{T}$. The evaluation of the chameleon ABO-TDF behaves exactly as the

ABO-TDF with $b = T(H_k(u,v))$ as its branch input. Consequently, the set of lossy branches of the chameleon ABO-TDF is made up of the pre-images of all lossy branches of the ABO-TDF, i.e., $\{(u,v) : T(H_k(u,v)) = b^*, b^* \in \mathcal{B}^*\}$, with $\mathcal{B}^*$ the set of lossy branches of the ABO-TDFs. The chameleon property of the chameleon ABO-TDFs inherits from that of chameleon hash functions and the security of the chameleon ABO-TDFs inherits mainly from the security and the property of "hidden lossy branches" of the ABO-TDFs.

Construction 1. *Let* $\left(\mathsf{HGen}, H_k, H_k^{-1}\right)$ *describe a family of chameleon hash functions with* $H_k : \mathcal{U} \times \mathcal{V} \to \mathcal{Y}$, *and* $\left(\mathsf{G}_{abo}, \mathsf{F}_{abo}, \mathsf{F}_{abo}^{-1}\right)$ *describe a family of* (n,k)-*ABO-TDFs with* $\mathcal{B}$ *the set of branches. Let* $\mathcal{T}$ *describe a family of collision-resistant hash functions mapping* $\mathcal{Y}$ *to* $\mathcal{B}$. *Then, a family of* (n,k)-*chameleon ABO-TDFs with branch set* $\mathcal{U} \times \mathcal{V}$ *can be constructed with the following algorithms* $\left(\mathsf{G}_{ch}, \mathsf{F}_{ch}, \mathsf{F}_{ch}^{-1}, \mathsf{CLB}_{ch}\right)$.

Sampling a function $\mathbf{G}_{ch}(1^\kappa)$: *Given a security parameter* $\kappa \in \mathbb{N}$, $T \xleftarrow{\$} \mathcal{T}$, $(k, td_1) \xleftarrow{\$} \boldsymbol{Hgen}(1^\kappa)$, $u^* \xleftarrow{\$} \mathcal{U}$, $v^* \xleftarrow{\$} \mathcal{V}$, *compute* $b^* = T(H_k(u^*, v^*))$. *Sample a function from the ABO-TDFs with* $(i', td_2, \mathcal{B}^*) \leftarrow \mathsf{G}_{abo}(1^\kappa, b^*)$. *Let* $\mathcal{S} = \{(u,v) : T(H_k(u,v)) = b^*, b^* \in \mathcal{B}^*\}$. *Return* $i = (i', H_k, T)$ *as the function index,* $td = (td_1, (u^*, v^*), td_2)$ *as the trapdoor, and* $\mathcal{S}$ *as the set of lossy branches.*

Evaluation of functions: *For all injective branch* (u,v), *define*

$$\mathsf{F}_{ch}(i, u, v, \cdot) := \mathsf{F}_{abo}(i', T(H_k(u,v)), \cdot).$$

Then, $\mathsf{F}_{ch}(i, u, v, \cdot)$ *computes an injective function if* $T(H_k(u,v)) \notin \mathcal{B}^*$, *and a lossy function if* $T(H_k(u,v)) \in \mathcal{B}^*$.

Inversion of injective functions: *On input a function index* i, *a branch* $(u,v) \notin \mathcal{S}$, *the trapdoor* $td = (td_1, (u^*, v^*), td_2)$, *and* $z = \mathsf{F}_{ch}(i, u, v, x)$, *the inverse function returns*

$$\mathsf{F}_{ch}^{-1}(i, u, v, td, z) := \mathsf{F}_{abo}^{-1}(i', T(H_k(u,v)), td_2, z).$$

Chameleon property(Computing a lossy branch): *On input the trapdoor* $td = (td_1, (u^*, v^*), td_2)$, *and* $u' \xleftarrow{\$} \mathcal{U}$, CLB_{ch} *computes* $v' = H_k^{-1}(u^*, v^*, td_1, u')$, *and return* (u', v'). *In formula,*

$$\mathsf{CLB}_{ch}(i, td, u') := H_k^{-1}(u^*, v^*, td_1, u').$$

When the range of the chameleon hash functions falls into the branch set of the ABO-TDFs, i.e, $\mathcal{Y} \subseteq \mathcal{B}$, the family $\mathcal{T}$ of collision-resistant hash functions can be omitted in the construction. We now state the security theorem of the above chameleon ABO-TDFs. The proofs will be given in the full version of the paper.

Theorem 1. *The above general construction of chameleon ABO-TDFs satisfies (1) indistinguishability between lossy branches and injective branches; (2) hidden lossy branches.*

5 Conclusion

In this paper, we showed a black-box construction of chameleon ABO-TDFs, which can transform any ABO-TDFs into chameleon ABO-TDFs with the help of chameleon hash functions, and possibly some collision-resistant hash functions. We can obtain the first chameleon ABO-TDFs based on the DDH assumption by instantiating the construction with the existing ABO-TDFs and chameleon hash functions. According to [12], these chameleon ABO-TDFs imply more efficient black-box construction of CCA-secure PKE in the standard model than that in [18].

Acknowledgement. We are grateful to the anonymous reviewers for their helpful comments. This work is partially funded by National Natural Science Foundation of China (No. 60873229) and Shanghai Rising-star Program (No. 09QA1403000), and also supported in part by A*STAR SERC Grant No. 102 101 0027 in Singapore.

References

1. Bellare, M., Hofheinz, D., Yilek, S.: Possibility and impossibility results for encryption and commitment secure under selective opening. In: Joux, A. (ed.) EUROCRYPT 2009. LNCS, vol. 5479, pp. 1–35. Springer, Heidelberg (2009)
2. Boldyreva, A., Fehr, S., O'Neill, A.: On notions of security for deterministic encryption, and efficient constructions without random oracles. In: Wagner, D. (ed.) CRYPTO 2008. LNCS, vol. 5157, pp. 335–359. Springer, Heidelberg (2008)
3. Boyen, X., Waters, B.: Shrinking the Keys of Discrete-Log-Type Lossy Trapdoor Functions. In: Zhou, J., Yung, M. (eds.) ACNS 2010. LNCS, vol. 6123, pp. 35–52. Springer, Heidelberg (2010)
4. Cachin, C., Micali, S., Stadler, M.A.: Computationally private information retrieval with polylogarithmic communication. In: Stern, J. (ed.) EUROCRYPT 1999. LNCS, vol. 1592, pp. 402–414. Springer, Heidelberg (1999)
5. Damgård, I., Jurik, M.: A generalisation, a simplification and some applications of Paillier's probabilistic public-key system. In: Kim, K.-c. (ed.) PKC 2001. LNCS, vol. 1992, pp. 119–136. Springer, Heidelberg (2001)
6. Freeman, D.M., Goldreich, O., Kiltz, E., Rosen, A., Segev, G.: More constructions of lossy and correlation-secure trapdoor functions. In: Nguyen, P.Q., Pointcheval, D. (eds.) PKC 2010. LNCS, vol. 6056, pp. 279–295. Springer, Heidelberg (2010)
7. Hemenway, B., Ostrovsky, R.: Lossy trapdoor functions from smooth homomorphic hash proof systems. In: ECCC, vol. 16(127) (2009)
8. Hemenway, B., Ostrovsky, R.: Homomorphic Encryption Over Cyclic Groups Implies Chosen-Ciphertext Security. Cryptology ePrint Archive, Report 2010/099 (2010)
9. Kiltz, E., Mohassel, P., O'Neill, A.: Adaptive trapdoor functions and chosen-ciphertext security. In: Gilbert, H. (ed.) EUROCRYPT 2010. LNCS, vol. 6110, pp. 673–692. Springer, Heidelberg (2010)
10. Kiltz, E., O'Neill, A., Smith, A.: Lossiness of RSA and the chosen-plaintext security of OAEP without random oracles (2009) (manuscript)

11. Krawczyk, H., Rabin, T.: Chameleon signatures. In: NDSS 2000. The Internet Society (2000)
12. Lai, J., Deng, R.H., Liu, S.: Chameleon All-But-One TDFs and Their Application to Chosen-Ciphertext Security. In: Catalano, D., Fazio, N., Gennaro, R., Nicolosi, A. (eds.) PKC 2011. LNCS, vol. 6571, pp. 228–245. Springer, Heidelberg (2011)
13. Mohassel, P.: One-time signatures and chameleon hash functions. In: Biryukov, A., Gong, G., Stinson, D.R. (eds.) SAC 2010. LNCS, vol. 6544, pp. 302–319. Springer, Heidelberg (2011)
14. Mol, P., Yilek, S.: Chosen-ciphertext security from slightly lossy trapdoor functions. Cryptology ePrint Archive, Report 2009/524 (2009)
15. Naor, M., Yung, M.: Universal one-way hash functions and their cryptographic applications. In: Proc. of 21st ACM Symposium on the Theory of Computing, pp. 33–43 (1989)
16. Nishimaki, R., Fujisaki, E., Tanaka, K.: Efficient non-interactive universally composable string-commitment schemes. In: Pieprzyk, J., Zhang, F. (eds.) ProvSec 2009. LNCS, vol. 5848, pp. 3–18. Springer, Heidelberg (2009)
17. Peikert, C., Vaikuntanathan, V., Waters, B.: A framework for efficient and composable oblivious transfer. In: Wagner, D. (ed.) CRYPTO 2008. LNCS, vol. 5157, pp. 554–571. Springer, Heidelberg (2008)
18. Peikert, C., Waters, B.: Lossy Trapdoor Functions and Their Applications. In: STOC, pp. 187–196. ACM, New York (2008)
19. Rosen, A., Segev, G.: Chosen-ciphertext security via correlated products. In: Reingold, O. (ed.) TCC 2009. LNCS, vol. 5444, pp. 419–436. Springer, Heidelberg (2009)
20. Shamir, A., Tauman, Y.: Improved online/Offline signature schemes. In: Kilian, J. (ed.) CRYPTO 2001. LNCS, vol. 2139, pp. 355–367. Springer, Heidelberg (2001)
21. Steinfeld, R., Pieprzyk, J., Wang, H.: How to strengthen any weakly unforgeable signature into a strongly unforgeable signature. In: Abe, M. (ed.) CT-RSA 2007. LNCS, vol. 4377, pp. 357–371. Springer, Heidelberg (2006)

PolyE+CTR: A Swiss-Army-Knife Mode for Block Ciphers

Liting Zhang[1], Wenling Wu[1], and Peng Wang[2]

[1] State Key Laboratory of Information Security
Institute of Software, Chinese Academy of Sciences, Beijing 100190, P.R. China
[2] Graduate University of Chinese Academy of Sciences, Beijing 100049, P.R. China
{zhangliting,wwl}@is.iscas.ac.cn, wp@is.ac.cn

Abstract. In this paper, we propose a new kind of mode of operation for block ciphers. By a single key, such a mode can protect data for privacy, authenticity and they both respectively, so we call it Swiss-Army-Knife mode. The purpose of SAK mode is to increase diversity of security services for a single key, thus we can provide different protections for data with different security requirements, without rekeying the underlying block cipher. As an example, we propose PolyE+CTR, an SAK mode that combines an authentication mode PolyE and a nonce-based encryption mode CTR in the authentication-and-encryption method. PolyE+CTR is provably secure with high efficiency.

Keywords: Block Cipher, Mode of Operation, Provable Security.

1 Introduction

Modes of operation for block ciphers are mechanisms that use block ciphers as underlying primitives to provide cryptographic protections for data security. Normally, there are three kinds of them. Authentication modes can protect data authenticity only and they are also called blockcipher-based message authentication codes, e.g. CMAC. Encryption modes can protect data privacy only, e.g. CTR, and authenticated encryption modes can protect data authenticity and data privacy both, e.g. CCM and GCM[1].

CONTRIBUTIONS. In this paper, we propose a new kind of modes of operation that is able to provide three different protections (for data authenticity, data privacy and they both respectively) with a single key, whereas the security of each of them is independent. Alternatively, such a mode can be seen as a combination of an authentication mode Auth, an encryption mode Enc and an authenticated encryption mode AE sharing the same key K. To protect data authenticity, we use Auth_K; to protect data privacy, we use Enc_K; and to protect the both, we use AE_K. With respect to security, these three protections should not only be secure as an individual mode, but also be secure as a whole — that is, they can work safely under the same key, without endangering each other. Due to its

X. Boyen and X. Chen (Eds.): ProvSec 2011, LNCS 6980, pp. 266–280, 2011.

multiple usages, we name such a mode as Swiss-Army-Knife (SAK) mode and will give a specific security definition later.

The target of SAK modes is to increase diversity of security services for a single key, providing optional security protections for different kinds of data. By an SAK, a database operator can use Auth_K to check the authenticity of publicly-known data (dates, room numbers, ...), use Enc_K to protect the privacy of secret data (guest names, ages, ...), and use AE_K to protect some secret and sensitive data (credit card numbers, ...). A mobile phone can ensure the authenticity for today's news by Auth_K, protect the privacy for emails by Enc_K, and protect the both in payments by AE_K. Similarly, a doctor can send his patients' medical records to hospital database by AE_K, and protects his working plans by Auth_K or Enc_K.

COMPARISON. Of course, we can use any Auth_{K_1}, Enc_{K_2} and AE_{K_3} with three independent keys K_1, K_2 and K_3 to do the above things, and we can even get K_1, K_2 and K_3 from a master key K by $K_1 = f_K(1)$, $K_2 = f_K(2)$ and $K_3 = f_K(3)$, where f is a subkey deriving function. Compared with this solution, the SAK mode saves key materials and rekeying for the underlying block ciphers, thus it reduces the burden of key management. Moreover, the SAK mode eliminates the possibility of security risks when two of the three keys are equal, which have been considered in related-mode attacks [18]. Such attacks are possible since some non-cryptographer users may take the same key in different applications.

Another solution is we can always use AE_K to get the protections, regardless of which specific security we need. Compared with this, the SAK mode can save computation load when only authentication or encryption is required, and this is especially desirable in some resource-restricted applications, such like mobile phones and smart cards.

A third substitution is to use tweakable block ciphers [14]. That is, we apply three different tweaks to block ciphers under modes Auth_K, Enc_K and AE_K (with the same key K). By security definition, tweakable block ciphers with the same key but different tweaks should be independently random, so the security of Auth_K, Enc_K and AE_K is equivalent to Auth_{K_1}, Enc_{K_2} and AE_{K_3} with three independent keys on the usual block ciphers. However, note that tweakable block ciphers runs slower than the usual block ciphers, since they are constructed from either iteratively calling the usual block ciphers [14,20] or modifying them by adding tweaks [12,17], such a solution offers lower efficiency.

Due to the advantage of using only one key, the security of SAK mode requires only PRP assumption on its underlying block cipher, this is weaker than both Related-Key PRP and PRP with different keys that the combination of Auth_{K_1}, Enc_{K_2} and AE_{K_3} requires in providing SAK services. Thus, the SAK mode is stronger in this sense. Furthermore, by carefully designing, the SAK modes may run faster or save computational resources, providing high efficiency.

OUR PROPOSAL. As an instance, we propose PolyE+CTR, an SAK mode that is based on an authentication mode PolyE and a nonce-based encryption mode CTR. Its authenticated encryption part is obtained by combining PolyE and

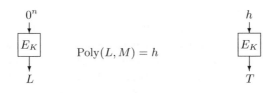

Fig. 1. PolyE+CTR used for Authentication

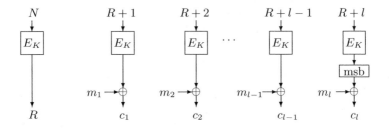

Fig. 2. PolyE+CTR used for Encryption

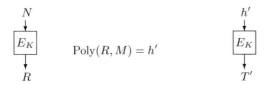

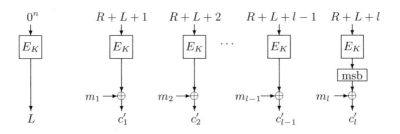

Fig. 3. PolyE+CTR used for Authenticated Encryption

CTR in authentication-and-encryption (A&E) method. See figures 1, 2 and 3 for illustrations.

PolyE takes the hash-then-encrypt strategy — applies a keyed polynomial hash function Poly to messages first, and then uses block cipher E to encrypt the hash values; at last, it outputs the ciphertexts as tags. The hash function key is obtained by $L = E_K(0^n)$. Nonce-based CTR uses $R + 1$ as the initial counter to get long enough random strings, and then outputs the ciphertexts by XORing them to messages, where $R = E_K(N)$ and N is the non-zero nonce that would be used for only once. The A&E method is one of the three generic composition methods used to construct AE modes from Auth and Enc, whose security has been formally discussed by Bellare and Namprempre [5]. Despite of their negative results on it, the A&E method works here because PolyE is PRF-secure and our specific design ensures the whole security.

In the following, we list some distinguishing features of PolyE+CTR,

1. single keyed for three services;
2. highly efficient — this comes from parallel framework of A&E method, parallel structure of CTR and fast implementations for PolyE;
3. PRF-secure in PRP assumption — all the outputs of PolyE+CTR$_E$ are pseudorandom when E is a PseudoRandom Permutation, and the whole security is upper bounded by the normal $O(\sigma^2)/2^n$ bound, where σ is the total number of blocks of all queries;
4. on-line — the mode can start to work without knowing the lengths of messages.
5. no need for blockcipher decryptions;
6. simplicity — in both structure and padding rule, no necessity for encoding messages.

RELATED WORKS. Different variants of the same primitive are usually strongly related, and so is their security under the same key. Thus, to increase diversity of security services (or levels) for a primitive is not an easy task. The authors of block cipher SQUARE used to suggest conservative users increase the number of rounds in a straightforward way without adaptation of key schedule [11], but Wu gave related-cipher attacks to show the security flaws in variants of SQUARE under the same key [23]. Cook et al presented an elastic block cipher that can encrypt plaintexts of lengths from n to $2n$ bits, where n is the block size of a traditional block cipher [10]. However, it is found that their elastic network can not hold pseudorandomness in the elastic applications, and so is their elastic block cipher [24]. A successful case is tweakable block cipher, initially proposed by Liskov, Rivest and Wagner to provide variability for block ciphers without rekeying [14]. Despite of some negative results [8,22], tweakable block ciphers have been widely accepted in the design of block ciphers and modes of operation [12,17,20,6,16].

2   Notations and Security Definitions

2.1   Notations

Denote $\{0,1\}^d$ as the set containing all bit strings of length d, and $\{0,1\}^*$ as the set containing all bit strings. For two bit strings a, b of equal length, $a \oplus b$ stands for their bit-wise XOR. For any two bit strings a and b, $a||b$ is their concatenation. Sometimes we write ab if there is no confusion. "+" and "×" are addition and multiplication operators over $GF(2^n)$ respectively, and we alternatively treat an n-bit string a as a number in $GF(2^n)$. For a bit string $M \in \{0,1\}^*$, $|M|$ stands for its length in bits and $m_1 m_2 \cdots m_l \leftarrow$ **Partition**(M) means we divide M into l successive parts, where $|m_i| = n$ $(1 \leq i < l)$ and $|m_l| \leq n$. For $d \leq |M|$, **msb**(M, d) is the most significant d bits in M. By $K \xleftarrow{\$} \mathcal{K}$ we mean a secret key K is selected from key space $\mathcal{K}$ uniformly at random.

Definition 1. *An SAK mode of operation for block ciphers is a single-keyed mode that can use block ciphers to protect data for privacy, authenticity and they both respectively, whereas the security of these three services are independent.*

2.2 Security Definition for SAK Modes

With a single key, an SAK mode can do the jobs by Auth, Enc and AE together, so its security should be at least as well as the three offers. In the following, we first review security definitions for Auth, Enc and AE respectively, and then combine them together to give a formal security definition for SAK modes.

UNFORGEABILITY FOR AUTH. Given a random key K, the security of Auth_K is evaluated by how unforgeable it is. Normally, an adversary $\mathcal{A}$ has access to $\text{Auth}_K(\cdot)$, and it can query with any message M in Auth's domain, getting the corresponding tag $T \leftarrow \text{Auth}_K(M)$. Finally, $\mathcal{A}$ is asked to make a forgery — output a pair (M', T') such that $T' = \text{Auth}_K(M')$ and M' was never queried to $\text{Auth}_K(\cdot)$ before. $\mathcal{A}$'s advantage is evaluated by $\mathbf{Adv}^{\text{mac}}_{\text{Auth},\mathcal{A}} = \Pr[\mathcal{A} \text{ forges}]$, and the security of Auth is evaluated by $\mathbf{Adv}^{\text{mac}}_{\text{Auth}}(t, q, \mu) = \max_{\mathcal{A}}\{\mathbf{Adv}^{\text{mac}}_{\text{Auth},\mathcal{A}}\}$, where the maximum is taken over all the adversaries spending at most time t, asking at most q queries, whose total length is at most μ bits [4].

INDISTINGUISHABILITY FROM RANDOM BITS UNDER CPA FOR ENC. Here we adopt a strong definition given by Rogaway, which considers the security of nonce-based symmetric encryptions in a setting that the adversaries other than the encryption schemes control the nonces [21]. With a random key K, $\text{Enc}_K(\cdot, \cdot)$ is compared with a random function $R(\cdot, \cdot)$ that for any nonce N and any message M in Enc's domain, $R(N, M)$ is a random string of length $|\text{Enc}_K(N, M)|$. Formally, an oracle $\mathcal{O}(\cdot, \cdot)$ is selected as either $\text{Enc}_K(\cdot, \cdot)$ or $R(\cdot, \cdot)$ with equal probability. A *nonce-respecting* adversary $\mathcal{A}$ (who never repeats a nonce) has access to $\mathcal{O}(\cdot, \cdot)$, and can query it with a new nonce N and any message M in Enc's Domain, getting the corresponding ciphertext $\mathcal{O}(N, M)$. At last, $\mathcal{A}$ is asked to determine $\mathcal{O}(\cdot, \cdot)$ is whether $\text{Enc}_K(\cdot, \cdot)$ or $R(\cdot, \cdot)$. Concretely, $\mathcal{A}$'s advantage is evaluated by $\mathbf{Adv}^{\text{ind\$}}_{\text{Enc},\mathcal{A}} = |\Pr[\mathcal{A}^{\text{Enc}_K(\cdot,\cdot)} = 1] - \Pr[\mathcal{A}^{R(\cdot,\cdot)} = 1]|$, and the security of Enc is evaluated by $\mathbf{Adv}^{\text{ind\$}}_{\text{Enc}}(t, q, \mu) = \max_{\mathcal{A}}\{\mathbf{Adv}^{\text{ind\$}}_{\text{Enc},\mathcal{A}}\}$, where the maximum is taken over all the adversaries spending at most time t, asking at most q queries with total length at most μ bits.

SECURITY FOR AE. Since it can provide both privacy and authenticity protections, the security of AE is usually defined in two aspects. Formally, an oracle $\mathcal{O}(\cdot, \cdot)$ is selected as $\text{AE}_K(\cdot, \cdot)$ or $R(\cdot, \cdot)$ with equal probability. Here, $R(\cdot, \cdot)$ is a random function that for any nonce N and any message M in AE's domain, $R(N, M)$ is a random string of length $|AE_K(N, M)|$ (the total length of ciphertext and tag). A *nonce-respecting* adversary $\mathcal{A}$ has access to $\mathcal{O}(\cdot, \cdot)$, and can query it with a new nonce N and any message M in AE's Domain, getting the corresponding ciphertext and tag by $\mathcal{O}(N, M)$. With respect to privacy, we define it in a similar way as we defined for Enc, i.e. $\mathbf{Adv}_{AE}^{priv}(t, q, \mu) = \mathbf{Adv}_{AE}^{ind\$}(t', q, \mu')$, except that here $\mathcal{A}$ can get not only the ciphertexts but also the tags. With respect to authenticity, the definition is also similar, i.e. $\mathbf{Adv}_{AE}^{auth}(t, q, \mu) = \mathbf{Adv}_{AE}^{mac}(t', q, \mu')$. Here, $\mathcal{A}$ can get not only the ciphertexts but also the tags, and $\mathcal{A}$ has to make a forgery (N', M', T') against $AE_K(\cdot, \cdot)$, where $T' = AE_K(N', M')$ and (N', M') was never queried to $AE_K(\cdot, \cdot)$ before. Notice that N' in the forgery is not necessarily an un-used nonce — the forgery may still be valid even if N' collides with a nonce used in the previous queries.

SECURITY FOR SAK. Base on the above, we give a security definition for a nonce-based SAK mode $F(\text{Auth}, \text{Enc}, \text{AE}) : \mathcal{K} \times \text{Nonce} \times \text{Domain} \to \text{Nonce} \times \text{Auth\_Tags} \times \text{Enc\_Ciphertexts} \times \text{AE\_Tags} \times \text{AE\_Ciphertexts}$, which consists of three modes Auth, Enc and AE. $F(\text{Auth}, \text{Enc}, \text{AE})$ will be compared with a set of random functions $R(R_{\text{Auth}}, R_{\text{Enc}}, R_{\text{AE}})$, where $R_{\text{Auth}}, R_{\text{Enc}}, R_{\text{AE}}$ are three independently random functions. The basic idea is, for any *nonce-respecting* adversary $\mathcal{A}$ making a query $N \in \text{Nonce}$ and $M \in \text{Domain}$, we let it get all the outputs from $\text{Auth}_K(\cdot, \cdot)$, $\text{Enc}_K(\cdot, \cdot)$ and $AE_K(\cdot, \cdot)$. After querying some times, $\mathcal{A}$ is asked to make a distinguishing attack against $\text{Enc}_K(\cdot, \cdot)$ from $R_{\text{Enc}}(\cdot, \cdot)$, or $AE_K(\cdot, \cdot)$ from $R_{\text{AE}}(\cdot, \cdot)$, or make a forgery attack against either $\text{Auth}_K(\cdot, \cdot)$ or $AE_K(\cdot, \cdot)$. The forgery attempt is allowed for only once. Formally, consider the following experiments.

With respect to privacy, we define two experiments as follows,

Experiment $\mathbf{Exp}_{F,\mathcal{A}}^{\text{sak}-\text{priv}-1}$

$\quad K \xleftarrow{\$} \mathcal{K}$;

$\quad$ if $\mathcal{A}$ makes the i-th query (N^i, M^i), do

$\quad\quad$ return $T^i \leftarrow \text{Auth}_K(N^i, M^i)$ to $\mathcal{A}$;

$\quad\quad$ return $C^i \leftarrow \text{Enc}_K(N^i, M^i)$ to $\mathcal{A}$;

$\quad\quad$ return $(T'^i, C'^i) \leftarrow AE_K(N^i, M^i)$ to $\mathcal{A}$;

$\quad$ until $\mathcal{A}$ stops and outputs d, return d.

and

Experiment $\mathbf{Exp}_{F,\mathcal{A}}^{\text{sak}-\text{priv}-0}$

$\quad$ if $\mathcal{A}$ makes the i-th query (N^i, M^i), do

$\quad\quad$ return $T^i \leftarrow R_{\text{Auth}}(N^i, M^i)$ to $\mathcal{A}$;

$\quad\quad$ return $C^i \leftarrow R_{\text{Enc}}(N^i, M^i)$ to $\mathcal{A}$;

$\quad\quad$ return $(T'^i, C'^i) \leftarrow R_{\text{AE}}(N^i, M^i)$ to $\mathcal{A}$;

$\quad$ until $\mathcal{A}$ stops and outputs d, return d.

Then let

$$\begin{cases} \mathbf{Adv}_{F,\mathcal{A}}^{\text{sak}-\text{priv}} = |\Pr[\mathbf{Exp}_{F,\mathcal{A}}^{\text{sak}-\text{priv}-1} = 1] - \Pr[\mathbf{Exp}_{F,\mathcal{A}}^{\text{sak}-\text{priv}-0} = 1]|, \\ \mathbf{Adv}_F^{\text{sak}-\text{priv}}(t, q, \mu) = \max_{\mathcal{A}}\{\mathbf{Adv}_{F,\mathcal{A}}^{\text{sak}-\text{priv}}\}, \end{cases}$$

where the maximum is taken over all the adversaries spending at most time t, asking at most q queries with total length at most μ bits.

With respect to authenticity, we define

Experiment $\mathbf{Exp}_{F,\mathcal{A}}^{\text{sak}-\text{auth}}$

$K \xleftarrow{\$} \mathcal{K}$;

if $\mathcal{A}$ makes the i-th query (N^i, M^i), do

$\qquad T^i \leftarrow \text{Auth}_K(N^i, M^i)$; return T^i to $\mathcal{A}$;

$\qquad C^i \leftarrow \text{Enc}_K(N^i, M^i)$; return C^i to $\mathcal{A}$;

$\qquad (T'^i, C'^i) \leftarrow \text{AE}_K(N^i, M^i)$; return (T'^i, C'^i) to $\mathcal{A}$;

until $\mathcal{A}$ stops and forges against either $\text{Auth}_K(\cdot, \cdot)$ *or* $\text{AE}_K(\cdot, \cdot)$;

if the forgery is valid, then return 1 else return 0.

Let

$$\begin{cases} \mathbf{Adv}_{F,\mathcal{A}}^{\text{sak}-\text{auth}} = \Pr[\mathbf{Exp}_{F,\mathcal{A}}^{\text{sak}-\text{auth}} = 1], \\ \mathbf{Adv}_{F}^{\text{sak}-\text{auth}}(t', q', \mu') = \max_{\mathcal{A}} \{ \mathbf{Adv}_{F,\mathcal{A}}^{\text{sak}-\text{auth}} \}, \end{cases}$$

where the maximum is taken over all the adversaries spending at most time t', asking at most q' queries with total length at most μ' bits.

If both $\mathbf{Adv}_{F}^{\text{sak}-\text{priv}}(t, q, \mu)$ and $\mathbf{Adv}_{F}^{\text{sak}-\text{auth}}(t', q', \mu')$ are sufficiently small, we say the nonce-based SAK mode $F(\text{Auth}, \text{Enc}, \text{AE})$ is secure.

Here, to make up a secure SAK mode, Auth has to be PRF-secure, otherwise adversaries may break the privacy against $\text{Enc}_K(\cdot, \cdot)$ or $\text{AE}_K(\cdot, \cdot)$ by the outputs from $\text{Auth}_K(\cdot, \cdot)$. Similarly, the tags from $\text{AE}_K(\cdot, \cdot)$ also have to be PRF-secure. According to the analysis in [3], PRF-secure tags achieve both integrity for plaintexts (INT-PTXT) and integrity for ciphertexts (INT-CTXT). PRF security has been common since many MACs are proved to reach such a level when their underlying primitives are pseudorandom, like HMAC [2], PMAC [9] and OMAC [13].

There are some other security definitions for Auth, Enc and AE respectively, so readers can make another security definition for their SAK by combining them together, on the condition that SAK should be keyed for only once.

3   Specification of PolyE+CTR

PolyE+CTR is a nonce-based SAK mode for block cipher E, and its key space equals to E's key space, i.e. $\mathcal{K} = \mathcal{K}_E$. By a random key $K \xleftarrow{\$} \mathcal{K}$ and a new *non-zero* nonce $N \in \{0,1\}^n \backslash \{0^n\}$, it can deal with any message $M \in \{0,1\}^*$, outputting the ciphertext $C \in \{0,1\}^{|M|}$ and tag $T \in \{0,1\}^n$. Concretely, PolyE+CTR is defined as in Fig. 4, and its Poly and CTR parts are defined in Fig. 5.

It should be noted that not only the key K, but also the values L, R and h should be carefully stored in secrecy. By properly selecting parameters, the polynomial hash function Poly can reach very high speed [7].

There are some circumstances that message M (needs authenticated encryption) is associated with extra data A (only needs authentication other than encryption) [19]. To adopt this, we can just put $A\|M$ into the authentication part

for Authentication	
Tag Generation	Tag Verification
Input: plaintext $M \in \{0,1\}^*$.	**Input:** plaintext $M \in \{0,1\}^*$, tag $\overline{T} \in \{0,1\}^n$.
01. $L \leftarrow E_K(0^n)$;	01. $L \leftarrow E_K(0^n)$;
02. $h \leftarrow \mathrm{Poly}(L, M)$;	02. $h \leftarrow \mathrm{Poly}(L, M)$;
03. $T \leftarrow E_K(h)$;	03. $T \leftarrow E_K(h)$;
04. **return** T.	04. if $\overline{T} = T$ **return** 1 else **return** 0.

for Encryption	
Encryption	Decryption
Input: nonce $N \in \{0,1\}^n \setminus \{0^n\}$	**Input:** nonce $N \in \{0,1\}^n \setminus \{0^n\}$.
plaintext $M \in \{0,1\}^*$.	ciphertext $C \in \{0,1\}^*$.
01. $R \leftarrow E_K(N)$;	01. $R \leftarrow E_K(N)$;
02. $\mathrm{KS} \leftarrow \mathrm{CTR}(R, |M|)$;	02. $\mathrm{KS} \leftarrow \mathrm{CTR}(R, |C|)$;
03. $C \leftarrow \mathrm{KS} \oplus M$;	03. $M \leftarrow \mathrm{KS} \oplus C$;
04. **return** N, C.	04. **return** M.

for Authenticated Encryption	
Encryption	Decryption
Input: nonce $N \in \{0,1\}^n \setminus \{0^n\}$	**Input:** nonce $N \in \{0,1\}^n \setminus \{0^n\}$, tag $\overline{T'} \in \{0,1\}^n$.
plaintext $M \in \{0,1\}^*$.	ciphertext $C' \in \{0,1\}^*$.
01. $L \leftarrow E_K(0^n)$;	01. $L \leftarrow E_K(0^n)$;
02. $R \leftarrow E_K(N)$;	02. $R \leftarrow E_K(N)$;
03. $h' \leftarrow \mathrm{Poly}(R, M)$;	03. $h' \leftarrow \mathrm{Poly}(R, M)$;
04. $T' \leftarrow E_K(h')$;	04. $T' \leftarrow E_K(h')$;
05. $\mathrm{KS}' \leftarrow \mathrm{CTR}(R + L, |M|)$;	05. $\mathrm{KS}' \leftarrow \mathrm{CTR}(R + L, |C'|)$;
06. $C' \leftarrow \mathrm{KS}' \oplus M$;	06. $M \leftarrow \mathrm{KS}' \oplus C'$;
07. **return** N, T', C'.	07. if $\overline{T'} = T'$ **return** M else **return** $\perp$.

Fig. 4. Specification of PolyE+CTR

Poly(S, M)	CTR(Counter, Length)
01. $M \leftarrow M \| 10^{n-1-(|M| \bmod n)}$;	01. $l \leftarrow \lceil \mathrm{Length}/n \rceil$;
02. $m_1 m_2 \cdots m_l \leftarrow \mathbf{Partition}(M)$;	02. **for** $i \leftarrow 1$ **to** l **do**
03. $h \leftarrow S$;	03. $\mathrm{KS}_i \leftarrow E_K(\mathrm{Counter} + i)$;
04. **for** $i \leftarrow 1$ **to** l **do**	04. **end for**
05. $h \leftarrow (h + m_i) \times S$;	05. $\mathrm{KS} \leftarrow \mathrm{KS}_1 \| \mathrm{KS}_2 \| \cdots \| \mathrm{KS}_l$;
06. **end for**	06. $\mathrm{KS} \leftarrow \mathrm{msb}(\mathrm{KS}, \mathrm{Length})$;
07. **return** h.	07. **return** KS.

Fig. 5. Specifications of Poly and CTR

(PolyE), and put M into the encryption part (CTR). In such a case, the outputs consist of the extra data A, the tag T and the ciphertext C. For convenience of decryption, these three values should be easy to distinguish in transition.

4   Security Analysis of PolyE+CTR

Now we prove the sak-security of PolyE+CTR. First, we give a information-theoretic result saying that PolyE+CTR$_P$ is sak-secure, where P is a random permutation over $\{0,1\}^n$. Concretely, we have

Theorem 1. *For any nonce-respecting adversary making at most q queries with total length no more than $\sigma < 2^{\frac{n-7}{2}}$ blocks, whose forgery length is no more than σ blocks, we have*

$$
\begin{cases}
\mathbf{Adv}^{\mathrm{sak-priv}}_{\mathrm{PolyE+CTR}_P} \leq \frac{10\sigma^2+40q\sigma+23q^2+4\sigma+9q}{2^{n+1}}, \\
\mathbf{Adv}^{\mathrm{sak-auth}}_{\mathrm{PolyE+CTR}_P} \leq \frac{48\sigma^2+80q\sigma+23q^2+84\sigma+55q+34}{2^{n+1}}.
\end{cases}
$$

Proof. For any *nonce-respecting* adversary, suppose it makes q queries (N^1, M^1), (N^2, M^2), $\cdots$, (N^q, M^q), where $N^i \in \{0,1\}^n \setminus \{0^n\}$, $N^i \neq N^j$ and $M^i \in \{0,1\}^*$ for $1 \leq i < j \leq q$. Without loss of generality, we assume $M^i = M^i_1 \| M^i_2 \| \cdots \| M^i_{l_i}$ with $|M^i_j| = n$ $(1 \leq j < l_i)$ and $|M^i_{l_i}| \leq n$. Let g be a random function from $\{0,1\}^n$ to $\{0,1\}^n$ and PolyE+CTR$_g$ denotes for PolyE+CTR with underlying primitive g.

We first prove that by the help of nonce and our "Secret Values Sharing" trick, the inputs to g have a sufficiently small probability to collide, so the outputs from g have a close-to-1 probability to be random bits. Notice that all the inputs to g are included in one of the following sets,

1. $\mathrm{Set}_1 = \{0^n\}$;
2. $\mathrm{Set}_2 = \{N^i, 1 \leq i \leq q\}$;
3. $\mathrm{Set}_3 = \{h^i = \mathrm{Poly}(L, M^i), 1 \leq i \leq q\}$;
4. $\mathrm{Set}_4 = \{h'^i = \mathrm{Poly}(R^i, M^i), 1 \leq i \leq q\}$;
5. $\mathrm{Set}_5 = \{R^i + j, 1 \leq i \leq q, 1 \leq j \leq l_i\}$;
6. $\mathrm{Set}_6 = \{R^i + L + j, 1 \leq i \leq q, 1 \leq j \leq l_i\}$.

Since $N^i \in \{0,1\}^n \setminus \{0^n\}$ and $N^i \neq N^j$ for $1 \leq i < j \leq q$, we directly have the elements in Set_1 and Set_2 are pairwise distinct. Furthermore, we hope $L = g(0^n)$ satisfies the following two conditions,

1. $\mathrm{Poly}(L, M^i) \notin \mathrm{Set}_1 \cup \mathrm{Set}_2$, $1 \leq i \leq q$;
2. $R^i + j1 \neq R^i + L + j2$, $1 \leq i \leq q$, $1 \leq j1, j2 \leq l_i$.

The above two conditions imply $q(q+1)$ and $\sum_{i=1}^q l_i^2$ inequalities about L respectively. Solving these inequalities, we get there are at least $2^n - \sum_{i=1}^q ((l_i + 2)(q + 1) + l_i^2)$ L making them hold. Since g is a random function and $L = g(0^n)$, the probability of the above two conditions hold is at least $1 - \frac{\sum_{i=1}^q ((l_i+2)(q+1)+l_i^2)}{2^n}$. The following analysis is based on this event occurs. For $R^1 = g(N^1)$, we hope it satisfies

1. $\mathrm{Poly}(R^1, M^i) \notin \mathrm{Set}_1 \cup \mathrm{Set}_2 \cup \mathrm{Set}_3$, $1 \leq i \leq q$;
2. $R^1 + j \notin \mathrm{Set}_1 \cup \mathrm{Set}_2 \cup \mathrm{Set}_3$, $1 \leq i \leq q$, $1 \leq j \leq l_1$;
3. $R^1 + L + j \notin \mathrm{Set}_1 \cup \mathrm{Set}_2 \cup \mathrm{Set}_3$, $1 \leq i \leq q$, $1 \leq j \leq l_1$;

4. $\mathrm{Poly}(R^1, M^1) \notin \{R^1 + j, 1 \leq j \leq l_1\} \cup \{R^1 + L + j, 1 \leq j \leq l_1\}$.

The above four conditions imply $2q+1$, $(2q+1)l_1$, $(2q+1)l_1$ and $2l_1$ inequalities about R^1 respectively. Solving these inequalities, we get there are at least $2^n - (l_1 + 2)(2q + 1) + (2q + 1)l_1 + (2q + 1)l_1 + 2l_1(l_1 + 2)$ R^1 making them hold. Since g is a random function and $R^1 = g(N^1)$, the probability of the above four conditions hold is at least $1 - \frac{(2q+1)(3l_1+2)+2l_1(l_1+2)}{2^n}$. The following analysis is based on this event occurs.

Similarly, for $R^i = g(N^i)$, we hope it satisfies

1. $\mathrm{Poly}(R^i, M^i) \notin \mathrm{Set}_1 \cup \mathrm{Set}_2 \cup \mathrm{Set}_3$;
2. $R^i + j \notin \mathrm{Set}_1 \cup \mathrm{Set}_2 \cup \mathrm{Set}_3, 1 \leq j \leq l_i$;
3. $R^i + L + j \notin \mathrm{Set}_1 \cup \mathrm{Set}_2 \cup \mathrm{Set}_3, 1 \leq j \leq l_i$;
4. $\mathrm{Poly}(R^i, M^i) \notin \{R^i + j\} \cup \{R^i + L + j\}, 1 \leq j \leq l_i$;
5. $\mathrm{Poly}(R^i, M^i) \notin \mathrm{Set}_7$;
6. $R^i + j \notin \mathrm{Set}_7, 1 \leq j \leq l_i$;
7. $R^i + L + j \notin \mathrm{Set}_7, 1 \leq j \leq l_i$;

where $\mathrm{Set}_7 = \{\mathrm{Poly}(R^u, M^u), 1 \leq u < i\} \cup \{R^u + v, 1 \leq u < i, 1 \leq v \leq l_u\} \cup \{R^u + L + v, 1 \leq u < i, 1 \leq v \leq l_u\}$. The above seven conditions imply $2q+1$, $(2q+1)l_i$, $(2q+1)l_i$, $2l_i$, $(i-1)+2(l_1+l_2+\cdots+l_{i-1})$, $l_i((i-1)+2(l_1+l_2+\cdots+l_{i-1}))$ and $l_i((i-1)+2(l_1+l_2+\cdots+l_{i-1}))$ inequalities about R^i respectively. Solving these inequalities, we get there are at least $2^n - (l_i+2)(2q+1) + (2q+1)l_i + (2q+1)l_i + 2l_i(l_i+2) + (l_i+2)((i-1)+2(l_1+l_2+\cdots+l_{i-1})) + l_i((i-1)+2(l_1+l_2+\cdots+l_{i-1})) + l_i((i-1)+2(l_1+l_2+\cdots+l_{i-1}))$ R^i making them hold. Since g is a random function and $R^i = g(N^i)$, the probability of the above seven conditions hold is at least $1 - \frac{(3l_i+2)(2q+i+2(l_1+l_2+\cdots+l_{i-1}))+2l_i(l_i+2)}{2^n}$. The following analysis is based on this event occurs until we finish evaluating $R^q = g(N^q)$.

Denote NoColl_q as the event that all the inputs to g are distinct. Then, the probability for NoColl_q to occur is at least

$$
\begin{aligned}
\Pr[\mathrm{NoColl}_q] &\geq (1 - \frac{\sum_{i=1}^{q}((l_i+2)(q+1)+l_i^2)}{2^n}) \\
&\times \prod_{i=1}^{q}(1 - \frac{(3l_i+2)(2q+i+2\sum_{j=1}^{i-1} l_j)+2l_i(l_i+2)}{2^n}) \\
&\geq 1 - \frac{3\sigma^2 + 14q\sigma + 7q^2 + \sigma + 3q}{2^n},
\end{aligned}
$$

where $\sigma = l_1 + l_2 + \cdots + l_q$.

Then, for the privacy of $\mathrm{Poly+CTR}_g$, we have

$$
\begin{aligned}
\mathbf{Adv}_{\mathrm{PolyE+CTR}_g}^{\mathrm{sak-priv}} &= |\Pr[\mathbf{Exp}_{\mathrm{PolyE+CTR}_g}^{\mathrm{sak-priv-1}} = 1] - \Pr[\mathbf{Exp}_{\mathrm{PolyE+CTR}_g}^{\mathrm{sak-priv-0}} = 1]| \\
&= |\Pr[\mathbf{Exp}_{\mathrm{PolyE+CTR}_g}^{\mathrm{sak-priv-1}} = 1 \cap \mathrm{NoColl}_q] \\
&\quad + \Pr[\mathbf{Exp}_{\mathrm{PolyE+CTR}_g}^{\mathrm{sak-priv-1}} = 1 \cap \overline{\mathrm{NoColl}_q}] \\
&\quad - \Pr[\mathbf{Exp}_{\mathrm{PolyE+CTR}_g}^{\mathrm{sak-priv-0}} = 1 \cap \mathrm{NoColl}_q] \\
&\quad - \Pr[\mathbf{Exp}_{\mathrm{PolyE+CTR}_g}^{\mathrm{sak-priv-0}} = 1 \cap \overline{\mathrm{NoColl}_q}]|.
\end{aligned}
$$

Notice that when NoColl_q happens, all the outputs of Poly+CTR_g are random bits because g is a random function from $\{0,1\}^n$ to $\{0,1\}^n$. So we have $\Pr[\mathbf{Exp}_{\text{PolyE+CTR}_g}^{\text{sak-priv-1}} = 1|\text{NoColl}_q] - \Pr[\mathbf{Exp}_{\text{PolyE+CTR}_g}^{\text{sak-priv-0}} = 1|\text{NoColl}_q] = 0$, which implies $\Pr[\mathbf{Exp}_{\text{PolyE+CTR}_g}^{\text{sak-priv-1}} = 1 \cap \text{NoColl}_q] - \Pr[\mathbf{Exp}_{\text{PolyE+CTR}_g}^{\text{sak-priv-0}} = 1 \cap \text{NoColl}_q] = 0$.

According to this, the following holds,

$$
\begin{aligned}
\mathbf{Adv}_{\text{PolyE+CTR}_g}^{\text{sak-priv}} &= |\Pr[\mathbf{Exp}_{\text{PolyE+CTR}_g}^{\text{sak-priv-1}} = 1 \cap \overline{\text{NoColl}_q}] \\
&\quad - \Pr[\mathbf{Exp}_{\text{PolyE+CTR}_g}^{\text{sak-priv-0}} = 1 \cap \overline{\text{NoColl}_q}]| \\
&\leq \Pr[\overline{\text{NoColl}_q}] \\
&\leq \frac{3\sigma^2 + 14q\sigma + 7q^2 + \sigma + 3q}{2^n}.
\end{aligned}
$$

Next, applying the PRP/PRF switching lemma [4] and notice that we have called the underlying primitive of PolyE+CTR for $2\sigma + 3q + 1$ times, we get

$$
\mathbf{Adv}_{\text{PolyE+CTR}_P}^{\text{sak-priv}} \leq \frac{10\sigma^2 + 40q\sigma + 23q^2 + 4\sigma + 9q}{2^{n+1}}.
$$

With respect to authenticity, we consider the following three cases:

1. the adversary makes a forgery (M', T') against $\text{Auth}_K(\cdot)$, the authentication part of $\text{PolyE} + \text{CTR}_g$, where $M' \notin \{M^1, M^2, \cdots, M^q\}$;
2. the adversary makes a forgery (N', M', T') against $\text{AE}_K(\cdot, \cdot)$, the authenticated encryption part of $\text{PolyE} + \text{CTR}_g$, where $N' \notin \{N^1, N^2, \cdots, N^q\}$;
3. the adversary makes a forgery (N', M', T') against $\text{AE}_K(\cdot, \cdot)$, where $N' \in \{N^1, N^2, \cdots, N^q\}$.

Without loss of generality, we assume M' has c blocks.

For the first two cases, we treat M' as the $q + 1^{\text{th}}$ query in the analysis. Concretely, in the first case, we select any $N'' \notin \{N^1, N^2, \cdots, N^q\}$, and put (N'', M') into $\text{PolyE} + \text{CTR}_g$; in the second case, we directly put (N', M') into $\text{PolyE} + \text{CTR}_g$. Denote NoColl_{q+1} as the event that all the inputs to g are distinct. Then, according to the previous analysis, the probability for NoColl_{q+1} to occur is at least

$$
\begin{aligned}
\Pr[\text{NoColl}_{q+1}] &\geq (1 - \frac{\sum_{i=1}^{q+1}((l_i + 2)(q+1) + l_i^2)}{2^n}) \\
&\quad \times \prod_{i=1}^{q+1}(1 - \frac{(3l_i + 2)(2q + i + 2\sum_{j=1}^{i-1} l_j) + 2l_i(l_i + 2)}{2^n}) \\
&\geq 1 - \frac{3\tilde{\sigma}^2 + 14\tilde{q}\tilde{\sigma} + 7\tilde{q}^2 + \tilde{\sigma} + 3\tilde{q}}{2^n},
\end{aligned}
$$

where $\tilde{\sigma} = \sigma + c$ and $\tilde{q} = q + 1$.

Notice that NoColl_{q+1} occurs implies all the outputs of g in $\text{PolyE} + \text{CTR}_g$ are random bits, and we have no restriction on the $q + 1^{\text{th}}$ query M' — this implies, for any $q + 1^{\text{th}}$ message (including the forgery made by the adversary), the following holds,

$$
\begin{aligned}
\mathbf{Adv}^{\text{sak-auth}}_{\text{PolyE+CTR}_g} &= \Pr[\mathbf{Exp}^{\text{sak-auth}}_{\text{PolyE+CTR}_g} = 1] \\
&= \Pr[\mathbf{Exp}^{\text{sak-auth}}_{\text{PolyE+CTR}_g} = 1 \cap \text{NoColl}_{q+1}] \\
&\quad + \Pr[\mathbf{Exp}^{\text{sak-auth}}_{\text{PolyE+CTR}_g} = 1 \cap \overline{\text{NoColl}_{q+1}}] \\
&\leq \frac{1}{2^n} + \Pr[\overline{\text{NoColl}_{q+1}}] \\
&\leq \frac{3\tilde{\sigma}^2 + 14\tilde{q}\tilde{\sigma} + 7\tilde{q}^2 + \tilde{\sigma} + 3\tilde{q} + 1}{2^n},
\end{aligned}
\tag{1}
$$

where inequality (1) is obtained by the relationship between MAC and PRF [4], and notice that here adversary is allowed to make a forgery against either $\text{Auth}_K(\cdot, \cdot)$ or $\text{AE}_K(\cdot, \cdot)$ for only once.

For the third case, without loss of generality, we assume $N' = N^q$. Of course, this implies $M' \neq M^q$. For any such pair (N', M'), we start by re-evaluating $R^q = g(N^q)$ and show that the probability for the outputs of $\text{PolyE} + \text{CTR}_g$ are random strings is still close to 1.

We select $L = g(0^n)$ and $R^i = g(N^i)$ for $1 \leq i \leq q - 1$ as before, and require $R^q = g(N^q)$ to satisfy the following conditions,

1. $\text{Poly}(R^q, M^q) \notin \text{Set}_1 \cup \text{Set}_2 \cup \text{Set}_3$;
2. $R^q + j \notin \text{Set}_1 \cup \text{Set}_2 \cup \text{Set}_3$, $1 \leq j \leq l_q$;
3. $R^q + L + j \notin \text{Set}_1 \cup \text{Set}_2 \cup \text{Set}_3$, $1 \leq j \leq l_q$;
4. $\text{Poly}(R^q, M^q) \notin \{R^q + j\} \cup \{R^q + L + j\}$, $1 \leq j \leq l_q$;
5. $\text{Poly}(R^q, M^q) \notin \text{Set}_7$;
6. $R^q + j \notin \text{Set}_7$, $1 \leq j \leq l_q$;
7. $R^q + L + j \notin \text{Set}_7$, $1 \leq j \leq l_q$;
8. $\text{Poly}(R^q, M') \notin \text{Set}_1 \cup \text{Set}_2 \cup \text{Set}_3$;
9. $\text{Poly}(R^q, M') \notin \{R^q + j\} \cup \{R^q + L + j\}$, $1 \leq j \leq l_q$;
10. $\text{Poly}(R^q, M') \neq \text{Poly}(R^q, M^q)$;
11. $\text{Poly}(R^q, M') \notin \text{Set}_7$.

The last four requirements ensure that $\overline{h}' = \text{Poly}(R^q, M')$ is a new input to random function g, then its output (T' corresponding to N' and M') would be random.

Due to the last 4 conditions, the above 11 conditions imply at most $(2q + 1)(c + 2) + 2l_q(c + 2) + 1 \times \max\{c + 2, l_q + 2\} + ((q - 1) + 2 \sum_{j=1}^{q-1} l_j)(c + 2) = (c+2)(3q+2\sigma) + \max\{c+2, l_q+2\}$ more bad points than the previous evaluation of R^q in privacy analysis. Denote NoColl' as the event that in q queries, all the inputs to g are distinct and in the forgery, $\overline{h}'$ is a new input to g. Assuming $c \leq \sigma$, then the probability for NoColl' to occur is at least

$$
\begin{aligned}
\Pr[\text{NoColl}'] &\geq \Pr[\text{NoColl}_q] \times (1 - \frac{(c+2)(3q+2\sigma) + \sigma + 2}{2^n}) \\
&\geq 1 - \frac{5\sigma^2 + 17q\sigma + 7q^2 + 6\sigma + 9q + 2}{2^n}.
\end{aligned}
$$

Similar as before, in such a case we have

$$\mathbf{Adv}_{\mathrm{PolyE+CTR}_g}^{\mathrm{sak-auth}} = \Pr[\mathbf{Exp}_{\mathrm{PolyE+CTR}_g}^{\mathrm{sak-auth}} = 1]$$

$$\leq \frac{1}{2^n} + \Pr[\overline{\mathrm{NoColl'}}]$$

$$\leq \frac{5\sigma^2 + 17q\sigma + 7q^2 + 6\sigma + 9q + 3}{2^n}.$$

Comparing the above with the results of the first two cases and assuming $c \leq \sigma$, we finally get $\mathbf{Adv}_{\mathrm{PolyE+CTR}_g}^{\mathrm{sak-auth}} \leq \frac{16\sigma^2 + 28q\sigma + 7q^2 + 28\sigma + 17q + 11}{2^n}$. Then, applying the PRP/PRF switching lemma [4] and notice that we have called the underlying primitive of PolyE+CTR for no more than $4\sigma + 3q + 4$ times, we get $\mathbf{Adv}_{\mathrm{PolyE+CTR}_P}^{\mathrm{sak-auth}} \leq \frac{48\sigma^2 + 80q\sigma + 23q^2 + 84\sigma + 55q + 34}{2^{n+1}}$. □

If we replace the random permutation P by a PRP-secure block cipher E, the following complexity-theoretic result holds,

Theorem 2. *If $E : \mathcal{K}_E \times \{0,1\}^n \to \{0,1\}^n$ is a PRP-secure block cipher, then for any nonce-respecting adversary making at most q queries with total length no more than $\sigma < 2^{\frac{n-7}{2}}$ blocks, whose forgery length is no more than σ blocks, we have*

$$\begin{cases} \mathbf{Adv}_{\mathrm{PolyE+CTR}_E}^{\mathrm{sak-priv}}(t,q,\mu) \leq \frac{10\sigma^2 + 40q\sigma + 23q^2 + 4\sigma + 9q}{2^{n+1}} + \mathbf{Adv}_E^{\mathrm{PRP}}(t',q',\mu'), \\ \mathbf{Adv}_{\mathrm{PolyE+CTR}_E}^{\mathrm{sak-auth}}(t,q,\mu) \leq \frac{48\sigma^2 + 80q\sigma + 23q^2 + 84\sigma + 55q + 34}{2^{n+1}} + \mathbf{Adv}_E^{\mathrm{PRP}}(t'',q'',\mu''), \end{cases}$$

where $t' = O(t)$, $t'' = O(t)$, $q' = 2\sigma + 3q + 1$, $q'' = 4\sigma + 3q + 4$, $\mu' = \mu + O(q)$ and $\mu' = \mu + O(q)$.

5   Comparison to Current Modes

To provide authentication, encryption or authenticated encryption, many modes of operation for block ciphers have been designed; however, their functionalities are limited to only one of the three. The SAK mode is the first that can provide different functionalities with a single key.

McGrew and Viega propose an AE mode GCM [15], which also combines PolyE and CTR, but in the encryption-then-authentication method. Furthermore, GCM is recommended by NIST [1], and is suggested to provide either authenticated encryption (GCM) or authentication (GMAC) service. By separating the nonces in GCM, GMAC, and CTR, and by adjusting the IV generation of the CTR mode, it is feasible to turn them into a SAK mode whose efficiency seems to be comparable to PolyE+CTR. However, PolyE+CTR is still a better choice because it uses a single nonce in providing three different services. On the other hand, if we use the same nonce (IV) in GCM and GMAC (which is strictly forbidden in [15] and [1]), related-mode attack works on them — an output (IV, A, C, T) from GCM_K is a valid forgery $(IV, A||C, T)$ against GMAC_K, because GMAC works in situations when "the data to be authenticated is included in A (the associated data) and the plaintext has zero length", as suggested by its authors [15].

6 Conclusions

We propose the notion of Swiss-Army-Knife mode of operation for block ciphers, with security definition and an instance. By a single key, the SAK mode can secure data with three different protections, thus it reduces the burden of key management for usual modes of operation and allows optional protections for different kinds of data, without rekeying its underlying block cipher. As an example, PolyE+CTR is proposed with provable security and high efficiency.

Acknowledgments. The authors would like to thank the anonymous referees at both Provsec 2011 and FSE 2011 for their valuable comments. Furthermore, this work is supported by the National Natural Science Foundation of China (No. 60873259, and No. 60903219) and the Knowledge Innovation Project of The Chinese Academy of Sciences.

References

1. —: Special Publication 800-38 Series. Recommendation for Block Cipher Modes of Operation. National Institute of Standards and Technology, http://csrc.nist.gov/groups/ST/toolkit/BCM/current_modes.html
2. Bellare, M.: New proofs for NMAC and HMAC: Security without collision-resistance. In: Dwork, C. (ed.) CRYPTO 2006. LNCS, vol. 4117, pp. 602–619. Springer, Heidelberg (2006)
3. Bellare, M., Goldreich, O., Mityagin, A.: The power of verification queries in message authentication and authenticated encryption. Cryptology ePrint Archive, Report 2004/309 (2004), http://eprint.iacr.org/
4. Bellare, M., Kilian, J., Rogaway, P.: The security of cipher block chaining. In: Desmedt, Y.G. (ed.) CRYPTO 1994. LNCS, vol. 839, pp. 341–358. Springer, Heidelberg (1994)
5. Bellare, M., Namprempre, C.: Authenticated encryption: Relations among notions and analysis of the generic composition paradigm. In: Okamoto, T. (ed.) ASIACRYPT 2000. LNCS, vol. 1976, pp. 531–545. Springer, Heidelberg (2000)
6. Bellare, M., Ristenpart, T., Rogaway, P., Stegers, T.: Format-preserving encryption. In: Jacobson Jr., M.J., Rijmen, V., Safavi-Naini, R. (eds.) SAC 2009. LNCS, vol. 5867, pp. 295–312. Springer, Heidelberg (2009)
7. Bernstein, D.J.: The poly1305-AES message-authentication code. In: Gilbert, H., Handschuh, H. (eds.) FSE 2005. LNCS, vol. 3557, pp. 32–49. Springer, Heidelberg (2005)
8. Black, J.A., Cochran, M., Shrimpton, T.: On the impossibility of highly-efficient blockcipher-based hash functions. In: Cramer, R. (ed.) EUROCRYPT 2005. LNCS, vol. 3494, pp. 526–541. Springer, Heidelberg (2005)
9. Black, J., Rogaway, P.: A block-cipher mode of operation for parallelizable message authentication. In: Knudsen, L.R. (ed.) EUROCRYPT 2002. LNCS, vol. 2332, pp. 384–397. Springer, Heidelberg (2002)
10. Cook, D.L., Keromytis, A.D., Yung, M.: Elastic block ciphers: the basic design. In: Bao, F., Miller, S. (eds.) ASIACCS, pp. 350–352. ACM, New York (2007)
11. Daemen, J., Knudsen, L.R., Rijmen, V.: The block cipher SQUARE. In: Biham, E. (ed.) FSE 1997. LNCS, vol. 1267, pp. 149–165. Springer, Heidelberg (1997)

12. Goldenberg, D., Hohenberger, S., Liskov, M., Schwartz, E.C., Seyalioglu, H.: On tweaking luby-rackoff blockciphers. In: Kurosawa, K. (ed.) ASIACRYPT 2007. LNCS, vol. 4833, pp. 342–356. Springer, Heidelberg (2007)
13. Iwata, T., Kurosawa, K.: OMAC: One-key CBC MAC. In: Johansson, T. (ed.) FSE 2003. LNCS, vol. 2887, pp. 129–153. Springer, Heidelberg (2003)
14. Liskov, M., Rivest, R.L., Wagner, D.: Tweakable block ciphers. In: Yung, M. (ed.) CRYPTO 2002. LNCS, vol. 2442, pp. 31–46. Springer, Heidelberg (2002)
15. McGrew, D.A., Viega, J.: The security and performance of the galois/Counter mode (GCM) of operation. In: Canteaut, A., Viswanathan, K. (eds.) INDOCRYPT 2004. LNCS, vol. 3348, pp. 343–355. Springer, Heidelberg (2004)
16. Minematsu, K.: Beyond-birthday-bound security based on tweakable block cipher. In: Dunkelman, O. (ed.) FSE 2009. LNCS, vol. 5665, pp. 308–326. Springer, Heidelberg (2009)
17. Mitsuda, A., Iwata, T.: Tweakable pseudorandom permutation from generalized feistel structure. In: Baek, J., Bao, F., Chen, K., Lai, X. (eds.) ProvSec 2008. LNCS, vol. 5324, pp. 22–37. Springer, Heidelberg (2008)
18. Phan, R.C.-W., Siddiqi, M.U.: Related-mode attacks on block cipher modes of operation. In: Gervasi, O., Gavrilova, M.L., Kumar, V., Laganá, A., Lee, H.P., Mun, Y., Taniar, D., Tan, C.J.K. (eds.) ICCSA 2005. LNCS, vol. 3482, pp. 661–671. Springer, Heidelberg (2005)
19. Rogaway, P.: Authenticated-encryption with associated-data. In: Atluri, V. (ed.) ACM Conference on Computer and Communications Security, pp. 98–107. ACM, New York (2002)
20. Rogaway, P.: Efficient instantiations of tweakable blockciphers and refinements to modes OCB and PMAC. In: Lee, P.J. (ed.) ASIACRYPT 2004. LNCS, vol. 3329, pp. 16–31. Springer, Heidelberg (2004)
21. Rogaway, P.: Nonce-based symmetric encryption. In: Roy, B., Meier, W. (eds.) FSE 2004. LNCS, vol. 3017, pp. 348–359. Springer, Heidelberg (2004)
22. Wang, P., Feng, D., Wu, W.: On the security of tweakable modes of operation: TBC and TAE. In: Zhou, J., López, J., Deng, R.H., Bao, F. (eds.) ISC 2005. LNCS, vol. 3650, pp. 274–287. Springer, Heidelberg (2005)
23. Wu, H.: Related-cipher attacks. In: Deng, R.H., Qing, S., Bao, F., Zhou, J. (eds.) ICICS 2002. LNCS, vol. 2513, pp. 447–455. Springer, Heidelberg (2002)
24. Zhang, L., Wu, W., Zhang, L., Li, Y.: A note on cook's elastic block cipher. In: Li, W., Susilo, W., Tupakula, U.K., Safavi-Naini, R., Varadharajan, V. (eds.) ASIACCS, pp. 380–383. ACM, New York (2009)

Security of Practical Cryptosystems Using Merkle-Damgård Hash Function in the Ideal Cipher Model

Yusuke Naito[1], Kazuki Yoneyama[2], Lei Wang[3], and Kazuo Ohta[3]

[1] Mitsubishi Electoric Corporation
[2] NTT Information Sharing Platform Laboratories
[3] The University of Electro-Communications

Abstract. In this paper, we clarify the security of practical cryptosystems with hash functions based on key derivation functions (KDFs). We use the indifferentiability framework in order to discuss the security because the indifferentiability from Random Oracle (and its variants) guarantees that cryptosystems remain secure even if Random Oracles (ROs) are instantiated with hash functions. Though previous works on the indifferentiability of Merkle-Damgård (MD) hash functions focus on stand-alone hash functions, there is no work which focuses on MD hash functions with KDFs. Many cryptosystems need longer output lengths of hash functions than stand-alone hash functions and KDFs are used to generate longer digests as specified in PKCS #1 v2.1 and IEEE P1363. Specifically, we obtain the following results. We denote the MD hash function using Stam's type-II compression function by MD-SCFII and MD-SCFII with KDFs by KDF-MD-SCFII.

- Cryptosystems secure in the pub-RO model (FDH, PSS, Fiat-Shamir, and so on): Dodis *et al.* proposed the indifferentiability from pub-RO to prove the security of these cryptosystems using MD-SCFII while did not consider the KDF structures. So we propose a different framework, indifferentiability from privleak-RO. Using this framework and their result, we show that these cryptosystems using KDF-MD-SCFIIs are secure.
- Encryption schemes secure in the RO model (OAEP, RSA-KEM, PSEC-KEM, ECIES-KEM and so on): The encryption schemes are secure in the "fixed inputl length" RO model because the input lengths of ROs from the encryption schemes are fixed. We show that this fact guarantees the security of the encryption schemes using KDF-MD-SCFII.

1 Introduction

The Random Oracle (RO) Methodology is a well known methodology for designing efficient cryptosystems and many important cryptosystems have been designed on the RO methodology. For example, RSA-OAEP [3], RSA-PSS [3], RSA-KEM [27], PSEC-KEM [27], and ECIES-KEM [27], which are standardized in RSA's PKCS #1 V2.1 or ISO 18033-2, are designed by this methodology.

X. Boyen and X. Chen (Eds.): ProvSec 2011, LNCS 6980, pp. 281–296, 2011.

When proving security, hash functions are viewed as ROs. When implementing a cryptosystem, ROs are replaced with cryptographic hash functions such as SHA-2 family and SHA-1 [24]. However, there are two problems in order to instantiate RO into a hash function. One is known separation results. Since there are several separation results for ROs and cryptographic hash functions, e.g., [9], the heuristic evidence of the methodology is questionable. The other is output lengths of hash functions. Many secure cryptosystems in the RO model actually require a non-standard hash function as an instantiation of RO. For example, the output length may be larger than standard sizes of hash functions (e.g., a signature scheme needs at least 1024-bits). Indeed, RSA's PKCS #1 V2.1, IEEE P1363 or ISO 18033-2 specifies to use *Key Derivation Functions* (KDF) to support arbitrary output lengths. Thus, practically, ROs may be instantiated hash functions with KDFs; therefore, we have to consider security under such an instantiation.

In order to fill the theoretical gap of the separation results, Maurer, Renner and Holenstein introduced the indifferentiability framework [22] and later Coron, Dodis, Malinaud, and Puniya applied the framework to hash functions, called indifferentiability from RO [13]. While the underlying primitive P (e.g. compression function) is idealized, if hash function H^P, is indifferentiable from RO, the security of cryptosystems in single-stage games (e.g., IND-CCA, EUF-CMA and many other security games) is preserved when RO is replaced with H^P. The Merkle-Damgård (MD) structure is the most famous hash construction. Many popular hash functions, e.g., SHA-1, SHA-256 and SHA-512 which are published as FIPS standard, employ the blockcipher-based MD structure and many blockcipher-based MD hash functions are collision resistance in the Ideal Cipher Model (ICM) [5], e.g., the SHA-family uses the Davies-Meyer mode which is collision resistance in the ICM. However, any of the MD hash functions is not indifferentiable from RO due to the extension attack [13]. Coron *et al.*, thus, examined indifferentiability of *modified* blockcipher-based MD hash functions (e.g., prefix-free MD, chopped MD) from ROs and obtained positive results. Moreover, they (briefly) considered indifferentiability of hash functions with KDFs. They showed that modified MD hash functions with a kind of KDFs (KDF2) is also indifferentiable from RO. However, due to the state of differentiability, there is no guarantee as to the security of cryptosystems when RO is replaced with the *original* MD hash functions. This leaves an open question whether cryptosystems can be securely instantiated when RO is replaced with the original blockcipher-based MD hash functions.

Dodis, Ristenpart and Shrimpton answered the question for several cryptosystems [16,17]. They proved that FDH [2], PFDH [12], Fiat-Shamir [18], BLS [7], PSS [4], a variant of Boneh-Franklin IBE [10] and Boneh-Boyen IBE [8] are secure when RO is replaced with a MD hash function that uses the Stam's Type-II compression function [29] (MD-SCFII) in the ICM. Note that MD-SCFII includes many popular hash functions (e.g., SHA-family hash functions) because SCFII includes 8 Group-1 PGV schemes (including the Davies-Meyer mode) and all Group-2 PGV schemes [26,5]. Their observation uses the Weakened Random

Oracle (WRO) approach. This approach states that for a hash function H defining a WRO such that H is indifferentiable from WRO and, then, proving the security of cryptosystems in the WRO model. They defined public-use Random Oracle (pub-RO) and proved the security of the above cryptosystems by using pub-RO. We call these cryptosystems "pub-RO secure cryptosystems". In addition, Naito, Yoneyama, Wang and Ohta showed that by other WROs: Traceable RO (TRO) and Extension Simulatable RO (ERO), several encryption schemes such as OAEP, variants of OAEP and RSA-KEM are secure when RO is replaced with the MD hash function using a fixed input length RO (FILRO) [23].

Motivating Problem. While several cryptosystems are secure when RO is replaced with MD hash functions [16,17,23], the security of cryptosystems based on KDFs were not discussed. Those include MGF1 specified in RSA's PKCS #1 V2.1 [21] and the scheme specified in IEEE P1363 [19]. For example, ISO 18033-2 and RFC 4055 contain several cryptosystems proved in the RO model such as RSA-OAEP and specify SHA-family hash functions in ISO 10118-3 and FIPS 180-2 to instantiate ROs. So the security discussion for cryptosystems using KDF-based SHA-type hash functions is important in practice. We thus focus on the more practical situation than the previous works [16,17,23]; we discuss the security of the following cryptosystems when RO is replaced with KDFs using MD-SCFII (KDF-MD-SCFII).

1. Pub-RO cryptosystems: Dodis *et al.* proved that pub-RO secure cryptosystems are secure when RO is replaced with MD-SCFII, while they did not consider the KDF's structure. Thus the security of these cryptosystems using KDF-MD-SCFIIs remains unclear, since there might exist some attack based on the KDF's structure.
2. Encryption schemes: In previous works [17,23], KDF's structures are not considered. Moreover, since important encryption schemes such as OAEP [4], RSA-KEM [27], PSEC-KEM [27], ECIES-KEM [27] and many other encryption schemes are insecure in the pub-RO model [30,23] and SCFII is not indifferentiable from FILRO, the results of Dodis *et al.* [17] and Naito *et al.* [23] provide no support for the security of these cryptosystems using KDF-MD-SCFII (and MD-SCFII). Thus the security of these important encryption schemes remains unclear.

Security of Pub-RO Secure Cryptosystems Using KDF-MD-SCFII Hash Functions. Our first contribution is showing that the pub-RO secure cryptosystems are secure when RO is replaced with KDF-MD-SCFII in the ICM. To support the KDF structure, we propose a new approach, called indifferentiability from private interface leaking RO (privleak-RO). We show that KDFs using pub-RO are indifferentiable from privleak-ROs. Since MD-SCFII is indifferentiable from pub-RO [17], KDF-MD-SCFIIs are indifferentiable from privleak-ROs. We show that pub-RO secure cryptosystems are secure in the provleak-RO model. Note that this can be easily proven from the same discussion of the security of pub-RO cryptosystems in the pub-RO model (See Subsection

3.1). Consequently, the pub-RO secure cryptosystems using KDF-MD-SCFIIs are secure.

Security of Encryption Schemes. Our second contribution is showing that OAEP, RSA-KEM, PSEC-KEM, ECIES-KEM and many other encryption schemes (e.g. OAEP+ [28], SAEP [6], SAEP+ [6], and many other schemes [1,11,14,15,20,25]) are secure when RO is replaced with KDF-MD-SCFII in the ICM where the input lengths of hash functions from the encryption schemes are fixed.

These encryption schemes are secure in the "FIL"RO model. For example, output lengths of ROs in OAEP [4] are specified as k_0-bit and $(k - k_0)$-bit, and OAEP is proved in such FILRO model. There might be an encryption scheme which is proven in the variable input length RO. So we prove that these encryption schemes are secure in the FILRO model. We show that KDF-MD-SCFIIs are indifferentiable from FILROs. Consequently, these encryption schemes using KDF-MD-SCFIIs are secure.

2   Preliminaries

Notation. For two values x, y, $x \| y$ is the concatenated value of x and y. For some value y, $x \leftarrow y$ means assigning y to x. $\oplus$ is bitwise exclusive or. $|x|$ is the bit length of x. $\langle i \rangle$ is the value encoded as a string of i. For set (list) $\mathcal{T}$ and element W, $\mathcal{T} \leftarrow W$ means to insert W into $\mathcal{T}$ (if W is already inserted in $\mathcal{T}$, W is not inserted.). $\mathcal{C}_{d,n} = (E, D)$ be a ideal cipher where $E : \{0,1\}^d \times \{0,1\}^n \rightarrow \{0,1\}^n$ is an encryption oracle, $D : \{0,1\}^d \times \{0,1\}^n \rightarrow \{0,1\}^n$ is a decryption oracle, the key size is d bits and the cipher text size is n bits. $\mathcal{F}_b : \{0,1\}^* \rightarrow \{0,1\}^b$ is a random oracle. Random Oracle is denoted by RO. Ideal Cipher is denoted by IC. IC model is denoted by ICM.

Indifferentiability Framework [22]. The indifferentiability framework sometimes distinguishes between a private interface and a public interface (following terminology from [22]), writing $Q = (Q^{pub}, Q^{priv})$ to denote an ideal primitive Q that has the private interface Q^{priv} and the public interface Q^{pub}. A private interface is used exclusively by honest parties while a public interface is used by adversaries and simulators. For example, consider RO. Since RO is a "public" random function, which means that any party can access to it, RO has both interfaces.

Let H^P be a hash function that utilizes an ideal primitive $P = (P^{priv}, P^{pub})$. Note that simce H is not an adversary, namely it is an honest party, H has oracle access to P^{priv}. Let $Q = (Q^{priv}, Q^{pub})$ be a second ideal primitive. The definition of the indifferentiability from Q for H^P is as follows.

Definition 1. H^P is (t_A, t_S, ϵ)-indifferentiable from Q, if there exists S of running time at most t_S for any distinguisher A of running time at most t_A such that

$$|\Pr[A^{H^P, P^{pub}} \Rightarrow 1] - \Pr[A^{Q^{priv}, S^{Q^{pub}}} \Rightarrow 1]| \leq \epsilon$$

where S has oracle access to Q^{pub}.

$\mathrm{MD}^h(M)$
$\overline{z_0 \leftarrow IV;}$
Break $\mathsf{pad}(M)$ into d-bit blocks, $M_1||\cdots||M_l$;
for $i = 1, \ldots, l$ do $z_i \leftarrow h(z_{i-1}, M_i)$;
Ret z_l;

$\mathrm{SCF}^{\mathcal{C}_{d,n}}(v, m)$
$\overline{(k, x) \leftarrow C^{\mathrm{PRE}}(v, m);}$
$y \leftarrow E(k, x)$
Ret $w \leftarrow C^{\mathrm{POST}}(v, m, y)$;

Fig. 1. Merkle-Damgård   **Fig. 2.** Stam's Compression Function

The goal of the simulator is to simulate P^{pub} such that the relations among (H^P, P^{pub}) are hold in (Q^{priv}, S) as well. We say "H^P is indifferentiable from Q" or $H^P \sqsubset Q$ when ϵ is a negligible function of the security parameter k (for polynomially bounded t_A and t_S). If $H^P \sqsubset Q$, then Q may be replaced by H^P in any cryptosystem which is secure in a single-stage game, and the resulting cryptosystem is at least as secure in the P model as in the Q model.

Merkle-Damgård. Let $h : \{0,1\}^{d+n} \to \{0,1\}^n$ be a compression function using primitive P (more strictly h^P) and $\mathsf{pad} : \{0,1\}^* \to (\{0,1\}^d)^*$ be an injective function. We define a Merkle-Damgård (MD) hash function MD^h in Fig.1 where IV is an n-bit initial value.

Generalized Rate-1 Blockcipher-Based Compression Function [29]. Stam [29] generalized rate-1 blockcipher-based compression functions [5,26]. He considered compression functions $\mathrm{SCF}^{\mathcal{C}_{d,n}}$ that, on the input of the chaining variable $v \in \{0,1\}^n$ and the message block $m \in \{0,1\}^d$, operates as Fig.2 where $C^{\mathrm{PRE}} : \{0,1\}^n \times \{0,1\}^d \to \{0,1\}^d \times \{0,1\}^n$ and $C^{\mathrm{POST}} : \{0,1\}^d \times \{0,1\}^n \times \{0,1\}^n \to \{0,1\}^n$ are functions called preprocessing and post-processing, respectively. He also defined auxiliary post-processing function $C^{\mathrm{AUX}} : \{0,1\}^d \times \{0,1\}^n \times \{0,1\}^n \to \{0,1\}^n$ such that $C^{\mathrm{AUX}}(k, x, y) = C^{\mathrm{POST}}(v, m, y)$. He defined a Type-II scheme: SCF is the Type-II scheme if: 1) C^{PRE} is bijective, 2) for all v, m $C^{\mathrm{POST}}(v, m, \cdot)$ is bijective, and 3) for all k, the inverse map $C_1^{-\mathrm{PRE}}(k, \cdot)$ is bijective. Here the map $C_1^{-\mathrm{PRE}} : \{0,1\}^d \times \{0,1\}^n \to \{0,1\}^n$ is defined by $C_1^{-\mathrm{PRE}}(k, m) = v$ where $(v, m) = C^{-\mathrm{PRE}}(k, x)$. By SCFII, we denote the Type-II scheme. SCFII includes the Group-2 PGV schemes and 8 Group PGV schemes (e.g. Davies-Meyer). The Davies-Meyer has $C^{\mathrm{PRE}}(v, m) = (m, v)$, $C^{\mathrm{POST}}(v, m, y) = v \oplus y$ and $C^{\mathrm{AUX}}(k, x, y) = x \oplus y$.

KDFs [27]. KDFs are specified in RSA's PKCS #1 V2.1, IEEE P1363 and ISO 18033-2. Since SHA-256 and many other hash functions do not support arbitrary output length, KDFs are used when extending the output lengths of hash functions. The definiton of KDFs is as follows. Let $H : \{0,1\}^* \to \{0,1\}^n$ be a hash function. When the output length is expanded from n bits to mn bits, KDF1, KDF2 and KDF3 are defined by

- $\mathsf{KDF1}_m\text{-}H(M) = H(M||\langle 0 \rangle)||H(M||\langle 1 \rangle)||\ldots||H(M||\langle m-1 \rangle)$
- $\mathsf{KDF2}_m\text{-}H(M) = H(M||\langle 1 \rangle)||H(M||\langle 2 \rangle)||\ldots||H(M||\langle m \rangle)$
- $\mathsf{KDF3}_m\text{-}H(M) = H(\langle 0 \rangle||M)||H(\langle 1 \rangle||M)||\ldots||H(\langle m-1 \rangle||M)$

Note that the length of $\langle j \rangle$ is defined when implementing the KDF function. In our discussion, we don't case the length. The description of KDF1 is equal to MGF1 used in several standards [21,19]. The description of KDF2 is discussed in [13]. The description of KDF3 is equal to the 1996 Bellare-Rogaway RO instantiation [4].

Indifferentiability from pub-RO [16,17]. Since the MD hash functions are not indifferentiable from ROs, which means that ROs are not replaced by the hash functions, they proposed pub-RO, which is a weaker ideal primitive than RO, and analyzed them by using it. Dodis *et al.* showed that the MD hash function using SCFII is indifferentiable from pub-RO. Then the indifferentiability framework guarantees that pub-RO can be replaced by the hash function in any cryptosystem, and the resulting cryptosystem is at least as secure under the hash function as in the pub-RO model [22].

Pub-RO consists of RO $\mathcal{F}_b$ and Leak Oracle (LO) $\mathcal{F}_{leak}$ that leaks the hash list of the lazily-sampled RO. The description of the lazily-sampled pub-RO is as follows. Let F_b be a (initially everywhere $\perp$) hash table and L_{leak} be a list that records all input-output pairs of $\mathcal{F}_b$.

$\underline{\mathcal{F}_b(M)}$
001 If $\mathsf{F}_b[M] \neq \perp$, ret $\mathsf{F}_b[M]$;
002 $\mathsf{F}_b[M] \xleftarrow{\$} \{0,1\}^n$;
003 $L_{leak} \leftarrow (M, \mathsf{F}_b[M])$;
004 Ret $\mathsf{F}_b[M]$;

$\underline{\mathcal{F}_{leak}()}$
011 Ret L_{leak};

When the output lenth of RO is b bits, we write it by pub-RO$_b$. In this model, pub-RO$_b^{priv} = \mathcal{F}_b$ and pub-RO$_b^{pub} = (\mathcal{F}_b, \mathcal{F}_{leak})$. Thus, when proving the security of a cryptosystem $\mathcal{C}$ in the pub-RO model, $\mathcal{C}$ has oracle access to $\mathcal{F}_b$ and an adversary has oracle access to $(\mathcal{F}_b, \mathcal{F}_{leak})$.

They found that FDH [2], PFDH [12], Fiat-Shamir [18], BLS [7], PSS [4], a variant of Boneh-Franklin IBE [10] and Boneh-Boyen IBE [8] are also secure in the pub-RO model because all input of hash functions in these schemes are published to adversaries and so LO does not help the adversaries. We call the cryptosystems "pub-RO secure cryptosystems".

3   Security of Pub-RO Secure Cryptosystems Using KDF-MD-SCFIIs

Let MD-SCFII be the the MD hash function using SCFII and KDFi-MD-SCFII be KDFi using MD-SCFII. In this section, we prove that the pub-RO secure cryptosystems are secure when RO is replaced by KDF1-MD-SCFII the ICM. Note that since KDF2 and KDF3 have the similar structure to KDF1 (the differences are only the position of counters and the counting rule), the KDF2 and KDF3 proofs can be obtained by the trivial extension of the KDF1 proof.

To prove the security, we propose an indifferentiability from private interface leaking RO (privleak-RO) which is a new weakened RO. We show that KDF1-pub-RO$\sqsubset$ privleak-RO. Since MD-SCFII $\sqsubset$ pub-RO [17], KDF1-MD-SCFII $\sqsubset$

privleak-RO. The security of the pub-RO secure cryptosystems can be proven in the privleak-RO model from the same discussion as [16,17] (See Subsection 3.1). The results yield the result that the pub-RO secure cryptosystems are secure when RO is replaced by KDF1-MD-SCFII.

If we can prove that KDF1-MD-SCFII $\sqsubset$ pub-RO, then the pub-RO cryptosystems using KDF1-MD-SCFII are secure. However, in this approach, we must consider the structures of KDF1, MD and SCFII at the same time and so the indifferentiability proof is very complex. Since MD-SCFII $\sqsubset$ pub-RO, we might be able to avoid the MD and SCFII structures by pub-RO. However, this approach cannot be used; in Appendix A, we show that KDF1-pub-RO is not indifferentiable from pub-RO. Intuitively, since RO of pub-RO has public and private interfaces, no one can know whether a value in L_{leak} is defined on the private interface or the public interface. The attack uses this fact. So we define privleak-RO to avoid the differentiable attack.

3.1 Privleak-RO

Privleak-RO consists of RO $\mathcal{F}_b = (\mathcal{F}_b^1, \mathcal{F}_b^2)$ and a private interface leak oracle $\mathcal{F}_{privleak}$. $\mathcal{F}_{privleak}$ leaks all input-output pairs of $\mathcal{F}_b^1$. The description is as follows. F_b is a (initially everywhere $\perp$) table and $L_{privleak}$ is a list in which all input-output pairs of $\mathcal{F}_b^1$ are stored.

<table>
<tr><td>

$\mathcal{F}_b^1(M)$

001 If $\mathsf{F}_b[M] \neq \perp$,
002     $L_{privleak} \leftarrow (M, \mathsf{F}_b[M])$;
003   Ret $\mathsf{F}_b[M]$;

004 $\mathsf{F}_b[M] \xleftarrow{\$} \{0,1\}^b$;
005 $L_{privleak} \leftarrow (M, \mathsf{F}_b[M])$;
006 Ret $\mathsf{F}_b[M]$;

</td><td>

$\mathcal{F}_b^2(M)$

011 If $\mathsf{F}_b[M] \neq \perp$, ret $\mathsf{F}_b[M]$;
012 $\mathsf{F}_b[M] \xleftarrow{\$} \{0,1\}^b$;
013 Ret $\mathsf{F}_b[M]$;

$\mathcal{F}_{privleak}()$

021 Ret $L_{privleak}$;

</td></tr>
</table>

When the output length of RO is b bits, we denote it by privleak-RO$_b$. We then define the private interface and the public interface by privleak-RO$_b^{priv} = \mathcal{F}_b^1$ and privleak-RO$_b^{pub} = (\mathcal{F}_b^2, \mathcal{F}_{privleak})$. For the hash function $H^P : \{0,1\}^* \rightarrow \{0,1\}^b$, the indifferentiability from privleak-RO is as follows.

Definition 2. H^P is (t_A, t_S, ϵ)-indifferentiable from privleak-RO$_b$, if there exists S of running time at most t_S for any distinguisher A of running time at most t_A such that

$$|\Pr[A^{H^P, P^{pub}} \Rightarrow 1] - \Pr[A^{\mathcal{F}_b^1, S^{\mathcal{F}_b^2, \mathcal{F}_{privleak}}} \Rightarrow 1]| \leq \epsilon \qquad (1)$$

where S has oracle access to $(\mathcal{F}_b^2, \mathcal{F}_{privleak})$.

If $H^P \sqsubset$ privleak-RO$_b$, then privleak-RO$_b$ may be replaced by H^P in any cryptosystem which is secure in a single-stage game, and the resulting cryptosystem is at least as secure in the P model as in the privleak-RO$_b$ model. Note that when considering the security of a cryptosystem $\mathcal{C}$ in the privleak-RO$_b$, $\mathcal{C}$ (honest party) has oracle access to $\mathcal{F}_b^1$ and an adversary has oracle access to

($\mathcal{F}_b^2, \mathcal{F}_{privleak}$). Since for the security of the pub-RO secure cryptosystems in the RO model adversaries can know all pairs of the hash list of the RO, in the privleak-RO model the additional function $\mathcal{F}_{privleak}$ does not help the attacks to the pub-RO secure cryptosystems. So the pub-RO cryptosystems are secure in the privleak-RO model. This is the same discussion of the security of the pub-RO cryptosystems in the pub-RO model [17].

3.2   Indifferentiability Results for KDFs

Theorem 1. $\mathsf{KDF1}_m\text{-pub-RO}_n \sqsubset \text{privleak-RO}_{nm}$ where $t_S = t_A + \mathcal{O}(q^2)$ and $\epsilon = 0$ where A can make queries to $(\mathsf{KDF1}_m\text{-pub-RO}_n, \mathcal{F}_n, \mathcal{F}_{leak})$ or $(\mathcal{F}_{nm}^1, S^{\mathcal{F}_{nm}^2, \mathcal{F}_{privl}})$ at most q times.
$\mathsf{KDF2}_m\text{-pub-RO}_n \sqsubset \text{privleak-RO}_{nm}$ where $t_S = t_A + \mathcal{O}(q^2)$ and $\epsilon = 0$ where A can make queries to $(\mathsf{KDF2}_m\text{-pub-RO}_n, \mathcal{F}_n, \mathcal{F}_{leak})$ or $(\mathcal{F}_{nm}^1, S^{\mathcal{F}_{nm}^2, \mathcal{F}_{privl}})$ at most q times.
$\mathsf{KDF3}_m\text{-pub-RO}_n \sqsubset \text{privleak-RO}_{nm}$ where $t_A, t_S = t_A + \mathcal{O}(q^2)$ and $\epsilon = 0$ where A can make queries to $(\mathsf{KDF3}_m\text{-pub-RO}_n, \mathcal{F}_n, \mathcal{F}_{leak})$ or $(\mathcal{F}_{nm}^1, S^{\mathcal{F}_{nm}^2, \mathcal{F}_{privl}})$ at most q times.

We give the proof of $\mathsf{KDF1}_m\text{-pub-RO}_n \sqsubset \text{privleak-RO}_{nm}$ in Subsection 3.3. Since KDF2 and KDF3 have the almost same structure as KDF1, we can straightforwardly prove that $\mathsf{KDF2}_m\text{-pub-RO}_n \sqsubset \text{privleak-RO}$ and $\mathsf{KDF3}_m\text{-pub-RO}_n \sqsubset \text{privleak-RO}$ by the same proof. So we omit these proofs.

Thus the pub-RO secure cryptosystems are secure when using KDF-MD-SCFIIs because those can be used instead of privleak-RO (from Theorem 1 and the result that MD-SCFII$\sqsubset$ pub-RO [17].) and the pub-RO secure cryptosystems are secure in the privleak-RO model.

3.3   Proof of Theorem 1

Consider the experiment. A interacts with $(\mathsf{KDF1}_m\text{-}\mathcal{F}_n, \mathcal{F}_n, \mathcal{F}_{leak})$ or $(\mathcal{F}_{mn}^1, S_{\mathcal{F}_n}, S_{leak})$ where $S_{\mathcal{F}_n}$ is a simulator of $\mathcal{F}_n$ and S_{leak} is a simulator of $\mathcal{F}_{leak}$. We define a simulator $S = (S_{\mathcal{F}_n}, S_{leak})$ in Fig. 3. Let F_S be a (initially everywhere $\perp$) list that stores all input-output values of $S_{\mathcal{F}_n}$. In this proof, we assume that the length of the counter used in KDF1 is u bits. For nm bit value w, we denote n-bit blocks of w by $w_0, \ldots, w_{m-1}$, that is $w = w_0||\ldots||w_{m-1}$. For $v + u$-bit value w, we denote the first v-bit value and the last u-bit value by $w_{(u)}$ and $w_{[u]}$, respectively. We define $S_{\mathcal{F}_n}$ such that it is consistent with $\mathcal{F}_{nm}^1$, that is for any M $\mathsf{KDF1}_m\text{-}S_{\mathcal{F}_n}(M) = \mathcal{F}_{nm}^1(M)$. Since a last u bit value of an input of $\mathcal{F}_n$ in $\mathsf{KDF1}_m\text{-}\mathcal{F}_n$ is one of $\{\langle 0 \rangle, \ldots, \langle m-1 \rangle\}$, on a query x where $x_{[u]} \in \{\langle 0 \rangle, \ldots, \langle m-1 \rangle\}$ the output is defined by using $\mathcal{F}_{mn}^2$ and on other type queries the outputs are defined by a random choice. We define S_{leak} such that it leaks input-output pairs of $S_{\mathcal{F}_n}$ and pairs defined from $\mathcal{F}_{privleak}$.

We give a proof using the game sequences Game 0, Game 1, ..., Game 6 that are shown in Figs. 4, 5, 6, 7, 8 and 9. Without loss of generality, we assume that

$S_{\mathcal{F}_n}(M)$	$S_{privleak}()$
101 If $\mathsf{F}_S[M] \neq \perp$, ret $\mathsf{F}_S[M]$;	111 $(M^1, w^1), \ldots, (M^j, w^j) \leftarrow \mathcal{F}_{privleak}()$;
102 If $M_{[u]} = \langle t \rangle \in \{\langle 0 \rangle, \ldots, \langle m-1 \rangle\}$,	112 For $i = 1, \ldots, j$ and $t = 0, \ldots, m-1$,
103 $\quad w \leftarrow \mathcal{F}_{mn}^2(M_{(u)})$;	113 $\quad L_S \leftarrow (M^i || \langle t \rangle, w_t^i)$;
104 $\quad \mathsf{F}_S[M] \leftarrow w_t$;	114 Ret L_S;
105 Else $\mathsf{F}_S[M] \leftarrow \{0,1\}^n$;
106 $L_S \leftarrow (M, \mathsf{F}_S[M])$;
107 Ret $\mathsf{F}_S[M]$;

Fig. 3. Simulator

$\mathcal{O}_0(M)$	choose-$\mathcal{F}_n(X)$
201 For $j = 0, \ldots, m-1$	231 If $\mathsf{F}[X] = \perp$, $\mathsf{F}[X] \overset{\$}{\leftarrow} \{0,1\}^n$;
202 $\quad w_j \leftarrow$ choose-$\mathcal{F}_n[M||\langle j \rangle]$;	232 $L_S \leftarrow (X, \mathsf{F}[X])$;
203 Ret $w_0 || \cdots || w_{m-1}$;	233 Ret $\mathsf{F}[X]$;
$\mathcal{O}_1()$
211 Ret L_S;
$\mathcal{O}_2(X)$
221 Ret choose-$\mathcal{F}_n(X)$;

Fig. 4. Game 0

$\mathcal{O}_0(M)$	choose-$\mathcal{F}_n(X)$
301 For $j = 0, \ldots, m-1$	331 If $X_{[u]} = \langle t \rangle \in \{0, \ldots, m-1\}$,
302 $\quad w_j \leftarrow$ choose-$\mathcal{F}_n(M||\langle j \rangle)$;	332 $\quad$ For $j = 0, \ldots, m-1$
303 Ret $w_0 || \cdots || w_{m-1}$;	333 $\quad\quad$ If $\mathsf{F}_j[X_{(u)}] = \perp$, $\mathsf{F}_j[X_{(u)}] \overset{\$}{\leftarrow} \{0,1\}^n$;
$\mathcal{O}_1()$	334 $\quad w \leftarrow \mathsf{F}_t[X_{(u)}]$;
311 Ret L_S;	335 Else
$\mathcal{O}_2(X)$	336 $\quad\quad$ If $\mathsf{F}[X] = \perp$, $\mathsf{F}[X] \overset{\$}{\leftarrow} \{0,1\}^n$;
321 Ret choose-$\mathcal{F}_n(X)$;	337 $\quad w \leftarrow \mathsf{F}[X]$
	338 $L_S \leftarrow (X, w)$;
	339 Ret w;

Fig. 5. Game 1

distinguisher A does not repeat a query to the oracles. In each game, A interacts with oracles $\mathcal{O}_0, \mathcal{O}_1$, and $\mathcal{O}_2$. Let Gi be the event that A outputs 1 in Game i.

Game 0. Choose-$\mathcal{F}_n$ is a lazy-sampled RO. In this oracle, (initially everywhere $\perp$) table F and (initially empty) list L_s are used. $\mathcal{O}_0$ is KDF1$_m$-$\mathcal{F}_n$, $\mathcal{O}_1$ is $\mathcal{F}_{leak}$ and $\mathcal{O}_2$ is $\mathcal{F}_n$. This game is the pub-RO scenario and thus $\Pr[G0] = \Pr[A^{\mathsf{KDF}1_m\text{-}\mathcal{F}_n, \mathcal{F}_n, \mathcal{F}_{leak}} \Rightarrow 1]$.

Game 1. In this game, we modify the subroutine choose-$\mathcal{F}_n$. We use new (initially everywhere $\perp$) tables F_j ($j = 0, \ldots, m-1$) in addition to table F.

$\mathcal{O}_0(M)$
401 For $j = 0, \ldots, m-1$
402     $w_j \leftarrow$ choose-$\mathcal{F}_n(M\|\langle j\rangle)$;
403 Ret $w_0\|\cdots\|w_{m-1}$;

$\mathcal{O}_1()$
411 Ret L_S;

$\mathcal{O}_2(X)$
421 Ret choose-$\mathcal{F}_n(X)$;

choose-$\mathcal{F}_n(X)$
431 If $X_{[u]} = \langle t\rangle \in \{0, \ldots, m-1\}$,
432   If $\mathsf{F}^*[X_{(u)}] = \bot$, $\mathsf{F}^*[X_{(u)}] \overset{\$}{\leftarrow} \{0,1\}^{mn}$;
433   For $j = 0, \ldots, m-1$
434   If $\mathsf{F}_j[X_{(u)}] = \bot$, $\mathsf{F}_j[X_{(u)}] \leftarrow \mathsf{F}^*[X_{(u)}]_j$;
435     $w \leftarrow \mathsf{F}^*[X_{(u)}]_t$;
436 Else
437   If $\mathsf{F}[X] = \bot$, $\mathsf{F}[X] \overset{\$}{\leftarrow} \{0,1\}^n$;
438     $w \leftarrow \mathsf{F}[X]$;
439 $L_S \leftarrow (X, w)$;
440 Ret w;

Fig. 6. Game 2 and Game 3

$\mathcal{O}_0(M)$
501 For $j = 0, \ldots, m-1$
502     $w_j \leftarrow$ choose-$\mathcal{F}_n(0, M\|\langle j\rangle)$;
503 Ret $w_0\|\cdots\|w_{m-1}$;

$\mathcal{O}_1()$
511 Ret L_S;

$\mathcal{O}_2(X)$
521 If $X_{[u]} = \langle t\rangle \in \{\langle 0\rangle, \ldots, \langle m-1\rangle\}$,
522   Ret choose-$\mathcal{F}_n(1, X)$;
523 Else ret choose-$\mathcal{F}_n(2, X)$;

choose-$\mathcal{F}_n(s, X)$
531 If $s \neq 2$,
532   If $\mathsf{F}^*[X_{(u)}] = \bot$, $\mathsf{F}^*[X_{(u)}] \overset{\$}{\leftarrow} \{0,1\}^{mn}$;
533     $w \leftarrow \mathsf{F}^*[X_{(u)}]_t$; $//\langle t\rangle = X_{[u]}$
534 Else
535   If $\mathsf{F}[X] = \bot$, $\mathsf{F}[X] \overset{\$}{\leftarrow} \{0,1\}^n$;
536     $w \leftarrow \mathsf{F}[X]$
537 $L_S \leftarrow (X, w)$;
538 Ret w;

Fig. 7. Game 4

$\mathcal{O}_0(M)$
601 If $\mathsf{F}^*[M] = \bot$, $\mathsf{F}^*[M] \overset{\$}{\leftarrow} \{0,1\}^{mn}$;
602 For $j = 0, \ldots, m-1$,
603     $L_S \leftarrow (M\|\langle j\rangle, \mathsf{F}^*[M]_j)$;
604 Ret $\mathsf{F}^*[M]$;

$\mathcal{O}_1()$
611 Ret L_S;

$\mathcal{O}_2(X)$
621 If $X_{[u]} = \langle t\rangle \in \{\langle 0\rangle, \ldots, \langle m-1\rangle\}$,
622   Ret choose-$\mathcal{F}_n(1, X)$;
623 Else ret choose-$\mathcal{F}_n(2, X)$;

choose-$\mathcal{F}_n(s, X)$
631 If $s = 1$,
632   If $\mathsf{F}^*[X_{(u)}] = \bot$, $\mathsf{F}^*[X_{(u)}] \overset{\$}{\leftarrow} \{0,1\}^{mn}$;
633     $w \leftarrow \mathsf{F}^*[X_{(u)}]_t$; $//\langle t\rangle = X_{[u]}$
634 If $s = 2$,
635   If $\mathsf{F}[X] = \bot$, $\mathsf{F}[X] \overset{\$}{\leftarrow} \{0,1\}^n$;
636     $w \leftarrow \mathsf{F}[X]$
637 $L_S \leftarrow (X, w)$;
638 Ret w;

Fig. 8. Game 5

These tables are used if $X_{[u]} \in \{\langle 0\rangle, \ldots, \langle m-1\rangle\}$, and table F is used otherwise. This modification clearly does not affect the view of A. So $\Pr[G0] = \Pr[G1]$.

$\mathcal{O}_0(M)$

701 If $\mathsf{F}^*[M] = \perp$, $\mathsf{F}^*[M] \xleftarrow{\$} \{0,1\}^{mn}$;
702 $T \leftarrow (M, \mathsf{F}^*[M])$;
703 Ret $\mathsf{F}^*[M]$;

$\mathcal{O}_1()$

711 $(M^1, w^1), \ldots, (M^i, w^i) \leftarrow T$;
712 For $j = 1, \ldots, i$ $t = 0, \ldots, m-1$,
713    $L_S \leftarrow (M^j \| \langle t \rangle, w_t^j)$;
714 Ret L_S;

$\mathcal{O}_2(X)$

721 If $X_{[u]} = \langle t \rangle \in \{\langle 0 \rangle, \ldots, \langle m-1 \rangle\}$,
722   Ret choose-$\mathcal{F}_n(1, X)$;
723 Else ret choose-$\mathcal{F}_n(2, X)$;

choose-$\mathcal{F}_n(s, X)$

731 If $s = 1$,
732   If $\mathsf{F}^*[X_{(u)}] = \perp$, $\mathsf{F}^*[X_{(u)}] \xleftarrow{\$} \{0,1\}^{mn}$;
733    $w \leftarrow \mathsf{F}^*[X_{(u)}]_t$; $//\langle t \rangle = X_{[u]}$
734 If $s = 2$,
735   If $\mathsf{F}[X] = \perp$, $\mathsf{F}[X] \xleftarrow{\$} \{0,1\}^n$;
736    $w \leftarrow \mathsf{F}[X]$
737 $L_S \leftarrow (X, w)$;
738 Ret w;

Fig. 9. Game 6

Game 2 (Boxed Procedures Included). In this game, we modify the procedure of the case that $X_{[u]} \in \{\langle 0 \rangle, \ldots, \langle m-1 \rangle\}$ in the subroutine choose-$\mathcal{F}_n$. $\mathsf{F}_1[X_{(u)}], \ldots, \mathsf{F}_m[X_{(u)}]$ are defined in line 432 in advance. These values are stored in a new (initially everywhere $\perp$) table F^*. In line 435 the output is defined by $\mathsf{F}^*[X_{(u)}]_t$. Note that $\mathsf{F}^*[X_{(u)}] = \mathsf{F}^*[X_{(u)}]_0 \| \cdots \| \mathsf{F}^*[X_{(u)}]_{m-1}$ where $|\mathsf{F}^*[X_{(u)}]_t| = n$ for $t = 0, \ldots, m-1$. Since $\mathsf{F}^*[X_{(u)}]_t = \mathsf{F}_t[X_{(u)}]$, these modifications does not affect the view of A. Thus $\Pr[G1] = \Pr[G2]$.

Game 3 (Boxed Procedures Removed). In this game, we remove boxed procedures (line 433 and line 434). Since tables $\mathsf{F}_0, \ldots, \mathsf{F}_{m-1}$ are not used in other procedures, this modification does not affect the view of A. Thus $\Pr[G2] = \Pr[G3]$.

Game 4. In this game, we modify $\mathcal{O}_2$ and choose-$\mathcal{F}_n$. Inputs of choose-$\mathcal{F}_n$ are two values. The first value s is that $s = 0$ if choose-$\mathcal{F}_n$ is called in $\mathcal{O}_0$, $s = 1$ if choose-$\mathcal{F}_n$ is called in $\mathcal{O}_2$ and $X_{[u]} \in \{\langle 0 \rangle, \ldots, \langle m-1 \rangle\}$, and $s = 2$ if choose-$\mathcal{F}_n$ is called in $\mathcal{O}_2$ and $X_{[u]} \notin \{\langle 0 \rangle, \ldots, \langle m-1 \rangle\}$. Since when $s = 0$ or $s = 1$ $X_{[u]} \in \{\langle 0 \rangle, \ldots, \langle m-1 \rangle\}$ and Lines 531-533 are executed, these modifications do not affect the view of A. Thus $\Pr[G3] = \Pr[G4]$.

Game 5. In this game, we hard-code choose-$\mathcal{F}_n$ in lines 602-603 in $\mathcal{O}_0$ and remove the case of $s = 0$ in choose-$\mathcal{F}_n$. This modification does not affect the view of A. Thus $\Pr[G4] = \Pr[G5]$.

Game 6. This is the final game. We modify $\mathcal{O}_0$ and $\mathcal{O}_1$. We remove line 602-603 and all input-output pairs are stored in a new table T. Lines 602-603 are moved to lines 712-713. Since no A can see these procedures, these modifications don't affect the view of A. Thus $\Pr[G5] = \Pr[G6]$.

In Game 6, $\mathcal{O}_0$ is equal to $\mathcal{F}_{mn}^1$. $\mathcal{O}_1$ is equal to S_{leak}. $\mathcal{F}_{mn}^2$ is hard-coded in lines 732-733. Thus $\mathcal{O}_2$ is equal to $S_{\mathcal{F}_n}$ and $\Pr[G6] = \Pr[A^{\mathcal{F}_{mn}^1,S} \Rightarrow 1]$. The proof is completed. □

4   The Security of Encryption Schemes Using KDF-MD-SCFIIs

In this section, we consider the security of cryptosystems from which input lengths to hash functions are fixed. Such cryptosystems are OAEP, RSA-KEM, PSEC-KEM, ECIES-KEM and many other encryption schemes. We call such cryptosystems "FIL-cryptosystems". We prove that the cryptosystems using KDFi-MD-SCFII ($i = 1, 2, 3$) are secure in the ICM.

Since the FIL-cryptosystems are secure in the fixed input length RO (FILRO) model, we prove that for $i = 1, 2, 3$, KDFi-MD-SCFII $\sqsubset$ FILRO in the next subsection. There might be a FIL-cryptosystem which is proven in the variable input length (VIL) RO model. So in Subsection 4.2, we prove that the above encryption schemes are also secure in the FILRO model. The indifferentiability from FILRO is as follows.

Definition 3. *Let* $\mathcal{F}_{a,b} : \{0,1\}^a \rightarrow \{0,1\}^b$ *be FILRO. Let* $H^P : \{0,1\}^* \rightarrow \{0,1\}^b$ *be a hash function using an ideal primitive* P. H^P *is* (t_A, t_S, ϵ)-*indifferentiable from FILRO, if there exists* S *of running time at most* t_S *for any distinguisher* A *of running time at most* t_A *such that*

$$|\Pr[A^{H^P,P^{pub}} \Rightarrow 1] - \Pr[A^{\mathcal{F}_{a,b},S^{\mathcal{F}_{a,b}}} \Rightarrow 1]| \leq \epsilon$$

where the length of A*'s queries to* H^P *is restricted by* a *bits.*

In the indifferentiability from FILRO, the length of the distinguisher's queries to the private interface (queries to FILRO and KDFi-MD-SCFII) is restricted because we consider reducibility from "FIL"RO to KDFi-MD-SCFII. Please note that for a cryptosystem $\mathcal{C}$ which is secure in the FILRO model, when FILRO is replaced by KDFi-MD-SCFII, adversaries can treat the variable length input to KDFi-MD-SCFII. (Please see Theorem 1 of [22] for the relation of the interfaces between the indifferentiability proof and the security proof of a cryptosystem) So this proof considers reducibility from FILRO to "VIL" KDFi-MD-SCFII. Consequently, the above encryption schemes are secure when FILRO is replaced by KDFi-MD-SCFII.

4.1   Indifferentiability of KDFi-MD-SCFII from FILRO

Since it is known that KDFs using RO is equal to RO, namely, KDFi_m-$\mathcal{F}_{a,n}$ $\sqsubset$ $\mathcal{F}_{a,nm}$ ($i = 1, 2, 3$), we prove that $\mathrm{MD}^{\mathrm{SCFII}^{\mathcal{C}_{d,n}}} \sqsubset \mathcal{F}_{a,n}$. If this holds, we can conclude that KDFi_m-$\mathrm{MD}^{\mathrm{SCFII}^{\mathcal{C}_{d,n}}} \sqsubset \mathcal{F}_{a,nm}$ ($i = 1, 2, 3$).

Lemma 1. $\text{MD}^{\text{SCFII}^{\mathcal{C}_{d,n}}} \sqsubseteq \mathcal{F}_{a,n}$ where for any t_A, $t_S = t_A + \mathcal{O}((q_E + q_D)^2)$

$$\epsilon \leq \frac{3(lq_H + q_E + q_D)^2 + (lq_H + q_E)^2 + 2(lq_H + q_E + q_D) + q_E^2 + 2(q_E + q_D)(q_E + q_D + 1)}{2^{n+1}}$$

where A can make queries to $\text{MD}^{\text{SCFII}^{\mathcal{C}_{d,n}}} / \mathcal{F}_n$ at most q_H times where the length of the query is a-bits and A can make queries to E/S_E and D/S_D at most q_E and q_D times, respectively. l is the block length to calculate the output of $\text{MD}^{\text{SCFII}^{\mathcal{C}_{d,n}}}$ for an a-bits input.

The proof of Lemma 1 can be proven by using the technique in [13] but differs in several aspects (in this proof distinguisher's queries are restricted). The proof is given in the full version.

4.2   The Security of Encryption Schemes in the FILRO Model

We call a cryptosystem, from which the input lengths of ROs are fixed, "FIL-cryptosystem". In this section, we show that any FIL-cryptosystem which is secure in the VILRO model is secure in the FILRO model.

To prove the security, we consider the following RO $\mathcal{F}'_{a,b}$. $\mathcal{F}'_{a,b}$ consists of $\mathcal{F}^{FIL}_{a,b} : \{0,1\}^a \to \{0,1\}^b$ and $\mathcal{F}^{VIL}_b : \{0,1\}^* \to \{0,1\}^b$.

$\mathcal{F}^{FIL}_{a,b}(M)$	$\mathcal{F}^{VIL}_b(M)$
01 If $\mathsf{F}_b[M] \neq \perp$, ret $\mathsf{F}_b[M]$;	11 If $\mathsf{F}_b[M] \neq \perp$, ret $\mathsf{F}_b[M]$;
02 $\mathsf{F}_b[M] \xleftarrow{\$} \{0,1\}^n$;	12 $\mathsf{F}_b[M] \xleftarrow{\$} \{0,1\}^n$;
03 Ret $\mathsf{F}_b[M]$;	13 Ret $\mathsf{F}_b[M]$;

Then $\mathcal{F}'^{priv}_{a,b} = \mathcal{F}^{FIL}_{a,b}$ and $\mathcal{F}'^{pub}_{a,b} = \mathcal{F}^{VIL}_b$. When considering a cryptosystem in the $\mathcal{F}'_{a,b}$ model, the cryptosystem uses $\mathcal{F}^{FIL}_{a,b}$ and adversaries have oracle access to $\mathcal{F}^{VIL}_b$.

Since the lengths of RO queries from FIL-cryptosystems are fixed, if FIL-cryptosystems are secure in the VILRO model, these are secure in the $\mathcal{F}'_{a,b}$ model. Note that the values a and b are determined by the description of the cryptosystem.

We show that $\mathcal{F}_{a,b} \sqsubseteq \mathcal{F}'_{a,b}$ as follows. Note that $\mathcal{F}^{priv}_{a,b} = \mathcal{F}_{a,b}$ and $\mathcal{F}^{pub}_{a,b} = \mathcal{F}_{a,b}$.

Lemma 2. $\mathcal{F}_{a,b} \sqsubseteq \mathcal{F}'_{a,b}$ where $t_S = t_A + \mathcal{O}(q)$ and $\epsilon = 0$ where A can make queries to $(\mathcal{O}_1, \mathcal{O}_2)$, which is $(\mathcal{F}^{FIL}_{a,b}, \mathcal{F}^{VIL}_b)$ or $(\mathcal{F}_{a,b}, S^{\mathcal{F}_{a,b}})$ at most q times.

From the lemma 2, any FIL-cryptosystem secure in the $\mathcal{F}'_{a,b}$ model is secure in the FILRO model. Since any FIL-cryptosystem secure in the RO model is secure in the $\mathcal{F}'_{a,b}$ model, the FIL-cryptosystem is secure in the FILRO model.

Proof (Lemma 2). First, we define a simulator S.

294 Y. Naito et al.

$$\underline{\mathcal{F}_{a,b}(M)}$$
11 If $\mathsf{F}_{a,b}[M] \neq \perp$, ret $\mathsf{F}_{a,b}[M]$;
12 $\mathsf{F}_{a,b}[M] \xleftarrow{\$} \{0,1\}^n$;
13 Ret $\mathsf{F}_{a,b}[M]$;

$$\underline{S(M)}$$
01 If $\mathsf{F}_S[M] \neq \perp$, ret $\mathsf{F}_S[M]$;
02 If $|M| = a$, $\mathsf{F}_S[M] \leftarrow \mathcal{F}_{a,b}(M)$;
03 Else $\mathsf{F}_S[M] \xleftarrow{\$} \{0,1\}^b$;
04 Ret $\mathsf{F}_S[M]$;

$\mathsf{F}_{a,b}$ is a (initially everywhere $\perp$) table which is used to realize FILRO $\mathcal{F}_{a,b}$. F_S is a (initially everywhere $\perp$) table which is stored the output of S.

If both $\mathcal{F}_{a,b}[M]$ and $\mathcal{F}_S[M]$ are defined, $\mathcal{F}_{a,b}[M] = \mathcal{F}_S[M]$. So the output distribution of $(\mathcal{F}_{a,b}, S^{\mathcal{F}_{a,b}})$ is equal to $(\mathcal{F}_{a,b}^{FIL}, \mathcal{F}_b^{VIL})$. Thus no A can distinguish between them. □

References

1. Abe, M., Kiltz, E., Okamoto, T.: Chosen Ciphertext Security with Optimal Ciphertext Overhead. In: Pieprzyk, J. (ed.) ASIACRYPT 2008. LNCS, vol. 5350, pp. 355–371. Springer, Heidelberg (2008)
2. Bellare, M., Rogaway, P.: Random Oracles are Practical: A Paradigm for Designing Efficient Protocols. In: ACM Conference on Computer and Communications Security, pp. 62–73 (1993)
3. Bellare, M., Rogaway, P.: Optimal Asymmetric Encryption. In: De Santis, A. (ed.) EUROCRYPT 1994. LNCS, vol. 950, pp. 92–111. Springer, Heidelberg (1995)
4. Bellare, M., Rogaway, P.: The Exact Security of Digital Signatures - How to Sign with RSA and Rabin. In: Maurer, U.M. (ed.) EUROCRYPT 1996. LNCS, vol. 1070, pp. 399–416. Springer, Heidelberg (1996)
5. Black, J.A., Rogaway, P., Shrimpton, T.: Black-Box Analysis of the Block-Cipher-Based Hash-Function Constructions from PGV. In: Yung, M. (ed.) CRYPTO 2002. LNCS, vol. 2442, pp. 103–118. Springer, Heidelberg (2002)
6. Boneh, D.: Simplified OAEP for the RSA and Rabin Functions. In: Kilian, J. (ed.) CRYPTO 2001. LNCS, vol. 2139, pp. 275–291. Springer, Heidelberg (2001)
7. Boneh, D., Lynn, B., Shacham, H.: Short Signatures from the Weil Pairing. In: Boyd, C. (ed.) ASIACRYPT 2001. LNCS, vol. 2248, pp. 514–532. Springer, Heidelberg (2001)
8. Boneh, D., Boyen, X.: Efficient Selective-ID Secure Identity-Based Encryption Without Random Oracles. In: Cachin, C., Camenisch, J.L. (eds.) EUROCRYPT 2004. LNCS, vol. 3027, pp. 223–238. Springer, Heidelberg (2004)
9. Canetti, R., Goldreich, O., Halevi, S.: The Random Oracle Methodology, Revisited (Preliminary Version). In: STOC, pp. 209–218 (1998)
10. Canetti, R., Halevi, S., Katz, J.: A forward-secure public-key encryption scheme. J. Cryptology 20(4), 265–294 (2007)
11. Chevallier-Mames, B., Phan, D.H., Pointcheval, D.: Optimal Asymmetric Encryption and Signature Paddings. In: Ioannidis, J., Keromytis, A.D., Yung, M. (eds.) ACNS 2005. LNCS, vol. 3531, pp. 254–268. Springer, Heidelberg (2005)
12. Coron, J.-S.: Optimal Security Proofs for PSS and Other Signature Schemes. In: Knudsen, L.R. (ed.) EUROCRYPT 2002. LNCS, vol. 2332, pp. 272–287. Springer, Heidelberg (2002)
13. Coron, J.-S., Dodis, Y., Malinaud, C., Puniya, P.: Merkle-Damgård Revisited: How to Construct a Hash Function. In: Shoup, V. (ed.) CRYPTO 2005. LNCS, vol. 3621, pp. 430–448. Springer, Heidelberg (2005)

14. Coron, J.-S., Joye, M., Naccache, D., Paillier, P.: Universal Padding Schemes for RSA. In: Yung, M. (ed.) CRYPTO 2002. LNCS, vol. 2442, pp. 226–241. Springer, Heidelberg (2002)
15. Dodis, Y., Freedman, M.J., Jarecki, S., Walfish, S.: Versatile padding schemes for joint signature and encryption. In: ACM Conference on Computer and Communications Security, pp. 344–353 (2004)
16. Dodis, Y., Ristenpart, T., Shrimpton, T.: Salvaging Merkle-Damgård for Practical Applications. In: Joux, A. (ed.) EUROCRYPT 2009. LNCS, vol. 5479, pp. 371–388. Springer, Heidelberg (2009)
17. Dodis, Y., Ristenpart, T., Shrimpton, T.: Salvaging Merkle-Damgård for Practical Applications. ePrint 2009/177 (2009)
18. Fiat, A., Shamir, A.: How to Prove Yourself: Practical Solutions to Identification and Signature Problems
19. IEEE. P1363: Standard specifcations for public-key cryptography
20. Komano, Y., Ohta, K.: Efficient Universal Padding Techniques for Multiplicative Trapdoor One-Way Permutation. In: Boneh, D. (ed.) CRYPTO 2003. LNCS, vol. 2729, pp. 366–382. Springer, Heidelberg (2003)
21. RSA Laboratories. PKCS #1 v2.1: RSA cryptography standard (June 14, 2002)
22. Maurer, U.M., Renner, R.S., Holenstein, C.: Indifferentiability, Impossibility Results on Reductions, and Applications to the Random Oracle Methodology. In: Naor, M. (ed.) TCC 2004. LNCS, vol. 2951, pp. 21–39. Springer, Heidelberg (2004)
23. Naito, Y., Yoneyama, K., Wang, L., Ohta, K.: How to Confirm Cryptosystems Security: The Original Merkle-Damgård Is Still Alive! In: Matsui, M. (ed.) ASIACRYPT 2009. LNCS, vol. 5912, pp. 382–398. Springer, Heidelberg (2009)
24. National Institute of Standards and Technoloty. FIPS PUB 180-3 Secure Hash Standard. In: FIPS PUB (2008)
25. Phan, D.H., Pointcheval, D.: OAEP 3-Round:A Generic and Secure Asymmetric Encryption Padding. In: Lee, P.J. (ed.) ASIACRYPT 2004. LNCS, vol. 3329, pp. 63–77. Springer, Heidelberg (2004)
26. Preneel, B., Govaerts, R., Vandewalle, J.: Hash Functions Based on Block Ciphers: A Synthetic Approach. In: Stinson, D.R. (ed.) CRYPTO 1993. LNCS, vol. 773, pp. 368–378. Springer, Heidelberg (1994)
27. Shoup, V.: A Proposal for an ISO Standard for Public Key Encryption (version 2.1) (2001)
28. Shoup, V.: OAEP reconsidered. In: Kilian, J. (ed.) CRYPTO 2001. LNCS, vol. 2139, pp. 239–259. Springer, Heidelberg (2001)
29. Stam, M.: Blockcipher-Based Hashing Revisited. In: Dunkelman, O. (ed.) FSE 2009. LNCS, vol. 5665, pp. 67–83. Springer, Heidelberg (2009)
30. Yoneyama, K., Miyagawa, S., Ohta, K.: Leaky Random Oracle (Extended Abstract). In: Baek, J., Bao, F., Chen, K., Lai, X. (eds.) ProvSec 2008. LNCS, vol. 5324, pp. 226–240. Springer, Heidelberg (2008)

A   Differentiable Attack for KDFs Using pub-RO

We only show that KDF1-pub-RO is not indifferentiable from pub-RO as follows. Similarly, the cases of KDF2 and KDF3 can be proven.

Consider the experiment of indifferentiability of $\mathsf{KDF1}_m$-pub-RO$_n$ from pub-RO$_{nm}$. A distinguisher interacts with $(\mathsf{KDF1}_m\text{-}\mathcal{F}_n, \mathcal{F}_n, \mathcal{F}_{leak})$ or $(\mathcal{F}_{nm}, S)$ where $S = (S_{\mathcal{F}}, S_{leak})$ has oracle access to pub-RO$_{nm}^{pub} = (\mathcal{F}_{nm}, \mathcal{F}_{leak})$

and simulates $\mathcal{F}_n$ and $\mathcal{F}_{leak}$ respectively. Let $(\mathcal{O}_H, \mathcal{O}_{\mathcal{F}}, \mathcal{O}_{leak})$ be $(\mathsf{KDF1}_m\text{-}\mathcal{F}_n, \mathcal{F}_n, \mathcal{F}_{leak})$ or $(\mathcal{F}_{nm}, S_{\mathcal{F}}, S_{leak})$. We define the following distinguisher A. Let q be the most minimum value in $\{q_H/2, q_{\mathcal{F}}, q_{leak}\}$ where q_H is the maximum number of queries to $\mathcal{O}_H$ made by A, $q_{\mathcal{F}}$ is is the maximum number of queries to $\mathcal{O}_{\mathcal{F}}$ made by A, and q_{leak} is is the maximum number of queries to $\mathcal{O}_{leak}$ made by A.

1. For $i = 1, \ldots, q$
   (a) $j \xleftarrow{\$} \{0,1\}$;
   (b) $M \xleftarrow{\$} \{0,1\}^{ns}$ such that $1 \le s$;
   (c) Makes a query $M||\langle 0 \rangle$ to $\mathcal{O}_{\mathcal{F}}$ and receives w;
   (d) If $j = 0$, makes a query M to $\mathcal{O}_H$ and receives z;
   (e) Makes a query to $\mathcal{O}_{leak}$ and receives the list L;
   (f) If $j = 1$, makes a query M to $\mathcal{O}_H$ and receives z;
   (g) If $z_1 \ne w$, return 1; $// z = z_1||z_2||\ldots||z_m$ and $|z_t| = n$ $(t = 1, \ldots, m)$.
   (h) If $j = 0$ and there does not exist $(M||\langle 1 \rangle, z_2)$ in L, return 1;
2. Return 0;

When A interacts with $(\mathsf{KDF1}_m\text{-}\mathcal{F}_n, \mathcal{F}_n, \mathcal{F}_{leak})$, A clearly outputs 0 with probability of 1. Consider the case that A interacts with $(\mathcal{F}_{nm}, S)$. Let M be a value defined in the step 1-b. When S does not query M to $\mathcal{F}_{nm}$ in the step 1-c, the probability that A outputs 1 is non-negligible due to the step 1-g. This implies that S should query M to $\mathcal{F}_{nm}$ in the step 1-c and the pair (M, z) should be stored in the list L_{leak} of pub-RO$_{nm}$, when the step 1-e is executed. Then, in the step 1-e, S does not know whether A queries M to $\mathcal{F}_{nm}$ in the step 1-d because j is chosen uniformly from $\{0,1\}$. Note that if $j = 0$, pairs $(M||\langle 0 \rangle, z_1), (M||\langle 1 \rangle, z_2), \ldots, (M||\langle m-1 \rangle, z_m)$ should be stored in L, and if $j = 1$, only the pair $(M||\langle 0 \rangle, z_1)$ should be stored in L.[1] Since S does not know j and so does not know whether $(M||\langle 1 \rangle, z_2)$ should be stored, A outputs 1 in the step 1-h with probability of almost 1 by the loop. So $\mathsf{KDF1}_m$-pub-RO$_n$ is not indifferentiable from pub-RO$_{nm}$.

---

[1] When $(\mathcal{O}_H, \mathcal{O}_{\mathcal{F}}, \mathcal{O}_{leak}) = (\mathsf{KDF1}_m\text{-}\mathcal{F}_n, \mathcal{F}_n, \mathcal{F}_{leak})$, if $j = 0$, pairs $(M||\langle 0 \rangle, z_1), (M||\langle 1 \rangle, z_2), \ldots, (M||\langle m-1 \rangle, z_m)$ is stored in L with probability 1, and if $j = 1$, only the pair $(M||\langle 0 \rangle, z_1)$ should be stored in L with probability 1.

Key-Dependent Message Security for Division Function: Discouraging Anonymous Credential Sharing*

Xianhui Lu[1], Bao Li[1], Qixiang Mei[2], and Haixia Xu[1]

1. State Key Laboratory of Information Security, Graduate University of Chinese Academy of Sciences, Beijing, 100049, China
2. School of Information, Guangdong Ocean University, Zhanjiang, 524088, China
{xhlu,lb,hxxu}@is.ac.cn, nupf@163.com

Abstract. Key-dependent message (KDM) security means that the encryption scheme remains secure even encrypting $f(sk)$, where f is an efficient computable function chosen by the adversary and $sk = sk_1, \cdots, sk_n$ are private keys. We concentrate on a special case that the function f is a division function. Namely, the messages of the form sk_i/sk_j are encrypted. We prove that if a public key encryption (PKE) scheme is IND-CPA (chosen plaintext attacks) secure and has the properties of public-key blinding and secret-key homomorphism, then it is KDM secure for division function (KDM-div secure). For concrete scheme, we show that the hybrid ElGamal scheme is KDM-div secure based on the decisional Diffie-Hellman (DDH) assumption in the standard model. We show that KDM-div secure scheme is useful in the design of anonymous credential systems.

Keywords: Public-key encryption, Key-dependent message security, Decisional Diffie-Hellman assumption.

1 Introduction

A PKE (Public Key Encryption) scheme is KDM [3] (Key Dependent Message) secure w.r.t. function set F if $\mathrm{E}_{pk_i}(f(sk_1, \cdots, sk_n))$ is indistinguishable from $\mathrm{E}_{pk_i}(0)$, where (pk_i, sk_i) is the public key and private key pair, $\mathrm{E}_{pk_i}(m)$ denotes encrypt m with pk_i, $f \in F, i \in [n]$.

A special case of KDM security, called circular security which was proposed by Camenisch and Lysyanskaya [2], means that KDM security holds for a "circular encryption" $I = (\mathrm{E}_{pk_1}(sk_2), \cdots, \mathrm{E}_{pk_{n-1}}(sk_n), \mathrm{E}_{pk_n}(sk_1))$. Circular security has particular interest because of its "all-or-nothing" property: if an individual A, who publishes I, reveals one of his secret keys sk_i to another user B, B can know all other secret keys $sk_1, ..., sk_n$ by decrypting ciphertexts of I.

---

* Supported by the National Natural Science Foundation of China (No.61070171), the National Basic Research Program of China(973 project) (No.2007CB311201) and the Postdoctoral Science Foundation of China (No.20100480514).

X. Boyen and X. Chen (Eds.): ProvSec 2011, LNCS 6980, pp. 297–308, 2011.

Circular secure encryption has an application to an anonymous credential system [2] because the "all-or-nothing" property discourages A from delegation of his secret keys to B. However, known circular secure encryption scheme relies on the random oracle [2,3], is impractical [7,14], or is based on lattice [9] (and therefore requires a large public key). The most practical circular secure encryption in the standard model was proposed by Malkin, Teranishi, and Yung [16]. In [16], the authors showed that the Paillier-based ElGamal is KDM secure w.r.t polynomial functions.

1.1 Our Contribution

We propose a new method to construct a PKE scheme with the "all-or-nothing" property and achieve an efficient PKE scheme with this property in the standard model. Specifically, our results comprised three parts.

First, we show that KDM security w.r.t division function satisfies "all-or-nothing" property. We call this case KDM-div security. Concretely, KDM-div security means that the scheme remains secure even when the messages of the form sk_i/sk_j are encrypted. Similar as circular encryption, we can construct a "divided" circular encryption $I' = (E_{pk_1}(sk_2/sk_1), \cdots, E_{pk_n}(sk_1/sk_n))$. It is clear that if an individual A, who publishes I', reveals one of his secret keys sk_i to another user B, B can know all other secret keys $sk_1, \cdots, sk_n$ by decrypting ciphertexts of I'.

Second, we give a sufficient condition for a PKE to be KDM-div secure. We prove that if a PKE scheme is IND-CPA (chosen plaintext attacks) secure and has the properties of public-key blinding and secret-key homomorphism, it is KDM-div secure. The main idea is that, the simulator S, in the security proof, sets $sk_i = xa_i$ (implicitly, through setting the corresponding public key by using the homomorphic property), where x is unknown to S, a_i is a random element selected by S. Then it follows that $sk_i/sk_j = a_i/a_j$, which means that S can compute $E_{pk_k}(sk_i/sk_j)$ even if she does not know the secret x. Hence, the simulator S can simulate the view of an adversary without knowing the secret x and therefore can embed some intractable problem into (the public data corresponding to) x.

Third, we show that the hybrid ElGamal scheme satisfied this sufficient condition in the standard model. As a result, we find a highly efficient scheme (hybrid ElGamal scheme) which satisfies "all-or-nothing" property in the standard model.

In [16], Malkin, Teranishi, and Yung proposed a general transformation which converted a KDM secure PKE w.r.t. a function set F into another KDM secure PKE w.r.t. a function set $f/g|f, g \in F$, and they showed that the Paillier-based ElGamal was KDM secure w.r.t. sk_i, Hence, the scheme converted from the Paillier-based ElGamal is KDM secure w.r.t. sk_i/sk_j. Since the Paillier-based ElGamal scheme is based on $Z^*_{N^s}$, where $s \geq 2$, $N = pq$, p, q are large prime numbers. Our solution is considerably more efficient than the scheme of Malkin et.al.

1.2   Related Works

Motivation for KDM Security. The danger of encrypting key-dependent messages was noted more than two decades ago by Micali, Rackoff and Sloan [1]. They also pointed out that in the designing of cryptographic protocols, one would often like to be able to transmit self-encrypted ciphertexts. For instance, if that type of messages were allowed, one would have a trivial solution to the problem of verifiable secret sharing. However, for a long period of time the encryption of key-dependent messages was seen as an abuse of encryption scheme and not taken into account by cryptographers. Over the last decade, it was found that the plaintext do depend on the private key in several cases. The first case, just as Micali, Rackoff and Sloan [1] had pointed out, key-dependent message encryption may be helpful in the designing of cryptographic protocols. For example, circular encryption is useful in the construction of anonymous credential systems [2]. The second case is that encryption schemes are viewed as abstract symbols in the designing of high-level protocols, say, E denotes encryption and D denotes decryption. From this viewpoint there is nothing obviously "abuse" with $E(D)$, and so we had better allow the adversary to get such ciphertexts in the formal definition of security. This case was observed by Black, Rogaway and Shrimpton [3], who proposed a new definition of security named as KDM security which is stronger than circular security [2]. The third case is that the encryption of key-dependent messages really happens unexpectedly in practical applications. When the IEEE p1619 standard group was developing the standard for sector level encryption, they were informed the possibility that the implementation of disk encryption in Windows Vista could store to the disk an encryption of its own secret key when the operating system goes to hibernate (the information in memory including the secret key itself will be encrypted and dumped to the disk).

KDM Security for Symmetric Encryption. Backes, Pfitzmann and Scedrov [4] extended KDM security to the active attack model of symmetric encryption by proposing two definitions named as AKDM (Adaptive Key-Dependent Message) and DKDM (Dynamic Key-Dependent Message). Halevi and Krawczyk [5] concentrated on the key dependent security of deterministic symmetric schemes such as PRFs (Pseudo-Random Functions) and block ciphers. Hofheinz and Unruh [6] proposed KDM secure symmetric encryption schemes in the standard model. The price they paid was that they only achieved a relaxed notion of the original KDM security [3] (the adversary can only query the encryption oracle at most $p(k)$ times). Bellare and Keelveedhi provided a comprehensive treatment of the security of authenticated encryption (AE) in the presence of key-dependent data, considering the four variants of the goal arising from the choice of universal nonce or random nonce security and presence or absence of a header.

KDM Security in the Case of Active Attacks. Backes, Dürmuth and Unruh [8] extended the KDM security to the case of adaptive corruptions and active attacks, and proved that OAEP encryption scheme meets their new definition.

Camenisch, Chandran and Shoup [10] showed the construction of PKE scheme that simultaneously provides KDM security and IND-CCA2 (adaptive chosen ciphertext attack) security (KDM-CCA2). They showed that by applying the Naor-Yung double encryption paradigm, one can combine any KDM-CPA secure scheme with any IND-CCA2 secure scheme, along with an appropriate non-interactive zero-knowledge proof, to obtain a KDM-CCA2 secure scheme.

KDM Security w.r.t Functions beyond Affine Function. Brakerski, Goldwasser and Kalai [12] proposed the construction of KDM secure schemes for degree-d polynomial functions. Barak, Haitner, Hofheinz and Ishai [13] proposed a KDM secure PKE scheme that allows the adversary to access encryptions of arbitrary efficient functions of the secret keys. However, the number of the public keys and the functions are bounded. Recently, Applebaum [15] removed these restrictions.

The Impossibility of KDM Security. Haitner and Holenstein [11] studied the possibility of constructing KDM secure encryption schemes. They showed that there exists no fully-black-box reduction from an encryption scheme that is key-dependent input secure against every poly(n)-wise independent family of hash functions to one-way permutations. The authors also showed that there exists no reduction with strongly-black-box proof of security from a key-dependent inputs encryption scheme to any secure cryptographic assumptions.

1.3   Outline

In section 2 we review the definition of public key encryption scheme, IND-CPA security, public-key blinding, secret-key homomorphism, DDH assumption and one-time symmetric key encryption scheme. In section 3 we prove that if a public key encryption scheme is IND-CPA secure and has the properties of public-key blinding and secret-key homomorphism, then it is KDM-div secure. In section 4 we prove that the hybrid ElGamal scheme is KDM-div secure based on DDH assumption under the standard model. Finally we give the conclusion in section 5.

2   Definitions

In describing probabilistic processes, we write $x \xleftarrow{R} X$ to denote the action of assigning to the variable x a value sampled according to the distribution X. If S is a finite set, we simply write $s \xleftarrow{R} S$ to denote assignment to s of an element sampled from uniform distribution on S. If A is a probabilistic algorithm and x an input, then $A(x)$ denotes the output distribution of A on input x. Thus, we write $y \xleftarrow{R} A(x)$ to denote of running algorithm A on input x and assigning the output to the variable y.

2.1   Public Key Encryption Scheme

A public key encryption scheme consists the following algorithms:

- PKE.G(l): A probabilistic polynomial-time key generation algorithm takes as input a security parameter l and outputs a public key and a private key (pk, sk). We write $(pk, sk) \leftarrow$ PKE.G(l)
- PKE.E(pk, m): A probabilistic polynomial-time encryption algorithm takes as input a public key pk and a message m, and outputs a ciphertext c. We write $c \leftarrow \mathrm{E}_{pk}(m)$
- PKE.D(sk, c): A decryption algorithm takes as input a ciphertext c and a private key sk, and outputs a plaintext m. We write $m \leftarrow \mathrm{D}_{sk}(c)$.

We require that for all (pk, sk) output by PKE.G(l), all $m \in M$ (M denotes the message space), and all c output by $\mathrm{E}_{pk}(m)$ we have $\mathrm{D}_{sk}(c) = m$.

2.2   IND-CPA Security

A public key encryption scheme is secure against chosen plaintext attacks (IND-CPA secure) if the advantage of any adversary in the following game is negligible in the security parameter l:

- **Setup:** The adversary queries a key generation oracle. The key generation oracle computes $(pk, sk) \leftarrow$ PKE.G(l) and responds with pk.
- **Challenge:** The adversary submits two messages m_0, m_1 with $|m_0| = |m_1|$. On input m_0, m_1 the encryption oracle computes:

$$b \xleftarrow{R} \{0, 1\}; c^* \leftarrow \mathrm{E}_{pk}(m_b)$$

  and responds with c^*.
- **Guess:** Finally, the adversary outputs a guess b'.

We say the adversary succeeds if $b' = b$. The adversary's advantage is defined as $\mathrm{Adv}_{\mathcal{A}}^{\mathrm{cpa}} = |\Pr[\mathcal{A}(\mathrm{E}_{pk}(m_0)) = 0] - \Pr[\mathcal{A}(\mathrm{E}_{pk}(m_1))) = 0]|$.

2.3   Public-Key Blinding and Secret-Key Homomorphism

We review the definition of public-key blinding and secret-key homomorphism introduced in [7]. Let (pk, sk) be a pair of public key and private key of a public key encryption scheme π, $c = \mathrm{E}_{pk}(m)$ be an encryption of a message m.

Public-key Blinding: We say π has the property of public-key blinding if there exists a function $\mathrm{blind}_r()$ that $\mathrm{blind}_r(pk)$ is an uniformly random public key for sk, where r is a random value.

Secret-key Homomorphism: We say π has the property of secret-key homomorphism if there exist two function $\mathcal{F}_s()$ and $\mathcal{G}_s()$ that we can get a new key pair (pk', sk') and a ciphertext $c' = \mathrm{E}_{pk'}(m)$ as follows:

$$s \xleftarrow{R} \mathcal{SK}; pk' \leftarrow \mathcal{F}_s(pk); sk' \leftarrow sk \cdot s; c' \leftarrow \mathcal{G}_s(c),$$

where $\mathcal{SK}$ is the space of private key.

2.4 Decisional Diffie-Hellman Assumption

Let G be a group of large prime order q, g is a generator of G, consider the following experiment:

$\text{Exp}_{G,A}^{\text{ddh}}$:

$$(x, y, z) \xleftarrow{R} Z_q^*, W_1 \leftarrow g^z, W_0 \leftarrow g^{xy}, b \xleftarrow{R} \{0, 1\},$$

$$b' \leftarrow A(g, g^x, g^y, W_b), \text{return } b'.$$

We define the advantage of A as

$$\text{Adv}_A^{\text{ddh}} = |\Pr[b' = 0|b = 0] - \Pr[b' = 0|b = 1]|.$$

We say that the DDH assumption holds if $\text{Adv}_A^{\text{ddh}}$ is negligible for all polynomial-time adversaries A.

2.5 One-Time Symmetric Key Encryption Scheme

A one-time symmetric key encryption scheme SKE consists of two algorithms:

- SKE.E(k, m): The deterministic, polynomial-time encryption algorithm takes as input a key k, and a message m, and outputs a ciphertext χ. We write $\chi \leftarrow$ SKE.E(k, m)
- SKE.D(k, χ): The deterministic, polynomial-time decryption algorithm takes as input a key k, and a ciphertext χ, and outputs a message m. We write $m \leftarrow$ SKE.D(k, χ)

We require that for all $k \in \{0, 1\}^{kLen}$, $kLen$ denotes the length of the key of SKE, and for all $m \in \{0, 1\}^*$, we have:

$$\text{SKE.D}(k, \text{SKE.E}(k, m)) = m.$$

A SKE scheme is secure against passive attacks if the advantage of any probabilistic polynomial-time adversary A in the following game is negligible in the security parameter $kLen$:

- **Setup:** The challenger randomly generates an appropriately sized key $k \in \{0, 1\}^{kLen}$.
- **Challenge:** The adversary queries the encryption oracle with two messages (m_0, m_1), $|m_0| = |m_1|$. A bit b is randomly chosen and the adversary is given a "challenge ciphertext" $\chi^* \leftarrow$ SKE.E(k, m_b).
- **Guess:** Finally, A outputs a guess b'.

The adversary's advantage in the game above is defined as $\text{Adv}_A^{\text{pa}} = |\Pr[b' = 0|b = 0] - \Pr[b' = 0|b = 1]|$. If a SKE scheme is secure against passive attack we say it is IND-PA secure.

3   KDM-div Security

A public key encryption scheme is KDM-div secure if the advantage of any adversary in the following game is negligible in the security parameter l:

- **Setup:** The challenger runs PKE.G(l) n times and obtains $(pk_i, sk_i), i = 1, \cdots, n$. It sends $(pk_1, \cdots, pk_n)$ to the adversary.
- **Challenge:** The adversary repeatedly issues queries (j_1, j_2, i), where $1 \leq j_1, j_2, i \leq n$. With each query, the challenger sends $E_{pk_i}(m_{jb})$ to the adversary, where $m_{j0} = \{0\}^{l_m}, m_{j1} = sk_{j_1}/sk_{j_2}, l_m = |m_{j1}|, j = 1, \cdots, q_e, q_e$ is the total number that the adversary queries, $b \in \{0, 1\}$ is a random bit selected by the challenger (note that the challenger chooses b only once).
- **Guess:** Finally, the adversary outputs b' as the guess of b.

The adversary's advantage is defined as $\text{Adv}_A^{\text{div}} = |\Pr[b' = 0|b = 0] - \Pr[b' = 0|b = 1]|$.

Now we give the formal description of how to get the KDM-div security from IND-CPA security.

Theorem 1. *A public key encryption scheme is KDM-div secure assuming that: (1) it is IND-CPA secure, (2) it has the properties of public-key blinding and secret-key homomorphism. To be concrete, for any adversary A against the scheme running for time Time_A, there exists an adversary B with*

$$\text{Adv}_B^{\text{cpa}} = \frac{1}{q_e} \text{Adv}_A^{\text{div}}$$

and $\text{Time}_B = \text{Time}_A + \mathcal{O}(q_e \cdot \text{Time}_E)$, where Time_E is the time for one encryption operation of the scheme.

Let π be a public key encryption scheme and has the properties public-key blinding and secret-key homomorphism. Suppose an adversary A can break the KDM-div security of π with the advantage of $\text{Adv}_A^{\text{div}}$. To prove the theorem we construct an adversary B to break the IND-CPA security of π.

We begin by describing some hybrid experiments associated to B. For $0 \leq J \leq q_e$, experiment $\text{Exp}(J)$ is described as follows:

1. Run the key generation algorithm n times and obtain n key pairs (pk_i, sk_i), $i = 1, \cdots, n$. Send $(pk_1, \cdots, pk_n)$ to the adversary A.
2. In the jth query, the adversary queries with (j_1, j_2, i), where $1 \leq j_1, j_2, i \leq n$. If $j \leq J$, the challenger encrypts m_{j0} using pk_i, if $j > J$ the challenger encrypts m_{j1} using pk_i. Then The challenger sends the ciphertext to the adversary A. Here $m_{j0} = \{0\}^{l_m}, m_{j1} = sk_{j_1}/sk_{j_2}, l_m = |m_{j1}|$.
3. The adversary A returns b'.

Let $\Pr[\text{ExpH}(J) = 0]$ denote the probability that experiment $\text{ExpH}(J)$ returns 0. We have that:

$$\begin{aligned} \text{Adv}_A^{\text{div}} &= |\Pr[b' = 0|b = 0] - \Pr[b' = 0|b = 1]| \\ &= |\Pr[\text{ExpH}(q_e) = 0] - \Pr[\text{ExpH}(0) = 0]|. \end{aligned} \tag{1}$$

Now we give the description of $\mathcal{B}$. The adversary $\mathcal{B}$ gets pk from an IND-CPA challenger, randomly selects $1 \leq J \leq q_e$ and runs as follows:

Key Generation: For $i = 1, \cdots, n$ $\mathcal{B}$ runs the following key generation algorithm:

$$(s_i, x_i) \xleftarrow{R} \mathcal{SK}, pk_i \leftarrow blind_{s_i}(\mathcal{F}_{x_i}(pk)).$$

The public key that $\mathcal{A}$ sees is $pk_1, \cdots, pk_n$, $\mathcal{B}$ knows $(x_1, \cdots, x_n)$ and $(s_1, \cdots, s_n)$. According to the property of public-key blinding and secret-key homomorphism, $(pk_1, \cdots, pk_n)$ are uniformly random public keys, the private key for pk_i is $(sk \cdot x_i)$, where sk denotes the private key for pk.

Challenge: In the challenge step, for the jth query (j_1, j_2, i) sets:

$$m_{j0} = 0^{|m_{j1}|},$$

$$\begin{aligned} m_{j1} &= sk_{j_1}/sk_{j_2} \\ &= (sk \cdot x_{j_1})/(sk \cdot x_{j_2}) \\ &= (x_{j_1})/(x_{j_2}). \end{aligned}$$

Then computes c_j as follows:

If $j < J$: $c_j \leftarrow \mathrm{E}_{pk_i}(m_{j0})$

If $j = J$: send (m_{j0}, m_{j1}) to the IND-CPA challenger, get the challenge ciphertext $c^* = \mathrm{E}_{pk}(m_{jb})$. Set $c_j \leftarrow \mathcal{G}_{x_i}(c^*)$. According to the property of secret-key homomorphism, we have that:

$$c_j = \mathcal{G}_{x_i}(c^*) = \mathcal{G}_{x_i}(\mathrm{E}_{pk}(m_{jb})) = \mathrm{E}_{pk_i}(m_{jb}).$$

If $j > J$: $c_i \leftarrow \mathrm{E}_{pk_i}(m_{j1})$

Then, $\mathcal{B}$ sends c_j to the adversary $\mathcal{A}$.

Guess: Finally, when $\mathcal{A}$ returns b', $\mathcal{B}$ outputs b' too.

The advantage of $\mathcal{B}$ in breaking the IND-CPA security of scheme π is:

$$\begin{aligned} \mathrm{Adv}_{\mathcal{B}}^{\mathrm{cpa}} &= |\Pr[\mathcal{B}(\mathrm{E}_{pk}(m_0)) = 0] - \Pr[\mathcal{B}(\mathrm{E}_{pk}(m_1)) = 0]| \\ &= \frac{1}{q_e}|\sum_{i=1}^{q_e}(\Pr[\mathcal{B}(\mathrm{E}_{pk}(m_0)) = 0|J = i] - \Pr[\mathcal{B}(\mathrm{E}_{pk}(m_1)) = 0|J = i])| \\ &= \frac{1}{q_e}|\sum_{i=1}^{q_e}(\Pr[\mathrm{ExpH}(i) = 0] - \Pr[\mathrm{ExpH}(i-1) = 0])| \\ &= \frac{1}{q_e}|\Pr[\mathrm{ExpH}(q_e) = 0] - \Pr[\mathrm{ExpH}(0) = 0]| \\ &= \frac{1}{q_e}\mathrm{Adv}_{\mathcal{A}}^{\mathrm{div}}. \end{aligned}$$

(2)

The adversary $\mathcal{B}$ encrypts q_e ciphertexts in the challenge stage. So we have:

$$\mathrm{Time}_{\mathcal{B}} = \mathrm{Time}_{\mathcal{A}} + \mathcal{O}(q_e \cdot \mathrm{Time}_{\mathrm{E}}).$$

This completes the proof of theorem 1.   □

3.1 Application

In [2] Camenisch and Lysyanskaya showed the construction of anonymous credential systems by using circular encryption. In the case of circular encryption [2] private keys are encrypted to form a "key cycle":

$$E_{pk_1}(sk_2), \cdots , E_{pk_n}(sk_1).$$

That is, each private key $sk_{(i \mod n)+1}$ is encrypted by the public key pk_i, where n is the number of key pairs. In anonymous credential systems, circular encryption is used to discourage users from delegating their private keys. If one of the private keys is leaked, then all of the other private keys can be computed from the "key cycle".

It is clear that KDM-div secure schemes can also be used for this purpose. That is, we use $(E_{pk_1}(sk_2/sk_1), \cdots , E_{pk_n}(sk_1/sk_n))$ instead of the original "key cycle". If sk_i is leaked, then we can get $sk_{(i \mod n)+1}$ as follows:

$$sk_{(i \mod n)+1}/sk_i \leftarrow D_{sk_i}(E_{pk_i}(sk_{(i \mod n)+1}/sk_i)),$$

$$sk_{(i \mod n)+1} \leftarrow (sk_{(i \mod n)+1}/sk_i) \cdot sk_i.$$

Likewise, all of the other private keys can be computed.

4 Hybrid ElGamal Is KDM-div Secure

In this section we prove that the hybrid version of ElGamal is KDM-div secure. First we review the hybrid version of ElGamal.

- **Key Generation:** Assume that G is a group of order q, where q is a large prime number.

$$g \xleftarrow{R} G, x \xleftarrow{R} Z_q^*, h \leftarrow g^x, pk \leftarrow (g, h), sk \leftarrow x.$$

- **Encryption:** To encrypt a message $m \in \{0, 1\}^*$, the encryption algorithm computes:

$$r \xleftarrow{R} Z_q^*, u \leftarrow g^r, k \leftarrow H(h^r), e \leftarrow SKE.E(k, m), c \leftarrow (u, e).$$

- **Decryption:** To decrypt the ciphertext (u, e), the decryption algorithm computes:

$$k \leftarrow H(u^x), m \leftarrow SKE.D(k, e).$$

Here $H : G \rightarrow \{0, 1\}^{kLen}$ is a universal hash function, SKE is an IND-PA secure one-time symmetric key encryption scheme, $kLen$ is the length of the key of SKE.

We now prove formally that the hybrid ElGamal scheme is KDM-div secure based on the DDH assumption.

Theorem 2. *The hybrid ElGamal encryption scheme is KDM-div secure assuming that: (1) DDH assumption holds in G, (2) SKE is an IND-PA secure one-time symmetric encryption scheme. To be specific, for any adversary $\mathcal{A}$ against the KDM-div security of the scheme, there exists an adversary $\mathcal{B}_1$ that can solve the DDH problem with*

$$\mathrm{Adv}_{\mathcal{B}_1}^{\mathrm{ddh}} = \frac{1}{2}\left(\frac{1}{q_e}\mathrm{Adv}_{\mathcal{A}}^{\mathrm{div}} - \mathrm{Adv}_{\mathcal{B}_2}^{\mathrm{pa}}\right).$$

The theorem follows from the facts:

1. **IND-CPA security:** It is well known that the hybrid ElGamal encryption scheme is IND-CPA secure based on the DDH assumption and the IND-PA security of SKE.

$$\mathrm{Adv}_{\mathcal{B}}^{\mathrm{cpa}} = 2\mathrm{Adv}_{\mathcal{B}_1}^{\mathrm{ddh}} + \mathrm{Adv}_{\mathcal{B}_2}^{\mathrm{pa}}. \tag{3}$$

2. **Public-key blinding:** Let $pk = (g, g^x)$ be a public key for the secret key $sk = x$. Then $blind_s(g, g^x) = (g^s, g^{xs})$ is an uniformly random public key for sk, where $s \in Z_q^*$ is a random element.

3. **Secret-key homomorphism:** Let $pk = (g, h) = (g, g^x)$ be a public key for the secret key $sk = x$, $c = (u, e) = (g^r, \mathrm{SKE.Encrypt}(\mathrm{H}(h^r), m))$ be an encryption of message m. Define $\mathcal{F}_s(g, h) = (g, h^s)$ and $\mathcal{G}_s(u, e) = (u^{1/s}, e)$. For random element $s \in Z_q^*$, we can get a new key pair (pk', sk') and the ciphertext $c' = \mathrm{E}_{pk'}(m)$ as follows:

$$pk' = \mathcal{F}_s(g, h) = (g, h^s) = (g, g^{x \cdot s}),$$

$$sk' = sk \cdot s = x \cdot s,$$

$$c' = \mathcal{G}_s(u, e) = (u^{1/s}, e) = (g^{r/s}, \mathrm{SKE.Encrypt}(\mathrm{H}((h^s)^{r/s}), m)).$$

According to theorem 1 we can get that:

$$\mathrm{Adv}_{\mathcal{B}_1}^{\mathrm{ddh}} = \frac{1}{2}(\mathrm{Adv}_{\mathcal{B}}^{\mathrm{cpa}} - \mathrm{Adv}_{\mathcal{B}_2}^{\mathrm{pa}})$$
$$= \frac{1}{2}(\frac{1}{q_e}\mathrm{Adv}_{\mathcal{A}}^{\mathrm{div}} - \mathrm{Adv}_{\mathcal{B}_2}^{\mathrm{pa}}).$$

This completes the proof of theorem 2. □

5   Conclusion

We proved that if a public key encryption scheme is IND-CPA secure and has the properties of public-key blinding and secret-key homomorphism, then it is KDM-div secure. For concrete scheme, we proved that the hybrid ElGamal scheme is KDM-div secure based on DDH assumption in the standard model. We showed that KDM-div secure public key encryption scheme is useful in the construction of anonymous credential systems.

Acknowledgement. We thank anonymous Provsec2011 reviewers for helpful comments and pointing out the papers of BGK09 [12] (new version on TCC2011), MTY2011 [16] and BK2011 [17].

References

1. Micali, S., Rackoff, C., Sloan, R.: The notion of security for probabilistic cryptosystems. SIAM J. on Computing (April 1988)
2. Camenisch, J., Lysyanskaya, A.: Efficient non-transferable anonymous credential system with optional anonymity revocation. In: Pfitzmann, B. (ed.) EUROCRYPT 2001. LNCS, vol. 2045, pp. 93–118. Springer, Heidelberg (2001)
3. Black, J., Rogaway, P., Shrimpton, T.: Encryption-Scheme Security in the Presence of Key-Dependent Messages. In: Nyberg, K., Heys, H.M. (eds.) SAC 2002. LNCS, vol. 2595, pp. 62–75. Springer, Heidelberg (2003)
4. Backes, M., Pfitzmann, B., Scedrov, A.: Key-dependent message security under active attacks - brsim/uc-soundness of symbolic encryption with key cycles. In: CSF, pp. 112–124. IEEE Computer Society, Los Alamitos (2007)
5. Halevi, S., Krawczyk, H.: Security under key-dependent inputs. In: Ning, P., De Capitani di Vimercati, S., Syverson, P.F. (eds.) ACM Conference on Computer and Communications Security, pp. 466–475. ACM, New York (2007)
6. Hofheinz, D., Unruh, D.: Towards Key-Dependent Message Security in the Standard Model. In: Smart, N.P. (ed.) EUROCRYPT 2008. LNCS, vol. 4965, pp. 108–126. Springer, Heidelberg (2008)
7. Boneh, D., Halevi, S., Hamburg, M., Ostrovsky, R.: Circular-Secure Encryption from Decision Diffie-Hellman. In: Wagner, D. (ed.) CRYPTO 2008. LNCS, vol. 5157, pp. 108–125. Springer, Heidelberg (2008)
8. Backes, M., Dürmuth, M., Unruh, D.: OAEP Is Secure under Key-Dependent Messages. In: Pieprzyk, J. (ed.) ASIACRYPT 2008. LNCS, vol. 5350, pp. 506–523. Springer, Heidelberg (2008)
9. Applebaum, B., Cash, D., Peikert, C., Sahai, A.: Fast Cryptographic Primitives and Circular-Secure Encryption Based on Hard Learning Problems. In: Halevi, S. (ed.) CRYPTO 2009. LNCS, vol. 5677, pp. 595–618. Springer, Heidelberg (2009)
10. Camenisch, J., Chandran, N., Shoup, V.: A Public Key Encryption Scheme Secure against Key Dependent Chosen Plaintext and Adaptive Chosen Ciphertext Attacks. In: Joux, A. (ed.) EUROCRYPT 2009. LNCS, vol. 5479, pp. 351–368. Springer, Heidelberg (2009)
11. Haitner, I., Holenstein, T.: On the (Im)Possibility of key dependent encryption. In: Reingold, O. (ed.) TCC 2009. LNCS, vol. 5444, pp. 202–219. Springer, Heidelberg (2009)
12. Brakerski, Z., Goldwasser, S., Kalai, Y.: Black-box circular-secure encryption beyond affine functions. In: Ishai, Y. (ed.) TCC 2011. LNCS, vol. 6597, pp. 201–218. Springer, Heidelberg (2011), http://eprint.iacr.org
13. Barak, B., Haitner, I., Hofheinz, D., Ishai, Y.: Bounded Key-Dependent Message Security. In: Gilbert, H. (ed.) EUROCRYPT 2010. LNCS, vol. 6110, pp. 423–444. Springer, Heidelberg (2010), http://eprint.iacr.org/
14. Brakerski, Z., Goldwasser, S.: Circular and Leakage Resilient Public-Key Encryption Under Subgroup Indistinguishability (or: Quadratic Residuosity Strikes Back). In: Rabin, T. (ed.) CRYPTO 2010. LNCS, vol. 6223, pp. 1–20. Springer, Heidelberg (2010), http://eprint.iacr.org

15. Applebaum, B.: Key-Dependent Message Security: Generic Amplification and Completeness. In: Paterson, K.G. (ed.) EUROCRYPT 2011. LNCS, vol. 6632, pp. 527–546. Springer, Heidelberg (2011), http://eprint.iacr.org
16. Malkin, T., Teranishi, I., Yung, M.: Efficient Circuit-Size Independent Public Key Encryption with KDM Security. In: Paterson, K.G. (ed.) EUROCRYPT 2011. LNCS, vol. 6632, pp. 507–526. Springer, Heidelberg (2011)
17. Bellare, M., Keelveedhi, S.: Authenticated and misuse-resistant encryption of key-dependent data. In: Rogaway, P. (ed.) CRYPTO 2011. LNCS, vol. 6841, pp. 610–629. Springer, Heidelberg (2011), http://eprint.iacr.org/2011/269

Randomness Leakage in the KEM/DEM Framework

Hitoshi Namiki[1], Keisuke Tanaka[2], and Kenji Yasunaga[2]

[1] Ricoh Co., Ltd., Tokyo
[2] Tokyo Institute of Technology

Abstract. Recently, there have been many studies on constructing cryptographic primitives that are secure even if some secret information leaks. In this paper, we consider the problem of constructing public-key encryption schemes that are resilient to leaking the randomness used in the encryption algorithm. In particular, we consider the case in which public-key encryption schemes are constructed from the KEM/DEM framework, and the leakage of randomness in the encryption algorithms of KEM and DEM occurs independently. For this purpose, we define a new security notion for KEM. Then we provide a generic construction of a public-key encryption scheme that is resilient to randomness leakage from any KEM scheme satisfying this security. Also we construct a KEM scheme that satisfies the security under the decisional Diffie-Hellman assumption.

1 Introduction

Recently, many studies have been devoted to construct encryption schemes that are secure even if some of the secret information leaks [4,7,1,11,2,3]. In [4,7,1,11,2], they mainly considered the case of leaking a secret key. In particular, studies in [1,11,2] considered the case that any of the secret-key information leaks, and the restriction is only the amount of the leaked information. This leakage model captures many realistic attacks including side-channel attack and cold-boot attack [8]. Naor and Segev [11] also studied the case of leaking the randomness used in the key generation algorithm. They proved that their proposed encryption scheme, which is resilient to the secret-key leakage, is also resilient to the leakage of the randomness used in the key generation algorithm.

Bellare et al. [3] considered the case of leaking the randomness used in the encryption algorithm. Their definition of leaking the randomness is different from those of other studies of information leakage. They considered the case that random strings are sampled from not a uniformly random distribution but an entropically guaranteed distribution.

In this work, we investigate the possibility of constructing public-key encryption schemes that are secure even if the randomness information used in the encryption algorithm leaks. The restriction we consider is only the amount of the leaked information.

First we define the security notions of public-key encryption in the presence of the leakage of the randomness used in the encryption algorithm. The definitions

X. Boyen and X. Chen (Eds.): ProvSec 2011, LNCS 6980, pp. 309–323, 2011.

are similar to those of the secret-key leakage introduced in [1,11]. We define two randomness-leakage attacks, *a priori randomness-leakage attack* and *a posteriori randomness-leakage attack*. In the a priori randomness-leakage attack, the adversary can obtain the leakage information on the randomness before she receives a public key. In the a posteriori randomness-leakage attack, the adversary can obtain the leakage information after receiving the public key. Then we show that a secure public-key encryption scheme against a priori randomness-leakage attack can be constructed from any secure public-key encryption scheme. This is proved by a similar argument to the case of key leakage in [11]. However, for the a posteriori randomness-leakage attack, we show that no public-encryption scheme can achieve the security. This situation is contrast to the case of secret-key leakage. Indeed, it is shown that a secure scheme for key leakage can be constructed from any hash proof system [11]. The results are summarized in Table 1, in which we compare the results of randomness leakage with that of key leakage.

Table 1. Comparison between Key Leakage and Randomness Leakage

Timing of leakage	Key leakage	Randomness leakage
Before receiving the public key	IND-CPA PKE [11]	IND-CPA PKE
After receiving the public key	Hash Proof Systems [11]	Impossible
After receiving the ciphertext	Impossible [1]	Impossible

Next, we focus on public-key encryption schemes based on the framework of key-encapsulation mechanism (KEM) and data-encapsulation mechanism (DEM). Since no scheme can achieve the randomness-leakage resilience if the leakage occurs after the adversary receives the public key, we restrict the way of leakage as follows. (1) The leakage of randomness used in KEM and that in DEM occurs independently, and (2) the leakage of randomness used in DEM occurs after the adversary selected two challenge messages. The situation of the first condition arises when the computation of KEM and that of DEM are implemented by two independent computer chips. The second condition is due to some technical reason. Hence, removing the second condition can be considered future work of this study. Regarding the leakage amount, we restrict the amount of the randomness leakage only for the encryption of KEM, and not for DEM. Namely, the adversary can learn the entire random bits used in the encryption of DEM. Note that we allow an encryption algorithm of DEM to be randomized, while it is usually deterministic.

To construct a public-key encryption scheme secure against randomness leakage attack, we define a new security notion for KEM. We call it *the entropic security against randomness-leakage attack*. A KEM scheme is entropically secure against randomness-leakage attack if there are fake public-keys such that the distribution of real public-keys and that of fake public-keys are computationally indistinguishable, and if a fake key is used instead of a real key, the symmetric key has high entropy even if the randomness leakage occurs. Then, we provide a generic construction of a public-key encryption scheme that is resilient to randomness leakage from any KEM scheme that is entropically secure against randomness-leakage attack.

Also we construct a KEM scheme that is entropically secure against randomness-leakage attack under the decisional Diffie-Hellman (DDH) assumption. The scheme is a simple variant of the ElGamal KEM scheme.

In Table 2, we summarize the results of information leakage on public-key encryption schemes. Note that the scheme proposed in this work is the first scheme that achieves the security against randomness leakage after receiving the public key.

Table 2. Information Leakage in Public-Key Encryption Schemes

References	Leakage information	Assumption	Timing of leakage
[1]	Secret key	LWE	After receiving the public key
[11]	Secret key	HPS	After receiving the public key
[3]	Randomness	Lossy TDF	Before receiving the public key
This work	Randomness	DDH	After receiving the public key

Related Work. The key-leakage security in which the adversary can learn any information on the secret key was first formalized by Akavia, Goldwasser, and Vaikuntanathan [1]. In addition, they showed that Regev's lattice-based scheme is resilient to the key leakage. Naor and Segev [11] extended the notion of [1], and they proposed a general construction of public-key encryption schemes that are resilient to key leakage based on universal hash proof systems. In addition, they applied the notion of leakage to the randomness used in the key-generation algorithm. Alwen, Dodis, and Wichs [2] constructed varieties of key-leakage resilient public-key cryptosystems, such as identification, signature, and authenticated key agreement. Recently, Halevi and Lin [9] have studied a realizable security of public-key encryption schemes in which the leakage occurs after the adversary receives the ciphertext.

There are several studies related to the leakage of the randomness used in the encryption algorithm. Bellare et al. [3] considered the situation in which the randomness used in the encryption algorithm is not uniformly random, but is entropically guaranteed. They introduced a security notion such that even if the randomness is not chosen uniformly at random, the scheme is secure as long as the joint distribution of the message and the randomness has high entropy. Note that the distribution of the randomness is chosen without using the information on the public key, which is different from the setting of our work.

Kamara and Katz [10] studied another type of randomness leakage in symmetric-key encryption. In their setting, the adversary can control the randomness of the ciphertext except that of the challenge ciphertext.

There are other formalization of information leakage. Dizembowski and Pietrzak [7] considered the key leakage under the assumption that only the computation leaks information, and constructed leakage-resilient stream-ciphers. Dodis, Tauman Kalai, and Lovett [6] studied symmetric-key encryption schemes under key-leakage attack. They considered the leakage of the form $f(sk)$, where sk is the secret key and f is any exponentially-hard one-way function, and do not restrict the entropy of the secret key.

2   Preliminaries

In this section, we present notions, definitions, and tools that are used in our constructions. Let n be the security parameter on all of the schemes in this paper, and U_t the uniform distribution over $\{0,1\}^t$, where $t \in \mathbb{N}$. For a distribution X, we write $x \leftarrow X$ to indicate that x is chosen according to X. We say an algorithm is PPT if it runs by a probabilistic polynomial-time Turing machine.

2.1   The Decisional Diffie-Hellman Assumption

Let $\mathcal{G}(1^n)$ be a group sampling algorithm which, on input 1^n, outputs a tuple of $\mathbb{G} = (p, G, g)$ where p is a prime, G is a group of order p, and g is a generator of G.

The decisional Diffie-Hellman (DDH) assumption is that the ensembles $\{(\mathbb{G}, g_1, g_2, g_1^r, g_2^r)\}_{n \in \mathbb{N}}$ and $\{(\mathbb{G}, g_1, g_2, g_1^{r_1}, g_2^{r_2})\}_{n \in \mathbb{N}}$ are computationally indistinguishable, where $\mathbb{G} \leftarrow \mathcal{G}(1^n)$, the elements g_1, g_2 are randomly selected generator of G, and $r, r_1, r_2 \in \mathbb{Z}_p$ are chosen independently and uniformly at random.

2.2   Randomness Extraction

The *statistical distance* between two random variables X and Y over a finite domain Ω is $\Delta(X, Y) := \frac{1}{2} \sum_{\omega \in \Omega} |\Pr[X = \omega] - \Pr[Y = \omega]|$. We say that two variables are ϵ-*close* if their statistical distance is at most ϵ. The *min-entropy* of a random variable X is $H_\infty(X) := -\log(\max_x \Pr[X = x])$. The min-entropy is a standard notion of entropy used in cryptography since it measures the worst case predictability of X. We also use the *average min-entropy* defined as follows:

$$\tilde{H}_\infty(X|Y) := -\log\left(E_{y \leftarrow Y}\left[2^{-H_\infty(X|Y=y)}\right]\right).$$

The average min-entropy represents the optimal predictability of X, given knowledge of Y. The following lemma was proved by Dodis, Ostrovsky, Reyzin, and Smith [5], which will be used in this paper.

Lemma 1. *Let $r \in \mathbb{R}$. If Y has 2^r possible values and Z is any random variable, then for a random variable X, $\tilde{H}_\infty(X|(Y, Z)) \geq H_\infty(X|Z) - r$.*

We use a strong randomness extractor as a main tool in our constructions. The following definition naturally generalizes the standard definition of strong extractors to the setting of the average min-entropy.

Definition 1. *A function* $\mathsf{Ext} : \{0,1\}^k \times \{0,1\}^t \to \{0,1\}^m$ *is an average-case* (n, ϵ)-*strong extractor if for all the pairs of random variables (X, I) such that $X \in \{0,1\}^k$, and $\tilde{H}_\infty(X|I) \geq n$, it holds that*

$$\Delta((\mathsf{Ext}(X, U_t), U_t, I), (U_m, U_t, I)) \leq \epsilon.$$

Dodis et al. proved the following variant of the leftover hash lemma. Any family of pairwise independent hash functions is indeed an average-case strong extractor [5].

Lemma 2. *Let* X, Y *be random variables such that* $X \in \{0,1\}^n$ *and* $\tilde{H}_\infty(X|Y) \geq k$. *Let* $\mathcal{H}$ *be a family of pairwise independent hash functions from* $\{0,1\}^n$ *to* $\{0,1\}^m$. *Then for* $h \in \mathcal{H}$ *chosen uniformly at random, it holds that*

$$\Delta((Y, h, h(X)), (Y, h, U_m)) \leq \epsilon$$

as long as $m \leq k - 2\log(1/\epsilon)$.

2.3 The KEM/DEM Framework

We present the framework of key-encapsulation mechanism (KEM) and data-encapsulation mechanism (DEM). The KEM/DEM paradigm is a simple way of constructing efficient and practical public-key encryption schemes. KEM is used as public-key encryption used for encrypting a random symmetric key K together with its ciphertext. The symmetric key is used for encrypting the message using DEM. A formal definition of KEM and DEM is as follows:

Definition 2. *Key encapsulation mechanism is a tuple of PPT algorithms* $KEM = (\mathsf{KEM.Gen}, \mathsf{KEM.Enc}, \mathsf{KEM.Dec})$ *such that*

$\mathsf{KEM.Gen}$: *On input a security parameter* 1^n, *output a pair of keys* (pk, sk).

$\mathsf{KEM.Enc}$: *On input a public key* pk *and a random string* r *from some underlying randomness space, output a ciphertext* c *and a symmetric key* K.

$\mathsf{KEM.Dec}$: *On input a secret key* sk *and a ciphertext* c, *output a symmetric key* K.

It is required that for any $(pk, sk) \leftarrow \mathsf{KEM.Gen}(1^n)$ *and any random string* r,

$$\mathsf{KEM.Dec}(sk, c) = K,$$

where $(c, K) \leftarrow \mathsf{KEM.Enc}(pk, r)$.

Definition 3. *Data encapsulation mechanism is a tuple of PPT algorithms* $DEM = (\mathsf{DEM.Gen}, \mathsf{DEM.Enc}, \mathsf{DEM.Dec})$ *such that*

$\mathsf{DEM.Gen}$: *On input a security parameter* 1^n, *output a symmetric key* K.

$\mathsf{DEM.Enc}$: *On input a symmetric key* K, *a message* m, *and a random string* r, *output a ciphertext* c.

$\mathsf{DEM.Dec}$: *On input a symmetric key* K *and a ciphertext* c, *output a message* m.

Note that we define $\mathsf{DEM.Enc}$ as a randomized algorithm, while it is usually deterministic. We provide a KEM/DEM construction in Section 5 in which the encryption algorithm of DEM is randomized.

In this paper, we only consider the case in which a public-key encryption scheme is constructed from KEM/DEM paradigm. KEM is used for exchanging a symmetric key K. The message is encrypted using DEM with the symmetric key K. Thus, a public-key encryption scheme can be written as a tuple of five PPT algorithms $(\mathsf{KEM.Gen}, \mathsf{KEM.Enc}, \mathsf{KEM.Dec}, \mathsf{DEM.Enc}, \mathsf{DEM.Dec})$.

3 Randomness Leakage in Public-Key Encryption

Akavia et al. [1] introduced the security of public-key encryption schemes in the presence of secret-key leakage. We formalize the security in the presence of randomness leakage based on their notion. In particular, we consider the leakage of the randomness used in the encryption algorithm.

We define two randomness-leakage attacks, *a priori randomness-leakage attack* and *a posteriori randomness-leakage attack*. In the a priori randomness-leakage attack, the adversary can have access to the leakage oracle before she obtains a public key. In the a posteriori randomness-leakage attack, the adversary can have access to the leakage oracle after she obtains the public key.

3.1 A Priori Randomness-Leakage Attack

Let $\Pi = (\mathsf{Gen}, \mathsf{Enc}, \mathsf{Dec})$ be a public-key encryption scheme, and $\ell(n)$ the length of the randomness used in the encryption algorithm Enc, where n is the security parameter. The leakage oracle, denoted by $\mathsf{RandLeak}(r)$, takes as input a function $f : \{0,1\}^{\ell(n)} \to \{0,1\}^*$ and outputs $f(r)$, where r is the randomness used in Enc. We call the adversary A is an *a priori $\lambda(n)$-randomness-leakage adversary* if the sum of the output length of $\mathsf{RandLeak}$ that A queries is at most $\lambda(n)$, and f is chosen by A before she receives the public key. Note that, although we may consider adaptive leakage, in which the adversary can access to the leakage oracle adaptively, it does not affect our definitions of randomness leakage as discussed in [1].

Definition 4. *A public-key encryption scheme $\Pi = (\mathsf{Gen}, \mathsf{Enc}, \mathsf{Dec})$ is a priori $\lambda(n)$-randomness-leakage resilient if for any PPT a priori $\lambda(n)$-randomness-leakage adversary $A = (A_1, A_2, A_3)$, it holds that*

$$\mathsf{Adv}_{\Pi,A}^{\mathsf{apriori}}(n) := \left| \Pr\left[\mathsf{Expt}_{\Pi,A}^{\mathsf{apriori}}(0) = 1\right] - \Pr\left[\mathsf{Expt}_{\Pi,A}^{\mathsf{apriori}}(1) = 1\right] \right|$$

is negligible in n, where the experiment $\mathsf{Expt}_{\Pi,A}^{\mathsf{apriori}}(b)$ is defined as follows.

1. *$(pk, sk) \leftarrow \mathsf{Gen}(1^n)$.*
2. *Choose $r \leftarrow U_{\ell(n)}$.*
3. *$st_1 \leftarrow A_1^{\mathsf{RandLeak}(r)}(1^n)$.*
4. *$(m_0, m_1, st_2) \leftarrow A_2(pk, st_1)$ such that $|m_0| = |m_1|$.*
5. *$c \leftarrow \mathsf{Enc}(pk, m_b, r)$.*
6. *$b' \leftarrow A_3(c, st_2)$.*
7. *Output b'.*

We provide a construction of public-key encryption scheme that is resilient to a priori randomness-leakage attack based on any IND-CPA secure scheme. The construction is similar to that of [1] for the case of the secret-key leakage.

Construction 5 *Let* $\Pi = (\mathsf{Gen}, \mathsf{Enc}, \mathsf{Dec})$ *be a public-key encryption scheme,* $\ell(n)$ *the length of the random string used in* Enc*, and* $\mathsf{Ext} : \{0,1\}^{k(n)} \times \{0,1\}^{t(n)} \rightarrow \{0,1\}^{\ell(n)}$ *an average-case extractor. The scheme* $\Pi^* = (\mathsf{Gen}^*, \mathsf{Enc}^*, \mathsf{Dec}^*)$ *is defined as follows.*

Gen^*: *On input* 1^n*, choose* $s \leftarrow U_{t(n)}$*, compute* $(pk, sk) \leftarrow \mathsf{Gen}(1^n)$*, and output* $PK = (pk, s)$ *and* $SK = sk$.

Enc^*: *On input a message* m *and a public key* $PK = (pk, s)$*, choose* $r \leftarrow U_{k(n)}$ *and output* $\mathsf{Enc}(pk, m, \mathsf{Ext}(r, s))$.

Dec^*: *On input a ciphertext* c *and a secret key* $SK = sk$*, output* $\mathsf{Dec}(sk, c)$.

Theorem 1. *Let* $\Pi = (\mathsf{Gen}, \mathsf{Enc}, \mathsf{Dec})$ *be an IND-CPA secure public-key encryption scheme and* $\mathsf{Ext} : \{0,1\}^{k(n)} \times \{0,1\}^{t(n)} \rightarrow \{0,1\}^{m(n)}$ *an average-case* $(k(n) - \lambda(n), \epsilon(n))$*-strong extractor for some negligible function* $\epsilon(n)$*. Then, the encryption scheme* Π^* *is a priori* $\lambda(n)$*-randomness-leakage resilient.*

Proof. We show that for any adversary A, there exists an adversary A' such that

$$\mathsf{Adv}_{\Pi^*, A}^{\mathrm{apriori}}(n) \leq \mathsf{Adv}_{\Pi, A'}^{\mathrm{CPA}}(n) + 2\epsilon(n),$$

where the $\mathsf{Adv}_{\Pi, A'}^{\mathrm{IND-CPA}}(n)$ the advantage of A' in the IND-CPA game with Π. Consider the following experiment $\mathsf{Expt}_{\Pi, A}(b)$:

1. $(pk, sk) \leftarrow \mathsf{Gen}(1^n)$, choose $r \leftarrow U_{k(n)}$, $s \leftarrow U_{t(n)}$, and $z \leftarrow U_{m(n)}$. Let $PK = (pk, s)$ and $SK = sk$.
2. $st_1 \leftarrow A_1^{\mathsf{RandLeak}(r)}(1^n)$.
3. $(m_0, m_1, st_2) \leftarrow A_2(PK, st_1)$ such that $|m_0| = |m_1|$.
4. $c \leftarrow \mathsf{Enc}(pk, m_b, z)$.
5. $b' \leftarrow A_3(c, st_2)$.
6. Output b'.

From Definition 4 and the triangle inequality, it follows that

$$\mathsf{Adv}_{\Pi^*, A}^{\mathrm{apriori}}(n) = \left| \Pr\left[\mathsf{Expt}_{\Pi^*, A}^{\mathrm{apriori}}(0) = 1\right] - \Pr\left[\mathsf{Expt}_{\Pi^*, A}^{\mathrm{apriori}}(1) = 1\right] \right|$$

$$\leq \left| \Pr\left[\mathsf{Expt}_{\Pi^*, A}^{\mathrm{apriori}}(0) = 1\right] - \Pr\left[\mathsf{Expt}_{\Pi, A}(0) = 1\right] \right|$$

$$+ \left| \Pr\left[\mathsf{Expt}_{\Pi, A}(0) = 1\right] - \Pr\left[\mathsf{Expt}_{\Pi, A}(1) = 1\right] \right|$$

$$+ \left| \Pr\left[\mathsf{Expt}_{\Pi, A}(1) = 1\right] - \Pr\left[\mathsf{Expt}_{\Pi^*, A}^{\mathrm{apriori}}(1) = 1\right] \right|.$$

The experiment $\mathsf{Expt}_{\Pi, A}(b)$ is identical to the experiment $\mathsf{Expt}_{\Pi^*, A}^{\mathrm{apriori}}(b)$, except for the fact that Enc uses a truly random input z, not $\mathsf{Ext}(r, s)$. Note that, from Lemma 1, given the information of $f(r)$, the average min-entropy of r is at least $(k - \lambda)$. Therefore the average-case strong extractor guarantees that the statistical distance between the view of the adversary in these two experiments is at most $\epsilon(n)$. This implies that $\left| \Pr\left[\mathsf{Expt}_{\Pi, A}(b) = 1\right] - \Pr\left[\mathsf{Expt}_{\Pi^*, A, F}^{\mathrm{apriori}}(b) = 1\right] \right| \leq \epsilon(n)$ for $b \in \{0, 1\}$. Since $\mathsf{Expt}_{\Pi, A}(b)$ is the same as the IND-CPA experiment $\mathsf{Expt}_{\Pi, A}^{\mathrm{IND-CPA}}(b)$, we can construct the IND-CPA adversary A' for which $\left| \Pr\left[\mathsf{Expt}_{\Pi, A}(0) = 1\right] - \Pr\left[\mathsf{Expt}_{\Pi, A}(1) = 1\right] \right| \leq \mathsf{Adv}_{\Pi, A'}^{\mathrm{CPA}}(n)$.

3.2   A Posteriori Randomness-Leakage Attack

In this section, we define a posteriori randomness-leakage attack. Consequently, we show that there is no public-key encryption scheme that is a posteriori randomness-leakage resilient even if the leakage information is only one bit.

We define the security in a similar way as in Definition 4. An adversary A is called *a posteriori* $\lambda(n)$*-randomness-leakage adversary* if the sum of the output lengths of RandLeak is at most $\lambda(n)$, and a leakage function f is chosen by A before receiving the challenge ciphertext.

Definition 6. *A public-key encryption scheme* $\Pi = (\mathsf{Gen}, \mathsf{Enc}, \mathsf{Dec})$ *is a posteriori* $\lambda(n)$-*randomness-leakage* resilient *if for any PPT a posteriori* $\lambda(n)$-*randomness-leakage adversary* $A = (A_1, A_2)$, *it holds that*

$$\mathsf{Adv}_{\Pi,A}^{\mathrm{aposteriori}}(n) := \left| \Pr\left[\mathsf{Expt}_{\Pi,A}^{\mathrm{aposteriori}}(0) = 1\right] - \Pr\left[\mathsf{Expt}_{\Pi,A}^{\mathrm{aposteriori}}(1) = 1\right] \right|$$

is negligible in n. *The experiment* $\mathsf{Expt}_{\Pi,A}^{\mathrm{aposteriori}}(b)$ *is defined as follows:*

1. $(pk, sk) \leftarrow \mathsf{Gen}(1^n)$.
2. *Choose* $r \leftarrow U_{\ell(n)}$.
3. $(m_0, m_1, st_1) \leftarrow A_1^{\mathsf{RandLeak}(r)}(pk)$ *such that* $|m_0| = |m_1|$.
4. $c \leftarrow \mathsf{Enc}(pk, m_b, r)$.
5. $b' \leftarrow A_2(c, st_1)$.
6. *Output* b'.

We show that no public-key encryption scheme achieves Definition 6. We construct an adversary A' that breaks the a posteriori randomness-leakage resilience, where $\lambda(n) = 1$. The strategy of A' is as follows. First, A' makes two challenge messages m_0, m_1 arbitrary, and randomly chooses $1 \leq i \leq d(n)$, where $d(n)$ is the maximum length of the possible ciphertexts. Then A' asks the leakage oracle with $f(\cdot) = \{\text{the } i\text{-th bit of the output of } \mathsf{Enc}(pk, m_1, \cdot)\}$. After A' receives the challenge ciphertext c, she checks whether the i-th bit of c and $f(r)$ are the same or not. If they are, she outputs 1, and otherwise outputs 0. There exists at least one position where the ciphertext of m_0 and that of m_1 are different because of the correctness of the scheme. If i is such a position, then A' can correctly predict the challenge message. The probability it occurs is at least $1/d(n)$, which is a lower bound of the probability $\Pr\left[\mathsf{Expt}_{\Pi,A'}^{\mathrm{aposteriori}}(0) = 0\right]$. On the other hand, $\Pr\left[\mathsf{Expt}_{\Pi,A'}^{\mathrm{aposteriori}}(1) = 1\right] = 1$. Thus,

$$\begin{aligned}
\mathsf{Adv}_{\Pi,A}^{\mathrm{aposteriori}}(n) &= \left| \Pr\left[\mathsf{Expt}_{\Pi,A}^{\mathrm{aposteriori}}(0) = 1\right] - \Pr\left[\mathsf{Expt}_{\Pi,A}^{\mathrm{aposteriori}}(1) = 1\right] \right| \\
&= \left| \left(1 - \Pr\left[\mathsf{Expt}_{\Pi,A'}^{\mathrm{aposteriori}}(0) = 0\right]\right) - 1 \right| \\
&\geq \frac{1}{d(n)},
\end{aligned}$$

which is non-negligible.

4   Randomness Leakage in KEM/DEM

In this section, we define randomness-leakage attack for KEM/DEM-based public-key encryption schemes. As discussed in Section 3, there is no public-key encryption that achieves a posteriori randomness-leakage. Therefore, we restrict the leakage of randomness such that the leaking of random bits used in KEM.Enc and DEM.Enc occur independently. Also when the adversary chooses two challenge messages, she is not allowed to access to the leakage information of random bits in DEM.Enc.

We describe the formal definition of the randomness-leakage attack in KEM/DEM. The randomness-leakage oracle for KEM.Enc, denoted by Leak, takes as input a function $f : R \rightarrow \{0,1\}^*$ and outputs $f(r)$, where R is the domain of the randomness used in KEM.Enc and r is the random bits generated in KEM.Enc. We restrict the function f to be efficiently computable. The leakage oracle for DEM.Enc, denoted by Leak', takes as input a function $g : R' \rightarrow \{0,1\}^*$ and output $g(r')$, where R' is the domain of the randomness used in DEM.Enc and r' is the random bits generated in DEM.Enc. We restrict the amount of the leaked bits for r but not for r'. Namely, the adversary can learn the entire random bits r', which are generated in DEM.Enc. We call an adversary A is a $\lambda(n)$-*randomness-leakage adversary* if the sum of the output length of Leak that A queries is at most $\lambda(n)$.

Definition 7. *A   public-key   encryption   scheme Π =* (KEM.Gen, KEM.Enc, KEM.Dec, DEM.Enc, DEM.Dec) *is* IND-CPA *secure against $\lambda(n)$-randomness-leakage attack if for any PPT $\lambda(n)$-randomness-leakage adversary $A = (A_1, A_2)$ it holds that,*

$$\mathsf{Adv}_{\Pi,A}^{\mathsf{RandLeak}}(n) := \left| \Pr[\mathsf{Expt}_{\Pi,A}^{\mathsf{RandLeak}}(0) = 1] - \Pr[\mathsf{Expt}_{\Pi,A}^{\mathsf{RandLeak}}(1) = 1] \right|$$

is negligible in n, where $\mathsf{Expt}_{\Pi,A}^{\mathsf{RandLeak}}(b)$ is defined as follows.

1. *$(pk, sk) \leftarrow$ KEM.Gen(1^n).*
2. *Choose $r \in R$ uniformly at random.*
3. *$(c, K) \leftarrow$ KEM.Enc(pk, r).*
4. *$(m_0, m_1, st_1) \leftarrow A_1^{\mathsf{Leak}(r)}(pk, c)$ such that $|m_0| = |m_1|$.*
5. *Choose $r' \in R'$ uniformly at random.*
6. *$d \leftarrow$ DEM.Enc(m_b, K, r').*
7. *$b' \leftarrow A_2^{\mathsf{Leak'}(r')}(d, st_1)$.*
8. *Output b'.*

Note that the ciphertext c generated by KEM.Enc is given to the adversary before she submits the challenge messages m_0 and m_1. This means the above definition captures a stronger security than the standard KEM/DEM framework. The randomness r' in DEM.Enc leaks only after the adversary chose the challenge messages.

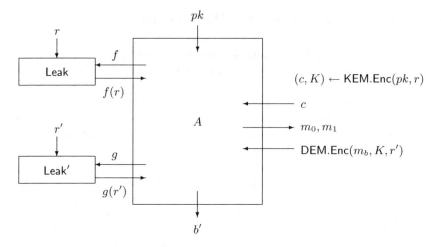

Fig. 1. Experiment $\mathsf{Expt}_{\Pi,A}^{\mathsf{RandLeak}}(b)$

5   Randomness-Leakage Resilient Schemes from Entropically-Secure KEM

In this section, we first define a new security notion for KEM. Then, we construct a public-key encryption scheme that is IND-CPA secure against randomness-leakage attack from any KEM scheme satisfying this security.

For a KEM scheme, we require that the symmetric key K still has high average min-entropy even if the adversary knows the public key pk, the ciphertext c, and any partial information $f(r)$ of the random string r. We consider a distribution PK^* that is computationally indistinguishable from the real distribution of pk, where pk is generated from the encryption algorithm of KEM. Given $pk^* \in PK^*, c^*,$ and $f(r)$, we require that K^* has enough entropy, where (c^*, K^*) is generated according to $\mathsf{KEM.Enc}(pk^*, r)$ and f is an arbitrary efficiently computable function whose output length is restricted.

Definition 8. *A KEM scheme* $(\mathsf{KEM.Gen}, \mathsf{KEM.Enc}, \mathsf{KEM.Dec})$ *is* $\kappa(n)$-*entropically secure against* $\lambda(n)$-*randomness-leakage attack if there exists an efficiently samplable distribution* PK^* *that is computationally indistinguishable from the distribution* $\{pk \mid (pk, sk) \leftarrow \mathsf{KEM.Gen}(1^n)\}$, *and*

$$\tilde{H}_\infty(K^* | pk^*, c^*, f(r)) \geq \kappa(n),$$

where $pk^* \leftarrow PK^*, (c^*, K^*) \leftarrow \mathsf{KEM.Enc}(pk^*, r),$ *and* f *is an arbitrary efficiently computable function whose output length is at most* $\lambda(n)$.

We can construct a public-key encryption scheme secure against randomness-leakage attack from any KEM scheme satisfying Definition 8.

Theorem 2. *Let* $\mathsf{Ext} : G \times \{0,1\}^t \rightarrow \{0,1\}^m$ *be an average-case* $(\kappa(n), \epsilon(n))$-*strong extractor for some negligible function* $\epsilon(n)$. *Let*

(KEM.Gen, KEM.Enc, KEM.Dec) *be a KEM scheme that is* $\kappa(n)$*-entropically secure against* $\lambda(n)$*-randomness-leakage attack. Then, the following scheme* $\Pi^* = ($KEM.Gen*, KEM.Enc*, KEM.Dec*, DEM.Enc*, DEM.Dec*) *is a public-key encryption scheme that is IND-CPA secure against* $\lambda(n)$*-randomness-leakage attack.*

Construction 9 *The algorithms* KEM.Gen*, KEM.Enc*, *and* KEM.Dec* *are the same as* KEM.Gen, KEM.Enc, *and* KEM.Dec, *respectively. The algorithms* DEM.Enc*, DEM.Dec* *are defined as follows.*

DEM.Enc***:** *On input a symmetric key* K *and a message* $M \in \{0,1\}^m$, *choose* $r' \in \{0,1\}^t$ *uniformly at random. Output the ciphertext*

$$d = (\mathsf{Ext}(K, r') \oplus M, r').$$

DEM.Dec* *On input a symmetric key* K *and a ciphertext* $d = (d_1, d_2)$, *output the message*

$$M = \mathsf{Ext}(K, d_2) \oplus d_1.$$

Proof (Proof of Theorem 2). We define the experiments $\mathsf{Expt}_{\Pi^*,A}^{\mathsf{RandLeak}^*}(b)$ and $\mathsf{Expt}_{\Pi^*,A}(b)$ for $b \in \{0,1\}$ as follows.

$\mathsf{Expt}_{\Pi^*,A}^{\mathsf{RandLeak}^*}(b)$:

1. Choose pk^* from PK^*, where PK^* is the distribution defined in Definition 8.
2. Choose $r \in R$ uniformly at random, where R is the domain of the randomness used in KEM.Enc*.
3. $(c^*, K^*) \leftarrow$ KEM.Enc$^*(pk^*, r)$.
4. $(m_0, m_1, st_1) \leftarrow A_1^{\mathsf{Leak}(r)}(pk^*, c^*)$ such that $|m_0| = |m_1|$.
5. Choose $r' \in R'$ uniformly at random, where R' is the domain of the randomness used in DEM.Enc*.
6. $d \leftarrow$ DEM.Enc$^*(m_b, K^*, r')$.
7. $b' \leftarrow A_2^{\mathsf{Leak}'(r')}(d, st_1)$.
8. Output b'.

$\mathsf{Expt}_{\Pi^*,A}(b)$:

1. Choose pk^* from PK^*.
2. Choose $r \in R$ uniformly at random.
3. $(c^*, K^*) \leftarrow$ KEM.Enc$^*(pk^*, r)$.
4. $(m_0, m_1, st_1) \leftarrow A_1^{\mathsf{Leak}(r)}(pk^*, c^*)$ such that $|m_0| = |m_1|$.
5. Choose $r' \in R'$ uniformly at random.
6. Choose $r^* \leftarrow U_m$, and set $d = (r^* \oplus m_b, r')$.
7. $b' \leftarrow A_2^{\mathsf{Leak}'(r')}(d, st_1)$.
8. Output b'.

Using the triangle inequality, for any adversary A it holds that

$$\mathsf{Adv}_{\Pi^*,A}^{\mathsf{RandLeak}}(n)$$

$$= \left| \Pr[\mathsf{Expt}_{\Pi^*,A}^{\mathsf{RandLeak}}(0) = 1] - \Pr[\mathsf{Expt}_{\Pi^*,A}^{\mathsf{RandLeak}}(1) = 1] \right|$$

$$\le \left| \Pr[\mathsf{Expt}_{\Pi^*,A}^{\mathsf{RandLeak}}(0) = 1] - \Pr[\mathsf{Expt}_{\Pi^*,A}^{\mathsf{RandLeak}^*}(0) = 1] \right| \quad (1)$$

$$+ \left| \Pr[\mathsf{Expt}_{\Pi^*,A}^{\mathsf{RandLeak}^*}(0) = 1] - \Pr[\mathsf{Expt}_{\Pi^*,A}(0) = 1] \right| \quad (2)$$

$$+ \left| \Pr[\mathsf{Expt}_{\Pi^*,A}(0) = 1] - \Pr[\mathsf{Expt}_{\Pi^*,A}(1) = 1] \right| \quad (3)$$

$$+ \left| \Pr[\mathsf{Expt}_{\Pi^*,A}(1) = 1] - \Pr[\mathsf{Expt}_{\Pi^*,A}^{\mathsf{RandLeak}^*}(1) = 1] \right| \quad (4)$$

$$+ \left| \Pr[\mathsf{Expt}_{\Pi^*,A}^{\mathsf{RandLeak}^*}(1) = 1] - \Pr[\mathsf{Expt}_{\Pi^*,A}^{\mathsf{RandLeak}}(1) = 1] \right| . \quad (5)$$

We first show an upper bound on the terms (1) and (5). Note that, the difference between $\mathsf{Expt}_{\Pi^*,A}^{\mathsf{RandLeak}}(b)$ and $\mathsf{Expt}_{\Pi^*,A}^{\mathsf{RandLeak}^*}(b)$ is only the distribution of choosing public keys. Since the distribution PK^* and $\{pk \mid (pk, sk) \leftarrow \mathsf{KEM.Gen}(1^n)\}$ are computationally indistinguishable, there is some negligible function $\mathsf{AdvComp}(n)$ that is an upper bound on both (1) and (5).

Second, we show an upper bound on (2) and (4). The difference between $\mathsf{Expt}_{\Pi^*,A}(b)$ and $\mathsf{Expt}_{\Pi^*,A}^{\mathsf{RandLeak}^*}(b)$ is only the mask string for m_b, which is $\mathsf{Ext}(K^*, r')$ and r^*, respectively. From the assumption of Theorem 2, we have that $\tilde{H}_\infty(K^* \mid pk^*, c^*, f(r)) \ge \kappa(n)$. Since r' is chosen from U_t and Ext is an average-case $(\kappa(n), \epsilon(n))$-strong extractor, the adversary can distinguish the distribution between $(\mathsf{Ext}(K^*, r'), r', pk^*, c^*, f(r))$ and $(r^*, r', pk^*, c^*, f(r))$ with probability at most $\epsilon(n)$. Thus, $\epsilon(n)$ is an upper bound on both (2) and (4).

Finally, we show the term (3) is equal to zero. The difference between $\mathsf{Expt}_{\Pi^*,A}(0)$ and $\mathsf{Expt}_{\Pi^*,A}(1)$ is the message m_b for $b \in \{0, 1\}$. Since m_b is masked by a uniformly random string r^*, the experiments $\mathsf{Expt}_{\Pi^*,A}(0)$ and $\mathsf{Expt}_{\Pi^*,A}(1)$ are the same. Thus, (3) is equal to zero.

Therefore, we have that $\mathsf{Adv}_{\Pi^*,A}^{\mathsf{RandLeak}}(n) \le 2(\mathsf{AdvComp}(n) + \epsilon(n))$, which is negligible in n.

6   The Construction of Entropically-Secure KEM

In this section, we provide a construction of entropically secure KEM based on the DDH assumption.

Construction 10 *Let G be a group of prime order p, and $\lambda(n)$ a leakage parameter. Then, the KEM scheme* $(\mathsf{KEM.Gen}, \mathsf{KEM.Enc}, \mathsf{KEM.Dec})$ *is defined as follows.*

$\mathsf{KEM.Gen}$: *On input a security parameter 1^n, choose $x_1 \in \mathbb{Z}_p$ and $g_1, g_2 \in G$ uniformly at random. Output a pair of keys (pk, sk) as*

$$pk = (g_1, g_2, g_1^{x_1}, g_2^{x_1}), \qquad sk = x_1.$$

KEM.Enc : *On input a public key* $pk = (g_1, g_2, pk_1, pk_2)$, *choose* $r_1, r_2 \in \mathbb{Z}_p$ *uniformly at random, and output the ciphertext* c *and the symmetric key* K *as*

$$c = g_1^{r_1} g_2^{r_2}, \qquad K = (pk_1)^{r_1} (pk_2)^{r_2}.$$

KEM.Dec : *On inputs a secret key* sk *and a ciphertext* c, *output the symmetric key as*

$$K = c^{sk}.$$

The correctness of the scheme immediately follows since if $c = g_1^{r_1} g_2^{r_2}$, $pk_1 = g_1^{x_1}$ and $pk_2 = g_2^{x_1}$, then $K = (pk_1)^{r_1} (pk_2)^{r_2} = (g_1^{x_1})^{r_1} (g_2^{x_1})^{r_2} = (g_1^{r_1} g_2^{r_2})^{x_1} = c^{x_1}$.

Next, we show the security of the scheme.

Theorem 3. *The KEM scheme defined in Construction 10 is* $(\log p - \lambda(n))$-*entropically secure against* $\lambda(n)$-*randomness-leakage attack under the DDH assumption.*

Proof. We need to show that there exists a distribution PK^* such that PK^* is computationally indistinguishable from the distribution $\{pk \,|\, pk \leftarrow \text{KEM.Enc}(1^n)\}$, and that $\tilde{H}_\infty(K^*|pk^*, c^*, f(r^*)) \geq \log p - \lambda(n)$, where $pk^* \leftarrow PK^*$, $(c^*, K^*) \leftarrow \text{KEM.Enc}(pk^*, r)$, and f is an arbitrary efficiently-computable function whose output length is at most $\lambda(n)$.

We define PK^* as follows.

PK^*: Choose $x_1, x_2 \in \mathbb{Z}_p$ with $x_1 \neq x_2$ and $g_1, g_2 \in G$ uniformly at random. Then output $pk^* = (g_1, g_2, g_1^{x_1}, g_2^{x_2})$.

It follows from the DDH assumption that the distribution PK^* and the distribution $\{pk \,|\, pk \leftarrow \text{KEM.Enc}(1^n)\} = \{(g_1, g_2, g_1^{x_1}, g_2^{x_1}) \,|\, x_1 \in \mathbb{Z}_p, g_1, g_2 \in G\}$ are computationally indistinguishable.

Next, we show that $\tilde{H}_\infty(K^*|pk^*, c^*, f(r^*)) \geq \log p - \lambda(n)$. If pk^* is chosen from PK^*, then the distribution $\{K^* \,|\, (c^*, K^*) \leftarrow \text{KEM.Enc}(pk^*, r)\}$ is equal to the following distribution $\mathcal{K}^*$.

$\mathcal{K}^*$: Choose $x_1, x_2, r_1, r_2 \in \mathbb{Z}_p$ with $x_1 \neq x_2$ and $g_1, g_2 \in G$ uniformly at random, and compute $c^* = g_1^{r_1} g_2^{r_2}$ and $K^* = (g_1^{x_1})^{r_1} (g_2^{x_2})^{r_2}$. Then output K^*.

We show that, given pk^* and c^*, the distribution $\mathcal{K}^*$ is the uniform distribution on G. To prove this fact, we show that, given pk^* and c^*, for any $K^* \in G$, there is a unique pair $(r_1, r_2) \in \mathbb{Z}_p \times \mathbb{Z}_p$ that satisfies $g_1^{r_1} g_2^{r_2} = c^*$ and $(g_1^{x_1})^{r_1} (g_2^{x_2})^{r_2} = K^*$. We can write $g_2 = g_1^\alpha, c^* = g_1^{y_1}$, and $K^* = g_1^{y_2}$ for some $\alpha, y_1, y_2 \in \mathbb{Z}_p$. Then it holds that $c^* = g_1^{y_1} = g_1^{r_1 + \alpha r_2}$ and that $K^* = g_1^{y_2} = g_1^{x_1 r_1 + \alpha x_2 r_2}$. Hence, we have two equations $y_1 = r_1 + \alpha r_2$ and $y_2 = x_1 r_1 + \alpha x_2 r_2$. Since $x_1 \neq x_2$ and $\alpha \neq 0$ (otherwise, g_2 is not a generator of G), there is a unique solution (r_1, r_2) of these equations.

From the above, we have that $H_\infty(K^*|pk^*, c^*) = \log p$. Then it follows from Lemma 1 that $\tilde{H}_\infty(K^*|pk^*, c^*, f(r)) \geq H_\infty(K^*|pk^*, c^*) - \lambda(n) = \log p - \lambda(n)$.

In summary, from Theorems 2 and 3, we can construct a public-key encryption scheme secure against randomness-leakage attack.

Theorem 4. *Let G be a group of prime order p, and* $\mathsf{Ext} : G \times \{0,1\}^t \to \{0,1\}^m$ *an average-case* $(\log p - \lambda(n), \epsilon(n))$*-strong extractor for some negligible function $\epsilon(n)$. Then, the following public-key encryption scheme $\Pi = (\mathsf{KEM.Gen}, \mathsf{KEM.Enc}, \mathsf{KEM.Dec}, \mathsf{DEM.Enc}, \mathsf{DEM.Dec})$ is IND-CPA secure against $\lambda(n)$-randomness-leakage attack under the DDH assumption.*

$\mathsf{KEM.Gen}$: *On input a security parameter 1^n, choose $x_1 \in \mathbb{Z}_p$ and $g_1, g_2 \in G$ uniformly at random, and output the public key $pk = (g_1, g_2, g_1^{x_1}, g_2^{x_1})$ and the secret key $sk = x_1$.*

$\mathsf{KEM.Enc}$: *On input a public key $pk = (g_1, g_2, pk_1, pk_2)$, choose $r_1, r_2 \in \mathbb{Z}_p$ uniformly at random, and output the ciphertext $c = g_1^{r_1} g_2^{r_2}$ and the symmetric key $K = (pk_1)^{r_1} (pk_2)^{r_2}$.*

$\mathsf{KEM.Dec}$: *On inputs a secret key sk and a ciphertext c, output the symmetric key $K = c^{sk}$.*

$\mathsf{DEM.Enc}$: *On input a symmetric key K and a message $M \in \{0,1\}^m$, choose $r' \in \{0,1\}^t$ uniformly at random, and output the ciphertext $d = (\mathsf{Ext}(K, r') \oplus M, r')$.*

$\mathsf{DEM.Dec}$: *On input a symmetric key K and a ciphertext $d = (d_1, d_2)$, output the message $M = \mathsf{Ext}(K, d_2) \oplus d_1$.*

Acknowledgments. This work was supported in part by NTT Information Sharing Platform Laboratories and Grant-in-Aid for Scientific Research.

References

1. Akavia, A., Goldwasser, S., Vaikuntanathan, V.: Simultaneous Hardcore Bits and Cryptography against Memory Attacks. In: Reingold, O. (ed.) TCC 2009. LNCS, vol. 5444, pp. 474–495. Springer, Heidelberg (2009)
2. Alwen, J., Dodis, Y., Wichs, D.: Leakage-Resilient Public-Key Cryptography in the Bounded-Retrieval Model. In: Halevi, S. (ed.) CRYPTO 2009. LNCS, vol. 5677, pp. 36–54. Springer, Heidelberg (2009)
3. Bellare, M., Brakerski, Z., Naor, M., Ristenpart, T., Segev, G., Shacham, H., Yilek, S.: Hedged public-key encryption: How to protect against bad randomness. In: Matsui, M. (ed.) ASIACRYPT 2009. LNCS, vol. 5912, pp. 232–249. Springer, Heidelberg (2009)
4. Canetti, R., Dodis, Y., Halevi, S., Kushilevitz, E., Sahai, A.: Exposure-Resilient Functions and All-or-Nothing Transforms. In: Preneel, B. (ed.) EUROCRYPT 2000. LNCS, vol. 1807, pp. 453–469. Springer, Heidelberg (2000)
5. Dodis, Y., Ostrovsky, R., Reyzin, L., Smith, A.: Fuzzy extractors: How to generate strong keys from biometrics and other noisy data. SIAM J. Comput. 38(1), 97–139 (2008)
6. Dodis, Y., Tauman Kalai, Y., Lovett, S.: On cryptography with auxiliary input. In: Mitzenmacher, M. (ed.) Proceedings of the 41st Annual ACM Symposium on Theory of Computing, STOC 2009, Bethesda, MD, USA, May 31 - June 2, pp. 621–630. ACM, New York (2009)
7. Dziembowski, S., Pietrzak, K.: Leakage-resilient cryptography. In: 49th Annual IEEE Symposium on Foundations of Computer Science (FOCS 2008), Philadelphia, PA, USA, pp. 293–302. IEEE Computer Society, Los Alamitos (2008)

8. Halderman, J. A., Schoen, S.D., Heninger, N., Clarkson, W., Paul, W., Calandrino, J.A., Feldman, A.J., Appelbaum, J., Felten, E.W.: Lest we remember: Cold boot attacks on encryption keys. In: USENIX Security Symposium, pp. 45–60 (2008)
9. Halevi, S., Lin, H.: After-the-Fact Leakage in Public-Key Encryption. In: Ishai, Y. (ed.) TCC 2011. LNCS, vol. 6597, pp. 107–124. Springer, Heidelberg (2011)
10. Kamara, S., Katz, J.: How to Encrypt with a Malicious Random Number Generator. In: Nyberg, K. (ed.) FSE 2008. LNCS, vol. 5086, pp. 303–315. Springer, Heidelberg (2008)
11. Naor, M., Segev, G.: Public-Key Cryptosystems Resilient to Key Leakage. In: Halevi, S. (ed.) CRYPTO 2009. LNCS, vol. 5677, pp. 18–35. Springer, Heidelberg (2009)

Generalized Learning Problems and Applications to Non-commutative Cryptography[*]
(Extended Abstract)

Gilbert Baumslag[1], Nelly Fazio[1], Antonio R. Nicolosi[2],
Vladimir Shpilrain[1], and William E. Skeith III[1]

[1] The City College of CUNY
gilbert.baumslag@gmail.com, {fazio,wes}@cs.ccny.cuny.edu,
shpil@groups.sci.ccny.cuny.edu
[2] Stevens Institute of Technology
nicolosi@cs.stevens.edu

Abstract. We propose a generalization of the *learning parity with noise* (LPN) and *learning with errors* (LWE) problems to an abstract class of group-theoretic learning problems that we term *learning homomorphisms with noise* (LHN). This class of problems contains LPN and LWE as special cases, but is much more general. It allows, for example, instantiations based on non-abelian groups, resulting in a new avenue for the application of combinatorial group theory to the development of cryptographic primitives. We then study a particular instantiation using relatively free groups and construct a symmetric cryptosystem based upon it.

Keywords: Learning with errors, Post-quantum cryptography, Non-commutative cryptography, Burnside groups.

1 Introduction

MOTIVATION. One of the pillars of the modern reductionist approach to cryptography, as exemplified *e.g.*, in [17,18], has been the focus on explicit computational assumptions, precisely phrased in the language of probabilistic modeling. The resulting separation of cryptographic mechanisms from their underlying conjectured-hard problems has been instrumental to the development of a proper formalization of security for disparate cryptographic notions, and for the establishment of connections and elucidation of relations among crypto primitives.

Despite their fundamental role in the theory of cryptography, there is little variety in the family of intractability assumptions. Most of the cryptographic constructs which are used in practice today either rely on a small handful of computational assumptions related to factoring and discrete logs (*e.g.*, RSA, Diffie-Hellman), or lack a well-defined assumption altogether (*e.g.*, AES, and

---

[*] Full version available at [7]. Supported in part by NSF grants CNS 1117675/1117679.

X. Boyen and X. Chen (Eds.): ProvSec 2011, LNCS 6980, pp. 324–339, 2011.
© Springer-Verlag Berlin Heidelberg 2011

any of the SHA functions). A number of alternatives have surfaced, beginning with elliptic curve cryptosystems [31,27] and more recently with lattice-based constructions [1,2]. Both have turned out to provide revolutionary advances in the theory. Elliptic curves led to the development of identity based cryptosystems [37,11,12], and lattices have recently led to the development of the first fully homomorphic cryptosystems [14,38,15,16].

In this paper, we seek to tap into new sources of computational hardness. Inspired by the recent success of the *learning parity with noise* (LPN [26,10]) and *learning with errors* (LWE [36,30]) problems as a platform for a variety of cryptographic applications, we pursue a generalization of these problems into an abstract class of hard *group-theoretic learning* problems. Besides being of interest in its own right, this generalization opens the way to a new approach for basing cryptography on combinatorial group theory. The rich algebraic structure of non-abelian groups compares favorably with the rigid structure of cyclic groups. Moreover, no efficient quantum algorithms are known for most computational problems in combinatorial group theory, which provides substantial motivation for pursuing this direction of research.

Besides enriching the set of viable intractability assumptions and providing a plausible alternative for post-quantum cryptography, our approach brings into play tools and ideas that have traditionally not found much application in cryptography. For example, in Section 4 we develop an instantiation of our abstract group-theoretic learning problem from the theory of groups with exponent k, or *Burnside groups*. We hope that the computational properties of these mathematical objects will spark further work to develop new applications of group theory to cryptography.

A number of attempts to apply combinatorial group theory to cryptography exist in the literature (see below for a survey). Earlier efforts aimed at capitalizing on the algorithmic unsolvability of many of the standard computational problems in combinatorial group theory (*e.g.*, the *word problem*, the *conjugacy problem* and the *membership problem*). These attempts, however, overestimated the relevance of problems that are unsolvable in the *worst-case* for cryptographic purposes. Our approach instead suggests new group-theoretic problems and efficiently sampleable distributions on which it is reasonable to conjecture that these problems remain difficult *on average*.

NON-COMMUTATIVE CRYPTOGRAPHY. In 1984, Wagner and Magyarik [39] proposed the first construction of a group-theoretic asymmetric cryptosystem based on the hardness of the word problem for finitely-presented groups and semigroups. In a nutshell, their idea parallels that of Goldwasser and Micali [19]: rather than distinguishing between quadratic residues and non-residues, the underlying problem is to distinguish two words in a finitely presented group G.

The Wagner-Magyarik cryptosystem has been cryptanalyzed in a number of works, including [21,23,8]. The breakdown in the security was not caused by a weakness of the word problem for groups, but rather it stemmed from a general lack of precision when describing the system and the assumptions on which it was founded. This absence of proper formalization has been characteristic of a number of the early approaches to applying group theory to cryptography [20]. For example, as noted in [8], the description of the protocol in [39] is quite ambiguous, and many design choices were left unspecified. More precisely, the authors failed to provide polynomial time algorithms to generate system parameters (*e.g.*, the group G), as well as the public and private keys, and also failed to provide a complete description of the decryption algorithm. Formal definitions of security were also lacking. When left with this level of ambiguity, formal security analysis is impossible.

A more recent proposal was the work of Anshel *et al.* [4], which can use essentially any non-abelian group as the platform. In their original paper, the authors adopted braid groups. However this choice made the protocol susceptible to various attacks, some of them quite successful (*e.g.*, [13]; see also [33] for a survey).

Perhaps it is not surprising that many of the early attempts to employ non-abelian groups in cryptographic protocols were lacking in precision. The transition from finite abelian groups to non-abelian (possibly infinite) groups for cryptographic purposes is not a small step. Very little is known regarding problems in the theory of non-abelian groups with high average-case complexity, let alone about problems that additionally could support public-key operations. To move a discussion of security to the setting of infinite groups is more difficult still. To begin with, many of the fundamental definitions of security (*e.g.*, [19]) are phrased in terms of probability. Probabilistic analysis for finite groups is readily manageable because the uniform distribution over, say, a finite cyclic group is easy to sample given just a generator and an estimate of the order. For infinite groups, it is even unclear what the corresponding concept of the uniform distribution is, let alone how one goes about sampling it. An attempt toward defining a suitable analogue of the uniform distribution on infinite groups has been recently made by Lee [28], who proposed the notion of *right invariance*, and observed that all previous concrete cryptographic constructions on infinite groups have failed to achieve it.

LPN/LWE. Roughly speaking, the LPN and LWE problems are about learning a certain function by sampling a "noisy" oracle[1] for its input / output behavior. Early research on these problems appears in [10] and [36], respectively. Both problems exhibit attractive self-reducibility properties, giving strong evidence to support the hypothesis that natural randomized versions of these problems are intractable. For LWE, there is more evidence still: the works of [36,35] demonstrate reductions to LWE from worst-case lattice problems. The self-reducibility arguments for these problems are very algebraic, which perhaps suggests that the generalizations we propose may enjoy similar properties when instantiated with other classes of groups. Such a development could produce an exciting new source of problems in group theory which are difficult on average.

---

[1] Here, "noisy" refers to the fact that the oracle may perturb the correct output according to some random variable whose probability distribution is known.

OUR CONTRIBUTIONS. Our main result is the generalization of the *learning parity with noise* (LPN) and *learning with errors* (LWE) problems to an abstract class of learning problems. At high level, we generalize the LWE setting of linear functions over vectors spaces to the context of homomorphisms between groups. This yields conjectured hard problems where the computational task is the recognition of noisy samples of (*preimage, image*) pairs for a hidden homomorphism versus random pairs of elements from the relevant domain and codomain.

The resulting abstract class of group-theoretic learning problems contains the LPN and LWE problems as special cases, but is much more general. It allows, for example, instantiations based on non-abelian groups: Another important component of our work is the development of a learning assumption based on free Burnside groups of exponent 3.

As an application, we propose a symmetric cryptosystem whose provable security can be rigorously analyzed and established based on the conjectured hardness of our Burnside learning problem. This is, to the best of our knowledge, the first time that the computational properties of Burnside groups have been employed for cryptographic purposes.

ORGANIZATION. Section 2 provides a brief review of basic group-theoretic notions. The proposed generalized learning problem is described in Section 3. Section 4 develops a combinatorial instantiation from free Burnside groups of exponent 3. A symmetric cryptosystem based on Burnside is reported in Section 5.1. Attaining asymmetric encryption is substantially more involved: a possible approach toward this goal is outlined in Section 5.2.

2   Review of Relevant Group-Theoretic Notions

FREE GROUPS. If X is a subset of a group G, let $X^{-1} = \{x^{-1} \mid x \in X\}$. An expression w of the form $a_1 \ldots a_n$ ($n \geq 0$, $a_i \in X \cup X^{-1}$) is termed a **word** or an X-**word**. Such an X-word is said to be **reduced** if $n > 0$ and no subword $a_i a_{i+1}$ takes either of the forms xx^{-1} or $x^{-1}x$. If F is a group and X is a subset of F such that X generates F and every reduced X-word is different from 1_F, then one says that F is a **free group**, freely generated by the set X, and refers to X as a **free set** of generators of F, and writes F as $F(X)$. A key property of a free group F freely generated by a set X is that for every group H, every mapping θ from X into H can be extended uniquely to a homomorphism θ_* from F into H. If θ_* is a surjection, and if K is the kernel of θ_*, then the quotient group F/K is isomorphic to H. If R is a subset of F, then in the event that K is generated by all of the conjugates of the elements of R, we express this by writing $H = \langle X; R \rangle$ and term the pair $\langle X; R \rangle$ a **presentation** of H (notice that the mapping θ is usually implicit).

RELATIVELY FREE GROUPS. If F is a free group and K a normal subgroup of F, then the factor group F/K is called **relatively free** if K is **fully invariant**, *i.e.*, if $\alpha(K) \leq K$ for any endomorphism α of F. If $x_1, \ldots, x_n$ are free generators of F, then $x_1 K, \ldots, x_n K$ are called relatively free generators of F/K, and typically

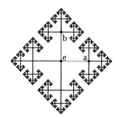

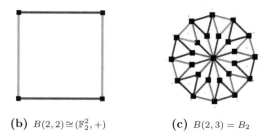

(a) Free group, $F(a, b)$　　　　**(b)** $B(2, 2) \cong (\mathbb{F}_2^2, +)$　　　　**(c)** $B(2, 3) = B_2$

Fig. 1. Cayley graphs for various groups

denoted simply by $x_1, \ldots, x_n$ when there is no risk of confusion. Let E_n denote a relatively free group of rank n, *i.e.*, $F_n = F(x_1, \ldots, x_n)$ and $E_n = F_n/K$ for some fully invariant K. One key property of such a group is that any set map on its generators into E_n can be extended to an endomorphism of E_n. Hence, one is immediately equipped with an exponential number of homomorphisms, provided that the image is non-trivial.

CAYLEY DISTANCE. Finitely generated groups can also be viewed as geometric objects via the notion of the **Cayley graph**. The Cayley graph of a group G relative to a particular set of generators has the group elements as vertexes, and an edge between two vertexes if and only if multiplication by a generator (or its inverse) translates one to the other. Figure 1 depicts Cayley graphs for few simple groups, including the 27-element *Burnside* group $B(2, 3)$ of exponent 3 with 2 generators. (Burnside groups are discussed in Section 4.) The **Cayley distance** between two group elements is defined as the length of the shortest path between the corresponding nodes in the Cayley graph. The maximum Cayley distance between any two elements in the graph is the **diameter** of the Cayley graph. The **Cayley norm** of an element x, denoted $\|x\|$, is its distance from the identity element in the Cayley graph. We remark that $\max_{x \in G}(\|x\|)$ corresponds precisely to the diameter.

COMMUTATORS. In non-abelian groups, the **commutator** of two group elements a, b, denoted $[a, b]$, is the group element satisfying the identity $ab = ba[a, b]$, that is, $[a, b] = a^{-1}b^{-1}ab$. Starting with the generators $x_1, \ldots, x_n$ of the group as the recursive basis, one obtains an ordered sequence of **formal commutators** by combining two formal commutators a, b into the formal commutator $[a, b]$. The **weight** of a formal commutator is defined by assigning weight 1 to the generators, and defining the weight of $[a, b]$ as the sum of the weights of a and b. The weight imposes a partial order on formal commutators, which is typically made total by assuming an arbitrary ordering among formal commutators of any given weight greater than 1, and by adopting the lexicographical order among the generators.

CENTER. The **center** of a group G, denoted $Z(G)$, is the set of all elements that commute with every element of G.

3 Generalized Learning Problems

We begin by reviewing the learning with errors problem, and we then generalize it to a novel abstract group-theoretic problem concerning learning with respect to a "noisy" oracle.

3.1 Learning with Errors (LPN/LWE)

The problem of *learning from noisy examples* has been considered by Angluin and Laird [3], and subsequently by Kearns [26] and Blum, Kalai, and Wasserman [10]. Informally, the problem is to deduce a particular function by sampling the input / output behavior in the presence of noise (*i.e.*, some of the outputs are incorrect). Of particular interest is the problem of *learning vectors from parity with noise* (LPN) [10], which may be stated as follows. Let Ψ be a distribution on $\mathbb{F}_2$. Let $\mathbf{s}$ and $\{\mathbf{a}_i\}_{i=1}^m$ be randomly chosen vectors, $\mathbf{s}, \mathbf{a}_i \in \mathbb{F}_2^n$, and let $\{e_i\}_{i=1}^m$ be independent samples from Ψ. Define $b_i = \mathbf{s} \cdot \mathbf{a}_i + e_i$ for $i = 1, \ldots, m$, where $\cdot$ denotes the inner product. The problem is then to determine $\mathbf{s}$ given $\{(\mathbf{a}_i, b_i)\}_{i=1}^m$. In general, this problem is believed to be computationally intractable. The best known algorithm is only slightly sub-exponential ($2^{\mathcal{O}(n/\log n)}$, due to [10]).

More generally, one may consider the same problem on vector spaces over finite fields other than $\mathbb{F}_2$. The case of $\mathbb{F}_p$ under zero-mean/low-variance discrete Gaussian noise was considered by Regev and termed *learning with errors* (LWE) problem [36]. Therein, Regev showed a quantum reduction from worst-case lattice problems (*e.g.*, the shortest vector problem), which gives further support to the conjecture that these problems are intractable. When the noise parameter is greater than $\sqrt{n}$, the best known algorithm for solving this problem was demonstrated in [10] and requires $2^{\mathcal{O}(n)}$ time. When the noise parameter is smaller than $\sqrt{n}$, the recent work of [6] has demonstrated a subexponential time algorithm using certain linearization techniques.

We also mention a variant of the LWE problem, recently proposed by Lyubashevsky *et al.* in [30] to improve the ratio of the entropy of the noisy images over that of their preimages. In the setting of [30], termed *ring-LWE*, the noisy samples have the form $(a, b) \in R \times R$, where R is a ring of algebraic integers in a suitable number field, $b \approx a \cdot s$ for a secret random ring element s, and $\cdot$ denotes multiplication in R.

3.2 Learning Homomorphisms with Noise (LHN)

The class of functions at play in the LWE problem is the class $\{\lambda_{\mathbf{s}}\}_{\mathbf{s} \in \mathbb{F}_p^n}$ of linear functionals from $\mathbb{F}_p^n$ into $\mathbb{F}_p$. By algebraic abstraction, we may replace arbitrary homomorphisms between groups for the linear functionals thus translating the learning problem from the setting of vector spaces to that of arbitrary groups. We describe the resulting generalization below.

For every $n \in \mathbb{Z}^+$, let G_n and P_n be groups (with the operation written multiplicatively). Let Γ_n, Ψ_n, and Ξ_n be distributions on G_n, P_n, and $G_n \times P_n$, respectively. Intuitively, Γ_n determines how preimages are sampled, and will usually be uniform; Ψ_n is the error distribution on the codomain; and Ξ_n is a sort of "base" distribution which is independent of any homomorphism and will also be uniform in most finite cases. Finally, let Φ_n be a distribution on the set $\mathrm{hom}(G_n, P_n)$ of homomorphisms from G_n to P_n. Furthermore, assume that Γ_n, Ψ_n, Ξ_n and Φ_n are efficiently sampleable. Let $\varphi \xleftarrow{\$} \Phi_n$ and define a distribution $A_\varphi^{\Psi_n}$ on $G_n \times P_n$ whose samples are preimage / distorted image pairs (a, b) where $a \xleftarrow{\$} \Gamma_n$ and $b = \varphi(a)e$ for $e \xleftarrow{\$} \Psi_n$. Figure 2 depicts the above generalization.

Fig. 2. Generalizing learning problems from vector spaces (LWE, left) to arbitrary groups (LHN, right)

We now formulate search and decision versions of a general problem which we term *learning homomorphisms with noise* (or for brevity, LHN).

Definition 1 (LHN-Search). *Given an $A_\varphi^{\Psi_n}$-oracle, the LHN-search problem is to recover φ.*

Definition 2 (LHN-Decision). *The LHN-decision problem is to distinguish $A_\varphi^{\Psi_n}$ from Ξ_n.*

For the search problem, the corresponding assumption is that for all probabilistic polynomial time algorithms W and for every polynomial p, we have:

$$\Pr\left[\varphi' = \varphi \mid \varphi' \leftarrow W^{A_\varphi^{\Psi_n}}(1^n)\right] < \frac{1}{p(n)}$$

where the probability is over the random choices of $\varphi \xleftarrow{\$} \Phi_n$ and over the random coins of the attacker W and of the oracle $A_\varphi^{\Psi_n}$. The corresponding assumption for the decision problem is simply that $A_\varphi^{\Psi_n} \underset{\mathrm{PPT}}{\approx} \Xi_n$.

Note that this is a proper generalization of the standard LWE problem [36], with $G_n = \mathbb{F}_p^n$, $P_n = \mathbb{F}_p$, Φ_n uniform on the linear functionals from $\mathbb{F}_p^n$ into $\mathbb{F}_p$, Γ_n uniform on $\mathbb{F}_p$, Ξ_n uniform over $G_n \times P_n$, and where Ψ_n corresponds to a zero-mean discrete Gaussian over $\mathbb{F}_p$ of suitable variance. At the same time, casting the assumption into abstract terms facilitates the formulation of new learning problems that leverage the potential hardness of group-theoretic settings other than the usual ones of cyclic groups and vector spaces. In particular, we will discuss an instantiation from combinatorial group theory in Section 4.

3.3   Looking for Instantiations of LHN: What Makes LPN/LWE Hard?

To gain insight as to what ingredients are required in the more general context, and to understand what properties one might need of a candidate group-theoretic setting to serve as a platform for the abstract LHN problem, we begin with some general observations on the standard LWE problem. First, we note that part of what makes LWE difficult in the standard vector space case is that $\mathbb{F}_p^n$ is a *free module*. Not only does this afford one with an exponential space of secret keys ($|\hom(\mathbb{F}_p^n, \mathbb{F}_p)| = p^n$); in some sense, it also maximizes the difficulty of learning with errors: Given a single noisy image $\varphi(\mathbf{a}_i) + e_i$, *every* choice of noise e_i produces a value that can be plausibly explained as the true image $\bar{\varphi}(\mathbf{a}_i)$ of some homomorphism $\bar{\varphi}$. Consequently, one must collect many samples in order to rule out any given potential value of the hidden homomorphism φ. Even once enough equations have been obtained to uniquely constrain φ, it is not clear which path to take to distill this large set of equations down to φ, leading to an essentially exponential number of choices to be considered. This is in sharp contrast with the setting of arbitrary finite groups, where $|\hom(G_n, P_n)|$ may not be exponential, and furthermore, one could potentially detect the presence of error from but a single sample (a, b) if, for example, the order of b does not divide the order of a.

From the above discussion, the setting of free groups arises as a seemingly natural alternative to vector spaces. As for the case of $\mathbb{F}_p^n$, instantiating LHN over free groups results in a huge space of possible keys (homomorphisms). Other similarities with vector spaces, however, are not easy to derive. First, free groups are infinite, which adds non-trivial complications to the sampling process, and makes it cumbersome to even formally state the abstract learning problem in this case. Second, multiplication in free groups is a rather transparent operation. For example, the analogue of the subset sum problem (a crucial ingredient that is often paired with the LPN/LWE assumptions, and used *e.g.*, in the cryptosystem of [36]) admits an efficient algorithm in the setting of free groups (see *e.g.*, [29, Proposition I.2.21]), which makes it rather unsuitable for cryptographic applications.

We contend, however, that suitable analogues of $\mathbb{F}_p^n$ might be found by restricting attention to certain sub-classes of groups, like *relatively free groups*. As mentioned in Section 2, these groups enjoy many of the desirable properties that free groups exhibit: they are, for instance, equipped with exponentially many homomorphisms into any non-trivial group, and thus provide adequate key space for the LHN problem. In contrast to free groups, they can also be chosen to be finite, thus avoiding many of the complications that come with free groups. In the next section, we describe an infinite class of finite relatively free groups: The free Burnside groups of exponent 3.

4   An Instantiation from Combinatorial Group Theory

We now put forth a new intractability assumption by instantiating LHN with a certain class of finite non-abelian groups. We begin with some background and basic facts on the class of groups in question, and then discuss their computational properties and choice of parameters suitable for instantiating the LHN problem.

4.1   Burnside Groups

For a positive integer k, consider the class of groups for which all elements x satisfy $x^k = 1$. Such a group is said to be of *exponent* k. We will be interested in a certain family of such groups called the *free Burnside groups of exponent* k, which are in some sense the "largest." The free Burnside groups are uniquely determined by two parameters: the number of generators n, and the exponent k. We will denote these groups by $B(n, k)$:

Definition 3 (Free Burnside group). *For any* $n, k \geq 0$, *the* Burnside group *of exponent* k *with* n *generators is defined as*

$$B(n, k) = \langle \{x_1, \ldots, x_n\}; \{w^k \mid \text{ for all words } w \text{ over } x_1, \ldots, x_n\} \rangle.$$

The question of whether $B(n, k)$ is finite or not is known as the *bounded Burnside problem*. For sufficiently large k, $B(n, k)$ is generally infinite [25]. For small exponents, it is known that $k \in \{2, 3, 4, 6\}$ yields finite groups for all n. (We remark that with the exception of $k = 2$, these are non-trivial results.) For other small values of k (most notably, $k = 5$), the question remains open.

For the purposes of this paper, we will be interested primarily in groups of exponent 3; hence in what follows we will denote $B(n, 3)$ simply by B_n for brevity. Next, we review some important facts about B_n (see [24,22] for a fuller account).

NORMAL FORM OF B_n. Each B_n-element can be written uniquely as an ordered sequence of (a subset of) generators (or their inverses[2]), appearing in lexicographical order, followed by (a subset of) the commutators of weight 2 (or their inverses), and finally by (a subset of) the commutators of weight 3 (or their inverses):

$$\prod_{i=1}^{n} x_i^{\alpha_i} \prod_{i<j} [x_i, x_j]^{\beta_{i,j}} \prod_{i<j<k} [x_i, x_j, x_k]^{\gamma_{i,j,k}}$$

where all $\alpha_i, \beta_{i,j}, \gamma_{i,j,k} \in \{0, 1, -1\}$ for all $1 \leq i < j < k \leq n$, and $[x_i, x_j, x_k] = [[x_i, x_j], x_k]$.

ORDER OF B_n. From the above normal form, it follows that B_n has exactly $3^{n+\binom{n}{2}+\binom{n}{3}}$ elements.

HOMOMORPHISMS FROM B_n TO B_r. There are $3^{n\left(r+\binom{r}{2}+\binom{r}{3}\right)}$ homomorphisms from $B_n \to B_r$. This follows immediately from the order of B_r and from the fact

---

[2] Note that $x^{-1} = x^2$ in B_n, as B_n has exponent 3.

that B_n is a free object in the category of groups of exponent 3 with generating set of size n.

We also have the following lemma regarding the diameter of B_n (for a proof see [7]):

Lemma 1. $\exists \tau_n \in B_n$ such that $\|\tau_n\| \in \Omega(\frac{n^3}{\log n})$.

4.2 Computational Aspects of Burnside Groups

In order for the Burnside groups to be of use in cryptography, at a minimum, they must have a concise representation, and the group operation must be efficiently computable. We demonstrate here that both criteria are met. First, we note that as described above, each element of B_n has a unique normal form as a product of the generators and certain commutators. Hence by storing an array of the exponents (each of which is in the set $\{0, 1, -1\}$) we can uniquely represent an element. The size of the array is cubic in n.

As for the group operation, this can be computed simply by concatenating two normal forms, and then reducing the resulting word back into normal form. This process, referred to as the *collection process*, takes cubic time (see [24], chap. 11) in the length of the input (which is itself cubic in n). However, all commutators of weight 3 are in the center $Z(B_n)$ of B_n, and hence there is no need to expand them and apply the collection process—one can simply add the corresponding exponents modulo 3. Furthermore, since all commutators of weight 4 are trivial (see [24], chap. 18), we know that $[B_n, B_n]$ is commutative. Hence, we can again avoid the collection process when moving the weight-2 commutators amongst themselves, and in cubic time, we can reduce the expression to a "nearly" normal form consisting of a product of at most $2n$ generators (or their inverses) followed by commutators in normal form. Therefore we need only to apply the collection process on linear input, and so the overall running time of computing the product is indeed $\mathcal{O}(n^3)$. Inverses can also be computed over B_n in at most cubic time by a similar (yet somewhat simpler) collecting process.

The last and most challenging computational aspect of B_n relates to its *geodesics*—the computation of distances in the Cayley graph. For the applications we introduce here, it will suffice to compute the *norm* (*i.e.*, the distance to the identity of the group).

In general, geodesics in the Cayley graph is a difficult problem. In some cases, it is known to be NP-hard [32].[3] However, this is not as troubling as it seems. We need only to compute norms in the codomain group P_n, which is generally small, and does not necessarily grow with the security parameter (although it may grow with a correctness parameter). For the case of the free Burnside group B_r, one possible solution is to perform a breadth-first search of the Cayley graph, storing the norm of every element in a table. This process will begin to become infeasible around $r = 5$. However, even with this small number of generators, the diameter

---

[3] One entertaining example is that of the Rubik's cube group, whose diameter was demonstrated to be 20 in 2010 via a distributed computing project which required 35 CPU-years.

is large enough to properly decode for many interesting error distributions Ψ_n. For the general case, geodesics in the Cayley graph of B_n might be efficiently computable (perhaps up to small approximation factors) making use of a number of commutator identities. We do not consider this in detail here, but will address this problem seperately.

4.3   Instantiating LHN over Burnside Groups

Here we propose a concrete instantiation from Burnside groups, which we subsequently denote by B_n-LHN. Set $G_n \doteq B_n$ and $P_n \doteq B_r$, where $2 \le r \le 4$. Let $\Gamma_n \doteq \mathbf{U}(B_n)$ and $\Xi_n \doteq \mathbf{U}(B_n \times B_r)$. The error distribution Ψ_n on B_r is constructed by taking a randomly ordered product of the generators, raised to random exponents. More precisely, its probability mass function is:

$$\forall e \in B_r, \qquad \Pr_{E \xleftarrow{\$} \Psi_n} [E = e] = \Pr_{\mathbf{v} \xleftarrow{\$} \mathbb{F}_3^r, \sigma \xleftarrow{\$} S_r} \left[e = \prod_{i=1}^{r} x_{\sigma(i)}^{v_i} \right] \qquad (1)$$

where the x_i's are the generators of B_r, the v_i's are the components of $\mathbf{v}$, and S_r denotes the symmetric group on r letters. Since $x^2 = x^{-1}$ in B_r, the norm $\|e\|$ of a Ψ_n-sample e is at most r. (Some intuition for this choice of Ψ_n is discussed at the end of this Section.) For any given secret homomorphism φ, the above choices completely describe the distribution $A_\varphi^{\Psi_n}$. As for the distribution Φ_n from which φ is drawn, we simply let $\Phi_n \doteq \mathbf{U}(\mathrm{hom}(B_n, B_r))$. Note that since B_n is a relatively free group, any mapping of its n generators uniquely extends to a homomorphism. Hence, to sample Φ_n, it suffices to select random B_r-images for the n generators of B_n. Note that for $2 \le r \le 4$, elements of B_r take at most 3 bytes, and thus storing φ requires just linear space.

Figure 3 summarizes the choice of groups and distributions for the B_n-LHN problem.

G_n	P_n	Γ_n	Ξ_n	Ψ_n	Φ_n
B_n	B_r	$\mathbf{U}(B_n)$	$\mathbf{U}(B_n \times B_r)$	$\left[\mathbf{v} \xleftarrow{\$} \mathbf{U}(\mathbb{F}_3^r), \sigma \xleftarrow{\$} S_r : \prod_{i=1}^{r} x_{\sigma(i)}^{v_i} \right]$	$\mathbf{U}(\mathrm{hom}(B_n, B_r))$

Fig. 3. Choice of groups and distributions for the B_n-LHN problem

Choice of Parameters. To determine suitable choice of parameters for the B_n-LHN instantiation described above, here we consider known approaches to attacking the assumption. First, observe that the key space is rather large: $|\mathrm{hom}(B_n, B_r)| = 3^{\Theta(nr^3)}$, and so even small choices of n and r will defeat a brute-force attack. In terms of a distinguishing attack, we derive below an interesting connection to LWE with $p = 3$, based on the projection onto the commutator-factor (*cf.* Figure 4).

$$\rho_n : B_n \to B_n/[B_n, B_n] \cong (\mathbb{F}_3^n, +)$$
$$\rho_r : B_r \to B_r/[B_r, B_r] \cong (\mathbb{F}_3^r, +)$$

$$
\begin{array}{ccc}
B_n & \xrightarrow{\ \varphi\ } & B_r \\
\downarrow{\scriptstyle \rho_n} & & \downarrow{\scriptstyle \rho_r} \\
(\mathbb{F}_3^n, +) & \xrightarrow{\ \varphi'\ } & (\mathbb{F}_3^r, +)
\end{array}
$$

Fig. 4. Projection of B_n and B_r onto the commutator-factor

Computationally, ρ_n amounts to just retaining the exponent-tuple corresponding to the generators in the normal form of a B_n-element. One easily verifies that ρ_n and ρ_r transform the distribution $A_\varphi^{\Psi_n}$ from an B_n-LHN instance to a new distribution, $A_{\varphi'}^{\Psi'_r}$ over $\mathbb{F}_3^n \times \mathbb{F}_3^r$, which presents us with a problem very similar to the standard LWE with $p = 3$. (Even with $r > 1$, the resulting problem is polynomial-time equivalent to the standard version; see *e.g.*, [5], Lemma 4.2.) Notably, the resulting noise distribution Ψ'_n for the LWE-like instance is just the abelianization of Ψ_n, which by construction amounts to a random r-tuple of $\mathbb{F}_3$-exponents (*cf.* Equation (1)). Thus, applying the commutator-factor transformation yields an LWE-like instance where the noisy distribution is *identical* to the random one, and so the instance is impossible to break. Nevertheless, in light of this connection with LWE, it seems prudent to pick values for n that would also make LWE hard. The best algorithm for this setting is currently the one of [10], and requires time $2^{\mathcal{O}(n/\log n)}$, which suggests values of n in the few hundreds.

Remark 1. Regarding the error distribution, we remark that the support of Ψ_n should never be contained in a proper normal subgroup of P_n, else an adversary may be able to "factor out" the noise to mount a distinguishing attack. Note that for the standard LWE/LPN problems, as well as the error distribution we propose for B_n-LHN in Equation (1), this issue does not arise because the support of Ψ_n generates all of P_n.

Regarding the choice of r, as discussed above, $r = 4$ will suffice, as this permits an exhaustive, breadth first search of the Cayley graph. For each element of B_r, a geodesic representative (or just the norm) can be stored in a moderately-sized table (≈ 14MB) for future use. We stress that only one pre-computation is required for the lifetime of the system.

We note also that there is still much flexibility in the choice of Ψ_n; random walks of variable length, perhaps according to a similar distribution as that of [9], may also be appropriate. Additionally, we remark that one may consider altogether different metrics on the group, *e.g.*, taking a normal form for the elements and then using the Hamming metric on the resulting vector of exponents. The distribution Ψ_n could then correspond to explicitly corrupting part of the description of $\varphi(a)$. However, the former approach using the Cayley graph seems to have much more promise for application to an asymmetric setting—we discuss this further in the following section.

5   Applications

5.1   A Group-Based Symmetric Cryptosystem

In this section, we present a symmetric cryptosystem based on the hardness of learning Burnside homomorphisms with noise (B_n-LHN cf. Section 4.3). Proofs of the following theorems are provided in [7].

Precomputation: Run breadth-first search on the Cayley graph of B_r, recording the norm of each element. We stress that this procedure need only be done once for the lifetime of the system.

Key-Gen(n): Run the setup algorithm for B_n-LHN to select a random homomorphism φ from the set of homomorphisms from B_n into B_r, and set the shared key SK $\doteq \varphi$. Using the table generated in the precomputation phase, select an element $\tau \in B_r$ of maximal norm. Given the lower bound from Lemma 1, we know that $\|\tau\| = \Omega(r^3/\log r)$.

Encrypt(SK, t): To encrypt a bit t, select $(a, b) \overset{\$}{\leftarrow} A_\varphi^{\Psi_n}$, compute $b' \doteq b\tau^t (= \varphi(a)e\tau^t)$, and output the ciphertext $c \doteq (a, b')$.

Decrypt(SK, (a, b')): Compute $e' = \varphi(a)^{-1} \cdot b'$ and output $t = 0$ if and only if $\|e'\| \leq r$.

Theorem 1 (Correctness)

If $(a, b') \overset{\$}{\leftarrow}$ Encrypt(SK, t), then Decrypt(SK, (a, b')) = t.

Remark 2. For the case of small r, we must take more care. Note that from the proof of Lemma 1, we have more precisely that $\|\tau\| \geq \left\lceil \frac{r + \binom{r}{2} + \binom{r}{3}}{\log_3 2r} \right\rceil$. Hence if $r = 4$, then our lower bound for $\|\tau\|$ is 8, which presents a small problem, since the maximal norm element from the support of Ψ_n is of norm 4. Such an element will be sampled from Ψ_n with probability $\frac{16}{81}$, and hence in this case, we simply remark that correctness can be amplified by sending multiple encryptions. The Decrypt algorithm will then output 0 if $\|\varphi(a)^{-1} \cdot y\|$ is ever less than 4, 1 if it is ever greater, and $\perp$ if it is always 4. We also remark that the elementary lower bounds from Lemma 1 are likely not tight, in which case there is no need for the amplification. Even for $r = 4$, if $\|\tau\| = 9$ rather than 8, the scheme above would attain correctness with probability 1, making amplification unnecessary.

Theorem 2 (Security). *If the B_n-LHN-Decision problem is hard, then the above cryptosystem is IND-CPA secure.*

5.2   Towards Group-Based Asymmetric Cryptosystems

There are several remaining obstacles to basing asymmetric cryptography on B_n-LHN. The primary issue is in providing a means of sampling the distribution $A_\varphi^{\Psi_n}$ without knowledge of the secret φ. In cryptosystems like that of [36], this was accomplished via computing the sum over a random subset of known samples from the distribution. However, note that commutativity seems critical for this to be effective:[4] if $\{(a_i, b_i)\}_{i=1}^m$ are samples (so $b_i = \varphi(a_i) + e_i$, where e_i are "small") and $S \subset [m]$, then $\sum_{i \in S} b_i = \sum_{i \in S}(\varphi(a_i) + e_i) = \varphi\left(\sum_{i \in S} a_i\right) + \sum_{i \in S} e_i$.

---

[4] We adopt below additive notation, as it is more natural for the LPN/LWE setting.

It follows that, if $|S|$ is not too large, $\sum_{i \in S} b_i$ will remain close to the true image $\varphi(\sum_{i \in S} a_i)$. In the non-abelian case, $\prod(\varphi(a_i)e_i)$ is not generally equal to $\prod \varphi(a_i) \prod e_i$, and so it is not necessarily true that $\prod(\varphi(a_i)e_i)$ remains close to $\varphi(\prod a_i)$ just because the norm of $\prod e_i$ is small.

We briefly mention some possible approaches toward bypassing this issue. A first workaround might be to consider only abelian P_n. However, this makes the problem somewhat less interesting, since applying the factor-commutator transformation to $A_\varphi^{\Psi_n}$ would then produce a new distribution over abelian groups which likely is not any more difficult to distinguish from uniform as the original (assuming that $\Gamma_n = \mathbf{U}(G_n)$ and $\Xi_n = \mathbf{U}(G_n \times P_n)$ as usual).[5] So it would seem that to consider only abelian P_n is to rule out non-abelian groups altogether.

A more promising approach might be to place additional constraints on the distribution Ψ_n. By careful selection of the error terms, one might be able to guarantee that the resulting product behaves well in the sense that commutators involving $e \overset{\$}{\leftarrow} \Psi_n$ are small in comparison to the diameter of P_n. However, we remark that the naïve method of forcing the support of Ψ_n to be contained in $Z(P_n)$ is flawed: the commutator-factor transformation then produces a distribution without noise, which will typically be easy to distinguish from random via standard linear algebra techniques. More generally, as discussed in Section 4, the support of Ψ_n should never be contained in a proper normal subgroup of P_n. Note that in our instantiation of B_n-LHN using free Burnside groups, the support of Ψ_n generates all of P_n.

6   Conclusions and Future Work

In this paper, we put forth a generalization of the learning parity with noise and learning with errors problems, moving from linear functionals over vector spaces to homomorphisms between arbitrary (possibly non-abelian) groups. We also developed an instantiation of our abstract group-theoretic learning problem from the theory of Burnside groups, and proposed the first cryptographic applications of these groups in the form of a symmetric cryptosystem.

Our work broadens the family of cryptographically useful intractability assumptions. It also raises several research questions, ranging from specific issues like estimating the most suitable choice of parameters, to broader problems like devising alternate instantiations of our learning problem. Other related lines of inquiry to be investigated in future work include: 1) applying the techniques of [34] to extend the symmetric scheme to efficiently encrypt multiple bits; 2) adapting our Burnside-based cryptosystem to the asymmetric setting; 3) improving existing algorithms for computing over Burnside groups (e.g., to compute the Cayley norm); and 4) assessing the hardness of learning homomorphisms with noise over Burnside groups by designing sub-exponential distinguishing attacks.

---

[5] This follows primarily from the fact that for any epimorphism $\psi : G \to P$ of groups, $\psi(\mathbf{U}(G)) = \mathbf{U}(P)$, but also requires the assumption that the commutator subgroup $[G_n, G_n]$ can be efficiently sampled, or that some other means exist for sampling the fibers of the projection $G_n \to G_n/[G_n, G_n]$.

Acknowledgement. We are grateful to Hugo Krawczyk for suggesting a cleaner acronym for our generalized learning assumption.

References

1. Ajtai, M.: Generating hard instances of lattice problems (extended abstract). In: Proceedings of the Twenty-Eighth Annual ACM Symposium on the Theory of Computing, pp. 99–108. ACM, New York (1996)
2. Ajtai, M., Dwork, C.: A public-key cryptosystem with worst-case/average-case equivalence. In: STOC 1997, pp. 284–293 (1997)
3. Angluin, D., Laird, P.: Learning from noisy examples. Machine Learning 2(4), 343–370 (1988)
4. Anshel, I., Anshel, M., Goldfeld, D.: Non-abelian key agreement protocols. Discrete Applied Mathematics 130(1), 3–12 (2003)
5. Applebaum, B., Cash, D., Peikert, C., Sahai, A.: Fast cryptographic primitives and circular-secure encryption based on hard learning problems. In: Halevi, S. (ed.) CRYPTO 2009. LNCS, vol. 5677, pp. 595–618. Springer, Heidelberg (2009)
6. Arora, S., Ge, R.: New algorithms for learning in presence of errors (2011) (manuscript)
7. Baumslag, G., Fazio, N., Nicolosi, A.R., Shpilrain, V., Skeith, III, W. E.: Generalized learning problems and applications to non-commutative cryptography. Cryptology ePrint Archive, Report 2011/357 (2011), http://eprint.iacr.org/2011/357
8. Birget, J.C., Magliveras, S.S., Sramka, M.: On public-key cryptosystems based on combinatorial group theory. Tatra Mountains Mathematical Publications 33, 137–148 (2006)
9. Blass, A., Gurevich, Y.: Matrix transformation is complete for the average case. SIAM Journal on Computing 24(1), 3–29 (1995)
10. Blum, A., Kalai, A., Wasserman, H.: Noise-tolerant learning, the parity problem, and the statistical query model. J. ACM 50, 2003 (2003)
11. Boneh, D., Franklin, M.: Identity-based encryption from the weil pairing. SIAM J. of Computing 32(3), 586–615 (2003)
12. Cocks, C.: An identity based encryption scheme based on quadratic residues. In: Honary, B. (ed.) Cryptography and Coding 2001. LNCS, vol. 2260, pp. 360–363. Springer, Heidelberg (2001)
13. Garber, D., Kaplan, S., Teicher, M., Tsaban, B., Vishne, U.: Probabilistic solutions of equations in the braid group. Advances in Applied Mathematics 35, 323–334 (2005)
14. Gentry, C.: Fully homomorphic encryption using ideal lattices. In: STOC 2009: Proceedings of the 41st Annual ACM Symposium on Theory of Computing, pp. 169–178. ACM, New York (2009)
15. Gentry, C.: Toward basing fully homomorphic encryption on worst-case hardness. In: Rabin, T. (ed.) CRYPTO 2010. LNCS, vol. 6223, pp. 116–137. Springer, Heidelberg (2010)
16. Gentry, C., Halevi, S., Vaikuntanathan, V.: i-hop homomorphic encryption and rerandomizable yao circuits. In: Rabin, T. (ed.) CRYPTO 2010. LNCS, vol. 6223, pp. 155–172. Springer, Heidelberg (2010)
17. Goldreich, O.: Foundations of Cryptography, vol. 1. Cambridge Univ. Press, Cambridge (2001)

18. Goldreich, O.: Foundations of Cryptography, vol. 2. Cambridge Univ. Press, Cambridge (2004)
19. Goldwasser, S., Micali, S.: Probabilistic encryption. JCSS 28(2), 270–299 (1984)
20. Gonzalez-Vasco, M.I., Magliveras, S., Steinwandt, R.: Group Theoretic Cryptography. Chapman and Hall/CRC, United States (to appear, 2012)
21. Gonzalez-Vasco, M.I., Steinwandt, R.: Reaction attacks on public key cryptosystems based on the word problem. Applicable Algebra in Engineering, Communication and Computing 14(5), 335–340 (2002)
22. Gupta, N.: On groups in which every element has finite order. Amer. Math. Month. 96, 297–308 (1989)
23. Hall, C., Goldberg, I., Schneier, B.: Reaction attacks against several public-key cryptosystem. In: Varadharajan, V., Mu, Y. (eds.) ICICS 1999. LNCS, vol. 1726, pp. 2–12. Springer, Heidelberg (1999)
24. Hall, M.: The Theory of Groups. Macmillan Company, New York (1959)
25. Ivanov, S.V.: The free Burnside groups of sufficiently large exponents. Internat. J. Algebra Comput. 4(1-2), ii+308 (1994)
26. Kearns, M.: Efficient noise-tolerant learning from statistical queries. Journal of the ACM, 392–401 (1993)
27. Koblitz, N.: Elliptic curve cryptosystems. Mathematics of Computation 48(177), 203–209 (1987)
28. Lee, E.: Right-invariance: A property for probabilistic analysis of cryptography based on infinite groups. In: Lee, P.J. (ed.) ASIACRYPT 2004. LNCS, vol. 3329, pp. 103–118. Springer, Heidelberg (2004)
29. Lyndon, R., Schupp, P.: Combinatorial Group Theory. Classics in Mathematics. Springer, Heidelberg (2001)
30. Lyubashevsky, V., Peikert, C., Regev, O.: On ideal lattices and learning with errors over rings. In: Gilbert, H. (ed.) EUROCRYPT 2010. LNCS, vol. 6110, pp. 1–23. Springer, Heidelberg (2010)
31. Miller, V.S.: Use of elliptic curves in cryptography. In: Williams, H.C. (ed.) CRYPTO 1985. LNCS, vol. 218, pp. 417–426. Springer, Heidelberg (1986)
32. Myasnikov, A., Roman'kov, V., Ushakov, A., Vershik, A.: The word and geodesic problems in free solvable groups. Trans. Amer. Math. Soc. 362, 4655–4682 (2010)
33. Myasnikov, A., Shpilrain, V., Ushakov, A.: Group-Based Cryptography. Birkhäuser Verlag, Switzerland (2008)
34. Peikert, C., Vaikuntanathan, V., Waters, B.: A framework for efficient and composable oblivious transfer. In: Wagner, D. (ed.) CRYPTO 2008. LNCS, vol. 5157, pp. 554–571. Springer, Heidelberg (2008)
35. Peikert, C.: Public-key cryptosystems from the worst-case shortest vector problem: extended abstract. In: STOC, pp. 333–342 (2009)
36. Regev, O.: On lattices, learning with errors, random linear codes, and cryptography. In: STOC, pp. 84–93. ACM Press, New York (2005)
37. Shamir, A.: Identity-based cryptosystems and signature schemes. In: Blakely, G.R., Chaum, D. (eds.) CRYPTO 1984. LNCS, vol. 196, pp. 47–53. Springer, Heidelberg (1985)
38. van Dijk, M., Gentry, C., Halevi, S., Vaikuntanathan, V.: Fully homomorphic encryption over the integers. In: Gilbert, H. (ed.) EUROCRYPT 2010. LNCS, vol. 6110, pp. 24–43. Springer, Heidelberg (2010)
39. Wagner, N.R., Magyarik, M.R.: A public key cryptosystem based on the word problem. In: Blakely, G.R., Chaum, D. (eds.) CRYPTO 1984. LNCS, vol. 196, pp. 19–36. Springer, Heidelberg (1985)

A Novel Framework for Protocol Analysis*

Kristian Gjøsteen, George Petrides, and Asgeir Steine

NTNU, Trondheim, Norway

Abstract. We describe a novel reformulation of Canetti's Universal Composability (UC) framework for the analysis of cryptographic protocols. Our framework is different mainly in that it is (a) based on systems of interactive Turing machines with a fixed communication graph and (b) augmented with a global message queue that allows the sending of multiple messages per activation. The first feature significantly simplifies the proofs of some framework results, such as the UC theorem, while the second can lead to more natural descriptions of protocols and ideal functionalities.

Keywords: Protocol Security, Universal Composability.

1 Introduction

Canetti's Universal Composability framework [2] has become a popular model for analysing cryptographic protocols (for another more or less equivalent model see [5]). Analysis begins by defining a so-called ideal functionality that encapsulates some desired functionality and security properties in the form of a trusted third party. If the protocol is in a specific sense indistinguishable from the functionality, we say that the protocol realises the functionality. If the functionality has the desired functional and security properties, then so will the protocol.

The most interesting property of Canetti's framework is that of composability, where any ideal functionality can be replaced by a subprotocol that realises it. Ideal functionalities are typically much easier to work with than cryptographic protocols, so this replacement can simplify analysis.

We note that ideal functionalities are also used to provide ideal models for the facilities that underlie protocols, such as communication networks, common reference strings, random oracles and out-of-band key agreement.

One interesting feature of Canetti's approach is a strong preference for studying the single-session case, since this significantly simplifies analysis. The multi-session analysis follows from the single-session case by composing multiple instances. For many protocols, however, this approach is quite simply not feasible (see [3] for one example). In other cases, multi-session analysis may result in tighter concrete results.

Some drawbacks of Canetti's framework are more apparent in the setting of anonymous communications. One such drawback is that all protocol machines

---

* Funded by the Norwegian Research Council's VERDIKT programme project 183195.

X. Boyen and X. Chen (Eds.): ProvSec 2011, LNCS 6980, pp. 340–347, 2011.

must agree on a unique session identifier before the execution. This is awkward because the anonymity requirements explicitly forbid most obvious approaches for agreeing on session identifiers.

Another drawback is the way the activation of interactive Turing machines (ITMs) is handled. When an ITM wants to send a message to another ITM, it has to write the message to the appropriate communication tape and stop its execution. The message recipient is activated, but the sender cannot control when itself will be reactivated.

Our contribution. In this short paper, we briefly describe a reformulation of Canetti's framework that we have developed based on our ongoing work with practical anonymous communication protocols. Additionaly, we define the notions of emulation and realisation, and sketch the proof of the usual composition theorem from [2]. For more details and illustrative examples we refer the reader to the full version of the paper, to appear in the Journal of Internet Services and Information Security.

There are two main differences between our formulation and that of Canetti:

- Canetti uses a very dynamic setting, where instances of ITMs come into existence as needed. Instead, we consider a fixed system of ITMs with communication regulated by a fixed communication graph.
- We augment Canetti's system of activation with a message queue, where ITMs can submit multiple messages into the queue for later delivery. Moreover, ITMs can send messages to themselves and, therefore, also reactivate themselves.

Since we use a fixed system of ITMs and a fixed communication graph, we shall usually let our protocol machines handle multiple sessions. As we have already argued, this is already necessary for some protocols, and may have other advantages as well.

The main advantage of adding a message queue is to get simpler and more natural protocol descriptions. In the field of anonymous communications, this also gives us quite natural solutions to certain problems that seem difficult to solve in Canetti's framework.

A final advantage of our formulation is that it significantly simplifies proofs of framework results. For instance, the proof of our composition theorem is essentially contained in the drawing given in Fig. 1. We follow the concrete security approach of [1], which we believe is essential for practical applications. Canetti uses local resource bounds on the parts of the system that imply global resource bounds for the entire system. Instead, we consider systems that "usually terminate", without exceeding global resource bounds. In our experience, this simplifies many arguments significantly.

Overview. Section 2 provides the basic definitions for systems and partial systems of ITMs. In Sect. 3 we introduce the notion of indistinguishable systems and partial systems, and state some basic results about indistinguishability. Finally, in Sect. 4 we define the notion of emulation and state our composition theorem.

1.1   Definitions

Our graphs will be undirected multigraphs with loops. A *graph* is a tuple (V, E, λ), where V is a set of vertices, E is a set of edges and λ is a function that assigns an unordered pair of vertices to every edge.

An *interactive Turing machine* (ITM) is a Turing machine with one working tape and five other tapes: random, input, incoming communication, output, and outgoing communication. The first three are read-only, the latter two are write-only. The ITM may enter a special *wait state*, in which processing temporarily stops, but may be resumed later from the same state. We refer the reader to [4] for more information.

2   Systems of Interactive Turing Machines

A *system* $\Sigma = (V, E, \lambda, v_0, M)$ consists of a *communication graph* (V, E, λ), a distinguished *initial vertex* $v_0 \in V$ and a function M that assigns an ITM to each $v \in V$ (denoted by M_v). The communication graph can have parallell edges, and we shall assume that every vertex has a loop.

A *partial system* $\Pi = (W, F, \lambda', N, X, \kappa)$ consists of a graph (W, F, λ'), a function N that assigns an ITM to each $v \in W$ (denoted by N_v), a set X of *external* edges (disjoint from the *internal* edges F) and a function $\kappa : X \to W$ that assigns a vertex to every external edge.

A partial system is *initial* if a vertex is designated as initial. Two partial systems are *interchangeable* if they have identical external edges, and they are either both initial or both not initial.

Two partial systems $\Pi_1 = (W_1, F_1, \lambda'_1, N_1, X_1, \kappa_1)$ and $\Pi_2 = (W_2, F_2, \lambda'_2, N_2, X_2, \kappa_2)$ are *composable* if they are not both initial and have disjoint vertex and edge sets. Their *composition*, denoted by $\Pi_1 \odot \Pi_2$, is the partial system $\Pi_3 = (W_3, F_3, \lambda'_3, N_3, X_3, \kappa_3)$, where:

- $W_3 = W_1 \cup W_2$,
- $F_3 = F_1 \cup F_2 \cup (X_1 \cap X_2)$,
- $\lambda'_3(e) = \begin{cases} \lambda'_1(e) & \text{if } e \in F_1, \\ \lambda'_2(e) & \text{if } e \in F_2, \\ \{\kappa_1(e), \kappa_2(e)\} & \text{if } e \in X_1 \cap X_2, \end{cases}$
- $N_{3,v} = \begin{cases} N_{1,v} & \text{if } v \in W_1, \\ N_{2,v} & \text{if } v \in W_2, \end{cases}$
- $X_3 = (X_1 \cup X_2) \setminus (X_1 \cap X_2)$, and
- $\kappa_3(e) = \begin{cases} \kappa_1(e) & \text{if } e \in X_1, \\ \kappa_2(e) & \text{if } e \in X_2. \end{cases}$

If either Π_1 or Π_2 is initial, then so is $\Pi_1 \odot \Pi_2$. If $\Pi_1 \odot \Pi_2$ is initial and has no external edges then it is a system and we say that Π_1 *completes* Π_2 (and vice versa).

Remark 1. Given two interchangeable partial systems, a third partial system may be composable with only one of them due to conflicts with vertices or internal edges in the other. For the same reason, several other natural and desirable operations, such as the composition of a partial system with itself, are forbidden by the above constructions.

The simple solution to this technical problem is to rename edges. We shall assume that such renaming can be done without cost. Also, trivial renaming will typically go unmentioned.

2.1   Execution Model

An *execution* of a system $\Sigma = (V, E, \lambda, v_0, M)$ works with the following state:

- For each vertex $v \in V$, one instance of the ITM M_v.
- A message queue Q containing tuples $V \times E \times \{0, 1\}^*$.

When the execution starts, any input to the system is written to the input tape of the M_{v_0} instance, which is then activated. Whenever an instance of an ITM M_v enters its wait state, the execution proceeds as follows:

- *Queuing a message.* If M_v has written a tuple (queue, e, m) to its communication tape and $\lambda(e) = \{v, v'\}$ for some $v' \in V$ then add (v, e, m) to Q and reactivate M_v.
- *Handing over.* If M_v has written (hand$-$over, e, m) to its communication tape and $\lambda(e) = \{v, v'\}$ then write (e, m) to the incoming communication tape of $M_{v'}$ and activate $M_{v'}$.
- *Delivering a message.* If M_v did not write to its communication tape and (v', e, m) is the first entry in Q with $\lambda(e) = \{v', v''\}$ then remove the entry from the queue, write (e, m) to the incoming communication tape of $M_{v''}$ and activate $M_{v''}$.
- *Default activation.* If M_v did not write to its communication tape, $v \neq v_0$ and Q is empty then activate M_{v_0}.
- *Termination.* If $v = v_0$ and M_v has halted after writing a (possibly empty) string x to its output tape then copy x to the system's output tape and stop.

Remark 2. Note that queuing messages via loop edges allows for some degree of controlled self-reactivation.

Resource Bounds. There is no requirement that an execution must terminate. However, we shall mainly be interested in systems that with high probability terminate, in which case it is interesting to consider the time required before termination. We define the total execution time of a system to be the sum of the execution time of all the ITMs plus the cost of managing activation and the message queue. Apart from execution time, there are other interesting resource measures in protocol analysis, such as the number of sessions run or the number of corrupted parties.

344   K. Gjøsteen, G. Petrides, and A. Steine

In general, for some tuple of resource bounds $R = (r_1, \ldots, r_n)$, we shall say that a system is (R, δ)-*bounded* or $(r_1, \ldots, r_n, \delta)$-*bounded* if the probability that the system terminates without exceeding any of the resource bounds in R is at least $1 - \delta$.

2.2 Protocols

The notion of a system of ITMs described above is very general. Our next aim is to discuss how protocols fit into this general system. For this, we shall define two notions, those of *protocol machine* and *ideal functionality*.

Protocol machines and *ideal functionalities* are ITMs that expect to be attached to vertices in a communication graph with a loop and specific number of incident non-loop edges. An ideal functionality will distinguish a special *attacker edge* and consider the remaining edges as *input/output (i/o) edges*. A protocol machine will distinguish up to three classes of edges: one or more *i/o edges*, zero or more *subprotocol edges* and zero or one *corruption edge*.

Remark 3. The interpretation of this is as follows. A protocol machine is attached to a vertex in a communication graph and receives instructions over its i/o edges directing its operation. If the protocol produces output, this is sent out via the i/o edges. A protocol machine can delegate work to and communicate with subprotocol machines via its subprotocol edges.

An attacker may be able to corrupt the protocol machine in various ways. In this case, the attacker will send special messages to the protocol machine over its corruption edge, and the protocol machine will respond according to its programming.

An ideal functionality either models an ideal subprotocol or some idealisation of some feature a protocol relies on, such as a physical communications network. The i/o edges play the same role as for protocol machines.

Protocol machines and ideal functionalities are organised in a layered hierarchical fashion with protocol machines above their subprotocol machines and ideal functionalities at the bottom. This is made formal by the notion of *protocol system*, which is a non-initial partial system satisfying:

1. All the ITMs are either protocol machines or ideal functionalities.
2. Every corruption and attacker edge is external.
3. Any non-external edge is considered an i/o edge by one of its incident ITMs and a subprotocol edge by the other.
4. If every edge in the graph is considered to be directed from the ITM that considers it as a subprotcol edge to the ITM that considers it as an i/o edge, then the communication graph has no cycles except for trivial cycles made up of loop edges.

If no ITM considers an external edge to be a subprotocol edge, we say that the protocol system is *closed*. Two protocol systems are *composable* if they are composable as partial systems and the composition is again a protocol system.

Remark 4. Traditionally, the equivalent of a closed protocol system is assumed to interact with a partial system composed of an environment and an attacker. In our formulation, a closed protocol will be composed with an initial partial system (the environment) so that it forms a system. Informally, we may consider part of the environment to be the attacker.

Remark 5. It will be useful to assume that every protocol machine is given an "identity", and every ideal functionality associates an "identity" with each i/o edge. These identities must be consistent, in the sense that subprotocol and parent protocol machines have the same identities, and the identity the ideal functionality associates to an i/o edge corresponds to the identity of any protocol machine attached via that edge.

3   Indistinguishability

The notion of indistinguishability is central in cryptography, and we shall define two notions of indistinguishability for systems and partial systems.

A distinguisher is an algorithm that provides input to an unknown system and then tries to say something about the system based on its output.

Formally, a *distinguisher* $D = (D_1, D_2)$ is a pair of algorithms such that D_1 outputs a string and a state, while D_2 takes a string and a state as input and outputs 0 or 1. An execution of D with a system Σ proceeds in three steps: Firstly D_1 is run and outputs x and a state. Secondly the system gets x as input to an execution and outputs y. Finally D_2 is given y and the state as input and outputs 0 or 1.

Remark 6. Since systems are not guaranteed to terminate, the same holds for distinguisher executions. However, if the system execution terminates, the distinguisher execution will also terminate.

We say that a distinguisher interacting with a system is (R, δ)-bounded if the above execution does not exceed the resource bounds in R except with probability δ. Note that we consider the time used to be not just the time used for the system execution, but also the time used by the distinguisher algorithms.

3.1   Definition of Indistinguishability of Systems

Let Σ_1 and Σ_2 be two systems, D a distinguisher and R_1 and R_2 resource bounds. Let E_i be the event that the execution of D with Σ_i outputs 1, and let G_i be the event that the execution of D with Σ_i terminates without exceeding the resource bound R_i. Note that D interacting with Σ_i is (R_i, δ_i)-bounded if $\Pr[\neg G_i] \leq \delta_i$.

The *distinguishing advantage* of D with respect to the resource bounds R_1 and R_2 is defined to be

$$\mathrm{Adv}(D, \Sigma_1, \Sigma_2; R_1, R_2) = |\Pr[E_1 \wedge G_1] - \Pr[E_2 \wedge G_2]| \ .$$

A system Σ_1 is $(R_1, \delta_1, R_2, \delta_2, \epsilon)$-*indistinguishable* from Σ_2 if for any D the following holds:

1. If (D, Σ_1) is (R_1, δ_1)-bounded then (D, Σ_2) is (R_2, δ_2)-bounded.
2. $\text{Adv}(D, \Sigma_1, \Sigma_2; R_1, R_2) \leq \epsilon$.

Remark 7. This notion of indistinguishability need not be symmetric.

Next, we define a similar notion of unbounded indistinguishability. The *unbounded distinguishing advantage* of D is defined to be

$$\text{Adv}(D, \Sigma_1, \Sigma_2) = |\Pr[E_1] - \Pr[E_2]| \ .$$

We say that Σ_1 and Σ_2 are ϵ-*indistinguishable* if any distinguisher D has unbounded distinguishing advantage at most ϵ.

Remark 8. If two systems are ϵ-indistinguishable, it is easy to show that for any input distribution, the probability that the executions terminate may differ by at most ϵ.

These notions of indistinguishability for systems carry over in a natural way to partial systems. Let Π_1 and Π_2 be interchangeable partial systems. We say that Π_1 is $(R_1, \delta_1, R_2, \delta_2, \epsilon)$-*indistinguishable* (respectively ϵ-*indistinguishable*) from Π_2 if for any partial system Π_3 that completes Π_1, we have that $\Pi_1 \odot \Pi_3$ is $(R_1, \delta_1, R_2, \delta_2, \epsilon)$-indistinguishable (respectively ϵ-indistinguishable) from $\Pi_2 \odot \Pi_3$ as systems.

3.2 Basic Results

We have a limited form of transitivity for indistinguishability. This follows from the fact that if two systems are distinguishable then one or both must be distinguishable from any third system.

Theorem 1 (Transitivity). *Let Π_1, Π_2 and Π_3 be interchangeable partial systems, such that Π_1 is $(R_1, \delta_1, R_2, \delta_2, \epsilon)$-indistinguishable from Π_2, and Π_2 is $(R_2, \delta_2, R_3, \delta_3, \epsilon')$-indistinguishable from Π_3. Then Π_1 is $(R_1, \delta_1, R_3, \delta_3, \epsilon + \epsilon')$-indistinguishable from Π_3.*

It is clear that if we have two indistinguishable partial systems and compose them with the same partial system, the resulting (partial) systems are indistinguishable.

Theorem 2 (Composition). *Let Π_1 and Π_2 be partial systems, and suppose Π_1 is $(R_1, \delta_1, R_2, \delta_2, \epsilon)$-indistinguishable from Π_2. Let Π_3 be any partial system that completes Π_1. Then $\Pi_1 \odot \Pi_3$ is $(R_1, \delta_1, R_2, \delta_2, \epsilon)$-indistinguishable from $\Pi_2 \odot \Pi_3$.*

4 Composition Theorem

A protocol is said to be secure if it is in some sense indistinguishable from an appropriate ideal functionality. When this secure protocol is used as a subprotocol, the following theorem proves that analysis of the parent protocol can be done using the ideal functionality abstraction, possibly a major simplification.

Let Π_1 and Π_2 be protocol systems with the same external i/o edges. We say that Π_1 $(R_1, \delta_1, R_2, \delta_2, \epsilon)$-*emulates* Π_2 if there exists a partial system $\mathcal{S}$ such that Π_1 and $\Pi_2 \odot \mathcal{S}$ are interchangeable, and Π_1 is $(R_1, \delta_1, R_2, \delta_2, \epsilon)$-indistinguishable from $\Pi_2 \odot \mathcal{S}$. In such case, we call $\mathcal{S}$ a *simulator*.

If the partial system Π_2 consists of a single ideal functionality $\mathcal{F}$, we say that Π_1 $(R_1, \delta_1, R_2, \delta_2, \epsilon)$-*realises* Π_2.

Theorem 3. *Let Π_1, Π_2 and Π_4 be closed protocol systems and let Π_3 be a protocol system composable with Π_1 and Π_2. If Π_1 $(R_1, \delta_1, R_2, \delta_2, \epsilon)$-emulates Π_2 and $\Pi_2 \odot \Pi_3$ $(R_2, \delta_2, R_3, \delta_3, \epsilon')$-emulates Π_4 then $\Pi_1 \odot \Pi_3$ $(R_1, \delta_1, R_3, \delta_3, \epsilon + \epsilon')$-emulates Π_4.*

The proof essentially relies on the transitivity theorem above, and a visual version of it is given in Fig. 1. The technicalities encountered in the corresponding proof of [2] are avoided due to our use of a fixed communication graph and global resource bounds.

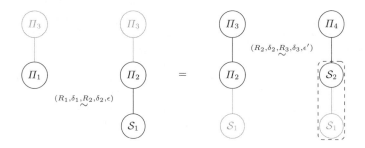

Fig. 1. Proof of Theorem 3. The bold parts of the diagram contain the indistinguishability assumptions. Theorem 2 says that adding the faded parts does not affect indistinguishability. The result follows from transitivity and taking the subsystem enclosed by the dashed lines as the required simulator.

References

1. Bellare, M., Desai, A., Jokipii, E., Rogaway, P.: A Concrete Security Treatment of Symmetric Encryption. In: FOCS 1997, pp. 394–403. IEEE Press, Los Alamitos (1997)
2. Canetti, R.: Universally Composable Security: A New Paradigm for Cryptographic Protocols, Report 2000/067, IACR ePrint Archive (2005)
3. Gjøsteen, K., Kråkmo, L.: Universally Composable Signcryption. In: López, J., Samarati, P., Ferrer, J.L. (eds.) EuroPKI 2007. LNCS, vol. 4582, pp. 346–353. Springer, Heidelberg (2007)
4. Goldreich, O.: Foundations of Cryptography. Cambridge University Press, Cambridge (2001)
5. Pfitzmann, B., Waidner, M.: A Model for Asynchronous Reactive Systems and its Application to Secure Message Transmission. In: Symposium on Security and Privacy, pp. 184–200. IEEE Press, Los Alamitos (2001)

Taxonomical Security Consideration of Authenticated Key Exchange Resilient to Intermediate Computation Leakage[*]

Kazuki Yoneyama[1] and Yunlei Zhao[2]

[1] NTT Information Sharing Platform Laboratories, Tokyo, Japan
yoneyama.kazuki@lab.ntt.co.jp
[2] Software School, Fudan University, Shanghai, China
yunleizhao@gmail.com

Abstract. SMQV authenticated key exchange scheme was stated to be secure against leakage of intermediate computations, i.e., secure in the seCK model. However, in this paper, we show errors in the security proof of SMQV. The found errors proceed from a failure in a simulation of leakage of intermediate computations. Moreover, we identify flaws in the security proofs of the underlying building tools of both SMQV and FHMQV, showing that both SMQV and FHMQV are not proven secure *even in the traditional CK model*. Then, we consider the cause of difficulty to prove security in the seCK model and classify previous Diffie-Hellman type authenticated key exchange schemes in the sense of achievable security levels. As a result, unfortunately, known schemes fall into hard to prove or insecure. Accordingly, we suggest that Diffie-Hellman type schemes provably secure in the seCK model are hard (or highly subtle) to achieve. Therefore, this paper clarifies the technical limitations (or high subtleties) of Diffie-Hellman type schemes for achieving provable security in the seCK model against leakage of intermediate computations.

Keywords: authenticated key exchange, intermediate computation leakage, seCK model, Diffie-Hellman.

1 Introduction

According to increase of threats of physical attacks to security devices or softwares (e.g., malwares, side channel attacks [1], fault attacks [2] and cold boot attacks [3]), resilience to the leakage of secret data upon cryptosystems receives many attentions. In the context of authenticated key exchange (AKE), how to capture leakage resilience has been studied in many security models like the Canetti-Krawczyk (CK) model [4], the extended CK (eCK) model [5] and the strengthened eCK (seCK) model [6] beyond the initial Bellare-Rogaway model [7]. These models capture leakage of various kinds of secret information like the static secret key and session-specific state information.

---

[*] The second author is partly supported by a grant from the Major State Basic Research Development (973) Program of China (No. 2007CB807901) and a grant from the National Natural Science Foundation of China NSFC (No. 61070248).

X. Boyen and X. Chen (Eds.): ProvSec 2011, LNCS 6980, pp. 348–365, 2011.

Table 1. Specifications of previous AKE schemes

	Public hash value	Secret exponent	Secret signature
MQV [18]	$D = 2^l + (X \mod 2^l)$ $E = 2^l + (Y \mod 2^l)$	$x + Da$	$(YK_B^E)^{x+Da}$
HMQV [17]	$D = H'(X,B), E = H'(Y,A)$	$x + Da$	$(YK_B^E)^{x+Da}$
CMQV [10]	$D = H'(X,A,B)$ $E = H'(Y,A,B)$	$H(x,a),$ $H(x,a) + Da$	$(YK_B^E)^{H(x,a)+Da}$
UP [11]	$D = H(X), E = H(Y)$	$x + a, x + Da$	$(YK_B^E)^{x+a}, (YK_B)^{x+Da}$
YZ [19]	$C = H'(A,K_A,Y)$ $D = H'(B,K_B,X)$ $E = H'(X,Y)$	$Ca + Ex$	$K_B^{Dx}Y^{Ca+Ex}$
FHMQV [20]	$D = H'(X,Y,A,B)$ $E = H'(Y,X,A,B)$	$x + Da$	$(YK_B^E)^{x+Da}$
SMQV [6]	$D = H'(X,Y,A,B)$ $E = H'(Y,X,A,B)$	$Dx + a$	$(Y^E K_B)^{Dx+a}$
FS [13]	c (constant number)	$x + a, x + ca$	$(YK_B)^{x+a}, (YK_B^c)^{x+ca}$
KFU [12]	none	$x + a_1, x + a_2$	$(YK_{B_1})^{x+a_1}, (YK_{B_2})^{x+a_2}$
KEA+ [21]	none	none	Y^a, K_B^x
NAXOS [5]	none	$H(x,a)$	$Y^a, K_B^{H(x,a)}, Y^{H(x,a)}$
Oka [14]	$D = H_1(A,B,Y_1,Y_2,Y_3)$ $E = H_2(B,A,X_1,X_2,X_3)$	$a_1 + Da_3, a_2 + Da_4,$ Ex	$Y_1^{a_1+Da_3}Y_2^{a_2+Da_4}.$ $Y_3^{x_3}K_{B_1}^x K_{B_2}^{Ex}$
MO [15]	$C = H_1(A,B,X_1,X_2,X_3,Y_1,Y_2,Y_3)$ $D = H_2(A,B,X_1,X_2,X_3,Y_1,Y_2,Y_3)$ $E = H_3(A,B,X_1,X_2,X_3,Y_1,Y_2,Y_3)$	$a_1 + Ca_3, a_2 + Ca_4,$ $Dx, Ea, a_5 + Ea_7,$ $a_6 + Ea_8$	$Y_1^{a_1+Ca_3}Y_2^{a_2+Ca_4}.$ $Y_3^{x_3}K_{B_1}^x K_{B_2}^{Dx}K_{B_3}^a K_{B_4}^{Ea}.$ $K_{B_5}^{a_5+Ea_7}K_{B_6}^{a_6+Ea_8}$

A is an initiator and B is a responder. Secret exponents and secret signatures in the table are for A. KFU is a scheme called "Protocol 1" in [12] and FS is a scheme called "Example 2" in [13]. All schemes except KFU, Oka and MO include a static secret key a, a static public key $K_A = g^a$, an ephemeral secret key x and an ephemeral public key $X = g^x$ for A, and a static secret key b, a static public key $K_B = g^b$, an ephemeral secret key y and an ephemeral public key $Y = g^y$ for B. For the details of KFU, Oka and MO, please see [12,14,15]. H and H' are hash functions modeled as a random oracle. H_1, H_2 and H_3 are (target) collision resistance hash functions.

For example, the eCK model is known to be able to provide strong resilience to leakage of both ephemeral and static secret. In two-party AKE schemes, a party keeps a static secret key and publishes a static public key in advance, and for a session the party chooses an ephemeral secret key (i.e., session-specific randomness), exchanges an ephemeral public key and generates a common session key finally. In the eCK model, an adversary can reveal any non-trivial combination of ephemeral and static secret keys. Though it is known that the CK model and eCK model are incomparable [8,9] in adversarial capability about leakage of secret information, the eCK model simply defines leakage resilience and so handy to prove security. Thus, various AKE schemes [5,10,11,12,13,14,15,16] are constructed to aim to be secure in the eCK model. All known AKE schemes secure in the eCK model are Diffie-Hellman (DH) type; that is, a party sends an ephemeral public key, computes a secret exponent and a secret signature, and finally generates a session key. For example, in HMQV [17], static secret keys are a and b, static public keys are $K_A = g^a$ and $K_B = g^b$, ephemeral secret keys are x and y, ephemeral public keys are $X = g^x$ and $Y = g^y$, secret exponents are $x + Da$ and $y + Eb$ where D and E are publicly computable hash values, secret signatures are

$(YK_B^E)^{x+Da}$ and $(XK_A^D)^{y+Eb}$, and session keys are computed by applying secret signatures to a random oracle. Table 1 shows specifications of known DH type AKE schemes.

Recently, Sarr et al. [6] claimed that the eCK model is still not enough because, besides ephemeral secret keys, intermediate computations (i.e., secret exponents and secret signatures) may be also leaked as a session-specific information practically. Hence, they proposed the seCK model in order to capture the leakage of the result of intermediate computations. Moreover, they introduced a (DH type) AKE scheme named SMQV and proved that SMQV is secure in the seCK model.

Our Contribution. Firstly, though Sarr. et al. gave a security proof of SMQV in the random oracle model, unfortunately, we point out an error in their security proof. The error occurs in the case that an adversary poses the query to reveal the result of intermediate computations (i.e., secret exponents or secret signatures) to a session related to the test session. In this case, the simulator cannot return the correct answer without knowledge of an unknown secret. The found error means that SMQV cannot be proved to be secure if the adversary has the power to reveal secret exponents or secret signatures; that is, SMQV cannot get over reveal of any result of intermediate computations. Moreover, we identify flaws in the security proofs of the underlying building tools of SMQV and FHMQV [20], showing that both SMQV and FHMQV [20] all are not proven secure *even in the CK model*.

Next, we discuss the cause in the proof error as follows. SMQV is designed to have a structure that to obtain any information of a secret signature in a session from secret exponents in different sessions is hard. Such a structure, originated from [19], prevents a reply attack that an adversary reveals a secret exponent in a session and sends the ephemeral public key in the session as that in a different session (the target session) executed by same parties. If secret exponents in different sessions are identical, the adversary can obtain the secret signature in the target session. Since almost all DH type AKE schemes [18,17,10,11,12,13,14] have the structure that secret exponents in some kind of distinct sessions are identical, the reply attack is effective. SMQV adapts a structure originated from [19], where the public hash values D and E fully hash (i.e., uniquely determined for each session) all of session information such as identities of parties and ephemeral public keys. Thus, such a strategy (originated from [19]) is a nice idea to be secure AKE schemes against leakage of the result of intermediate computations. However, as already observed in [19,22], not all instantiations (particularly the YZ-MQV variants proposed in [19]) from such a strategy are provable secure *in the traditional CK model*. In particular, we identify the proof errors with SMQV and HMQV. Uniqueness of secret exponents interfere the simulation to the query to reveal the result of intermediate computations. Specifically, though there exists a case that the simulator must fix a secret exponent in the simulation, the fixed secret exponent corresponds to the session chosen by the adversary with only negligible probability because the adversary can adaptively change the session to be sent and a secret exponent in a session must be different from that in different sessions. It is in a dilemma.

We conclude that it is hard or highly subtle to avoid both the reply attack and the proof error as stated above in DH type AKE schemes if an adversary is allowed to reveal the result of intermediate computations (even if only either of secret exponent and secret signature may be leaked). Indeed, the construction based on the strategies like

YZ-MQV and SMQV/FHMQV is no hope to achieve provable security in the seCK model, actually even in the traditional CK model, by the above discussions. However, constructions based on another strategy might be provable, perhaps. Thus, we do a taxonomical consideration of security of previous DH type AKE schemes in the seCK model. Specifically, we can classify schemes in achievable security levels as follows; the first level is 'secure', the second level is 'hard to prove', the third level is reveal of session keys (i.e., 'insecure') and the fourth level is reveal of static secret keys (i.e., 'total break'). Unfortunately, we find that there is no scheme that has been provably secure in the seCK model. The protocols of rYZ, srYZ, YZ-MQV-1,YZ-MQV-2, FH-MQV, SMQV and NAXOS enter into the second level. The protocols of MQV, HMQV, YZ, sYZ, KFU, and KEA+ enter into the third level. And, unfortunately, CMQV, UP, FS, Oka and MO enter into the fourth level. Therefore, our results show a technical limitation or the high subtleties of DH type AKE schemes for achieving provable security in the seCK model.

Related Works. The work [19] proposed a general protocol structure, called general YZ (gYZ), for DH type AKE between two players A (of public-key $K_A = g^a$ and ephemeral public-key $X = g^x$) and B (of public-key $K_B = g^b$ and ephemeral public-key $Y = g^y$). The shared DH-secret (from which the session-key is derived) of gYZ is defined as follows: $SK_A = K_B^{Fa+Dx} Y^{Ca+Ex} = K_A^{Fb+Cy} X^{Db+Ey} = SK_B$, where SK_A (computed by A) and SK_B (computed by B) satisfy, roughly speaking, the following general conditions:

- C, D, E, F are hash values that are publicly computable from the session-tag (A, K_A, B, K_B, X, Y), and the session-tag is committed to (C, D, E, F) in the sense that inputs of C, D, E, F include all components in the session-tag.
- The values K_A^{Fb+Cy} and X^{Db+Ey} (resp., K_B^{Fa+Dx} and Y^{Ca+Ex}) are non-malleably independent, no matter how a malicious B (resp., A) does.

Under the general structure of gYZ, the work [19] proposed the following instantiations of gYZ, which are very carefully designed to be provably secure in the CK model.

YZ. $C = H(A, K_A, Y), D = H(B, K_B, X), E = H(X, Y), F = 0$, where $H : \{0,1\}^* \to \mathbb{Z}_p^*$ is a hash function.
Single-hash YZ (sYZ). $C = D = 1, E = H(A, K_A, B, K_B, X, Y), F = 0$.
Robust YZ (rYZ). $C = H(A, K_A, B, K_B, Y), D = H(A, K_A, B, K_B, X), E = H(A, K_A, B, K_B, X, Y), F = H(A, K_A, B, K_B)$.
Single-hash rYZ (srYZ). $C = D = F = 1, E = H(A, K_A, B, K_B, X, Y)$.

Besides provable security in the CK-model, the protocols of YZ, sYZ and rYZ also enjoy the following advantageous features beyond (H)MQV (more advantages of the YZ protocol family are discussed in [19,22,23]):

On-line Optimal Efficiency. Specifically, for all the protocols of YZ,sYZ and rYZ, each player can perform only one on-line exponentiation that is optimal for DH type AKE. With the computation of B as an example, the value K_A^{Fb+Cy} can be off-line pre-computed by B, as the inputs of F and C do not include X.

Remark 1. We remark that, if the family of YZ protocols work in the off-line pre-computation model, only the values K_A^{Fb+Cy} (rather than the exponent $Fb + Cy$ itself) and the exponent $Db + Ey$ can be leaked to the adversary. That is, for the above YZ protocols working in Implementation Mode II of the seCK model, the values $Y, K_A^{Fb+Cy}, Db + Ex$ are computed by the tamper-proof device, where Y and K_A^{Fb+Cy} are off-line pre-computed by the tamper-proof device during its idle time. The values $(Y, K_A^{Fb+Cy}, Db + Ex)$ are given to the host machine, who then computes the session key. Note that the on-line efficiency of the host machine in YZ-KE is optimal, i.e., only one exponentiation, while that of (H)MQV is about 1.5 exponentiations. It is shown in [23] that the above YZ-KE protocol family supports Mode II of the seCK model.

Deniability of YZ and sYZ. YZ and sYZ enjoy the deniability property, which is very desirable for AKE protocols. Specifically, the session key can be merely computed from the ephemeral secret keys x and y.

Post-ID Computability of YZ. The value X^{Db+Ey} can be computed by B without knowing its peer's identity information.

The work [19] also identified some attacks against (H)MQV, and then proposed (in Page 11-14, and Claims 30-31 in [19]) some fixing approaches within the general structure of gYZ [1]

YZ-MQV-1. $C = H(A, K_A, B, K_B, X, Y), D = H(C), E = 1, F = CD$, which corresponds to $SK_B = (XK_A^C)^{y+Db}$.

YZ-MQV-2. $D = H(A, K_A, B, K_B, X, Y), C = H(D), E = CD, F = 1$, which corresponds to $SK_B = (X^D K_A)^{Cy+b}$.

YZ-MQV-3. $C = H(A, K_A, X, pub_1), D = H(B, K_B, Y, pub_2), E = 1, F = CD$, which corresponds to $SK_B = (XK_A^C)^{Db+y}$, where pub_1 and pub_2 are some (possibly empty) subset of the set of components included in the session tag and other public values related to the session run.

YZ-MQV-4. $C = H(B, K_B, Y, pub_2), D = H(A, K_A, X, pub_1), E = CD, F = 1$, which corresponds to $SK_B = (X^C K_A)^{b+Dy}$.

Remark 2. It is easy to check that all the protocols of YZ, sYZ, rYZ, srYZ, YZ-MQV-1, YZ-MQV-2, YZ-MQV-3, YZ-MQV-4, FHMQV and SMQV can be instantiated from gYZ. In particular, FHMQV (resp., SMQV) can be instantiated from YZ-MQV-3 (resp., YZ-MQV-4), by setting $pub_1 = (B, K_B, Y)$ and $pub_2 = (A, K_A, X)$. It was observed in [19,23] that the security analysis of (H)MQV and YZ-KE intrinsically cannot be extended to YZ-MQV protocol variants, which particularly implies that the security proof of FHMQV and SMQV are also flawed. We will make clear clarifications later.

---

[1] In [19], only the protocol variant of YZ-MQV-4 is named YZ-MQV there, while other protocols variants are only listed without names. Here, for presentation simplicity, we rename all the proposed fixing approaches listed and implied in [19].

2   Preliminaries

2.1   Implementation Modes for AKE

In this section, we discuss two ways to implement executions of AKE schemes in order to consider possible leakages according to the seCK model. In this paper, we focus on DH type AKE schemes; thus, we discuss specifically for DH type.

We suppose a standard setting that a party executes an AKE protocol through his (not always secure) host machine with some build-in tamper-proof module (e.g., smart cards and some tamper-proof area of storage). In almost implementations of AKE schemes, the static secret key SSK is required to be stored in the tamper-proof module, and so we can consider that it is not leaked except corruption of the party. Moreover, top-level computations (i.e., computations using value of the static secret key directly) should be executed in the tamper-proof module because direct value of the static secret key should not be given to the host machine of the party. On the other hand, there are two ways to deal with the ephemeral secret key ESK and to derive the session key SK.

One is called implementation *mode I*. In this mode, the host machine chooses the ephemeral secret key ESK (in idle time), computes the ephemeral public key EPK, receives the ephemeral public key of the peer, and inputs ephemeral public keys of both parties and the static public key SPK of the peer to the tamper-proof module. Upon receiving these, the tamper-proof module executes all other intermediate computations (i.e., secret exponents Exp and secret signatures Sig) to derive the session key SK. Thus, intermediate computations are also hidden from adversaries in the mode I though the ephemeral secret key may be leaked by some factor (e.g., a malware in the host machine reveals randomness or a pseudo random generator implemented in the system is poor).

The other is called implementation *mode II*. In this mode, the ephemeral secret key ESK is chosen by the tamper-proof module and top-level computations which need value of the static secret key SSK and the ephemeral secret key ESK directly are also executed in the tamper-proof module. For (H)MQV, the tamper-proof module for user $\hat{A}$ computes $(X = g^x, x + DA)$. For YZ-KE, the tamper-proof module computes $(X = g^x, K_B^{Dx}, Ca + Ex)$. Note that the value of K_B^{Dx} can be off-line pre-computed by the tamper-proof module of YZ-KE during its idle time, and thus the host machine only needs to perform one exponentiation in computing the session-key. On the other hand, secret signature Sig is computed by the host machine. Since the (non-idle time) computational cost of intermediate computations is higher than that of the top-level computations, the mode II can reduce the cost for the tamper-proof module than the mode I.

Fig. 1 depicts the mode I and the mode II where solid lines mean interactions with an external peer and dashed lines mean local computations. From the perspective of possible leakage, we need different security models corresponding to the mode I and the mode II. In the mode I, an adversary may obtain the ephemeral secret key but cannot obtain the result of intermediate computations. Thus, the eCK model [5] and the seCK model are suitable for the mode I. On the other hand, in the mode II, an adversary may obtain the result of intermediate computations (i.e., secret exponents and secret signatures) but cannot obtain the ephemeral secret key. Thus, the eCK model cannot capture

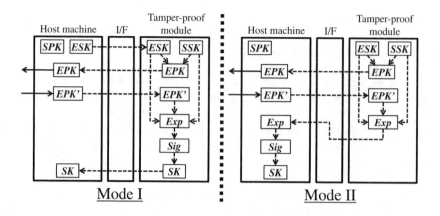

Fig. 1. Two implementation modes for DH type AKE

the mode II. The seCK model allows an adversary to reveal the result of intermediate computations and so can capture the mode II. Therefore, the seCK model is stronger than the eCK model.

2.2 seCK Security Model for Diffie-Hellman Type AKE

In this section, we recall the seCK security model (specifying DH type).

Syntax. An AKE scheme consists of the following algorithms. We denote a party by P modeled as a probabilistic polynomial-time Turing machine.

Setup. The setup algorithm **Setup** takes a security parameter κ as input, and outputs a public parameter *params*, i.e., **Setup**$(1^\kappa) \rightarrow params$.

Key Generation. The key generation algorithm **KeyGen** takes *params* and P, and outputs a static secret key SSK_P and a static public key SPK_P corresponding to P, i.e., **KeyGen**$(params, P) \rightarrow (SSK_P, SPK_P)$.

Key Exchange. The party A and the party B share a session key by performing the following n-pass protocol.

A starts the protocol by computing the 1st message m_1 by the algorithm **Message**, that takes *params*, A, B, SSK_A, SPK_A and SPK_B, and outputs 1st message m_1. A sends m_1 to the other party B.

For $i = 2, ..., n$, upon receiving the $(i - 1)$th message m_{i-1} from the other party $\bar{P}$ ($\bar{P} = B$ or A), the party P ($P = A$ or B) computes the ith message by algorithm **Message**, that takes *params*, $P, \bar{P}, SSK_P, SPK_P, SPK_{\bar{P}}$ and the sent and received messages $m_1, ..., m_{i-1}$, and outputs the ith message m_i, i.e., **Message**$(params, P, \bar{P}, SSK_P, SPK_P, SPK_{\bar{P}}, m_1, ..., m_{i-1}) \rightarrow m_i$. The party P sends m_i to the other party $\bar{P}$ ($\bar{P} = B$ or A).

Upon receiving or after sending the final nth message m_n, P computes a session key by algorithm **SessionKey**, that takes *params*, $P, \bar{P}, SSK_P, SPK_P, SPK_{\bar{P}}$ and the sent and received messages $m_1, ..., m_n$, and outputs a session key SK, i.e., **SessionKey** $(params, P, \bar{P}, SSK_P, SPK_P, SPK_{\bar{P}}, m_1, ..., m_n) \rightarrow SK$.

Session. An invocation of a protocol is called a *session*. A session is activated with an incoming message of the forms $(\mathcal{I}, A, B)$ or $(\mathcal{R}, B, A, m_1)$, where $\mathcal{I}$ and $\mathcal{R}$ are role identifiers. If A was activated with $(\mathcal{I}, A, B)$, then A is called the session *initiator*. If B was activated with $(\mathcal{R}, B, A, m_1)$, then B is called the session *responder*. After activated with an incoming message of the forms $(\mathcal{I}, A, B, m_1, \dots, m_{k-1})$ from the responder B, the initiator A outputs m_k, then may be activated next by an incoming message of the forms $(\mathcal{I}, A, B, m_1, \dots, m_{k+1})$ from the responder B. After activated by an incoming message of the forms $(\mathcal{R}, B, A, m_1, \dots, m_k)$ from the initiator A, the responder B outputs m_{k+1}, then may be activated next by an incoming message of the forms $(\mathcal{R}, B, A, m_1, \dots, m_{k+2})$ from the initiator A. Upon receiving or after sending the final nth message m_n, both parties A and B compute a session key SK.

If A is the initiator of a session, the session is identified by sid $= (\mathcal{I}, A, B, m_1)$, $(\mathcal{I}, A, B, m_1, m_2, m_3), \dots, (\mathcal{I}, A, B, m_1, \dots, m_n)$. If B is the responder of a session, the session is identified by sid $= (\mathcal{R}, B, A, m_1, m_2), (\mathcal{R}, B, A, m_1, m_2, m_3, m_4), \dots, (\mathcal{R}, B, A, m_1, \dots, m_n)$. We say that a session is *completed* if a session key is computed in the session. The *matching session* of a completed session $(\mathcal{I}, A, B, m_1, \dots, m_n)$ is a completed session with identifier $(\mathcal{R}, B, A, m_1, \dots, m_n)$ and vice versa.

Adversary. The adversary $\mathcal{A}$ that is modeled as a probabilistic polynomial-time Turing machine who controls all communications between parties including the session activation by performing the following queries.

- Send(message): The message has one of the following forms: $(\mathcal{I}, A, B, m_1, \dots, m_k)$, or $(\mathcal{R}, B, A, m_1, \dots, m_{k+1})$. The adversary obtains the response from the party.

Revealing secret information of parties is captured via the following queries.

- SesRev(sid): The adversary obtains the session key for the session sid if the session is completed.
- EphRev(sid): The adversary obtains the ephemeral secret key associated with the session sid. This query is only allowed when sid follows the mode I.
- IntRev(sid): The adversary obtains the intermediate computation result associated with the session sid. This query is only allowed when sid follows the mode II. In DH type AKE schemes, IntRev can be subdivided to two queries as follows:
  - ExpRev(sid): The adversary obtains the secret exponent associated with the session sid.
  - SigRev(sid): The adversary obtains the secret signature associated with the session sid.
- StaRev(P): The adversary learns the static secret key corresponding to P. This query represents corruption of parties.
- Establish(P, SPK_P): This query allows the adversary to register a static public key SPK_P on behalf of the party P; the adversary totally controls that party. If a party is established by Establish(P, SPK_P) query issued by the adversary, then we call the party P *dishonest*. If not, we call the party *honest*.

Freshness. For the security definition, we need the notion of freshness.

Definition 1 (Freshness). *Let* $\mathsf{sid}^* = (\mathcal{I}, A, B, m_1, \ldots, m_n)$ *or* $(\mathcal{R}, B, A, m_1, \ldots, m_n)$ *be a completed session between an honest party A and B. If the matching session exists, then let* $\overline{\mathsf{sid}}^*$ *be the matching session of* sid^*. *We say* sid^* *to be __fresh__ if none of the following conditions hold:*

1. *The adversary issues a* $\mathsf{SesRev}(\mathsf{sid}^*)$ *or* $\mathsf{SesRev}(\overline{\mathsf{sid}}^*)$ *query if* $\overline{\mathsf{sid}}^*$ *exists,*
2. sid^* *follows the mode I,* $\overline{\mathsf{sid}}^*$ *exists and follows the mode I, and the adversary makes either of the following queries*
   - *both* $\mathsf{StaRev}(A)$ *and* $\underline{\mathsf{EphRev}}(\mathsf{sid}^*)$, *or both* $\mathsf{StaRev}(B)$ *and* $\mathsf{EphRev}(\overline{\mathsf{sid}}^*)$,
3. sid^* *follows the mode I,* $\overline{\mathsf{sid}}^*$ *exists and follows the mode II, and the adversary makes either of the following queries*
   - *both* $\mathsf{StaRev}(A)$ *and* $\underline{\mathsf{EphRev}}(\mathsf{sid}^*)$, *or* $\mathsf{IntRev}(\overline{\mathsf{sid}}^*)$,
4. sid^* *follows the mode I,* $\overline{\mathsf{sid}}^*$ *does not exist and the adversary makes either of the following queries*
   - *both* $\mathsf{StaRev}(A)$ *and* $\mathsf{EphRev}(\mathsf{sid}^*)$, *or* $\mathsf{StaRev}(B)$,
5. sid^* *follows the mode II,* $\overline{\mathsf{sid}}^*$ *exists and follows the mode I, and the adversary makes either of the following queries*
   - $\mathsf{IntRev}(\mathsf{sid}^*)$, *or both* $\underline{\mathsf{StaRev}}(B)$ *and* $\mathsf{EphRev}(\overline{\mathsf{sid}}^*)$,
6. sid^* *follows the mode II,* $\overline{\mathsf{sid}}^*$ *exists and follows the mode II, and the adversary makes either of the following queries*
   - $\mathsf{IntRev}(\mathsf{sid}^*)$ *or* $\mathsf{IntRev}(\overline{\mathsf{sid}}^*)$,
7. sid^* *follows the mode II,* $\overline{\mathsf{sid}}^*$ *does not exist and the adversary makes either of the following queries*
   - $\mathsf{IntRev}(\mathsf{sid}^*)$ *or* $\mathsf{StaRev}(B)$.

Security Experiment. For the security definition, we consider the following security experiment. Initially, the adversary $\mathcal{A}$ is given a set of honest parties, and makes any sequence of the queries described above. During the experiment, $\mathcal{A}$ makes the following query.

- $\mathsf{Test}(\mathsf{sid}^*)$: Here, sid^* must be a fresh session. Select random bit $b \in \{0, 1\}$, and return the session key held by sid^* if $b = 0$, and return a random key if $b = 1$.

The experiment continues until $\mathcal{A}$ makes a guess b'. The adversary *wins* the game if the test session sid^* is still fresh and if $\mathcal{A}$'s guess is correct, i.e., $b' = b$. The advantage of $\mathcal{A}$ in the experiment with the AKE scheme Π is defined as

$$\mathsf{Adv}_{\Pi}^{\mathrm{AKE}}(\mathcal{A}) = \Pr[\mathcal{A} \; wins] - \frac{1}{2}.$$

We define the security as follows.

Definition 2 (seCK Security [6]). *We say that an AKE scheme Π is secure in the seCK model, if the following conditions hold:*

1. *If two honest parties completing matching sessions, then, except with negligible probability, they both compute the same session key.*
2. *For any probabilistic polynomial-time adversary $\mathcal{A}$, $\mathsf{Adv}_{\Pi}^{\mathrm{AKE}}(\mathcal{A})$ is negligible.*

3 SMQV Revisited

In this section, we show an error in the security proof of SMQV [6]. Then, we discuss possibility to fix the proof error.

3.1 SMQV Scheme

First, we recall the protocol of SMQV. For simplicity, we omit "(mod p)" in this paper when computing the modular exponentiation. "$s \in_R S$" means randomly choosing an element s of a set S.

Setup: For input a security parameter κ, choose p, G and g, where G is a cyclic group of order κ-bit prime p with a generator g. Let $H_1 : \{0, 1\}^* \to \mathbb{Z}_p$ and $H_2 : \{0, 1\}^* \to \{0, 1\}^\kappa$ be hash functions. Then, output a public parameter $params :=$ (p, g, G, H_1, H_2).

KeyGen: For input P, choose at random the static secret key $r \in_R \mathbb{Z}_p$, compute $K_P = g^r$, and output the static secret key $SSK_P := r$ and the static public key $SPK_P := K_P$ for P.

Exchange: We suppose that the party A is the session initiator and the party B is the session responder. A has the static secret key $SSK_A = a$ and publishes the static public key $SPK_A = K_A = g^a$, and B has the static secret key $SSK_B = b$ and publishes the static public key $SPK_B = K_B = g^b$. Then, A sends to B the ephemeral public key EPK_A and B sends to A the ephemeral public key EPK_B. Finally, both parties A and B compute the shared key SK.

1. First, A chooses at random the ephemeral secret key $ESK_A := x \in_R \mathbb{Z}_p$ and computes the ephemeral public key $EPK_A := X = g^x$. Next, A sends (EPK_A, A, B) to B.
2. Upon receiving EPK_A, B chooses at random the ephemeral secret key $ESK_B := y \in_R \mathbb{Z}_p$ and computes the ephemeral public key $EPK_B := Y = g^y$. Next, B sends (EPK_B, B, A) to A.
   B computes the shared secret as follows: First, B computes $D = H_1(X, Y, A, B)$ and $E = H_1(Y, X, A, B)$. Next, B sets $\sigma = (X^D K_A)^{Ey+b}$ and the session key $SK = H_2(A, B, EPK_A, EPK_B, \sigma)$, and completes the session.
3. Upon receiving EPK_B, A computes the shared secret as follows: First, A computes $D = H_1(X, Y, A, B)$ and $E = H_1(Y, X, A, B)$. Next, A sets $\sigma = (Y^E K_B)^{Dx+a}$ and the session key $SK = H_2(A, B, EPK_A, EPK_B, \sigma)$, and completes the session.

In the mode II, the generation of ESK and the computations of the exponents g^x (resp. g^y) and $Dx + a$ (resp. $Ey + b$), i.e., top-level computations, are executed in the tamper-proof module, but all remaining computations are executed in the host machine. Note that g^x (resp. g^y) can be computed in idle time and so the computation in non-idle time is just $Dx + a$ (resp. $Ey + b$). Thus, an adversary can obtain g^x (resp. g^y) publicly, $Dx + a$ (resp. $Ey + b$) as the secret exponent by an ExpRev query and $(Y^E K_B)^{Dx+a}$ (resp. $(X^D K_A)^{Ey+b}$) as the secret signature by a SigRev query to any session other than the test session. In the non-idle time computation, SMQV does not need any modular exponentiation.

Design Principle of SMQV. As the YZ-MQV protocol variants [19], SMQV is intentionally designed as secret exponents in distinct sessions are different in order to prevent the following reply attack (we call this attack Atk1) indicated in [24,6].

1. activate a session by parties A and B, pose ExpRev to the session and obtain the secret exponent $Dx + a$.
2. activate another session by parties A and B again, send the ephemeral public key X of A in the first session to B as the ephemeral public key of A in the second session.

Then, the secret exponent $Dx+a$ in the first session is different from $D'x+a$ in the second session even if x is reused because D differ from D' when B's ephemeral public keys Y and Y' in two sessions are different. Since B chooses the ephemeral secret keys y and y' randomly, Y coincides with Y' with negligible probability. In AKE schemes such as MQV, HMQV and CMQV exponents are identical as Table 1. The adversary can know the session key in the second session with the result of intermediate computations in the first session because the adversary can reuse the leaked exponent in the first session into the exponent in the second session. Obviously, these AKE schemes cannot be proved in the seCK model.

Public hash values D and E in SMQV are designed to include both parties' ephemeral public keys X and Y and both parties' IDs as appeared in Table 1. Thus, if which component is different, the hash value becomes different; therefore, SMQV is resilient to Atk1.

3.2   Error in Security Proof

Strategy of Original Proof. Sarr et al. gave a proof that SMQV is secure in the seCK model under the gap Diffie-Hellman (GDH) assumption in the random oracle model directly.[2] We focus on the case of that a fresh session by parties A and B follows the mode II and the test session of A has no matching session of B (this event corresponds to E.2.2 in their proof.). We briefly show a sketch of the proof in [6].

The simulator S is given an instance of the computational Diffie-Hellman (CDH) problem $U = g^u$ and $V = g^v$, and embeds U into the static public key K_B and V into the ephemeral public key of the test session. S must simulates the hash query, the Send query, the SesRev query, EphRev query, IntRev query and StaRev query from an adversary $\mathcal{A}$. The most subtle point in this proof is to simulate the Send query to initiate B as the initiator (the responder is P) in a session other than the test session. In order to fix the simulated world into the real experiment without knowing the static secret key of B, S sets the ephemeral public key $X = (g^r U^{-1})^{D^{-1}}$, where $r, D \in \mathbb{Z}_p$ are chosen randomly and D is registered in the hash list as $H_1(X, *, B, P)$. If the hash query (X, Z, B, P) is posed later, S returns D. Also, if the IntRev query to this session is posed, S returns r. Finally, S can obtain $g^{(Dv+a)(Ey+u)}$ from the hash list and extract g^{uv} with the forking lemma [25].

Problem in Direct Proof. The problem exists in the case of that a fresh session by parties A and B follows the mode II and the test session of A has no matching session of B (this event corresponds to E.2.2 in their proof.). Then, the simulator S has to embed one of the CDH instance (i.e., U or V) into the static public key K_B in order to extract

---

[2] The proof is in the full version of [6] (report 2010/237 in the Cryptology ePrint Archive).

the answer of the CDH problem from σ. We propose an attack Atk2. An adversary $\mathcal{A}$ poses queries in the following order and makes $\mathcal{S}$ not be able to simulate correctly.

1. pose Send(I, B, P_i) and obtain X_i for $1 \leq i \leq N$, where P_i is a party other than A and B, and N is an arbitrary polynomial number in the security parameter.
2. pose an arbitrary number of queries (X_i, Z_i, B, P_i) to the random oracle H_1 and obtain outputs $\{h_i\}$, where $Z_i \in G$ is distinct for each query and denote $\{Z_i\}$ as the set of queried Z_i.
3. randomly choose $Z_i' \in \{Z_i\}$ and pose Send(I, B, P_i, X_i, Z_i').
4. pose IntRev(I, B, P_i, X_i, Z_i') for $1 \leq i \leq N$ and obtain results of intermediate computations.

As in their proof, a possible strategy of $\mathcal{S}$ is to return $X_i = (g^r K_B^{-1})^{1/D_i}$ where $r, D_i \in \mathbb{Z}_p$ are randomly chosen values and to embed D_i into $H_1(X_i, Z_i', B, P_i)$. r is implicitly defined as the secret exponent in this session (i.e., $r = Dx + b$). If this simulation was correctly done, $\mathcal{S}$ could successfully simulate by returning $(X_i, r, (Z_i'^{E_i} K_{P_i})^r)$ to IntRev(I, B, P_i, X_i, Z_i'). However, since $\mathcal{S}$ must embed D_i into $H_1(X_i, Z_i', B, P_i)$ before Z_i' is decided by Send(I, B, P_i, X_i, Z_i'), $\mathcal{S}$ must guess Z_i' queried by Send from $\{Z_i\}$ for all i because each D_i can be embedded only one of outputs of H_1. Even if $\mathcal{S}$ guesses the random oracle query corresponding to Z_i' and embeds D_i into there, the success probability becomes negligible because the potential adversarial strategies of $\mathcal{A}$ are exponentially many, which thus cannot be handled by the polynomial time simulator. For example, $\mathcal{A}$ poses two queries (X_1, Z_{11}, B, P_1) and (X_1, Z_{12}, B, P_1) to the random oracle and poses either of outputs $(h_{11}$ and $h_{12})$ of the random oracle as the Send query. In this case, $\mathcal{S}$ correctly guesses whether either of Z_{11} and Z_{12} will be sent with probability $1/2$. If $\mathcal{A}$ repeats this procedure for parties P_1 to P_N, then the number of queries to the random oracle is $2N$. Since N is a polynomial number, $\mathcal{A}$ can pose $2N$ queries in the polynomial time. On the other hand, $\mathcal{S}$ correctly guesses sent values for all parties with probability $1/2^N$; that is, only negligible probability. Thus, $\mathcal{S}$ cannot simulate all IntRev(I, B, P_i, X_i, Z_i') queries without knowing the discrete logarithm b of K_B and so the proof fails. Note that if IntRev query is limited to either of ExpRev and SigRev, $\mathcal{S}$ cannot simulate correctly. In the case that SigRev is prohibited, $\mathcal{S}$ cannot return the correct secret exponent to ExpRev(I, B, P_i, X_i, Z_i') as long as $\mathcal{S}$ succeeds to guess, because the secret exponent must be $r + (D' - D)x = D'x + b$ for $D' = H_1(X_i, Z_i', B, P_i)$ but $\mathcal{S}$ does not know x. In the case that ExpRev is prohibited, also, $\mathcal{S}$ cannot return the correct secret signature to SigRev(I, B, P_i, X_i, Z_i') as long as $\mathcal{S}$ succeeds to guess, because the secret signature must be $(Z_i'^E K_{P_i})^{r+(D'-D)x} = (Z_i'^E K_{P_i})^{D'x+b}$ for $D' = H_1(X_i, Z_i', B, P_i)$ but $\mathcal{S}$ does not know x. Therefore, if a part of intermediate computations of SMQV in the mode II is executed in the tamper-proof module, it is not a help to prove security in the seCK model. We remark that Atk2 is not an explicit attack to SMQV, which is only a counterexample against the proof strategy in [6]. Thus, we cannot say SMQV is "insecure" now.

Problem in Security of Underlying Signature. We can show the other view of the flaw in the security proof of SMQV.

The security proof of SMQV, conducted in [6], critically depends on the security of interactive signature schemes (FXCR-1 and FDCR-1). However, the proof details of FXCR-1 and FDCR-1 are not given in [6]. It is only briefly mentioned in [6] that the security of FXCR-1 and FDCR-1 can be obtained similarly as that of another interactive signature schemes (FXCR and FDCR) presented in [20] for FHMQV.

The security proof of FXCR in [20] only considers the security of FXCR with the signer B as the protocol responder and, more importantly, the value Y cannot be leaked to an adversary before generating signatures involving Y (in the actual session run in which Y is sent as ephemeral public-key). This has already significantly limited the provable security guarantee of FHMQV and SMQV. Specifically, we suppose that the value Y is off-line pre-computed (which is most common and realistic in practice) and exposed to the adversary before the actual session run involving Y, then the security proofs of FHMQV/SMQV have already been invalidated, which contradicts the claims made in [20,6] on the security advantage of FHMQV/SMQV over HMQV.

More importantly, for the security of FXCR when the signer B is protocol initiator, which implies that the value Y will be first sent to the adversary and then the adversary poses the Send query with X. As the value Y is known to the adversary (before sending X), the adversary can pose (X, Y, m) for arbitrary X before making the FXCR signature query w.r.t. (X, Y, m). Such subtleties are buried in the security proofs of FHMQV and SMQV, which are over sketchy and vague than the analysis of HMQV and (s)YZ. The proof of FDCR is directly based on that of FXCR. As the proof of FXCR is limited, so is FDCR. The security of FHMQV in the CK model is based on that of FDCR; thus, the proof of FHMQV is influenced by the security limit of FDCR. Specifically, in the case that the test session has no matching session, the security proof of FHMQV is also invalidated by Atk2. Therefore, FHMQV cannot be proved by the strategy in [20] and is hard to prove *even in the CK model*.

The proof of SMQV is based on the security of FXCR-1 and FDCR-1, which is only mentioned that can be obtained similarly from that of FXCR and FDCR. FXCR-1 and FDCR-1 also inherit the limit of FXCR and FDCR. Thus, SMQV is also hard to prove *even in the CK model*.

3.3   Discussion about Solution

From the proof error we have found, it is clear that the security of SMQV is not proven in the seCK model by the strategy in [6]. Our next interest is whether we can achieve a scheme which is secure in the seCK model and does not need any modular exponentiation in the non-idle time computation. Here, we discuss possibility of such a scheme.

The proof error pointed out in Sec. 3.2 is caused by the reason that the simulator S cannot arrange r and D_i against Atk2. Since D is an output of the random oracle H_1, S can embed an arbitrary random number D as the output. In the above possible strategy of S, (x, b, D) must be fixed before IntRev query. Only r is not fixed and S may be able to return an arbitrary value as r for IntRev query. However, since r is bound by (x, b, D) for the relation $r = Dx + b$ in advance, r does not coincide with the secret exponent if S fails to guess the embedding point of D in H_1 queries. In this case, the secret exponent is only computable with r and x (or b); but S does not know x nor b. Accordingly, how to avoid the proof error is classified as follows:

Correct Guess. If S could correctly guess Z'_i which $\mathcal{A}$ poses $\text{Send}(\mathcal{I}, B, P_i, X_i, Z'_i)$ for all i, S succeeded by returning r to $\text{IntRev}(\mathcal{I}, B, P_i, X_i, Z'_i)$ query. However, as we discussed in Sec. 3.2, there is an exponential number of combinations of H_1

and Send queries for the polynomial number of P_i; thus, S succeeds with only negligible probability.

Making Secret Exponent Adjustable. We consider the case that D is chosen randomly and the secret exponent is different from r. In this case, S can correctly return the answer to IntRev query if the secret exponent is computable without knowing x or b.

The first way cannot be achieved but the second way remains to be achieved. Thus, we discuss possibility of the second way hereafter.

Simplistically, if secret exponents in different sessions by same parties may be identical or related such as MQV and HMQV, secret exponents are computable without knowing x or b. For example, we suppose that the form of a secret exponent is $Dx + Db$. In this case, S can return $X = (g^r K_B^{-1})$ (i.e., $r = x + b$) and the secret exponent is defined as rD' where $D' = H_1(X, Z_i', B, P_i)$. Thus, S can simulate the secret exponent without knowing x or b. Naturally, such a scheme which secret exponents in different sessions may be identical or related is insecure against Atk1 as Sec. 3.1.

Thus, independence of the secret exponent from that in another session is mandatory to prevent Atk1. However, uniqueness also prevent the simulation according to Atk2. One idea is to make the simulator be able to control secret exponents to be related according to Atk2 in the simulation but secret exponents are independent in the real protocol. Specifically, it is to modify exponents $Dx + a$ and $Ey + b$ to $D_1x + D_2a$ and $E_1y + E_2b$ with an additional random oracle H_2 where $D_1 = H_1(X, Y, A, B)$, $D_2 = H_2(X, Y, A, B)$, $E_1 = H_1(Y, X, A, B)$ and $E_2 = H_2(Y, X, A, B)$. This modified scheme is implied by rYZ in [19,23]. In this modification, $D_1x + D_2a$ in a session is independent from $D_1'x + D_2'a$ in another session like SMQV. Also, in the simulation, the simulator can manage $D_1x + D_2a$ to be related from $D_1'x + D_2'a$ by programming outputs of H_1 and H_2. Indeed, according to Atk2, the simulator returns $X = g^r K_B^{-D}$ where $r, D \in_R \mathbb{Z}_p$. For $H_1(X, Z, B, P)$ and $H_2(X, Z, B, P)$ queries, the simulator adjusts $D_1 = H_1(X, Z, B, P)$ and $D_2 = H_2(X, Z, B, P)$ to keep the relationship that $D_2/D_1 = D$ for any pair (D_1, D_2). Thus, if the adversary poses an arbitrary number of queries to the random oracle, the simulator can simulate $\mathsf{Send}(\mathcal{I}, B, P, X, Z')$ and $\mathsf{IntRev}(\mathcal{I}, B, P, X, Z')$ queries for any $Z' \in \{Z\}$.

However, the strategy of the simulation has a fatal error as follows: D_1 and D_2 keep the relationship that $D_2/D_1 = D$. Thus, if either value is chosen randomly, then the other has to be deterministically decided. In the simulation, outputs of random oracles have to be uniformly random. Otherwise, the adversary will distinguish the simulation environment from the real experiment. As a result of the discussion, a DH type AKE scheme which is *provably* secure in the seCK model is hard to achieve with the YZ-MQV/SMQV strategies.

Another resort is to allow a minimum modular exponentiation in the non-idle time computation. For example, NAXOS has Y^a in the secret signature but a is, obviously, not contained in the secret exponent. Thus, Y^a must be computed in the tamper-proof module in non-idle time in the mode II. However, other components ($B^{H(x,a)}$ and $Y^{H(x,a)}$) are able to be computed in the host machine. Hence, NAXOS allows one modular exponentiation in the non-idle time computation. In the next section, we will also discuss the security of NAXOS.

4   Classification of Security Levels in seCK Model

From the discussion in Sec. 3.3, to prove security of DH type AKE schemes in the seCK model is hard. However, achievable security levels may be different by schemes with the mode II. There may be no explicit attack for a scheme while security of the scheme is hard to prove or even unprovable. On the other hand, there may be a serious attack like the total break of a scheme. Thus, in this section, we classify previous DH type AKE schemes in Table 1 in the sense of achievable security levels in the seCK model.

Firstly, from our first result in Sec. 3.2, security of YZ-MQV-2 and SMQV is hard to prove in the seCK model due to Atk2; but, we cannot find an explicit attack. YZ-MQV-1 (resp., FHMQV) can be regarded as an analogy of YZ-MQV-2 (resp., SMQV), and is also hard to prove in the seCK model due to Atk2. Thus, YZ-MQV-1, YZ-MQV-2, SMQV and FHMQV enter into a same security level: 'hard to prove'.

Secondly, MQV, HMQV and KFU are insecure in the seCK model because the session key of a session is derived from a secret exponent in another session due to Atk1. An another insecurity of HMQV against intermediate computation leakage is also pointed out in [24]. In the seCK model, the adversary can pose the StaRev query to the owner and the peer of test session from the freshness condition. We can break the security of KEA+ by the following attack: Firstly, the adversary poses StaRev(A) and StaRev(B), and obtains a and b. Then, for the test session sid* by A and B, the adversary derives the secret signature (Y^a, X^b) with a and b, and obtains the session key. Thus, KEA+ also falls into insecure in the sense of reveal of the session key. Also, in the seCK model, the adversary can pose the EphRev query to the owner and the peer of test session from the freshness condition. We can break the security of YZ and sYZ by the following attack in Mode I: Firstly, the adversary poses EphRev(sid) and EphRev($\overline{\text{sid}}$), and obtains x and y. Then, for the test session sid by A and the matching session $\overline{\text{sid}}$ by B, the adversary derives the secret signature $K_B^{Dx} K_A^{Cy} g^{Exy}$ with x and y, and obtains the session key. Thus, YZ and sYZ also fall into insecure in the sense of reveal of the session key. Therefore, MQV, HMQV, YZ, sYZ, KFU and KEA+ enter into a same security level: 'insecure'.

Remark 3. Recall that the YZ and sYZ protocols were very carefully designed to enjoy the deniability property, as well as the post-ID computability for YZ. The deniability and post-ID computability properties are highly desirable for AKE to preserve players' privacy. From our view, YZ and sYZ achieve better balance between security and efficiency than rYZ and srYZ. This also indicates the limits of seCK model for achieving AKE protocols with the deniability and post-ID computability properties.

Thirdly, we find that CMQV, UP, FS, Oka and MO have more serious weakness in the seCK model than 'insecure' schemes. The adversary can obtain the static secret key without StaRev query by using IntRev query. For CMQV, if the adversary pose IntRev query to a session, then $H(x, a)$ and $H(x, a) + Da$ are obtained. Since D is publicly computable, the adversary can obtain the static secret key a. For UP, if the adversary pose IntRev query to a session, then $x + a$ and $x + Da$ are obtained. Since D is publicly computable, the adversary can obtain the static secret key a. For FS, if the adversary pose IntRev query to a session, then $x + a$ and $x + ca$ are obtained. Since c is public constant number, the adversary can obtain the static secret key a. For Oka, if the adversary pose

Table 2. Security classification of DH type AKE schemes in the seCK model

Secure	Hard to prove	Insecure	Total break
none	YZ-MQV-1 [19] (even for CK security)	MQV [18]	CMQV [10]
	YZ-MQV-2 [19] (even for CK security)	HMQV	UP [11]
	FHMQV [20] (even for CK security)	YZ [19]	FS [13]
	SMQV [6] (even for CK security)	sYZ [19,22]	Oka [14]
	NAXOS [5]	KFU [12]	MO [15]
	rYZ [19]	KEA+ [21]	
	srYZ [19]		

IntRev query to some two sessions executed by same parties, then $(a_1 + Da_3, a_2 + Da_4, Ex)$ and $(a_1 + D'a_3, a_2 + D'a_4, E'x)$ are obtained. Since D and D' are publicly computable, the adversary can obtain a part of the static secret key (a_1, a_2, a_3, a_4). Though a_0 (the other part of the static secret key) is not obtained, the adversary can impersonate party ID_A because the session key can be derived from only (a_1, a_2, a_3, a_4). For MO, if the adversary pose IntRev query to some two sessions executed by same parties, then $(a_1 + Ca_3, a_2 + Ca_4, Dx, Ea, a_5 + Ea_7, a_6 + Ea_8)$ and $(a_1 + C'a_3, a_2 + C'a_4, D'x, E'a, a_5 + E'a_7, a_6 + E'a_8)$ are obtained. Since C, C', D, D', E and E' are publicly computable, the adversary can obtain the static secret key $(a, a_1, a_2, a_3, a_4, a_5, a_6, a_7, a_8)$. To obtain the static secret key without StaRev means that the adversary can freely impersonate any party because such a reveal of the static secret key does not interfere with the freshness condition. Therefore, CMQV, UP and FS enter into a same security level: 'total break'.

Next, we consider the security of NAXOS. In the mode I, the seCK model is identical to the eCK model; thus, NAXOS is also secure in the seCK model. In the mode II, the secret exponent $H(x, a)$ in a session can be revealed by the IntRev query and $H(x, a)$ is reused in another session by Atk1. Then, the adversary can know $B^{H(x,a)}$ and $Y^{H(x,a)}$ in the secret signature in the target session. However, Y^a is not known because the adversary is not allowed to reveal a or y from the freshness condition. Thus, it seems that the IntRev query does not help the adversary; but, unfortunately, NAXOS also has a hurdle to prove security. We consider Atk2 again. Though the simulator cannot return the secret exponent to $IntRev(\mathcal{I}, B, P_i, X_i, Z'_i)$ correctly in SMQV and FHMQV, the simulator can do in NAXOS because the secret exponent $H(x, b)$ does not depend on Z'_i in $Send(\mathcal{I}, B, P_i, X_i, Z'_i)$. However, the simulator cannot return the secret signature to $IntRev(\mathcal{I}, B, P_i, X_i, Z'_i)$ correctly. The secret signature includes Z'^b_i. The simulator cannot know b and $\log Z'_i$, and cannot handle X_i in order to adjust Z'^b_i because Z'^b_i is independent from X_i. Therefore, though there may be no explicit attack, we cannot prove security of NAXOS in the seCK model and NAXOS enters into the level 'hard to prove'. We note rYZ and srYZ seem to be not suffered from the above security proof hurdle.

Finally, we consider the security rYZ and srYZ. Different from YZ and sYZ, for rYZ and srYZ in Mode I of the seCK model, the exposures of x and y are not helpful to compute the session-key, as the value g^{ab} is involved with rYZ and srYZ. On the other hand, for rYZ and srYZ (with off-line pre-computation) in Mode II of the seCK model, the security proof hurdle discussed about underlying signature is not applicable to rYZ and srYZ (note also that rYZ and srYZ have already been provably secure in the CK model). However, the other hurdle (i.e., Atk2) can be also applicable to rYZ and srYZ;

thus, we cannot prove security of rYZ and srYZ in the seCK model and rYZ and srYZ enter into the level 'hard to prove'.

Table 2 shows the resultant security classification of known DH type AKE schemes.

5   Conclusion

We find errors of the proofs of SMQV and FHMQV. Thus, SMQV and FHMQV are not proven secure in the seCK model (moreover, even in the CK model). Also, we consider a taxonomical classification of security of previous DH type AKE schemes in the seCK model. Unfortunately, known schemes fall into hard to prove or insecure. In the present state of affairs, the seCK model is almost meaningless because there is no scheme which *provably* satisfies it. Thus, a remaining problem of future works is to finalize possibility of a provably secure scheme in the seCK model: to come up with a concrete scheme with rigorous security proof or to show rigorous impossibility. One way is to further analyze the (slight variants of) rYZ and srYZ (by additionally applying the transformation methods mentioned in [19][3] and possibly additionally applying the NAXOS transformation on ephemeral secret-key generation). Another possible way is to construct AKE schemes based on other type of hard problems like the factoring problem.

References

1. Kocher, P.C., Jaffe, J., Jun, B.: Differential Power Analysis. In: Wiener, M. (ed.) CRYPTO 1999. LNCS, vol. 1666, pp. 388–397. Springer, Heidelberg (1999)
2. Boneh, D., DeMillo, R.A., Lipton, R.J.: On the Importance of Checking Cryptographic Protocols for Faults. In: Fumy, W. (ed.) EUROCRYPT 1997. LNCS, vol. 1233, pp. 37–51. Springer, Heidelberg (1997)
3. Halderman, J.A., Schoen, S.D., Heninger, N., Clarkson, W., Paul, W., Calandrino, J.A., Feldman, A.J., Appelbaum, J., Felten, E.W.: Lest We Remember: Cold Boot Attacks on Encryption Keys. In: 17th USENIX Security Symposium, pp. 45–60 (2008)
4. Canetti, R., Krawczyk, H.: Analysis of Key-Exchange Protocols and Their Use for Building Secure Channels. In: Pfitzmann, B. (ed.) EUROCRYPT 2001. LNCS, vol. 2045, pp. 453–474. Springer, Heidelberg (2001)
5. LaMacchia, B.A., Lauter, K., Mityagin, A.: Stronger Security of Authenticated Key Exchange. In: Susilo, W., Liu, J.K., Mu, Y. (eds.) ProvSec 2007. LNCS, vol. 4784, pp. 1–16. Springer, Heidelberg (2007)
6. Sarr, A.P., Elbaz-Vincent, P., Bajard, J.-C.: A New Security Model for Authenticated Key Agreement. In: Garay, J.A., De Prisco, R. (eds.) SCN 2010. LNCS, vol. 6280, pp. 219–234. Springer, Heidelberg (2010)
7. Bellare, M., Rogaway, P.: Entity Authentication and Key Distribution. In: Stinson, D.R. (ed.) CRYPTO 1993. LNCS, vol. 773, pp. 232–249. Springer, Heidelberg (1994)

---

[3] The method is, for mutual fairness, to require the responder to first commit to its ephemeral public-key (e.g, by sending $C = H(A, K_A, B, K_B, Y)$) before the initiator sends its ephemeral public-key X. This method ensures that the responder cannot set its ephemeral public-key based on its peer's ephemeral public-key, but results in a three-move variant.

8. Cremers, C.J.F.: Session-state Reveal Is Stronger Than Ephemeral Key Reveal: Attacking the NAXOS Authenticated Key Exchange Protocol. In: Abdalla, M., Pointcheval, D., Fouque, P.-A., Vergnaud, D. (eds.) ACNS 2009. LNCS, vol. 5536, pp. 20–33. Springer, Heidelberg (2009)
9. Cremers, C.J.F.: Examining Indistinguishability-Based Security Models for Key Exchange Protocols: The case of CK, CK-HMQV, and eCK. In: ASIACCS 2011, pp. 80–91 (2011)
10. Ustaoglu, B.: Obtaining a secure and efficient key agreement protocol from (H)MQV and NAXOS. Des. Codes Cryptography 46(3), 329–342 (2008)
11. Ustaoglu, B.: Comparing *sessionStateReveal* and *ephemeralKeyReveal* for diffie-hellman protocols. In: Pieprzyk, J., Zhang, F. (eds.) ProvSec 2009. LNCS, vol. 5848, pp. 183–197. Springer, Heidelberg (2009)
12. Kim, M., Fujioka, A., Ustaoğlu, B.: Strongly Secure Authenticated Key Exchange without NAXOS' Approach. In: Takagi, T., Mambo, M. (eds.) IWSEC 2009. LNCS, vol. 5824, pp. 174–191. Springer, Heidelberg (2009)
13. Fujioka, A., Suzuki, K.: Designing Efficient Authenticated Key Exchange Resilient to Leakage of Ephemeral Secret Keys. In: Kiayias, A. (ed.) CT-RSA 2011. LNCS, vol. 6558, pp. 121–141. Springer, Heidelberg (2011)
14. Okamoto, T.: Authenticated Key Exchange and Key Encapsulation in the Standard Model. In: Kurosawa, K. (ed.) ASIACRYPT 2007. LNCS, vol. 4833, pp. 474–484. Springer, Heidelberg (2007), http://eprint.iacr.org/2007/473/
15. Moriyama, D., Okamoto, T.: An eCK-Secure Authenticated Key Exchange Protocol without Random Oracles. In: Pieprzyk, J., Zhang, F. (eds.) ProvSec 2009. LNCS, vol. 5848, pp. 154–167. Springer, Heidelberg (2009)
16. Huang, H., Cao, Z.: An ID-based Authenticated Key Exchange Protocol Based on Bilinear Diffie-Hellman Problem. In: ASIACCS 2009, pp. 333–342 (2009)
17. Krawczyk, H.: HMQV: A High-Performance Secure Diffie-Hellman Protocol. In: Shoup, V. (ed.) CRYPTO 2005. LNCS, vol. 3621, pp. 546–566. Springer, Heidelberg (2005)
18. Law, L., Menezes, A., Qu, M., Solinas, J.A., Vanstone, S.A.: An Efficient Protocol for Authenticated Key Agreement. Des. Codes Cryptography 28(2), 119–134 (2003)
19. Yao, A.C., Zhao, Y.: Method and Structure for Self-Sealed Joint Proof-of-Knowledge and Diffie-Hellman Key-Exchange Protocols. In: PCT Patent (that is the PCT version of the Chinese patent No. 200710047344.8 filed in, with the Chinese patent file as the priority reference). Number PCT/CN2008/072794 (August 2007)
20. Sarr, A.P., Elbaz-Vincent, P., Bajard, J.-C.: A secure and efficient authenticated diffie–hellman protocol. In: Martinelli, F., Preneel, B. (eds.) EuroPKI 2009. LNCS, vol. 6391, pp. 83–98. Springer, Heidelberg (2010)
21. Lauter, K., Mityagin, A.: Security Analysis of KEA Authenticated Key Exchange Protocol. In: Yung, M., Dodis, Y., Kiayias, A., Malkin, T. (eds.) PKC 2006. LNCS, vol. 3958, pp. 378–394. Springer, Heidelberg (2006)
22. Yao, A.C., Zhao, Y.: A New Family of Practical Non-Malleable Diffie-Hellman Protocols. CoRR abs/1105.1071 (2011)
23. Yao, A.C., Zhao, Y.: A New Family of Practical Non-Malleable Protocols. Cryptology ePrint Archive 2011/035 (this is the academic paper version of the patent file PCT/CN2008/072794) (2011)
24. Basin, D., Cremers, C.: Modeling and Analyzing Security in the Presence of Compromising Adversaries. In: Gritzalis, D., Preneel, B., Theoharidou, M. (eds.) ESORICS 2010. LNCS, vol. 6345, pp. 340–356. Springer, Heidelberg (2010)
25. Pointcheval, D., Stern, J.: Security proofs for signature schemes. In: Maurer, U.M. (ed.) EUROCRYPT 1996. LNCS, vol. 1070, pp. 387–398. Springer, Heidelberg (1996)

Gateway-Oriented Password-Authenticated Key Exchange Protocol with Stronger Security

Fushan Wei[1,2,*], Chuangui Ma[1], and Zhenfeng Zhang[2]

[1] Zhengzhou Information Science and Technology Institute,
Zhengzhou 450002, China
[2] State Key Laboratory of Information Security, Institute of Software, Chinese
Academy of Sciences, Beijing 100190, China
`weifs831020@163.com`, `chuanguima@sina.com`,
`zfzhang@is.iscas.ac.cn`

Abstract. A gateway-oriented password-based authenticated key exchange (GPAKE) is a three-party protocol, which allows a client and a gateway to establish a common session key with the help of an authentication server. To date, most of the published GPAKE protocols have been subjected to undetectable on-line dictionary attacks. The security models for GPAKE are not strong enough to capture such attacks. In this paper, we define a new security model for GPAKE, which is stronger than previous models and captures desirable security requirement of GPAKE. We also propose an efficient GPAKE protocol and prove its security under the DDH assumption in our model. Our scheme assumes no pre-established secure channels between the gateways and the server unlike previous schemes, but just authenticated channels between them. Compared with related schemes, our protocol achieves both higher efficiency and stronger security.

Keywords: Password-based authentication, Gateway, DDH, Security model.

1 Introduction

1.1 Password-Based Authenticated Key Exchange

Password-based authenticated key exchange (PAKE) protocols allow users to securely establish a common key over an insecure open network only using a low-entropy and human-memorable password. PAKE protocols are widely used for user authentication and secure communications in real applications, such as internet banking and remote user authentication. Over the years, there

* This work was supported in part by the National High Technology Research and Development Program of China (No. 2009AA01Z417), the National Natural Science Foundation of China (60873261) and Key Scientific and Technological Project of Henan Province (No. 092101210502).

X. Boyen and X. Chen (Eds.): ProvSec 2011, LNCS 6980, pp. 366–379, 2011.
© Springer-Verlag Berlin Heidelberg 2011

have been a great deal of research on efficient and provably secure password-based authenticated key exchange protocols in the two-party or n-party settings [1,2,3,4,5,6,7,8,9,10,11,12].

In practice, a password is usually chosen from a small set of possible values (for example, 4 or 8 characters such as natural language phrase). Due to the low entropy of passwords, PAKE protocols are susceptible to so-called *dictionary* attacks. In dictionary attacks, an adversary tries to break the security of a protocol by exhaustive search. Dictionary attacks can be classified into three types [10] : on-line, off-line, and undetectable on-line dictionary attacks. In on-line dictionary attacks, an attacker first guesses a password, and tries to verify the password using responses from a server in an on-line manner. On-line password dictionary attacks can be easily detected and thwarted by counting access failures. In off-line password dictionary attacks, an adversary tries to determine the correct password without the involvement of the honest parties based on information obtained during previous executions of the protocol. Thus, the attacker can freely guess a password and then check if it is correct without limitation in the number of guesses. The last type is undetectable on-line dictionary attacks, where a malicious insider tries to verify a password guess in an on-line manner. However, a failed guess cannot be detected by the honest client or the server. The malicious insider participates in the protocol legally and undetectably many times to get sufficient information of the password. Among these attacks, on-line dictionary attacks are unvoidable when low entropy passwords are used, so the goal of PAKE protocols is to restrict the adversary to on-line dictionary attacks only. In other words, off-line and undetectable on-line dictionary attacks should not be possible in a PAKE protocol. Nevertheless, undetectable on-line dictionary attacks are always more difficult to be found than off-line ones in the design of password-based protocols, especially in that of three-party PAKE cases, so that some three-party PAKE protocols are still susceptible to the undetectable attacks even if they are claimed to be provably secure [3,5].

1.2   Related Work

In order to address practical scenarios in which the service provider is actually composed of two distinct entities, one being the direct interlocutor of the client and the other being a back-end server capable of checking the identity of the client, Abdalla et al. put forward the notion of gateway-oriented password-based authenticated key exchange (GPAKE) in 2005 [1]. A GPAKE protocol enables a client to establish an authenticated session key with a gateway via the help of an authentication server. The server and the client previously share a password for authentication, but a session key is generated between the gateway and the client. The client sends information to the gateway in an encrypted form for authentication. The gateway just forwards it to the authentication server and gets back the decision on whether or not the authentication is really successful. In their work, in addition to the usual notion of semantic security of the session key, two other security goals are considered: key privacy with respect to curious servers and password protection with respect to gateways. The former says that the session key should remain indistinguishable from random, even with respect to an honest-but-curious server that knows the passwords of all the users. The latter states that the gateway should not learn any information about the passwords of clients from the authentication server. In 2006, Byun et al. [7] showed that the GPAKE protocol by Abdalla et al. was vulnerable to an undetectable on-line dictionary attack. A malicious gateway can iteratively guess a password and verify its guess without being detected by the server. They also proposed a countermeasure for the attack by exploiting MAC of keying material sent to the authentication server from the client. In 2008, Shim [13] showed that Byun's countermeasure was still insecure against the same undetectable on-line dictionary attack contrary to the claim in [7] that it was. In addition, Shim also designed its enhanced version (S-GPAKE) by using a symmetric encryption algorithm to overcome the attack. Nevertheless, Yoon et al. [15] pointed out that the S-HPAKE protocol was inefficiently and incorrectly designed. Although the protocols [13,15] are presumed to be secure against undetectable on-line dictionary attacks, they are lack of rigorous reduction. Recently, Abdalla et al. [4] presented an anonymous variant of the original GPAKE protocol [1] with similar efficiency. They also provided a new model having stronger security which captured all the security goals in a single security game. The new security model allowed corruption of the participants. They proved the security of the new protocol in the enhanced security model. However, partially due to user anonymity, the new protocol is still subject to undetectable on-line dictionary attacks. Undetectable on-line dictionary attack is a threatening attack to GPAKE protocols and should be taken care of. Until now, to the best of our knowledge, there is no formal treatment of undetectable on-line dictionary attacks in GPAKE protocols.

1.3   Our Contribution

In this paper, we define a new security model of GPAKE to capture desirable security requirements of GPAKE protocols, especially the resistance to undetectable on-line dictionary attacks. Our model is based on the security model of GPAKE by Abdalla et al. [4] and the recent formal model of 3PAKE by Yoneyama [14]. It can be seen as a combination of the two models. The new model is stronger than the one by Abdalla et al. [4] since it additionally captures the resistance to undetectable on-line dictionary attacks. However, it is actually weaker than the one by Yoneyama [14]. This is because our model is in the same setting as [1,4], i.e., the authentication between the client and the server is done only by the password, without using the public key cryptosystem.

We also construct a new GPAKE scheme based on OMDHKE scheme in [6]. We let the client and the server execute the OMDHKE protocol to generate a common secret key, and then use the secret key to authenticate the key material between the client and the gateway. In this way, the authenticators between the client and the server will leak no information of the password to the gateway, and the session key established between the client and the gateway is private to the server. To make our protocol more efficient, the key material of the client is re-used both in server authentication and session key establishment. Furthermore, we prove that our scheme is secure in the sense of our model in the random oracle model under the DDH assumption. Compared with other GPAKE schemes, our protocol is quite efficient in terms of computation while achieving stronger security.

The remainder of this paper is organized as follows. In Section 2, we recall the communication model and present the new security model. We describe our protocol and prove its security in Section 3. In Section 4, we compare the efficiency and security of our protocol with related schemes. We conclude this paper in Section 5.

2   Security Model

In this section, we first overview the security requirements of the GPAKE protocol, and then define a security model of GPAKE based on the security models of [4,14] in order to capture strong security properties, especially resistance to undetectable on-line dictionary attacks. We will prove security of our protocol in this model.

2.1   Overview

A GPAKE protocol allows a client to establish an authenticated session key with a gateway via the help of an authentication server, where the authentication is done by the means of a short password. The password is known to both the client and the authentication server, but not the gateway. While the communication channel between the gateway and the authentication server is usually assumed to be authenticated and private, the channel connecting the client to the gateway may be insecure and under the control of an adversary.

The main security goal of the GPAKE protocol is to securely generate a session key between the client and the gateway without leaking information about the password to the gateway. As there may be a number of different attacks on GPAKE protocols, it is hard to give an accurate definition of security goal. However, it is desirable that a GPAKE protocol should have the following security properties [14]:

- **Known-Key Security (KS):** The adversary cannot distinguish random value from the real session key although it has learned some other session keys.
- **Forward Secrecy (FS):** The session keys established before the compromise of the long-term key (including passwords) are still indistinguishable from random values.
- **Key Privacy against Honest-but-Curious Server (KP):** The session key established between the client and the gateway via the help of the server cannot be distinguished from a random value by the passive server.
- **Resistance to Basic Impersonation (BI):** An adversary cannot impersonate a client unless it gets the password of the client.

- **Resistance to Unknown-Key Share (UKS):** Any insider including the server cannot interfere with the session key establishment between a client C and a gateway G such that at the end of the attack both parties compute the same session key, but have different views of whom the peer is. UKS attack represents both an authentication failure and a vulnerability to known-key attacks.
- **Resistance to Off-Line Dictionary Attacks:** There is no successful adversary (including the gateway) as follows: an adversary guesses a password and verifies its guess using the eavesdropped information. Since no participant of the honest client or the server is required, these attacks are hard to notice.
- **Resistance to Undetectable On-Line Dictionary Attacks:** There is no successful adversary (including the gateway) as follows: an adversary guesses a password and verifies its guess in an on-line transaction and a failed guess cannot be detected by the honest client or the server.

2.2 Security Model

Protocol Participants. The participants in a gateway-oriented password-based key exchange are the client $C \in \mathcal{C}$, the gateway $G \in \mathcal{G}$ and the authentication server $S \in \mathcal{S}$. We denote by $\mathcal{U}$ the set of all participants (i.e., $\mathcal{U} = \mathcal{C} \cup \mathcal{G} \cup \mathcal{S}$) and by U a non-specific participant in $\mathcal{U}$. For simplicity, we assume there is only one server S.

Communication. The channel between the client and the gateway is assumed to be insecure and under the control of the adversary. Unlike previous model, we don't require the channel between the gateway and the server to be private and authenticated. Instead, we only assume the channel between the gateway and the server is authenticated and established by symmetric secret key. We also assume *indirect communication structure*, which means that the client cannot communicate with the server directly, the communication between the client and the server should be relayed by the gateway.

Long-Lived keys. Each client $C \in \mathcal{C}$ holds a password pw_C. Each server $S \in \mathcal{S}$ holds a vector of passwords $pw_S = \langle pw_C \rangle_{C \in \mathcal{C}}$ with an entry for each client. pw_C is called the long-lived key of client C. Since we assume the authenticated channel between the gateway and the server is established by a symmetric secret key, the symmetric secret key is the long-lived key of the gateway, and the long-lived key of the server consists of pw_S and the symmetric secret key.

The adversary's capabilities are modeled through queries. During the execution, the adversary may create several concurrent instances of a participant. Let U^i denote the instance i of a participant U. The list of oracles available to the adversary are as follows:

- $Execute(C^i, G^j, S^t)$: This query models passive attacks in which the attacker eavesdrops on honest executions among a client instance C^i, a gateway instance G^j and a server instance S^t. The output of this query consists of the messages that were exchanged during the honest execution of the entire protocol.

- $Send(U^i, U'; m)$: This query models an active attack, where the adversary chooses the message m and sends it to the instance U^i in the name of U'. The adversary gets back the message U^i should produce upon receiving such a message m.

Since we assume *indirect communication structure*, the adversary cannot send messages to the client in the name of the server and vice-versa. For simplicity, we use $Send(U^i, m)$ if there is no ambiguity who the sender is. Furthermore, because of the authenticated channels between the gateways and the server, if the adversary does not know the symmetric secret key shared between the gateway and the server, the receipt will not accept a message that has not really been sent by the legitimate sender. The $Send$ oracle can be further divided into the following four types:

- $SendClient(C^i, m)$: This query models an active attack against the client instance C^i, in which the adversary chooses the message m and sends it to the client instance C^i in the name of the gateway. The output of this query is the message that the participant instance C^i would generate upon receipt of the message m.

- $SendServer(S^t, m)$: This query models an active attack against the server instance S^t, in which the adversary chooses the message m and sends it to the server instance S^t in the name of the gateway. The message m will be ignored if the adversary does not know the secret key used to establish the channel between the gateway and the server. The output of this query is the message that the server instance S^t would generate upon receipt of the message m.

- $SendGateway(G^j, C; m)$: This query models an active attack against the gateway instance G^j, in which the adversary chooses the message m and sends it to the gateway instance G^j in the name of the client C. The output of this query is the message that the gateway instance G^j would generate upon receipt of the message m.

- $SendGateway(G^j, S; m)$: This query models an active attack against the gateway instance G^j, in which the adversary chooses the message m and sends it to the gateway instance G^j in the name of the server S. The message m will be ignored if the adversary does not know the secret key used to establish the channel between the gateway and the server. The output of this query is the message that the gateway instance G^j would generate upon receipt of the message m.

- $SessonKeyReveal(U^i)$: This query models misuses of session keys. If the session key of the instance U^i is not defined, then return the undefined symbol $\bot$. Otherwise, return the session key held by the instance U^i.

- $StaticKeyReveal(U)$: This query models leakage of the static secret of U. The output of this query consists of the static secret key of U. If U is a client, then the adversary learns the password of U; If U is a gateway, the adversary gets the secret key used to establish the authenticated channel, which means that the adversary gets access to the authenticated channels between the gateway and the server; If U is the server, then the adversary learns all the passwords stored into the server and gets access to the authenticated channels between the server and all the gateways.

Note that, this query does not give the adversary full control of U or revealing any ephemeral secret information.

- $EphemeralKeyReveal(U^i)$: This query models leakage of ephemeral key used by instance U^i. The output of this query consists of the ephemeral key of the instance U^i.
- $EstablishParty(C, pw_C)$: This query models an adversary to register a password pw_C on behalf of a client. In this way, the adversary totally controls the client. Clients against whom the adversary did not issue this query are called *honest*.
- $Test(U^i)$: This query is used to measure the semantic security of the session key of instance U^i, if the latter is defined. If the key is not defined, return the undefined symbol $\perp$. Otherwise, return either the session key held by instance U^i if $b = 1$ or a random key of the same size if $b = 0$, where b is the hidden bit selected at random prior to the first call. Note that, this query is only allowed once at any time during the experiment.
- $TestPassword(C, pw_C')$: This query does not model the adversarial ability, but the protection of the password. If the guessed password pw_C' is just the same as the client $C's$ password pw_C, then return 1. Otherwise, return 0. Note that, this query is only allowed once at any time during the experiment.

2.3   Security Notions

We give the main definitions in the following. The definition approach of partnering uses session identifications and partner identifications. The session identification is the concatenation of all the messages of the conversation between the client and the gateway instances before the acceptance. Two instances are partnered if they hold the same non-null session identification.

Definition 1. (Partnering) *A client instance C^i and a gateway instance G^j are said to be partnered if the following conditions are met: (1) Both C^i and G^j accept; (2) Both C^i and G^j share the same session identification; (3) The partner identification for C^i is G^j and vice-versa; (4) No instance other than C^i and G^j accepts with a partner identification equal to C^i or G^j.*

The adversary is only allowed to perform tests on *fresh* instances. Otherwise, it is trivial for the adversary to guess the hidden bit b. The freshness notion captures the intuitive fact that a session key is not trivially known to the adversary.

Definition 2. (Freshness in Semantic Security) *A client instance C^i or a gateway instance G^j is fresh, if the instance and its partnered instance of the session are honest, and none of the following conditions hold:*
  1. The adversary reveals the session key of C^i or of G^j.
  2. The adversary asks no $SendClient(C^i, m)$ or $SendGateway(G^j, m)$. Then the adversary either makes the queries:

- $EphemeralKeyReveal(C^i)$ or
- $EphemeralKeyReveal(G^j)$.

3. *The adversary asks $SendClient(C^i, m)$ or $SendGateway(G^j, m)$ query. then the adversary either makes queries:*

- $StaticKeyReveal(C)$ or
- $StaticKeyReveal(S)$ or
- $StaticKeyReveal(G)$ or
- $EphemeralKeyReveal(C^l)$ for any session l or
- $EphemeralKeyReveal(S^t)$ for any session t or
- $EphemeralKeyReveal(G^j)$.

Consider an execution of the key exchange protocol $\mathcal{P}$ by the adversary $\mathcal{A}$ in which the latter is given access to *Execute*, *Send*, *SessionKeyReveal*, *StaticKeyReveal*, *EstablishParty*, *EphemeralKeyReveal* oracles, as well as to *Test* oracle calls to fresh instances. The goal of the adversary is to guess the value of the hidden bit b used by the *Test* oracle. Let *Succ* denote the event in which the adversary successfully guesses the hidden bit b used by *Test* oracle.

Definition 3. (Semantic Security) *The advantage of an adversary $\mathcal{A}$ in violating the AKE semantic security of the protocol $\mathcal{P}$, when passwords are uniformly drawn from a dictionary $\mathcal{D}$, is defined as*

$$Adv_{\mathcal{P},\mathcal{D}}^{ake}(\mathcal{A}) = 2 \cdot Pr[Succ] - 1.$$

The advantage function of the protocol $\mathcal{P}$ is defined as

$$Adv_{\mathcal{P},\mathcal{D}}^{ake}(t, R) = max\{Adv_{\mathcal{P},\mathcal{D}}^{ake}(\mathcal{A})\}$$

where maximum is over all $\mathcal{A}$ with time-complexity at most t and using resources at most R (such as the number of oracle queries).

A GPAKE protocol $\mathcal{P}$ is said to be semantically secure if the advantage $Adv_{\mathcal{P},\mathcal{D}}^{ake}(t, R)$ is only negligibly larger than $kn/|\mathcal{D}|$, where n is number of active sessions and k is a constant.

Now, we consider the notion of password protection. Beyond the notion of semantic security, the notion of password protection is needed because we have to consider security for passwords against attacks performed by malicious insiders such as a malicious gateway. As noted before, undetectable on-line password guess by a malicious gateway is a threatening attack to the password of the client and should be thwarted. The goal of password protection is that any attacker (including the malicious gateway) cannot get any information of the password via *Execute* queries and cannot do much better than eliminating one password with a *Send* query. Furthermore, a failed guess of the password will be detected by the target participant.

Consider an execution of the key exchange protocol $\mathcal{P}$ by the adversary $\mathcal{A}$ in which the latter is given access to *Execute*, *Send*, *SessionKeyReveal*,

374   F. Wei, C. Ma, and Z. Zhang

StaticKeyReveal, *EstablishParty*, *EphemeralKeyReveal* oracles, as well as to *TestPassword* oracle. The goal of the adversary is to guess the password of the victim client. Let $Succ^{pw}$ denote the event that $TestPassword(C)$ outputs 1. Next, we define the freshness in password protection and the password protection security.

Definition 4. (Freshness in Password Protection) *The password of a client C is said to be fresh if C is honest, and none of the following conditions hold:*

- *$StaticKeyReveal(C)$ or*
- *$StaticKeyReveal(S)$ or*
- *$EphemeralKeyReveal(C^i)$ for any session i or*
- *$EphemeralKeyReveal(S^t)$ for any session t.*

Definition 5. (Password Protection Security) *The advantage of an adversary $\mathcal{A}$ in violating the password protection security of the protocol $\mathcal{P}$, when passwords are uniformly drawn from a dictionary $\mathcal{D}$, is defined as*

$$Adv_{\mathcal{P},\mathcal{D}}^{pw}(\mathcal{A}) = Pr[Succ^{pw}].$$

The advantage function of the protocol $\mathcal{P}$ is defined as

$$Adv_{\mathcal{P},\mathcal{D}}^{pw}(t, R) = max\{Adv_{\mathcal{P},\mathcal{D}}^{pw}(\mathcal{A})\}$$

where maximum is over all $\mathcal{A}$ with time-complexity at most t and using resources at most R (such as the number of oracle queries).

A GPAKE protocol $\mathcal{P}$ achieves password protection security if the advantage $Adv_{\mathcal{P},\mathcal{D}}^{pw}(t, R)$ is only negligibly larger than $kn/|\mathcal{D}|$, where n is number of Send queries which messages are found as "invalid" by the target participant and k is a constant.

Note that when define the freshness (Def.2 and Def.4), the adversary is not allowed to get access to ephemeral key of the client or the server. This is because the authentication between the client and the server is done only by password. Given the ephemeral key of the client or the server, the target password is easily derived by an off-line dictionary attack since the authenticators are deterministically depends on the client's (server's) ephemeral key, the password and communication received from the other party. Leakage of the ephemeral key of the client or the server will lead to leakage of the client's password. However, the ephemeral key of the gateway has nothing to do with the password, and the leakage of the ephemeral key will only lead to the leakage of the session key.

Our model covers several attacks to the GPAKE protocols. With a similar analysis as in [14], we can see that the semantic security captures the security of KS,FS, KP, BI and UKS. For example, the security of KS is represented as condition 1 of definition 2, i.e., the adversary can obtain session keys excepts the test session. The security of KP with respect to honest but curious server is represented as condition 2 of definition 2, i.e., the adversary can get static and ephemeral keys of the server but no *SendClient* or *SendGateway* query to the test session. For more details, refer to [14]. The password protection security captures resistance to different kinds of dictionary attacks. It is worth mentioning that our model can capture the undetectable on-line dictionary attacks by a malicious gateway. On one hand, the adversary can get the static and the ephemeral keys of the gateway, and the knowledge of the static of the gateway allows the adversary to impersonate the gateway at will. On the other hand, we use "invalid" messages to capture the number of the attacks performed by a malicious gateway. Usually, "invalid" message means the message which is not derived according to the protocol description. However, the target participant should be able to distinguish the valid messages from invalid ones. If there is no specification for what kind of messages are invalid in the description of the protocol, then we take all the messages to be valid even if some of them are fabricated by the adversary. For an on-line impersonation of the malicious gateway, if the authentication server will not be able to detect the attack, then the message faked by the gateway will not be labeled as "invalid".

3 Proposed GPAKE Protocol

In this section, we describe our GPAKE protocol and present its security results.

3.1 Description

Let p, q be large primes with $q|(p-1)$ and $\mathbb{G}_q$ be the multiplicative subgroup of F_p^* of order q. Let g be a generator of $\mathbb{G}_q$. $H_i : \{0,1\}^* \rightarrow \{0,1\}^k (i = 0, 1, 2)$ are hash functions modeled as random oracles, where k is a sufficiently large security parameter. $\mathcal{G} : \{0,1\}^* \rightarrow \mathbb{G}_q$ is a full domain hash function modeled as a random oracle. The protocol runs among a client C, a gateway G and an authentication server S. In the proposed system, it was assumed that the communication channel between G and S was authenticated by a symmetric secret key. Both C and G wished to agree on a common session key with the help of the trusted server S. In the proposed GPAKE protocol, we let the server S initiate the protocol. This is reasonable because in real applications there is always a Hello message used to announce the presence of a client on the network. The detailed steps of the proposed GPAKE protocol, as shown in Fig.1, were described as follows:

1. S chooses a random number $r \in Z_q^*$, computes $R = g^r$, $PW = \mathcal{G}(C, G, pw)$ and $R^* = R \cdot PW$, then sends (C, R^*) to G. Upon receiving (C, R^*), G just forwards (G, R^*) to C.
2. Upon receiving (G, R^*), C first computes $PW = \mathcal{G}(C, G, pw)$ and $R = R^*/PW$, then chooses a random number $x \in Z_q^*$, computes $X = g^x$ and $K_{CS} = R^x$. Finally, C generates the authenticator $\alpha = H_1(C, G, S, X, R^*, K_{CS})$ and sends (C, X, α) to G.
3. Upon receiving (C, X, α), G chooses a random number $y \in Z_q^*$, computes $Y = g^y$, and then sends (C, X, Y, α) to S.

4. Upon receiving (C, X, Y, α), S first computes $K_{CS} = X^r$, then uses K_{CS} to verify the validity of α. If α is invalid, S labels the message as invalid and terminates the protocol. Otherwise, S computes $\beta = H_1(C, G, S, X, R^*, Y, K_{CS})$ and sends (C, β) to G.

5. Upon receiving (C, β), G computes the Diffie-Hellman key $K = X^y = g^{xy}$ and generates a session key $sk = H_0(C, G, X, R^*, Y, K)$. Finally, G computes $Auth_G = H_2(C, G, X, R^*, Y, K)$ and sends $(G, Y, \beta, Auth_G)$ to C.

6. Upon receiving $(G, Y, \beta, Auth_G)$, C first uses K_{CS} to verify the validity of β. If β is invalid, C labels the message as invalid and terminates the protocol. Otherwise, C also computes the Diffie-Hellman key $K = Y^x = g^{xy}$, and then checks if $Auth_G$ is equal to $H_2(C, G, X, R^*, Y, K)$. If the check is successful, then C generates the session key $sk = H_0(C, G, X, R^*, Y, K)$ and accepts the session.

Finally, C and G could use the common session key $sk = H_0(C, G, X, R^*, Y, K)$ in upcoming private communication.

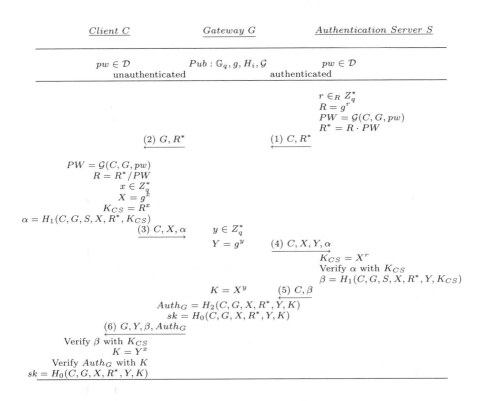

Fig. 1. The proposed GPAKE protocol

3.2   Security

In this section, we prove the security of our protocol within the formal model of security given in Section 2. Due to lack of space, we omit the proof of the Theorems. In our analysis, we assume the intractability of the DDH problem.

DDH Assumption [14]. Let p, q be large primes with $q|(p-1)$ and $\mathbb{G}_q$ be the multiplicative subgroup of F_p^* of order q. Let g be a generator of $\mathbb{G}_q$. We can define the DDH assumption by defining two experiments, $Exp_{\mathbb{G}}^{ddh-real}(\mathcal{I})$ and $Exp_{\mathbb{G}}^{ddh-rand}(\mathcal{I})$. For a distinguisher $\mathcal{I}$, inputs (g, g^u, g^v, Z) are provided, where u, v are drawn at random from Z_q^*. $Z = g^{uv}$ in $Exp_{\mathbb{G}}^{ddh-real}(\mathcal{I})$ and $Z = g^w$ in $Exp_{\mathbb{G}}^{ddh-rand}(\mathcal{I})$, where $w \in_R Z_q^*$. We say that DDH assumption holds on $\mathbb{G}_q$ if the maximus value of $Pr[Exp_{\mathbb{G}}^{ddh-real}(\mathcal{I}) = 1] - Pr[Exp_{\mathbb{G}}^{ddh-rand}(\mathcal{I}) = 1]$ over all $\mathcal{I}$ within polynomial time is negligible.

Semantic Security. As the following theorem states, our protocol achieves semantic security as long as the DDH problem is intractable.

Theorem 1. *Assuming the DDH problem is hard in $\mathbb{G}_q$, then our scheme satisfies semantic security in Sec. 2.3.*

Server Password Protection. As the following theorem shows, our protocol achieves password protection security as long as the DDH problem is intractable.

Theorem 2. *Assuming the DDH problem is hard in $\mathbb{G}_q$, then our scheme satisfies password protection security in Sec. 2.3.*

4   Performance Analysis

In this section, we compare the security properties and efficiency of the proposed protocol with other GPAKE protocols, which are summarized in Table 1. With respect to computation, we only consider modular exponentiation because this is the most expensive type of computation. Let "e" stand for "modular exponentiation". Since the protocols [7,13,15] assume a secure 2-party PAKE protocol was executed between the client and the server, we instantiate these protocols using very efficient 2-party PAKE protocol in [8]. We denote UODA, FS, DDH and PCDDH as the undetectable on-line dictionary attack, forward security, Decisional Diffie-Hellman assumption and Password-based Chosen-basis Decisional Diffie-Hellman assumption [1], respectively.

We can see from Table 1 that our protocol is quite efficient in terms of computation. Our protocol needs 7 modular exponentiations in total. Although Adballad's protocol [1] is slightly efficient than our protocol in computation cost (6 modular exponentiations in total), their protocol fails to achieve resistance to undetectable on-line dictionary attacks and forward security. In terms of communication, Abdalla's protocols [1,4] only need 4 messages, which is more efficient than our protocol. However, their protocols are subject to undetectable on-line dictionary attacks. To make their protocols immune to such attacks, at least two message flows should be added (the client sends the authentication message to the gateway and gateway forwards it to the server).

The protocols [7,13,15] have no security reduction. Although the protocols [13,15] are presumed to be secure against undetectable on-line dictionary attacks, without the proof of security, we cannot be assured of the security properties of these protocols. Another advantage of our protocol is that proof of its security relies on simple and standard DDH assumption, while the security of protocols [1,4] also relies on PCDDH assumption, which is not as standard as DDH assumption.

Table 1. Comparisons of efficiency and security

Protocols	Computation			Messages	UODA	FS	Assumptions
	Client	Gateway	Server				
ACFP[1]	2e	2e	2e	4	N	N	DDH,PCDDH
AIP [4]	4e	3e	3e	4	N	Y	DDH,PCDDH
BLL [7]	4e	2e	4e	8	N	N	unproven
Shim [13]	4e	2e	4e	8	Y	N	unproven
YY [15]	4e	2e	4e	9	Y	N	unproven
Our protocol	3e	2e	2e	6	Y	Y	DDH

5   Conclusion

In this paper, we investigate the design of efficient GPAKE protocol which can resist undetectable on-line dictionary attacks. First, we proposed a new stronger security model of GPAKE which captures desirable security requirements. Next, we proposed an efficient GPAKE protocol in the same setting as Abdalla's protocols [1,4] and prove its security in the sense of our definition. Finally, we compare the efficiency and security properties of our protocol with related schemes. The comparison shows that our protocol achieve both higher efficiency and stronger security.

References

1. Abdalla, M., Chevassut, O., Fouque, P.A., Pointcheval, D.: A simple threshold authenticated key exchange from short secrets. In: Roy, B. (ed.) ASIACRYPT 2005. LNCS, vol. 3788, pp. 566–584. Springer, Heidelberg (2005)
2. Abdalla, M., Chevassut, O., Pointcheval, D.: One-time verifier-based encrypted key exchange. In: Vaudenay, S. (ed.) PKC 2005. LNCS, vol. 3386, pp. 47–64. Springer, Heidelberg (2005)
3. Abdalla, M., Fouque, P., Pointcheval, D.: Password-based authenticated key exchange in the three-party setting. In: Vaudenay, S. (ed.) PKC 2005. LNCS, vol. 3386, pp. 65–84. Springer, Heidelberg (2005)
4. Abdalla, M., Izabachene, M., Pointcheval, D.: Anonymous and transpanent gateway-based password-authenticated key exchange. In: Franklin, M.K., Hui, L.C.K., Wong, D.S. (eds.) CANS 2008. LNCS, vol. 5339, pp. 133–148. Springer, Heidelberg (2008)

5. Abdalla, M., Pointcheval, D.: Interactive Diffie-Hellman assumptions with applications to password-Based Authentication. In: S. Patrick, A., Yung, M. (eds.) FC 2005. LNCS, vol. 3570, pp. 341–356. Springer, Heidelberg (2005)

6. Bresson, E., Chevassut, O., Pointcheval, D.: New security results on encrypted key exchange. In: Bao, F. (ed.) PKC 2004. LNCS, vol. 2947, pp. 145–158. Springer, Heidelberg (2004)

7. Byun, J.W., Lee, D.H., Lim, J.I.: Security analysis and improvement of a gateway-oriented password-based authenticated key exchange protocol. IEEE Communications Letters 10(9), 683–685 (2006)

8. Bellare, M., Pointcheval, D., Rogaway, P.: Authenticated key exchange secure against dictionary attacks. In: Preneel, B. (ed.) EUROCRYPT 2000. LNCS, vol. 1807, pp. 139–155. Springer, Heidelberg (2000)

9. Canetti, R., Halevi, S., Katz, J.: Universally composable password-based key exchange. In: Cramer, R. (ed.) EUROCRYPT 2005. LNCS, vol. 3494, pp. 404–421. Springer, Heidelberg (2005)

10. Ding, Y., Horster, P.: Undetectable on-line password guessing attacks. ACM Operating Systems Review 29, 77–86 (1995)

11. Gennaro, R., Lindell, Y.: A framework for password-based authenticated key exchange. In: Biham, E. (ed.) EUROCRYPT 2003. LNCS, vol. 2656, pp. 524–543. Springer, Heidelberg (2003)

12. Wang, W., Hu, L.: Efficient and provably secure generic construction of three-party password-based authenticated key exchange Protocols. In: Barua, R., Lange, T. (eds.) INDOCRYPT 2006. LNCS, vol. 4329, pp. 118–132. Springer, Heidelberg (2006)

13. Shim, K.A.: Cryptanalysis and enhancement of modified gateway-oriented password-based authenticated key exchange protocol. IEICE Trans. Fundamentals E91-A(12), 3837–3839 (2008)

14. Yoneyama, K.: Efficient and strongly secure password-based server aided key exchange. In: Chowdhury, D.R., Rijmen, V., Das, A. (eds.) INDOCRYPT 2008. LNCS, vol. 5365, pp. 172–184. Springer, Heidelberg (2008)

15. Yoon, E.j., Yoo, K.Y.: An optimized gateway-oriented password-based authenticated key exchange protocol. IEICE Trans. Fundamentals E93-A(4), 850–853 (2010)

TMQV: A Strongly eCK-Secure Diffie-Hellman Protocol without Gap Assumption

Jiaxin Pan and Libin Wang⋆

School of Computer, South China Normal University,
Guangzhou 510631, China
csplator@gmail.com, lbwang@scnu.edu.cn

Abstract. In this paper, we propose an authenticated key exchange (AKE) protocol under the computational Diffie-Hellman (CDH) assumption with respect to the strengthened eCK-security (seCK-security) of Sarr *et al.*. To date, many AKE protocols either are provably secure under a rather strong and non-standard assumption named as the gap Diffie-Hellman (GDH) assumption, or fall to practical attacks on the intermediate result leakage which can be captured by the seCK model. In order to remove the gap assumption and achieve stronger security requirements, we present the TMQV protocol using the twinning technique and the MQV key derivation method. With the help of trapdoor test theorem, TMQV is provably seCK-secure under the standard CDH assumption in the random oracle model. Compared with the related works, TMQV achieves not only stronger security but also higher implementation efficiency with weaker cryptographic assumptions.

Keywords: Strengthened eCK model, authenticated key exchange, Diffie-Hellman assumption, trapdoor test.

1 Introduction

Motivation. Authenticated key exchange (AKE) protocols are cryptographic protocols by which two parties that communicate over a public network can generate a common session key. After the invention of the (extended) Canetti-Krawczyk (CK and eCK) models [2,8] for AKE security, many authenticated Diffie-Hellman (DH) protocols have been formally proven secure. The security proofs for these protocols (e.g. HMQV [7], CMQV [15] and NAXOS [8]) requires an external decisional DH (DDH) oracle to verify the DH value, and then the gap assumption [11] seems to be essential for them. Moreover, many existing AKE protocols are shown to be insecure against the intermediate result leakage [4,16,13,14]. Thus, it is interesting to design an authenticated DH key exchange protocol admits stronger security but without the gap assumption.

Trapdoor test method of Cash *et al.* [3] allows us to implement an effective decision oracle for the twin DH (TDH) problem without knowing any of the

---

⋆ Corresponding author.

X. Boyen and X. Chen (Eds.): ProvSec 2011, LNCS 6980, pp. 380–388, 2011.
© Springer-Verlag Berlin Heidelberg 2011

corresponding discrete logarithms. The TDH problem, given a random triple (X_1, X_2, Y) of finite cyclic group elements, outputs the DH results of (X_1, Y) and of (X_2, Y).

It is a non-trivial task to embed the trapdoor test method in the AKE security proof and do verification without a DDH oracle. On one hand, the gap DH (GDH) assumption is stronger than the TDH assumption, and, more important, the decision oracle for TDH problem is very different from that used in the AKE proof. The decision oracle involved in the AKE proof allows *fully* adversarial access to the DDH predicate which on the adversary chosen input $(\tilde{X}, \tilde{Y}, \tilde{Z})$ returns 1 if $\tilde{Z}$ is the DH value of $\tilde{X}$ and $\tilde{Y}$, while the TDH decision oracle only provides *partially* adversarial access to the TDH predicate which, on input $(X_1, X_2, \tilde{Y}, \tilde{Z}_1, \tilde{Z}_2)$ where $\tilde{Y}, \tilde{Z}_1$ and $\tilde{Z}_2$ are adversary chosen and X_1 and X_2 are from the problem instance, returns 1 if both $\tilde{Z}_1$ is the DH value of $(X_1, \tilde{Y})$ and $\tilde{Z}_2$ is the DH value of $(X_2, \tilde{Y})$.

On the other hand, resilience to the leakage on intermediate results in computing session keys is a desired requirement for the authenticated DH protocol. In practice, an AKE protocol is always implemented using an untrusted host machine together with a computationally limited tamper-resistant device, which stores the static private keys. For many authenticated DH protocols, the computation of intermediate results is more costly than that of ephemeral public keys. To enhance the protocol implementation efficiency safely, we require the protocol is secure against the intermediate result leakage and compute the intermediate result in the host machine, while the ephemeral public key is pre-computed in the device's idle time.

Unfortunately, many existing AKE protocols without the gap assumption (e.g. NAXOS+ [9], HC [5] and KFU2 [6]) are insecure against the intermediate result leakage. That is to say the intermediate results of these protocols must be computed in the tamper-resistant device's non-idle time. What is worse, for these AKE protocols, the computation of intermediate results is much more costly than that of ephemeral public keys. For example, NAXOS+ requires 4 exponentiations for a session key, but only 1 exponentiation for an ephemeral public key. Thus, designing an AKE protocol resilient to the intermediate result leakage without the gap assumption is of not only theoretical interest but also practical values.

Contribution. According to the aforemention challenges, a twinning variant of MQV, named as TMQV, is proposed.

To capture the intermediate result leakage formally, we recall the strengthened eCK (seCK) model of Sarr *et al.* [14]. Three attempts in designing AKE protocols without the gap assumption are due to NAXOS+ [9] and to HC [5] and to KFU2 [6]. Unfortunately, these protocols does not consider the intermediate result leakage and we show the insecurity of these AKE protocols in the seCK model formally.

Motivated by the seCK-insecurity of these protocols, we enhance the MQV key derivation method by binding the session identifiers to the shared secrets, and apply the twinning technique to compute the static keys and the shared secrets in order to remove the gap assumption. With the help of the trapdoor test theorem, TMQV is provably secure under the standard CDH assumption in the seCK model.

Unlike the HMQV, CMQV and SMQV [14] proof, TMQV does not need the GDH assumption or KEA1 [1], and admits higher security than HMQV and CMQV. In addition, TMQV does not use NAXOS trick. As claimed in [16, Sect. 4.3] and [10, Sect. 3], the protocols based on NAXOS trick can not guarantee their security against the leakage on the discrete logarithm of the ephemeral public key. Finally, compared with the related works (especially for NAXOS+, HC and KFU2), TMQV achieves stronger security and higher implementation efficiency with weaker cryptographic assumptions.

Organization. Section 2 analyzes the seCK-insecurity of some AKE protocols. Section 3 proposes TMQV protocol combined with its design rationales and security result and protocols comparison. We draw a conclusion in Section 4. Note that, for the description of seCK model, the readers can refer to the full version of our paper or the original paper of Sarr et al. [14].

2   seCK-Insecurity of Some AKE Protocols

In order to motivate the design of seCK-secure DH protocol without the gap assumption, we cryptanalyze NAXOS+ [9] and HC [5] and KFU2 [6] which are AKE protocols based on the standard CDH problem with respect to the ephemeral private key leakage.

Here we present a key compromise impersonation (KCI) attack and a secret replication (SR) attack on KFU2 [6] using oracle queries defined in Approach 2 of the seCK model. These attacks can be easily extended to the other two (i.e. NAXOS+ and HC). We do not describe these protocols here and recommend the original papers for the readers.

KCI Attack. Resistance to the KCI attack guarantees the disclosure of an honest user $\hat{A}$'s static private key does not enable an adversary to impersonate other uncorrupted entities to $\hat{A}$. KFU2 falls to the KCI attack:

1. The adversary $\mathcal{M}$ issues StaticKeyReveal($\hat{A}$) to learn the static private key (a_1, a_2) of party $\hat{A}$; $\mathcal{M}$ chooses $(a_1', a_2') \xleftarrow{\$} \mathbb{Z}_q^* \times \mathbb{Z}_q^*$ $(a_1' \neq a_1$ and $a_2' \neq a_2)$ and computes $(A_1', A_2') = (g^{a_1'}, g^{a_2'})$ and registers a party $\hat{A}'$ $(\hat{A}' \neq \hat{A})$ and the corresponding static public key (A_1', A_2') through Establish query.
2. $\mathcal{M}$ issues Send($\hat{A}, \hat{B}$) to initiate $\hat{A}$ who creates a session sid as an initiator with the honest peer $\hat{B}$ and returns $(\hat{B}, \hat{A}, X)$. Then $\mathcal{M}$ records the ephemeral public key X.
3. $\mathcal{M}$ issues Send($\hat{B}, \hat{A}', X$) to initiate $\hat{B}$ who creates a session sid' as a responder with the peer $\hat{A}'$. $\hat{B}$ computes the ephemeral public key $Y = g^y$ $(y \xleftarrow{\$} \mathbb{Z}_q^*)$ and the shared secrets $Z_1' = (XA_1')^{y+b_1}$, $Z_2' = (XA_1')^{y+b_2}$, $Z_3' = (XA_2')^{y+b_1}$ and $Z_4' = (XA_2')^{y+b_2}$. During this computation $\mathcal{M}$ issues InterReveal(sid') to get (Z_1', Z_2', Z_3', Z_4'). $\hat{B}$ returns $(\hat{A}', \hat{B}, X, Y)$ and completes the session $sid' = (\mathcal{R}, \hat{B}, \hat{A}', Y, X)$ with session key $SK' = H(Z_1', Z_2', Z_3', Z_4', X, Y, \hat{A}', \hat{B})$.

4. $\mathcal{M}$ issues $\mathsf{Send}(sid, (\hat{A}, \hat{B}, X, Y))$ to $\hat{A}$ and $\hat{A}$ computes $Z_1 = (YB_1)^{x+a_1}$, $Z_2 = (YB_2)^{x+a_1}$, $Z_3 = (YB_1)^{x+a_2}$ and $Z_4 = (YB_2)^{x+a_2}$ and completes the session $sid = (\mathcal{I}, \hat{A}, \hat{B}, X, Y)$ with session key $SK = H(Z_1, Z_2, Z_3, Z_4, X, Y, \hat{A}, \hat{B})$.

5. $\mathcal{M}$ can compute (Z_1, Z_2, Z_3, Z_4) correctly according to the relations $Z_1 = Z_1' \cdot (YB_1)^{a_1-a_1'}$, $Z_2 = Z_2' \cdot (YB_2)^{a_1-a_1'}$, $Z_3 = Z_3' \cdot (YB_1)^{a_2-a_2'}$ and $Z_4 = Z_4' \cdot (YB_2)^{a_2-a_2'}$. Session sid is fresh, since sid and sid' are non-matching and sid is locally unexposed and no $\mathsf{StaticKeyReveal}(\hat{B})$ is issued. $\mathcal{M}$ chooses sid as the test session and breaks the seCK-security of sid easily. That is to say $\mathcal{M}$ successfully impersonates any uncorrupted party $\hat{B}$ to party $\hat{A}$ to compute a common session key after revealing $\hat{A}$'s static private key.

The attack shown as above can be easily extended to NAXOS+ and HC: $\mathcal{M}$ executes Step 1 to 4 faithfully according to the definitions of NAXOS+ and HC except for the relation between the secrets of two non-matching sessions sid and sid' in Step 5: for NAXOS+, $Z_1 = B^a$, $Z_2 = Y^a$, $Z_3 = Z_3'$ and $Z_4 = Z_4'$ (where $Z_1 = \mathsf{CDH}(A, B)$, $Z_2 = \mathsf{CDH}(A, Y)$, $Z_3 = \mathsf{CDH}(X, B)$ and $Z_4 = \mathsf{CDH}(X, Y)$), and for HC, $Z_1 = Z_1'$, $Z_2 = Z_2'$, $Z_3 = Z_3' \cdot Y^{a_1-a_1'}$ and $Z_4 = Z_4' \cdot Y^{a_2-a_2'}$. In addition, we recognize a trivial attack on HC using $\mathsf{InterReveal}$ query: by issuing $\mathsf{InterReveal}$ query on any session in $\hat{B}$, $\mathcal{M}$ gets y, $y + b_1$ and $y + b_2$, and then $\mathcal{M}$ figures out (b_1, b_2) and impersonates $\hat{B}$ without issuing $\mathsf{StaticKeyReveal}(\hat{B})$.

The KCI attack is possible since the shared secrets of these protocols are not related to the identifiers of the participants in the protocol execution. As a result of that, the adversary $\mathcal{M}$ can act as a dishonest party $\hat{A}'$ in the middle and forward the messages between $\hat{A}$ and $\hat{B}$. At the end of the execution, $\hat{A}$ and $\hat{B}$ compute the similar secrets with non-matching peers' static public keys. Since $\mathcal{M}$ knows the static private keys of $\hat{A}$ and $\hat{A}'$, according to the property of the CDH problem, $\mathcal{M}$ can extract $\hat{A}$'s secret from $\hat{B}$'s secret successfully.

SR Attack. The SR attack was proposed firstly by Cremers [4]. In the attack, the adversary forces two non-matching sessions with the same communication parties to establish similar shared secrets. Then $\mathcal{M}$ can compute the shared secret of the test session from that of the non-matching session. SR attacks differ from KCI attacks shown as above in the sense that $\mathcal{M}$ does not learn the static private key of any party. The SR attack on KFU2 is shown as follows:

1. $\mathcal{M}$ issues $\mathsf{Send}(\hat{A}, \hat{B})$ to initiate $\hat{A}$ who creates a session sid as an initiator and returns $(\hat{B}, \hat{A}, X)$. Then $\mathcal{M}$ records $\hat{A}$'s ephemeral public key X.

2. $\mathcal{M}$ issues $\mathsf{Send}(\hat{B}, \hat{A})$ to initiate $\hat{B}$ who creates a session sid' as an initiator and returns $(\hat{A}, \hat{B}, Y)$. Then $\mathcal{M}$ records $\hat{B}$'s ephemeral public key Y.

3. $\mathcal{M}$ issues $\mathsf{Send}(sid', (\hat{B}, \hat{A}, Y, X))$ to $\hat{B}$ and $\mathsf{Send}(sid, (\hat{A}, \hat{B}, X, Y))$ to $\hat{A}$. Then, $\hat{B}$ computes the shared secret as $Z_1' = (XA_1)^{y+b_1}$, $Z_2' = (XA_2)^{y+b_1}$, $Z_3' = (XA_1)^{y+b_2}$ and $Z_4' = (XA_2)^{y+b_2}$. $\hat{A}$ computes the shared secret as $Z_1 = (YB_1)^{x+a_1}$, $Z_2 = (YB_2)^{x+a_1}$, $Z_3 = (YB_1)^{x+a_2}$ and $Z_4 = (YB_2)^{x+a_2}$. We can see $Z_1 = Z_1'$, $Z_2 = Z_3'$, $Z_3 = Z_2'$ and $Z_4 = Z_4'$, and $sid = (\mathcal{I}, \hat{A}, \hat{B}, X, Y)$ and $sid' = (\mathcal{I}, \hat{B}, \hat{A}, Y, X)$.

4. $\mathcal{M}$ issues $\mathsf{InterReveal}(sid')$ to get (Z_1', Z_2', Z_3', Z_4') and computes the secret (Z_1, Z_2, Z_3, Z_4) of sid according to the relation described in Step 3.

5. Session sid is fresh, since sid and sid' are non-matching and sid is locally unexposed and no StaticKeyReveal($\hat{B}$) is issued. $\mathcal{M}$ issues Test(sid) and guesses the private bit involved in Test query correctly.

The attack shown as above can be easily extended to NAXOS+ and HC: $\mathcal{M}$ executes Step 1, 2, 4 and 5 according to the definition of NAXOS+ and HC except the relation between the secrets of two non-matching sessions in Step 3; for NAXOS+, $Z_1 = Z'_1$, $Z_2 = Z'_3$, $Z_3 = Z'_2$ and $Z_4 = Z'_4$, and for HC, $Z_1 = Z'_3$, $Z_2 = Z'_4$, $Z_3 = Z'_1$ and $Z_4 = Z'_2$.

The SR attack is possible since the shared secrets of these protocols are not bound to the corresponding sessions, and then the adversary can easily force two non-matching sessions with similar secrets.

These attacks conclude, for NAXOS+ and HC and KFU2, the shared secrets should be computed in the computationally limited tamper-resistant device (by their insecurity against the intermediate result leakage), while the ephemeral public keys can be computed in the untrusted host machine (by their eCK-security). In order to reduce the tamper-resistant device's computational effort and achieve higher AKE security, it is interesting to design an AKE protocol based on CDH with security against the leakages on the intermediate result and the ephemeral private key respectively.

3   Proposed AKE Protocol: TMQV

We present several design rationales of TMQV before its definition.

Prevent KCI and SR attacks. Hashing the session identifiers into the exponents of the corresponding secrets (i.e. d and e in TMQV) can make the secrets of two non-matching sessions independent, due to the properties of non-matching session definition and the hash function (which is modeled as a random oracle). The independence makes KCI and SR attacks impossible. Moreover, as shown formally in the full version, TMQV is provably seCK-secure.

Remove the gap assumption. In the TMQV initialization procedure, we apply the twinning technique to compute the static keys appropriately such that the trapdoor test method can be used in the security reduction, and thus the simulator can answer the DDH oracle faithfully (except with negligible probability) and solve the CDH problem easily. That is equivalent to say the security of TMQV is provable without the GDH assumption and admits weaker cryptographic assumptions. Compared with the related methods to remove the gap assumption (e.g. NAXOS+, HC and KFU2), TMQV is more effective (see Section 3.3).

Avoid the NAXOS trick. We avoid the use of the controversial NAXOS trick [8] in the ephemeral public key derivation, which is recommended by Ustaoglu [16, Sect. 4.3] and Moriyama et al. [10, Sect. 3]. In the design of TMQV, we derive the ephemeral public key for a party following the original Diffie-Hellman protocol, and improve the secret derivation method of MQV by the twin static key: the secret for party $\hat{A}$ is computed as $(\sigma_1, \sigma_2) = (\mathsf{CDH}(XA_1^d, YB_2^e), \mathsf{CDH}(XA_2^d, YB_1^e))$. Without the knowledge of x and (a_1, a_2), an entity can not learn $(\mathsf{DLOG}(XA_1^d), \mathsf{DLOG}(XA_2^d))$ and figure out (σ_1, σ_2).

3.1 Protocol Description

TMQV is a two-pass AKE protocol. Let $\lambda \in \mathbb{N}$ be the security parameter and $\mathbb{G} = \langle g \rangle$ be a cyclic group of prime order q with $|q| = \lambda$ and H_1 and H_2 be two hash functions modeled as random oracles. H_1 outputs integers of length $|q|/2$. This output length provides the best trad-off between security and performance [7, Remark 4.2]

We compute the twin static key of a party: the static private key of party $\hat{A}$ is $(a_1, a_2) \overset{\$}{\leftarrow} \mathbb{Z}_q^* \times \mathbb{Z}_q^*$ (where $\mathbb{Z}_q^* = [1, q-1]$) and the static public key is $(A_1, A_2) = (g^{a_1}, g^{a_2})$; similarly, the static private key of $\hat{B}$ is (b_1, b_2) and the static public key is $(B_1, B_2) = (g^{b_1}, g^{b_2})$. As usual, we require a certificate binds the static public key to the corresponding party. A graphical description of TMQV is shown in Figure 1.

Public Information: $\mathbb{G}$, (A_1, A_2), (B_1, B_2), H_1, H_2 Private Information: (a_1, a_2), (b_1, b_2)		
Party $\hat{A}$		Party $\hat{B}$
$x \overset{\$}{\leftarrow} \mathbb{Z}_q^*$ $X = g^x$	$\hat{B}, \hat{A}, X$ $\longrightarrow$	Verify $X \in \mathbb{G}^*$?
		$y \overset{\$}{\leftarrow} \mathbb{Z}_q^*$
Verify $Y \in \mathbb{G}^*$?	$\longleftarrow$ $\hat{A}, \hat{B}, X, Y$	$Y = g^y$
$d = H_1(\mathcal{I}, \hat{A}, \hat{B}, X, Y)$		$d = H_1(\mathcal{I}, \hat{A}, \hat{B}, X, Y)$
$e = H_1(\mathcal{R}, \hat{B}, \hat{A}, Y, X)$		$e = H_1(\mathcal{R}, \hat{B}, \hat{A}, Y, X)$
$s_{1a} = x + da_1, \sigma_1 = (YB_2^e)^{s_{1a}}$		$s_{1b} = y + eb_2, \sigma_1 = (XA_1^d)^{s_{1b}}$
$s_{2a} = x + da_2, \sigma_2 = (YB_1^e)^{s_{2a}}$		$s_{2b} = y + eb_1, \sigma_2 = (XA_2^d)^{s_{2b}}$
$K_{\hat{A}} = H_2(\sigma_1, \sigma_2, \hat{A}, \hat{B}, X, Y)$		$K_{\hat{B}} = H_2(\sigma_1, \sigma_2, \hat{A}, \hat{B}, X, Y)$

Fig. 1. An honest execution of TMQV

3.2 Security

A detailed reductionist proof will be presented in the full version to show the seCK-security of TMQV without the GDH assumption. In the proof, we embed the CDH instance in the static public key or the ephemeral public key appropriately according to the freshness of the test session, and use the trapdoor test theorem [3] to remove the gap assumption due to the twin static keys; and we also have a patch in the proof to treat a special kind of attackers using the derandomization technique.

3.3 Protocols Comparison

Table 1 provides a comparison between TMQV and some well accepted AKE protocols in the random oracle model. The comparison focuses on the efficiency (numbers of exponentiations and hash computation per party) and the security (security model, cryptographic assumption and tightness of security reduction). "#Exp-s" and "#Exp-e" and "#Exp-ss" denote the numbers of exponentiations used to compute the static public keys and ephemeral public keys and shared secrets respectively. Note that, for TMQV, #Exp-ss is counted as 1.5 exponentiations for σ_1 (0.5 for e-exponent and 1 for s_{1a}-exponent) and 1.5 exponentiations for σ_2. All protocols are assumed to perform public key validation, so it is left out efficiency. The number of exponentiations is counted in the naive way without accounting for possible improvements. "#Hash" denotes the number of hash computation. We say a security reduction *is* tight if the forking lemma [12] is not used in the reduction, otherwise the security reduction is *not* tight. The advantages of TMQV are shown:

Table 1. Protocols Comparison

Protocol	#Exp-s	#Exp-e	#Exp-ss	#Hash	Model	Assumption	Tight
HMQV [7]	1	1	1.5	3	CK (not seCK)	GDH, KEA1 [1]	no
CMQV [15]	1	1	2	4	eCK (not seCK)	GDH	no
SMQV [14]	1	1	1.5	3	seCK	GDH	no
NAXOS [8]	1	1	3	2	eCK (not seCK)	GDH	yes
NAXOS+ [9]	1	1	4	2	eCK (not seCK)	CDH	yes
HC [5]	2	1	4	2	eCK (not seCK)	CDH	yes
KFU2 [6]	2	1	4	1	eCK (not seCK)	CDH	yes
TMQV	2	1	3	3	seCK	CDH	no

Higher Security Level. TMQV not only achieves higher security level but also is more practical than NAXOS+ and HC and KFU2 which are also based on CDH. TMQV is provably seCK-secure while the other three are shown to be seCK-insecure. The seCK-security achieves both theoretical and practical advantages and encompass the eCK-security.

TMQV requires less exponentiations in computing the shared secret. #Exp-ss of TMQV is 3, since computing σ_1 requires 1.5 exponentiations (0.5 for e-exponentiation and 1 for s_{1a}-exponentiation) and computing σ_2 requires 1.5 exponentiations. More hash computation is required for TMQV. As it is known to us, the hashing is much more efficient than the exponentiation. Although TMQV requires one more exponentiation in computing the static public key than NAXOS+, but the computation of the shared secret is more costly than that of the static public key. For $s(\lambda) > 1$ sessions, NAXOS+ requires $s(\lambda) - 1$ more exponentiations than TMQV.

TMQV can follow different implementation approaches to improve its efficiency, while NAXOS+ and HC and KFU2 can not. For these four protocols, the computation of shared secrets is more costly than that of ephemeral public keys. Implementation efficiency of TMQV can be significantly enhanced following Approach 2 in the seCK model, but that is not the case for the other three due to their insecurity against the intermediate result leakage.

Weaker Cryptographic Assumptions. Amongst the provably secure MQV variants, TMQV admits weaker assumptions with comparable security level. As shown in [13, Sect. 2] and [14, Sect. 4], HMQV and CMQV are not ephemeral secret exponent leakage resilient. That is to say HMQV and CMQV are both seCK-insecure. For SMQV, TMQV achieves the same security level but weaker assumptions.

NAXOS-Trick-Free Design. TMQV is a NAXOS-trick-free design, while NAXOS, NAXOS+ and HC compute the ephemeral public keys using the NAXOS trick. Ustaoglu [16] and Moriyama *et al.* [10] claimed that security proofs of the protocol using NAXOS trick can not guarantee the security against the leakage on the discrete logarithm of the ephemeral public key. Moreover, it is not difficult to see NAXOS can not meet the seCK-security.

4   Conclusion

We have proposed an authenticated Diffie-Hellman protocol, TMQV, by utilizing the twinning technique and the key derivation method of MQV. TMQV is provably secure in the strengthened eCK model under the standard computational Diffie-Hellman (CDH) assumption. The implementation efficiency of TMQV can be significantly reduced, while the related protocols can not. Compared with the related works, TMQV admits the strengthened security and enhanced efficiency with weaker and more standard cryptographic assumptions. On the negative side, the security reduction of TMQV is not tight, since the forking lemma is essential. It is interesting to consider an appropriate modification to the shared secret derivation of MQV in order to construct a tight reduction under the CDH assumption.

Acknowledgments. We would like to thank the anonymous reviewers for their valuable comments, and Augustin P. Sarr for helpful discussions on improving the security proof.

References

1. Bellare, M., Palacio, A.: The knowledge-of-exponent assumptions and 3-round zero knowledge protocols. In: Franklin, M. (ed.) CRYPTO 2004. LNCS, vol. 3152, pp. 273–289. Springer, Heidelberg (2004)
2. Canetti, R., Krawczyk, H.: Analysis of key-exchange protocols and their use for building secure channels. In: Pfitzmann, B. (ed.) EUROCRYPT 2001. LNCS, vol. 2045, pp. 453–474. Springer, Heidelberg (2001)
3. Cash, D., Kiltz, E., Shoup, V.: The twin Diffie-Hellman problem and applications. Journal of Cryptology 22(4), 470–504 (2009)
4. Cremers, C.J.: Session-state reveal is stronger than Ephemeral Key Reveal: Attacking the NAXOS authenticated key exchange protocol. In: Abdalla, M., Pointcheval, D., Fouque, P.-A., Vergnaud, D. (eds.) ACNS 2009. LNCS, vol. 5536, pp. 20–33. Springer, Heidelberg (2009)

5. Huang, H., Cao, Z.: Strongly secure authenticated key exchange protocol based on computational Diffie-Hellman problem. Cryptology ePrint Archive, Report 2008/500 (2008), http://eprint.iacr.org/

6. Kim, M., Fujioka, A., Ustaoglu, B.: Strongly secure authenticated key exchange without NAXOS' approach. In: Takagi, T., Mambo, M. (eds.) IWSEC 2009. LNCS, vol. 5824, pp. 174–191. Springer, Heidelberg (2009)

7. Krawczyk, H.: HMQV: A high-performance secure Diffie-Hellman protocol. In: Shoup, V. (ed.) CRYPTO 2005. LNCS, vol. 3621, pp. 546–566. Springer, Heidelberg (2005), http://eprint.iacr.org/2005/176

8. LaMacchia, B., Lauter, K., Mityagin, A.: Stronger security of authenticated key exchange. In: Susilo, W., Liu, J.K., Mu, Y. (eds.) ProvSec 2007. LNCS, vol. 4784, pp. 1–16. Springer, Heidelberg (2007)

9. Lee, J., Park, J.H.: Authenticated key exchange secure under the computational Diffie-Hellman assumption. Cryptology ePrint Archive, Report 2008/344 (2008), http://eprint.iacr.org/

10. Moriyama, D., Okamoto, T.: An eCK-secure authenticated key exchange protocol without random oracles. In: Pieprzyk, J., Zhang, F. (eds.) ProvSec 2009. LNCS, vol. 5848, pp. 154–167. Springer, Heidelberg (2009)

11. Okamoto, T., Pointcheval, D.: The gap-problems: a new class of problems for the security of cryptographic schemes. In: Kim, K.-c. (ed.) PKC 2001. LNCS, vol. 1992, pp. 104–118. Springer, Heidelberg (2001)

12. Pointcheval, D., Stern, J.: Security arguments for digital signatures and blind signatures. Journal of Cryptology 13(3), 361–396 (2000)

13. Sarr, A.P., Elbaz-Vincent, P., Bajard, J.-C.: A secure and efficient authenticated Diffie-Hellman protocol. In: Martinelli, F., Preneel, B. (eds.) EuroPKI 2009. LNCS, vol. 6391, pp. 83–98. Springer, Heidelberg (2010)

14. Sarr, A.P., Elbaz-Vincent, P., Bajard, J.-C.: A new security model for authenticated key agreement. In: Garay, J.A., Prisco, R.D. (eds.) SCN 2010. LNCS, vol. 6280, pp. 219–234. Springer, Heidelberg (2010), http://eprint.iacr.org/2010/237

15. Ustaoglu, B.: Obtaining a secure and efficient key agreement protocol from (H)MQV and NAXOS. Designs, Codes and Cryptography 46(3), 329–342 (2008)

16. Ustaoglu, B.: Comparing SessionStateReveal and EphemeralKeyReveal for Diffie-Hellman protocol. In: Pieprzyk, J., Zhang, F. (eds.) ProvSec 2009. LNCS, vol. 5848, pp. 183–197. Springer, Heidelberg (2009)

Strongly Secure One Round Authenticated Key Exchange Protocol with Perfect Forward Security

Hai Huang

Zhejiang Sci-Tech University,
Hangzhou, Zhejiang, 310018, China
haihuang1005@gmail.com

Abstract. So far, there exist no two-pass authenticated key exchange protocols which are provably secure in the eCK model and meanwhile achieve perfect forward security against active adversary in one round.

The paper proposes a new two-pass (one round) authenticated key exchange protocol which enjoys following desirable properties. **First**, our protocol is shown secure in the eCK model under the gap Diffie-Hellman (GDH) assumption. Moreover, our protocol does not use the NAXOS transformation, the drawback of which will be discussed in the introduction. **Second**, under the same assumption, we prove that our protocol achieves perfect forward security against active adversary in one round.

To the best of our knowledge, our proposal is the first two-pass (one round) authenticated key exchange protocol provably secure in the eCK model and achieving perfect forward security against active adversary.

Keywords: Authenticated key exchange, eCK model, Perfect forward security, Provably secure.

1 Introduction

Key exchange (KE) protocol enables two parties, Alice (A) and Bob (B), to establish a shared session key over an insecure channel. Since the classic Diffie-Hellman (DH) key exchange protocol is only secure against a passive adversary, much of work has been dedicated to armor the DH protocol against active, man-in-the-middle attacks. This is the goal of authenticated key exchange (AKE) in which both parties are assured that no other parties aside from their intended peers may learn the shared session key. Since the traditional trial-and-error design method has led to the situation that the protocols have been broken or the flaws in the protocols have taken many years to discover, the attentions have been focused on the development of rigorous security models for authenticated key exchange.

LaMacchia, Lauter and Mityagin [8] presented a new security model for authenticated key exchange protocols, the enhanced Canetti-Krawczyk (eCK)

X. Boyen and X. Chen (Eds.): ProvSec 2011, LNCS 6980, pp. 389–397, 2011.

model. To achieve eCK security, they introduce so called NAXOS transformation which requires that the ephemeral public key X is computed as $X = g^{H(x,a)}$ instead of $X = g^x$, where x, a are ephemeral private key and static private key respectively. However, it seems that NAXOS transformation does not prevent the leakage of the ephemeral DH exponents. In some scenarios, we do not guarantee that leakages on DH exponents can not occur [9]. On the other hand, constructing the authenticated key exchange protocol secure in the eCK model without NAXOS transformation has its advantages. For example, it can reduce the risk of leakage of the static private key and use of the random oracle [6].

An important property not captured by the eCK model for the two-pass AKE protocols is perfect forward security (PFS) against active adversary. Recall that PFS guarantees that the leakages on the static private keys of both parties involved do not compromise the previously established session keys by these parties. However, as observed in [7], no two-pass AKE protocols with basic DH message can achieve PFS, if the adversary is *actively* involved with the choice of the DH messages X, Y at a session. So the best the two-pass AKE protocols with the DH messages can achieve is the weak form of perfect forward security (wPFS), which guarantees security against the passive adversary.

Based on Okamoto-Tanaka's work [3], Gennaro, Krawczyk and Rabin propose an ID-based two-pass AKE protocol called mOT [4], the PFS security against active adversary of which is proved under a non-standard knowledge of exponent assumption (KEA1) [1]. However, mOT protocol does not resist the ephemeral key query attack, i.e, mOT protocol is insecure in the eCK model. In fact, the design of two-pass AKE protocol with PFS secure against the ephemeral key query attack is one of the open problems in [4].

1.1 Our Contributions

While there have already been some two-pass AKE protocols [8,10,5,6] provably secure in the eCK model, *none* of them achieve perfect forward security against active adversary. Although it is possible to transform a two-pass AKE protocol provably secure in the eCK model into a three-pass AKE protocol with perfect forward security against active adversary by adding two messages [7], the resulting protocol has a higher round-complexity.

This paper proposes a new two-pass (one round) authenticated key exchange protocol in the eCK model with PFS property. Our protocol enjoys following desirable properties. **First**, without the NAXOS transformation our protocol is shown secure in the eCK model under the gap Diffie-Hellman (GDH) assumption. **Second**, under the same assumption, we prove that our two-pass (one round) protocol achieves perfect forward security against active adversary.

To the best of our knowledge, our proposal is first two-pass (one round) AKE protocol which is provably secure in the eCK model and achieves perfect forward security against active adversary.

2 Strongly Secure One Round Authenticated Key Exchange Protocol with Perfect Forward Security

In this section, we propose a new one round AKE protocol with perfect forward security. The security proofs for eCK-security and PFS property are shown in section 3 and 4 respectively.

2.1 Protocol Setup

Let the value κ be the security parameter. Let $\mathbb{G} = \langle g \rangle$ be a cyclic group of order q in which decisional Diffie-Hellman (DDH) problem can be efficiently solved. Let $g \in \mathbb{G}$ be a generator and $\mathbb{G}^*$ be the non-identity elements set of $\mathbb{G}$. Let $h : \{0,1\}^* \to \mathbb{G}^*, H : \{0,1\}^* \to \{0,1\}^\kappa$ be two hash functions. The party Alice($\hat{A}$)'s static private key is a and its static public key is $A = g^a$. Similarly, the party Bob($\hat{B}$)'s static private key is b and its static public key is $B = g^b$.

2.2 Protocol Description

The protocol runs between Alice and Bob. Its description is given in Fig. 1.

1. Alice($\hat{A}$) chooses an ephemeral private key $x \in \mathbb{Z}_q$ at random, computes the ephemeral public key $X = g^x$ and sends $X, c_1 = h(X)^a$ to $\hat{B}$.
2. Bob($\hat{B}$) chooses an ephemeral private key $y \in \mathbb{Z}_q$ at random, computes the ephemeral public key $Y = g^y$ and sends $Y = g^y, c_2 = h(Y)^b$ to $\hat{A}$.
3. Upon receiving X, c_1, $\hat{B}$ verifies $X \in \mathbb{G}^*$ and checks if $(g, h(X), A, c_1)$ is a valid Diffie-Hellman tuple. If so, $\hat{B}$ computes $sk = H((XA)^{y+b}, sid)$, where $sid = (\hat{A}, \hat{B}, X, c_1, Y, c_2)$. Then, $\hat{B}$ keeps sk as the established session key.
4. Upon receiving Y, c_2, $\hat{A}$ verifies $Y \in \mathbb{G}^*$ and checks if $(g, h(Y), B, c_2)$ is a valid Diffie-Hellman tuple. If so, $\hat{A}$ computes $sk = H((YB)^{x+a}, sid)$, where $sid = (\hat{A}, \hat{B}, X, c_1, Y, c_2)$. Then, $\hat{A}$ keeps sk as the established session key.

$\hat{A}$ $(A = g^a)$	$\hat{B}$ $(B = g^b)$
$x \leftarrow_R \mathbb{Z}_q, X = g^x$	$y \leftarrow_R \mathbb{Z}_q, Y = g^y$
$c_1 = h(X)^a$	$c_2 = h(Y)^b$
$\xrightarrow{\quad X, c_1 \quad}$	
$\xleftarrow{\quad Y, c_2 \quad}$	
$\mathrm{DDH}(g, h(Y), B, c_2) \overset{?}{=} 1$	$\mathrm{DDH}(g, h(X), A, c_1) \overset{?}{=} 1$
If it does not verify, then aborts	If it does not verify, then aborts
$sk = H((YB)^{x+a}, sid)$	$sk = H((XA)^{y+b}, sid)$
where $sid = (\hat{A}, \hat{B}, X, c_1, Y, c_2)$	where $sid = (\hat{A}, \hat{B}, X, c_1, Y, c_2)$

Fig. 1. Strongly Secure One Round Authenticated Key Exchange Protocol with Perfect Forward Security

2.3   Rationale

Our protocol follows the DH values plus signature paradigm. However, it should be noted that using the generic signature is not sufficient. Indeed, to make the protocol eCK-secure, the signature have to comply with following two restrictions: First, the signature scheme should be deterministric. Otherwise, the leakage on the ephemeral private key will destroy the security of the protocol as observed in [8]. Second, the static public key should be of the form $X=g^x$. Otherwise, it is difficult to combine the static public key and ephemeral public key, which is crucial to avoiding NAXOS transformation. To the best of our knowledge, the BLS signature [2] is a nice (and probably only) instantiation of such special signature. Thus, our protocol uses the BLS signature plus DH paradigm.

3   Security Proof

Theorem 1. *Suppose that the GDH assumption for group* $\mathbb{G}$ *holds, h, H are hash functions modeled as random oracles, then the proposed scheme in Fig. 1 is a secure authenticated key exchange protocol in the eCK model.*

Proof. Assume that the adversary succeeds with non-negligible probability in the eCK model[1]. Following the standard approach, we use it to build an algorithm to solve GDH problem. The proof starts with the fact: Since the input to the key derivation function $H(\cdot)$ includes all exchanged information contained in *sid* and H is modeled as random oracle, we know that two different sessions necessarily have two different session keys except with negligible probability, and the only way for the adversary to succeed is by computing the value $\mathrm{GDH}(XA, YB)$, which is called forging attack.

The rest of this section is mainly devoted to the analysis of the forging attack. According to the freshness definition, we consider separately two complementary subcases below:

CASE 1: No honest party owns a matching session to the Test session.

CASE 2: The Test session has a matching session owned by another honest party.

3.1   The Analysis of CASE 1

In this case, it suffices to discuss the following two subcases:

CASE 1.1: The adversary issues a StaticKeyReveal query on party $\hat{A}$ and EphemeralKeyReveal query on party $\hat{B}$ communicating with party $\hat{A}$ (neither EphemeralKeyReveal query on the Test session nor StaticKeyReveal query on party $\hat{B}$ is allowed).

CASE 1.2: The adversary issues a EphemeralKeyReveal query on the Test session and EphemeralKeyReveal query on party $\hat{B}$ communicating with party

---

[1] Due to space limitations, we omit the description of the eCK model, the details of which are referred to [8].

$\hat{A}$ (neither StaticKeyReveal query on party $\hat{A}$ nor StaticKeyReveal query on party $\hat{B}$ is allowed).

CASE 1.1: To show that the success probability of the adversary is negligible, we will construct a GDH problem solver SIM that uses an adversary M who succeeds with non-negligible probability in the attack.

Input to SIM. The input to the SIM is a GDH problem instance $(U = g^u, V = g^v)$, where $u, v \in \mathbb{Z}_q$ and $U, V \in \mathbb{G}$. The goal of SIM is to compute $\text{GDH}(U, V) = g^{uv}$.

Guessed Test session. SIM guesses the adversary M will select one party denoted by $\hat{A}$ as the owner of the Test session and the other party denoted by $\hat{B}$ as the peer. Further, SIM guesses the adversary M will select the session $\Pi^s_{\hat{A}, \hat{B}}$ as the Test session. Note that the probability that the Test session is chosen by M is non-negligible. If this is not the case, SIM aborts.

Setup of SIM. SIM assigns static public key V for $\hat{B}$, and random static public/private key pairs for the remaining parties (including $\hat{A}$). This way, SIM knows all static private keys of parties except for $\hat{B}$.

Simulating the non-Test sessions. The adversary M can activate sessions between any two parties and insert its own messages into these sessions by either generating or scheduling the messages. The simulator SIM needs to respond the sessions on behalf of honest parties. Simulating the actions of any honest party other than $\hat{B}$ is simple as SIM knows their static private keys. Assume that $\hat{B}$ is a responder and $\hat{C}$ is the peer, and the messages it receives is of the form $\tilde{X}, \tilde{c}_1$ allegedly from $\hat{C}$. Whenever $\hat{B}$ is activated in a session, SIM first verifies that $\tilde{X} \in \mathbb{G}^*$ and calls its DDH oracle to check if $\text{DDH}(g, h(\tilde{X}), C, \tilde{c}_1) \overset{?}{=} 1$. If so, SIM chooses an ephemeral private key $\tilde{y} \in \mathbb{Z}_q$ at random, computes ephemeral public key $\tilde{Y} = g^{\tilde{y}}$, and sets $h(\tilde{Y})$ to be $g^{\tilde{r}}$, where $\tilde{r} \in \mathbb{Z}_q$. Then SIM sets the values $\tilde{Y}, \tilde{c}_2 = V^{\tilde{r}}$ as the outgoing messages.

Response to the static private key and session key queries (non-Test session). SIM can respond the static private key queries on any party except for $\hat{B}$. Likewise, the session key queries to these sessions owned by any party other than $\hat{B}$ can be easily responded by SIM as it knows the corresponding static private keys and generates the ephemeral private keys itself. However, sessions in which $\hat{B}$ is a participant are problematic since SIM does not know $\hat{B}$'s static private key. Again, assume that $\hat{B}$ is a responder and the peer is $\hat{C}$. Since SIM does not know $\hat{B}$'s static private key, it can not generate the session key itself. To respond the session key queries and keep the consistency of the random oracles H, SIM calls DDH oracles to check if $\text{DDH}(g, \tilde{X}C, \tilde{Y}V, \sigma) \overset{?}{=} 1$ where σ is the first element int H.

Response to the ephemeral private key queries. SIM can respond the ephemeral private key queries on any party including $\hat{B}$ as in the simulation SIM chooses the values for all the parties itself.

Simulating the Test session. When the adversary activates the Test session at $\hat{A}$, SIM acts as follows. Without loss of generality, assume that $\hat{A}$ is an initiator.

SIM computes $c_1 = h(U)^a$ and sets the outgoing message to be U, c_1. Upon receiving the message Y, c_2 allegedly from $\hat{B}$, SIM first verifies that $Y \in \mathbb{G}^*$ and calls its DDH oracle to check if $\mathrm{DDH}(g, h(Y), V, c_2) \overset{?}{=} 1$. If so, SIM waits for the adversary's next query, else it aborts.

Computing the forgery $GDH(U, V) = g^{uv}$. The goal of SIM is to compute $\mathrm{GDH}(U, V) = g^{uv}$. Below we show that whenever the adversary M succeeds in the forging attack SIM can compute $\mathrm{GDH}(U, V) = g^{uv}$. Assume that the outgoing message of the Test session is $X = U, c_1$ and the incoming message is Y, c_2 allegedly from $\hat{B}$. Indeed, to succeed in the forging attack it must be that the adversary M queries the first element σ of the form $(YB)^{x+a} = (YV)^{u+a}$ in H. In order to compute U^v, the value Y must be eliminated from σ (SIM knows the value a). However, without knowing y, this elimination seems difficult. Fortunately, it can be shown that the message Y can not be generated by the adversary itself except with negligible probability. In other words, if there is an adversary who correctly generates a message Y, c_2 itself with non-negligible probability, we can construct a GDH problem solver $\overline{SIM}$ that uses the adversary. The action of $\overline{SIM}$ is as follows: With the input U, V, setting the static private key of party $\hat{B}$ to be V, $\overline{SIM}$ responds the adversary's queries in the same way as SIM. Finally, if the adversary generates a message Y, c_2 itself, then $\overline{SIM}$ calls its DDH oracle to check if $\mathrm{DDH}(g, h(Y), V, c_2) \overset{?}{=} 1$, where $h(Y)$ is set to be U. If so, $\overline{SIM}$ outputs c_2 which equals $\mathrm{GDH}(U, V) = g^{uv}$.

Now we learn that Y must have been generated by SIM on behalf of party $\hat{B}$. Then Y can be easily eliminated from $(YB)^{x+a} = (YV)^{u+a}$ as SIM knows y. Denote the first element in H by σ. SIM proceeds as follows.

$$(\sigma/(YV)^a)/U^y = ((YV)^{u+a}/(YV)^a)/U^y = (YV)^u/U^y = U^v.$$

This contradicts the GDH assumption. The proof for **CASE 1.1** and **CASE 2** will be presented in the full version of the paper.

4   Proof of PFS Property

In the section, under the same GDH assumption, we prove that our protocol enjoys perfect forward security (PFS) against the active adversary, the definition of which will be presented in the full version. Our proof does not use any additional assumption, e.g. KEA1 assumption and is thus comparatively straightforward. To show that the success probability of the adversary M is negligible, we will construct a GDH problem solver SIM that uses an adversary M who succeeds with non-negligible probability in the attack.

Input to SIM. The input to the SIM is a GDH problem instance $(U = g^u, V = g^v)$, where $u, v \in \mathbb{Z}_q$ and $U, V \in \mathbb{G}$. The goal of SIM is to compute $\mathrm{GDH}(U, V) = g^{uv}$.

Guessed Test session. SIM guesses the adversary M will select one party denoted by $\hat{A}$ as the owner of the Test session and the another party denoted by $\hat{B}$ as the peer. Further, SIM guesses the adversary M will select the session $\Pi^s_{\hat{A}, \hat{B}}$

as Test session. Note that the probability that the Test session is chosen by M is non-negligible. If this is not the case, SIM aborts.

Setup of SIM. According to the definition of PFS game, the adversary M can issue StaticKeyReveal query on neither party $\hat{A}$ nor party $\hat{B}$ *before* the Test session is complete. However, M is allowed to reveal the static private keys of party $\hat{A}$ and $\hat{B}$ after the Test session is complete. To deal with StaticKeyReveal query, SIM assigns random static public/private key pairs for *all* the parties (including $\hat{A}$ and $\hat{B}$) itself. This way, SIM knows all the static private keys of parties.

Simulating the non-Test sessions. Simulating the actions of any honest party other than $\hat{B}$ is simple as SIM knows their static private keys. But since the incoming message of the Test session may be generated or scheduled from other sessions of party $\hat{B}$, the simulation for the sessions of party $\hat{B}$ is slightly different. Specifically, to prove PFS against the active attack, the GDH instance V must be embedded into the outgoing messages of *each* session of the party $\hat{B}$ (and instance U is embedded into the outgoing messages of the Test session). Assume that $\hat{B}$ is a responder and $\hat{C}$ is the peer, and the messages $\hat{B}$ receives is of the form $\tilde{X}, \tilde{c}_1$ allegedly from $\hat{C}$. Whenever $\hat{B}$ is activated in a session, SIM first verifies that $\tilde{X} \in \mathbb{G}^*$ and calls its DDH oracle to check if $\mathrm{DDH}(g, h(\tilde{X}), C, \tilde{c}_1) \overset{?}{=} 1$. If so, SIM chooses $\tilde{t}_i \in \mathbb{Z}_q$ at random, computes ephemeral public key $\tilde{Y} = V^{\tilde{t}_i}$, and sets the values $\tilde{Y}, \tilde{c}_2 = h(\tilde{Y})^b$ as the outgoing messages.

Response to the static private key and session key queries (non-Test session). SIM can respond these queries since it knows the static private keys of all the parties.

Response to the ephemeral private key queries. Since the definition of PFS stipulates that the adversary is not allowed to make any EphemeralKeyReveal query, if these happen, SIM aborts.

Simulating the Test session. When the adversary activates the Test session at $\hat{A}$, SIM acts as follows. Without loss of generality, assume that $\hat{A}$ is an initiator. SIM computes $c_1 = h(U)^a$ and sets the outgoing message to be U, c_1. Upon receiving the message Y, c_2 allegedly from $\hat{B}$, SIM first verifies that $Y \in \mathbb{G}^*$ and calls its DDH oracle to check if $\mathrm{DDH}(g, h(Y), B, c_2) \overset{?}{=} 1$. If so, SIM waits for the adversary's next query, else it aborts.

Computing the forgery $GDH(U, V) = g^{uv}$. The goal of SIM is to compute $GDH(U, V) = g^{uv}$. Below we show that whenever the adversary M succeeds in the forging attack SIM can compute $GDH(U, V) = g^{uv}$. Assume that the outgoing message of the Test session is U, c_1 and the incoming message is Y, c_2 allegedly from $\hat{B}$. As shown by $\overline{SIM}$ in CASE 1.1, the message Y, c_2 can not be generated by the adversary itself except with negligible probability. Thus, it must be that the message Y, c_2 have been scheduled by the adversary from other sessions of party $\hat{B}$. That is to say, the value Y, c_2 must have been generated by SIM itself with the form $Y = V^{t_i}$ and $c_2 = h(Y)^b$. Denote the first element in H by σ. With value t_i, SIM proceeds as follows.

$$\overline{\sigma} = (\sigma/(YB)^a)/U^b = ((YB)^{u+a}/(YB)^a)/U^b = (YB)^u/U^b = Y^u$$

Then,

$$(\overline{\sigma})^{t_i^{-1}} = (Y^u)^{t_i^{-1}} = (V^{t_i u})^{t_i^{-1}} = U^v$$

This contradicts the GDH assumption.

5   Comparison of Protocols

In Table 1 we compare our protocol with several popular AKE protocols in term of efficiency, security model and underlying hardness assumptions, etc. For simplicity, we do not take into account subgroup validation and speedup trick that may be applicable. The "E" denote the exponentiation in $\mathbb{G}$ and "E_N" denote the exponentiation in the RSA group. The CK_{HMQV} denotes modified Canetti-Krawczyk security which captures CK model, KCI, wPFS and ephemeral key query. $CK_{HMQV\text{-}C}$ captures CK_{HMQV} model, PFS. The KEA1 stands for Knowledge of Exponent Assumption [1]. RSA and GDH stand respectively for RSA and gap Diffie-Hellman assumptions.

Table 1. Comparison of Protocols

Protocol	Computation	Round	Security Model	Assumption	NAXOS Transformation
NAXOS [8]	4E	1	eCK	GDH	Y
CMQV [10]	3E	1	eCK	GDH	Y
HMQV [7]	3E	1	CK_{HMQV}	GDH,KEA1	N
HMQV-C [7]	3E	3	$CK_{HMQV\text{-}C}$	GDH	N
mOT[4]	$2E_N$	1	CK,PFS	RSA,KEA1	N
Our scheme	3E+1DDH	1	eCK,PFS	GDH	N

Compared with the NAXOS, CMQV and HMQV protocols, all of which only achieve weak perfect forward security (wPFS), the main advantage of our scheme is that it achieves perfect forward security (PFS). On the other hand, to be secure in the eCK model the former two protocols use the NAXOS transformation while our scheme does not. Compared with HMQV-C protocol which achieves perfect forward security (PFS), our scheme has lower round complexity (within one round). While mOT protocol achieves perfect forward security (PFS) within one round, it does not resist the ephemeral key query, i.e, mOT is insecure in the eCK model. Compared to it, our scheme is provably secure in the eCK model and meanwhile achieves perfect forward security (PFS).

6   Conclusions

Although there have already been some two-pass AKE protocols provably secure in the eCK model, *none* of them achieve perfect forward security against active adversary. On the other hand, while mOT protocol achieves PFS security against active adversary within one round, it is not secure against the ephemeral key query attack, i.e, insecure in the eCK model.

This paper proposes a new two-pass (one round) authenticated key exchange protocol in the eCK model with PFS property. Our protocol provably enjoys following desirable properties. First , without the NAXOS transformation our protocol is shown secure in the eCK model under the gap Diffie-Hellman (GDH) assumption. Second, under the same assumption, we prove that our two-pass (one round) protocol achieves perfect forward security against active adversary.

To the best of our knowledge, our proposal is the first two-pass (one round) AKE protocol which is provably secure in the eCK model and achieves perfect forward security against active adversary.

Acknowledgments. The author would like to thank the anonymous reviewers for their valuable comments. This work was supported in part by the Zhejiang Provincial Natural Science Foundation of China (Grant No. Y1110157), and Science Foundation of Zhejiang Sci-Tech University (Grant No. 1007827-Y).

References

1. Bellare, M., Palacio, A.: The knowledge-of-exponent assumptions and 3-round zero-knowledge protocols. In: Franklin, M. (ed.) CRYPTO 2004. LNCS, vol. 3152, pp. 273–289. Springer, Heidelberg (2004)
2. Boneh, D., Lynn, B., Shacham, H.: Short signatures from the weil pairing. In: Boyd, C. (ed.) ASIACRYPT 2001. LNCS, vol. 2248, pp. 514–532. Springer, Heidelberg (2001)
3. Okamoto, E., Tanaka, K.: Key distribution systems based on identification information. IEEE Journal on Selected Areas in Communications 7(4), 481–485 (1989)
4. Gennaro, R., Krawczyk, H., Rabin, T.: Okamoto-tanaka revisited: Fully authenticated diffie-hellman with minimal overhead. In: Zhou, J., Yung, M. (eds.) ACNS 2010. LNCS, vol. 6123, pp. 309–328. Springer, Heidelberg (2010)
5. Huang, H., Cao, Z.: Strongly secure authenticated key exchange protocol based on computational diffie-hellman problem. In: Inscrypt 2008, Full version available at Cryptology ePrint Archive, Report 2008/500 (2008)
6. Kim, M., Fujioka, A., Ustaoglu, B.: Strongly secure authenticated key exchange without naxos' approach. In: Takagi, T., Mambo, M. (eds.) IWSEC 2009. LNCS, vol. 5824, pp. 174–191. Springer, Heidelberg (2009)
7. Krawczyk, H.: HMQV: A high-performance secure Diffie-Hellman protocol. In: Shoup, V. (ed.) CRYPTO 2005. LNCS, vol. 3621, pp. 546–566. Springer, Heidelberg (2005)
8. LaMacchia, B.A., Lauter, K., Mityagin, A.: Stronger security of authenticated key exchange. In: Susilo, W., Liu, J.K., Mu, Y. (eds.) ProvSec 2007. LNCS, vol. 4784, pp. 1–16. Springer, Heidelberg (2007)
9. Sarr, A.P., Elbaz-Vincent, P., Bajard, J.-C.: A new security model for authenticated key agreement. In: Garay, J.A., De Prisco, R. (eds.) SCN 2010. LNCS, vol. 6280, pp. 219–234. Springer, Heidelberg (2010)
10. Ustaoglu, B.: Obtaining a secure and efficient key agreement protocol from (H)MQV and NAXOS. Des. Codes Cryptography 46(3), 329–342 (2008)

Author Index